# The Therapeutic
# Use Of
# Child's Play

# THE
# THERAPEUTIC
# USE OF
# CHILD'S PLAY

### Edited by
### Charles Schaefer

## JASON ARONSON INC.
*Northvale, New Jersey*
*London*

To Anne Anastasi,
mentor and friend

New printing 1990
**Library of Congress Cataloging in Publication Data**
Main entry under title:
The Therapeutic use of child's play.

    Includes bibliographies and index.
    1. Play Therapy. I. Schaefer, Charles E. [DNLM:   1.   Play therapy.    WM450 T398]
RJ505.P6T48           618.9'28'9165                   75-9556
ISBN 0-87668-209-3

Manufactured in the United States of America. Jason Aronson Inc. offers books and cassettes. For information and catalog write to Jason Aronson Inc., 230 Livingston Street, Northvale, New Jersey 07647.

# CONTENTS

# Part II    Major Approaches To The Therapeutic Use Of Play

# Preface

The purpose of this book is to provide a broad introduction to the use of child's play for therapeutic purposes. Since the turn of the century, clinicians have approached play activity in a variety of ways; and the aim of this volume is to present both past pioneering insights and present new directions. Eclectic in scope, this book attempts to offer a fair representation of the diverse viewpoints while inviting the reader to select the therapeutic principles that are most compatible with his personal style and orientation.

This book grew out of my experiences as a supervisor of clinical interns at a residential treatment center for children. I found that the students had a narrow view of play approaches in that they tended to equate play therapy with Axline's nondirective method. Since the students found it impractical to locate the materials in my list of recommended readings, I decided to compile this volume of basic writings.

In regard to my criteria for selecting articles, I relied mainly on my judgment of both intrinsic excellence and practical value. I also gave preference to "classic" articles by the original authors. Although all-inclusiveness was impossible, I sought broad coverage of key theories and techniques. I regret that unavoidable limitations of space and, in some instances, unavailability of reprint rights, meant certain valuable articles could not be included. This volume does not attempt to offer a critical evaluation of any of the principles or techniques described herein, because well-controlled evaluation studies of different approaches to child psychotherapy are just beginning to appear in the literature. The author hopes that a future volume of research findings will help resolve the question of what techniques work best with what children in what circumstances . . . and why.

In reviewing the literature on play therapy I found new, provocative, and ingenious theories and techniques appearing continually over the past seventy years. A major goal of this volume, then, is to convey some of the sense of excitement and wonder I experienced as I became engrossed in these profoundly important studies. Since play therapy is an area still largely unexplored, I hope that this book will also serve as a catalyst for innovations in both clinical practice and research.

This book is intended for use by both beginning and experienced child therapists. In particular, clinicians in the fields of psychology, psychiatry, social work, occupational therapy, school counseling, and special education should profit from reading this book. The references listed at the end of the articles point the way for more in-depth reading of select topics.

I would like to thank the authors and the journal editors who agreed to let these writings be reproduced. Specific notations appear in the Acknowledgments section.

## Preface to Second Printing

The response to the first printing of this book has been most encouraging. The reviews in professional journals have been consistently positive, especially in regard to the comprehensiveness, clear format, and practical usefulness of this volume. The book has been chosen by three major book clubs and has been adopted as the main text for courses on play therapy by many colleges and universities. Such a strong and continuing interest in this volume seems to underscore the fact that play therapy is an integral part of virtually all major approaches to understanding and treating the emotional and behavioral problems of children.

Charles E. Schaefer, Ph.D.
The Children's Village
Dobbs Ferry, N.Y. 10522

# PART I
# Understanding
# Child's Play

# Introduction

Children's play was a neglected topic until the turn of this century. At the present time, however, there is no dearth of theories about the nature and functions of play behavior. The purpose of this chapter is to provide a basic understanding of the role of play in child development. Although play theorists differ in the emphasis they place on certain functions of play, they all highlight the fundamental importance of play for a child's growth and maturation. It seems clear, for example, that the processes of socialization and self-actualization have their roots in a child's play activities. A basic insight into the nature of play, then, seems essential for the clinician who wishes to use play effectively in therapy.

Perhaps the most influencial theorists on play are Freud and Piaget. Some of their basic concepts on play are discussed in the articles by Pulaski and Walder. It is interesting to note that both Freud and Piaget point out that a principal function of play is adaptive, i.e., to help a young child gradually assimilate and gain mastery over unpleasant experiences. The functional relationship between play and cognitive development is outlined by Sutton-Smith, while the article by Florey relates the play phenomenon to theories of intrinsic motivation and presents a classification scheme of play development. The two articles by Frank discuss, from a transactional perspective, the crucial importance of play for a child's personality development and social adaptation. The final article by Slobin reviews the major theoretical explanations of play and reaches some conclusions about the basic purpose and function of play. The reader who wishes to deepen his understanding of the psychology of play is referred to the excellent texts by Millar[1] and by Herron and Sutton-Smith[2].

[1]Millar, S. *The Psychology of Play*. Baltimore: Penguin Books, 1968.
[2]Herron, R. E. & Sutton-Smith, B. *Child's Play*. New York Wiley, 1971.

The power of play in helping children gain mastery over various forms of emotional turmoil has been very well described in the psychodynamic and psychoanalytic literature. After thoroughly analyzing the adaptive value of play, Erik Erikson concluded that playing out a troublesome situation is the most natural autotherapeutic method that childhood offers[1]. This concept is particularly evident in the approach of the nondirective play therapists who give a child almost complete freedom to work out his problems by himself through the medium of play.

The literature on play has indicated that emotionally disturbed children differ from normal children more in the quality of their play than in the content of play. Thus, normal children tend to show as many hostile themes toward their parents in play as the disturbed children, but the intensity of the hostility exhibited by the disturbed child is much greater. Moreover, the emotionally disturbed child's response to play tends to be more variable and unreliable than that of the normal child. It is also noteworthy that the anxious, fearful child tends to show less activity, vigor, and creativity in his play, while the autistic child tends to play in a repetitive, ritualistic, emotionally-detached, and often bizarre manner. Diagnostically, then, the child therapist can gain a great deal of valuable information about a child's level of emotional and social development by carefully observing him at play. In this regard, a major diagnostic advantage of play is that it can be used to assess the reactions of a child to a wide variety of concrete, emotionally arousing situations that are very difficult to reproduce otherwise, particularly in a medium that is both natural and enjoyable to the child.

[1]Erikson, E. H. Studies in the interpretation of play: I. Clinical observation of play disruption in young children. *Genetic Psychology Monographs*, 1940, 22, 557-671.

# The Role of Play in Cognitive Development

BRIAN SUTTON-SMITH

Our interest here is in research investigations of play as a form of cognitive variation seeking. A useful lead is provided by the work of Lieberman (1965). She was interested in relations between children's playfulness and their creativity. Her subjects were ninety-three kindergarten children from middle-class homes attending five kindergarten classes in three New York schools. The children were rated on playfulness scales which included the following characteristics:

1. *How often does the child engage in spontaneous physical movement and activity during play?* This behavior would include skipping, hopping, jumping, and other rhythmic movements of the whole body or parts of the body like arms, legs, or head, which could be judged as a fairly clear indication of exuberance.

2. *How often does the child show joy in or during his play activities?* This may be judged by facial expression such as smiling, by verbal expressions such as saying "I like this" or "This is fun" or by more indirect vocalizing such as singing as an accompaniment of the activity; e.g., "choo, choo, train go along." Other behavioral indicators would be repetition of activity or resumption of activity with clear evidence of enjoyment.

3. *How often does the child show a sense of humor during play?* By "sense of humor" is meant rhyming and gentle teasing ("glint-in-the-eye" behavior), as well as an ability to see a situation as funny as it pertains to himself or others.

4. *While playing, how often does the child show flexibility in his interaction with the surrounding group structure?* This may be judged by the child joining different groups at any one play period and becoming part of them and their play activity, and by being able to move in and out of these groups by his own choice or by suggestion from the group members without aggressive intent on their part.

A factor analysis of the results led Lieberman to conclude that these scales tapped a single factor of playfulness in these children. But the finding to which we wish to call attention in the present case is the significant relation which was found between playfulness and ability on several creative tasks. That is, children who were rated as more playful were also better at such tasks as: (a) suggesting novel ideas about how a toy dog and a toy doll could be changed to make them more fun to play with; (b) giving novel plot titles for two illustrated stories that were read and shown to the children; and (c) giving novel lists of animals, things to eat, and toys. Unfortunately, the problem with Lieberman's work, as well as with much other work involving creativity measures, is that intelligence loads more heavily on the separate variables of playfulness and creativity than these latter variables relate to each other. Consequently, we cannot be sure whether the findings reflect a distinctive relation between playfulness and creativity or whether these variables are two separate manifestations of intelligence as measured by conventional intelligence tests.

And yet it seems to make sense that the variations in response which constitute playful exercise should be similar to the required variations in response on creativity tests. In other words, these two variables appear to be structurally similar. Our confidence that this may indeed be the case is bolstered by some recent work of Wallach & Kogan (1965) who found that if they gave their creativity tests in a situation in which the subjects were free from usual test pressures, they did indeed obtain creativity scores which were in the main statistically distinct from conventional intelligence test scores. Their conditions for producing these results were individual testing, a complete freedom from time pressures, and a *game-like approach* to the task. The experimenters were introduced to the subject as visitors interested in children's games, and for several weeks prior to testing, spent time with the children in an endeavor to heighten this impression. From this work, Wallach & Kogan concluded that creativity is indeed something different from conventional intelligence and that its manifestation is facilitated in a playful atmosphere. In consequence it may be concluded that if playfulness and creativity co-vary as Lieberman discovered, it is not a function of their separate relations to intelligence.

## Play and Novel Repertoires

What then is the functional relation between the two? While there are various possibilities, only one will be presented here as the concern is more with research than it is with theory. The viewpoint taken is that when a child plays with particular objects, varying his responses with them playfully, he increases the range of his associations for those particular objects. In addition, he discovers many more uses for those objects than he would otherwise. Some of these usages may be unique to himself and many will be "imaginative," "fantastic," "absurd," and perhaps "serendipitous." Presumably, almost anything in the child's repertoire of responses or cognitions can thus be combined with anything else for a novel result, though we would naturally expect recent and intense experiences to play a salient role. While it is probable that most of this associative and combinatorial activity is of no utility except as a self-expressive, self-rewarding exercise, it is also probable that this activity increases the child's repertoire of responses and cognitions so that if he is asked a "creativity" question involving similar objects and associations, he is more likely to be able to make a unique (that is, creative) response. This is to say that play increases the child's repertoire of responses, an increase which has potential value (though no inevitable utility) for subsequent adaptive responses.

In order to test this relation, the writer hypothesized that children would show a greater repertoire of responses for those toys with which they had played a great deal than for those with which they had played less. More specifically, it was hypothesized that both boys and girls would have a greater repertoire of responses with objects for their own sex than for opposite sex objects. In order to control for differences in familiarity, like and opposite sex toys were chosen that were familiar to all subjects. Four toys were selected that had been favorites during the children's year in kindergarten. The girls' toys were dolls and dishes; the boys' were trucks and blocks. It was expected that as they had all known and seen a great deal of all of these toys throughout the year, they would not differ in their familiarity with the toys, as measured by their descriptions of them, but that they would differ in their response variations with these toys as measured by their accounts of the usages to which the toys could be put. Nine boys and nine girls of kindergarten age were individually interviewed, and the investigator played the "blind" game with them. That is, of each toy, he asked, pretending that he was blind: "What is it like?" (description), and "What can you do with it?" (usage). Each child responded to each toy. The interviews were conducted in a leisurely manner, the longest taking forty-five minutes and the most usages given for one object being seventy-two items. The results were that the sexes did not differ from each other in their descriptions of the four objects. Both sexes did differ, however, in the total number of usages given for each toy and the number of unique usages. Boys were able to give more usages and more unique usages for trucks and blocks than they could give for dolls and dishes, although they had not differed between the two sets in their descriptions. Similarly, the girls displayed a larger repertoire for the objects with which they had most often played, dolls and dishes, than for trucks and blocks which had also been in the kindergarten all year, but with which they had not played extensively (Sutton-Smith, 1967).

As the number of responses was not related to intelligence, and as the children showed equal familiarity with all objects (as judged by their descriptions), it seemed reasonable to interpret their response to this adaptive situation (asking them questions) as an example of the way in which responses developed in play may be put to adaptive use when there is a demand. This principle may apply to games as well as play. While most of the activities that players exercise in games have an expressive value in and for themselves, occasionally such activities turn out to have adaptive value, as when the subject, a healthy sportsman, is required in an emergency to run for help, or when the baseball pitcher is required to throw a stone at an attacking dog, or when the footballer is required to indulge in physical combat in war, or when the poker player is required to consider the possibility that a business opponent is merely bluffing. In these cases, we need not postulate any very direct causal connection between the sphere of play and the sphere of adaptive behavior, only the general evolutionary requirement that organisms or individuals with wider ranges of expressive characteristics, of which play is but one example, are equipped with larger response repertoires for use in times of adaptive requirement or crisis. This appears to be true phylogenetically (Welker, 1961). The finding that the variety of games (Roberts and Sutton-Smith, 1962) and the complexity of art (Barry, 1957) have increased with cultural evolution is consonant with such a point of view on the cultural level.

## Play and the Representational Set

But there is perhaps an even more essential way in which play might be related to cognition. Beginning with the representational play of two-year-olds, there develops a deliberate adoption of an "as if" attitude towards play objects and events. The child having such an attitude continues to "conserve" imaginative identities throughout the play in spite of contraindicative stimuli. This cognitive competence is observable both in solitary play, social games, and in the children's appreciation of imaginative stories. Yet it is not until five to seven years of age that children can conserve the class identities of such phenomena as number, quantity, space, and the like, despite contraindicative stimuli. Paradoxically the factor which prevents children from conservation of class identities appears to be the very stimulus bondedness which they are able to ignore in their play. The question can be raised, therefore, as to whether the ability to adopt an "as if" or representational set in play has anything to do with the ability to adopt representative categories on a conceptual level. The only available data are correlational in nature, but again they show a correspondence between the status of the play and the status of the cognition. In Sigel's studies of cognitive activity, lower-class children who exhibited an inability to categorize in representational terms were also impoverished in their play, showing a high frequency of motoric activity, minimal role playing, and block play of low elaboration (Sigel and McBane, 1966). The evidence suggests the possibility that play may not only increase the repertoire of available responses, but that, where encouraged, it may also heighten the ease with which representational sets can be adopted towards diverse materials.

The difficulty with the studies so far cited, however, is that we cannot be sure whether play merely expresses a pre-existing cognitive status of the subjects or whether it contributes actively to the character of that status. That is, is the play constitutive of thought or merely expressive of thought? More simply, does the player learn anything by playing?

## Play as Learning

The view that something is learned by play and games has long been a staple assumption in the "play way" theory of education and has been revived amongst modern educators under the rubric of game simulation (Bruner, 1965; Meier and Duke, 1966). Evidence for effects of particular games on particular learnings are few, although where research has been carried out, it seems to be of confirming import. Research with games involving verbal and number cues seems to show that games result in greater improvement than occurs when control groups receive the same training from more orthodox workbook procedures (Humphrey, 1965, 1966). Similarly, research with games requiring the exercise of a variety of self-controls seems to indicate social improvements in the players (Gump and Sutton-Smith, 1955; Sutton-Smith, 1955; Redl, 1958; Minuchin, Chamberlain, and Graubard, 1966). As an example of this type of field research, the present investigator used a number game to induce number conservation in young children between the ages of 5-0 and 5-7 years. The game known traditionally as "How many eggs in my bush?" is a guessing game in which the players each hide a number of counters within their fist, and the other player must guess the number obscured. If he guesses correctly, the counters are his. The players take turns and the winner is the player who finishes up with all the counters. Each player begins with about ten counters. Children in the experimental group showed a significant improvement from a pre- to post-test on number conservation as compared with children in the control group. The game apparently forced the players to pay attention to the cues for number identity or they would lose, be cheated against, be laughed at, and would certainly not win (Sutton-Smith, 1967).

Given these demonstrations that learning can result as a consequence of game playing, we are perhaps in a better position to interpret those other studies of games which show that continued involvement in games is correlated with important individual differences in player personality and cognitive style. For example, a series of studies has been carried out with the game of Tick Tack Toe (Sutton-Smith, Roberts, et al., 1967). Tick Tack Toe is the most widespread elementary game of strategy and is a game in which players compete to see who can get three crosses or circles in a row on a grid-shaped diagram. A series of studies with this game has shown that children who are better players are indeed very different from those who are losers. More importantly, distinctions have been established between those who tend to win on this game and those who tend to draw. Although these children do not differ in intelligence, they do differ in a number of other ways. Boys who are winners are also perceived as "strategists" by their peers on a sociometric instrument. They are better at arithmetic; they persevere at intellectual tasks; they are rapid at making decisions. Boys who are drawers, on the other hand, are less independent, more dependent on parents and teachers for approval, and more conventional in their intellectual aspirations. Girls who are winners are aggressive and tomboyish, whereas girls who are drawers are withdrawing and ladylike. These results support the view that there are functional interrelations between the skills learned in games and other aspects of player personality and cognitive style.

Similarly, cross-cultural work with games seems to show that games are tied in a functionally enculturative manner to the cultures of which they are a part. Thus, games of physical skill have been shown to occur in cultures where there is spear-throwing and hunting. The older tribal members introduce and sustain these games which have a clearcut training value.

Games of chance occur in cultures where there is punishment for personal achievement and an emphasis upon reliance on divinatory approaches to decision-making (Roberts and Sutton-Smith, 1966); games of strategy occur in cultures where the emphasis is on obedience and diplomacy as required in class and intergroup relations and warfare (Roberts, Sutton-Smith, & Kendon, 1963).

Still, all this research, though it implies functional relations between games and culture patterns, and between games and cognitive styles is like the pedagogic research mentioned above. The latter clearly demonstrates that one can gain a pedagogic and cognitive advantage by use of games for training purposes, but the research is weak insofar as it does not allow us to draw conclusions concerning the particular facets of the games that have the observed influence. The multi-dimensional character of play and of games makes it difficult to specify the key variables which are effective in bringing about the cognitive changes. We do not know yet what interaction between player desire to win and attention to the correct cues brings about the demonstrated learning. This is a subject for future research.

In conclusion, the intent of the present account has been to indicate that there is evidence to suggest that play, games, and cognitive development are functionally related. But the relation, it has been stressed, is a loose one. Play, like other expressive characteristics (laughter, humor, and art), does not appear to be adaptive in any strictly utilitarian sense. Rather, it seems possible that such expressive phenomena produce a superabundance of cognitions as well as a readiness for the adoption of an "as if" set, both of which are potentially available if called upon for adaptive or creative requirements. Given the meagerness of research in this area, however, it is necessary to stress that these are conclusions of a most tentative nature.

## References

Aldrich, N. T., "Children's Level of Curiosity and Natural Child-Rearing Attitudes," Paper presented at Midwestern Psychol. Assn., Chicago, May 1965.

Beach, F. A., "Concepts of Play in Animals," *Amer. Natur.*, 1945, **79**, 523–541.

Berlyne, D. C., *Conflict, Arousal and Curiosity*, New York: McGraw-Hill, 1960.

———, "Laughter, Humor, and Play," in G. Lindzey and E. Aronson (Eds.). *Handbook of Social Psychology*, (2nd Ed.), in press.

Bruner, J. S., "Man: A Course of Study," *Educational Services Inc. Quarterly Report*, 1965, **3**, 85–95.

de Grazia, S., *Of Time, Work, and Leisure*, New York: Twentieth Century Fund, 1962.

Erikson, E. H., *Childhood and Society*, New York: Norton, 1963.

Gilmore, J. B., "Play: a special behavior," in R. N. Haber (Ed.), *Current Research in Motivation*, New York: Holt, Rinehart and Winston, 1965.

Goffman, I., *Encounters*, Indianapolis: Bobbs-Merrill, 1961.

Gump, P. V. and Sutton-Smith, B., "The 'It' Role in Children's Games," *The Group*, 1955, **17** 3–8.

Hunphrey, J. H., "Comparison of the Use of Active Games and Language Workbook Exercises as Learning Media in the Development of Language Understandings and Third-Grade Children," *Percept. Mot. Skills*, 1965, **21** 23-26.

———, "An Exploratory Study of Active Games in Learning of Number Concepts by First-Grade Boys and Girls," *Percept. Mot. Skills*, 1966, **23** 341-342

Hurlock, E. B., "Experimental Investigations of Childhood Play," *Psychol. Bull.*, 1934, **31**, 47-66.

Levin, H. & Wardwell, Eleanor, "The Research Uses of Doll Play," *Psychol. Bull.*, 1962, **59**, 27-56.

Lieberman, J. N., "Playfulness and Divergent Thinking: An Investigation of Their Relationship at the Kindergarten Level," *J. Genet. Psychol.*, 1965, **107**, 219-224.

Marshall, H., "Children's Plays, Games, and Amusements," in C. Murchison (Ed.), *Handbook of Child Psychology*, Worcester: Clark Univ. Press, 1931, 515-526.

Marshall, Helen R. & Shwu, C. H., "Experimental Modification of Dramatic Play," Paper presented at the Amer. Psychol. Assn., New York, Sept. 1966.

Maw, W. H. & Maw, E. W., "Personal and Social Variables Differentiating Children with High and Low Curiosity," *Cooperative Research Project* No. 1511, Wilmington: Univ. of Del., 1965, 1-181.

Mead, George H., *Mind, Self, and Society*, Chicago: Univ. of Chicago Press, 1934.

Meier, R. L. & Duke, R. D., "Game Simulation for Urban Planning," *J. Amer. Institute of Planners*, 1966, **32**, 3-18.

Minuchin, Patricia, Chamberlain, P., & Graubard, P. A., "A Project to Teach Learning Skills to Disturbed Delinquent Children," Paper presented at the 43rd Annual Meeting of the Amer. Orthopsych. Assn., San Francisco, April 1966.

Piaget, J., *Play, Dreams, and Imitation in Childhood*, London: Heinmann, 1951.

Redl, F., "The Impact of Game Ingredients on Children's Play Behavior," *Fourth Conference on Group Process*. New York: Josiah Macy, Grant Foundation, 1958, 33-81.

Rheingold, Harriet L., *Maternal Behavior in Mammals*, New York: John Wiley, 1933.

Roberts, J. M. & Sutton-Smith, B., "Child Training and Game Involvement," *Ethnology*, 1962, **1**, 166-185.

———, "Cross-Cultural Correlates of Games of Chance," *Behav. Sci. Notes*, 1966, **3**, 133-144.

Roberts, J. M., Sutton-Smith, B., & Kendon, A., "Strategy in Folk-Tales and Games," *J. Soc. Psychol.*, 1963, **61**, 185-199.

Sigel, I. E. & McBane, B., "Cognitive Competence and Level of Symbolization Among Five-Year-Old Children," Paper read at Amer. Psychol. Assn., New York, Sept. 1966.

Sutton-Smith, B., "A Game of Number Conservation," Unpublished manuscript, Bowling Green State Univ., 1967.

———, *The Games of New Zealand Children,* Berkeley: Univ. of Calif. Press, 1959.

———, "Novel Signifiers in Play," *Merrill-Palmer Quarterly,* 1968, **14**, 159-160.

———, "The Psychology of Games," *National Education,* 1955, Pt. 1, 228-229 & Pt. 2, 261-263 (Journal of New Zealand Educational Inst.).

Sutton-Smith, B., Roberts, J. M., *et al.,* "Studies in an Elementary Game of Strategy," *Genet. psychol. Monogr.,* 1967, **75**, 3-42.

Sutton-Smith, B., Rosenberg, B. G., and Morgan, E., "The Development of Sex Differences in Play Choices During Preadolescence," *Child Developm.,* 1963, **34**, 119-126.

Wallach, M. A. & Kogan, N., *Modes of Thinking in Young Children,* New York: Holt, Rinehart and Winston, 1965.

Welker, W. I., "An Analysis of Exploratory and Play Behavior in Animals," in D. W. Fiske & S. R. Maddi (Eds.), *Functions of Varied Experience,* Homewood, Ill.: Dorsey, 1961.

# Play Symbolism in
# Cognitive Development

MARY ANN PULASKI

Compared with other areas of human development very little attention has been given to the nature and function of children's make-believe play. Some writers such as Mark Twain and A. A. Milne, author of *Winnie the Pooh*, have given us delightful descriptions of the fantasy play of children, but by and large most adults tend to tolerate, ignore, or actively criticize it. The nineteenth-century educators, Froebel and Pestalozzi, were aware of the importance of imaginative play in early childhood, but their influence was counteracted by that of Montessori, who frowned upon fantasy as "a somewhat unfortunate pathological tendency of early childhood" (Hill, in Garrison, 1926, p. xiv). Her materials were designed to suppress fantasy and imaginative play. Children should not make believe, Montessori declared: "To encourage them along such lines was to encourage defects of character" (Gross & Gross, 1965). The fact that Montessori's theories and materials are enjoying such a revival today makes one wonder whether they may be contributing to a decrease in fantasy play.

## Theories of Play

Probably the most influential theory of play was that of Sigmund Freud (1962) who felt that the creative processes of adults grew out of their childhood fantasies. He hypothesized that thought originates when an infant is deprived of something he wants very badly, such as his mother's breast. When his need becomes so great that he cannot stand it, he "hallucinates" an image of the breast which helps to comfort him and make the delay endurable until she comes to nurse him. Thus for Freud, thought and imagery grew out of deprivation and a need for wish fulfillment. His followers have continued to see fantasy and make-believe play as an expression of unfulfilled needs, or an acting out of anxieties and conflicts. Practically every play therapist has a doll house and a family of dolls, and reams have been written about the traumatic family situations which have been acted out by children during make-believe play in the therapist's office. Even the learning theorists such as Sears and his associates have come to see make-believe play as an outlet for antecedent frustrations. This "catharsis" theory of play, which also includes the need to master anxiety-provoking situations by playing them out over and over again, has dominated our attitudes toward make-believe play for half a century.

**Piaget's "Ludic Symbolism"**

But what Freud overlooked was the joy and delight that children show when they are playing their make-believe games. Anyone who has ever watched a group of children absorbed in playing house or cops and robbers, knows that they are having a perfectly wonderful time! This Piaget did not miss, and this is why he gave the name "ludic symbolism" to children's make-believe play. *Ludus* is Latin for play or jest — the root word in *ludicrous* — and the term symbolism refers to the as-if quality of make-believe, wherein a stick is used as if it were a gun or leaves and acorns are used as if they were plates and cups. In other words, the hallmark of make-believe play is the ability to use objects as symbols for other objects or people not immediately present and to act out the fantasy with a sense of joy and delight.

It is because of its symbolic function that play is so important, according to Piaget, in the child's cognitive development. Play bridges the gap between concrete experience and abstract thought. In make-believe play the child is still dealing in a sensory-motor way with concrete objects, but the objects are symbols for something else of which the child is thinking. Sometimes the connection is obvious, but sometimes it is quite remote. A rag doll is an obvious substitute for a baby, but when Piaget's daughter, Jacqueline, (at 1 yr., ll mos., or 1:11) slid a shell along the top of a box, Piaget had no idea what it represented until she said, "Cat on a wall."

There are two ways, according to Piaget, in which the child attempts to cope with the many new experiences of his pre-school years. One is imitation; by mimicking the words and actions of the adults around him, the child learns to speak and to behave as his family does. Imitation appears very early in infancy and appears to be an effort to accommodate to the environment. Babies will cry when they hear other babies cry or smile in response to smiling faces. Later on they play peek-a-boo or produce sounds that approximate their parents' words, such as "da-da" or "bye-bye." In imitation the child seems to be making a serious effort to master new activities by mimicking the people around him. To use Piaget's terms, accommodation takes precedence over assimilation in the effort to adapt to new experiences.

But when the baby begins to repeat his actions just for the fun of it, and to laugh and crow as he does it, he is discovering the joy of play. During the sensory-motor period most play is characterized by repeated motor patterns accompanied by smiles and laughter. Piaget has described how his son Laurent, who was learning to push aside his father's hand in order to reach a toy, was having such a good time pushing his father that he forgot all about the toy! His interest was transferred from the goal of the activity to the activity itself, and he was enjoying the functional pleasure of play for its own sake (Piaget, 1962, p. 92).

Near the end of the sensory-motor period simple motor games give way to make-believe games characterized by the emergence of ludic symbolism. Jacqueline at one year, three months saw a fringed cloth whose edges reminded her of her pillow. She lay down and pretended to go to sleep, laughing all the time. Five months later she pretended to eat a piece of paper, saying "Very nice!" Lucienne, at about the same age, pretended to drink out of a box, and then held it to the mouths of all who were present. In all these activities the objects used were symbolic of something else not actually present. Piaget felt that games such as these helped the child to express himself imaginatively and eventually to develop a rich and creative intellectual life.

## Piaget's Classification

Of course Piaget was aware that there are other types of play which he discussed in some detail, seeking to explain the evolution of play and why it disappears in later years. He concluded that there are three main categories of play: practice games, symbolic games and games with rules. Practice games appear first and are an outgrowth of the imitative activities of the sensory-motor period: pitching pebbles, stringing beads, jumping rope and so forth. Such games may lead to improved motor performance or they may develop into symbolic games, such as building a castle out of sand. As children grow older and become more socialized, the practice games may become games with rules, such as hopscotch or marbles. Piaget felt that games with rules are essentially social, and since they persist even among adults, perhaps this is the explanation of what happens to children's play; it dies out in later years in favor of socialized games. There are also constructive games such as building or weaving, but Piaget regarded these not really as games so much as a bridge between play and work, merging imperceptibly into the practical skills of adult life.

## Make-Believe Play

Most of Piaget's interest centered upon symbolic or make-believe games, which are both imitative and imaginative and which "imply representation of an absent object" (Piaget, 1962, p. 111). This kind of play is at its peak between the ages of two (the end of the sensory-motor period) and four. Piaget as usual carefully classified into types and sub-types all the developments he observed in children's play. Type I included the projection of the earliest symbolic schemata onto new objects. Jacqueline moved from pretending she was asleep to making her doll and her bear go to sleep. Lucienne pretended to telephone, and then made her doll telephone, and finally used all kinds of things, such as a leaf, instead of a real telephone receiver.

In the following months the children began to use their own bodies to represent other people or things. Piaget called this Type II behavior. Jacqueline at two years old moved her finger along the table and said "Finger walking — horse trotting." Lucienne played that she was the postman, or her godmother, or "Therese with her velvet hat." At four, she stood quite still beside Piaget one day imitating the sounds of bells. "I asked her to stop," wrote Piaget, "but she went on. I then put my hand over her mouth. She pushed me away angrily, but still keeping very straight, and said: 'Don't. I'm a church' (the belfry)" (1962 p. 125). Here we see clearly how Lucienne was using her own straight little body to represent the steeple and reproducing the sound of the bells with her voice.

In Type III there appears the transposition of whole scenes, instead of isolated bits, and long, complicated episodes of play-acting sometimes sustained over periods of time. At around two and a half Jacqueline pretended to prepare a bath for Lucienne, using an empty box for the bath and a blade of grass as a thermometer. She plunged the thermometer into the bath, and finding it too hot, she waited a moment and tested it again. "That's all right, thank goodness!" she said, and then pretended to undress Lucienne, garment by garment, without actually touching her.

About a month later Jacqueline pretended to be walking a baby to sleep, talking to it as she held it in her arms. A week later, as she played the same game, she stopped talking when anyone came near. From a distance Piaget could hear her saying things like, "Now we're going for a walk." Already Jacqueline's make-believe play was becoming a secret inner experience.

At this stage of symbolic play, children often invent imaginary companions. At four, Jacqueline had a dwarf and later a Negress named Marécage. Piaget feels that children create these characters "to provide a sympathetic audience or a mirror for the ego" (1962, p. 131). They become playmates, inseparable companions, and sometimes even take on the moral authority of the parents to make the children behave. Children may refer to them quite openly or whisper to them as secret companions. Piaget feels that just as Jacqueline stopped talking out loud and interiorized her make-believe play, so these imaginary companions may become interiorized as daydreams.

What Piaget calls compensatory play is also included in his discussion of Type III. This involves doing in make-believe what is forbidden in reality. He describes Jacqueline at 2:4 going through the motions of pouring water with an empty cup after she had been forbidden to play in the real washtub. At 2:7 she wanted to carry Lucienne, who was then a newborn baby. When her mother told her she could not carry the baby yet, Jacqueline folded her arms and announced that she had the baby — there were two babies. Then she rocked and talked to the imaginary baby, and even said she was the baby when she was scolded for screaming with temper, thus excusing her behavior. By the time she was four, Jacqueline had a well-developed imagination, and whenever she was restricted in any way, she could make up a "compensatory" tale in which the direction of her desires was clear. When she was angry at her father she announced that Marécage (her imaginary friend) "has a horrid father. He calls her in when she's playing. Her mother chose badly." When she was told to take a nap, Jacqueline said, "Marécage never lies down in the afternoon; she plays all the time." Clearly, she was working out in her make-believe play what was forbidden in reality.

## Therapeutic Value

This of course is very close to the Freudian view of play in which emotion is acted out in gradual degrees, so that it becomes bearable. Play therapy is frequently concerned with reliving experiences of hospitalization, death, or other trauma of childhood. In so doing, children gradually reduce their fearful feelings thus making the situations more tolerable. This is the usual explanation of why children enjoy horror movies on TV. They know the scene is not real, that they can turn it off at will, so they are able to cope with the horror and master their own fear in slow degrees. In the following observation Jacqueline shows how a child acts and learns to live with the unpleasant realities of life.

At 3:11 Jacqueline was impressed by the sight of a dead duck which had been plucked and put on the kitchen table. The next day I found Jacqueline lying motionless on the sofa in my study, her arms pressed against her body and her legs bent: "What are you doing, J? Have you a pain? Are you ill?" "No, I'm the dead duck."

At 4:6, I knocked against J's hands with a rake and made her cry. I said how sorry I was, and blamed my clumsiness. At first she didn't believe me, and went on being angry as though I had done it deliberately. Then she suddenly said, half appeased: "You're Jacqueline and I'm daddy. There!" (She hit my fingers.) "Now say: 'You've hurt me.'" (I said it.) "I'm sorry, darling. I didn't do it on purpose. You know how clumsy I am," etc. In short, she merely reversed the parts and repeated my exact words (1962, page 134).

## Assimilation and Accommodation

These make-believe forms of play, as Piaget has pointed out, represent "pure assimilation." The child is free to interpret and even distort reality as he pleases, without having to conform to the demands of the real world as in imitation. The young child at this age is still very egocentric in his thinking, and is also subjected to more parental demands than at any time in his life. Constantly he hears, "No no." "Don't touch." "Stay out of the street." "Don't get dirty." "Time for bed." He must be toilet-trained, learn to talk correctly, and use proper table manners. Piaget does not say this, but it is my feeling that at this age the child's life is polarized around his efforts to adapt to reality and thus please his parents (imitative accommodation) and his efforts to escape from those demands and satisfy his own ego through his make-believe play (symbolic assimilation). As the accommodation to reality becomes easier, the polarity between these two processes decreases. Gradually they converge in increasingly well-adapted functioning, until the child's play becomes almost indistinguishable from his daily reality.

We see this during the second half of the preoperational period, when symbolic games begin to lose their importance. It is not that they decline so much as that they come closer and closer to reality as the child accommodates to a greater and greater extent to the world around him. Piaget notes that after the age of four, symbolic games become much more orderly, as opposed to the incoherence of earlier games. The child is improving in language skills, and also emerging from the egocentric world of his own needs into the world of reality. He notices how events follow each other in time and space, and his stories become much more precise and coherent.

Another characteristic of play at this age is that it reproduces an increasingly precise imitation of reality. There is "increasing attention to exact detail in the material constructions which accompany these games: houses, cots, tables, kitchens, drawings and models" (1962, p. 136). This is the time when little girls delight in doll houses complete to the tiniest pots and pans, and boys like realistic forts and guns. Their play becomes increasingly a replica of reality, not only on the level of the setting and properties, but also on the level of what happens in their games. From about five and a half onward, Jacqueline constructed an entire village which she called Ventichon. She, and later Lucienne, spent hours acting out real-life scenes in the lives of its inhabitants—weddings family visits, dinner parties, and so on. The little girls began to play "permanent parts as mothers of families with numerous children, grandparents, cousins, visitors etc., the husbands being rather in the background. 'Mrs. Odar' and 'Mrs. Anonzo,' etc., thus became the starting point of new cycles, analogous to those of the preceding stages, but much closer to reality, always true to life and with scenery and buildings which became more and more elaborate" (1962, p. 138).

## Socialized Play

A third characteristic that Piaget notes is that after the age of four or five symbolic play becomes increasingly social. *Collective symbolism* is his term for play in which children take different parts and act them out with an awareness of each other, as in the cases of Mrs. Odar and Mrs. Anonzo above. This is in contrast to the symbolic play of younger children, which tends to be carried on alone, even when the child is in the company of others. As in parallel play, in which the preschool child plays beside another child without playing with him, so early symbolic play is usually carried on individually, using dolls or a much younger child who passively carries out his role, without really understanding or taking part in it. ("You can be the baby and sleep in the carriage," four-year-old girls will say to a much younger child.) But Piaget traces the way in which this sort of imaginary parallel play evolves into group play with each child taking a different role and reacting to the others involved. The following delightful observation shows clearly how Jacqueline at four was ready for a collective socialized game, while Lucienne, who was only two, was not.

At 4:7 J. did her utmost to stage a scene with a car ride; L., who was 2:2 was in process of constructing a bed, and said 'Brr' to show that she was taking part in the movement of the car, but did not stop her own game. What followed was for L. a confused medley of the two games, while J. perseveringly arranged the parts. J. came off victorious, and made L. the wife of a doll, "You're the wife of this husband. Yes," and herself another lady. (J.) "We're two ladies in a car." (L.) "Are you in a car, madam?" (J.) "Yes, and I'm throwing your husband and your child through the window." (She threw the doll away.) But L. went and got it and forgot the game (1962, p. 139).

After the age of seven or eight there is a definite decline in symbolic play, according to Piaget. This age marks the emergence of concrete operations; it also coincides with increased interest in school, and in socialized activities and games with rules. The symbolic games lessen as socialization progresses until by eleven or twelve (period of formal operations) they disappear or are transformed into daydreams (internal) or dramatics (external).

## Intellectual and Creative Activity

Symbolic play seems to end with childhood; we have seen how the ludic symbols imitate reality even more closely. As the child accommodates better to the outer world, he has less occasion to assimilate reality to his personal inner needs, thereby distorting it. For the well-adapted child, play is no longer very different from intellectual activity. Piaget traces this transition from symbolic games to spontaneous creative activity in the play of his son Laurent, who like his sisters created an imaginary village. At about seven, he began to make maps of the country where this village was and to imagine all sorts of people who lived there and the adventures they had. After the age of eight the imaginary characters disappeared, but the careful, detailed maps grew into cartographic models. During an illness that year Laurent worked out descriptions of the climate in different zones of his country, which he called Siwimbal. At nine his interest advanced to real maps of all parts of Europe. Finally, when he was about ten, Laurent's symbolic play appeared on another plane. His maps were quite correct and objective, but the boy now became fascinated with the study of history and reconstructed the costumes, furniture, and architecture of various periods. He dressed tiny toy animals in the costumes of the Middle Ages, the Renaissance, or the eighteenth century. He and a school friend went carefully through the literature on each period so that they could make their reproductions exactly. Here symbolic play began to merge with intellectual and artistic creativity. As Piaget says, "One needs to have seen a little monkey in a wig, a three-cornered hat, silk breeches and lace ruffles, in an eighteenth-century setting made of cardboard, in order to understand the pleasure that two eleven-year-old boys can find in spending their leisure time in evoking the spirit of the past" (1962, p. 141). In this description we see clearly how the ludic symbol has developed into "an image whose purpose is no longer assimilation to the ego but adaptation to reality" (1962, p. 142). Laurent's activities no longer represent private fantasy but socialized study. The long period of childhood is at an end.

What happens then to fantasy, the lovely private world of make-believe, when childhood is left behind? We have said that some of it is "interiorized" in daydreams but Piaget feels much of it goes to enrich developing intellectual interests, such as Laurent's study of historical periods.

"Creative imagination," he states at the end of his discussion, " . . . does not diminish with age but . . . is gradually reintegrated in intelligence, which is thereby correspondingly broadened" (1962, p. 289).

### Experimental Studies

It has been almost thirty years since Piaget published his theories about children's play in French. They appeared in English in 1951 and have stimulated new interest in this subject. Just recently a number of new books on children's play and fantasy have appeared. Herron and Sutton-Smith have brought out a collection of papers called *Child's Play* (1971), which reviews all aspects of children's play from the street games to sex differences. Eric Klinger of the University of Minnesota has written *The Structure and Functions of Fantasy* (1971) which examines the relationship between children's symbolic play, adolescent fantasies, and the dreams, both daydreams and night dreams, of adults. The most recent book called *The Child's World of Make-Believe: Experimental Studies of Imaginative Play* (1973) is by Jerome L. Singer of Yale University. Along with an interesting explanation of Singer's theoretical rationale, there are four chapters written by his doctoral students, describing their experimental studies in this area under his supervision. Since my dissertation was a part of this research, I should like to describe briefly the theoretical position of its authors.

Dr. Singer is a clinical psychologist who theorizes that the ability to make believe and to daydream is a cognitive skill which helps people to be more flexible in solving problems, and better able to postpone immediate gratification in favor of long range goals. His interest in children's make-believe play has developed gradually out of his studies of daydreaming

(1966) which he has been conducting for the past twenty years. In one such experiment he found that there was significant difference in waiting ability between high-fantasy and low-fantasy children. He divided forty little boys aged six to nine, into two groups on the basis of tests and interviews in which he asked questions about their favorite games, their parents' reading habits, what they played when alone, and whether they had ever had an imaginary companion. He ended up with nineteen boys classified as "high-fantasy" subjects, and twenty-one as "low-fantasy," with no significant difference in IQ's between the groups. He told the children he was looking for "space men of the future" who would have to be able to stand long periods of solitary confinement. Then he asked the boys to sit or stand still quietly for fifteen minutes, and measured the time that elapsed before they became restless. In another procedure, he asked the boys to stay still as long as they could, and signal when they had had enough. The results were very interesting. Although the mean waiting time was only about six minutes, the high-fantasy boys were able to wait significantly longer than the low-fantasy group in both situations. The ones who lasted longer were those who turned the situation into a fantasy game and made believe they were flying rockets or blasting off into space.

A consideration of the personality and family characteristics of these groups revealed interesting differences. The high-fantasy children tended to be the older children in their families, with close relationships with their parents, particularly their fathers, though there was no significant difference in how much their parents read to them. The boys had been asked to make up stories, and the high-fantasy group's stories were rated as more creative and imaginative than those of the low-fantasy group. There were also clinical differences in the two groups which suggested a difference in life style. To quote Singer, the tendency toward fantasy behavior "seems to be a dimension of experience and exploration available to most children but one whose richness and frequency of employment grows from a set of optional conditions including parental interest and acceptance of imagination, availability of adults for identification, and opportunity or occasion for practice of fantasy by being alone" (1973, p. 73).

In view of the number of complaints in the schools today about hyperactive children with short attention spans who are highly distractable and cannot concentrate on school work, the implications of this study are very interesting. If the ability to make believe and fantasize helps children to sit still and concentrate on their own thoughts, perhaps we should be actively encouraging this in schools today as a cognitive skill.

This imaginative experiment is only one of many which Singer has conducted or directed in an effort to study make-believe play in a systematic way with appropriate scientific controls. I will mention some others only briefly. My own study was an attempt to show that simple unstructured play materials would evoke much more imaginative make-believe play than would highly structured materials such as ready-made costumes or Barbie and GI Joe dolls with all their clothes and accessories complete. I used kindergarten, first- and second-grade children as subjects, divided into groups of equal intelligence. Half the children were judged to have high predispositions to fantasy (on the basis of tests and interviews similar to Singer's) and the other half were rated low in fantasy. I was very much surprised to find that the structure of the toys made very little difference; by the age of five the high-fantasy children were already playing in an imaginative, original way with all the toys, structured or not. The low-fantasy youngsters, on the other hand, fooled around manipulating all the toys, and their make-believe stories were more concrete and closely related to their daily lives. On a half a dozen measures such as the number of fantasy themes, the organization and variety of these themes, their distance from real life situations, the concentration of the subjects, and their flexibility in switching to new activities when interrupted — on all these measures the high-fantasy children scored significantly higher than the low-fantasy group. These results suggest that children's fantasy predisposition may be already pretty well formed by the age of five, and that children low in fantasy may be much less creative and flexible in their thinking, concentrate less well, and stick to concrete ordinary themes when asked to make up a story. Again, the implication is that if children who have predisposition to fantasy can function so much more imaginatively and flexibly, and can organize and concentrate on their subjects so much better, perhaps we can find a way to foster and encourage these fantasy skills.

## Effects of Adult Modeling

It begins to appear that the predisposition to fantasy is part of one's general life style from preschool years, and that it represents a dimension of human skill or competence available for the enhancement and enrichment of life. If the ability to engage in fantasy or make-believe play is such a useful and valuable skill, how can we help our children to attain it? Let me sketch for you very briefly two studies on the effects of modeling to increase fantasy and make-believe play. In the first, Joan Freyberg selected eighty disadvantaged kindergarten children in New York City whose parents had little education and were economically hard-pressed. She divided them into high- and low-fantasy groups and a control group and then had all the children systematically observed during a free play period. Then she gave eight training sessions in small groups to all but the controls, during which she used pipe cleaner people, Playdoh, blocks and Tinker Toys to act out small plots and engage in make-believe adventures. She encouraged the children to adopt roles, act out stories, and make their own sound effects. She used four main themes, but she encouraged each child to make up his own story. In the beginning she had to do most of the story-telling, but as the children caught on they took the initiative and the plots took all sorts of spontaneous, original and sometimes surprising turns.

At the end of a month, both experimental groups had improved significantly in the imaginativeness of their play as well as in the expression of positive emotions and the degree of concentration shown in their play. The control group, which had had eight sessions manipulating jigsaw puzzles and Tinker Toys, showed no change. The high-fantasy group improved more than the low-fantasy group in imaginativeness and concentration but not in affect, indicating that both groups really enjoyed the training. Two months later the children were still playing with greater imaginativeness and improved verbal communication, as well as more spontaneity, and increased attention span. Thus it was dramatically shown that by modeling and direct teaching Freyberg was able to effect marked changes in these children's functioning despite long-term lack in experiental background and cognitive development.

The second modeling study was conducted by Sybil Gottlieb with older elementary and junior high students. She showed them abstract sound and color films which she either interpreted realistically or used as the basis for a fantasy story. Then she showed another film and asked the students to write their own interpretation. She found the junior high school youngsters much less susceptible to the modeling effects than the elementary children, who showed a significant difference in their responses to the fantasy and realistic interpretations. The junior high school students who had been classified as having a high predisposition to fantasy wrote original imaginative stories regardless of which kind of model they were exposed to, while the low-fantasy group were much more concrete, realistic and conventional in their responses. These results support the notion, that the ability to make-believe and fantasize is part of one's personality organization; it is a skill that develops with age and becomes a part of one's cognitive lifestyle.

These last two studies show clearly the effectiveness of an adult model in helping children to develop make-believe stories and imaginative thought. Undoubtedly parents and teachers have been doing this more or less consciously for years, which is why even young children can be shown to have developed high levels of fantasy predisposition. There is other research described by Smilansky (1968) in Israel and El'Konin (1971) in Russia which implies that adult models are not only desirable but necessary to help children carry out make-believe play. Piaget believes that it develops by itself in the course of the child's intellectual development but he was working with his own bright, privileged children, and probably served as an unconscious model as well. If models are necessary or helpful, as the research seems to indicate, then it behooves us all to be aware of what kind of modeling we are doing and what subtle signs of approval or disapproval we may be giving. Whether in teaching or nursing or therapy or just the daily business of child-rearing, we are constantly either encouraging or discouraging children in the use of imaginative original ways of thinking and problem-solving.

## Summary and Conclusions

To summarize, let me say once more that in the view of Piaget and other cognitive psychologists today, make-believe play is an intrinsic part of normal growth. "It represents an effort to organize the (child's) available experience and at the same time utilize motor and cognitive capacities to their fullest" (Singer, 1973, p. 23). We have seen that it is associated with verbal fluency, waiting ability, increased concentration, positive affect, flexibility, originality, and imagination. Since it appears to be such a useful, creative skill, what can we do to encourage and foster it?

For one thing, children need privacy and time to themselves to think over and replay their experiences. It is difficult to make believe with the TV blasting or a mother constantly checking up on you. For another, they need an environment that is not too structured or well-ordered, so that they develop greater flexibility in using the materials at hand. I belong to a generation that used to play in the attic on rainy days, dressing up in old clothes and putting on all sorts of dramatic skits with appropriate sound effects. Children need a variety of interesting playthings which can be used in a number of different ways. I remember an old bathtub on legs which was used to represent anything from a pirate ship to the crater of a volcano.

Not only do children need time and opportunity and materials, they need wealth of content for their make-believe play. This generally comes from being read to or having stories told to them by an appreciative adult. There have been many beloved story-tellers throughout history from

Aesop to Uncle Remus. It may be that television is providing much of the material for children's fantasy play in this generation. I personally think TV time should be limited and kept under strong parental supervision, but in homes where parents do not read to their children it may be filling a much-needed gap. Singer feels strongly that television has had great impact upon the cognitive and fantasy development of poor children. Educated parents have always passed on legends, myths, fairy tales, and poems to their youngsters, but the children of working class people may not have been exposed to such a broad range of stimulation. "In this sense, then, television has tremendously widened the horizons of the poor and provided them with a great deal of material that can be used in the course of make-believe and indeed may even have stimulated greater tendencies toward make-believe play than might have been in evidence in the past" (Singer, 1973, p. 43). The same would apply to the culturally deprived children one sees these days even in families of comparative affluence.

Only time and research will tell us whether Singer is correct, but it certainly appears that children tend to play out in fantasy what they see on TV, particularly in an accepting environment. If parents and teachers enter into and encourage make-believe play instead of shaming or making fun of it, the child is much more likely to develop this skill. If not, the adult can help him, beginning even in infancy with make-believe games like "Patty-cake" or "This little piggy went to market." We have already discussed the importance of adults as models in make-believe games, charades, or role-playing. Richard deMille feels this is so important that he has written a book called *"Put Your Mother on the Ceiling"* (1967). It is written mainly for teachers, to help them develop their children's imagination through fantasy games. The teacher may start with having each child visualize his mother; then picture her in a red dress; then in the corner of the classroom and so on, until he has her floating up to the ceiling. This kind of teaching might be very effective with poor or culturally deprived children, and certainly could not hurt even imaginative youngsters from enriched backgrounds.

In closing, I would like to make a final plea that children be allowed to enjoy the magical world of childhood. In this age of too many things and not enough time, let us not push and drag and harass our children to accommodate to a world that many of us find increasingly unsatisfying. Let us give them time and privacy and respect, as they play out their fantasies and dream their daydreams and try to bring imagination and understanding and maybe even a little romance to this tired old world. We could all use it.

## References

deMille, R., *Put Your Mother on the Ceiling: Children's Imagination Games*, New York: Walker & Co., 1967.

El'Konin, D., "Symbolics and its function in the play of children," in R. Herron & B. Sutton-Smith (eds.) *Child's Play*, New York: Wiley, 1971.

Freud, S., "Creative Writers and Daydreaming," in J. Strachey (ed.) *The Standard Edition of the Complete Psychological Works of Sigmund Freud*, London: Hogarth, 1962, Vol. IX.

Garrison, Charlotte, *Permanent Play Materials for Young Children*, New York: Scribner, 1926.

Gross, R. & Gross, B., "Let the Child Teach Himself," *New York Times Magazine*, May 16, 1965, p. 34.

Herron, R. E. & Sutton-Smith, B., *Child's Play*, New York: Wiley, 1971.

Klinger, E. *Structure and Functions of Fantasy*, New York: Wiley, 1971.

Piaget, J. *Play, Dreams and Imitation in Childhood*, New York: Norton, 1962.

Pulaski, Mary Ann, *Understanding Piaget: An Introduction to Children's Cognitive Development*, New York: Harper & Row, 1971.

———, "Play as a Function of Toy Structure and Fantasy Predisposition," *Child Development*, 1970, 41, 531–537.

Singer, J. L., *Daydreaming: An Introduction to the Experimental Study of Inner Experience*, New York: Random House, 1966.

———, *The Child's World of Make-Believe: Experimental Studies of Imaginative Play*, New York: Academic Press, 1973.

Smilansky, S., *The Effects of Sociodramatic Play on Disadvantaged Preschool Children*, New York: Wiley, 1968.

# Play in Personality Development

LAWRENCE K. FRANK

This approach to personality development emphasizes the processes whereby the individual organism becomes a human being, learning to live in a social order and in a symbolic cultural world. Thereby we may observe the child from birth on, growing, developing and maturing, while engaged in establishing, maintaining, and transforming all his idiomatic relations with the world and with himself.

These processes of maturation and personality development involve several steps or phases which are never separate and distinct actually, but may be distinguished for purposes of discussion, always remembering that they are taking place in an intact functioning organism, more or less concomitantly and continuously, as he faces his life tasks (14).

## Learning to Delay Gratification

Thus we see the newborn infant, arriving with all the wisdom of the body derived from his mammalian ancestors, beginning to relate himself to the world initially through his basic organic needs and functional capacities. He carries on his unremitting intercourse with the environment by breathing, ingesting food, eliminating waste, sleeping, maintaining his internal environment in a dynamic, ever-changing equilibrium that is repeatedly disturbed by hunger, cold, shock and pain, deprivation of bodily tactual contacts (9). Adults expect, and may coerce him, if necessary, to transform these organic needs and functional capacities into goal-seeking, purposive conduct addressed to deferred or symbolic consummations, thereby establishing new ways of relating himself to the world by a reciprocal, circular process.

Thus hunger is transformed into appetite for specific kinds of food, in customary utensils at more or less scheduled feedings; elimination into regular evacuations at specific times and places; sleep into prescribed naps and bedtimes. The baby thereby surrenders some of his physiological autonomy and self-regulation, becoming increasingly responsive in his functional processes to the external world and its requirements as he transforms organic needs into purposive strivings. His eating is regulated, not by his changing blood-sugar level, but by family meals; his elimination is governed, not by pressures internally, but by the designated place and time; his sleep by parental schedules.

Thus the child is freed from coercion by his own organic needs and can increasingly replace early patterns by more mature patterns that enable him to cope with the world purposefully. At the same time he builds up his expectations of the world according to his experience of being cared for, protected, and loved. He develops confidence in the world insofar as his needs and expectations are fulfilled. With this confidence, or lack of confidence, he faces the demands and denials, the patterning of his living, and transformation of his needs. As his bodily integrity is respected, he develops an image of himself that reflects the world as a place to trust, or otherwise. In this transition from the organic to the cultural-social, the infant becomes a human being who will, under favorable treatment, eagerly seek to live in the world of adults in his own idiomatic way.

Since the infant's capacity for homeostasis is not yet well developed, his internal stabilization is only slowly established within these patterns imposed by adults and thereby is often warped or skewed in development. Within the first year of life, the infant may be compelled to relinquish his autonomous organic functioning and accept a regimen of living that may be imposed too early and may be often not suitable to his organism and idiomatic functional capacities.

In these transformations of organic needs and functionings, this relinquishing of organic autonomy to accept social patterning and regulations of his physiological functioning, we may observe the first steps in the process of maturation — a process of repeated relinquishing and supersedure of an earlier pattern of functioning or conduct, by another pattern more appropriate to the growing, developing, aging individual. This process offers one clue to the understanding of personality development as an ongoing process of maturation which may be stunted or distorted or prematurely overdeveloped.

**Functional Capacities**

One of the basic functional capacities of the infant is to react emotionally by accelerating, intensifying and augmenting his normal physiological processes, mobilizing his many reserves when provoked as a way of relating himself to painful or threatening situations. Since this capacity for emotional reaction is primitive and strong in most infants, he may be unable to relinquish such reactions, resisting the attempts of adults to pattern and transform them. If adults continually provoke such emotional reactions by their maltreatment or neglect of the infant, he may develop chronic affective responses (11).

Another basic functional capacity (and an organic need) is for close tactual bodily contacts which apparently all young mammals require and receive in licking, nuzzling, cuddling, caressing and petting, with close bodily contacts with the mother (23). It has been observed how caressing and even vigorously patting a baby soothes him when disturbed and apparently fosters all his physiological functioning.

Since the child must give up his close bodily contacts with the mother and learn to accept her voice as a surrogate for her touch, reluctance or inability to surrender this tactual relation may compromise his maturation. A persistent attachment to mother on this organic tactual level may hamper his going out into the world. He may fail to transform his relation to mother from an organic to a symbolic process which is essential if he is to meet the world with confidence in her continued, but absent, love and reassurance and if he is to seek adult tactual fulfillments later. The transformation of this tactual need and its satisfaction through successive surrogates seems to be crucial in the maturation of the personality, especially in adolescence.

If the infant is permitted to live fully and freely on this sensorimotor, functional level, then eating, eliminating, sleeping, tactual-cutaneous contacts will be experienced as necessary organic fulfillments which will later yield to the prescribed or expected transformations into goal-seeking, purposive conduct as suggested above. If these organic processes are denied or interfered with, they may be prematurely patterned and invested with emotional or affective significance. For example, eating may become, like elimination, a way of fighting mother or pleasing her, or sleep may be similarly disturbed. What should be a flexible functional process becomes prematurely "committed" and therefore less available for more mature transformation later. The infant needs to transform his native impulsive behavior into orderly, patterned conduct, observing the inviolability of things and persons and places. This calls for transformation of parental prohibitions into self-administered inhibitions. The child is expected to learn to say "no" and "don't" to himself and to refrain from prohibited actions. Likewise, the child is required to perform a variety of prescribed actions, such as cleanliness, grooming, manners, masculine or feminine conduct, and so on, renouncing his naive, impulsive behavior for these socially required patterns. Here again we see how the child is expected to relinquish his direct relations with the world of actual things and events and learn to live in a world defined by parents in terms of what he may, may not, must and must not do, in all the varied activities of living. He must learn to do this autonomously when not under adult supervision, guided by some idea or concept, however rudimentary. These lessons are basic patterns of social order, involving respect for private property and for the integrity of the person of others, social inventions of far-reaching significance for social order and interpersonal relations. The child concomitantly alters his perception of the world and his conduct responsive to that altered perception which requires both inhibition and performance according to the prescriptions of social order, especially the masculine or feminine role.

In these experiences the child begins to learn language, first responding to verbal directions and later learning to speak (26). He then learns that every thing and every person has a name and a meaning which he practices repeatedly and he begins to ask questions and to make assertions. Here we see another example of how a basic physiological function of breathing is transformed into a socialized, symbolic practice of speaking for communication which later becomes established in inner speech, fantasy and thinking. Moreover, we see the child beginning to accept words as surrogates for actuality and especially for the close tactual contacts he has previously sought: the child begins to accept mother's voice, often at a distance, as equivalent for her physical caresses or her physical punishments.

These are steps in the child's introduction to the symbolic cultural world of meanings, values, and deferred or symbolic consummations in which adults live and carry on their life careers. The child learns, or is deliberately taught by adults, the various concepts by which the flux of experience is made more or less stable (12), orderly, and meaningful and by which the child's conduct will be increasingly guided as he relinquishes his naive relations to the world of actuality and learns to relate himself to this conceptual world according to various beliefs and expectations he shares with others. Here again we have largely neglected this process of conceptualization in personality development on the theory that thinking and reasoning are governed primarily by wish fulfillment, pleasure seeking, etc., and so can be largely ignored, while focusing upon impulses, emotional reactions and striving for fulfillment of desires. But it seems clear that through conceptualization, the child patterns his perceptions, guides his conduct, and alters his emotional reactions as he learns to live and relate himself to our cultural world. Moreover, the confusions and conflicts he may engender in his early conceptual framework may persist as he assimilates whatever he learns into these preconceptions, thereby patterning his conduct and relations.

## Transactional Relationship

In this approach we may observe how the infant or child utilizes a variety of modes of functioning — bodily contacts, eating, eliminating, sleeping, emotional reactions, all his sensorimotor capacities for his initial relations with the world. As his development brings increasing capacities and new demands and opportunities, he progressively replaces these organic patterns with a variety of uniquely human patterns. Thus he builds up a selective awareness, patterned perceptions, and the purposive, goal-seeking conduct which the world, as it is uniquely perceived by him, makes necessary and appropriate for him. Speech, cognition, focused affective responses, and motor activities are learned patterns for these relations, which are essentially circular, reciprocal transactions. This means that the child's activities are to be viewed as neither exclusively governed by internal events or needs, processes, or self-acting impulses, instincts, etc., nor controlled by external stimuli, causes, or other concepts of reaction or interaction. Rather we are confronted with a circular process as the way the child sees, hears, touches, thinks and fantasies and feels the world according to its meaning. He is then responsive to that self-created life space, his "private world," in his idiomatic personal ways.

Each child, it seems evident, builds up his own private frame of reference, his idiomatic ideas and concepts, more or less consonant with the consensual public world of others (that we call reality), but often warped, distorted, and always infused with emotional reactions and chronic persistent affective responses as his idiosyncratic relation to that life space (8). Thus we may view the child as learning to live overtly in this adult consensual world but maintaining his own private world of meanings and values, of feelings and emotional reactions which he increasingly guards from others.

Since these various steps and stages, here very briefly and inadequately described, involve many denials, deprivations, frustrations, and coercions, the child learns every lesson and each new way of relating himself, with emotional coloring or affective response that he experienced during his initial learning. That is to say, how he reacted to adults and others initially as a functioning organism when relinquishing and transforming these patterns (as we have earlier described) may become an established mode or reaction so that he perceives the world in terms not only of the ideas and conduct he is expected to exhibit, but with the emotional provocations and affective meanings which they now present to him as he perceives them.

Thus we should emphasize that in the process of personality development, the child matures by continually altering his awareness of the world, continually patterning his perception of people and situations according to their changing meanings and significance for him.

This conception of the process of personality development should be recognized as essentially a transactional process (1,3) as distinguished from self-action (animism, demonology, instincts, or libido); from reaction (cause and effect, or stimulus and response, acting upon inert bodies); from interaction (billiard-ball or other inert-particle collisions). In the transactional process, the organism-personality selectively invests or imputes meanings to the world, while actively seeking or creating the situations in which he can function, finding thereby occasions for fulfillment of his transformed organic functional requirements. Thus the child is not inert, waiting to be motivated or driven by some internal force or impulse, or external cause or instinct. He is active, and increasingly he learns to prepare for and seek occasions for eating, for evoking elimination, for sleep, and his ever changing relations with people. He soon advances beyond the purely infantile dependence of accepting or rejecting what is offered, learns to act toward the world according to what he idiomatically perceives, interprets, and then feels and acts toward events and people.

The child learns to maintain a precarious equilibrium between himself and the public consensual world where in order to be accepted and to pursue his purposes, he must conform to some extent while guarding and maintaining, often at an excessive psychological cost, his own idiosyncratic private world. It seems clear that the early discovery of the not-me is of a highly idiomatic not-me (my mother, my bottle, my crib), and then only slowly and often reluctantly does he relinquish this private not-me to recognize and accept the consensual public world of not-me. Moreover, the kind of consensual public world he learns to recognize and deal with, including adults' treatment of himself, is the reciprocal of his image of the self; with every alteration in his awareness, perception, affective response, concepts and skills for relating himself to that world and to people, he revises his image of the self and often the emotional and affective coloring of his private world.

Indeed, we may say that the young child's eager explorations of the world, especially when he walks and manipulates things purposefully, serve to discover himself, establishing a new image of himself. Then he revises it as he learns to relate himself in new ways and patterns and evokes new relations of people with him. Once a child begins to invest situations and people with meanings, to impute affective significance to the world, he can "make-believe," pretend, fantasy almost anything. His relations to the world will be governed by these idiomatic beliefs and feelings unless and until he replaces them.

Some children may have difficulty in relinquishing their direct, primary, sensorimotor relations with the world (16, 21); others may not be able to replace their highly idiomatic not-me with the prescribed social-cultural norms (reality), and try to live with two competing or alternating sets of ideas and concepts (22). Some children may negotiate these transitions effectively except for one specific area or aspect, of their relationships with the world. Indeed, we might say that a child's neurosis is his personal, idiomatic version of a culture or social pattern which, not being sufficiently general to permit socially patterned relations, requires ever-increasing effort to defend and maintain. The "repetitive core of the neurosis," to use Lawrence Kubie's phrase, may be viewed as this strongly fixated, idiomatic relation with the world arising from the patterned perception, activity, and feeling which the child has not been able to relinquish for a more mature relation, involving a concomitant, reciprocal transformation of the world and of himself.

This continuous, never ending process of relating himself transactionally to the world embraces all his basic physiological functions and sensory processes, his awareness, perception, cognition, motor activity, emotional reactions and affective responses, his interpersonal and group relations and social conduct. By viewing the organism — personality as engaged in these varied and ever-changing relations, we can begin to unify our conception of human development and replace many now anachronistic assumptions and obsolete conceptions (especially the still static ideas often disguised by "dynamic" terminology) with genuinely dynamic conceptions of circular transactional processes more congruous with the emerging new climate of opinion.

## Origins of Normal and Abnormal Personalities

Accordingly, it is suggested that we recognize that the same basic processes, operating in different children, at different times and in different situations and relations, may produce very different products, as revealed in the variety of personalities. Likewise, different processes may produce equivalent products. This conception definitely rejects the idea of unvarying cause and effect, multiple causation and their variants as applicable to the study of identified human personalities. It also renounces the belief in various instincts, impulses, emotions, motives, wishes and desires, whereby we retain the older idea of self-action (an animistic survival) when concerned with the problems of human personality development in a social-cultural world. We can fruitfully utilize the conception of transactional process in a field and see the child at play engaged in dynamic, circular, reciprocal relationships wherein he learns to live in the social-cultural world, to face "reality" (the consensual world of our social-cultural traditions and patterns), develop "object relations" (7), but always as idiomatic creations of greater or less congruity with the prescribed norms of our social order. We may then view personality as this highly individualized way of carrying on these idiomatically patterned processes through which each person continually maintains his life space, guards his private world while participating more or less adequately in maintaining our social life. The neurotic and psychotic may be regarded then as products of the same process which, under more favorable conditions, may produce the healthy personality. In this way, we may begin to formulate a generalized theory of personality not exclusively concerned with the psychopathological.* Likewise, we may be able to translate the idea of the organism-personality "as a whole" into more than a verbal assertion by discovering how the organism-personality functions, not by separate, isolated parts or forces or self-acting entities, but by continually relating himself internally and overtly, by the variety of processes, capacities, skills, techniques, and patterns of which the human is capable (11). These dynamic relations and their transformations provide the understanding we seek of how the individual exists and continually functions as an organism all through his life but becomes a human personality who engages in purposive striving as he seeks the goals and symbolic fulfillments in and through which his organic capacities have been transformed for human conduct and social living.

We may in this way recognize that many neurotic persons are, as so often asserted, engaged in a constant search for tension reduction, but that the healthy maturing personality enjoys and seeks the building up of tensions, the deliberate deferment of gratifications or consummations, the postponement of a climax and the acceptance of symbolic, deferred fulfillments since that is the uniquely human way of life as contrasted with sheer organic existence which is apparently a search for immediate consummation and tension reduction. Thus we can recognize the

*For many years medicine was based upon pathology and only within more recent decades, through physiology, endocrinology, and related disciplines, has been able to develop a more generalized and inclusive theory of organic functioning which may produce pathology but can also provide healthy functioning and reveal the strengths and potentialities of the organism which the physician can invoke for the patient's recovery from illness.

immense variety of signs, signals, and symbols which the human personality accepts as surrogates for actuality and learns to deal with purposefully. We also can recognize that the human personality utilizes ideas, concepts, and beliefs as his way of ordering and equalizing or stabilizing (12) the ever-changing events of the world and enabling him to relate himself productively (*e.g.*, tools and technology) and aesthetically.

Likewise, we may better understand that the neurotic and psychotic reveal the many hazards of human living, the costs of maintaining a cultural world which imposes such difficult conceptual confusions upon growing individuals who may utilize ideas and concepts as defenses and escapes which others use as instrumentalities for living.

## Functions of Play

When we approach play with this orientation and regard the child's play as his way of exploring and experimenting, while he builds up or establishes his idiomatic relations with the world and himself, we may note some significant aspects or phases of play that merit further study. We might say that in play the child is learning to learn: he is discovering how he can come to terms with the world, cope with life tasks, master various skills, techniques and symbolic processes in his way; then, having gained confidence in himself and his capacity to relate himself to the world, as he sees and feels it, he is ready to learn other tasks and accept less congenial patterns.

We may observe play as revealing the process of personality development whereby the child learns and repeatedly rehearses these varied transformations by exploring, manipulating, utilizing objects, animals, people, events as occasions for creating his own life space while increasingly capable of living in the consensual world. All play is creative even if it becomes stunted, warped, distorted, because the child is actively constituting his individualized, more or less unique, life space by imposing forms, meaning, significance upon situations, and relating himself to those self-imposed meanings in his idiosyncratic way. Slowly, and often reluctantly, but also often eagerly, the child strives to master the perplexities, the confusions and conflicts and the skills for living in the grown-up world. In his play he assumes or takes an ever-changing array of roles, especially the masculine or feminine role, as offering access to and practice in the adult world, abandoning and rejecting them freely since he is not yet committed to any one as a child.

Perhaps we think of the child's activities as play because we realize that he is still more or less tentative and uncommitted, still capable of exploration and revision, of renouncing and replacing, of manipulating objects, events, people with less restriction than the adult who may have only a limited area of free play and less uncommitted potentialities for new patterns and relations.

## Growth Through Play

The child in his play relates himself to his accumulating past by continually reorienting himself to the present through play: He rehearses his past experiences, assimilating them into new perceptions and patterns of relating himself and by this process he advances into the future, repeatedly revising his time perspective so long as his past can be freely reorganized. When any of his early experiences resist this reorganization as too painful or difficult to manage or recall, their emotional affective concomitants may persist as increasingly incongruous and so compromise his capacity for maturation.

It may be said that adult living is largely play, but we no longer recognize it as such since the adult has largely ceased to reorganize his past and is "committed" to the more or less specific and often rigidly patterned "make-believe" fantasies and symbolic goals of his social-cultural group, unable to play other games freely, or take on new roles as the child does. Adult leisure time and recreational pursuits often provide more or less conventionalized roles in which adults can "escape" from their usual patterns and customary expectations of the inevitable, as in gambling.

Thus, in the changing play of the child we may observe the persistence of early patterns while he explores for and learns the new pattern which will replace the earlier one as he strives to mature. He may exhibit much repetition, endlessly varying and elaborating or suddenly appearing in a new role and relationship to the world. If we remember that this involves the concomitant alteration of the child and of his environment as he perceives it and is responsive to what he perceives, we will see that this circular process of development and maturation may be initiated internally or externally, sometimes the developing child reaching or striving for a new relationship, sometimes the world evoking what was ready to emerge.

In this way the child is continually discovering himself anew, revising his image of himself as he can and must, with each alteration in his relations with the world. Likewise, in his play the child attempts to resolve his problems and conflicts, manipulating play materials and often adult materials as he tries to work through or play out his perplexities and confusions. While he soon learns to guard his speech and resort to unvoiced speech for verbal manipulations and fantasies (25), he will usually naively expose these otherwise concealed feelings and beliefs in play, unless, as Erik Erikson (4,5,6) suggested earlier, his play is interrupted by his inability to cope with these crises in his private world. If he had a fairly stable and dependable relation with adults, especially parents, he freely passes back and forth between play fantasy and the actual world, taking roles (2) and playing parts — truck driver, policeman, fireman, soldier, outlaw, without relinquishing his role as mother's and father's boy while he explores these various possibilities. So long as he can enjoy the full potentialities of his prolonged infancy as a human child, retain this flexibility and plasticity, engage fully in living at each stage of his maturation, he can take roles and develop his varied capacities, live spontaneously and, with little or no difficulty, renounce what has been the very acme of childish delight as he accepts new roles, learns new patterns and new relations, with a revised image of himself.

In his play we may observe various *themes* (5) or *schemas* (21) in which his immediate concerns are focused and more or less symbolically played out. The degree to which he can utilize symbols reveals his increasing capacity for transforming his infantile organic needs and direct primary sensorimotor relations to the patterns of our adult world, using ideas and concepts and symbols for transforming his functions and establishing new relations to the increasingly orderly, meaningful world he is learning to perceive and respond to. This calls for the capacity to sustain, build up, and defer the release of tensions which are essentially enhanced or augmented physiological functional responses to events. The child uses his own symbolic play for communicating with himself, especially the self of his early primary sensorimotor experiences that he must progressively renounce to live in the adult world. Often, as Margaret Lowenfeld has shown, in his play world he reveals this "forgotten self" and re-establishes communication, as artists and poets often do, with his "primary processes" (17).

## Play and Symbolism

It seems clear that in observing children's play we must recognize "equivalent stimuli." As Heinrich Kluver (15) has pointed out, learning to live in a symbolic world of meanings, symbols, and goal values involves the capacity to accept equivalents (surrogates) of widely varying dimensions and divergence from the actual world and cultural norms, but having equivalent meaning for the individual. Moreover, in all human learning, there appears to be a process of attenuation of the symbol which becomes increasingly minimal or abstract or nonrepresentative, merging into a variety of surrogates which the human personality can invest with the full meaning that was originally learned from actuality. At the same time these symbols may evoke a variety of relations that have similar purposes.

It may be useful here to think of play as a figurative language, recognizing that the child's play reveals equivalents of almost all our familiar figures of speech — metaphor, analogy, metonymy, hyperbole, synecdoche, onomatopeia, and so on. And it is also to be noted that children's spontaneous play is usually accompanied by verbalizations of more or less appropriate words and especially the special sounds that accompany the play activity; for example, *choo-choo*. These vocalizations apparently reinforce the child's imputation of meanings to play materials and situations as if the sound effects helped to create the context for transforming play materials into their play roles.

By the sounds he makes, he may increase his mastery of situations: voicing the noise, the loud bangs, the piercing screeches, the repetitive sounds of terrifying objects. He learns to face these with increasing self-confidence as he plays out his relations to the adult world. Here we see the process whereby the child accepts the not-me world of actuality, by learning to relate himself to that world through various modes of activity and response which he develops as his idiomatic way of putting order and meaning into the actual world and dealing with those meanings as his way of stabilizing and equalizing the flux of experiences.

There is, of course, endless play with sounds and words, again with continual rejection of earlier patterns for more mature words and enunciations, just as there are endless motor activities from birth on (18), continual play with the body, with the accessible objects and persons (mother's face, breast, and hands), which gradually become patterned, oriented, and ever more effectively established relations with the world. In all these experiences the child utilizes whatever may be available as materials for his play as one pole or focus of this circular reciprocal transactional process in which he is both agent and respondent.

## Analogical and Digital Processes

Children's play likewise exhibits both analogical and digital processes, as the child copes with problems and conflicts analogically and also learns later to deal with events digitally. For example, the child manipulates words, sounds, playthings, as he endeavors to work out and resolve a perplexing or confusing problem. His resolution of that problem is not a neat, precise, or quantitative answer or mastery of the situation actually. Like using a slide rule, he approximates the answers and develops a pattern for dealing with such situations that can be utilized more generally. At the same time he may face a task in playing where he must advance, step by step, adding, subtracting, digitally, like an adding machine which gives an exact answer to a very special problem and a method of more limited application.

Language and artistic creations are analogical while arithmetic and logic are digital processes which quite early in life may be preferentially utilized by a child, with apparently an increasing bias toward the analogical on the part of those whose bisexuality is toward the female-feminine end of that gamut and whose developing relations to the world are thereby oriented and patterned.

## Adult Participation and Acceptance

As we observe children's play, we may note two alternating phases — those play activities of an imaginative dramatic character in which they use available objects, blocks, chairs, or play toys as instruments in the play schema in which they solicit, even demand, adult participation: they want the adult to enter in and take part in their play drama as if finding enhanced meaning and fulfillment because the adult gives additional meaning to their play performance. Then, alternately, they will attempt to rehearse what adults do, transforming available materials into make-believe autos, gas stations, tools, various utensils, etc. But in "pretending" or rehearsing make-believe adult activities and use of tools, etc., the child seeks to live in the adult world for a time, withdrawing whenever he gets weary, bored, or frustrated by its refractoriness or difficult requirements.

The adult's participation, his sharing in the make-believe, reassures the child that his play is valid and meaningful, gives him strength to cope with it, shows him that he has adult approval to go on striving for mastery of that play situation. Adults communicate more effectively than through language by their participation in the child's play, sharing or encouraging the childish and fumbling manipulations and intense concern with the symbolic or analogical significance of the play activity. This also occurs when the adult reads or tells a story, sharing a fantasy with the child, reassuring and protecting the child as he confronts difficulties and dangers, feeling strengthened by the adult participation.

Adult acceptance of a child's fantasy may thus help him to relinquish his idiomatic private ideas and expectations for the more actual adult concepts and practices; without this adult approval, he may cling to and vigorously defend his infantile ideas and by so much refuse or fail to mature. Apparently imaginary playmates continue longer when the child does not share them (except perhaps twins). Thinking of the child's eagerness to live in the adult world, to follow their patterns and share their ways, may give more understanding than the customary interpretation of this as identification which seems to occur when the child feels he is not accepted or his childish play is not approved and so he must try to be, not himself but what his parents demand or expect or hopefully will admire.

### Individuality vs. Conformity

In a somewhat similar way, we may recognize how the child alternates between his idiomatic individualized perception and patterned activity, playing out his fantasy and feelings and his slowly learned relations, and then exhibiting, sometimes reluctantly, a conformity to adult social prescriptions which he finds he must increasingly utilize in order to communicate, negotiate, attain his goals and fulfill his purposes. In play activities, especially creative and dramatic play, a child may find and productively utilize the possibilities for idiomatic expression, thus maintaining one area in which he can be an individual, can channel some of his functional capacities into personally fulfilling experiences while exhibiting the prescribed norms of performance demanded by social life. These areas of free play may be of crucial significance insofar as they offer avenues or fields of expressing emotional reactions and affective responses in more mature patterns as he gives up the naive outbursts of anger and rage, of direct aggressive or retaliatory action toward others. He finds in words, in gestures, in dramatic play, in manipulation of plastic and graphic material, etc., increasingly more mature expressions of his emotional reactions without having to repress these or become anesthetic (20). Since these are difficult transitions, the child may require prolonged play experiences under understanding, but not necessarily interpreting, adults in order to attain these more mature patterns.

Early in life, each child with his unique capacities and requirements begins to develop his idiomatic way of coping with the life tasks as they appear to him. While he may successively revise, alter, and replace his earlier patterns with new ones, these will continue to be idiomatic equivalents of what he has relinquished. Thus we can observe persistence with change, continuity of the identifiable personality through successive transformations, as the child tries to mature while maintaining his individuality. This process, especially the difficulties, conflicts, confusions, and triumphs the child experiences, is revealed in his play, especially his spontaneous play when he does not feel observed and is not interrupted or unduly restricted.

Sometimes a child who is outwardly apathetic or seemingly withdrawn may, in a congenial and encouraging play situation, emerge with increasingly spontaneous participation, as if waiting for such a favorable opportunity to escape from his own self-imposed restriction. Similarly, an aggressive, destructive child in a play situation offering little opportunity or provocation may discover new ways of relating himself to others through more cooperative play. Children, and especially those "withdrawn" and those over-aggressive, may need to translate their private world and feelings into play situations, to make these more or less "objective," outside themselves, so they can deal with them, begin to alter and revise them toward the patterns of the consensual world.

## Rite of Passage

Sometimes a child's play serves as a sort of ritual with its own internal order and symbolic performance as he strives to establish a difficult, new relation with the world involving more conception of time, rhythm and cycles, and space and their implications, antecedents, and consequences, etc. (13), as well as those involving personal relations, sharing, taking turns, giving as well as taking, cooperating in a group activity. In these ways we may see how difficult it is for the child to renounce his direct, primary sensorimotor relations to the world (16, 17) and replace them with conceptually patterned conduct and the reciprocal circular process of social-cultural living. In these transitions the child reveals his essential unity as an organism-personality and his versatility, as he often tries his total repertory of response-relations, organic, emotional and motor, verbal, conceptual, and symbolic, gradually learning, if not stunted or blocked, to attain a more or less coherent, congruent set of patterns for these enlarging response-relations as he develops and matures. Children need order and boundaries, clearly stated but appropriately timed and formulated definitions of the world, with which to build up their private worlds and accept our conceptions and patterns of conduct, with permission to react emotionally while they gradually achieve more stable relations with the world which does not involve these acute disturbances.

## Uniquely Human Aspects of Play

Play, while observable in many very young organisms and in older members of the primate group, is almost uniquely human, expressive of man's possession of the largest "uncommitted" portions of the nervous system and brain and the long infancy and prolonged adolescence of man, all of which make possible his capacity for living in a symbolic world wherein he can strive for the essentially human goal values that give human living its unique significance. For generations children have grown, developed, matured, playing their way to adult living, interrupted, diverted, and channeled by various kinds of educational procedures. Today as the "unseen hand" of cultural traditions becomes less coercive and less directive, we must recognize in play the possibilities for providing intentionally planned opportunities for children to learn how to live in a social order and a cultural world (13), which they can and must renew and reorient in the light of the new understandings and the new insights we are developing for meeting the persistent tasks of life, for fostering the healthy personalities who alone can undertake such a tremendous labor (10).

One clue we may find to this problem is in recognizing and respecting the integrity of the individual child as a unique organism and potential personality who must find his way to maturity, at his own rate of progress, with his individualized capacities and limitations. Respecting and cherishing the dignity of the child from birth on so that we do not invade his integrity by neglect or coercion, we may through adequate provision for play give him what will enable him to mature and face life with courage, confidence in himself and the adequacy he can develop for participating in social order. Above all, through this kind of play activity we can help him to develop an image of himself that is congruous with the expectation and the responsibilities of a free social order in which each member must learn to bear the burdens of freedom and to live as an autonomous personality in a world of shared goal values. This kind of child-rearing and education calls for a profound faith in human nature and its potentialities (19) and the ability to recognize the unique organism-personality, striving to find his way in a perplexing world.

## References

1. Cantril, H., Ames, A., Hastorf, A. H., and Ittelson, W. H., "Psychology and Research," *Science*, 110; 461, 517, 1949.
2. Coutu, Walter, "Role Playing vs. Role Taking: An Appeal for Clarification," *American Sociology Review*, 16: 188–197, 1951.
3. Dewey, John and Bentley, Arthur, *Knowing and the Known*, Boston; Beacon Press, 1949.
4. Erikson, Erik, *Configurations in Play*. Psychiatric Quarterly, 6: 2, 1937.
5. ———, *Studies in Interpretation of Play*. Genetic Psychology Monographs, 22: 557–671, 1940.
6. ———, *Childhood and Society*, New York: Norton, 1950.
7. Fairbairn, W. Ronald, *Psychoanalytic Studies of the Personality*, London: Tavistock Publications, 1952.
8. Frank, Lawrence K., *Projective Methods*, Springfield, Ill.: Charles C. Thomas, 1948.
9. ———, Genetic Psychology and its Prospects, *American Journal of Orthopsychiatry*, 21: 506–522, 1951.
10. ———, *Nature and Human Nature: Man's New Image of Himself*, New Brunswick, N. J.: Rutgers University Press 1951.
11. ———, *Feelings and Emotions*, New York: Doubleday, 1954.
12. Goldstein, Kurt, *The Organism: A Holistic Approach to Biology*, New York: American Book Co., 1939.
13. Hartley, Ruth, Frank, L. K., and Goldenson, R., *Understanding Children's Play*, New York: Columbia University Press, 1952; also *New Play Experiences for Children* (pamphlet); *Growing Through Play* (pamphlet).
14. Havighurst, Robert J., *Developmental Tasks and Education*, Chicago: University of Chicago Press, 1948.
15. Kluver, Heinrich, "The Study of Personality and the Methods of Equivalent and Non-equivalent Stimuli," *Character and Personality*, 5: 91–112, 1936.
16. Lowenfeld, Margaret, *Play in Childhood*, London: Gollancz, 1935.
17. ———, World Pictures of Children, *British Journal of Medical Psychology*, 18: 65–101, 1939.
18. Mittelmann, Bela, "Psychodynamics of Motility," in *The Psychoanalytic Study of the Child*, Vol. IX. New York: International Universities Press, 1954.
19. Murphy, Gardner, "Human Potentialities." Journal of Social Issues, Suppl. Series No. 7, 4–19, 1953.
20. Peller, Lili, Models of Children's Play, *Ment. Hyg.*, 36: 66–89, 1953.
21. Piaget, Jean, *Play, Dreams and Imitation in Childhood*, New York: Norton, 1951.
22. Powdermaker, Florence, "Concepts Found Useful in Treatment of Schizoid and Ambulatory Schizophrenic Patients." *Psychiatry*, 15: 1, Feb. 1952.
23. Reyniers, J. A., "Germ-Free Life Studies," *Lobind Reports*, No. 1, 1948, and No. 2, 1949.
24. Schachtel, Ernest, "Dynamic Perception and the Symbolism of Form," *Psychiatry*, 4: 1, 79–96, Feb. 1941.
25. Vigotsky, L. S., "Thought and Speech." *Psychiatry*, 2: 1, 29–54, Feb. 1939.
26. Werner, Heinz and Caplan, Edith, "The Acquisition of Word Meanings: A Developmental Study," *Child Development Monograph* XV, Series No. 51, No. 1, 1950.

# Development Through Play

LINDA FLOREY

It is time to take out of hiding and present for reconsideration an important component of occupational therapy in pediatrics — the role of "playlady." For those of you who may not be familiar with this role, the occupational therapist, with little space and hardly any budget, purchased a large cart and filled it with all kinds of play materials. She used to make her rounds on the pediatric wards stopping by each bed, talking with each child, and attempting to find something that he might be interested in playing or making. Sometimes she pushed beds together so children could play checkers or showed them how to make pencil holders out of orange juice cans decorated with macaroni, and sometimes she just talked with them. The occupational therapist as playlady was a very significant person to the children but not a very important person on the medical team. The observation that Johnny and Jimmy had finally come to some agreement on the relative merits of diagonal and triple jumps and had managed to complete a whole game of checkers was not a valued piece of information. It was felt that the daily play of hospitalized children was not of sufficient concern to merit the attention of trained professionals. Anyone could provide for the play of children, and today we permit anyone and everyone to plan for the daily play of handicapped and hospitalized children.

This paper proposes that play become a legitimate area of concern and study in occupational therapy. It proposes that theories of intrinsic motivation provide a relevant frame of reference for the study of play itself and for a classification of play development.

## The Play Phenomenon

Play is one of the most commonplace of childhood phenomena, yet it is singularly difficult to define, describe, and delimit. As Slobin says, "when we examine a set of behaviors as outstanding as that of play, we find ourselves face-to-face with hundreds of years of attempts to understand human behavior."[1] What is known about play is found in the theories of play, theories of personality, theories of cognition and derives from such fields as philosophy, psychology, medicine, sociology, anthropology, and education.[2] It is known that play is a biological, psychological, and sociocultural phenomenon. It can facilitate development in a number of areas and can also reflect a level of development in these areas. To select any one approach to play necessitates some exclusion of other valuable inputs to our understanding, and to some extent it is a little like trying to describe a cake by its eggs alone. However, the quantity and variance in what is written about play require delimitation.

Theories of intrinsic motivation as the basis for the study of play have been selected. In a classification of play theories Slobin terms this approach a life-space orientation. By this he means that the focus of explanation is directed primarily to the person's interaction with objects and people in his world and the role of play in determining these.[1] This approach does not focus directly on a biological or sociocultural explanation, nor does it focus on psychoanalytic explanations of play.

## Intrinsic Motivation

The terms *intrinsic motivation* or *theories of intrinsic motivation* refer more to a position taken by a number of theorists than to any one theory. Broadly stated, an intrinsic motive refers to factors which are relatively independent of tissue need (hunger) and external agents with specific beneficent or noxious effects (pain).[3] Bruner defines a key property of these motives:

> An intrinsic motive is one that does not depend on reward that lies outside the activity it impels. Reward inheres in the successful termination of that activity or even in the activity itself.[4]

The theories of intrinsic motivation present important and necessary alternatives to ways of thinking about a number of behaviors with which the occupational therapist, for one, has always been concerned. These behaviors include visual exploration, grasping, crawling and walking, attention and perception, language and thinking, exploring novel objects and places, manipulating the surroundings, and producing effective changes in the environment. The theories address themselves to the motivation of such behaviors; they challenge the position that all of behavior, and these behaviors in particular, can be attributed to such drives as hunger, thirst, sex, the libido instinct, to the states of anxiety or fear, or as a consequence of secondary reinforcement.[5] [6] These behaviors are best conceptualized in a different way. The terminology used is different from author to author, and the strategies used in explication also are different. The theories include such proposals as Montgomery's exploration motive, Butler's visual exploration motive, Harlow's manipulation motive, Berlyne's curiosity motive, Hunt's motivation inherent in information processing, McClelland's achievement motive, and White's effectance energy.[5] [7]

The proponents of these models are not attempting to explain behaviors in the service of such forces as hunger, thirst, sex, fear, or aggression. They are attempting to explain behaviors that are ignored or inadequately conceptualized by orthodox drive or instinct positions.[5] As a consequence, they call attention to, and make important, considerations for the promotion of these behaviors. These theories have had great impact on theories of personality development, and methods of teaching.[4] [8] For the occupational therapist, they have tremendous implications for the way in which we view the play of the child.

## Play and Intrinsic Motivation

The play of the child is a behavioral manifestation of intrinsic motivation, and it becomes a critical arena for the development of competence.[5] [8] Robert White puts it in this way:

> . . . the many hours that infants and children spend in play are by no means wasted or merely recuperative in nature. Play may be fun, but it is also serious business in childhood. During these hours the child steadily builds up his competence in dealing with the environment.[8]

White has a great deal to say about the nature of play and how we might nurture it throughout development.[5] [8] [9] [10] These views are distilled into four main principles and these principles are related to clinical practice.

### Play as Learning.

Play can best be thought of as a learning process. Play is spare-time behavior that is selective, directed, persistent, and self-rewarding.[5] [10] It supports the everyday learning about people and objects in the environment and one's relationship to them. In referring to play, White states "it is one of the child's principal ways of finding out what effects he can have on his environment and what effects it is likely to have on him. Only by putting forth many and varied actions and by learning from the consequences can he become competently adapted to his world."[10] What the child learns in the course of his interactions contributes to his repertoire of skills and to his sense of competence or the degree to which he feels he can influence his human and nonhuman environment.

In the treatment of children, occupational therapists have traditionally used play activities to facilitate the child's acquisition of sensorimotor, perceptual-motor, and interpersonal skills.[11] But we somehow act as if the only important learning of these skills is accomplished in one-half-hour sessions in the occupational therapy clinic, or in the mother's direction of a home program. Play is spare-time learning that happens every day, day after day. This view of play requires that we stop thinking about the learning through play as if it occurred in one-half-hour blocks of time.

*Play as Action.*

Play involves feeling about, perceiving, thinking about, and acting on human and nonhuman objects. The action dimension in play is selected for the purpose of making an operational definition. This definition is serviceable when looking at a number of studies done on play development. These studies reflect qualitative changes in the actions children take at different ages.[12] Although these actions may or may not include what the mother or the playground leader encourages or how toy manufacturers intend that a toy be used, they are important to the child and deserve our respect.

*The Nurture of Play.*

There are certain kinds of environmental conditions that facilitate the play of the child and others that inhibit it. Some of the conditions inhibiting play are stresses such as hunger and anxiety and the association of play with isolation, fear, or pain. Conditions facilitating play are stimuli such as novelty and related variables, opportunities for exploration, repetition, and imitation of competent role models.[9] Occupational therapists might think of providing good play models as well as models for sportsmanship and craftsmanship. These conditions provide some specifications for examining the state of the play milieu.

Many homes, hospitals, and institutions devoted to the care of children are conspicuously lacking in their provision for and encouragement of play. In some hospitals a day room passes for a playroom and a television placed close to the ceiling is the only toy for a child. The importance of play and its significance for the growth of competence require that steps be taken to protect and nurture play throughout development.

*Constitutional Inhibition of Play.*

Constitutional factors may affect the degree to which a child is able to experience feelings of satisfaction as a result of his active efforts. According to White, "this could be the case if activity level were low and effort uncomfortable, or if coordination were poor so that the effects produced on the environment were not regular and repeatable."[9] To a great extent, White is describing our total patient population. The dysfunction that occupational therapists identify in their population has a pervasive effect on the child's performance in many situations. A child with a reading disability may also have a "playground disability" or a "cub scout disability." Sometimes a child manages to compensate for his deficits in awkward or unusual ways; however, these may represent his only way of achieving competence in such a situation.

Although the selected principles require that occupational therapists readjust or reaffirm their commitment to the play of children, at the same time these principles enrich our understanding and can enrich the quality of care provided to handicapped children.

## Development in Play

Many authors have carefully described both quantitative and qualitative changes in children's play at different ages or stages in development. G. Stanley Hall was the first to propose stages of play. The stages obtain from his recapitulation theory of play in which it is believed that the child goes through the phases of civilization in an effort to rid himself of primitive instincts. The stages correspond to the cultural stages in the development of races (animal, savage, nomad, agricultural, and tribal life stages).[2] This classification does recognize changes in play throughout development, but is neither valid nor relevant today.

Studies of development in play include a number of different approaches to the problem [13] [14] [15] [16] [17] [18] [19] [20]. Palmer, Markey, Hartley, *et al.*, divide play into a number of different behaviors and study changes in these behaviors at different ages. These include changes in sensory, movement, manual dramatic, and language behaviors, changes in water play, imaginative play, and the use of blocks, clay, and finger paint. Guanella and Jones describe different stages in children's use of such selected play materials as wheeled objects and blocks. Gesell's classification of developmental changes in children's play derives from a standardized observation of what children 15–60 months do with people and a specified set of objects. Hartley and Goldenson point to salient characteristics of play during each year, from birth to teen-age. A major contribution to understanding development in play is found in the work of Piaget. The specific content of play derives from the mental structure of the organism, and thus Piaget believes that play can only be classified according to the degree of mental complexity presented by each game. He identifies three distinct stages in play: practice games (2 months–2 years), symbolic games (2 years–7 years), games with rules (7 years–11 years).

## Classification of Play Development

Although the terminology and purposes of study are slightly different from author to author, the studies do describe the ways in which children deal with their environment at different ages. To tease out this information, a classification scheme was designed to select and order the content of the development studies.[12] The classification is here presented in two charts (Charts A and B). This scheme is based upon the definition of play as action on human and nonhuman objects. The objects of action (human and nonhuman) formed the two major categories. These categories were further divided in accordance with the types of objects that were specified in the development studies. The action of play was defined as an overt, observable motor response.

The human objects identified in the studies on play development were parents, peers, and the body itself. This last subcategory refers to responses that do not require anything except perhaps the surface of the floor or a chair — standing up and sitting down, then repeating the same thing again and again.

The nonhuman objects identified were grouped according to the possibilities they offered in changing their shape or form. Objects that seemed to change shape or form intrinsically when manipulated — paints, clay, sand, water — were called Type I. These would be creative or unstructured media. Type II objects seemed to change shape or form when combined with another like object or many dissimilar objects — beads, blocks, tinker toys, craft materials, constructional media. Toys such as rattles, balls, dolls, or play equipment didn't seem to change shape or form when manipulated and were called Type III objects.

CHART A

| | Birth - 6 Months | 6 - 12 Months | 1 - 2 Years | 2 - 3 Years | 3 - 4 Years | 4 - 5 Years |
|---|---|---|---|---|---|---|
| **HUMAN OBJECTS — PARENTS** | Visually fixates and follows; smiles | Pat-a-cake; differentiation of parents from strangers — shy with strangers | Chasing and hiding games; watching and following; imitating actions such as reading paper, holding cup, sweeping, dusting when parents demonstrate these | Asking to listen to stories, over and over without any change in wording | Not asking to hear same story word for word | Bragging, e.g., "I can do ____", asking "why" questions; listening to stories — fairy tales |
| **HUMAN OBJECTS — PEERS** | No play specific information reported | No play specific information reported | Solitary or onlooker (ignoring or watching); if in close contact, treating as objects, e.g., hitting, pushing | Parallel (playing alongside on same or different activity); fighting; pinching; defending play objects; taking object from another | Parallel; beginning to take turns | Enjoys being with other children; sharing materials; bragging and name calling |
| **HUMAN OBJECTS — SELF** | No play specific information reported | Practice of newly acquired motor skills, e.g., pulling self up and letting self down, locomoting | Practice of newly acquired motor skills, e.g., walking, standing up, sitting down, bending over, climbing | Practice of newly acquired motor skills, e.g., balancing, rolling | Identifying body with other people or things, e.g., "I am a bear", "I am a fireman" — does not ask for costumes for such action, may have imaginary friends | May have imaginary friends |
| **NON-HUMAN OBJECTS — TYPE I** | No play specific information reported | Splashes (with water) | Making marks and imitating scribbles; tasting; eating; smearing; placing on body; stepping on | Emptying and filling containers; splashing (with water); making marks and using many sheets of paper (with paint or crayons); tasting, putting on self, squishing through fingers; patting, pulling apart, extending effort beyond boundary of paper or surface; does not name product or ask to have it saved | Attending to results of efforts, e.g., "Look what I made" and naming of products; treating product as object itself and not a representation of object — likely to throw a clay ball | Intends to make something when begins although may end with different product; talking about what making; treating product as representation of object — not likely to throw a clay ball — product does not have to be a realistic representation; wanting to put name on product and wanting it saved |
| **NON-HUMAN OBJECTS — TYPE II** | Reaching; grasping; holding; mouthing; crude hand manipulation | Picking up; mouthing; banging; throwing | Pounding; throwing; taking in and out of containers; arranging and rearranging in space — building vertically or placing in rows; possessive; ending action — handing blocks when finished | Stringing beads; working puzzles; building vertically; placing in rows; building floor-like arrangement; massing arch; transporting in containers | Working puzzles; building wall like arrangement, floor like arrangement, arch, or solid structure (a wall of several thicknesses); using the form built in imaginative action | Naming what building although not intent on making product a realistic representation; wanting structures saved; collecting, e.g., variation of nature objects mainly |
| **NON-HUMAN OBJECTS — TYPE III** | Visually fixates and follows; reaching; grasping; holding; mouthing; crude hand manipulation | Picking up; mouthing; banging; shaking; throwing; taking out of containers | Pounding; twirling; throwing-picking up-throwing; handling more than one at a time; pulling; taking off; pulling apart; putting together; opening; closing; screwing-unscrewing; manipulating parts (knobs, dials); arranging and rearranging in space; possessive; ending action — handing toy when finished, tearing page out of book | Looking at and playing with the same object; manipulating parts; taking simple things apart or off; placing pegs in board; pushing and propelling over obstacles; kicking; climbing; imaginative action — ascribing action, e.g., making dolly eat, sleep, cry; making truck "start" | Fine motor action — hitting nail with hammer, dropping buttons through small openings; propelling over obstacles; imaginative action — identifying one object as another by speech before using in action, e.g., paper as blanket, shell as cup | Fine motor action — cutting, sewing on cards, gross motor action — arranging perilous feats for self, e.g., jumping; climbing jungle gym; imaginative action — identifying body with other people and wanting a few elements of costume; sequences more complex, e.g., more than one event (feeding, bathing dolly), or expansion of one event |

**CHART B**

| | | 5 - 6 Years | 6 - 7 Years | 7 - 8 Years | 8 - 9 Years | 9 - 11 Years |
|---|---|---|---|---|---|---|
| HUMAN OBJECTS | PARENTS | Asking "why" questions; wanting to know what to expect; wanting to listen to realistic stories as opposed to fairy tales | In listening to stories, has greater tolerance for fairy tales in the form of magic | Asking to listen to stories about heroes own age in setting he can recognize; opinions of group more important than opinions of parents; boys want some individual time with father; girls want some individual time with father | Rebelling against parents especially when group opinions conflict with parental ones | No play specific information reported |
| | PEERS | Cooperative (two or more working on same project); wanting playmates; playing group games in which everyone has a turn — no competition; imaginative action — roles differentiated, e.g., one plays mother, one plays baby | Wants to be with a group although there is little cooperation; important to obey customs of group — must act, look, talk like others; may tattle; game action — unable to put rules of game above need to win; learning to work as team in relay races; imaginative action — includes more than one or two children and often depends on leader; details in costume | Group is very important — a for or against age in which one is in or out of group; game action — rules apply to everyone except him; group games in which everyone has a chance to play; trading of objects, imaginative action — each group has organization and leader; imitation of reality; separation of sexes, e.g., girls-house, boys-war | Group is very important — must compete with others and conform to code; secrecy of gang important; game action — rules can still apply to everyone except him; imaginative action — done in group and reflect events outside of home and school; scouts or cubs important; trading of objects | Group is very important — joins many groups; game action — more conscious about rules and obeys them; competition is strong and plays for personal and team glory at the same time; imaginative action is rare |
| | SELF | No play specific information reported | No play specific information reported | No play specific information reported | No play specific information reported | No play specific information reported |
| NON-HUMAN OBJECTS | TYPE I | Attempting to make realistic representations; definitely wanting products saved and displayed; putting name on products | Attempting realistic representation | In a hurry for results — prefers crayons to paint as doesn't want to wait for paint to dry; concerned with realistic representation | Paints and uses casein; concerned with realistic representation | Making projects, e.g., clay modeling |
| | TYPE II | Constructing simple projects which can be completed within approximately 20 minutes — projects must be useful, e.g., potholders | Has trouble finishing any simple project — gets bogged down in middle; very critical of self in work | Sampling age — tries many different crafts and explores use of tools in relation to them; in a hurry for results so doesn't use best workmanship | Makes things that move and work; constantly overreaching self in projects — needs someone to help get materials and show procedures; exploring many processes in crafts, e.g., potato carving, stencils | Exploring many crafts, e.g., model making, weaving, woodworking, metal working, working with leather, carving, making baskets, sewing. Projects made must serve some usefulness |
| | TYPE III | Fine motor action — making mosaics; gross motor action — leaving earth with ropes in jumping; imaginative action — identifies body with other people and wanting whole costume; using miniature objects to represent real ones; attempting exact imitation of reality | Collecting items — quantity important; taking objects apart, e.g., clocks; speed important in sport activities, e.g., roller skating | Beginning to collect only certain items; gross muscle action — speed important; trying to improve physical skills and sampling new skills, e.g., swimming, archery, riding, skiing | Reads and chooses folk tales and legends — stories about everyday people in everyday situations; gross muscle action — gross muscle sports of hopscotch, roller skating, kite flying, wrestling; not ready for fine precision sports, e.g., tennis, golf; collecting according to individual interests | Exploring a variety of books, e.g., adventure fantasy, biography, mysteries, westerns, sports, animal, scientific; exploring a variety of sports — trying many and concentrating on a few and practicing those skills |

The action component of play was selected in order to define the phenomenon operationally. The action component refers to overt, observable motor responses to the six objects at the different ages used in the developmental studies. Play involved simultaneous response to human and nonhuman objects. It was not necessarily real or desirable to attempt to separate these responses, but for the purpose of the study, the following criterion was used: if the response required a human object in order that it occur at all (sharing, cooperating) it was placed in the human object category. If the response could be done alone, even if initially it required guidance or instruction by a person, it was placed in the nonhuman category.

The classification is certainly not a developmental test of play. Also it does not reflect all the behaviors in a child's play at different ages nor does it attempt to examine why children play differently at different ages. The classification attempts only to put down in a format some of the ways in which children act upon people and things at different ages. With proper procedures employed, it might become a useful tool for the observation of children's play.

To facilitate play throughout development a variety of objects are needed. At three years, a child may be perfectly content to play fireman with only a stick for a hose. At five or six years of age he says he needs a fireman's hat, badge, maybe a raincoat and a garden hose — and those materials should be available to him. Unfortunately there are no simple formulas or prescriptions for the selection of play materials or the nurturing of play throughout development. However, important guidelines are contained in the description of conditions which prompt intrinsic motivation, [5] [9] [21] in Montessori's description of the prepared environment,[22] in Takata's specifications for the play milieu,[23] in Michelman's provisions for creative play,[24] in Hartley and Goldenson's list of play materials,[15] and in many other writings on child behavior.

## Conclusion

"When a child cannot play, we should be as troubled as when he refuses to eat or sleep."[15] The significance of the everyday play of the child requires that professionals who work with children regard it as a respectable area of concern. When children are having difficulty in play, this is not the time to call in the volunteer or to dip into the bag of scrap materials. This is the time for the immediate attention of a professional, and it calls for his careful and studied examination of what might be going wrong.

**References**
1. Slobin, D. I., "The Fruits of the First Season; A Discussion of the Role of Play in Childhood," *Journal of Humanistic Psychology,* 4: 1, 1964.
2. Mitchell, E. and Mason, B., *The Theory of Play,* New York: A. S. Barnes Company, 1948.
3. Berlyne, D. E., "Notes on Intrinsic Motivation and Intrinsic Reward in Relation to Instruction" in *Learning about Learning* (a conference report monograph), Washington: U.S. Government Printing Office, 1966, pp. 105–110.
4. Bruner, J. S., *Toward a Theory of Instruction,* Cambridge: The Belknap Press of Harvard University Press, 1964.
5. White, R. W., "Motivation Reconsidered: The Concept of Competence," in *Readings in Child Behavior and Development* (2nd ed.), C. B. Stendler (ed.), New York: Harcourt Brace & World, Inc., 1964, pp. 164–191.
6. Haber, R. N., *Current Research in Motivation,* New York: Holt, Rinehart and Winston, Inc., 1967.
7. Cofer, C. and Appley, M., *Motivation: Theory and Research,* New York: John Wiley & Sons, Inc., 1964.
8. White, R. W., Competence and the Psychosocial Stages of Development, *Nebraska Symposium on Motivation,* M. Jones (ed.), Lincoln: University of Nebraska Press, 1960, pp. 97–138.
9. White, R. W., "Ego and Reality in Psychoanalytic Theory," *Psychological Issues Monograph* 11 (3): 1–196, 1963.
10. White, R. W., "The Experience of Efficacy in Schizophrenia, " *Psychiatry* 28: 199–211, 1965.
11. Willard, H. and Spackman, C., *Occupational Therapy,* 3rd ed., Philadelphia: J. B. Lippincott Company, 1963.
12. Florey, L., "A Developmental Classification of Play," Master's Thesis, Occupational Therapy Department, University of Southern California, 1968.
13. Gesell, A., *et al., The First Five Years of Life,* New York: Harper & Brothers, 1940.
14. Guanella, F. M., "Block Building Activities of Young Children," *Archives of Psychology,* 26 (174): 5–92, 1934.
15. Hartley, R. and Goldenson, R., *The Complete Book of Children's Play,* New York: Thomas Y. Crowell Company, 1963.
16. Hartley, R., *et al., Understanding Children's Play,* New York: Columbia University Press, 1952.
17. Jones T. D., "The Development of Certain Motor Skills and Play Activities in Young Children, *Child Development Monograph 26,* New York: Bureau of Publications, Teacher's College, Columbia University, 1939.
18. Markey, F. V., "Imaginative Behavior of Preschool Children," *Child Development Monograph 18,* New York: Bureau of Publications, Teacher's College, Columbia University, 1935.
19. Palmer, L., *Play Life in the First Eight Years,* Boston: Ginn & Company, 1916.
20. Piaget, J., *Play, Dreams and Imitation in Childhood,* London: Routledge & Kegan Paul Ltd., 1962.
21. Berlyne, D. E., *Conflict, Arousal & Curiosity,* New York: McGraw-Hill Book Company, Inc., 1960.
22. Orem, R. C. (ed.), *Montessori for the Disadvantaged,* New York: Capricorn Book Edition, 1968.
23. Takata, N., "Development of a Conceptual Scheme for Analysis of Play Milieu," Master's Thesis, Occupational Therapy Department, University of Southern California, 1968.
24. Michelman, S., "The Importance of Creative Play," Paper presented at Occupational Therapy Symposium, The Continuum of Skills from Play through Work, 1970.

# Validity of Play

LAWRENCE K. FRANK

Probably most of those who read these remarks are already convinced of the great importance of play in child development, not only in the early years but all through childhood and adolescence and in adult life as well. But how can we convince those who are indifferent or opposed to play and wish to focus the child's interest and activities on required learning and the development of academic competence? How can their understanding of child development be enlarged to recognize the child's urgent need for play? Can we show them that play is genuinely productive and necessary if the child is to master the often rigidly structured program set for children?

## Courses on Play

Do the schools of education which prepare teachers and administrators provide an initial orientation and understanding of play? Do the formal courses in child development neglect play because it has not been studied by current research methods and techniques to produce the kind of quantified findings on selected variables given in child development texts? If we are to hope for a reorientation and a recognition of the vital role of play, we should critically examine the courses and programs in our schools of education, recognizing the often unspoken disapproval of play, except perhaps of motor activities and competitive games on the playground.

## Spontaneity

While many young organisms engage in play, the human child finds in play the activities and the occasions for discovering himself, his strengths and his weaknesses, his skills and his interests, enabling him to learn to cope with situations and events appropriate to his size and strength. But, of special importance, through play the child exercises his spontaneity and his reactions and response to what he encounters and has selected for his activity.

Playing and the use of play materials, alone or with others, evoke his energies, focus his attention and direct his efforts on what is appropriate and congenial and, in so doing, foster his development as a young organism seeking to cope with the actual world he finds around him.

Since play, not only by children but by adults, is a universal activity, it may seem unnecessary to assert that play is valid. But within recent years there has been a strong movement to restrict the play of children, young and older, to adult-imposed patterns in order to promote formal learning, especially preparation for school. We need, therefore, to be reminded of the validity, indeed the imperative necessity, of play in human development.

Some perspective may be gained by recognizing that the child arrives as a young mammalian organism, with all the wisdom of the body, as Walter Cannon termed it — the varied inherited capacities for functioning as an organism which he must continually exercise in order to live, grow, develop, mature and learn. Recent studies have shown that those babies who, shortly after birth, are given opportunities for sensory and muscular activities develop and learn more than those who are neglected or deprived.

### Fruitful Learning

During the first five or six years of his life, the child is expected to learn to cope with the world, natural and human. He explores and manipulates and thus cumulatively learns about what and how . . . and also in these explorations, he discovers himself. He endlessly rehearses, primarily by direct contact with the world, his gradually enlarging awareness, his patterned perceptions and his growing repertory of skills. He also learns the names and meanings of what he encounters, not only by being told in words but by making those words personally meaningful through his actual contacts and manipulations.

With his sensory capacities, the child learns not only to look but to see, not only to hear but to listen, not only to touch but to feel and grasp what he handles. He tastes whatever he can get into his mouth and he begins to smell what he encounters. No program of teaching and adult instruction could adequately provide for his own personal observations, activities and direct knowing. But he can and will, if not handicapped, impaired or blocked, master these many experiences through continual play, as we call this seemingly nonpurposeful activity which is actually the most intensive and fruitful learning in his whole life cycle.

## Trial and Error

The world confronting the child is, as William James called it, a "great blooming confusion," which the child has to organize by putting into it some orderliness and meaning, some way of making situations and events understandable. The big adult world, the macrocosm, is too large, too complicated and often threatening to the child who cannot cope with it; and so he focuses upon the microcosmic world of play, as Erik Erikson stated some years ago, a world that he can encompass through toys and play materials. To these he imputes his often childish beliefs and expectations and also his feelings, but by repeated explorations he gradually relinquishes some of his more fantastic beliefs.

When he tries to make the world conform to his childish beliefs and expectations, he is repeatedly confronted with the actuality of situations and events, the ever-present threats and sometimes painful consequences. But he can do this restructuring of the world only if he is permitted and encouraged to try, to persist until he learns what can and cannot be done; and play provides a minimum of risks and penalties for mistakes. Play, as we see in many animals, is a way of learning by trial and error to cope with the actual world.

## Discovering Self

To live in the public world, the child must learn what is expected and consonant with the beliefs and expectations of his family, especially the symbol systems (primarily language) by which his society names, defines and interprets whatever it is aware of and has learned to perceive. But before he can or should relinquish his own highly individualized interpretations of the world and accept the prescribed social patterns, he needs a prolonged period of fantasy and make-believe in order to exercise his imagination and his spontaneity. He builds up his "as if" world and establishes his life space as his version of what he is told and expected to say and do. In this way he discovers himself (not self-expression, since he must first develop a self before he can express it).

We should always remember that everyone exists in a public world and carries on his life activities but, as noted above, each person creates his own life space, as Kurt Lewin called it, his selected version of the world, which both recognizes and ignores what others may emphasize and insist as necessary for adult living. By observing children at play, especially with miniature life toys, we often can see how they are building their life space by the way they select and reject, combine and separate, and manipulate play materials. They gradually learn the difference between my and thine and develop an image of the self as me, my and mine, the target of others' judgments and activities.

## Basic Patterns

Accordingly, it cannot be too strongly emphasized that play is of immense and crucial significance in development, when many of our unique human capacities are being evoked and put into practice, especially when many of the basic patterns for living as a human personality are being learned. How important these play experiences are has been shown by students of personality development and especially by those play therapists who are dealing with the stunted, warped and emotionally disturbed children, including the shut-in, nonresponsive, autistic children. Since these children cannot, or will not, speak they may be invited to use a variety of play materials wherein they disclose their private worlds and otherwise individualized "problems" by the way they manipulate play materials.

Through play — including not only play with playthings but spontaneous play and dramatizations as well — many children by themselves can resolve some of their perplexities and clarify their feelings. Soon after a child learns to speak, he stops making overt expressions of his thoughts and feelings as he realizes this is not often safe and may invite parental correction or punishment. Thus he develops his inner speech and begins to create his own private world; he assumes an identity as expressed by the I who is the speaker and actor and learns to perform various roles.

## Free Play

While play may be focused upon playthings and situations and people, it soon becomes concerned with ideas, concepts and assumptions by which the child carries on his many "thought experiments." So many of the most fruitful ideas in art and science have been developed by individuals who were free to consider new and unexplored possibilities which they later translated into more formal expression. They seem to have retained from childhood a capacity for creative thinking and imagination as testified by many of the most creative thinkers as having found their inspiration in what might be called idle fancy and nonlogical thinking — the free play of the mind.

But, unfortunately, while this capacity varies from child to child, it may be repressed and constricted in childhood by lack of experiences and encouragement to speak freely, to explore, to "make-believe" and to test out his own thinking by play experience.

## Imaginative Play

Especially important in play is the opportunity for a wide range of artistic, esthetic experiences — telling stories, spontaneous dramatization and role-playing, drawing, painting and modeling, group singing and playing simple instruments by which the child can learn rhythm and the use of his voice. Dancing, the dance drama translating a story into bodily movements, and simple group dances with chanting also foster imaginative play and provide experiences which contribute to the child's development.

The great importance of the arts in childhood is that they provide and can, if not rigidly imposed by misguided adults, foster and evoke creative activities — not masterpieces but rather the production of what the individual believes and feels as his own, not a copy of models, following set patterns. Those who grow up to become artistic in various media were the children who were encouraged to explore and experiment, to discover themselves with opportunities for developing their individualized potentialities. But all children need the arts as essential to their development as personalities, to enlarge their awareness and to cultivate their sensibilities for human living.

## Sources of Renewal

As the demands and constraints of social living grow and are imposed upon them, adolescents and adults may find sources for renewal and re-creation by nonrational experiences, as in play, often an elaboration of what they enjoyed in early life. Indeed the need for nonrational experiences, for living as an organism and functioning spontaneously, may become increasingly necessary if adults are to maintain mental health and find renewed strength for being rational when and as required. But unfortunately many adults have lost the capacity for play and seek passive entertainment and distractions which usually provide very temporary and inadequate relief from tensions and worries.

As the foregoing indicates, the schools often ignore and wholly neglect what the young child before academic schooling needs to develop as a personality, with some capacity for spontaneity and creative experiences. If the young child has had ample opportunities for play, he is likely to be better prepared for academic study and disciplined learning. If he has engaged in play without interference or interruption, he learns to perseverate, to engage in purposeful goal-seeking activities which he, as an individual, invests with his own meanings and values as he translates his personal capacities and often unsuspected potentialities into concerted and rewarding activities and relationships.

## Interpersonal Relations

Perhaps the most difficult learning confronting the child is concerned with his interpersonal relations, with adults and especially with other children, younger and older. Games with definite rules and imaginary boundaries provide repeated occasions for learning to recognize and to respect others, their property and their persons, and to inhibit the impulses and feelings that are not socially permissible.

But all this requires adequate space, facilities and play materials. And, above all, it requires understanding, empathic adults and older adolescents who will, when necessary, provide the definition of situations and the necessary restrictions, explain and interpret the possibilities whereby the child is helped to learn to live with others. Especially in the formal school years, children need play to relax and to release tensions in various ways when they have been immobilized for some time and have had to submit to an imposed but often unwelcome regimen.

## Pressure for Achievement

As Otto Rank remarked some years ago in his book, *Modern Education*, every generation uses children for its own purposes. Today the pressure for academic achievement, cognitive learning and preparation for the next grade seems to be an expression of this contemporary desire to exploit children for what is often self-defeating purposes. This is interpreted as necessary to provide trained, skilled and knowledgeable recruits for business and industry, for science and technology and for scholarship. As we are discovering, we may be highly successful in this program but foster unhappy and frustrated personalities who are neglectful or indifferent to human needs and feelings.

Many of our adolescents are expressing their discontent and even open revolt against the educational establishment which, according to many recent studies, exhibits a strong resistance to change. Many schools are unwilling or reluctant to give adequate time for play, for artistic activities and for nonacademic interests. They refuse to recognize that most of the basic learning for living and social life cannot be taught formally but must be learned through daily living, playing and enjoying the opportunities at each stage of the life cycle.

## Exploration Through Play

We should recognize that children from their earliest years are actively curious and exploratory and seek through play ways of coping with the world in their own individualized patterns. But unfortunately many are suppressed and robbed of their spontaneity and denied the opportunities they need for learning and growing. The integrity of the child as an organism-personality who through play comes to terms with the world and himself should be preserved. It is unfortunate that the term *play* has long been interpreted to mean idle and unproductive activity, for in truth it embraces a wide range of spontaneous and productive experiences.

**Suggested Readings**
Erikson, Erik, *Childhood and Society*, New York: W. W. Norton & Co., Inc., rev. ed., 1964.
Ghiselin, Brewster. *Creative Process*. New York: New American Library, 1952.
Hartley, Ruth, Frank, Lawrence and Goldenson, Robert. *Understanding Children's Play*. New York: Columbia University Press, 1952.
Hartley, Ruth and Goldenson, Robert, *The Complete Book of Children's Play*, New York: Cromwell Press, 1957 and 1963 (rev. ed., Apollo paperback, 1970).
Moustakas, Clark E. and Berson, Minnie, *The Young Child in School*. New York: Whiteside, Inc. and William Morrow & Co., 1956.
Murphy, Lois, *et al.*, *Widening World of Childhood: Paths Toward Mastery*, New York: Basic Books, Inc. 1962.

# Psychoanalytic Theory of Play

ROBERT WÄLDER

Children's play has been the subject of scientific discussion for many psychologists of various schools of thought. Child psychology, as it is taught in our universities, has occupied itself with the remarkable phenomenon that a considerable part of a growing child's day is taken up with play and has undertaken to make various contributions to the interpretation of this phenomenon. It will now be our endeavor to see what psychoanalysis has to contribute to the question of children's play.

Comparing the literature of academic psychology with the more casual psychoanalytic publications dealing with the subject, it will immediately be noticed that each draws attention to a different group of games. Academic psychology studies chiefly what one might designate "official" games of children — games which are typical and played by all children. In psychoanalytic literature, on the contrary, interest is chiefly centered on games of a different type — those of a more individual nature, to which the child clings for a certain time only. Naturally, it cannot be said that academic psychology is not interested in the individual games or that psychoanalysis is not concerned with the traditional, typical ones; but it is hardly possible to overlook the fact that the two place the stress differently.

The psychoanalytic theory of play is not able to supply a unitary explanation for the phenomenon called "play," by which all games and all manifestations arising from them can be interpreted. On the contrary, here, as is usually the case in psychoanalysis, a single phenomenon may have various meanings, may perform various functions and cannot be explained by a single general interpretation: in short, as we say in psychoanalysis, the phenomenon has a number of determinants. In the following discussion, we propose to study intensively those elements in the psychoanalytic play theory which are most characteristically psychoanalytic.

## Pleasure Principle

First of all, it may be stated of children's games, that they elaborate material which has been experienced by the child. This material may then, in the child's playing, be expressed in various ways. The incident experienced in reality may be given a different arrangement in play, but at all events the material is gathered from experience. For example, we see the child playing mother with a doll, or playfully representing father and mother with another child, or teacher and pupil, or policeman and robber, or the like. The material which becomes elaborated is at times derived from an experience such as an observed situation involving the mother and father, teacher and pupil, and so on. Hence, the pleasure principle is our first guide to the study of psychic phenomena. We consider a manifestation comprehensible when we see that it results in a gratification of a desire for pleasure. This is without doubt frequently the case in children's play. In the game with the doll, it is difficult not to recognize the nature of the gratification in the situation, namely, the child's wish to be a mother herself — a special case of a general principle found in many other games, the desire to be big and grown up. If the child, through experience, has once become acquainted with the happy situation of an automobile ride, or if his imagination has been stimulated by stories about it — if he then wishes to ride and realizes this wish in a game, we can immediately comprehend the meaning of the game. There is to be sure no explanation of why these particular wishes should find their materialization in a game; but the phenomenon is, at all events, aligned in the field of fantasy gratifications familiar to us from other sources, and its content, at least, is understandable.

These few examples indicate that in the playing of children, numerous gratifications of the desire for pleasure are demonstrable; that frequently or perhaps even always, play deals with some portion of a pleasurable situation, or with some of the determinants of its realization; that in fact much of children's play is a manifestation of the pleasure principle.

Now, however, a difficulty arises. Though on the one hand, it is evident that the pleasure principle will explain many circumstances in children's play, yet, on the other hand, one cannot help realizing that the child, in playing with extraordinary frequency reproduces or at least proceeds from situations which were in actual experience devoid of pleasure. As a simple illustration: A child was taken to a dentist. It had been very apprehensive concerning the dentist, from whom it had previously suffered tormenting pain. According to the pleasure principle, we should offhand suppose that the highly disagreeable situation, once it was fortunately in the past, would have been set aside and that the child would be only too glad to let the matter drop. The pleasure principle hardly prepares us to expect the return of this situation in play. Nevertheless, in reality, this often occurs. The child at home on the following day may play dentist, utilizing a doll or a conveniently available younger sister or brother. In this way, it is often precisely the highly unpleasurable situation which becomes material, or at any rate, a starting point for a subsequent game, which as a rule is played for a time and then gradually abandoned. Guided by the pleasure principle — which, for many other reasons, we confidently accept as the valid principle of psychic life — we arrive at a point which seems to contradict this principle, and we must ask how this can be.

## Functional Pleasure

A theory of K. Buhler, not referring exactly to this situation, but to a similar one, may be applicable here. According to Buhler, play cannot be explained by the idea of pleasurable gratification. But play is pleasurable and consequently, according to Buhler's theory, is connected with a form of pleasure other than the pleasure of gratification. Buhler speaks of the "functional pleasure"; i.e., of the pleasure experienced in pure performance without regard to the success of the activity. Gratification-pleasure represents pleasure in the success of an action, while functional pleasure represents the joy in the activity itself. The most vivid example of a functional pleasure is the playing of children. In play, we find joy in all the activities and functions involved in the development of the child. Play activities have for a time the teleological significance of an exercise preparatory for future functions, a belief formerly entertained by philosophers, for example, by Groos[1]; but the functional pleasure

[1]Without denying the teleological function of most games as preparation, there are indications that there are games in which a preparation can by no means be discovered; moreover, there are some which distinctly make for unpreparedness. To these latter, for example, belongs the game of playing baby. It sometimes happens that a child, in about its third year, plays at being a baby again and acts out a playful helplessness and inability to speak.This game is certainly not a constant occurrence, but, on the other hand, it is not so infrequent that it can be overlooked. It makes its appearance occasionally after the birth of a younger sister or brother. In this case, the purport of the game is obviously a wish fulfillment. The child wants to participate again in the advantages which the newborn child enjoys either in reality or in his eyes. The game is sometimes associated with the onset of enuresis. Without going into the details of such a manifestation, it is at least an example of the fact that all games do not necessarily signify a preparation.

represents the experimental evidence that such preparation does take place.

Within the confines of this paper, it is not possible to discuss this theory exhaustively, and only a few references to it can be made here. The fact that pleasure can be derived from performance, independently of its success, meets with no doubt. But in such pleasure two components are to be differentiated. One component may again be called gratification pleasure, if in the activity itself a decided gratification is embodied;[2] for example, in the activity of playing at being the parents, the gratification of being big and grown up oneself, and of being father or mother; a second component independent of this might well represent the functional pleasure in its true sense. The existence of such a functional pleasure may be granted without reservation. There is no reason for doubting its existence, and it may play a role, particularly during the period of growth of the organism — that is to say, in childhood. Although we grant the existence of this sort of pleasure, nevertheless functional pleasure does not seem to us sufficient to explain the above-mentioned games in which the material was a disagreeable experience; and specifically, it seems insufficient on the following grounds: Functional pleasure is purely formal and, from its very definition, not dependent on the occurrences in which it was experienced. But the content of play is manifestly not a matter of indifference. Again and again one sees that precisely certain games suddenly occur to the child, to be abandoned later on. There is no justification for the assumption that the child's playing the game at this particular time is a coincidence and requires no further explanation. Why, to return to our illustration, on the day following the child's experience with the dentist, which threw him out of equilibrium, is the game of dentist played? Why does this game persist for, let us say, a fortnight, and why does it then desist completely? If this game could be so completely explained by the idea of functional pleasure that there was nothing to be added, then one theme would be interchangeable with another, and the content of one game replaceable by another. If this were the case, the child in our illustration would be ready, instead of playing "dentist," to play any other game bearing some similarity to this game in respect of the function involved. But this interchangeability of content

---

[2]The fatal equivocation resident in the word *gratification* (Befriedigung) is inconvenient in this connection. On the one hand it means "to attain peace" or "to come to rest," on the other, in a broader sense every pleasurable realization — for example, in the expression "gratification in work." Psychoanalysis uses the word in the broader sense throughout. It has, however, nothing to do with the metapsychological question as to whether gratification in the last analysis represents the equalizing of tension in the psychic system — as was formerly assumed — or whether it represents an excitation process, as has been supposed since the publication of Freud's paper, *The Economic Principle in Masochism.*

does not exist. Indeed a particular game is given preference at a particular time. The content is not a matter of indifference and is not interchangeable. Therefore a theory of formal pleasure is not sufficient to give us a thorough understanding of phenomena which are also quite definite in respect of content. The games of the type mentioned above have, in addition, a characteristic course which can likewise not be explained by the assumption of a functional pleasure. Thus, to go back to our illustration, the child plays at being a dentist repeatedly and very enthusiastically for several days, then the theme appears more and more rarely, is accompanied by less affect and finally disappears; if it reappears occasionally, this has, generally speaking, certain definite precipitating causes. The course of the game's intensity and affective content produces the impression that here an affect is being discharged, or better, that an affective residue, left over from the experience itself, is gradually being assimilated.

## Repetition Compulsion

This brings us to the Freudian theory of children's play and its principal function in the child's life. Before we present this theory, a short digression into one chapter of relevant psychoanalytic theory must be permitted us: study of the repetition compulsion. After this theoretical digression we may turn to our subject proper — the psychoanalytic study of children's play.

In the life of human beings there are repetitions of many kinds. It happens quite often that an individual repeatedly does the same thing, or that, over and over again, he lives through the same experience. Not all repetitions occurring in human life but only a quite definite group of them can be regarded as manifestations of the repetition compulsion, according to the psychoanalytic meaning of the term. When a person creates the same situation over and over because he is seeking a gratification which he never finds (the Don Juan type), the fact that he is "repeating" is obvious. Such a repetition is not to be explained by the repetition compulsion, however, but rather by the constant striving for a particular goal and by the frustration of each attempt to attain it. A different kind of repetition may be observed in the constantly renewed efforts toward accomplishments made by a severely inhibited individual. Here also the impression of repetition arises, yet this phenomenon also is explicable through its psychic setting, and the repetition compulsion need not be invoked as an explanation. Another type of repetition arises through mental rigidity and impoverishment — a type which appears, for example, in senile dementia. One could probably thus differentiate numerous other types of repetition in psychic life, of which each has its individual explanation but which nevertheless do not involve the specific repetition process which psychoanalysis regards as due to the "repetition compulsion."

By this repetition compulsion proper we understand the process described as follows: the individual has been through a specific experience, which was too difficult or too large for him to assimilate immediately. This unabsorbed, or incompletely absorbed experience weighs heavily upon his psychic organization and calls for a new effort at handling and for a reexperience. This experience has two aspects. Considered as a process of the id, that is, in so far as the individual is passive and lives in accordance with forces within himself, it is a compulsion which influences him and drives him to reexperience. This process has an active side as well; considered as a process of the ego, it represents at the same time the ego's attempt to assimilate the experience more completely through renewing and thereby gaining the mastery over it. The repetition compulsion, therefore, is Janus-faced. In one way, it is a fate to which we are subjected, in another way, an active attempt to master this fate. The whole process is perhaps best compared — if the comparison is permissible — to the rumination of certain animals. The morsel is too large to be digested at one time and the undigested meal remains in the stomach. It must be chewed again if it is to be digested. This process, too, if one is willing to hazard carrying the comparison so far, has two sides: the pressure of the undigested meal is, so to speak, the passive, id component, and digestion by the act of chewing the cud, the ego component of the process. The point at which our analogy finally forsakes us is this: to chew the cud once or several times (in the organic example) is sufficient, while in the repetition compulsion a very frequently repeated chewing occurs, in one case more frequently, in another less frequently; and in some cases, as we shall see, assimilation is never properly complete in spite of persistent rumination.

The two aspects of the repetition compulsion, its Janus face, may also be described in another way. During the repetition, the individual passes over from passivity to activity and in this manner psychically masters the impressions which were originally received in a merely passive way. Freud has repeatedly described this feature of the repetition compulsion. Thus, he says:

> The ego which has passively experienced the trauma, now actively repeats an enfeebled reproduction of it, hoping that in the course of this, it will be able through its own action to direct it. We know that the child takes the same attitude to all impressions painful

to him, reproducing them in the form of a game; through this manner of proceeding from passivity to activity he seeks to master mentally the impressions received from life.[3]

With more particular reference to children's play, the same idea is expressed in an even earlier paper, to which we shall return in our subsequent discussion:

> We see the children repeat in their play everything that has made a great impression on them in actual life, that they thereby abreact the strength of the impression, and so to speak make themselves masters of the situation.[4]

> In the play of children we seem to arrive at the conclusion that the child repeats even the unpleasant experiences because through his own activity he gains a far more thorough mastery of the strong impression than was possible by mere passive experience. Every fresh repetition seems to strengthen this mastery for which the child strives. . . .[5]

And to give one more quotation:

> The relation of activity and passivity deserves special attention. In every field of mental activity, and not in the realm of sexuality alone, it is easy to observe that a passively received impression provokes an active response in the child. It, itself, tries to do that which was done to it or with it. This process is part of the work it must undertake to master its environment; it may even lead the child to a painstaking repetition of the very impressions which, because of their unpleasant content, it has every reason to avoid. Children's play also serves as a method of adding an active counterpart to the passive experience. After the doctor has pried open a struggling child's mouth, looked down its throat, and finally departed, the child plays doctor and repeats the vigorous procedure on a small sister or brother, who is then quite as helpless as it, itself, had been with the doctor. This unmistakably shows a disinclination to be passive and a preference for the active role. This swing from passivity to activity varies in different children, and may even be absent altogether. From the child's behavior we can judge the relative strength of the masculinity or femininity which will one day appear in its sexuality.[6]

As I have said, the passages quoted explicitly refer to the theory of children's play, which we may now consider. We have up to now been

[3]Freud: *Hemmung, Symptom und Angst.* Ges. Schr. XI, 110.
[4]Freud: *Beyond the Pleasure Principle*, 15.
[5]*Loc. cit*, 43.
[6]Freud: *Concerning the Sexuality of Woman.* This Quarterly I, 202. 1932.

formulating the psychological processes in those phenomena which psychoanalysis describes under the concept of repetition compulsion, and stating the remarkable double position that the repetition occupies, as a pressure *a tergo* and an assimilative attempt on the part of the ego.

All of this is based on an assumption concerning the relationship of the psychic organism to the outer world. Psychoanalysis assumes that the psychic organism is able to ingest and assimilate the stimulations of the outer world in small doses only, if so quantitative a figure of speech may be used. If, in a given unit of time, the excitations of the outer world impinge upon the individual excessively, the ability to absorb them fails and the mechanism of the repetition compulsion comes into play. The stimuli not disposed of exert a pressure and must be dealt with repeatedly and, so to speak, belatedly, must be divided into small portions.

The repetition compulsion, then, purely empirically, is not a blind primal impulse which demands, "Repeat!" It is a pressure exerted by unfinished processes, and it is a constant striving to assimilate. The reality of its empirical existence is hardly open to dispute; proof for it is constantly found in everyday events.

### Assimilation Function

After this digression into the theory of the repetition compulsion, we are prepared to discuss the psychoanalytic solution of the previously mentioned problems of children's play. In all those cases in which the child's play originates in disagreeable experiences, the pleasure principle does not enable us to appreciate why, instead of letting these painful matters sink into desuetude, the child continues to busy itself with them, nor why these experiences which it elaborates into games are too difficult for its immediate carrying capacity. The experience at the dentist's, in our illustration, was an onslaught of more events in a relatively brief interval of time than could be endured by the immature, untempered, extraordinarily plastic and responsive psychic organism of the child. The capacity for assimilation, naturally, very much depends on age. As one grows older, the ego becomes stronger, and consequently the capacity to endure difficulties grows; the difficult experiences of the past function as preparations for future tolerance (a sort of hardening). With an increasing rigidity of the personality, the protective crust against outer excitations becomes denser and less permeable (this becomes especially conspicuous in old age, but is already indicated in adult life), and with the diminishing plasticity the receptivity and readiness of the individual to react decline. All these circumstances, along with many others, contribute toward the fact that, infinitely more often than an adult, a child is confronted with experiences which he cannot immediately assimilate. To the psychic organism just establishing its existence, for which everything is still novel — some things attractively pleasant, many things painful and menacing — excessive stimulation (trauma as it might be called in a certain sense) is plainly a normal experience, while in the life of the adult it surely constitutes the exception. This, probably, is one of the reasons why the abreaction of traumatic experiences by games plays so important a role precisely in childhood. That the child not only experiences trauma more frequently than the adult but also — just because all its strength is engaged in growth — the child is in an incomparably better position to surmount it, is fortunately true, but is extraneous to our discussion. The fact is not altered that traumatic stimulation in childhood is the general rule.

According to the conclusions arrived at by psychoanalysis, play may be a process like a repetition compulsion, by which excessive experiences are divided into small quantities, reattempted and assimilated in play. To return to the problem mentioned at the start — namely, why unpleasant experiences so often constitute the material of games — we may say that although these experiences are unpleasant, they were at the same time too difficult. Play may now be characterized as a method of constantly working over and, as it were, assimilating piecemeal an experience which was too large to be assimilated instantly at one swoop. Buhler is quite aware that unpleasurable experiences are repeated in play but believes that this takes place only after the experiences have been freed of their painful quality. He says:

> The fact that unpleasurable happenings find an echo in the play of children has markedly impressed Freud. The fact, as such, is completely and readily evident. Indeed, Groos observed it and aptly described it as follows: The pain in an experience must be overcome before the experience can be repeated and enjoyed in play. This is true for adults and children too. Let us suppose that the child was once bitten by a dog, or that I burnt its finger on a candle. Nothing in the world will induce the child to repeat this experience in reality or in play, until the situation is inwardly settled, and the child on a fresh occasion feels reassured and superior to the situation.[7]

The difference between Buhler's view and the psychoanalytic view is due to a question as to the facts. The contrary thesis of psychoanalysis would be accurately worded as follows: A painful experience is repeated

[7]Buhler, K.: *Die Krise der Psychologie*. 1. Aufl., Jena 1927, 189 f.

in play not after it has been overcome and mastered, but before, while it is still unmastered; and it is eventually mastered because of the playful repetition itself.

Thereby, play becomes aligned with assimilative procedures which operate by repetition, of which others also exist in the psychic life. Furthermore, according to psychoanalytical theory, play has in this way a teleological function as well. This function is not so much the preparation for future activities in adult life as it is the assimilation of the mass of excitations from the outer world, which affect the organism too severely or too suddenly to permit of their immediate disposal.

## Assimilative Processes

The assimilative process in play can take place in various ways, and probably various types could be differentiated. First of all the simple fact that the child reproduces in playing a passively received experience, a transformation from passivity to activity, is significant. In one group of games, in addition, the child adopts another role than the one played in reality; if in real life, it was the sufferer or a frightened spectator, it becomes in play the active party, the rescuer or the *deus ex machina*. In this group, then, the turning from passivity to activity is emphasized by the choice of role; the illustration of the dentist is to the point here. In another group, the child changes the outcome of the situation experienced and furnishes it with a different solution. Presumably it is possible to differentiate other such types of assimilative processes.

As has been previously pointed out, still other assimilative processes or attempts occur on the pattern of the mechanism of the repetition compulsion, which play a significant role in adult life. The simplest example might be an adult who has been through some unusually difficult experience and who is constantly occupied in his thoughts with this experience, or who talks about it incessantly for a period of time — sometimes forever. This process, too, is under the sway of the repetition compulsion, as we have described it. The unassimilated invasion of reality into the psychic organism has the same disturbing effect as a foreign body. That which is not disposed of harasses the individual and demands that it be tackled again; the ego at the same time through dealing with the experience anew attempts to assimilate it. Here again we see the Janus face of the repetition compulsion turned both to the id and the ego.

Mourning also belongs to the assimilative processes in the category of repetition compulsions. The loss of a beloved person is a painful experience. At the moment of the loss there is pain but as yet no grief. We know from Freud that gradual severing from the beloved, lost object takes place, achieved, obviously, through the mechanism of reality testing, which informs us repeatedly that the loved object is no longer accessible. Mourning is the suffering entailed by this task of separation. This task, however, is accomplished under the sway of the repetition compulsion. The lost object constantly comes to mind, fresh accesses of ungratified affection are freshly painful. In this constantly repeated resurgence of the painful experience a gradual assimilation occurs simultaneously with the course of normal grief. The affect fades away little by little.

The dreams of war neurotics and traumatic neurotics present another example of such processes. The terrifying experience of being shelled, or of the other traumata from which traumatic neuroses result, returns repeatedly in dreams. From the standpoint of the pleasure principle this would be incomprehensible, nor can it be explained by the wish-fulfillment theory of dreams. The process is the same as in the previous examples; it is subject to the repetition compulsion: the trauma insists on returning because it has not been assimilated, and, at the same time, the ego strives to conquer the experience.

To a certain critic, the close similarity of children's play to the traumatic neuroses sounded dubious. The interpretation on one and the same principle of such severely pathological phenomena as the dreams of a war neurotic and of a manifestation so delightful and vital as children's play appeared to carry this principle *ad absurdum*. We believe that this objection is unjustified; both instances have in common, that they are dealing with an attempt to assimilate an overwhelming situation. On the other hand, the two cases differ inordinately in regard to the success of the processes. In one case the attempt fails and in spite of all repetitions, assimilation does not take place, while in the other a relatively satisfactory assimilation of the occurrence is attained.

## Unique Characteristics of Play

With the recognition that play belongs to the group of gradually progressive assimilative processes which are spurred on by the repetition compulsion, play, at least in respect of this one determination — and in our opinion, its most crucial one — has been clearly classified; but not all the problems pertaining to it are solved. For there are other processes of this sort, as we have seen from a number of examples, and we must ask what distinguishes play from them. At first glance, one would be inclined to say that play has a blissful and unreal quality which distinguishes it from the others; and perhaps the *differentia specifica* of games may be defined on this basis. Play, as a fundamental and purposeful phenomenon is encountered only in children, that is, during a period of growth, in which the traumata of life touch the ascending limb of the vitality curve. This is also the time of extraordinary plasticity of both somatic and psychic material. It is certainly not yet possible to see this relationship with the desired degree of clarity, but apparently it is not mere chance that the abreactions in play are correlated with the stage of greatest plasticity of the psyche and that, seemingly, they presuppose a psychic substance which has not yet been completely structuralized. When this plasticity has dwindled and the possibilities have narrowed and made way for a well-formed reality, and when the diffuse amorphous psychic organism has become a structure, then, apparently, other less alluring procedures take the place of play.

Another specific characteristic of play, which even today may be stated somewhat accurately, is related to the quality of unreality. In children, the boundaries between reality and fantasy are still hazy; the two realms overlap occasionally. This crucial characteristic of the child's world, as is well known, did not always attract the attention even of observers schooled in analytical psychology, and it has not been made the subject of exhaustive psychological study. It is obviously this merging of reality and fantasy which makes possible the abreaction of an experience in play. It remains for us to indicate how our knowledge may find practical application in pedagogy. If it is true that an abreaction to traumatic experiences occurs in play, the teacher is in a position to help the child obtain this kind of abreaction. When the child has had a very disagreeable experience, which is productive of shock or anxiety, it is possible for the teacher to play the experience with the child and somewhat casually permit the game to end with an outcome different from the experience or with the child in a different role, thus assisting the child to effect a comparatively speedy assimilation.

## Additional Functions of Play

This discussion has not attempted an exhaustive treatment of the phenomenon of play, nor is it an exhaustive account of everything which psychoanalysis can contribute to the understanding of the subject. We have commented only on the one aspect of play in children which seems to psychoanalysis of most significance for its understanding. It contains in no way the assertion that every game, without exception, must be such an assimilation process or that these determinants should be accepted as the final ones in the understanding of every single game.

A simple example of a game not in harmony with this interpretation is the playful reaching out for all objects, which puts in its appearance during the latter months of the first year. This behavior is perhaps the first which may be regarded as a manifestation of the instinct of mastery. At this particular time the child has reached an age when it is slowly becoming aware of the world and when objects in the outer world lose the originally menacing character to which the primal, predominantly negative reactions of the child bear witness, so that the child finds pleasure in gaining mastery over more and more objects. The pleasure he feels in this is perhaps remarkably similar to the one designated by the term "functional pleasure," but we must not ignore the specific quality of mastery.[8]

An additional function of play becomes evident if we consider that during play the child ventures to take over in a permissible way, roles which are ordinarily prohibited by his education, and which later, once the super-ego has formed, are also forbidden by his own conscience. Play is thus a leave of absence from reality, as well as from the superego.[9] Thus, play also helps in assimilating the impositions of education, in a way other than the one described.

The striking parallels to the play of children appear to be, as previously mentioned, fantasy and daydream. The two cardinal functions which we believe can be found in play we also encounter in fantasies: instinctual gratification and assimilation of disagreeable experiences. To a large extent fantasies are manifestly wish fulfillments, be they successful love, wealth, satisfied ambition or power, or whatever a daydream can conjure up as having been realized. In certain fantasies, however, the other role is involved: in these, experiences of a painful and disagreeable nature are constantly revived and return; unassimilated material urges to be re-handled, and only in this manner can it be assimilated, slowly and in small doses. To be sure, in the case of fantasy, the first meaning, that of wish fulfillment, is infinitely more frequent, so that one can seldom point out illustrations of the second function of fantasy, whereas, in the case of play, its significance as a frolicsome abreaction is undoubtedly just as important and as frequent as that of the realized gratification of a wish. The difference seems to be based on a circumstance we have already discussed: the ubiquity of traumatic

---

[8]In the empirical sense one can confidently speak of an instinct of mastery, but by this term we do not mean the ultimate in the realm of instinct. From the standpoint of the theory of instincts, the mastery instinct, like all others, is a blending of love and destructive instinct which has been turned outwards and rendered harmless through love.

[9]I wish to thank Mr. E. Kris for this formulation, which seems to me a happy one.

experiences during the tender years and its relative rarity in the life of the adult, hardened and protected by various kinds of armor.

Here the question may be raised as to the psychological difference between play and fantasy. Some of Freud's observations seem to answer this question.

> Every playing child behaves like a poet, in that he creates a world of his own, or more accurately expressed, he transposes things into his own world according to a new arrangement which is to his liking. It would be unfair to believe that he does not take this world seriously; on the contrary, he takes his play very seriously, he spends large amounts of affect on it. The antithesis of play is reality, not seriousness. The child differentiates his play world from reality very well, in spite of all the affective cathexis, and gladly lets his imaginary objects and relationships depend upon the tangible and visible things of the real world. Only this dependence differentiates the "play" of children from "fantasying."[10]

Freud's answer, then, is that a child's fantasies occupy themselves with a real object, while in the case of an adult, reality is severed from the world of fantasy. This appertains to that intermingling of reality and the fantasy world which is a familiar and characteristic feature of the infantile mind. Fantasy woven about a real object is, however, nothing other than play.

## Summary

To summarize, the psychoanalytic contributions to the problem of play may be indicated by the following phrases: instinct of mastery; wish fulfillment; assimilation of overpowering experiences according to the mechanism of the repetition compulsion; transformation from passivity to activity; leave of absence from reality and from the superego; fantasies about real objects.

If we compare these with the contributions which we owe to academic psychology, and which one can couch approximately in these phrases — phylogenetic echoing of serious affairs; atavism; mimicry; excess energy; preparation for future functions; functional pleasure — without in the least questioning the value of this point of view for a comprehensive theory of play, one can hardly avoid the impression, that the psychoanalytic contributions are more valuable for an understanding

---

[10]Freud: *The Relation of the Poet to Day-Dreaming*, Collected Papers, IV.

of the individual child, its individual development, its difficulties, and its attempts at their solution. They teach us to regard play as a sign of the child's psychological situation, and they can give us leads as to how to intervene properly in childhood conflicts.

# The Role of Play in Childhood

DAN I. SLOBIN

*The child's toys and the old man's reasons*
*Are the fruits of the two seasons.*
*— William Blake*

We are somewhere in Europe. A noisy, energetic group of children is playing before us, laughing and screaming. If they speak German, they will tell us that they are playing *Fuchs ins Loch;* if they speak French, it will be *Mère Garuche;* in Hungarian it will be *śanta roka* (Pfeifer, 1919). The language is not important, for the game is the same. Let us watch the children. They have drawn a circle on the ground, and in the circle stands one child, both feet firmly planted on the ground, a knotted handkerchief in his hand. Let us call him the "fox," after the German-speaking version. The fox comes out of his "hole," hopping on one leg, chasing the other players, waving his handkerchief. As soon as this whip touches one of the fleeing children, the roles change. The new child becomes the hopping fox, and all of the others chase him with their little whips until he finds refuge in his hole, where he is safe until he sallies forth again to continue the game. And so it goes for hours.

After our casual observation, the question immediately arises: "Why are these children playing this game?" One is tempted to answer: "Because that's the way the children around here enjoy themselves," and move on to other topics. But this common-sense answer is as deceptively simple as it is inadequate. Under the aegis of Freud (1950), the psychoanalyst Dr. Sigmund Pfeifer (1919) stepped forward to point out the manifestation of infantile-erotic drives in this game, and, indeed, in all games:

... we can assume in advance, with great probability, that in the creation of such general forms of pleasureful activity as [*Fuchs ins Loch*] the main role has been played by the same forces as in typical dreams, myths, legends, and neuroses. (pp. 248-249)

Since Freud refers to this account as authoritative (1950, p. 12), let us examine it to see how far it takes us in answering our question. Pfeifer, following Freud's clue in *Totem and Taboo*,* considers the latent content of all play to be that of wish-fulfilment effected via the use of symbols. Thus the task of the psychoanalyst lies in interpreting the symbols — inevitably overdetermined — through which the playing child strives to gratify his repressed sexual wishes. He spends many pages interpreting the latent content of the game we have just described. The circle of refuge, the hole, is, of course, recognized as "the genital symbol with parental significance, above all the mother's lap, when the child is protected from all the dangers and difficulties of the external world, to which he is drawn by his love and his erotic interest, to which he always strives to return" (p. 249). The fox's presence in this hole represents incest, followed by the punishment of castration: he must hop on one leg when leaving the hole. This interpretation is shored up by an appeal to the role of "mother earth" in mythology. But, symbols being overdetermined, the fox's behavior upon leaving his refuge, although punished by castration, still has sexual significance:

> the single leg functions itself as a penis symbol, rhythmically coming in contact with the Mother-Imago "Earth," and the game, if only symbolically, has procured for the player the desired gratification, which he has consciously (*sic*) already renounced. (p. 253)

What of the other children in the game? Again, the symbolism is overdetermined, for the fox also represents the father, who vengefully wields his whip against the "brother-band" of players, they in turn scourging the new fox with equal passion. With the symbolic change of generations, the new fox takes over the role of the father and enters the "motherly circle."

This sort of interpretation goes on for many pages. The psychoanalytically trained reader can undoubtedly fill in many of the details by himself. Pfeifer concludes that in all of his examples he has "found the most powerful of infantile-erotic forces, the incest-complex, to be active as primum movens" (p. 262). The basic aim of play is the attainment of

---

*"In the case of the child who finds himself under analogous psychic conditions, without being as yet capable of motor activity, we have elsewhere advocated the assumption that he at first really satisfies his wishes by means of hallucinations. . . . Such a *representation* of the gratified wish [in primitives] is altogether comparable to the *play* of children, where it replaces the purely sensory technique of gratification." (Freud, 1961, pp. 95-96).

pleasure through the gratification of these drives. To him the latency period is not a vacuum in the sexual life of the individual, but a phase in which sexuality is expressed in play:

> The emergence of games with repressed content coincides with the beginning of the great thrust of childhood repression, and especially the typical games with "mythological" content fill approximately the time from the third year of life until puberty, where a sharp decline of play activity is manifested. (p. 281)

Does this completely answer our first question as to why these children are playing this game? I think not. Does the symbolism of this traditional group game explain the motivation of each individual player? Does this sort of interpretation help us at all to understand why little girls should play *Fuchs ins Loch*? Does it tell us anything about the universality or non-universality of this game? Does it tell us anything about the effect of this game on the future lives of the players — both privately and socially? Clearly, the problem is not exhausted by Pfeifer's analysis.

This introduction has, however, been useful. Often a close examination of a particular phenomenon serves to illuminate not only that phenomenon, but a variety of theoretical positions as well. When we examine a set of behaviors as outstanding as that of play, we find ourselves face-to-face with hundreds of years of attempts to understand human behavior. As soon as we push beyond the above analysis, we are struck by diversity and multiplicity — multiple meanings of the words "play" and "game," and multiple meanings of the question: "Why does the child play?" Before we go further, these multiplicities must be dealt with.

## Semantic Domain

I will not attempt to define the words "play" or "game," but will consider their general and variegated meanings in English to be applicable here. The interested reader is referred to Huizinga's comparative philological study of this semantic domain in his excellent book *Homo Ludens* (1955). It should be pointed out, however, that the theories considered in this paper are couched in a variety of languages. Among them, English is unique in employing two words of unrelated historical origin — *play* and *game* (cf. German *spielen* and *spiel*, French *jouer* and *jeu*, Russian *igrat* and *igra*, etc.). In all of these languages the terms have a wonderful variety of metaphoric extensions. The relatively small desk edition of the *American College Dictionary* lists fifty-five uses of the word *play* and eighteen of *game*. The four-volume *Dictionary of the Russian Language*, published by the Academy of Sciences of the U.S.S.R., devotes six page-columns to words derived from the root *igr*, corresponding to the words *play* and *game*. Such usage seems to attest to the widespread importance of playlike activities in human life.

The inability to define exactly the phenomenon under consideration will not, I believe, hamper us in our analysis. We are unable to define precisely most of the words we use in everyday speech, yet this in no way interferes with our ability to use them consistently. No one has pressed this point more forcefully than the great modern philosopher Ludwig Wittgenstein, and nowhere more eloquently than in his discussion of this very word — *game*. I take the liberty of quoting him here *in extenso*, for his discussion applies both to the general issue of the definability of words, and to the specific theme of this paper.

> 66. Consider for example the proceedings that we call "games." I mean board-games, card-games, ball-games, athletic contests, and so on. What is common to all of them? — Don't say: "There *must* be something common to them or they would not be called 'games' " — but *look and see* whether there is something common to all. — For if you look at them you will not see something common to *all*, but similarities, relationships, and a whole series of them at that. . . . Look for example at board games, with their multifarious relationships. Now go on to card games; here you find many correspondences with the first group, but many common features disappear, and others appear. When we pass next to ball-games, much that is common is retained, but much is lost. — Are they all *"amusing?"* Compare chess with "X's and O's." Or is there always winning and losing, or competition between players? Think of patience. In ball games there is winning and losing; but when a child throws his ball at the wall and catches it again, this feature has disappeared. Look at the roles played by skill and luck. And how different is skill in chess and skill in tennis. Think now of games like ring-a-ring-a-roses: Here is the element of amusement, but how many other characteristic features have disappeared! And we can go through the many, many other groups of games in the same way; can see how similarities crop up and disappear.
>
> And the result of this examination is: We see a complicated network of similarities which overlap and criss-cross. Sometimes overall similarities, sometimes similarities of detail.
>
> 67. I can think of no better word to characterize these similarities than "family resemblances": for the various resemblances between members of a family: build, features, color of eyes, gait, temperament, etc., etc. overlap and criss-cross in the same way. — And I will say: "games" form a family. . . .

69. Then how would we explain to someone what a game is? I believe we would describe *games* to him, and we could add to the description: "this, *and similar things*, are called 'games.'" And do we know any more about it ourselves? Is it only other people whom we cannot tell exactly what a game is? — But this is not ignorance. We do not know the boundaries because none have been drawn. ...

70. "But if the concept 'game' is uncircumscribed like that, you don't really know what you mean by a 'game.'" — When I give the description: "The ground was all covered with plants" — do you want to say I don't know what I am talking about until I can give a definition of a plant? (1960, pp. 324-325)

This interlude has been long, but I hope useful — both in delimiting the field and revealing the problems which would accompany further attempts at definition. We are now free to go back to our original question once more: "Why does the child play?" This question, like the word itself, is not a single entity. It must be broken up into a number of more specific questions:

1. Where does the energy expended in play come from?
2. What, if any, is the biological function of play?
3. Why does the child spend his time playing, as opposed to doing nothing or doing other things?
4. What is the child's motivation in choosing a given game or play activity?
5. Why does the child continue to play, once he has begun?
6. How does play aid the child in development? (What is the significance of childhood play for the future life of the individual?)
7. Why does the child's society provide him with a given sub-set of the set of all possible games? (Is this sub-set of game related to others aspects of the society?)

To the best of my knowledge, no one theorist had addressed himself to all of these sub-questions, although many have claimed to have answered the broader question conclusively. (See bibliography.) Each theorist seems to pick out one or several of these smaller issues, offering an explanation consonant with his general theory of behavior or focus of interest. It is thus that most of the "theories of play" are not mutually exclusive, but complementary. With the deletion of a few widely discredited theories (like Hall's "abreaction of ancestral instincts"), we should be able to fit most of the explanations into a "grand overview" of the problem of play. Rather than attempt to elevate one facet of play to a statement of its fundamental nature, we shall attempt to treat the significance of the phenomenon, like the significance of its name, as one of multiple meanings.

For purposes of exposition, explanations of play will be discussed under four headings, on the basis of the *focus of attention* of the explanation: (1) biologically oriented, (2) person-oriented, (3) lifespace-oriented, and (4) socioculturally oriented explanations. This scheme claims to be neither an exhaustive nor a sharp classification of explanations of play, for explanations vary in their breadth of focus. The terminology for the second and third headings is borrowed, of course, from Lewin (1933). By person-oriented explanations I mean those whose primary interest is in the tensional systems within the individual and the means by which these tensions are dealt with in play. This is thus an "intrapersonal" orientation. By lifespace-oriented explanations I mean those which are concerned primarily with the person's interaction with objects and people in his world, and the role of play in structuring and determining these "extrapersonal" aspects of behavior. The meanings of the first and fourth headings seem to be fairly unambiguous, and will be developed in the discussion below.

It will be useful to make one more point of definition before moving into the discussion. Following Piaget (1951), I would like to distinguish between three main categories of games:

1. *Practice games.* This is generally what we call "play" in English, as opposed to "games." The term will be used to refer to pleasureful exercise of physical skills.

2. *Symbolic games.* These are games made up by individual children and played alone, usually involving a good deal of make-believe and imitation.

3. *Games with rules.* These are social games, involving regulations imposed by the group and sanctions for the violation of the rules.

It should be noted that this is a hierarchy: symbolic games may involve physical skill, and games with rules, such as *Fuchs ins Loch,* may involve both symbolism and physical skill. I also believe that this is an ontogenetic sequence, the prelinguistic infant exercising newly acquired skills purely for *Funktionslust;* the preschool child inventing his own games; the school child entering into games with his peers.

Many of the theories considered below do not take account of all three levels of playing, but try either to explain one type of game alone, or to assimilate all three to one type.

## Explanations of Play

### 1. *Biologically oriented explanations*

A number of theorists have been interested in setting play in the framework of biological evolution (Beach, 1945; Colozza, 1895; Groos, 1901; Nissen, 1951; Spencer, 1901; Spuhler, 1959).

The earliest of such attempts was that of Herbert Spencer, who argued that animals higher on the evolutionary continuum do not spend all of their time and energy in getting food, and thus must use up "surplus energy" in other activities. This aspect of Spencer's theory was earlier proposed by the poet Schiller, who said:

> An animal works when the mainspring of his activity is a deficiency, and it plays when this mainspring is a wealth of energy, when superfluous life itself presses for activity. (1862, p. 105)

For this reason, the theory is often called the "Schiller-Spencer Theory of Surplus Energy," although Spencer carried it farther than Schiller's hint. He theorized that faculties which have been quiescent for some time of necessity push for expression, and concluded that

> play is . . . an artificial exercise of powers which, in default of their natural exercise, become so ready to discharge that they relieve themselves by simulated actions in place of real actions. (1901, p. 630)

There are a number of difficulties in accepting this approach as explanatory of all play. At best, it tells us why the child plays as opposed to doing nothing or doing other things, and attempts to explain the energy source of this activity. The use of the word "surplus" is somewhat puzzling — surplus from what? There is usually apparent circularity in this usage: energy is considered surplus if expended in play, and non-surplus if expended in work.

This "theory" does not help us to understand the choice of play activities, and it limits the range of activity to the exercise of a vaguely defined and outdated concept of a biologically fixed and localizable set of "faculties." It deals only with practice games, which are common to higher animals and man, and is helpful only in saying that children are very energetic and, having nothing else to do, spend their time playing. This is barely more than common sense and does not carry us very far. Going back to our game of *Fuchs ins Loch*, we know nothing more about the symbolism or the rules of the game; and we do not even know why the children continue to play for hours, even to the point of exhaustion.

For this last reason, the surplus-energy view has often been opposed by the so-call *Erholungstheorie*, or "recreation theory," attributed to Lazarus (Colozza, 1895; Groos, 1901). This view regards play as an opportunity for the relaxation and restoration of exhausted powers. Actually, these two interpretations are not contradictory; both could operate under different conditions. But neither explains the choice of game or play activity. It is merely stated that "there is playing."

Groos, the great nineteenth-century authority on play, added another dimension to this sort of theorizing (1901): He noted the increasing dependency period and decreasing importance of rigidly patterned instinctual behavior up the phylogenetic scale, and explained play in higher animals as a period of *Vorubung* ("pre-exercise") of skills which the organism needs later in life:

> Play is the agency employed to develop crude powers and prepare them for life's uses, and from our biological standpoint we can say: From the moment when the intellectual development of a species becomes more useful in the "struggle for life" than the most perfect instinct, will natural selection favour those individuals in whom the less elaborated faculties have more chance of being worked out by practice under the protection of parents — that is to say, those individuals that play. (p. 375) . . . In general I hold to the view that play makes it possible to dispense to a certain degree with specialized hereditary mechanisms by fixing and increasing acquired adaptations. (p. 395)

This theory deserves more attention than the other two nineteenth-century theories discussed above, since it was also endorsed by Freud (1958, pp. 101–104) and seems to have support from contemporary comparative psychology (Nissen, 1951), and anthropology (Spuhler, 1959). Spuhler points out an evolutionary trend "from built-in nervous pathways to neural connections over association areas (where learning and symboling can be involved) in the physiological control of activities like sleep, play, and sex" (1959, p. 7). And Nissen develops the point that:

> In biological-teleological terms, play serves the purpose of developing an equipment of perceptual and motor patterns in the higher mammals, whereas animals with an inherited repertory of perceptions and motor coordinations do not need this opportunity,

being already provided with such neural organizations. (1951, p. 359)

If interpreted broadly enough, this point can carry us beyond practice games to all games. Given a long dependency period and little instinctively patterned behavior, the human child must learn not only physical, but also social and symbolic skills. We have hit here upon one of the essential functions of play in human life, a function not adequately dealt with by surplus energy or reaction theories. We will follow this thread of the role of play in socialization throughout the rest of the paper.

The biological explanations have, however, only started us off in our discussion by telling us that human children *do* in fact play. Groos attempts to carry us a step further in dealing with the question of why children continue to play once they have begun. Referring to the surplus energy and recreation theories, he says:

> But we find on further examination that a game once begun is apt to be carried on to the utmost limit of exhaustion — a fact which it is superfluous to illustrate, and which is inexplicable by either of the theories in question. Therefore it is important to notice two . . . considerations which throw light on [this problem]. The first is circular reaction, that self-imitation which in the resultant of one's own activities finds ever anew the model for successive acts and the stimulus to renewed repetition. The second is the trance condition [*Rauschzustand*], which so easily ensues from such activity, and which is practically irresistible. (pp. 366–369)

It is at just this point that Freud enters the discussion, and we shall accordingly turn now to him.

2. *Person-oriented explanations*

In the course of his prolific career, Freud made many references to the phenomenon of play.* Almost all of his statements deal with the role of play in working out individual problems or in yielding individual pleasure, and thus we will discuss his contribution in the context of intrapersonal explanations.

*1905: *Wit and its Relation to the Unconscious;* 1908: *The Relation of the Poet to Daydreaming;* 1912-13: *Totem and Taboo;* 1919: *The Uncanny;* 1920: *Beyond the Pleasure Principle;* 1926: *Inhibitions, Symptoms, and Anxiety; The Question of Lay Analysis; On Female Sexuality.*

Freud's earliest remarks on play are to be found in *Wit and its Relation to the Unconscious*, first published in 1905. Here we find direct responses to the work of Groos, which had appeared six years earlier. In speaking of the acquisition of language, Freud accepts Groos' general interpretation:

> Play . . . appears in children while they are learning how to use words and connect thoughts; this playing is probably the result of an impulse which urges the child to exercise his capacities (Groos). (1958, p. 104)

He disagrees with Groos, however, on the interpretation of repetition in play. He explains repetition on the basis of the pleasure involved in rediscovering and recognizing the familiar. (It is interesting to note that this was also Aristotle's position in his *Poetics*.)

It was not until *Beyond the Pleasure Principle*, in 1920, that Freud examined in detail the problem of play and repetition. At one point in this work he explains the pleasure of repetition as one which stems from the reassuring knowledge of the stability of the world; the child finds joy in the knowledge of identity, in the ability to say, as William James put it, "thingambob again!"

> But children will never tire of asking an adult to repeat a game that he has shown them or played with them, till he is too exhausted to go on. And if a child has been told a nice story, he will insist on hearing it over and over again rather than a new one. . . . None of this contradicts the pleasure principle; the re-experiencing of something identical, is clearly in itself a source of pleasure. (1950, pp. 45–46)

Freud's argument, however, becomes especially important in the discussion of the role of the pleasure principle in the repetition of symbolic games which individual children invent themselves, as opposed to the practice games discussed by Groos or the games they play with adults. Freud sees such games as the ego's attempt to repeat actively a traumatic event which was earlier experienced passively, thereby gaining a belated mastery over the event. This interpretation immediately raises the problem of the repetition of unpleasant experiences, and Freud considers the possibility that such repetition goes "beyond the pleasure principle." He comes to the conclusion that, although play resembles repetition compulsions which do go beyond the pleasure principle, repetition in play is supported by other motives, such as mastery or revenge:

We are therefore left in doubt as to whether the impulses to work over in the mind some overpowering experience so as to make oneself master of it can find expression as a primary event, and independently of the pleasure principle. For, in the case we have been discussing, the child may, after all, only have been able to repeat his unpleasant experience in play because the repetition carried along with it a yield of pleasure of another sort but none the less a direct one. (1950, p. 16) . . . the compulsion to repeat, and instinctual satisfaction which is immediately pleasurable, seem to converge here into intimate partnership. (p. 25)

And, finally, Freud concludes:

In the case of children's play we seemed to see that children repeat unpleasurable experiences for the additional reason that they can master a powerful impression far more thoroughly by being active than they could by merely experiencing it passively. Each fresh repetition seems to strengthen the mastery they are in search of. (p. 45)

Freud's ideas about play are echoed in many places in the psychological literature. (See Fenichel, 1945; Erikson, 1950, 1959). The concept of play as a situation in which the ego can, in Erikson's terms, "deal with experience by creating model situations and . . . master reality by experiment and planning" (1950, p. 194) is the guiding principle of play therapy. Virginia Axline has just this interpretation of play in mind in saying:

Play therapy is based upon the fact that play is the child's natural medium of self-expression. It is an opportunity which is given to the child to "play out" his feelings and problems just as, in certain types of adult therapy, an individual "talks out" his difficulties. (1947, p. 9) . . . When he plays freely . . . he is expressing his personality. . . . He is releasing the feelings and attitudes that have been pushing to get out into the open. (p. 23)

This view is so strikingly similar to that of Friedrich Schiller that it is of interest to quote his statement of 1795:

In the midst of the terrible empire of energies [cf. id?] and in the midst of the holy empire of laws [cf. superego?] the drive of aesthetic creativity cultivated, unnoticed, a third, happy empire of play and of illusion, in which it removes from man the bonds of all relationships and frees him from all that is called constraint — in the physical as well as in the moral sphere. (1862, p. 109)

This is all we shall have to say about the role of play in resolving inner conflicts, although aspects of this problem will arise again in the following section. Until now, everything we have had to say about play fits into the scheme of orthodox psychoanalytic theory and represents most of what that theory has to say about our problem. How far have we come? Let us review the seven questions which we found lurking behind our original query — "Why does the child play?" (1) The energy comes from infantile-erotic drives which strive for expression. (2) The biological function of play is to allow for the reduction of tensions created by the repression or suppression of activities — either because they are socially reprehensible, or because the child is not yet capable of mastering his environment. (3) The child spends his time playing because he is cared for — he does not have to "struggle for existence" — and because he has many things to learn before he can begin to "struggle." (4) He chooses practice games because of the pleasure of exercising his capacities without anxiety. He invents symbolic games to master actively traumatic experiences endured passively. He partakes of group games with rules because they allow for symbolic resolution of his oedipal conflict. (5) He continues to play, once he has begun, either because recognition of a return of the familiar is pleasureful, or because repeated mastery of a problem is pleasureful. (6) We know very little about the significance of childhood play for the future life of the individual, except that the role of play in making childhood adjustments will have something to do with later adult adjustments. (7) We have no idea why games should differ from society to society. As a matter of fact, following the above argument, there should be no significant difference between societies as far as games are concerned. If the human drama — its myths, its symbols, its conflict — is universal, and if play is but an acting out of this drama, play, too, must be universal in character.

We see that psychoanalytic theory has not brought us to the end of our journey. It is precisely in what I have called the "extra-personal" aspects of play that this theory is weakest. It does not account for the observed fact, to be discussed below, that societies *do* in fact differ consistently in the sub-set of the set of all possible games which are played by their members. Nor does it deal with the fact that play, in addition to releasing tensions, has a great deal to do with structuring the individual's view of himself and his world.

Piaget's far-reaching analysis of *Play, Dreams, and Imitation in Childhood* (1951) attempts to deal with the same problems as psychoanalytic theory from a different point of view. We have already found his classification of games useful, and we will discuss his analysis of games with rules below. Like Freud, he accepts *Funktionslust* and mastery of conflicts as motivations for play. Just as Freud says that "the re-experiencing of something identical, is clearly in itself a source of pleasure," so does Piaget characterize play as activity in which "assimilation" predominates over "accommodation." That is to say that the playing child is more engaged in adopting experience and making it his own by fitting it into his schemata, than he is in changing his schemata to meet the demands of reality and experience. Thus play is seen as assimilation of reality to the ego.

Piaget insists, however, that children's use of symbolism can only be explained as being a function of the way in which they think in the stages of development which precede logical thought:

> . . . the formation of the symbol is not due to its content, but to the very structure of the child's thought. Wherever there is symbolism, in dreams, in the images of the half-sleeping state or in children's play, it is because thought, in its . . . elementary stages, proceeds by egocentric assimilation, and not by logical concepts. (p. 156)

He gives many convincing examples to prove his point, but I am not prepared to choose between this interpretation of symbolism and the Freudian. Although Piaget's study is very impressive, we are still left with some of the problems noted above.

### 3. *Lifespace-oriented explanations*

We turn now to those explanations of play which focus their attention on the child's interaction with objects and people in his world, and the role of play in structuring and determining these "extrapersonal" aspects of behavior. Among these explanations we find those of the "ego-psychologists."

*Play with others.* — Erikson has much to say about play in this light. He defines the field as follows:

> I would look at a play act as, vaguely speaking, a function of the ego, an attempt to bring into synchronization the bodily and social processes of which one is a part even while one is a self. (1950, p. 194)

This is the first discussion we have considered which pays specific attention to "social processes." Erikson follows the psychoanalytic tradition in considering symbolic games — play for oneself — as being aimed at mastery of conflicts and of motor skills. But he introduces play with others into his discussion also, and points out the role of group games in social adjustment:

> Finally, at nursery-school age playfulness reaches into the *macrosphere*, the world shared with others. First these others are treated as things, are inspected, run into, or forced to "be horsie." Learning is necessary in order to discover what potential play content can be admitted only to fantasy or only to autocosmic play; what content can be successfully represented only in the microcosmic world of toys and things; and what content can be shared with others and forced upon them. (p. 194)

This shift of emphasis draws our attention to the insight of George Herbert Mead (1934). Interaction in play with other children enables the child to develop both an idea of self and of "generalized other." The playing child shifts from one role to another (remember *Fuchs ins Loch*) and is forced to change his perspective. In group games with rules the player must know the roles of all the other players, as well as his own role, and must develop the ability to "take the role of the other" in order to predict what will happen next and adjust his behavior accordingly. The child begins to assess his abilities against those of others, and develop a self-image — an identity.

The playing youngster learns more than his own identity. By playing various adult roles, he must also learn the social rules, the norms which regulate that actor's behavior.

In addition, all of these games with rules are of great psychological interest in another aspect of personality development. The player must learn to submit to a rule even in those situations in which his immediate impulse would push him to a completely different behavior. He may play only one role at a time, and he must play it according to the rules. In the words of the Soviet psychologist Leontiev: "To master a rule — this means to master one's own behavior, to learn to regulate it, to learn to submit it to a given task." (1959, p. 404).

Piaget's careful study of the rules of marble games (1932) has shown in great detail what an important and difficult task this learning of rules is. He distinguished three stages in the development of the consciousness of rules:

> Before the intervention of adults or of older children there are in the child's conduct certain rules that we have called motor rules. But they are not imperative, they do not constitute duties but only spontaneous regularities of behavior. From the moment, however, that the child has received from his parents a system of commands,

rules and, in general, the world order itself seem to be morally necessary. In this way, as soon as the little child encounters the example of older children at marbles, he accepts these suggestions and regards the new rules discovered in this way as sacred and obligatory. (1932, p. 101)

Finally, in the highest stage, the children demonstrate an interest in rules for their own sake, realizing that rules are based on mutual consent, and can thus be altered.

It seems to me that these three functions of play — the learning of *identity roles, and rule-bound behavior* — are not sufficiently dealt with in the psychoanalytic analysis which we reviewed above. Nevertheless, we cannot ignore the psychodynamic aspects of play, either. Erikson is careful to point out that the elements of group games must have both common and unique meanings. A common game *may* have important unique meanings to some children, providing them with symbolic gratification of various desires. But the game certainly does not have the same symbolic meaning to all of the players, and may not even be used by all of them as a symbolic outlet. Thus some of the children playing *Fuchs ins Loch* may indeed find gratification of incestuous wishes, but others may satisfy aggressive desires by flailing their knotted handkerchiefs; still others may be primarily motivated by the prestige of playing with older children, and so on. I am convinced that a mono-motive, monolithic explanation of such complex behavior must be considered inadequate, despite its apparent simplicity. Alfred North Whitehead once said: "Seek simplicity, and distrust it."

*Play and Motivation.* — The simple, motor-motive, tension-reduction view of behavior has been attacked from many fronts recently. All of the talk about curiosity drives, exploratory drives, manipulatory drives, and so on is applicable to our problem. Such stimulus-seeking behavior is characteristic of much of play. Robert White takes these views and the problem of learning physical and social skills, and builds an impressive argument for the importance of "effectance motivation" and the development of competence:

> The theory that we learn what helps us to reduce our viscerogenic drives will not stand up if we stop to consider the whole range of what a child must learn in order to deal effectively with his surroundings. . . . Seen in this light the many hours that infants and children spend in play are by no means wasted or merely recuperative in nature. Play may be fun, but it is also a serious business in childhood. During these hours the child steadily builds up his competence in dealing with the environment. (1960, p. 102)

White's approach sums up the necessity of taking what I have called an "extra-personal" or "lifespace-oriented" frame of reference:

> I have no intention to dispute what Erikson, among others, have shown about symbolism in child's play and about erotic and aggressive preoccupations that lead to play disruption. But we lose, rather than gain, in my opinion, if we consider the child's *undisrupted* play, six hours a day, to be a continuous expression of libidinal energy, a continuous preoccupation with the family drama, *as if there could be no intrinsic interest in the properties of the external world and the means of coming to terms with it.* (Italics mine.) (1960, p. 113)

Piaget again presses this point when he speaks of play enabling the ego to assimilate reality — to develop concepts of the objective and social worlds (1951).

It is precisely this aspect of play that has always impressed educators, and men from Plato to Confucius to Locke, Froebel, Vygotsky, and Bruner have dealt with the importance of play in the process of learning. Closely related is all of the theorizing in psychology about the role of intrinsic motivation. Bruner has recently stressed the play aspect of learning in suggesting the hypothesis

> that cognitive operations are facilitated by a "game attitude" — a certain playfulness constrained by a sense of the rules. It may well be that a "game attitude" has the effect of denaturing or delibidinizing problem solving activity so that it is less interfered with by a sense of the consequences of success and failure. The evidence seems to indicate, however ambiguously, that "playing around with ideas pays off." (1961, p. 29).

I think we must conclude that individual play, by giving the child the opportunity to manipulate his world without the threat of severe loss or punishment, can help him both to work out his emotional problems and to learn about the world around him. And social play gives him the opportunity to develop ideas of his own identity, interaction with others, social roles, and the importance of rule-bound behavior. Thus it appears that, beginning with the initial achievement of mastering the object concept in infancy, it is through play that much of what we call "a civilized human being" is produced.

### 4. *Socioculturally oriented explanations*

The fact that different societies produce different sorts of "civilized human beings" brings us to the last main topic of discussion. At this point the sociologists and anthropologists join us, bringing their knowledge of the uses of play in various cultures of the world.

Obviously, games in which children act out social roles and events will vary from culture to culture, depending on the models available for imitation. Using John Whiting's concept of "status envy" (1960), however, we can go more deeply into this point. Whiting argues that a child will covertly practice those roles which seem to him to carry special privileges, but which he, because of his status as a child, cannot act out in reality. That is, a child will behave like a favoured individual in an attempt to get for himself the privileges associated with his status. The sum of these envied statuses make up the child's "optative identity." Following this reasoning, a study of those role models which are most frequently imitated by children in their play will yield valuable information about the child's view of social reality in various cultures. Thus aspects of the family and social structures influence the child's choice of play activities.

From here it is a short step to the fruitful consideration of games as models for other cultural activities. A. R. Anderson and O. K. Moore at Yale have developed the concept of "autotelic folk-model" to deal with this very important aspect of games (Anderson and Moore, 1960; Moore and Anderson, 1961). They make the point that human beings in society face three broad types of problems, or aspects of problem situations: (1) non-interactional problems, in which the human being manipulates the environment without being manipulated back; (2) interactional problems, in which the behavior of others must be taken into account; and (3) affective problems. The behavioral scientist must raise the question: How do people learn technique to handle these problems? (Cf. White's statement, quoted above, about "the whole range of what a child must learn in order to deal effectively with his surroundings.")

It is not enough to say that children learn from adults. Such problems often entail serious consequences and require a certain degree of skill before they can be dealt with well. Thus every society must have certain activities which serve as teaching devices. Anderson and Moore set down three conditions which such activities must satisfy: (1) They must be cut off from the more serious aspects of the society's activities. The rewards must not be too expensive, nor the consequences of error too serious. (2) Thus "the rewards in the learner's activities must be intrinsic, or inherent in the activity itself. Such activities we call *autotelic*: they contain their own goals, and sources of motivation." (3) The devices must help the child to learn the relevant techniques.

Although Anderson and Moore do not often use the term *play* to describe these activities, I think it is clear that they are addressing themselves to the same problems which we have considered. Their approach seems to me to be a useful one. We can fit our classification of games into their classification of universal problem situations: Practice games deal with non-interactional problems; symbolic games deal with affective problems; and games with rules deal with interactional problems. It is encouraging to find our classification system repeated in this guise, and it leads us to hope that such a classification of autotelic activities may be universal. This system allows us, I believe, to deal with all of the functions of play which we have discussed above. The fact that each of our major categories of games coincides with a general human problem area lends credence to the notion of games as models for more serious aspects of human behavior.

These play activities are called, by Anderson and Moore, "autotelic folk models" — i.e., "models in the pre-scientific culture, with the help of which members of a society learn about and 'play at' the workings of their society." A fascinating argument justifies the choice of games as models for more serious behavior. Both probability theory and game theory grew directly out of the study of activities which people engage in "for the fun of it," yet the striking fact is that these mathematical theories are also successful in dealing with "the more serious matters of survival and welfare." Thus it is quite plausible to suggest that "in acting autotelically we are 'modeling' our own more serious behavior" (1961, p. 4). Modern board games like "Monopoly" and "Diplomacy" are obvious examples. But the correspondence between games and cultural activities need not be so sharply drawn. Huizinga was so struck with this correspondence between play and other aspects of human life that he dubbed man *Homo Ludens*, finding the play element pervading all of the activities of man (1955).

Roberts, Arth, and Bush (1959), looking upon games in a similar light, went to the Yale Area Files and confirmed some very interesting ideas about games as models for other behavior. They classified games into three groups, somewhat similar to ours: (1) games of physical skill, in which self-reliance is learned; (2) games of strategy, in which social roles are learned; and (3) games of chance, in which responsibility and achievement are learned. They then looked for the following sorts of relationships between games and culture:

> If games are expressive models, they should be related to other aspects of culture and to variables which figure in expressive or projective mechanisms. More specifically, games of strategy which are models of social interaction should be related to the complexity of the social system; games of chance which are models of interaction with the supernatural should be linked with other expressive views of the supernatural; and there is a possibility that games of physical skill may be related to aspects of the natural environment. (pp. 599–600)

Social system, religion, and natural environment were found to be related to the presence of various sorts of games in a given society. For example, societies with high political integration and social stratification have many games of strategy, while societies low in these variables do not tend to have such games. Yet these variables were not related to the presence of games of skill in the societies examined. Thus the "macrosphere" which we look to for an understanding of children's play must be larger than the nursery-school group — it must include the social system, religion, natural environment, and probably additional aspects of the larger world in which children and their parents find themselves.

Roberts, Arth, and Bush quote unpublished data of Whiting, Lambert, and Child which show relations between games and child-rearing practices. For example, the presence of games of strategy was found to be positively associated with low permissiveness in child training, high severity of bowel training, and high reward for obedience behavior. Games of chance were not related to these variables, but to stress on responsibility and achievement behavior. Thus the sub-set of the set of all possible games which a society makes available to its members is also determined by the values and way of life of the society. We are faced with a web of causality far more complex than the simple explanation of Pfeifer that European children play *Fuchs ins Loch* in order to gratify symbolically their incestuous desires. This argument would be more convincing if it were limited to games which have been played at all times and in all places, but, even then, the Freudian explanation is no more economical than one based on universal and enduring aspects of the problem situations which human beings always face.

## Conclusions

It is now time to return to the question which arose at the outset of this review of what men have had to say about play. We had just watched a group of children playing *Fuchs ins Loch*, or *Mère Garuche*, or *śanta ťoka*, and we asked: "Why are these children playing this game?" On closer examination, it turned out that we had at least seven questions to answer. Have we made any progress?

1. *Where does the energy expended in play come from?* It comes from the same source as all of the energy which drives the body. It makes no sense to call it "surplus" — surplus from what? We only know that it is being expended in play. It is also unenlightening to speak of "infantile-erotic drives," or of libido, for if this energy is the only energy available to the body for *all* activity, play is not differentiated in its energy source.

Following the Freudian tripartite division of the psyche, however, we can say that the energy expended in play is at the service of the ego.

2. *What, if any, is the biological function of play?* If we wish, we may consider the reduction of psychic tensions to be a biological function of play. But, more generally, there does not seem to be a strictly biological function of all play, nor does this seem to be the most significant fact about human play. We can say that a certain amount of muscular exercise seems to be a basic need of the organism (Nissen, 1951). Thus the biological function of playing *Fuchs ins Loch* is one of exercise and, perhaps for some children, tension reduction.

3. *Why does the child spend his time playing, as opposed to doing nothing or doing other things?* The children we have been watching are human beings, who have a long dependency period, few rigidly patterned instinctive behaviors, and a great capacity to learn how to get along with their environment. They are not yet capable of supporting themselves and are nurtured by adults. For much of the time these European children playing before us are not only free of serious work obligations, but are expected to spend some of their time in play.

4. *What is the child's motivation in choosing a given game or play activity?* Individual differences make it impossible to answer this question. In the swarm of children chasing after the "fox," who knows how many different sorts of motivation impel them onward? I do not believe that we can accept any of the suggestions we have reviewed as *the* answer to this question. Certainly, the Freudian motive is one answer, but there are also needs for achievement, affiliation, power and so on. Many play activities are certainly pursued primarily for *Funktionslust*, although other motivations, such as mastery, may enter also.

5. *Why does the child continue to play, once he has begun?* There is, to be sure, a certain *Rauschzustand*, a certain "trance state," associated with such group games as the one we are considering. But there are also needs for achievement and affiliation involved in continuing to play in the group, and a host of other needs. Some children may indeed enjoy the repeated mastery of disturbing conflicts, as symbolized in the game. We are tempted to say that each child plays on because he is enjoying himself — but is this really true in every case?

6. *How does playing aid the child in development?* Certainly this game develops motor skill and coordination. It also develops social skills which are learned in the process of interacting with others. In order to play *Fuchs ins Loch* the children must learn the rules and follow them. They must learn to shift roles and change orientations quickly. To the extent that adjustments to childhood problems are made through this game, playing has some effect upon later adult adjustments.

7. *Why does the child's society provide him with a given sub-set of the set of all possible games?* (i.e., why is *Fuchs ins Loch* played in 20th-century Europe?) This is a difficult question to answer, for we do not know enough here about the history of this game or the sociocultural nature of the areas in which it is played. But we can be sure that there are many important sociocultural and environmental determinants, as well as interesting regional variations.

I hope we have advanced somewhat in our notion of why children play and what the significance of their playing may be. The question undoubtedly has more facets, but we have at least been able to place children's play in its psychological and sociocultural setting.

Let me conclude with the observation of a great inventor of mathematical and philosophical systems, Gottfried Wilhelm Leibnitz: "Die Menschen haben niemals grösseren Scharfsinn gezeigt als bei der Erfindung der Spiele." ("Man has never shown more keen sense than in his invention of games.")

## References

Anderson, A. R., and Moore, O. K., "Autotelic Folk-Models," American Sociological Association, Sociological Theory Section, New York, September, 1960; mimeographed.

Appleton, Lilla E., *A Comparative Study of the Play Activities of Adult Savages and Civilized Children*, Chicago: University of Chicago Press, 1910.

Axline, Virginia M., *Play Therapy*, Boston: Houghton Mifflin, 1947.

Beach, F. A., "Current Concepts of Play in Animals," *American Naturalist*, Vol. 79 (1945), pp. 523-54.

Bruner, J. S., "On Coping and Defending," Harvard University, no date; Ditto. (Published in French as "Affrontment et defense" in Journal de Psychologie, Vol. 1 [1961], pp. 33-56.)

———, "On Learning Mathematics," Harvard University, Center for Cognitive Studies, 1961: two chapters, Ditto.

———, *On Knowing : Essays for the Left Hand*, Cambridge, Mass.: Belknap Press of Harvard University Press, 1962.

Buytendijk, F. J. J., *Wesen und Sinn des Spiels*, Berlin : Kurt Wolff, 1933.

Callois, R., "The Structure and Classification of Games," *Diogenes*, 1955, No. 12, pp. 62-75.

Colozza, G. A., *Il Giuoco nella Psicologia e nella Pedagogia*, Naples : Ditta G. B. Paravia, 1895.

Drost, J. W. P., *Het nederlansch kinderspel vóór de zeventiende eeuw*, 's-Gravenhage : Martinus Nijhoff, 1914.

———, "Identity of the Life Cycle," *Psychological Issues*, Vol. 1 (1959), No. 1.

Erikson, E. H., *Childhood and Society*, New York : Norton, 1950.

Fenichel, O. *The Psychoanalytic Theory of Neurosis*, New York : Norton, 1945.

Freud, S., "Das Unheimliche," in *Ges. Werke*, XII, London : Imago, 1947.

———, "Hemmung, Symptome und Angst," *ibid.*, XIV, London : Imago, 1948.

———, "Nachwort zur 'Frage der Laienanalyse,' " *ibid.*

———, "Uber die weibliche Sexualitat," *ibid.*

———, *Beyond the Pleasure Principle*, New York : Liveright, 1950.

———, *Der Witz und seine Beziehung zum Unbewussten*, Frankfurt : Fischer, 1958.

———, "The Relation of the Poet to Daydreaming," in *On Creativity and the Unconscious*, New York : Harper, 1958.

———, *Totem und Tabu*, Frankfurt : Fischer, 1961.

Groos, K., *The Play of Man*, New York : Appleton, 1901.

Huizinga, J., *Homo Ludens: A Study of the Play-Element in Culture*, Boston : Beacon, 1955.

Leontiev, L. N., "Psikhologicheskie osnovy doshkol'noi igry" ["Psychological bases of pre-school play"], in *Problemy razvitiya psikhiki* [Problems of mental development]. Moscow : izd-vo APN FSFSR, 1959; pp. 384–406.

Lewin, K., "Environmental Forces," in C. Murchison (ed.), *A Handbook of Child Psychology*, 2d ed., rev. Worcester, Mass. : Clark University Press, 1933; pp. 590–625.

———, *A Dynamic Theory of Personality*, New York : McGraw-Hill, 1935.

Lowenfeld, Margaret, *Play in Childhood*, London : Gollancz, 1935.

Mead, G. H., *Mind, Self and Society from the Standpoint of a Social Behaviorist*, Chicago : University of Chicago Press, 1934.

Miller, N., *The Child in Primitive Society*, New York: Brentano's, 1928.

Moore, O. N., and Anderson, A. R., "Some Puzzling Aspects of Social Interaction," Yale University; mimeographed. (To be published in the Proceedings of the Small Groups Symposium held June 20-24, 1961, at Stanford University.)

Nissen, H. W., "Phylogenetic Comparison," in S. S. Stevens (ed.), *Handbook of Experimental Psychology*, New York: Wiley, 1951; pp. 347-386.

Pfeifer, S., "Ausserungen infantil-erotischer Triebe im Spiele: Psychoanalytische Stellungnahme zu den wichtigsten Spieltheorien," *Imago*, Vol. 4 (1919), pp. 247-282.

Piaget, J., *The Moral Judgment of the Child*, New York: Harcourt, Brace, 1932; chap. i, The Rules of the Game, pp. 1–103.

———, *Play, Dreams and Imitation in Childhood*, New York: Norton, 1951.

Pokrovskii, E. A., *Detskie igry premushchestvenno russkiya* [Children's games, mostly Russian], Moscow : Richter, 1895.

Roberts, J. M., Arth, M. J., and Bush, R. R., "Games in Culture," *American Anthropologist*, Vol. 61 (1959), pp. 597-605.

Sarbin, T. R., "Role Theory," in G. Lindzey (ed.), *Handbook of Social Psychology*, Reading, Mass. : Addison-Wesley, 1954; I, 223–258.

Schiller, F., "Ueber die astetische Erziehung des Menschen," in einer Reihe von Briefen, in Samt. Werke, XII, 1-112, Stuttgart : Cotta'scher Verlag, 1862.

Schlosberg, H., "The Concept of Play," *Psychological Review*, Vol. 54 (1947), pp. 229-231.

Spencer, H., *The Principles of Psychology*, New York : Appleton, 1901; Vol. II.

Spuhler, J. N., *The Evolution of Man's Capacity for Culture*, Detroit : Wayne State University Press, 1959.

Stern, W., *The Psychology of Early Childhood up to the Sixth Year of Age*, New York : Holt, 1930.

Vygotski, L. S., *Pedagogicheskaya psikhologiya : kratkii kurs* [Pedagogical psychology : Short course], Moscow : izd-vo Rabotnik Prosveshcheniya, 1926.

White, R. W., "Competence and the Psychosexual Stages of Development," in M. R. Jones (ed.), *Nebraska Symposium on Motivation, 1960*. Lincoln : University of Nebraska, 1960; pp. 97-141.

Whiting, J., "Sexual Identification and Cultural Patterns," (Lecture, Harvard University, Department of Social Relations, October 28, 1960.)

Wittgenstein, L., *Schriften*, Frankfurt : Suhrkamp, 1960.

# PART II
# Major Approaches to the Therapeutic Use of Play

# Introduction

Six theoretical approaches to the therapeutic use of play are presented in this chapter. The approaches are listed in historical sequence, beginning with the pioneering techniques of the psychoanalysts and ending with the recent applications of learning or behavioral principles to the playroom. Quite diverse in nature, the approaches explain the therapeutic changes that occur during the play session in terms of different psychological processes and levels of psychic functioning. Also noteworthy is the fact that while the analytic and release approaches to play place great emphasis on the content of the child's play during therapy, other schools of thought use play only as a medium for other interventions, such as setting limits on inappropriate behavior or developing relationships. For this reason the term "therapeutic use of play" seems to be a better way of classifying the six major approaches than the more common term "play therapy." All the approaches under the former classification consider child's play to be a natural and effective modality for eliciting and altering the problem behavior of children.

The psychoanalytic approach to play emphasizes the use of the therapist's interpretation of a child's words and actions, as well as the analysis of the transference relationship, to help the child achieve insight into his unconscious conflicts. The release approach, on the other hand, attempts to structure the play materials so as to assist the child to ventilate and work through his emotional conflicts. The relationship orientation of Axline[1] stresses the importance of creating a social climate wherein the therapist shows acceptance of the child and trust in the

[1]See Virginia Axline's book *Play Therapy*. New York: Ballantine, 1969.

child's ability to resolve his own problems. The play group approach for very young children as well as the activity group approach for preadolescents add the influence of group dynamics to the therapeutic process.[2] The limit-setting approach places great emphasis on the therapist's setting clear and enforceable rules regarding a child's unacceptable behavior in the playroom. The behavioral approach uses empirically derived principles of learning — e.g., reinforcement — to help the child and parents unlearn maladaptive behaviors.

With such a wide assortment of therapeutic play approaches to draw from, the clinician may find it extremely difficult to decide which strategy is best for an individual child. At the present time one has to rely more on clinical judgment and experience than research data to resolve this question. It has been the editor's experience that the analytic approach is best suited for children with neurotic disorders who have little insight into their intrapsychic conflict. The release approach has been used effectively to help children with pent-up hostility achieve catharsis and to assist children to ventilate their anxieties over traumatic events in their lives. The relationship approach seems particularly appropriate for encouraging the insecure, withdrawn child to gain self-confidence and trust in others. The play or activity group is clearly the method of choice for children with socialization problems, including shy and aggressive children. The limit-setting approach is best employed with undisciplined, impulsive children, while the behavioral approach is applicable to a broad-spectrum of behavior problems. The behavioral approach has proven especially effective with habit and conduct disorders.

There is still, however, a pressing need for well-controlled research studies to investigate the effectiveness of each of the major play approaches with different types of childhod disorders.

[2]For a comprehensive discussion of the play group approach see M. Schiffer's book *The Therapeutic Play Group*. New York: Grune & Stratton, 1969.

# PSYCHOANALYTIC

# The Psychoanalytic Play Technique

MELANIE KLEIN

In this paper, I shall briefly outline the steps by which the psychoanalytic play technique developed. In 1919, when I started my first case, some psychoanalytic work with children had already been done particularly by Dr. Hug-Hellmuth. However, she did not undertake the psychoanalysis of children under six, and although she used drawings and occasionally play as material she did not develop this into a specific technique.

At the time I began to work, it was an established principle that interpretations should be given very sparingly; and although psychoanalysts were endeavoring to explore the unconscious, with few exceptions they did not penetrate deeply into it. All this applied particularly to children. Moreover, at that time, and for some years to come, only children from the latency period onward were regarded as suitable for psychoanalysis.

## Basic Principles

My first patient was a five-year-old boy. I referred to him under the name Fritz in my first published paper (3). To begin with I thought it would be sufficient to influence the mother's attitude. I suggested that she should encourage the child to discuss freely with her the many unspoken questions which were obviously at the back of his mind and impeding his intellectual development. This had a good effect but his neurotic difficulties were not sufficiently alleviated, and it was soon decided that I should psychoanalyze him. In doing so I deviated from some of the rules so far established, for I interpreted what I thought to be most urgent in the material the child presented to me and found my interest focusing on his anxieties and the defenses against them.

The treatment was carried out in the child's home with his own toys. This analysis was the beginning of the psychoanalytic play technique, for Fritz expressed fantasies, anxieties, and defenses mainly by play, and I consistently interpreted its preconscious and unconscious meaning to him, with the result that additional material came up in his play. That is to say that I already used with this patient in essence the method of interpretation which became characteristic of my technique. This approach corresponds to a fundamental principle of psychoanalysis — free association. In interpreting not only the child's words but also his activities with his toys, I applied this basic principle to the mind of the child, whose play and varied activities, in fact his whole behavior, are means of expressing what the adult expresses predominantly by words. I was also guided from the beginning by two other tenets of psychoanalysis: the exploration of the unconscious as the main task of the psychoanalytic procedure and the analysis of the transference as the means of achieving this. I am here referring to one of the fundamental discoveries of Freud, that the patient transfers his early experiences and his feelings and thoughts in relation first to his parents and then to other people to the psychoanalyst and that it is by analyzing this transference that the past as well as the unconscious part of the mind can be explored.

## Phobias and Obsessions in a Girl of Two

Between 1920 and 1923, I gained further experience with other child cases, but a definite step in the development of play technique was the treatment of a child of two years and nine months, whom I psychoanalyzed in 1923. I have given some details of this child's case under the name Rita in my book *The Psycho-Analysis of Children* (7). Rita suffered from night terrors and animal phobias, was very ambivalent toward her mother, at the same time clinging to her to such an extent that she could hardly be left alone. She had a marked obsessional neurosis and was at times very depressed. Her play was inhibited and her inability to tolerate frustrations made her upbringing increasingly difficult. I was very doubtful how to tackle this case since the analysis of so young a child was an entirely new experiment. The first session seemed to confirm my misgivings. Rita, when left alone with me in her nursery, at once showed signs of what I took to be negative transference: she was anxious and silent and very soon asked to go out into the garden. I agreed and went with her — I may add, under the watchful eyes of her mother and aunt, who took this as a sign of failure. They were very surprised to see that Rita was quite friendly toward me when we returned to the nursery some ten to fifteen minutes later. The explanation of this change was that while we were outside, I had been interpreting her negative transference (this again being against the usual practice). From a few things she said and the fact that she was less frightened when we were in the open, I concluded that she was particularly afraid of something which I might do to her when she was alone with me in the room. I interpreted this, and referring to her night terrors, I linked her suspicion of me as a hostile stranger with her fear that a bad woman would attack her when she was by herself at night. When, a few minutes after this interpretation, I suggested that we should return to the nursery, she readily agreed. As I said, Rita's inhibition in playing was marked, and to begin with, she did hardly anything but occasionally dress and undress her doll. But soon I came to understand the anxieties underlying her obsessions and interpreted them. This case strengthened my growing conviction that a precondition for the psychoanalysis of a child is to understand and to interpret the fantasies, feelings, anxieties, and experiences expressed by play or, if play activities are inhibited, the causes of the inhibition.

As with Fritz, I undertook this analysis in the child's home and with her own toys; but during this treatment, which lasted only a few months, I came to the conclusion that psychoanalysis should not be carried out in the child's home. For I found that, although the child was in great need of help and the parents had decided that I should try psychoanalysis, the mother's attitude toward me was very ambivalent, and the atmosphere was on the whole hostile to the treatment. More important still, I found that the transference situation — the backbone of the psychoanalytic procedure — can only be established and maintained if the patient can feel that the consulting room or the playroom, indeed the whole analysis, is something separate from his ordinary home life. For only under such conditions is he able to overcome his own resistance against experiencing and expressing thoughts, feelings, and desires which are incompatible with convention and, in the case of children, felt to be in contrast to much of what they have been taught.

## A Girl of Seven who Disliked School

I made further significant observations in the psychoanalysis of a girl of seven, also in 1923. Her neurotic difficulties were apparently not serious, but her parents had for some time been concerned about her intellectual development. Although quite intelligent she did not keep up with her age group, she disliked school, and sometimes played truant.

The relation to her mother, which had been affectionate and trustful, had changed since she had started school: she had become reserved and silent. I spent a few sessions with her without achieving much contact. It had become clear that she disliked school; and from what she diffidently said about it, as well as from other remarks, I had been able to make a few interpretations which produced some material. But my impression was that I would not get much further in that way. In a session in which I again found the child unresponsive and withdrawn I left her, saying that I would return in a moment. I went into my own children's nursery, collected a few toys, cars, little figures, a few bricks, a train, put them into a box, and returned to the patient. The child, who had not taken to drawing or other activities, was interested in the small toys and at once began to play. From this play I gathered that two of the toy figures represented herself and a little boy, a schoolmate about whom I had heard before. It appeared that there was something secret about the activities of these two figures and that other toy people were resented as interfering or watching and were put aside. The activities of the two toys led to catastrophes, such as their falling down or colliding with cars. This was repeated with signs of mounting anxiety. At this point I interpreted, with reference to the details of her play, that some sexual activitiy seemed to have occurred between herself and her friend and that this had made her very frightened of being found out, and therefore distrustful of other people. I pointed out that while playing she had become anxious and seemed on the point of stopping her play. I reminded her that she disliked school and that this might be connected with the fear that the teacher would find out about her relation with her schoolmate and punish her. Above all she was frightened and therefore distrustful of her mother and she might feel the same way about me. The effect of this interpretation on the child was striking: her anxiety and distrust first increased but very soon gave way to obvious relief. Her facial expression changed; and although she neither admitted nor denied what I had interpreted, she subsequently showed her agreement by producing new material and by becoming much freer in her play and speech; also her attitude toward me became much more friendly and less suspicious. Of course the negative transference, alternating with the positive one, came up again and again; but from this session onward the analysis progressed well. Concurrently there were favorable changes, as I was informed, in her relation to her family, in particular to her mother. Her dislike of school diminished, and she became more interested in her lessons; but her inhibition in learning, which was rooted in deep anxieties, was only gradually resolved in the course of her treatment.

## Play Materials

I have described how the use of the toys which I kept especially for the child patient in the box in which I first brought them proved essential for her analysis. This experience, as well as others, helped me to decide which toys are most suitable for the psychoanalytic play technique. They are mainly little wooden men and women — usually in two sizes — cars, wheelbarrows, swings, trains, airplanes, animals, trees, bricks, houses, fences, paper, scissors, a not-too-sharp knife, pencils, chalks or paints, glue, balls and marbles, plasticine, and string. The small size of such toys, their number and variety, enable the child to express a wide range of fantasies and experiences. It is important for this purpose that the toys should be nonmechanical, and that the human figures, varying only in color and size, should not indicate any particular occupation. Their very simplicity enables the child to use them in many different situations, actual or fantasied, according to the material coming up in his play. The fact that the child can thus simultaneously present a variety of experiences and situations also makes it possible for us to arrive at a more coherent picture of the workings of his mind.

In keeping with the simplicity of the toys, the equipment of the playroom is very simple. It should not contain anything except what is needed for the psychoanalysis. It has a washable floor, running water, a table, a few chairs, a little sofa, some cushions, and a chest of drawers. Each child's playthings are kept locked in one particular drawer, and he therefore knows that his toys and his play with them, which is the equivalent of the adult's associations, will only be known to the psychoanalyst and to himself. The box in which I first introduced the toys to the little girl mentioned above turned out to be the prototype of the individual drawer, which is part of the private and intimate relation between analyst and patient, characteristic of the psychoanalytic transference situation.

I do not suggest that the psychoanalytic play technique depends entirely on this particular selection of play material. In any case, children often spontaneously bring their own toys, and the play with them enters as a matter of course into the analytic work. But I believe that on the whole the toys provided by the psychoanalyst should be of the type I have described; that is to say, simple, small, and nonmechanical.

Toys, however, are not the only requisites for a play analysis. I have already mentioned the running water. Many of the child's activities are at times carried out round the basin which is equipped with one or two small bowls, tumblers, and spoons. There are other occupations, such as drawing and painting, cutting out, writing, and repairing of broken toys.

At times the child plays games in which he allots roles to the psychoanalyst and himself; for instance, playing shop, doctor and patient, school, or mother and child. In such games, he often takes the part of the adult, thereby not only expressing his wish to reverse the roles, but also demonstrating how he feels the parents or other people in authority behave toward him or should behave. Sometimes he gives vent to his aggressiveness and resentment by being sadistic, in the role of parent, toward the child, represented by the psychoanalyst. The principle of interpretation remains the same whether the fantasies are presented by toys or by dramatization. For, whatever the material used, it is essential that the psychoanalytic principles underlying the technique should be applied. I have elsewhere given instances both of play with toys and of the games described above (4, 5, 7).

## Handling Aggression

Aggressiveness is expressed in various ways in the child's play, either directly or indirectly. Often a toy is broken; or when the child is more aggressive, attacks are made with knife or scissors on the table or on pieces of wood; water or paint is splashed about and the room generally becomes a battlefield. It is essential to enable the child to bring out his aggressiveness, but what counts most is to understand why at this particular moment in the transference situation destructive impulses come up and to observe their consequences in the child's mind. Feelings of guilt may very soon follow after the child has broken, for instance, a little figure. Such guilt refers not only to the actual damage done, but to what the toy stands for in the child's unconscious; e.g., a little brother or sister, or a parent. The interpretation has, therefore, to deal with these deeper levels as well. Sometimes we can gather from the child's behavior toward the psychoanalyst that not only guilt but also persecutory anxiety has been the sequel to his destructive impulses and that he is afraid of retaliation.

I have usually been able to convey to the child that I would not tolerate physical attacks on myself. This attitude not only protects the psychoanalyst, but is of importance for the analysis as well. For such assaults, if not kept within bounds, are apt to stir up excessive guilt and persecutory anxiety in the child and therefore add to the difficulties of the treatment. I have sometimes been asked by what method I prevented physical attacks, and I think the answer is that I was very careful not to inhibit the child's aggressive fantasies; in fact he was given opportunity to act them out in other ways, including verbal attacks on myself. Moreover, I did not show disapproval or annoyance at the child's aggressive desires and was usually able to interpret their deeper motives in time and thus to keep the situation under control. This was not always so; with some psychotic children I occasionally found it difficult to protect myself against their aggressiveness.

## Persecutory Anxiety

I found that the child's attitude toward a toy he has damaged is very revealing. He often puts aside such a toy, representing for instance a sibling or a parent, and ignores it for a time. This indicates dislike of the damaged object, due to the persecutory fear that the attacked person (represented by the toy) has become retaliatory and dangerous. The sense of persecution may be so strong that it covers up feelings of guilt and depression which are also aroused by the damage done. Or guilt and depression may be so strong that they lead to a reinforcing of persecutory feelings. However, one day the child may search in his drawer for the damaged toy. This suggests that by then the psychoanalyst has been able to diminish persecutory feelings, thus making it possible for the sense of guilt and the urge to make reparation to be experienced. When this happens we can also notice that a change in the child's relation to the particular sibling for whom the toy stood, or in his relations in general, has occurred; and this confirms that persecutory anxiety has diminished and that, together with the sense of guilt and the wish to make reparation, feelings of love, which had been impaired by excessive anxiety, have come to the fore. With another child, or with the same child at a later stage of the psychoanalysis, guilt and the wish to repair may follow very soon after the act of aggression; and tenderness toward the brother or sister, damaged in fantasy, may become apparent. The importance of such changes for character formation and relations to other people, as well as for mental stability, cannot be overrated.

It is an essential part of the interpretative work that it should keep in step with fluctuations between love and hatred, between happiness and satisfaction on the one hand, and persecutory anxiety and depression on the other. This implies that the psychoanalyst should not show disapproval of the child's having broken a toy; he should not, however, encourage the child to express his aggressiveness, nor suggest to him that the toy could be mended. In other words, he should enable the child to experience his emotions and fantasies as they come up. It was always part of my technique not to use educational or moral influence, but to keep to the psychoanalytic procedure only, which — in a nutshell — consists in understanding the patient's mind and in conveying to him what goes on in it.

### Interpreting the Unconscious

I shall now give a few more detailed illustrations of the psychoanalytic play technique. Here is a typical instance; a little boy in the first analytic session may put up a few toy figures and surround them, let us say, by bricks. I would conclude and interpret that the child shows a room and that the figures symbolize people. Such an interpretation effects a first contact with the child's unconscious. For through the interpretation he comes to realize that the toys stand in his mind for people and, therefore, that the feelings he expresses toward the toys relate to people; also that preceding the interpretation he had not been aware of this. He is beginning to gain insight into the fact that one part of his mind is unknown to him; in other words, that the unconscious exists. Moreover, it becomes clearer to him what the analyst is doing with him. All this implies that the analytic situation is being established. This does not, however, mean that the child would necessarily be able to express in intellectual terms what he is experiencing.

To return to my instance of the little figures representing people in a room. Next the psychoanalyst would try to find out who these people are meant to be, what their relation to each other is, and what they are supposed to be doing in that room. Let us assume that the child picks out as many toy figures as there are people in his family, which in this instance would be four. I would point out to him that the figures represent himself with his parents and his younger brother. The child may then take one of these figures and put it outside the space he had enclosed by bricks. Assuming that he has shown that this figure represents his younger brother, this gives an opening for the next step; namely, to understand why he makes him leave the room at that moment. Having been informed before the start of the psychoanalysis about the symptoms and difficulties of the child, as well as about his history, I might already know something about the relation between the patient and his brother. If I gathered from the play that the three people remaining in the room are father, mother, and the patient, I would interpret that at times he wanted his younger brother out of the way, wishing to remain alone with his parents and to be an only child as he had been before the birth of his brother. This might lead to his putting another of the toy people out of the supposed room — a figure standing for his father — which would lead me to interpret that there are times when he feels his father to be in the way and wants his mother all to himself. I might also have grounds to interpret that in this situation the analyst represented his mother whom he wished to devote herself exclusively to him. At any point in this sequence, even perhaps quite early, we might observe on the child's face that telling look, so convincing to the psychoanalyst, which shows clearly that the child has understood something about himself and that he feels this insight to be helpful and valuable.

It is very likely that the child while playing has said something which substantiates the conclusions the analyst drew from the play. He may also have expressed his disagreement. He may even have pushed away the toys and stopped playing, particularly in response to the interpretation dealing with his aggressiveness toward his brother or father. But by then the psychoanalyst has already gathered the content of the anxiety stirred up, and he would interpret the reasons why the child interrupted the play; he would also interpret the negative transference, according to which the psychoanalyst may have come to represent, for example, the angry father or the disappointing mother. Should the child, as often happens, resume his play after such an interpretation, he might produce the same material in a different way; this can be taken as a confirmation of the correctness of the interpretation given. The child might, for instance, begin to build with bricks; now the bricks represent people while the room is indicated by fences or other objects. Or he plays with cars or any other toys which in the context of the play can be seen to stand for people. He may also start a game in which he allots to the psychoanalyst symbolically the role of one of his family, thereby transferring his feelings from them into the relation with the analyst. In the course of his play he possibly refers to some happenings from his everyday life, which again throw light on the former play with the figures. All these activities and associations may present the same material by different means. But the anxiety and feelings of guilt, which in some cases lead to an interruption of the play or a change in it, sometimes introduce what appears to be an entirely different situation. Perhaps the child searches in his drawer for a toy which is soiled or damaged and cleans it thoroughly at the wash basin. In that context the analyst would gather and interpret that the child is expressing his anxious need to clean and restore his little brother whom he feels he has soiled and damaged by his hostile impulses.

These instances do not, of course, exhaust the range of the situations and experiences which a child may show by his play. Feelings of frustration and being rejected, jealousy of both father and mother, or of brothers and sisters, the aggressiveness accompanying such jealousy, the pleasure in having a playmate or ally against the parents, the feelings of love and hatred toward a newborn baby or one who is expected, as well as the ensuing anxiety, guilt, and urge to make reparation are some of the many emotional situations which may be expressed. We also find in the child's play the repetition of actual experiences and details of everyday life, often interwoven with his fantasies. It is revealing that sometimes very important actual events in his life fail to enter either into his play or into his associations and that the whole emphasis at times lies on apparently minor happenings. But these minor happenings are of great importance to him because they have stirred up his emotions and fantasies.

## Cases of Play Inhibition

I have already discussed the problem of children whose play is inhibited. Such inhibition does not always completely prevent them from playing but may soon interrupt their activities. For instance, a little boy was brought to me for one interview only. (There was a prospect of an analysis in the future, but at the time the parents were going abroad with him.) I had some toys on my table and he sat down and began to play, which soon led to accidents, collisions, people falling down whom he tried to stand up again. In all this he showed a good deal of anxiety, but since no treatment was yet intended, I refrained from interpreting. After a few minutes he quietly slipped out of his chair, and saying, "Enough of playing," went out. I believe from my experience that if this had been the beginning of treatment and I had interpreted the anxiety shown in his actions with the toys and the corresponding negative transference toward me, I should have been able to resolve his anxiety sufficiently for him to continue playing.

The next instance may help me to show some of the causes of a play inhibition. A boy aged three years nine months, whom I described under the name Peter (7), was very neurotic. To mention some of his difficulties: he seemed unable to play, could not tolerate any frustration, was timid, plaintive, and unboyish, yet at times aggressive and overbearing, very ambivalent toward his family, and strongly fixated on his mother. She told me that Peter had greatly changed for the worse after a summer holiday, during which, at the age of eighteen months, he shared the parents' bedroom and had the opportunity to observe their sexual intercourse. On that holiday he had become very difficult to manage, slept badly, and relapsed into soiling his bed at night, which he had not done for some months. He had been playing freely until then, but from that summer onward he stopped playing and became very destructive toward his toys; he could do nothing with them but break them. Soon afterward his brother was born, and this increased all his difficulties.

In the first session Peter started to play; he soon made two horses bump into each other and repeated the same action with different toys. He also mentioned that he had a little brother. I interpreted to him that the horses and the other things bumping together represented people — an interpretation which he first rejected and then accepted. He again bumped the horses together, saying that they were going to sleep, covered them up with bricks, and added, "Now they're quite dead; I've buried them." He put the motorcars front to rear in a row, which, as became clear later in the analysis, symbolized his father's penis, and made them run along, then suddenly lost his temper and threw them about the room, saying, "We always smash our Christmas presents straight away; we don't want any." Smashing his toys thus stood in his unconscious for smashing his father's genitals; in fact, during this first hour he broke several toys.

In the second session Peter repeated some of the material of the first hour, in particular the bumping together of cars, horses, etc., speaking again of his little brother, whereupon I interpreted that he was showing me how his mummy and daddy bumped their genitals together (using of course his word for genitals) and that he thought that their doing so caused his brother to be born. This interpretation produced more material, throwing light on his very ambivalent relation toward his little brother and toward his father. He laid a toy man on a brick which he called a "bed," threw him down, and said he was "dead and done for." He then re-enacted the same thing with two toy men, choosing figures he had already damaged. I interpreted that the first toy man stood for his father whom he wanted to throw out of his mother's bed and kill and that one of the two toy men was again the father and the other himself to whom his father would do the same. The reason he had chosen two damaged figures was that he felt that both his father and himself would be damaged if he attacked his father.

This material illustrates a number of points of which I shall mention only one or two. Because witnessing the sexual intercourse of his parents had made a great impact on his mind and roused strong emotions such as jealousy, aggressiveness, and anxiety, this was almost the first thing which Peter expressed in his play. There is no doubt that he no longer had any conscious knowledge of this experience, that it was repressed, and that only the symbolical expression of it was possible for him. I have reasons to believe that if I had not interpreted that the toys bumping together were people, he might not have produced the material which came up in the second hour. Furthermore, had I not, in the second hour, been able to show him some of the reasons for his inhibition in play by interpreting the damage done to the toys, he would very likely — as he did in ordinary life — have stopped playing after breaking the toys.

There are children who at the beginning of the treatment may not even play in the way Peter did, or the little boy who came for one interview only. But it is very rare for a child completely to ignore the toys laid out on the table. Even if he turns away from them he often gives the analyst some insight into his motives for not wishing to play. In other ways, too, the child analyst can gather material for interpretations. Any activity, such as using paper to scribble on or to cut out, every detail of behavior, such as changes in posture or in facial expression, can give a clue to what is going on in the child's mind, possibly in connection with what the psychoanalyst has heard from the parents about his difficulties.

### Children's Capacity for Insight

I have said much about the importance of interpretations for the play technique and have given some instances to illustrate their contents. This brings me to a question which I have often been asked: "Are young children intellectually able to understand such interpretations?" My experience and that of my colleagues has been that if the interpretations relate to the salient points in the material they are fully understood. Of course the child analyst must give his interpretations as succinctly and as clearly as possible and should also use the child's expressions in doing so. But if he translates into simple words the essential points of the material presented to him, he gets into touch with those emotions and anxieties which are the most operative at the moment; the child's conscious and intellectual understanding is often a subsequent process. One of the many interesting and surprising experiences of the beginner in child analysis is to find in even very young children a capacity for insight which is often far greater than that of adults. To some extent this is explained by the fact that the connections between conscious and unconscious are closer in young children than in adults and that infantile repressions are less powerful. I also believe that the infant's intellectual capacities are often underrated and that in fact he understands more than he is credited with.

I shall now illustrate what I have said by a young child's response to interpretation. Peter, of whose analysis I have given a few details, had strongly objected to my interpretation that the toy man he had thrown down from the "bed" and who was "dead and done for" represented his father. (The interpretation of death wishes against a loved person usually arouses great resistance in children as well as in adults). In the third hour Peter again brought similar material, but now accepted my interpretation and said thoughtfully, "And if I were a daddy and someone wanted to throw me down behind the bed and make me dead and done for, what would I think of it?" This shows that he had not only worked through, understood, and accepted my interpretation, but that he had also recognized a good deal more. He understood that his own aggressive feelings toward his father contributed to his fear of him and also that he had projected his own impulses onto his father.

The next instance was told me by one of my students. A little boy aged four had strongly objected in one analytic session to some of the analyst's interpretations of his play. At the beginning of the following session, he again presented play material identical with that of the previous day. Then he said to the analyst, "Now let's talk." To her question what they should talk about, he replied, "What you were telling about yesterday." The psychoanalyst went over the material of the previous day, repeating and elaborating her interpretations, to which he now listened with great attention and which he obviously accepted. The same child, in a later session, after some interpretations of his anxiety which had clearly produced much relief, coined a new term for his fears by saying in a thoughtful way, "What can you do with my afraidy-nesses?"

## Symbolic Language and Fantasy

It has already been pointed out in the introduction to this paper that my attention from the beginning focused on the child's anxieties and that it was by means of interpreting their contents that I found myself able to diminish anxiety. In order to do this, I made full use of the archaic language of symbolism, which I recognized to be an essential part of the child's mode of expression. As we have seen, the brick, the little figure, the car not only represent things which interest the child in themselves; but in his play with them they always have a variety of symbolical meanings as well, which are bound up with his fantasies, wishes, and actual experiences. This archaic mode of expression is also the language with which we are familiar in dreams, and it was by approaching the play of the child in a way similar to Freud's interpretations of dreams that I could get access to the child's unconscious. But we have to consider each child's use of symbols in connection with his own particular emotions and anxieties and in relation to the whole situation which is presented in the analysis; mere generalized translations of symbols are meaningless.

The importance I attributed to symbolism led me — as time went on — to theoretical conclusions about the process of symbol formation. Play analysis had shown that the capacity to use symbols enables the child to transfer not only interests but also fantasies, anxieties and guilt to objects other than people. Thus a great deal of relief is experienced in play, and this is one of the factors which make it so essential for the child. For instance, little Peter, to whom I referred earlier, pointed out to me, when I interpreted his damaging a toy figure as representing attacks on his brother, that he would not do that to his real brother — he would only do it to the toy brother. My interpretation of course made it clear to him that it was really his brother whom he wished to attack but the instance shows that only by symbolic means was he able to express his destructive tendencies in the analysis.

I have also arrived at the view that in children a severe inhibition of the capacity to form and use symbols, and so to develop fantasy life, is a sign of serious disturbance. I suggested that such inhibitions and the resulting disturbance in the relation to the external world and to reality are characteristic of schizophrenia (6,8). This conclusion has since influenced the understanding of the schizophrenic's mode of communication and has found its place in the treatment of schizophrenia.

One of the important points in my technique has always been the analysis of the transference. It is my experience that we are able to help the patient fundamentally by taking his desires and anxieties in our transference interpretations back to where they originated; namely, in infancy and in relation to his first objects. For, by reexperiencing early emotions and fantasies and understanding them in connection with his primal relationships — to his mother and father — he can, as it were, revise these early relations at their root and thus effectively diminish his anxieties.

It has been mentioned above how, since my earliest case, my interest has been centered on anxieties and the defenses against them. This emphasis on anxiety led me deeper and deeper into the unconscious and into the fantasy life of the child. My approach was also in contrast to the psychoanalytic point of view prevailing at that time — and for quite a long time to come — that interpretations should not be given frequently. This approach, therefore, involved a radical change in technique. I also ventured into new territory from another angle; the contents of fantasies and anxieties and the defenses against them, which I found in young children and interpreted to them, were at that time still largely undiscovered. In using this new technique I was faced with serious problems. The anxieties encountered when analyzing my first case were very acute; and although I was strengthened in my belief that I was working on the right lines by the relief which the interpretations again and again produced, the intensity of the anxieties which were being brought into the open was at times perturbing. At one such moment I sought advice from Dr. Karl Abraham. He replied that since my interpretations up to then had often produced relief and the analysis was obviously progressing, he saw no reason for changing my method of approach. I felt encouraged by his support and, as it happened, in the next few days the child's anxiety which had come to a head greatly diminished, and this led to further improvement. The conviction gained in this analysis strongly influenced the whole course of my analytic work.

## Development of Child Analysis

At the beginning of this paper, I mentioned how I evolved the psychoanalytic play technique. Having worked for five and half years in Berlin, I accepted an invitation from Dr. Ernest Jones and settled in London in 1926. He had always taken a lively interest in my work, and his support and the cooperation of a number of my British colleagues helped me to establish the psychoanalytic play technique in London, and this became part of what has often been called the "English school of psychoanalysis."

I should now like to say something about the development of child analysis in general. During the last three decades the psychoanalysis of children has steadily grown in importance and is now carried out all over the world. To this development, Anna Freud's work has greatly contributed. She started in Vienna in the twenties and has continued her practice and teaching in London since 1938. Her approach differs from mine in a number of fundamental points; but both lines of thought have deeply influenced psychoanalytic work with children wherever it is practiced.

In this context it is of interest that the play technique has not altered in principle since the time when I presented it in my *Psycho-Analysis of Children*. I myself am not psychoanalyzing children any more — I have not done so for some years — but I remain in close touch through my students and colleagues who are carrying on this work in its original form. I am glad to say that this technique has also had an effect on work with children in other fields, such as child guidance, education, and tests. The importance of play for the welfare and happiness of the child has, as we all know, been recognized by Froebel and has been widely accepted. Liberal educators who based their views on Froebel have ever since understood the importance of play for the child. But Susan Isaacs' work at the Malting-House School has given fresh impetus to educational activities and a new insight into educational needs in England. Her books about that experiment (1,2) have been widely read and have had a lasting effect on educational techniques in this country, especially where young children are concerned. Her approach was strongly influenced by her great appreciation of child analysis, in particular of play technique; and it is largely due to her that in England development in education and the psychoanalytic understanding of children have gone hand in hand.

I have mentioned the influence of play technique on child guidance. When in 1929, the first group of people about to take up child guidance in this country went to the United States to study American methods in order to introduce them here, they found that play with children was little used. From the beginning of the thirties onward, the psychoanalytic play technique has increasingly influenced the methods applied in child guidance clinics in this country and elsewhere.

One important result of the psychoanalysis of children, based on play technique, has been the greater understanding of the earliest stages of development, more especially of the role of fantasies, anxieties, and defenses in the emotional life of the young infant (9). Since in these infantile processes lie the fixation points of adult psychoses, this greater knowledge and the play technique by which it was acquired have opened up a new way of treating psychotic patients by psychoanalysis. This field, in particular the psychoanalysis of schizophrenic patients, needs much further exploration, but the work done in this direction by some of my colleagues seems to justify hopes for the future.

In the thirty-five years that have elapsed since play technique was evolved, its influence on the development of psychoanalysis has been profound; for the psychoanalytic play technique has greatly added to our knowledge of the infantile mind and thus to our understanding both of normal and abnormal adults.

### References

1. Isaacs, Susan, *Intellectual Growth in Young Children*, London: Routledge & Kegan Paul, 1930.
2. ———, *Social Development in Young Children*, London: Routledge & Kegan Paul, 1933.
3. Klein, Melanie, "The Development of a Child," *International Journal of Psychoanalysis*, 4: 1923. Also in *Contributions to Psycho-Analysis 1921–1945*. Hogarth Press, London, 1948.
4. ———, "Criminal Tendencies in Normal Children," *British Journal of Medical Psychology*, 7:1927. Also in *Contributions to Psycho-Analysis 1921–1945*.
5. ———, "Personification in the Play of Children," *International Journal Psychoanalysis*, 8: 1929. Also in *Contributions to Psycho-Analysis 1921–1945*.
6. ———, "The Importance of Symbol Formation in the Development of the Ego," *Ibid.*, 11: 1930. Also in *Contributions to Psycho-Analysis 1921–1945*.
7. ———, *The Psycho-Analysis of Children*, London: Hogarth Press, 1932.
8. ———, "Notes on Some Schizoid Mechanisms," *International Journal of Psychoanalysis*, 27:1946. Also in *Developments in Psycho-Analysis*, London: Hogarth Press, 1952.
9. ———, "Some Theoretical Conclusions Regarding the Emotional Life of the Infant," in *Developments in Psycho-Analysis*, London: Hogarth Press, 1952.

# The Role of Transference in the Analysis of Children

ANNA FREUD

Ladies and Gentlemen. I will go briefly over the ground covered at our last meeting.

We directed attention to the methods of the analysis of children; we remarked that we have to put the case history together from information furnished by the family, instead of relying exclusively upon that given by the patient; we became familiar with the child as a good dream-interpreter, and evaluated the significance of day dreams and imaginative drawings as technical auxiliaries. On the other hand I had to report that children are not inclined to enter into free association, and by this refusal oblige us to look for some substitute for this most essential of aids in the analysis of adults. We concluded with a description of one of these substitute methods, postponing its theoretical evaluation until today.

## Klein Play Method

The play technique worked out by Mrs. Melanie Klein is certainly valuable for observing the child. Instead of taking the time and trouble to pursue it into its domestic environment we establish at one stroke the whole of its known world in the analyst's room, and let it move about in it under the analyst's eye but at first without his interference. In this way we have the opportunity of getting to know the child's various reactions, the strength of its aggressive impulses or of its sympathies, as well as its attitude to the various things and persons represented by the toys. There is this advantage over the observation of real conditions, and the toy environment is manageable and amenable to the child's will, so that it can carry out in it all the actions which in the real world, so much bigger and stronger than itself, remain confined to a fantasy existence. All these merits make the use of the Klein play-method almost indispensable for familiarisation with small children, who are not yet capable of verbal self-expression.

Mrs. Klein however takes an important further step in the employment of this technique. She assumes the same status for these play-actions of the child as for the free associations of the adult patient, and translates as she goes along the actions undertaken by the child in this way into corresponding thoughts; that is to say, she tries to find beneath everything done in play its underlying symbolic function. If the child overturns a lamppost or a toy figure she interprets it as something of an aggressive impulse against the father; a deliberate collision between two cars as evidence of an observation of sexual union between the parents. Her procedure consists in accompanying the child's activities with translations and interpretations, which themselves — like the interpretation of the adult's free associations — exert a further influence upon the patient.

## Objection to Klein's Method

Let us examine the justification for equating the child's play activity with the adult's free association. The adult's ideas are "free," that is to say the patient has divested his thoughts of all direction and influence, but his attitude is nevertheless influenced by a certain consideration — that he who is associating has set himself to be analyzed. The child lacks this attitude. I think it is possible, as I have explained before, to give the children some idea of the purpose of analysis. But the children for whom Mrs. Klein has worked out her play-technique, in the first infantile period, are too young to be influenced in this way. Mrs. Klein considers it as one of the important advantages of her method that by it she is saved the necessity of such a preparation of the child. But if the child's play is not dominated by the same purposive attitude as the adult's free association, there is no justification for treating it as having the same significance. Instead of being invested with symbolic meaning it may sometimes admit of a harmless explanation. The child who upsets a toy lamppost may on its walk the day before have come across some incident in connection with such an object; the car collision may be reproducing some happening in the street; and the child who runs towards a lady visitor and opens her handbag is not necessarily, as Mrs. Klein maintains, thereby symbolically expressing its curiosity as to whether its mother's womb conceals another little brother or sister, but may be connecting some experience of the previous day when someone brought it a little present in a similar receptacle. Indeed with an adult we do not consider ourselves justified in ascribing a symbolic significance to every one of his acts or ideas, but only to those which arise under the influence of the analytical situation which he has accepted.

In reply to this objection to the Klein technique it may be said that a child's play is certainly open to the harmless interpretation just suggested, but why does it reproduce just those particular scenes with the lamppost or the cars? Is it not just the symbolic significance behind these observations which causes them to be preferred and reproduced before any others in the analytical hour? It is true, the argument may proceed, that the child lacks in its actions the purposive attitude of the analytical situation, which guides the adult. But perhaps it does not need it at all. The adult must renounce the guidance of his thoughts by a conscious effort of will and leave their direction entirely to his unconscious impulses. But the child may require no such deliberate modification of its situation. Perhaps it is at all times and in every piece of play entirely surrendered to the domination of its unconscious.

It is not easy to determine by an exchange of theoretical arguments the question of whether the equation of children's play with adults' free association is justifiable or not. This is obviously a matter for review in the light of practical experience.

### Transference vs. Attachment

Let us try criticism on another point. We know that Mrs. Klein utilizes for interpretation, besides the things which the child does with the toys provided, all its procedure towards the objects found in her room or towards her own person. Here again she follows strictly the example of adult analysis. We certainly feel justified in drawing into the analysis all the patient's behavior toward us during the visit, and all the little voluntary and involuntary actions which we observe him to perform. In this we are relying upon the state of transference in which he finds himself, which can invest even otherwise trivial behavior with symbolical significance.

Here the question arises as to whether a child finds itself in the same transference situation as the adult; in what manner and in what forms its transference impulses come to expression; and in what they lend themselves to interpretation. We have come to the important consideration, of *the role of transference as a technical expedient in the analysis of children.* The decision on this question will at the same time furnish fresh material to controvert or support Mrs. Klein's contention.

I explained in the first lecture how I took great pains to establish in the child a strong attachment to myself, and to bring it into a relationshp of real dependence on me. I would not have tried so hard to do this, if I had thought the analysis of children could be carried out without a transference of this kind. But the affectionate attachment, the positive transference as it is called in analytical terminology, is the prerequisite for all later work. The child in fact will only believe the loved person, and it will only accomplish something to please that person.

The analysis of children requires much more from this attachment than in the case of adults. There is an educational as well as an analytical purpose with which we shall later be concerned in more detail: successful upbringing always — not only in children's analysis — stands or falls with the pupil's attachment to the person in charge of it. And we cannot say in regard to the analysis of children that the establishment of a transference is in itself enough for our purpose, regardless of whether it is friendly or hostile. We know that with an adult we can get through long periods with a negative transference, which we turn to our account through consistent interpretation and reference to its origins. But with a child negative impulses towards the analyst — however revealing they may be in many respects — are essentially inconvenient, and should be dealt with as soon as possible. The really fruitful work always takes place with a positive attachment.

I have described the establishment of this affectionate tie during our discussion of the introductory phase to the analysis of children. Its expression in fantasies and small or larger actions is hardly distinguishable from the equivalent processes in adult patients. We are made to feel the negative reactions at every point where we attempt to assist a fragment of repressed material towards liberation from the unconscious, thereby drawing upon ourselves the resistance of the ego. At such a time we appear to the child as the dangerous and to-be-feared tempter, and we bring on ourselves all the expressions of hatred and repulsion with which at other times it treats its own forbidden instinctual impulses.

### Transference Fantasies in Children

I will give an account of a positive transference-fantasy from the six-year-old obsessional patient. The external occasion for it was furnished by myself, for I had visited her in her own home and stayed for her evening bath. She opened her visit on the next day with the words, "you visited me in my bath and next time I'll come and visit you in yours." Some while later she detailed for me the daydream which she had composed in bed before going to sleep, after I had gone away. I add her own explanatory asides in brackets.

"All the rich people did not like you. And your father who was very rich did not like you at all. (That means I am angry with your father, don't you think?) And you liked no one and gave lessons to no one. And my father and mother hated me and so did John and Billy and Mary and all the people in the world hated us, even the people we did not know, even the dead people. So you liked only me and I liked only you and we always stayed together. All the others were very rich but we two were quite poor. We had nothing, not even clothes for they took away everything we had. There was only the sofa left in the room and we slept on that together. But we were quite happy together. And then we thought we ought to have a baby. So we mixed a-a and cissies to make a baby. But then we thought that was not a nice thing to make a baby out of. So we began to mix flower-petals and things that gave me a baby. For the baby was in me. It stayed in me quite a long while (my mother told me that, that babies stay quite a long while in their mothers) and then the doctor took it out. But I was not a bit sick (mothers usually are, my mother said). The baby was very sweet and cunning and so we thought we'd like to be just as cunning and changed ourselves to be very small. I was "so" high and you were "so" high. (That is, I think because in our lesson last week we found out that I wanted to be like Billy and Mary.) And as we had nothing at all we started to make ourselves a house out of rose-leaves, and beds of rose-leaves and pillows and mattresses all out of rose-leaves sewn together. Where the little holes were left we put something white in. Instead of wall-paper we had the thinnest glass and the walls were carved in different patterns. The chairs were made of glass too but we were so light that we were not too heavy for them. (I think I left my mother out because I was angry with her for not coming to see me.)" Then there followed a detailed description of the furniture and all the things that were made for the house. The daydream was obviously spun out in this direction until she went to sleep, laying special emphasis on the point that our initial poverty was finally quite made up for and that in the end we had much nicer things than all the first mentioned rich people.

The same little patient at other times related how she was warned against me from within. The inner voice said, "Don't believe Anna Freud. She tells lies. She will not help you and will only make you worse. She will change your face too, so that you look uglier. Everything she says is not true. Just be tired, stay quietly in bed and don't go to her today." But she always told this voice to be silent and said to it that it should be told of first of all in the next appointment.

Another small patient envisaged me, at the time when we were discussing her masturbation, in all sorts of degrading roles — as a beggar, as a poor old woman, and once as just myself but standing in the middle of my room with devils dancing around me.

You will notice that we become the object towards which the patient's friendly or hostile impulses are directed, just as we do in the case of adults. It might seem from these examples that a child makes a good transference. Unfortunately that is not really true. The child indeed enters into the liveliest relations with the analyst, and evinces a multitude of reactions which it has acquired in the relationshp with its parents; it gives us most important hints on the formation of its character in the fluctuation, intensity, and expression of its feelings; but it forms no transference neurosis.

The analysts amongst you will know what I mean by this. The adult neurotic gradually transforms, in the course of analytic treatment, the symptom on account of which he sought this remedy. He gives up the old objects on which his fantasies were hitherto fixed, and centers his neurosis anew upon the person of the analyst. As we put it, he substitutes transference-symptom for his previous symptoms, transposes his existing neurosis, of whatever kind, into a transference-neurosis, and displays all his abnormal reactions in relation to the new transference person, the analyst. On this new ground, where the analyst feels at home, he can follow up with the patient the origin and growth of the individual symptoms; and on this cleared field of operations there then takes place the final struggle, for gradual insight into the malady and the discovery to the patient of the unconscious processes within him.

There are two possible reasons why this cannot be brought about in the case of a small child. One lies within the psychological structure of the child itself, the other in the child's analyst.

The child is not, like the adult, ready to produce a new edition of its love-relationships, because, as one might say, the old edition is not yet exhausted. Its original objects, the parents, are still real and present as love-objects — not only in fantasy as with the adult neurotic; between them and the child exist all the relations of everyday life, and all its gratifications and disappointments still in reality depend on them. The analyst enters this situation as a new person, and will probably share with the parents the child's love or hate. But there is no necessity for the child to exchange the parents for him, since compared to them he has not the advantages which the adult finds when he can exchange his fantasy-objects for a real person. Let us in this connection reconsider Mrs. Klein's method. She maintains that when a child evinces hostility towards her in the first visit, repulsing or even beginning to strike her, one may see in that a proof of the child's ambivalent attitude towards its mother. The hostile components of this ambivalence are merely displaced onto the analyst. But I believe the truth of the matter is different. The more tenderly a little child is attached to its own mother, the fewer friendly impulses it has towards strangers. We see this most clearly with the baby, who shows only anxious rejection towards everyone other than its mother or nurse. Indeed the converse obtains. It is especially with children who are accustomed to little loving treatment at home, and are not used to showing or receiving any strong affection, that a positive relationship is often most quickly established. They obtain from the analyst what they have up till now expected in vain from the original love objects.

On the other hand, the behavior of the children's analyst, as we have described him, is not such as to produce a transference that can be well interpreted. We know how we bear ourselves in the analysis of adults for this purpose. We remain impersonal and shadowy, a blank page on which the patient can inscribe his transference-fantasies, somewhat after the way in which at the cinema a picture is thrown upon an empty screen. We avoid either issuing prohibitions, or allowing gratifications. If in spite of this we seem to the patient forbidding or encouraging, it is easy to make it clear to him that he has brought the material for this impression from his own past.

But the children's analyst must be anything but a shadow. We have already remarked that he is a person of interest to the child, endowed with all sorts of interesting and attractive qualities. The educational implications which, as you will hear, are involved in the analysis, result in the child knowing very well just what seems to the analyst desirable or undesirable, and what he sanctions or disapproves of. And such a well-defined and in many respects novel personality is unfortunately a bad transference-object, of little use when it comes to interpreting the transference. The difficulty here is, as though, to use our former illustration, the screen on which a film was to be projected already bore another picture. The more elaborate and brightly-colored it is, the more will it tend to efface the outlines of what is superimposed.

## Importance of Home Environment

For these reasons the child forms no transference-neurosis. In spite of all its positive and negative impulses towards the analyst it continues to display its abnormal reactions where they were displayed before — in the home circle. Because of this the children's analyst is obliged to take into account not only what happens under his own eye but also what occurs in the real scene of the neurotic reactions; i.e. the child's home. Here we come to an infinity of practical technical difficulties in the analysis of children, which I only lay broadly before you without going into actual detail. Working from this standpoint we are dependent upon a permanent news-service about the child; we must know the people in its environment and be sure to some extent of what their reactions to the child are. In the ideal case, we share our work with the persons who are actually bringing up the child; just as we share with them the child's affection or hostility.

Where the external conditions, or the personalities of the parents, do not allow of such cooperative treatment, certain material for the analysis eludes us. On this account I had to conduct some analyses of children almost exlusively by means of dreams and daydreams. There was nothing interpretable in the transference and most of the day-to-day symptomatic neurotic material never became available to me.

But there are ways and means to bring about an equation of the child's situation to that of the adult (so much better suited for the carrying through of analysis); and so to force the child into a transference neurosis. This may become necessary where it is a case of severe neurotic illness in an environment hostile either to analysis or the child. In such a case the child would have to be removed from its family and placed in some suitable institution. As there is no such institution in existence at present we are at full liberty to imagine one, say a home supervised by the children's analyst himself, or  — less far-fetched — a school where psychoanalytical principles predominate and the work is attuned to cooperation with the analyst. In both cases a symptom-free period would first occur, in which the child accustoms itself to the new and favorable surroundings. The better it feels at this time, the more unapt and unwilling for analysis shall we find it. We shall probably do best to leave it quite undisturbed. Only when it has "acclimatised itself," that is to say when under the influence of the realities of everyday life it has formed an attachment to the new environment, beside which the original objects gradually pale; when it allows its symptoms to revive again in this new existence, and groups its abnormal reactions around new personages; when it has thus formed its tranference-neurosis — will it become analyzable once more.

In an institution of the first sort, managed by the children's analyst (and at present we cannot even judge whether such an arrangement is to be desired) it would then be a matter of an actual transference-neurosis in the sense of the adult's, with the analyst as focal object. In the other sort we should simply have artificially bettered the home environment, creating a substitute home which, so to say, allows us to see into it, as seems necessary for the analytical work, and the reactions of which towards the child we can control and regulate.

Thus the removal of the child from its home might appear to be the most practical solution. But when we come to consider the termination of a child's analysis, we shall see how many objections there are to it. By this expedient we forestall the natural development at a crucial stage, forcing the child's premature detachment from the parental objects at a time when it neither is capable of any independence in its emotional life, nor has at its disposal, owing to external circumstances, any freedom in the choice of new love-objects. Even if we insist on a very long duration for the analysis of children there still remains in most cases a hiatus between its termination and the development of puberty, during which the child needs education, protection, and guidance in every sense of the words. But what gives us any assurance that after we have secured a successful resolution of the transference the child will find of itself the way to the right objects? It returns home at a time when it has become a stranger there, and its further guidance is now perhaps entrusted to the very persons from whom we have forcibly detached it. On inner grounds it is not capable of self-reliance. We are thus placing it in a position of renewed difficulty, in which it will find again most of the original elements of its conflict. It can now take either once more the path to neurosis or, if this is closed to it by the successful outcome of the analytical treatment, the opposite line of open rebellion. From the purely therapeutical point of view this may seem an advantage; but from that of social adjustment which in the child's case matters most in the end, it is certainly none.

# Child's Growth in Play Therapy

ELISABETH F. HELLERSBERG

## Functional and Physical Aspects

It is a valid assumption that every serious problem causes an arrest of the child's growth process and that therapy aims to revive this process in an accelerated form (1,9). This is possible only when the functional and physical needs, as well as the mental and emotional ones, are understood and satisfied. By stressing some physical, developmental aspects of child therapy, it may be possible to broaden the understanding of the curative process beyond the decription of the influence the therapist alone exerts. In the past the strong emphasis on libido development has overshadowed the observation of the ego functions which characterize the child's changing psycho-physical needs. These needs are expressed in his play activities, in his relationship to the place of treatment, and to the objects presented to him, as well as in his relationship to the therapist. By play he makes or regains contact with the world, and thus, he tests and re-experiences his ego boundaries and ego strength. To understand the full meaning of play therapy for the child's total growth, more attention should be paid to the sensory and, particularly, tactile explorations of the child, his motor activity, and even occasional devotion to movements which appear nonsensical. The child's absorption in various games or building projects is also important. Each of these activities, properly observed, will broaden the understanding and deepen the interpretation of the therapeutic process.

What is said in the following is, therefore, not a new way of treating the child patient, but another way of evaluating and describing the established mode of treatment. By this emphasis on physical and developmental happenings, this paper wants to stimulate similar observations in therapy. The author aims at a more effective use of the psychoanalytic discoveries and believes that, for a child's therapeutic progress, the verbalized interpretation of his problems appear of minor importance (1,9); but essential is a therapist's enlightened and alert responsiveness to every single movement of the child in a very physical sense. For the neurotic child, the therapeutic method is different from that chosen to help the ego-weak or schizoid child. In this paper only the first is under study, leaving the observations of the schizoid child to a later publication.

## Initial Phase

To illustrate what I mean, let me begin with the initial phase of therapy and focus on the physical and functional aspects of its setting. The child has been in trouble before he comes for therapy, at least, he has noticed other adults' concern. Frequently, the child expects the therapist to be one of these eager, but unsuccessful people whose disapproval he has earned, people who tried in vain to change or to reform him (1, 2). In order to counteract such anticipations, his first entrance into the play-room should assure him of minimal interference on the part of the therapist. In an unobtrusive way the latter explains to the child that there are many things at his disposal which he can use as he likes. He gives the child ample time to approach the situation so that the patient does not feel intruded upon by a new adult. Whatever his age he should be exposed to toys or materials suitable for different developmental stages. Offering a variety and giving the child freedom for discovery, one rarely fails to produce a positive response. The child finds a new place where his troubles are forgotten and where he can explore his own suppressed needs. Such needs automatically come to light sooner or later. The touching of sand, the tense fingering of a book while probably studying the therapist, the throwing down of some puppets, any initial action, however arbitrary it may appear, should be considered as significant as the first dream brought to the initial analytical session in adult therapy. The less the child's first movements are influenced by the therapist, the more they may be interpreted as first steps to health and normal functioning. At this phase the therapist helps most, not by discussing the child's problems, but by fully identifying with the child and approving any mode expressing his needs. Thus the therapist becomes the nurturing agent to gratify these needs by means of what the playroom offers. In this way the first play hours become comparable to the first weeks of an infant's life. We may assume that the patient's capacity to accept human relationship is only latent. This capacity grows indirectly within the child, after he first discovers his own needs and searches for their satisfaction. If he finds something he enjoys touching or handling, he will have a positive and pleasant reaction. No demands are made upon him, and just "having a good time" turns almost, without fail, into liking the agency who grants the security for this new experience. Thus, the basis for trust and confidence in an interpersonal relationship is laid. The child must come to the realization that the therapeutic session is the time to reveal hidden and repressed needs and that he will have opportunity to pursue their gratification. By discovering his suppressed needs the patient becomes able to recapture those phases of his former development which he has not fully assimilated in his present, incomplete state of maturing. Such growth will be possible only if the therapist promotes a state of genuine spontaneity in the child and tries to maintain this state as far as possible. It is a common truth that without spontaneity no life develops, no growth can be secured (1, 6, 9). How to create or maintain a spontaneous spirit in a child is the very problem with which we are dealing. It is not merely one conflict from which the child is suffering, it is the total personality of the child which must be brought to full responsiveness.

## Developmental Needs

A frequently observed need is the sensory one, particularly a tactile contact with the material world. The child explores the surface, the texture of things, and also its properties. From the tactile he proceeds to the use of other senses, of taste, smell, sight, and hearing. Another basic need is the child's rediscovery of space, the relationship of his own body shape and capacity to the physical world and its spatial condition. A third definite phase in the child's therapeutic activity is shown by his urge to master something, to create or construct a miniature world, or to utilize some material such as clay, paint, wood, erector set, and so on, in order to make them yield to an idea. He wishes to build a town, a pioneer fortress or to make boats, guns, houses, airplanes, etc. These different types of child activities correspond to stages recognized by psychoanalytic doctrine as major phases of libidinal development in childhood; namely, the sensory, related to the oral phase, and the motor, to the anal phase. The child's wish to master engages his total organization just as does the genital phase (3).

To supplement the libidinal viewpoint I wish to throw light on the corresponding phases in the child's ego development during therapy. It is desirable for the therapist to recognize such phases, to understand their dynamic significance, and in reporting or interpreting therapy to give each incident and activity full credit. Later, in the case material, I shall demonstrate that these phases are not separated when dealing with a child beyond four years, but are intermingled in many parts of the actual, as well as the therapeutic growth process. Exploring matter is, for instance, not only the need of a one- to two-year-old child. It never ends in human life. Yet, I maintain, that such exploration bears particular meaning when it occurs in the sequence of the therapeutic hour. This is due to the fact that in the permissive atmosphere with the encourage-ment of an unknown protective person, the therapist, inner urges of the child are revived and set in motion. Automatically, they serve the tendency of growth which is dormant in every living organism (1, 9). On this assumption, it is possible to recognize the child's activities as manifestations of different stages in their rudimentary form and to regard each movement as instinctively and developmentally conditioned. The sequence of various manipulations, fully observed and understood, will reveal the whole breadth and uniqueness of the child's striving for new growth.

We could make better use of our therapeutic observations if all aspects of the child's normal development were better defined so that they could be brought closer to clinical consideration. However, as long as these two disciplines, the clinical and developmental theories of childhood, have not yet found a theoretical synthesis, a presentation like this must remain hypothetical (5).

### Sensory-Tactile, Exploratory Needs

When the child first explores his therapy room, one often observes his search for sensory-tactile contact with this new world. How important such contacts are can be learned by watching normal children. They continuously test out a new environment to satisfy their curiosity. In doing so they gain familiarity with their surroundings which contributes to their security. These are vital experiences which problem children need to repeat. Due to pressure from the outside, exerted by misunderstanding adults, or due to inner conditions which have hampered the child's alert curiosity in the past, many of our problem children have not had this opportunity. Freedom in tactile exploration is, in our understanding, the most concrete means to gain security in the playroom world. By exploring in therapy the child recaptures early primitive satisfactions. He finds a new link between himself and the surroundings, which, for the first time, answer fully to his desires. If, by these means, his mental curiosity and his need for object relation are satisfied, the playroom or the play hour becomes his own in a very important sense of the word. The relationship to the therapist as an agent who provides this gratification is then beyond any question. It is in this first phase that we can compare the development of affection through gratification of needs with the smiling infant after his hunger is stilled. Any interference at this phase by probing into the problems of the child or making him talk about his difficulty only delays the process. I received the strongest lesson in this direction from a boy of six years.

Dick was reported to have threatened his family, including a baby brother, grandparents, and mother, by throwing rocks at their home. The rage developed gradually. First he played noisily with wooden blocks. When he continued in spite of reprimand, the mother put him outdoors on a damp and chilly day. He then began to throw rocks at the door and windows, breaking several panes of glass. The mother called the police who consulted the psychiatrist. The latter referred the child to me for diagnosis and treatment. The father, returning from work, finally succeeded in calming down this completely frightened child.. He brought him to my office the following day. The facts elicited were that since infancy Dick had been severely restricted in all his activities and was never permitted to touch adult objects. The mother's parents who shared the household assumed that a child's actions are potentially harmful and destructive. These grandparents domineered the extremely immature and dependent mother whose very contradictory and confusing commands had contributed to the child's upset. When Dick came to me the first time he was still frightened, expecting punitive retaliation from an adult person. In the waiting room were some colorful stones on the mantel piece; and while the therapist was speaking with the father, the boy discovered the rocks on the shelf. Before Dick made any move himself, the therapist put some of the rocks down on the floor beside the wooden blocks he had been given earlier. The boy immediately took a rock and, somewhat fearfully, made a belligerent move as if to throw it. The therapist again encouraged him to play. After a while he slipped down until he lay flat on the ground. He rolled himself over the rocks, pushed them with his back, then with his hands and feet, until they were on the other side of the room. Then he rolled back with the rocks in front of him. He obviously wanted to feel their weight, texture, and consistency with all parts of his body. He seemed completely absorbed in this action and appeared to have forgotten the presence of father and therapist. The play with rocks on the floor was repeated for several hours in our interviews. Later it was interspersed by using blocks somewhat more meaningfully, as a two- to four-year-old would do: building towers or lining blocks up as a train. The father was advised to stay home from work for a few days. He gave all his attention to the child, who recovered

from his acute anxiety attack within ten days. Dick was then placed in a
kindergarten, where he used toys and other things with complete
freedom. First the teachers gave him special attention, but after a week
Dick was reported to fit well in the normal group. His uneasiness toward
his home still remained for a while. The family, as a result of guidance,
reformed their ideas about child-rearing. They learned to accept Dick and
permitted normal expression of his drives.

The accumulation of Dick's tension had, in my understanding,
something to do with his estrangement from his very physical world. His
rolling around over the rocks, his body contact with them created an
experience which the child had not had before. His quick recovery,
indicated by the gradual relaxation in the few hours of therapy, made him
sufficiently pliable to be introduced to a children's group. This change
was made possible because, through the object world and the satisfaction
found in it, he could accept his father's and my support and thus regain
new confidence in human relationships. Such situations in therapy are
not the exception. They are fairly common. It is this aspect of child
therapy which has been neglected in case reports. Similar physical
happenings are even more meaningful in the treatment of children
whose deficiency is not neurotic but one of the ego-structure.

## Muscular-Motor Needs

The next physical need we will discuss is the child's urge for moving
and discovering his body in relation to the space around him. In some
movements we observe a one- to three-year-old child's urge to find his
own body boundaries. He squeezes himself into small closets, cuddles on
a shelf after he removes the toys, jumps on the couch bouncing up and
down, proudly noticing how big he is and that he can jump from the
couch without falling. Other children want to test their energies. For
instance, a five-year-old child grabs a saw and tries to test his strength by
cutting wood. Another one wants to drive nails in a board. No concrete or
definite idea of what they wish to produce inspires these activities. They
just feel good when their muscular efforts make an impression upon the
substance. This pleasurable experience, is, no doubt, a form of tension
release. It also serves as a testing out of their body form and capacities
and brings to children the awareness of their physical and mental selves.
To illustrate this statement some events in the therapy of an eight-year-
old boy may be helpful.

Jimmy was treated by me in a public clinic, while his mother was
guided by a social worker. He was very inhibited in the beginning of
therapy and moved helplessly around the playroom. For several hours he

touched and then quietly put down things as if they contained poison. Finally, he took a board built for small children and hammered pegs in it. Then he turned it around and hammered the pegs out again. He continued this for quite a while and then announced, "This is what little children like to do." He went on banging harder and harder. This action brought forth an amazing change in his general behavior, which will become clear if we understand the events which preceded the boy's arrival in the clinic. Jimmy was a healthy and vigorous child from early infancy, but his activities were restricted, and his behavior molded to a smooth and sissy-like "goodness." His parents were foreign-born. It was the mother who particularly ruled the child by her superficial standards, based on her wish for social prestige. In this atmosphere Jimmy was first a perfect baby, but after six years he turned into a difficult child. When his wishes were not fulfilled he had bad temper tantrums. He became quite compulsive about things which were not done right for him. Then he became over-anxious with bad nightmares and finally developed a stubborn daytime enuresis. Each symptom of his neurosis could be traced to his mother's oversolicitous behavior, not releasing the boy out of her controlling power, until many normal growing needs were suppressed. The drive of an eight-year-old boy to be more independent was warped to such a degree that the world was full of fear to him, growing up was a threat, and the most infantile manifestaions, like daytime wetting, were used to attract his mother's attention. When he hammered the peg board, vital energies in his system came to life. Soon after, he started to play with miniature Indians and pioneers, toys which he dared not touch before. Several hours later, his projective play showed fully his pent-up aggression. Jimmy was articulate enough to discuss some difficulties he had; for instance, his enuresis, which disturbed him greatly. Yet, I believe, it was the friendly encouragement to express by actions his various boyish inclinations, for many years so badly neglected, which aroused a more spontaneous spirit within him and mobilized his development. He once said that only in mother's presence did he wet his pants. This was underlined by the therapist but not further stressed. There was a definite indication of oedipal attachment to the mother, but it was also obvious that the mother's own seductive trends interfered with Jimmy's development. He increasingly appreciated in himself his growing faculties. He showed no difficulty in identifying with his father as a male person who became a good friend to him, sharing with him sports and outdoor activities. Jimmy's enuresis diminished and later disappeared as the boy extended his interests into larger spaces beyond mother's solicitous supervision. In the last phase of therapy, he could put his pride and self-confidence to test by building an Indian camp which he took home piece by piece and put on his shelf. This was the world to which he now belonged, a man's world with which he identified himself. In the last two hours he made extensive plans and actual preparation for a wire communication line with his friend. They wanted to use a secret sign system which no adult could understand. His treatment took approximately fourteen months, once weekly; his mother, being guided by the social worker, needed a few weeks longer to become fully able to accept this vigorous and healthy son.

## Motor Constriction

We stress the need for such body release action in child therapy in order to re-create the flexibility lost in the former years and to help the child regain new fluidity and spontaneity, the basis of all growth.

The study and interpretation of such release by movement is particularly valuable in neurotic conditions which in adults are often diagnosed as obsessive or compulsive, but which also appear in younger children, such as Jimmy, to a milder degree. These symptoms are easily traceable to the attitudes of parents who, too early, set unusually high standards, thwarting the child's need for self-expression and self-enjoyment. Parents' restrictions of body activity are most crucial in the period between one and three. When practicing toilet training such parents demand from the child too much inner control; when confining him in playpens or exerting anxious supervision over all his actions, they deprive the child of vitally needed motions such as toddling, creeping, climbing, etc. His needs conflict with the parents' concept of his safety or with their exaggerated ideas about what is clean or dirty, good or bad. To shield himself against outer pressures and continuous demands, the child acquires a cramped control. This gradually affects his whole psycho-physical system and may later lead to that compulsive neurotic character structure in adults whose analytical treatment is a most arduous one. Often the patient requires years of therapy to bring back to him some of the freedom and spontaneity he lost in early years. By contrast, it seems easy to open up the chance for release action in children, a fact which places the child therapist in a very favorable position. Providing and channelizing freedom of action has a multiple meaning. First, the patient rids himself of some tension. When he mobilizes his needs for body activity he soon discovers a new Body-Self. This leads automatically to serious groping for new values in judging not only his Body-Self but also his rights and needs in relation to his environment. This development was noticeable in Jimmy. After having discovered his suppressed boyish aggression through body release, he committed many violations against mother's principles, without being chastised. However, it took him many months to do this without anxiety. It was highly significant that Jimmy, one day walking with his mother to the clinic, took a snowball and flung it against her back. This happened in the last phase of therapy. This self-assertion was a testing out of his own new Self, indicating to him the superiority of his needs and values over the oppressive power his mother had held over him in the past.

Often, the therapist becomes directly instrumental in leading the child to search for new values about himself. If he encourages the child's desire for free body movement and physical outlets, the therapeutic relationship becomes something more than merely nurturing and permissive. The child's action may endanger his health and safety, and the therapist naturally gives warning. The child becomes able to understand the therapist's protective attitude as a confirmation that the latter identifies with his infantile need to find outlets, but nevertheless does not wish to see the patient harmed. This makes the patient susceptible to reasoning. He discovers on a less infantile level, what his growing interests really are. He comprehends that he has to take responsibility for himself. This shift in the patient provides the basis for searching his own standard, for finding self-chosen controls and limitations in his behavior. Thus, the process of voluntary self-control, destroying the faulty superego forces, first begins on a completely physical level. After the child's body constrictions and his oppositional defenses are released, he becomes susceptible to new experiences. The child's contacts with the outer world widen, and he acquires new conceptions of reality, less laden with fear. Gradually, as the child's anxiety symptoms and defenses disappear, he discovers and also identifies himself with the needs of other children outside the playroom. In fact, it is the protective and free atmosphere which enables the child to develop new trust and confidence, first in the therapist, then in his own peers and adults. The symptomatology of the compulsive neurotic is here understood in relation to the child's early confinement in space, and the prohibition and control of his body activities, which extend automatically to the eliminatory function and give this type of neurosis its name.

Dr. Ernest Zierer, the art therapist in Hillside Hospital, Long Island, found some supporting evidence for the above statement through his research (10). If psychotic patients, with anal regressive symptoms, paint landscapes they often stratify one element above the other. (Four- to six-year-old children also do this.) Other patients paint the front object transparent, so that one can see the object behind it. Upon questioning they explain, "There is space between the objects. I have to show that there is space." Zierer concludes that anal regression has definite relation to confusion in spatial arrangement. The drawings of compulsive neurotics are characterized by overcrowding of the given space, an outer reflection of their inner condition. The compulsive neurotic and the psychotic with anal regression have one thing in common; namely, their conditioning in childhood. They were restricted in narrow realms, both physically and psychologically, at an age when their constitutional and developmental needs demanded free activities and the mobility of a growing organism. In consequence, the compulsive personality acquires rigid, ritualistic rules, the obsessional symptoms as well as the sadistic outlets. These may be considered safeguards to shield him from anxieties produced by uncertainties in himself. They also protect the patient from the challenge of unfamiliarity and the awareness of free spaces he was not permitted to enjoy in his childhood.

## Representational and Constructive Play

The sensory, tactile, and motor activities comprise the regressive needs expressed in play. A more complex aspect of child's play is usually characterized by imaginative or projective activity. He builds in life size or in miniature a representation of his own understanding of the environment by playing with dolls, miniature objects, or puppets. Sometimes he transforms the whole playroom into his house, street, or school, and often he re-enacts adult roles he has observed: his mother, teacher, the milkman, mailman, etc. (3). Developmentally speaking, this play serves as a means for the child to explore and understand the social world around him in relation to himself. It also allows him to project the emotional handicaps which have impaired his human relationships. Hence, this sort of play is highly important for diagnostic as well as therapeutic purposes. Yet, to the author's understanding, any sort of social conflict must be understood also in relation to earlier frustrations, like those expressed in sensory and muscular motor needs. It is a truism that all social problems have their origin in infancy. In fact, in any therapy one can observe not only the child's social conflicts, but also his need for physical regression, interspersed, as the child indulges in his representational and imaginative projection. In two cases which follow, the earlier residues of elementary needs will be emphasized, not because we believe that the physical developmental aspects of ego growth are more important than the libidinal ones, but because we see in the physical activities the beginning of the new growth process, a means to mobilize the child's social and libidinal development.

The construction of toys or other objects is the fourth category of child's play activity we shall discuss here. When the child employs a work bench and uses tools, he is mastering material and creating a replica of what he has seen in the adult world (3). In such construction, the child not only imitates an adult world as in the representational activity, he becomes identified with a grown-up person who produces his own objects. This is "work" and not merely play. He proves himself in his physical and also mental qualities. I mentioned before that representational and constructive play activities may well be compared to the genital phase of libidinal development. This point becomes particularly significant, when we observe the assimilation of earlier infantile drives in this constructive effort of producing an object by satisfying tactile and motor needs, or when the child projects his social world in a spatial reality around him. If the early ego stages which produced the sensory and motor needs are not fully consummated, the child's attempts toward constructive or projective activities are in vain. He obviously has not reached the developmental stage of mastering his genital phase. He pretends to build something, but he does not succeed. Often he squanders the material by mishandling it, or he is completely unrealistic in applying his energies or his reasoning. He cannot judge his capacity in relation to the idea he has in mind, nor can he choose or organize the proper material. The playful creation of a miniature world may be the first step to this object-building tendency, if one considers both activities in terms of the effects on ego growth. The construction of objects, fully accomplished by the child, gives him a great feeling of independence and mastery. From this viewpoint the comparison of the neurotic child here described with the schizoid personality is especially fruitful.

## Two Cases

1. John's parents were of Canadian descent, from families whose social prominence was of long standing. Both were oversensitive and physically weak. Various irresponsible nurses took care of the child in his infancy. When he was four, the father, an artist and always an erratic person, developed a brain tumor. This sickness caused many temper outbursts to which the child was often exposed. His mother, wavering between her obligation to the child and her husband, had acquired guilt feelings about almost everything which lay in the past. When she learned that her husband was incurable and faced with increasing personality aberrations, she decided upon a divorce. At the same time she brought the six-year-old John for diagnosis and treatment.

John was a well-built, sensitive child with a bearing that commanded respect. His symptoms were excessive masturbation, difficulty in falling asleep, bad appetite, continuous temper tantrums, mainly directed toward his mother, and incapacity to deal with playmates. Once he chased some children with a knife. The private school he attended had advised withdrawal until he recovered from his disturbance. The child's behavior had the character of a desperate reaction against the pressures exerted on him. These were caused, not only by the separation from his father for whom he preserved a real attachment, but also by his mother's guilt feelings, which caused her to shower the boy with attention, fondling him like a one-year-old infant. Once she said, "He is so beautiful I hardly can keep my hands off him." This worked on the child as a continuous sensual stimulation. It also burdened him with ambivalent feelings and even hatred toward his mother, as his own sexual desires conflicted with his strivings for self-respect and independence. His ego did not appear weakened like that of a psychotic child, but he seemed involved in an extreme struggle to maintain the integrity which a six-year-old boy needs.

John refused to enter the house where the playroom was located. When I met him outdoors, he displayed a belligerent tendency to run away or to do something violent. When I said, "Let's stay out here," he relaxed somewhat and looked up at a small tree. Guessing what he wanted, I told him, "You may climb it." This reduced his resistance still further. He went up into the tree with such agility and grace that one could not hesitate to praise him for that. He sat on a branch over my head. Sitting high in the tree, he was able to produce some positive feelings about himself. He slipped down the tree and wandered around the house to the nursery play yard where he found a three-year-old boy waiting for his mother. Both children played on the jungle gym and soon began digging in sand and packing it in a cart. John met this new friend on a perfect three-year-old level. The difference was only his greater strength in doing things and just this fact increased his self-confidence. When John came to the second interview, he immediately asked for the other boy who did not appear. John still refused to enter the house. He went to the backyard and worked with the shovel, packing a cart full of sand. Then he built a ramp to a huge box and wheeled the cart up. He was again higher than myself. I had given him a hand in moving the heavy cart. He proceeded to unload it by throwing the sand about with a shovel in a large circle. This fascinated him. Being higher up asserted his body power (sensory and motor needs satisfied). After the third hour, John at last entered the house. During that hour and several succeeding ones, he played in the sandbox but no longer like a three-year-old. He worked on a war game, in which he had all the miniature soldiers fight on his side, except three Indians which he designated as my army. He declared the three Indians "dead or alive" at will, showing his need to control his enemies. In the sand he built trenches and other fortifications with blocks. The caving-in of the sand was one of the tricks the material played on him, which he had to combat by putting up walls of wood (elementary physical needs satisfied). He finally landed in a sitting position in the sand box, legs under him, partially buried in sand, the war machine contraptions surrounding him. He called to me, "Won't you make some war machines, too?" When I screwed some erector set beams together, he immediately took them away, saying, "This machine is mine." He repeated this several times. Then came a long discussion about how smart he had to be to outsmart his enemies and not only to win by physical power. He became very fond of this sort of play. Once he said, "This is my hour," and he wished to come more frequently and for longer periods. The later phase of the war game was a space battle in the universe. His physical skill was supplemented by intelligent handling of structures, and this construction work absorbed him completely. His social relation to me became easy and firm, and he often called me Pal. At this time he permitted me more war material. I avoided being active and felt that John's need for warfare was fading away. Simultaneously, it was reported that his relations with others were improving; only rarely did he have temper tantrums. His concentration on work and play was fully established, and his excessive masturbation stopped. He was now ready to return to school, and we terminated treatment three months after he had started. John's mother, who also received help for two months from the same therapist, remarried a half year later, and John's introduction to this new situation was carefully guided by the therapist. Now, after three years, John's complete adjustment has been repeatedly confirmed.

2. Bill was ten years old, with a brother one and a half years younger. In contrast to this brother, who was well-accepted, Bill had the established reputation among his family, relatives, neighbors, and teachers, of being unmanageable, destructive, and utterly negativistic. He appeared to be a very worried child, tense and fearful. The stories about him did not quite fit the impression one got from the boy himself. In dealing with the mother, bad relations between her and the boy were observed. For years a battle had gone on between them which left the boy close to being wrecked in his feeling about himself. To escape the angry wrath of this misunderstood child the family occasionally left home over the weekend, locking up Bill completely alone in their house. There was hardly any area in Bill's life where he could present himself in an accepted way. His first move in our therapy room was characterized by fearful

compliance. He did not dare to make any exploration. He saw the erector set and started to build a gun. He soon gave up, because he could not manage the gun barrel and also would not accept help. Then a windmill was tried, and it was finished with assistance. In this first hour he realized that no demands were being made on him.

In the second hour he was more himself. He seized upon a puppet with the features of a well-known entertainer, and in an agitated voice he asked, "Is he alive or is he dead? If he is dead we bury him, that jerk!" Bill buried the puppet in a sandbox and banged on the top, then pulled the puppet out again, beat it, and buried it again. This puppet became the target of more abuse. It symbolized to him something that he wanted to depart from, either a part of himself, or his brother with whom he fought a life-long battle of sibling rivalry. Bill's sadistic trend was quite obvious. Sometimes he filled the rubber body with sand, went to the top floor of the house, and dropped it down on the ground after repeated spanking and shaking. While Bill was in this elated spirit of revenge against the world, he suggested making a fire to burn houses. There were folded paper houses, used by other children to represent little towns. After it was decided to do this in the sandbox for safety, he burned one after the other, jumping from one leg to the other with joy. After the sixth house was burned, the therapist said he should stop, because other children wanted to use the houses for play. He understood. From this hour it was certain that Bill could be given plenty of leeway, but nevertheless could stop without resentment, upon being told. This was a sign that the basis for a good relationship with the therapist had been laid.

His home environment was hard to influence, though his mother was frequently seen by the therapist and occasionally also his father. Their preconceived idea that naughtiness had to be fought by physical punishment was firmly established. It was clear to me after some weeks that Bill's behavior pattern could be reformed, but the parents had to gain belief in him too. I wanted to offer him a new start in a milieu uninfluenced by the parents' attitude. A director of a small private school was informed of his predicament in the family, and she good-heartedly promised cooperation. Bill was told that this situation would offer him a real chance. No attempt was made to hide my opinion about him and the difficulties he was having with his family. This school experience turned out most positive. The school's reports were full of praise. The teacher described him as a "very intelligent and over-sensitive child who needs much encouragement." "Very eager to please, etc." This was Bill's real nature. In that year he became an ardent student of music and was especially proficient in his church choir. The choirmaster, who also discovered him to be an unusually gifted boy, became a real friend to Bill.

His mother's response to the good reports was always, "Wait until the next month."

Bill's behavior in the therapy hour remained similar to that of the first two months. His need for regressive sensory-motor behavior was unlimited. He seized every opportunity for dashing around and romping. In the large mansion where the play therapy took place, he ran from the cellar to the top floor, often using the fire escape to come down. When this was forbidden, he stopped without protest. He explored every corner of the house, always searching for secret plotters or enemies in closets. He just could not believe that all this freedom was given to him and no punishment followed. Later Bill asked to be taken to the hills, where he enjoyed rock climbing. His relationship to the therapist remained a stable one throughout.

Most of Bill's behavior reflected the motility of a two- to four-year-old child. However, there were also many exploratory needs. His play with fire was one of these. When he discovered remnants of a chemistry set, he worked with everything so long that no tube, no chemical was left. Then he wished to build an explosive bomb. He filled an electric bulb with water and mixed the water with whatever he could get hold of: cleanser from the bathtub, sand, powder from finger paint, etc. He put the "bomb" in the fireplace, where a fire was burning. The bulb burst and extinguished the fire. Upon being given an objective explanation for this occurrence, Bill became quite curious and completely rational. After the emotional affect was over, he acted entirely as a boy of his own age.

It required a year for Bill to establish a more normal relation to his family. Then I felt he was ready for a more constructive experience. A smaller boarding school for boys was found which was willing to accept my interpretation of the boy's personality and his present developmental needs. In the next year I received from the school two enthusiastic reports stressing his fair sportsmanship, his intelligent devotion to learning, and his great advances in music.

## Comparison of the Two Cases

These two cases are typical of many others the author has experienced in her practice during the last twenty years. Both children were severely milieu-damaged. Bill was despised by his mother, who was blinded by her own neurotic condition; John, born into a sickly family situation, was shattered almost out of his senses by an erring mother who wanted to make good for her failure. Both boys were endowed with an extraordinary sensitivity and, exposed to their family conditions, offered a precarious diagnosis. Their ego consistency was strained to the breaking point. Both were average clinical cases in a heightened phase of their neurotic defenses.

What was the course of John's therapy? By his avoidance of the playroom he instinctively created the situation which permitted him to get down from his six-year-old level to a three-year-old one. Climbing the tree, throwing sand provided the elementary outlets which established an easier relationship with the therapist than he had anticipated. Later, sitting in the sand box, partially dug under with his knees, he created a war game where he could fight the therapeutic environment as he fought home and school before. His war games were less a shooting war than a plotting cold war, inventing better machinery. The conflicts between his sick father and himself, on the one hand, and his mother's faulty attempts to stimulate love responses in the child, on the other, were most confusing, because he could not see the fronts against which he could defend himself, while Bill saw his fronts quite clearly. Bill's defenses were a forward battle against any person in his environment, because they were all prejudiced and influenced by his mother's erroneous conception of him. His aggression, mixed with spells of moody defeat and misery, needed expansion in space, and a most primitive reconquest of his body feelings, in order to restore some self-integrity. His running and romping filled almost twelve months of therapy. The construction work in the beginning was mere compliance. He did not yet understand the therapeutic process and was not yet able to discover his own needs. Bill's physical energy directed against the rubber puppet seemed to be more important than a verbalization of this hate impulse. Once he tore off a smaller doll's head. He had to twist it several times. Finally he succeeded and threw the head in the fireplace where he had just started a fire. I watched him while he did this; and when he was through, I said, "You really had to do this," as if it were a harmless prank. It is my contention that the event itself is the release. One need not put a label on such situations in the heat of the child's excitement. The empathy of the therapist, expressed by his attitude, is the solution to the problem. If Bill would have destroyed more dolls, the therapist would have said the same to him as when he burned the six houses. It is this kind of full outlet which becomes a bridge to more social consideration. In the events of therapy this appears as simple as weaning an infant from the breast to the bottle when the mother enjoys his growing capacity.

John's social conflicts were tackled by sitting in the sandbox, playing competitive games with the therapist to find out who was smarter. In his fantasies he reached actually far beyond his age, pondering over technical up-to-date means of fighting enemies. He also used space cadets and other fantastic figures. If this boy had not been treated, he might have submerged himself in such symbolic fantasies, completely withdrawing from reality. Bill's desperate outbreaks, on the other hand, would have offered eventually serious conflicts with the social order, unloved and rejected as he was. The point here is that, whatever the basic conflicts of the children were, the type of play they chose, the activities, regressive or progressive, revealed the only possible way for them to solve their problems.

## Therapist's Role

By giving the above-developed aspects greater weight, the role of the therapist can be somewhat redefined. We mentioned already his nurturing attitude when he encourages the child to discover his needs and search for gratification. It is the nursing mother who promotes the first contact with reality. Tackling various objects while exploring the room, trying out some activity, enriches the child with new concrete experiences. The situation becomes more realistic when the therapist warns the child of some discomfort if he thoughtlessly pursues his aim. The warning must be in such a form that the child still realizes the full identification of the therapist with his own interests. At the same time the patient is motivated to search for more subtle gratifications. As child therapist one often encounters situations where one wishes to have the patient insured for possible physical damages. Yet, in many years of this kind of practice, no child ever got harmed. On the contrary, many children showed an awakening sense of responsibility combined with their awareness of the physical realities. The more spontaneity is developed for any activity, the easier it is for the therapist to check destructive tendencies either toward themselves, toward people, or toward play material. In this way the therapist moves toward the role of a conscious agent and mediator between the child and the world outside the playroom.

Here again, something happens which can be compared with the development from infancy to later childhood. At first, the nurturing parent is liked for his need gratification; later he becomes the representative of a group beyond the narrow confines of the two-way exchange of sympathy. The parent bridges this step by showing the child the positive gain he will make when meeting friends and moving in the realms of neighbors who also accept him. In therapy, likewise, the narcissistic self-demands change into something new; namely, the child's desire for mutuality and social give-and-take. This became obvious in John's therapy when he started to call the therapist Pal. Nurturing was no longer necessary. Cautioning to safeguard material or the interests of other people proves to the child that the therapist is identified, not only with the patient's needs, but also with the rules and requirements of a world outside the play hour. The proper timing of such a hint to the reality beyond the play hour is a very important point. While the therapy progresses, the question arises whether the child can take such suggestions or not. If not, the therapist has to sacrifice another paper house for burning, or another doll's head will be pulled off. From this point of view also, it must be stressed that the treatment of the neurotic child differs essentially from that of the schizoid child. The latter's reality-testing is the main object of therapy, while for the neurotic child our aim is to reduce or remodel his drives with his obligations towards a wider world, and the therapist must be the agent to accomplish this. When he first confirms the child's right to self-expression, he gradually makes the child choose his own way of limiting and controlling his impulses. The patient becomes able to develop a more subtle desire for satisfaction when he feels accepted by the therapist first, and then he strives to be accepted by the outer world beyond the playroom.

In this last phase the freedom of the child's own expressiveness is merged with the child's chosen self-control. When his social responses have improved and he gains the rewards of being accepted in his environment, the therapist can well, retrospectively, point out the meaning of these play hours, relative to the concrete conflict in which the child found himself. Now he is able to understand his former problems, and he will also understand that the purpose of all the fun and freedom he has experienced was a means to help him express what he was never able to express before. His new, voluntary adjustment to his environment was what he wanted more than just some "good times" in the play hours. It is easy to give the child the feeling that he himself chose this new order and social adaptation, just as an adult realizes that his therapy is actually a self-educating process, after his inner needs have been fully realized. This explains why the child, in his regained self-respect and self-confidence, finds it so easy to leave the therapist. There is hardly any good-bye. The child now feels as good about not coming to the play therapy, as he formerly felt eager to come. His urges and strivings are again turned toward the larger world of his home, friends, and school. His spontaneity is regained, and thus, he can now utilize anything that is offered him for further growth. His contacts with people and the outer world have been reestablished.

**References**
1. Allen, F. H., *Psychotherapy with Children*, New York: W.W. Norton & Co., 1942.
2. Despert, J. L., "Play Analysis in Research and Therapy," in *Modern Trends in Child Psychiatry*, New York: International Universities Press, 1945.
3. Erikson, E. H., *Childhood and Society*, New York: W. W. Norton & Co., 1950.
4. Freud, Anna, *The Psycho-Analytical Treatment of Children*, London: Image, 1950.
5. Hartman, H., "Psycho-Analysis and Developmental Psychology," in *The Psychoanalytical Study of the Child*, New York: International Universities Press, vol. V, 1950.
6. Meyer, A., "Spontaneity" in *The Commonsense Psychiatry of Dr. Adolf Meyer*, New York:
7. Piaget, Jean, *The Construction of Reality in the Child*, New York: Basic Books, 1954.
8. Schilder, P., "The Image and Appearance of the Human Body," *Psychological Monographs*, London: Kegan Paul, Trench, No. 4, 1945.
9. Whitaker, C. A. and T. Malone, *The Roots of Psychotherapy*, New York: Blakiston, 1953.
10. Zierer, E., "Developmental Aspects of the Body Space Concept," (Read in manuscript.).

# RELEASE

# Release Therapy

DAVID M. LEVY

There has been great interest and activity in recent years devoted to the study of the child's play as a basis for psychotherapy. Treating the child's problems by exploiting his own methods of treating him has a sound basis, analogous to a study of the cure of disease by determining the organism's own methods of protection. How does the small child handle his own emotional difficulties? It is well known that he uses imaginative play as an important method of getting rid of tensions arising out of anxiety. Presumably, if the child's behavior were appropriate during the event that caused anxiety, no tensional residues would have remained. When the child's method of dealing with anxiety is unsuccessful, symptoms indicating the presence and the severity of the disturbance are at hand. This is best illustrated in a group of children referred primarily because of night terrors or fears, or both.

In the group of thirty-five cases of release therapy which form the clinical substance of this paper, eleven were referred primarily because of night terrors or fears. The group of eleven comprises eight girls and three boys, age range being from two to nine. In these cases there was typically a specific event that precipitated the fear reaction. The problem in therapy became well defined — how to develop a method whereby the event could be restored in the child's play and thereby release the anxiety that the child had been unable to release by himself. Why had these children failed in their own efforts at abreacting anxiety, where others may have succeeded? The answer has to do with a number of factors — the strength of the stimulus is one, since fears are of varying intensity and duration. They also may be summated; that is, several events, each provoking fear, may occur simultaneously or in close time relation. Another factor has to do with the child's sensitivity to the stimulus. A fear stimulus may have a completely different effect at the age of two than at the age of eight. Moreover, a child may have been sensitized through a specific past experience that intensifies the response. A constitutional factor must also be considered. Here is an example. A boy aged seven years (Case 7), had two experiences in late infancy in which he was bound in blankets for a paracentesis of the eardrums, without anesthesia. The mother described the boy's struggles, attested by the movements of both arms and legs, the expression of fear, etc. Each experience was of more than a half hour's duration. Also at the age of seven, some boys bound him to a tree in Central Park with ropes. One of the boys picked up an ant and dropped it on his hand. That was part of the "torture." His nurse, who had been engaged in conversation with other nurses, looked up after a while and released her charge. He was referred for treatment about four months later because of night terrors of six weeks' duration. He would wake every night sobbing and recount dreams of torture, chiefly of being bound and gagged. But these night terrors were precipitated by an event that happened on the day that the first nightmare occurred. Frightening stories were told to the class by a teacher, especially one in which two knights drove nails through the hands of an innkeeper, pinning him against his own door.

Why the third of the series of events produced the nightmares and not the other two is not known. It is easy to understand, however, that in the three episodes the same type of experience was happening to the patient, so that the third experience, without the previous sensitizing experiences, presumably might not have caused so great an effect. The classroom story was played out in the first session in numerous versions. The boy had a nightmare as usual that night, but none in the past two months. There were four sessions in all. Though only two months have elapsed since treatment began, there is no question of the immediate therapeutic effect of such a method.

## Special Sensitivity

A somewhat more complicated example of special sensitivity to the fear-provoking experience is seen in Case 2, a girl aged three years, five months, referred because of generally fearful behavior and night terrors. These started at the age of eighteen months, immediately following sutures of a lacerated scalp due to an accident, done without anesthesia. After this experience she became fearful and tense but improved after several months. Six months after the first accident she was hospitalized and had three paracenteses of the eardrum. Following this she became fearful of everything and fought off the nurses and doctors. Again, improvement occurred until a tonsillectomy at the age of thirty months, after which the terrors became a nightly occurrence for six weeks, gradually diminishing in frequency to about once a week at the time of referral. This fearful attitude prevented social contacts with other children in the nursery group. So far we see, as in the previous case, a sensitivity to a special type of experience. In this case there was the additional factor that previous to the tonsillectomy she had been masturbating, had been warned about it, and was still struggling with the problem when the tonsillectomy occurred, demonstrated by her own activities in the playroom. The frightening aspects of the tonsillectomy can be seen, therefore, to involve a threat to the life of the child because of guilty sexual practices.

## Weighting of Events

The weighting of the event is well illustrated in Case 8, a girl aged seven years, eight months, referred because of night terrors and insomnia of three weeks' duration. She had gone to a movie in the afternoon; there were a number of frightening episodes, but the one which apparently affected the patient had to do with a scene in which a child released a trap door on which a woman was dancing. The woman was a prima donna who had taken the place of an older dancer whom the children loved. The dancer fell through the trap door and was crippled by the fall. The patient saw the movie in the afternoon and that night had a frightening dream from which she awoke screaming. Thereafter for three weeks, until referral, she was unable to fall asleep for hours. There were other events in this movie to which the patient apparently was unresponsive; for example, an attempt at suicide by drowning.

The fear-provoking episode in the movie was weighted by a number of experiences. The patient had on that very day visited her father, who had remarried. The second wife was well known to the patient since she had been a friend of the mother's. At the same time the patient was having difficulty with her governess. From the child's behavior in play therapy one could reconstruct the response of the child to the frightening episode as comprising the fright itself, as fright at any death-threatening experience, a hostility to the stepmother, to the governess and to the mother — the stepmother for living with her father, the governess for her severity, and her own mother for throwing her father out of the house. In a scene in which the trap door incident was reconstructed and the child kept throwing objects on the dancer who had fallen on the basement floor, she spoke about throwing them on her mother. After the first session the child slept through the night.

## Effectiveness of Release Therapy

This is as it should be, since cases selected for release therapy have in the main been uncomplicated; uncomplicated in the sense that the particular problems presented by the children were presumably not affected seriously by problems in the family relationship. Furthermore, they represent cases in which the forces that resolve anxiety can be quickly mobilized. In the series of eleven cases a therapeutic effect on the problem presented occurred in one of the first three sessions in all but two cases. In these two, therapeutic modification occurred by the sixth and eighth sessions respectively. In the eleven cases, follow-up studies are over periods varying from two weeks to five and one-half years. In two cases there were ten and fifteen sessions each; in the others the number of sessions varied from two to seven.

Of the remaining children in the entire series, five were referred primarily for tics, six for speech disturbance, four for temper tantrums or negativism and the remainder for miscellaneous reasons: refusal to accept femininity (three cases), hyperkinesis, nocturnal enuresis, inhibited behavior, reading difficulty, epilepsy, dementia (one each). The age range of the entire group was two to ten, the median age six, about two or three years lower than the median of the entire group of patients seen over that period.

Follow-up interviews for all cases have been made, at varying intervals. At the present time notations of adjustment are at hand for all children: nine, three to six years; sixteen, one to three years; and ten, two weeks to one year after treatment. Success (as noted specifically in the records appended) has occurred in all but three cases. Experimentally tried out in one case of epilepsy and one of dementia (organic?) the method failed.

## Criteria for Use

Ideally, the criteria for selecting children for release therapy are: (1) the presenting problem should be a definite symptom picture, precipitated by a specific event, in the form of a frightening experience, the birth of a younger sibling, the discharge of a governess, divorce of the parents, or the like. (2) The problems should not be of too long duration. The children are preferably ten years or younger. It is quite a different task treating a boy referred for fears at the age of fourteen and a boy with fears at the age of five. In the latter case the problems may be described as more specific, in the former as more closely integrated with the personality structure. The fears of many years duration have had their effect, for example, on all the boy's social relationships, on his handling of the problem of sex, even, perhaps, on intellectual function. In that type of case, release therapy as a complete method is distinctly inadequate. (3) Regardless of the age at the time of referral and the specificity of the problem, it is important that the child is suffering from something that happened in the past and not from a difficult situation going on at the time of treatment. Release therapy cannot be applied, for example, to a child suffering from the results of maternal rejection or overprotection. In such cases, the mother and not the child is the primary or even the exclusive object of therapy. It is assumed, when a child is under release therapy, that the family relationships are normal, giving a wide latitude to the meaning of that word, or at least, that the particular problem presented is not primarily related to the family situation at the time. An example is shown in cases in which the child shows tenseness, lack of affectionate response, fear of dirt or disorderliness based on a mother or governess who has been disciplinary too soon or too severely. In such a case efforts are first made to ensure the fact that a modification in regard to maternal behavior has been made or that the governess is out of the picture.

### Basic Principles

The methodologic principle of release therapy is in the use of the acting-out principle in play to the highest degree. Examples have already been given in cases of night terrors, in which the original pathogenic situation has to be recreated. Cases of tics may be used as examples in which the problem of restoring the act is no longer present, because the act, the tic, is there. I refer to those tics which represent the act as partially fulfilled or displaced. A boy aged eight years (Case 21) was referred for a variety of tics, including a mouth-opening tic, character-ized by frequent sudden involuntary wide opening and closing of the mouth. It represented an incompleted biting act. When played out on dolls, he bit the anal regions. All his tics had to do with sucking, biting, and sexual impulses. Another eight-year-old (Case 20) was referred for a finger smelling tic, consisting of innumerable sniffings of his right index finger. This was related to an inhibited rectal masturbation and "played out" by inserting his finger into slits made in dolls.

In release therapy the interpretive function of the therapist is reduced to a minimum and may be absent, especially in children age two, three, and four. In selecting cases for this discussion, some difficulty arose in classifying when interpretation appeared to be well mingled with a playing-out method. In cases of doubt, the method was considered interpretive-play rather than an acting-out technique (release therapy) and not included.

Examples of therapy without any interpretive activity are afforded by cases in which the play sessions are devoted entirely to release of destructive behavior, messy play, and general "naughtiness." There are twenty-three in the series in which there has been no interpretation. The younger children, ages two to five, were cured apparently without any knowledge of why they came or any relationship between the treatment and cure, so far as known. For example (Case 24), a girl aged two years, nine months, referred among other things for tantrums in which she would remain mute for about half an hour, and general lack of responsiveness to affection. In the nineteen sessions the activity consisted chiefly in throwing clay on the floor, stepping on it, playing with water, cutting, throwing, and hitting objects, at times spilling water on the floor and sitting in it — generally a return to infantile pleasure and release of aggression. Throughout the sessions, notes from the mother indicated a general increase in affectionate response, a more outgoing quality and a marked increase in speech. Release therapy in this type of child, by overcoming anxieties that had to do with dirt, orderliness, and hostile expressions, made possible an expansion of personality, presumably bound down by a discipline too early or too severe. The therapy is, then, a kind of dilatation process, designed to overcome a constricted personality. In such a case there is nothing to interpret. With the unfolding of personality, growth of the emotional life seems to be a rapid process. When release becomes inadequate and interpretations are felt to be essential, I don't know. I know certainly, in the older age group and in the more serious problems in younger children, as an exclusive or primary method, it does appear inadequate.

There are cases in which the important task of treatment is to give the child insight into its own motivation. In general, they represent cases in which the child is not suffering from the symptoms as much as from their exploitation. Inability to fall asleep for hours may be a symptom of anxiety, and hence be benefited by release therapy. It may, however, be a method, regardless of how it came about, by which the child, for example, exerts control over a parent. In the latter case, the play of this behavior through dolls is used chiefly as an aid to a simple insight therapy.

Again there are severe cases in which it is clear at once that the attitude of the child toward the therapist is too suspicious or too anxious to risk the rapidity of release therapy. Further, there are severe neuroses in children in which the problem of therapy is primarily psychoanalytic;

in which free play and interpretive therapy are essential technical considerations.

Though "free play," in the sense of the child's own selection of material and methods, is part of release therapy, it is characterized by what may be called a control situation, in the sense that the therapist may select the material and depict the plot, as in the sibling rivalry situation. The therapist supplies the main actors and the dramatic situation. The child is encouraged to work with the plot selected, add whatever other actors or scenes he wishes, and keep the play going. The same method holds for free and controlled play — the use of skills to keep the action going, to surrender the therapist's interpretive art to that of fulfilling the child's own function in the play — to keep the play moving whenever possible to its natural dramatic crescendo. This applies in a sense, even when methods of simple release are used as, for example, in repetitions of the act of bursting water-filled balloons — the repetitions are encouraged if need be until the child has apparently finished a cycle of activity. It is also important to stop quickly if any play is poorly tolerated, whether from anxiety or boredom, in fact, to stop all controlled play activity.

Release therapy may be used, of course, in combination with other methods. In using insight therapy, as previously mentioned, it may be wise to get release of feeling, especially of hostility, in a relationship play as a prelude to giving the child insight into the nature of his attitude. In various forms of psychoanalytic therapy it may likewise be used, as it actually is in certain phases. In Case 22, a boy aged eleven years, referred for impulsive, aggressive behavior, it was used for a short period only for the treatment of an eye-blinking tic.

## Handling Transference

The problem of handling the transference in release therapy, by which is meant the problem of utilizing the child's emotional response to the therapist, may be described in general as a process whereby the therapist enables the child to fulfill the therapeutic function of the play. From that point of view the therapist supplies the child with a safe stage on which to perform, the child's performance with the material being the assumed primary activity in this particular form of therapy. Naturally, this is possible only when the relation with the therapist is, at the least, sufficiently secure for the child to tolerate his presence in the playroom, to accept his activity in the play to the point of utilizing material and responding to it. The means of overcoming anxiety in the play is the momentum of the play itself as it is aided by the skill of the therapist in gauging the child's tolerance of the situation depicted, and in representing himself to the child as an adult who permits, in fact who enthusiastically endorses, the behavior released in play.

The most common form of activity on the part of the child with the therapist is to attack him in various ways. The child will, for example, spill water in his direction, threaten to throw things at him, in fact actually attack him. When such behavior occurs only occasionally, or playfully, nothing is made of it. When it seems important, dolls are used as in the play to depict the examiner on whom hostility can be spent in a manner similar to other play performance. Ordinarily, a direct attack on the examiner is forbidden and prevented by physically restraining the child if necessary, since the rule of the playroom is that the examiner be spared. At times this is interpreted as, for example: "You are angry at me because the brother smashed the baby." Such interpretation need not necessarily be made. When the child attacks an object, as in the sibling rivalry situation, and says, "You made me do it," I sometimes say, "Yes, I gave you the dolls to play with." I am not clear myself as to when I feel the need of making the interpretive comment, but in attempting to recall my own feelings in these situations, I think it occurs when the child's anxiety seems more acute than usual and it seems best at the time to attempt to allay it by interpreting the behavior. When a child becomes free in water play, after several sessions of inhibited behavior, there is a typically joyous type of performance, almost invariably accompanied by humming or singing. At this stage it is very likely that the child will try to spill water on me. I will then forbid it, with the words, "No, you are not allowed to do it on me," which seems to work. I think the attack on me in such instances represents a freedom of play to such a degree that an attack on the forbidding adult is released, a representation of feelings toward the restraining parental world. The behavior of the child in this situation is quite unlike that in which the child attacks me after it has attacked a doll personifying a member of the family. The latter, as has been previously demonstrated, occurs especially at that point in the sequence of play in which self-punishing behavior may occur.* It is a question at such a moment whether the therapist or the child itself will be attacked. When the examiner is attacked instead of the child, it represents, therefore, a projected self-punishment.

From the point of view of the transference problem, one can differentiate the simplest form of release therapy in which the child is

---

*Studies in Sibling Rivalry, David M. Levy. Monograph No. 2 of the American Orthopsychiatric Association Series.

intrigued by the play in the first session and evolves, in a way, its own therapeutic process, while the examiner stands by as a friendly property man who supplies the scenery for the stage and occasionally acts as prompter. Starting with a form of therapy in which the therapist has a minimal role to play, there are gradations of this role up to a maximum, when the forms of activity are largely in the relation to the therapist. When the transference problem as such becomes of major importance, the problem in treatment goes beyond the limits of release therapy.

It would seem that when the child leaves the playroom with little or no residue of anxiety, the examiner is liked. Otherwise he is disliked. This is clearly shown in Case 2, where the child reported to the mother that she liked the doctor after the third session and that she disliked him after the seventh. Knowledge of these projections is of special value in a therapy of brief duration and gives a clue to gauging its tempo. In the case of the child referred to, the depiction of a traumatic operation in which her guilt about masturbation was involved seemed to change, temporarily, her attitude toward the therapist. The latter is, in that sense, made responsible by the child for its discomfort. It was easy thereafter to slow up the therapy, indicating that the child's manipulation of play material can be controlled as an instrument of releasing tensions more readily than direct interpretation which, once made, cannot be recalled. Interpretation requires more skill in regard to the method of verbalizing it, timing it properly, and knowing when and if the child is ready for it.

Typically, the child leaves treatment in a state of positive transference. One might anticipate a precipitation of the symptoms when the therapy is ended for a patient who is unwilling to stop. Actually, this does not occur. It may be due to the nature of the therapy, to its brevity, the minimum of interpretive activity and, especially, to the flexibility of the child's personality. In Case 10 the patient said, "I love to come and I won't get well. I'll keep on staying awake so I can keep on coming." Nevertheless, she slept through that night. In the last session she expressed regret at not coming and didn't see why she couldn't come any longer. I told her she was cured, and there was no reason for it. I would infer from the fact that in none of these cases was there a return of symptoms within the period of follow-up that the play itself was missed more than the therapist.

## Forms of Release Therapy

In general, one can differentiate three forms of activities of release therapy in the playroom: (1) simple release, of aggressive behavior in throwing objects or of infantile pleasures in sucking water out of a nursing bottle, spilling water on the floor, sitting in it and slapping it; (2) release of feelings in standard situations, as in those depicting sibling rivalry, parents alone together, the nude boy and girl doll, and the like; (3) release of feelings in a specific play situation set up to resemble a definite experience in the life of the patient.

Finally, in all these techniques it must be emphasized there are no pat formulae; the methods are modified primarily by the therapist's immediate understanding of the child's own response.

## Case Summaries

In the following summaries the age of the child and the problem are given in the first paragraph, the number of sessions and general description of the methods of therapy in the second, progress and follow-up notes in the third. The cases are grouped according to the main referral symptom.

### Group I

Cases 1 to 11 inclusive. Referred primarily because of night terrors or fears: three boys, eight girls. Age range: two years, five months to nine years, one month. Average number of sessions: seven. Follow-ups: two months to five years, five months.

Case 1        An only child, a girl, aged two years, five months, was referred because of night terrors, onset two days before referral. She awoke frightened and screamed that there was a fish in her bed and refused to go back. The next night she started shrieking and screaming when put back to bed, shouting, "There's a fish in my bed." By advice of the pediatrist this was ignored. She continued screaming off and on for two and one-half hours. The night terror was related to a visit to a fish market on that very day. The fish merchant, who was fond of the child, lifted her up to see the fish.

A second complaint was stammering, which had its onset five months before referral, although speech had developed normally up to that time. The stammering consisted of a repetition chiefly of consonants; e.g., to quote the mother, "It was almost like agony in getting the letter out in 'hello.'" This would occur probably once every minute of conversation.

There were ten play sessions in all. A fish made of clay was introduced in the second session. To the question, why was the doll afraid of the fish, the answer was that the fish would bite, and the fish would go "in here," pointing to her eye, her ears, and finally, to her vagina. A few days before the night terror the patient had inquired about sex differences after seeing the father naked. Other than the introduction of the fish in various parts of the play sessions, the method was chiefly to facilitate her own type of play, whenever a difficulty in the play occurred. For example, she saw finger paint and wanted to play with it. I showed her how, but she wouldn't touch it with her finger, nor let me put a dot of paint on her hand. She said, "No, no, I don't like that — dirty, dirty." By playing with it myself and getting her to handle it gradually, she got to prefer it and started each session with, "I want to do paint." She played with it very freely, messed it on the floor, and on her legs. Similarly with water play, she got to drag a chair to the sink, playing with balloons, squirting water, breaking a baby doll, the latter becoming a frequent activity in the last two sessions.

Following her first appointment there was no change in behavior that could be related to it. Fear of the fish left after the third or fourth session and the stammering showed improvement after the sixth, disappearing two weeks before the last session. A follow-up was made seven months later. Improvement was maintained; patient was developing normally and making good contacts with other children. She remained an orderly child, though no longer so fussy.

Case 2        A girl, an only child, aged three years, five months, was referred because of generally fearful behavior, onset at eighteen months of age; night terrors occurring on the average of once every seven to ten days, onset at twenty-three months of age. The symptoms were related to an accident at eighteen months, laceration of the scalp requiring six stitches, done without anesthesia; otitis media at twenty-four months, requiring hospitalization and three paracenteses; and to a tonsillectomy at thirty months. Before the accident at eighteen months, the child was "fearful and high-spirited." After the accident she became fearful and tense, though this improved until she was hospitalized for the otitis. Then she was fearful of everything and fought the nurses and doctors. Again improvement occurred, until the tonsillectomy, after which the night terrors became almost a nightly occurrence for six weeks, gradually diminishing to the frequency given at the time of referral. The patient attended a nursery school where she held tightly to her toys and did not join in the activities of the other children.

There were fifteen sessions in all, covering a period of six weeks. In the first session she was quiet and timid. Of the activities presented — water play with balloons, clay, trains, amputation doll, and piercing partly blown balloons — she responded with enthusiasm only to the last item. One of her fears, that of being bitten by a frog, was introduced in the second session, and fear of torn objects treated by encouraging tearing activity and play with the amputation doll. A play of an operation was done in the third session and repeated in the fourth, fifth, seventh, and several other sessions, until the original experience was played out in full. That the various fears arising out of operation and hospital procedures were related to fears about her masturbation was demonstrated by her own activities in the playroom; *e.g.*, demonstrating how the frog scared her by putting its paw in a slit between a doll's legs, placing a tongue depressor in doll's mouth and then in its vagina, verbalizing the act in terms of her own masturbation and fears of the consequences — all repetitions of actual events during her illnesses and operations.

The grandmother reported that after the second session the patient was much more outgoing, talked more freely, and was friendly with the children at school. The statement of the governess was confirmed in an interview with the mother after the ninth session. She added that the child's behavior was in marked contrast to previous behavior. The child now waked happily, gaily singing. She played many games of "frowing" things away with her mother. After the second session the child told her mother I was like an uncle, a favorite uncle, and that she liked me. After session seven the child was "amazingly different." An interview with the teacher confirmed the previous observation. The child, though friendlier to children and the teacher, for the first time displaying response to their "warmth," still did not play with the others. Four months after the last session the symptoms had not recurred. She was getting along well with other children at school, however was considered "too highstrung" to take a nap with them and during nap-time was put in a room by herself. Mother debated about returning patient to treatment on this account but did not do so.

Case 3        A girl aged three years, nine months, the oldest of three children, was referred because of fears — of fire, of electric light plugs, of any person who limped, of the toilet in school, and on numerous occasions, of being touched. Onset was probably at eleven months, after accidentally breaking a toy, whereupon she scampered away and avoided that part of the room and all broken toys for several months.

Fears were related to a basic fear of being destroyed by touching, the kernel of all her fears, directly expressed by the patient. In the four sessions it was easy, through finger paint and water play, to carry her behavior into the breaking of objects. Play of mother touching the child's bed, and also play of burning paper in a steel basket were used. There were four sessions in all.

In the third session she pulled an electric plug from its socket and had already given proof at home that she was free of all symptoms except the fear of fire. This disappeared after the fourth session. A follow-up conversation with the mother twenty-one months following the last session indicated no return of fears; she showed interest in playing with the objects previously feared except in one instance when, about three months following the latest session she avoided contact for several hours with a girl who had a cast on her leg, though thereafter she played with her freely. She was doing good school work and had made a generally good social adjustment. There was recent evidence of sibling rivalry with the brothers.

Case 4        A boy aged four years, one month, the older of two children, was referred because of night terrors, timidity with children, negativism and sibling rivalry. The symptoms were all of three weeks's duration (except sibling rivalry) and were precipitated by a fight with a companion in which the patient was licked. Night terrors had occurred a year previously and for one month following the birth of the younger sibling, a girl.

Patient was to leave for the country at the end of the week. There were daily sessions for six days, comprising sibling rivalry situations in which there was quick release of primitive hostility against mother, baby, and breasts. Anxiety of falling into the toilet and crushing a baby doll that fell in, occurred in the fourth session.

Night terrors stopped after the second session. Follow-up interviews, nine months, twenty-two months, and four years, five months after treatment stopped, revealed a marked change in the sibling rivalry, first noted during treatment; a change from a jealous, hostile relationship to a protecting, friendly one. At school he became well adjusted, frequently exchanging home visits with children and showed good social initiative. School work was always superior. Negativism in the form of sulky disobedience and refusals were noted as modified in the first follow-up to an amiable, reasonable attitude, which continued. Night terrors recurred for a period of about five weeks, three years after treatment, following a change of governesses and measles with delirium and high fever the first three days. They occurred nightly the first two weeks and gradually decreased in intensity and frequency.

Case 5        Girl aged six years, three months, the oldest of three children, referred because of refusal to "do anything outside of her routine." The difficulty, attributed to fear, was an occasional problem for several years. It became a very frequent one following a tonsillectomy, two months before referral. The fear involved strangers, going out of the neighborhood, eating in restaurants, or even of missing any item in the routine of the day. The patient's marked "methodical" habits were well recognized at the age of three. Bowel and bladder control were established by the age of one year.

There were five sessions in all, three sessions of sibling rivalry play and especially messy play with chalk, clay, water and finger paint. The patient enacted through dolls the pleasure of enuresis. ("They wet the bed. They like to wet the bed. Now they have a water bed. They sleep right in the number one. They love it.") She scribbled on the wall, smeared paint, and dirtied her clothes. ("This is a dirty room. We can be dirty here. . . . We don't care if we get our clothes dirty, do we?") In the sibling rivalry play she attained a performance of "mild to moderate hostility" in five trials.

At the end of the first session the mother noticed that the patient was more relaxed. By the end of the third the patient went out places but at the end of the week again refused. The symptoms again cleared up after the fourth session. A follow-up with mother six months, and with grandmother nineteen months after the last session showed maintenance of progress, increased social activity and outgoing quality.

# Structured Play Therapy

GOVE HAMBRIDGE, Jr.

During some thirty years of clinical practice, David M. Levy worked out a series of play forms which he found useful in the treatment of children. Essentially what he did was to devise a series of specific stimulus situations which the child could then freely play out. I have taken the liberty of calling the overall technique "structured play therapy." Levy was interested in the technique as a research method, as in his "Studies in Sibling Rivalry," and also as a psychotherapeutic procedure, as in "Release Therapy." It is, however, unfortunate for students of the art of psychotherapy that he has not written more extensively on the subject from the clinical point of view. The present paper is a preliminary effort toward a systematic review of the use of structured play therapy in the larger framework of psychotherapy with children. My objectives are two: (1) to evaluate the technique critically in comparison with other techniques and (2) to stimulate trial of the technique by other therapists. Limitation of space makes it necessary to omit many valuable clinical illustrations, but these will be presented in another publication.

In the area of direct psychotherapy with children, the physician has at his disposal a number of techniques (see references). In large measure, the differences between these techniques depend on the nature of the therapist's activity during the sessions with the child. For instance, the therapist acts to focus attention, to stimulate further activity, to give approval, to gain information, to interpret, or to set limits. Structuring the play situation is a form of activity which can serve any of these functions. As a consequence, the technique should be used selectively with different patients and at different times during the treatment of one patient; with some, it should not be used at all.

The structured play situation is used as a stimulus to facilitate the independent creative free play of the child in treatment. The patient should already be acquainted with the playroom, which should in turn be supplied with materials of proven value from a clinical point of view. The child will then have the opportunity to choose other play materials beyond those which are given him at the outset of structured play. Lack of adequate facilities may vitiate the advantages of using play therapy. Since the child's own selection is an important and significant element in treatment, play therapy should not be conducted with limited materials.

## Types of Play Situations

New baby at mother's breast (sibling rivalry play).       This is the standard stimulus situation used by Levy in his classic experiments on sibling rivalry and the hostile act. The therapist provides a mother doll, a baby doll (preferably readily destructible and replaceable), and a self-doll, called in the play brother or sister, depending on the sex of the patient. The therapist inquires of the child if he knows what breasts are for, simultaneously modeling a clay breast and placing it in position on the mother doll. If necessary, the child is told briefly of the milk-giving function of the breast. He is then asked to make, and place in position, the mother doll's other breast. Then, while placing the mother doll in the chair and the baby in her lap sucking at the breast, the therapist says, "This is the mother and this is the baby. The brother (or sister) comes in and sees the baby for the first time. He sees the baby nursing at his mother's breast. What happens?" A further stimulus to the expression of hostility can be added by saying, "He sees that bad, bad, baby nursing at his mother's breast." This play situation is useful not only to facilitate the abreaction and working through of sibling rivalry and dependency conflicts, but also to check on a patient's progress during treatment. Thus, for comparative purposes, it is advantageous to use it in the standard form, so that one may compare the patient's handling of this situation from time to time.

Balloon bursting.       This type of play was devised by Levy for use in "release therapy." Its primary purpose is the activation of self-assertion in inhibited children through the release of suppressed or repressed aggression and hostility. In setting up this play, the therapist provides a large number of colored balloons of assorted sizes and shapes. He says, "Now we are going to play with balloons." He blows up a balloon and ties the end. It is very important that the first balloon be blown up only a little bit, so that when it breaks it does not make such a loud noise that the child is so frightened that he will not continue the play. Experience teaches that if the play is not introduced too early the child can usually be encouraged to break the first balloon. The therapist encourages the child to break balloons in any way he wishes. Stamping and jumping are most common. Special devices — nails, mallets, dart guns, etc. — should be available to the child for the playing out of specific problems or impulses. As the play progresses, the balloons are inflated closer to the bursting point. Later, if the child is able, he should inflate and tie the balloons himself. With more anxious children, it may be necessary to precede the balloon play with less startling forms of noise making, such as paper-rattling, participating in calling, shouting, and so on.

Peer attack.     This play may be useful for the resolution of conflicts involving a fear of retaliation, a guilt-born need to be punished, bullying behavior due to displaced hostility, or for the interruption of certain types of automatized patterns of social isolation. It may be presented in different ways, as illustrated by the following examples. With a self-doll and a peer doll of appropriate sex according to the historical context, the therapist says, "This boy meets another boy who walks up to him and, for no reason at all, hits him hard. What happens?" Or, "This boy for no reason at all says to the other one, 'You are no good.' What happens?"

Punishment or control by elders.     These two forms of play facilitate the therapeutic handling of problems in relationship to authority. Each is taken from an appropriate situation in the child's history, past or present. For children who have not made an adequate differentiation of the two situations, they may be used in sequence. The most common sources are from life at home and at school.

Separation.     This play is designed not only to offer an opportunity for the release and expressive mastery of separation anxiety and separation anger, but also to afford diagnostic information relative to the child's ability to orient himself in time. For this reason, separation for a definite time interval is specified. The therapist provides a mother doll and a self-doll and says to the patient, "The mother tells the boy (or girl) that she is going away and will be back this afternoon (or "tomorrow" or "next week," etc.). What happens?" Thus the child may play out a problem centering either about the idea "Will mother return?" or about uncertainty as to when mother will return.

Genital difference.     In this scene, the therapist uses two dolls. These may be play therapy dolls constructed with genitalia. Or they may be more readily obtainable and cheaper dolls modified at the time with clay. Clay is superior, not only because of ease of removal and replacement, but also because in this area plastic representation of fantasy promotes fuller impulse modification and ego mastery. One doll, the self-doll, is of the same sex as the patient; the other doll is of the opposite sex. This play form is used rather late in treatment, when it will be less threatening to the child, and then only if there is direct indication for its use. The therapist says, "This boy sees a girl naked for the first time. What happens?" Variations on this play are important. For after the therapist has presented the situation as just outlined a number of times, he may recognize that the boy patient is not as afraid of the impulses represented to him by this play — or of punishment for these impulses — as he is afraid of the girl's jealous attack upon his organ. If under circumstances such as these, the child does not spontaneously reorient the play, the therapist can restructure it as follows: "This girl sees the boy naked for the first time. What happens?" To emphasize the girl's activity, he asks, "What does she do?" I find it helpful in this play to provide water, balloons, and baby bottles with nipples, so that the child can play out fantasies regarding the function of the genital organs. This play often facilitates the working through of genital difference problems in boys, such as castration fear, prudery, fear of the girl's jealousy of his organ, and tabooed exploration. In girls, rejection of femininity, envy and fear of the male genital, castration fear, and hostility toward males are some of the problems which are appropriate for this play form.

The invisible boy (or girl) in the bedroom of his parents.      This type of play requires a mother doll, a father doll, and a self-doll; a bed for the parents may be used. I prefer not to introduce articles of furniture, but to leave this up to the child, who knows that they are available in the playroom. The therapist says, "Here is the boy, and here are his father and mother. They are asleep in their bedroom. The boy is invisible — nobody can see him. He goes into the bedroom. What happens?" Or, "What does he see?" "What does he hear?" "What does he do?" The therapist facilitates the unhindered play in whatever direction the child chooses, whether, for instance, this be primal scene play, competition with the parent of the same or opposite sex, or the elaboration of a fantasy of sexual activity as a battle between the parents.

Birth of a baby.      This calls for a hollow rubber doll with a pelvic opening. The doll must be large enough so that a small celluloid baby doll can be passed through the opening and be inside the mother before the play is introduced. A self-doll is not included in the original structuring of the play. To start the play, the therapist says, "This is a mother doll. There is a baby inside who is going to be born. What happens?" There are several alternative procedures. For example, the physician may hand the prepared mother doll to the patient, asking if the patient knows what it is. Again, the physician may pick up the mother doll and insert the baby doll through the pelvic opening as a means of starting the play. In any case, it is important for the patient actually to perform with the dolls the act of birth. The child often will suggest further variations on the play as he indicates the primacy of certain fears. Levy has told me that in his experience there are three major fears, the most common of which is associated with the question, "How does the baby get out?" The other two are associated with the questions, "How did the baby get there?" and "How does the baby live (stay alive) there?"

Acting out dream.        The handling of dream material or other fantasies brought in from the outside, as opposed to those produced in the therapeutic situation, can frequently be facilitated by the use of structured play. The therapist may select any part or all of the dream, as long as it does not become too complicated. For instance, a ten-year-old girl with a great deal of repressed rage at her mother reported in the third hour a long dream in a part of which a green witch captured her with the intent of killing her. At that point in treatment the basic conflict, of which this dream represented a graphic picture, was a major threat to this sensitive girl. Activation of this conflict purposely was delayed until the nineteenth hour, when the dream was set up as structured play. She immediately expressed overt hostility toward her mother and conflict about the feminine role. After this was worked through, the patient no longer saw adult women as witches and no longer felt that it might be preferable to be a boy.

Another use of structured play in relation to dreams is to externalize or make explicit the conflict implicit in a reality situation. The latter is portrayed verbally and the child is asked to show in action how the self-doll dreams about this situation.

Other individualized play.        Innumerable conflict situations, as they present themselves either in the history or other sources of data about the child, can be presented in dramatic form for play therapy.

Testing play.        The therapist may use structured play situations to test his hypotheses about the basis of some behavior, to test the accuracy of an interpretation before it is given and finally, to determine the significance of specific symbols which the child may produce in dreams, drawings, painting, modeling, or other creative activity. These techniques will be considered in a future publication.

### Introducing Structured Play

Any new technique of treatment should result in increased economy of effort and closer approximation to the desired result. Structured play therapy increases the specificity of treatment method in direct psychotherapy with children. Simultaneously, it saves time by not indulging in hours of diffuse, therapeutically unremunerative activity. There can, therefore, be nothing pedantic or compulsive in the selection of play forms: The therapist uses only those forms of play which are indicated. He re-creates in dramatic play an event, situation, or conflict which, he suspects, precipitated or now maintains the child's illness. The patient is encouraged to show what happens — not just talk about it. The sources of information for this are primarily the history (as given by parents, patient, or others), the child's spontaneous (free) play, the child's changes of previously structured play, relationship material, and the mother's interim report on behavior since the last session. The therapist does not, simply out of a compulsion for thoroughness or fear of incompleteness, use forms of play manifestly unrelated to the patient's problem.

The therapist introduces structured play when the therapeutic relationship has developed to a point where there will be neither anxiety nor acting out to an extent disruptive to treatment. This means that the child should have developed enough security in the relationship with the therapist so that structured play does not precipitate overwhelming anxiety. However, the therapist who becomes anxious can contribute to such a result. Anyone who is to use structured play must either possess or develop self-assurance in his ability to handle this form of treatment. To step into the free play situation with deftness and surety in such a way as to facilitate rather than to interfere with the continuity of the child's communication and relationship with the therapist is a skill which, to be sure, comes only with repeated experience and practice.

Of the many variables the therapist should assess in introducing structured play, there are three that deserve particular mention. The first is the child's integrative capacity in the face of externalized affect, such as anxiety, anger, and the various need tensions; a higher integrative capacity gives more latitude in the use of structured play. Flooding (a term introduced by Levy to refer to a massive and uncontrolled release of all kinds of uncompleted acts from the past), accompanied by acute regressive and disintegrative states, should be avoided either during the treatment session or on the outside as a result of treatment. Second is the nature of the play; some play forms, such as sibling rivalry play, are generally less threatening, while others, such as genital difference play, are more threatening. Individual differences will make some children more sensitive to certain dramatic presentations than to others. The third variable to assess is the capacity of the people in the environment to handle realistically the patient's change in behavior in reaction to treatment. The family is informed of the expected increase in aggressiveness of the child as a result of treatment and is told to maintain the usual restraints at home. The therapist's task in this regard is to pace treatment so that the parents' ability to handle the child at home is not overtaxed.

The appropriate use of any therapeutic tool is a concern of the physician at all times. Since Levy's 1938 and 1939 papers on release therapy, in which he developed clear-cut criteria for the use of the technique in certain specific situations, some conflicting reports have appeared in the literature about the use of structured play therapy. Cameron (6), in 1940, recommended structured play techniques to less skilled therapists on the theory that the free play of the child is more threatening to the therapist. In 1941, Newell (42) suggested a highly restricted use of structuring; namely, to start the play of the inhibited patient at the beginning of treatment. In 1948, Gerard (17) said the technique was too limited, by virtue of inflexibility, to be of value. Most of these differences can probably be explained by the therapeutic predilections of the various authors. On the other hand, Kanner (29) in 1948 indicated that many psychotherapists who work with children have incorporated a mixture of structured and free play techniques within the scope of their handling of patients. If it is true that this method is so widely used, and yet there is considerable difference of opinion about it, it behooves us to take a closer look at the characteristics and situations which could give rise to such differing experiences.

Therapeutic tools are used to aid the natural properties of growth and repair of the organism. If these proceed satisfactorily under more conservative measures, one does not use more radical ones. Consistent with this principle, although structured play is particularly suited to the release and mastery of repressed or developmentally by-passed and insufficiently lived-out affect, it is not used if the child makes adequate progress with the use of spontaneous play or verbal interaction. Just as the skilled surgeon knows when, where, how, and how much to use the scalpel for specific purposes, so must the medical psychotherapist know when, where, how, and how much to use structured play therapy. Thus the same instrument, when correctly used, is therapeutic; when it is incorrectly used, it is harmful. The correction of misuse, however, is not to reject the instrument, but to perfect the necessary skills. While limited knowledge is available in this direction, the great part of it is still to be gained through clinical investigation and research.

Part of the answer to this problem may lie in knowing when to push structured play in the face of resistance by the patient, a situation which puts the careful therapist in an apparent dilemma. While many child patients take to structured play immediately and with gusto, others put up various types of resistance. It is a situation similar to that of the internist who must administer an antibiotic in spite of side actions of the drug, and attain a therapeutically effective drug level; a lower level is less effective and lengthens treatment. The parallel in structured play therapy may be more serious, because the psychotherapist, out of painful experience, may be so scared to push his patient that he infects the patient with the atmosphere of uncertainty and thus provides a breeding ground for an even greater unnecessary prolongation of treatment. The patient's resistance may arise from any of a number of factors, such as simple opposition, anger, fear of self-exposure, or the arousal of automatized defensive maneuvers. The therapist has different methods of handling each. In the face of slight opposition, he may repeat the phrase "Then what happens?" On the other hand, he may be more permissive and encouraging if the child is more frightened than oppositional. If the fear is of self-exposure from the idea of the reality of the play, the therapist may say, "It is just a game," or "It is not the real thing." When the patient starts the play gingerly, the fact that play has been started at all can be commended by exclaiming, "Fine! Good!" Other useful phrases are, "Let him (her) do anything he wants," "He can do anything he wants," "You can do anything you want." One can go even farther to facilitate the play of the more hesitant child who needs permission by example from the authority figure. The physician can say, "Now we will do it together," and act out the drama with the child the first time. The greatest facilitation is obtained if the therapist actually "does it first" for the child. This somewhat ticklish procedure is not used until other methods have failed. It is wise for the physician to wait until he is well versed in the vagaries of the use of structured play before he tries this last method.

## Conducting Structured Play Therapy

This section of the paper deals with different problems in the conduct of psychotherapy once structured play has been introduced.

The ideal of the play therapist is to facilitate play, not to enter into play. He is a shifter of scenes. The consequence which arises from breaking the rule of the passive role of the therapist is that he may be seduced into going too far. He should keep out of the play except in order to facilitate it, in spite of the fact that the child, for purposes of his own defenses, will try to draw him into it. The inevitable complexity of this apparently simple principle can be illustrated by the following example. A boy, aged seven, was already in treatment for multiple fears. On return from summer vacation, his mother reported, "He got anxious when he started back to school after vacation. He was upset by the air-raid drills. His appetite went, he could not eat. At one drill, the assistant principal said, 'If you don't hurry, you will all be killed.' He was terribly upset and would not go to school." The mother left the room and the boy came in, carrying with him a toy airplane and a wooden truck with wooden men in it. Structured play. At an appropriate point, the therapist crashed the plane into the truck. The patient took over without being told, and in vigorous play knocked men out of the truck, saying, "They are scared. One jumps out just in time and runs to his house, scared." He talked with the therapist about air-raid drills. Structured play. Therapist moved the toy plane through the air as if it were zooming, diving, bombing. As it approached the patient, he became briefly literally terrified, then very excited. Quickly his attitude changed and he shot at the plane with the dart gun. He said he was afraid of bombs. He shot the plane down out of the sky many times. At last, he was exultant, no longer fearful.

In this case, the activity of the therapist is an example of the overdetermination of his role. His activity represented facilitation in relation to the play of the child. It was, in addition, a test of the child's anxiety, as important for the latter as it was for the therapist. The therapist did not exceed the patient's integrative capacity in the face of anxiety. The structured activity focused or sharpened the patient's anxiety, thus, both literally and figuratively, giving him the target at which to shoot. Once anxiety has been reduced in treatment, there are times when it is therapeutically indicated to raise the anxiety for a specific purpose. In this illustration, the purpose was to strengthen ego mastery through an intense corrective emotional experience.

The question often arises, "How many plays must you use in the treatment of a particular child?" Or, "Should you not always see that such and such a play is used?" Let me repeat that the selection of structured play is not rigid. For example, if no problem arises about the birth of a baby, that play form is not used. As a matter of fact, no play form is introduced unless there is prior evidence that its use will have direct bearing upon the resolution of the problems for which the child's treatment was undertaken. While structuring is occasionally a useful adjunct in the psychoanalysis of children, this technique alone is not adapted to that goal of psychoanalysis which is concerned with the completeness of treatment; namely, the working through of every complex of the patient.

Structured play is always followed by the free play of the patient. I have consistently observed that this play must eventually show certain characteristics if the patient is to achieve a maximum of abreactive value, impulse modification, and ego mastery. These characteristics are (a) direct physical manipulation of the dolls, as differentiated from simply telling what they do; (b) relatively complete absorption in the play so that the patient is practically oblivious of his surroundings; (c) playing out the primary impulses involved, as opposed to stopping play before the defenses have been worked through. Other things being equal, the single most important factor in arriving at these aims is repetition of the play.

Once structured play has been introduced, there are three major sequences from which the therapist may choose for the conduct of treatment. These may be diagrammed like this:

1. Structured play — free play.
2. Structured play — free play — repeat same structured play.
3. Structured play — free play — new structured play.

Each of the sequences is independent. They are not interdependent, nor are they necessarily sequential. The therapist may choose from among them after each presentation of structured play.

In the first sequence, structured play is used as a stimulus to free play for the purpose of assuring the patient's continued productive activity in treatment. The aim is also the facilitation of free play, but with the specific intent of focusing activity upon a particular problem, selected because of its probably etiologic importance. In this method, the therapist follows the patient's play to an appropriate end point, then reintroduces the same play. The sequence "structured play — play to end point" is repeated until the child fully tires of this play. This may take a long time, with many repetitions over several hours, seemingly endless to the therapist. In general, the child's play is at first characterized by defensive maneuvers. As these drop out, the various derived and then primary impulses are played out. When these have been fully expressed, the child becomes bored with the play. It is the therapist's responsibility to recognize whether this is true satiation, or whether the boredom itself is a defense. The patient may avoid the play before full therapeutic benefit has been derived. If there is overt or covert anxiety of excessive intensity, it will be necessary to leave this play and to return to it later. The therapist must estimate what price he pays for continuing the play against resistance. It is often preferable to continue the play in spite of resistance, and to analyze or work through the resistance either concomitantly at the verbal level, or later at the verbal or play activity levels. In the third sequence, the aim is again the facilitation of free play. The therapist follows the lead of the child in order to make the stimulus to play more appropriate to the child's conflict. These changes in the structured stimulus are frequently selected from the child's play after a previous stimulus. For instance, in one case of a boy, six years old, the historical evidence pointed quite clearly to a problem of sibling rivalry. When the therapist introduced the new baby at the mother's breast situation, the boy quickly brought the father into the picture and demonstrated that his problem was an oedipal one. This lead was followed in subsequent structured play therapy.

### Functional Significance of Structured Play

Psychotherapy today is more than an art. It is a clinical scientific procedure with ample room for personal experimentation. The need for quick, effective techniques is attested on all sides. Through psychoanalysis, we have learned to listen to patients and to recognize and utilize the latent content of their communication. We have passed through the exploratory phase when in our relative ignorance we had to track down every conflict a patient brought up. We leaven our ideal of the perfect therapeutic result with a recognition of the uncompromising limitations of reality. Our discipline has advanced to the point at which we can make explicit the problems of the patient entering treatment. The natural consequence of this is to focus our attention on these problems during treatment. Structuring of the play serves this function for the child patient. This enables patient and therapist to bring energy to bear where it will count, rather than to expend energy diffusely in random activity, which, although it may be highly informative for the therapist, is essentially doing little more than wasting the patient's time. It also serves the valuable function of requiring the therapist to arrive at a specific formulation and shows him quickly whether or not he is on the right track.

The functional significance, as well as certain aspects of the technique of the introduction and conduct of structured play therapy can best be illustrated by clinical material. The following is offered from this point of view.

Case 1.     This ten-year-old boy, the oldest of three siblings, was referred for treatment ostensibly because of school failure in the fourth grade, which he was repeating at the time of entering treatment. In addition, his mother, a quiet, friendly, self-assured woman, complained that he was afraid of needles and of going into an elevator alone, that he was too cautious, and that he was "too much of a mamma's boy." She said he would become panic-stricken if she were away from home. She said he was too fussy; he had to have clean underclothes and socks every day. On the other hand, she had to force him to wash his dirty hands before eating. She said he got along poorly with his siblings, being bossed and teased both by his sister, aged seven, and his brother, aged five. He had few friends. He was poor in sports. He was shy and isolated. He played alone with his tricycle or with his toys at home. The boy's father, a heavy-set, blustery, impulsively aggressive man, who was sure he knew the answers and who made little effort to conceal his low regard for psychiatry, said the boy was nervous and afraid, especially of dogs. He said the boy had peculiar habits; for instance, he had to go back and turn the light off five times or more. He said the main trouble was the boy's lack of confidence.

The mother said that she had made many mistakes in raising this boy. He was her first child, and she conformed completely to the recommendations of the pediatrician. The boy was on a rigid feeding schedule as an infant, often screaming with hunger for half an hour before food. Toilet training began at three months and was a battle from then on. He was three when his sister was born, and he was not even allowed to touch the baby, at which time he acquired the habit of biting people, excepting only his mother. At the age of five, he had a strep throat, immediately followed by the birth of his brother, and his being sent to kindergarten. Social withdrawal began at this time. At the age of six he entered first grade screaming because he could not see his mother. At the age of eight he had weekly injections for six months for "allergy — asthmatic wheeze, angioneurotic edema, and sinusitis." Fear of needles began at this time. At the age of ten he was very homesick at summer camp, lacked confidence, and was socially withdrawn. Two months later, he started to repeat fourth grade.

The patient was a well-developed, healthy, blond boy, shy, self-conscious, and very inhibited verbally. He did not know why he came for treatment. In the waiting room, his siblings were observed to be freely assertive and happy, and it was seen that they easily dominated the patient. He came on an average of twice a week; his mother was not in treatment. In the first seven hours, there was a gentle opening of release of affect by crayon drawing and finger painting. The patient was unable to make use of structured sibling rivalry play. (This is unusual and speaks for massive inhibition.) At the end of this period in treatment, he became "ornery" at home. During the subsequent twelve hours (eight through nineteen), balloon-bursting play almost exclusively dominated the picture. After a hesitant start in which the therapist blew up the balloons and tied them off, the patient became completely engrossed. Twice a week, for six weeks, he blew up balloons and filled them with air or water, then shot them or smashed them. Gradually, he personified the balloons, and then "killed them." Each hour, he would become oblivious of his surroundings, raging, stamping, jumping, giving orders, bursting balloon after balloon with a loud bang. At the end of this time, the mother reported that the patient was a lot more aggressive at home, primarily with her, but was still submissive to his younger sister, and still afraid of elevators. During the nineteenth hour, the patient looked very embarrassed when the subject of his mother's pregnancy came up. He said, "How can I tell if she is? I know      you can tell by the legs — no higher up." Therapist said, "By her tummy." After talking back and forth about the coming baby for a few minutes, the therapist introduced the baby doll into the situation as something that the patient could shoot at. He hesitated, and the therapist acted to give him an example, shooting the doll. The patient shouted, "You killed him!" He then went ahead and shot the baby doll himself. In a minute, he turned to balloons and wanted to insert things into them before inflating them. He put in pieces of paper; then he inflated some and shot them with excitement. He chose a large nail, named it "the soup," and threw it point first at the balloons. He rushed out at the end of the hour to see if he could ride down in the elevator alone. His younger brother shouted triumphantly, "He did it, he did it!"

The nineteenth hour has been presented in some detail because it represented a turning point in treatment. Up to this time, the patient had, with monotonous regularity, been playing the same game every hour ever since it had first been introduced by the therapist. Beginning with the nineteenth hour, the balloon play became less important to him.

In the twentieth hour, the patient for the first time did not reject the use of dolls to play out family battles. In the twenty-first hour, he started with balloons, but played mechanically, and in the twenty-second hour he stopped this play entirely in favor of dolls. In the twenty-fourth hour, the therapist reintroduced the standard sibling rivalry play. After some hesitation, the patient entered into vigorous play in which he introduced rivalry with the father. The parents were repeatedly killed. He announced in the twenty-sixth hour that his new baby sister had just been born. He expressed curiosity about how a baby is born. After the patient had talked about this for a while, the therapist again introduced sibling rivalry play. The patient represented some initial skirmishes among family members, in which the mother dropped the baby. He then said, "Now we will have a war." The big brother part was played by the patient, who treated the dolls as if they were his size and he were in the group, with fighting and yelling among all. Curiosity about the birth of a baby continued, and in the twenty-eighth hour, this structured play was introduced. He played through it several times, was encouraged by therapist to continue, but stopped. (At this point in treatment, it was felt that it was too early to push the patient to complete this play against his reluctance.) The next time he came in, he very proudly announced that he was riding the elevator alone at home.

The final phase of treatment started in the thirtieth hour, when the patient related a dream of separation anxiety involving his mother, in which after his mother left him, he jumped off a boat into the water and was scared. In the next hour, he went through the birth of a baby play four times with vigorous participation. While playing it he said, "The baby is safe in Mommy's stomach. I wish I was in it. Somebody put an arrow in Mommy's back. The baby comes out by its side — it was a mistake." On the final repetition, he said that the baby was coming out by its head. He immediately started talking about swimming in water. He gradually lost interest. At this point, structured genital difference play was introduced. The patient's first response was that (1) the boy couldn't really believe that there was a genital difference and (2) the boy was punished by his parents for any interest in this area. Later (hour thirty-two), in reference to this new play form, he said, "I am going to keep up with this play until it is all over." He played it out repetitively over and over again. In the thirty-sixth hour he introduced oedipal material, following which (hour thirty-seven) the therapist brought in the invisible boy in the bedroom of his parents as well as the genital difference play. For seven sessions the patient played out a classical oedipus situation and the concept of coitus as a fight.

Shortly after this, the patient's father reported that the boy's peculiar habits had ceased, that he was more self-confident, went out with children to play, and was no longer dominated by his siblings. The patient's mother concurred and added that it was much more troublesome to handle her son now that he was symptom free and self-assertive at home. Treatment was terminated at this time.

A year later, the mother reported that the patient had been slow in making new friends when the family moved to a new home. She complained that he tended to oppose her authority. His symptoms had not returned, and he was handling his siblings as well as he had at the termination of treatment. She complained of the boy's fear of criticism by his father and of the father's lack of understanding by being too hard on the boy. Two years after termination, the boy was seen. He had grown a lot. He was spontaneously friendly and made an easy relationship with the therapist. There was no evidence of return of symptoms. His relationships in the family and at school had remained improved.

Case 2.      This patient was referred for the treatment of persistent and intractable cardiospasm of three years' duration, which was by then threatening her very existence. She was a frail, wistful, ingratiating child of eleven years, physically little more than skin and bones. She had gained but seven pounds in the three years of her illness. She had always been a "good girl" who had been unable to cope with her two aggressive sisters, one older and the other younger. Her good behavior made her the favored child in the family. The diagnosis of cardiospasm was established radiographically two years before psychotherapy, a year after its onset at the time the child had had mumps. She had had only temporary relief at various times from sedatives, antispasmodics, and from a dilatation of the cardia one year previously. In the hospital, the physical and laboratory findings were all negative except for the esophagram. This showed a greatly dilated and moderately tortuous esophagus, spastic at the cardia. At the time she entered treatment, she felt hurt, lonely, different and was afraid of dying.

Eight sessions of interview therapy, carefully coordinated with a second surgical dilatation of the cardia, were held while the child was a bed patient in the hospital. These were pointed toward emotional evocation and the development of insight into the relationship between her personal experience of significant emotional stress and the simultaneous occurrence of her cardiospastic symptoms. This development was facilitated by the fact that interviews occurred at suppertime, and in talking about her feelings while eating the patient inevitably made the obvious connections. However, the patient did not work through the basic dependency and rivalry conflicts with their attendant reactions of fear and rage.

The second phase psychotherapy began after the patient was discharged from the hospital. The child came as an outpatient three times a week for five weeks and then twice a week until termination. She took easily to play with dolls. Structured play therapy was used repeatedly as a stimulus to play out conflicts centered about sibling rilry and dependency in the oral context. Central to this aspect of her treatment was a burning hostility, resentment, and envy of the younger sister's being fed. Guilt was handled by direct interpretation in addition to the implied acceptance by the therapist of her feelings through the presentation of the structured play situations and his permissiveness and encouragement as she played them out in her own way.

The cardiospastic symptoms did not recur. After two months of treatment she was lively, smiling, happy, relaxed. She was put on a trial vacation from treatment for two weeks; treatment was then terminated. eighteen months later, on follow-up interview, there had been no return of symptoms. Two and a half years after terminatim it was revealed that the child had occasional episodes of vomiting associated with emotional stress, but no regurgitation with cardiospasm. Follow-up esophagrams continued to show the same dilated and tortuous esophagus with slight retention at the cardia.

## Termination

In conclusion, I should like to make a few remarks about termination. I have presented a technique of psychotherapy which is oriented toward the attainment of specific goals in treatment. Consistent with this aim is termination when these goals have been reached. The goals are determined by the therapist's clinical judgment of the treatment necessary to resolve the conflicts which produce the disordered behavior for which the patient was referred. This is checked empirically during the course of treatment, so that the patient is discharged at the point of optimum therapeutic benefit. A frequent temptation, however, is to continue treatment beyond this point so that it becomes relatively interminable. There are severe objections to this, among them being the fact that the treatment becomes uncontrolled. The patient may suffer from overtreatment, and the physician does not learn what his patient is capable of doing on his own after the original objectives have been reached. Finally, the value of the follow-up study is diluted by virtue of blurring of the end point and the loss of objective criteria for scientific control. In the long run, the proof of progress in our field comes from good follow-up studies. Therefore, we should take special care that what we observe subsequently can be clearly related to what went before in treatment, and that we do not confuse the issue by introducing intercurrent and uncontrolled variables through unnecessary nonspecific procedures carried out with the "hope" of producing a better result.

## References

1. Ackerman, Nathan W., "Constructive and Destructive Tendencies in Children," *American Journal of Orthopsychiatry*, 7: 301-319, 1937.
2. Allen, Frederick H., *Psychotherapy with Children*, Norton: New York, 1942.
3. Bender, Lauretta and Adolf G. Woltmann, "Play and Psychotherapy," *Nervous Child*, 1: 17-42, 1941.
4. Bornstein, B. A., "Child Analysis," *Psychoanalytical Quarterly*, 4: 190-225, 1935.
5. Buseman, A., "Die Sprache der Fugend als Ausdruck der Entwicklungsrhythmik," Jena: Fischer, 1925. (Partial translation, National Institutes of Health, Bethesda, Maryland.)
6. Cameron, W. M., "The Treatment of Children in Psychiatric Clinics with Particular Reference to the Use of Play Techniques,"*Bulletin of the Menninger Clinic*, 4: No.6, 172-180, 1940.
7. Clothier, Florence, "The Treatment of the Rejected Child," *Nervous Child*, 3: 89-110, 1944.
8. Conn, Jacob H., "A Psychiatric Study of Car Sickness in Children," *American Journal of Orthopsychiatry*, 8: 130-141, 1938.
9. ———, "The Child Reveals Himself Through Play — The Method of the Play Interview," *Mental Hygiene*, 23, 49-69, 1939.
10. ———, "Children's Reactions to the Discovery of Genital Differences," *American Journal of Orthopsychiatry*, 10: 747-754, 1940.
11. Frank, Lawrence K., "Projective Methods for the Study of Personality," *Journal of Psychology*, 8: 389-413, 1939.
12. Freud, Anna; *The Psycho-Analytical Treatment of Children*,London: Imago Publishing Co., 1946.
13. Fries, Margaret E., "Play Technique in the Analysis of Young Children,"*Psychoanalytical Review*, 24: 233-245, 1937.
14. ———, "The Value of Play for a Child Development Study," *Understanding the Child*, 7: 15-18, 1938.
15. Gerard, Margaret W., "Child Analysis as a Technique in the Investigation of Mental Mechanisms," *American Journal of Psychiatry*, 94: 653-663, 1937.
16. ———, "Direct Treatment of the Pre-School Child," *American Journal of Orthopsychiatry*, 12: 50-55, 1942.

17. ——, "Direct Treatment of the Child," in *Orthopsychiatry, 1923-1948* (L. G. Lowrey and V. Sloane, eds.), pp. 494–523, New York: American Orthopsychiatric Assoc., 1948.
18. Gitelson, Maxwell, *et al.*, "Clinical Experience with Play Therapy," *American Journal of Orthopsychiatry*, 8: 466–478, 1938.
19. ——, Section on "Play Therapy," 1938. Ibid., 499–524.
20. Gitelson, Maxwell, "Direct Psychotherapy of Children," *Archives of Neurology and Psychiatry*, 43: 1208-1223, June 1940.
21. Hamilton, Gordon, *Psychotherapy in Child Guidance,* New York: Columbia Univ. Press, 1947.
22. Hawkins, Mary O'Neil, "Psychoanalysis of Children," *Bulletin of the Menninger Clinic,* 4: No. 6, 181-186, 1940.
23. Holmer, Paul, "The Use of the Play Situation as an Aid to Diagnosis," *American Journal of Orthopsychiatry*, 7: 523-531, 1937.
24. Isaacs, Susan, "The Nature and Function of Fantasy," *International Journal of Psychoanalysis*, 29: 73-97, 1948.
25. Jackson, Edith B., "Treatment of the Young Child in the Hospital," *American Journal of Orthopsychiatry*, 12: 56-63, 1942.
26. Jackson, Lydia and K. M. Todd, *Child Treatment and the Therapy of Play* (2nd ed.), New York: Ronald Press, 1950.
27. Jessner, Lucie, Gaston E. Blom and Samuel Kaplan, "The Use of Play in Psychotherapy in Children, *Mental Disorders,* 114, 175-177, 1951.
28. Kanner, Leo, "Play Investigation and Play Treatment of Children's Behavior Disorders," *Journal of Pediatrics*, 17, 533-546, 1940.
29. ———, *Child Psychiatry*, Springfield, Ill.: Charles C Thomas, 1948 (Chap. XVI, "Projective Methods," section on "lay," 228-234.)
30. Klein, Melanie, *The Psychoanalysis of Children* (3rd ed.), (transl. by Alix Strachey), London: Hogarth Press, 1949.
31. Levy, David M., "Notes on Psychotherapy," *Social Service Review,* 1: 78-83, 1927.
32. ——, "The Use of Play Technique as Experimental Procedure," *American Journal of Orthopsychiatry,* 3: 266–275, 1933.
33. ——, "Hostility Patterns in Sibling Rivalry," *Ibid.,* 6: 183–257, 1936.
34. ——, "Studies in Sibling Rivalry," Research Monograph No. 2, New York: American Orthopsychiatric Assoc., 1937.
35. ——, "Release Therapy in Young Children," *Psychiatry,* 1: 387–390, 1938.
36. ——, "Release Therapy in Young Children," *Child Study,* 16: 141–143, 1939.
37. ——, "Release Therapy," *American Journal of Orthopsychiatry,* 9: 713–736, 1939.
38. ——, "Control-Situation — Studies of Children's Responses to the Difference in Genitalia," *Ibid.,* 10: 755–762, 1940.
39. ——, "Psychotherapy and Childhood," *Ibid.,* 905–910.
40. Lippman, Hyman S., "Treatment of the Young Child in a Child Guidance Clinic," *American Journal of Orthopsychiatry*, 12: 42–49, 1942.
41. Liss, Edward, "Play Techniques in Child Analysis," *American Journal of Orthopsychiatry,* 6: 17–22, 1936.
42. Newell, H. Whitman, "Play Therapy in Child Psychiatry," *American Journal of Orthopsychiatry,* 11: 245–251, 1941.
43. Rank, Beata T., "The Therapeutic Value of Play," *Understanding the Child,* 7: 19–23, 1938.
44. Rogers, Carl R., *The Clinical Treatment of the Problem Child,* Boston: Houghton Mifflin, 1939.
45. Rogerson, C. H., *Play Therapy in Childhood,* London: Oxford University Press, 1939.
46. Simpson, Grete, "Diagnostic Play Interviews," *Understanding the Child,* 7: 6–10, 1938.
47. Solomon, J. C., "Active Play Therapy," *American Journal of Orthopsychiatry,* 8: 479–498, 1938.

48. ———, "Active Play Therapy: Further Explorations," *Ibid.*, 10: 763-781, 1940.
49. ———, "Treatment of Behavior and Personality Disorders of Children," *Archives of Pediatrics,* 58, 176-193, 1941.
50. Sylvester, Emmy, "Analysis of Psychogenic Anorexia and Vomiting in a Four-Year-Old Child," in *The Psychoanalytic Study of the Child,* Vol. 1, New York: International Universities Press, 1945.
51. Weiss-Frankl, Anni B., "Diagnostic and Remedial Play," *Understanding the Child*, 7: 3-5, 1938.

# RELATIONSHIP

# Play Therapy
# Procedures and Results

VIRGINIA M. AXLINE

A seven-year-old boy, in the middle of a play therapy session, cried out spontaneously, "Oh, every child just once in his life should have a chance to spill out all over without a 'Don't you dare! Don't you dare! Don't you dare!' " That was his way of defining his play therapy experience at that moment.

An eight-year-old girl suddenly stopped her play and exclaimed, "In here I turn myself inside out and give myself a shake, shake, shake, and finally I get glad all over that I am me."

A twelve-year-old boy who had a long record of delinquency stopped his play, sat down, and looked at the play therapist. He had had many stormy play sessions in this room.

"Strangest thing that ever happened to me," he commented slowly. "Dragged through one court lecture after another. End up coming here because I'm a no-good kid. What happens? Nothin'. Nothin', but time for me to spend as I want to spend it. Any way seems all right in here. So I'm used to squandering time, see? The faster it's over, the better I like it, see? Now all of a sudden I'm confused. I turn into a miser about my time. I want this to last, see? I can't understand it at all. I ask myself who is crazy here — you or me? How come, all of a sudden, no lectures? Has everybody finished all the yellin' and cussin' they had for me? Don't you know who you got in here? Don't you know I'm a no-good kid that'll probably end up killing somebody? Or what cooks?"

"It is baffling and difficult for you to understand how you do feel about all this," said the therapist.

"It don't really seem to matter what it is that's happening. You stay the same. I ain't suspicious of you any more. I think maybe you're crazy, see. Maybe you don't know about what people are really like — mean —

and I hate their guts. Maybe I'm crazy! Maybe in here we're both of us crazy, see?" He quickly went over to the table and with a sweep of his arm flung all the toys off the table onto the floor. He turned and looked defiantly at the therapist. "Well?" he demanded. "So what?"

"You say what," the therapist replied quietly.

The boy dug his hands through his hair, uttered a sound like a groan.

"I'm a tough kid, see?" he said with a trace of desperation in his voice. "I can't suddenly get soft spots deep inside of me. I can't get so — so slowed down I — I feel all my feelings!"

## Nature of The Therapeutic Experience

What is this experience which is known as psychotherapy? There are many different psychological rationales and methods. The overall objective is probably basic to all procedures; namely, to provide a relationship with the client that will enable him to utilize the capacities that are within him for a more constructive and happier life as an individual and as a member of society. The degree to which we achieve this varies greatly with individual cases. The method by which we seek to achieve the cooperative effort between the therapist and the client varies. This paper will deal with the writer's tentative conclusions that have grown out of the detailed study and analysis of many electrically recorded play therapy sessions, evaluations of the results at termination by parents, teachers, physicians, and follow-up studies.

It seems evident that individuals are learning something all of the time. It is a cumulative, integrative process. A baby is born into a completely new and different world of experience. With his first breath, he begins his long span of accumulating experiences. The first breath leads to the second breath — and while it is similar in process it is not identical. The third breath is different from the preceding ones because of the changes in lung capacity, the experience of breathing, the process of adjusting to the outer world. And this begins the individual's experience in a world of people and things. Life forces interact and the process of learning is under way.

Psychotherapy is a learning experience — a very complex, cumulative, integrative, personal involvement.

The individual's perceptions of himself and his relationships to his world are as uniquely the individual's as are his own heartbeats. Efforts may be made to increase our understanding of how experiences are perceived by the individual, and it may be possible to obtain a fairly close approximation of the individual's perceptions. However, the individual alone experiences the total impact of any personal involvement because he feels not single, isolated feelings of the moment but feelings that are created and colored by the affective accompaniment of his total experiences.

Certain descriptive words frequently used in discussions of behavior have become almost stereotyped concepts, lacking accuracy in functional use. For example, is it possible to feel hate without accompanying fear, inadequacy, threat? Does a feeling of guilt come naked and alone? Or does guilt emerge with attendant feelings of insecurity, inadequacy, fear? How does one determine which of the feelings is of greater significance to the individual? Or is this even necessary in order to provide a therapeutic experience for the individual — as *therapeutic experience* is defined in this paper?

In psychotherapy, we are dealing with emotionalized attitudes that have developed out of the individual's past experiencing of himself in relation to others. These emotionalized attitudes influence his perception of himself as either adequate or inadequate, secure or insecure, worthy of respect or not worthy of respect, having personal worth or deficient in this basic feeling. His perception then, in turn, determines his behavior. The individual's behavior at the moment seems to be his best efforts to maintain and defend his selfhood and so maintain a psychological identity and a resistance to threats against his personality. Consequently, the child who is emotionally deprived and who has had experiences that seem to form and reinforce feelings of inadequacy and lack of personal worth learns the kind of behavior that protects his self-esteem and lessens the impact of threats against his personality. He may withdraw from relationships with others in his effort to avoid further emotional abuse. He may refuse to behave in certain ways that are expected or demanded by others in order to maintain a self with integrity. He may be dominated and overwhelmed by his relationships with others that strive to take from him his claim to individuality without giving him the love and feelings of security and worthwhileness that he needs. He may seem to comply to the external pressures and to conform to demands made upon him. However, this type of behavior seems to be symptomatic of his underlying feelings of insecurity and inadequacy and does not have the integrated, purposeful self-involvement that leads to increasing psychological independence and maturity. He may react by hostile, aggressive rebellion. He may strike out at people and things in his world because of his reaction to a weakening concept of self-adequacy. The child who is extremely deprived emotionally shows this deficiency by his apathetic, overwhelming fear of his relationships that seems almost to paralyze him in his efforts to bring something of himself into a relationship with others.

In the past few years, there has been increasing awareness of a kind of behavior that is sometimes termed "pseudo mental retardation." The child's behavior resembles closely the kind of behavior that has been evaluated as indicating mental retardation. There is often lack of responsiveness, lack of progress along developmental lines, deficient social and emotional behavior. The studies that have been made in an attempt to check the validity of the diagnosis of many of these children through psychotherapeutic interviews have raised a significant question in the field of child psychology. These studies and exploratory work have indicated that often this type of behavior is a mask that a child who is emotionally deprived and who feels rejected and unloved and unwanted wears to protect himself. He does not know that this behavior only aggravates the attitudes toward him that create the behavior. It is not premeditated, rational behavior. It is defensive behavior. It is reinforced by the increasing pressures placed upon him where he finds himself more and more frequently in a situation where he is being "tested," put on trial, forced to face an almost endless probing in attempts to understand him, to help him, or to change him.

How can we explain the changes in the child's behavior in those cases where the child has received some form of psychotherapy — and in those cases where the parents have not been willing to participate in any kind of counseling or psychotherapy for themselves?

One ready explanation is that the child would have changed anyhow — that the passage of time alone brought this about. The answer to that explanation can be approached through research projects that have control groups. There is very little research of this kind at the present time.

Another explanation grows out of recorded, objectively observed analysis of therapeutic sessions of growing numbers of children with this behavior pattern. These observations, when followed by evaluation and assessment of the children's behavior after psychotherapy and at later follow-up periods, indicate a theoretical position that should be subjected to the rigors of research procedures to either support or deny the theory.

When such a child comes into a play therapy room and is confronted with a room full of toys — or a modified selection of toys — and the therapist tries to create the kind of experience that will enable the child to learn how he can function on his own, he is involved in a very complex, highly personal, emotional learning experience.

## Personal Characteristics of the Therapist

Procedures in the playroom vary greatly. There are, however, basic requirements for all therapists. They should have a genuine respect and interest in the child as a total person. They should have patience and understanding of the complexities of a child's inner world. They should know themselves well enough to be willing and able to serve the child's needs without emotional involvement. They should have sufficient objectivity and sufficient intellectual freedom to set up tentative hypotheses to check — with adequate flexibility to adjust their thinking and responses to further enhance the child's self-discovery. They should have sensitivity, empathy, a sense of humor, and a light touch because a child's work is variable, delicate, full of movement, lights, shadows, rhythm, poetry, and grace. The child is quick to respond to the attitudes of respect and love that are offered to him — not thrust upon him.

The child is far more accepting of others — is far more understanding and tolerant — than are his elders. He is without prejudice until he catches this attitude from those about him whose insecurity breeds fear and bias.

The therapist and the child meet in the playroom. It is a learning experience for both of them. It is a cooperative effort by which each one learns something that becomes an integral part of both of them.

This is a safety zone that communicates security to the child gradually because of the consistency of the therapist, the stability of the limitations, the friendly understanding, the gentle but firm emphasis on the child's frame of reference, and the patience that keeps out society's pressures to hurry. The child has the time to experience deeply and fully his ability to be a person in his own right through an increasing understanding of his feelings and attitudes and capacities to act and interact with honesty and forthrightness.

## Learning and Psychotherapy

If we accept the statement that individuals are learning something all of the time, we are forced to ask ourselves what it is they are learning. It is here that a great discrepancy becomes apparent. If we think of a learning experience as something that is taught, honesty bids us examine closely the relationship between what is taught and what is learned. It seems a probable assumption that people are learning something all of the time — only seldom, if ever, what "the teacher" thinks he is teaching.

Learning is a complex process. There are many psychological concepts and experiments that attempt to explain the process. We read about stimulus, response, reinforcement, extinction, conditioning, retention, forgetting, transference, generalization, discrimination, and other concepts.

In psychotherapy, the learning process is in evidence. It seems to be a cumulative, compound, integrative, affective experience that can be used to illustrate many learning theories. At the same time, it raises many questions as to the adequacy of any existing theory to explain conclusively the learning experience that occurs during psychotherapy.

In play therapy experiences, the child is given an opportunity to learn about himself in relation to the therapist. The therapist will behave in ways that he intends will convey to the child the security and opportunity to explore not only the room and the toys but himself in this experience and relationship.

If play therapy is an experience in self-exploration, self-in-relation-to-others, self-expansion, and self-expression, how can this be achieved and develop a generalization on the part of the child to accept not only himself but others as well, and to learn to use freedom with a sense of responsibility for that privilege? How is the child helped to learn self-understanding that grows into an attempt to understand others? How does the child learn to expand beyond self-centeredness to a recognition and appreciation of others?

If psychotherapy is to be an experience of social and emotional learning for the child, what procedures might facilitate this objective?

## Therapeutic Processes

There are many glib, overly simplified terms applied to the process of psychotherapy. The use of the term *permissiveness* has sometimes seemed to put a stamp of approval on completely uncontrolled behavior. It seems more appropriate to define *permissiveness* functionally as the oportunity to utilize the capacities within the individual for the expression of emotionalized attitudes and thoughts and feelings when channelized into symbolic, legitimate activities by the sensible use of limitations in the hope that the child learns responsible freedom of expression.

Limitations or boundaries that prevent the child from either attacking another person or destroying property seem to develop within the child a feeling of security and stability in the therapeutic relationship. If his emotionalized attitudes find outlet in an acceptable manner of externalizing them, it seems probable that he would learn to know his feelings objectively without adding guilt or fear or anxiety that might be precipitated by this lack of symbolic expression.

There needs to be sensitive communication between therapist and child. Here again the attitudes of the therapist show through. The communication seems to be more often on a nonverbal level than on a verbal one. If the therapist considers it important to emphasize the child's frame of reference, here will be an attempt to keep to a minimum any statements or comments that might try to interject the therapist's frame of reference. If the therapist hopes to help the child develop an honest awareness of his emotions, then the therapist will attempt to respond with sensitivity to the child's emotional expressions by a reflection of his expressed feelings, by simple acceptance of what the child says or does, by the manner in which he listens to the child, by the extent to which he is able to get right into the child's frame of reference.

When working with children in play therapy, the therapist must be able to accept the hypothesis that the child has reasons for what he does and that many things may be important to the child that he is not able to communicate to the therapist. It seems quite likely that the play therapy sessions offer the child the opportunity of experiencing affectively this relationship; and because of this present emotional experience, the child can gain much from it even though the therapist does not always know what is going on in the child's inner world — and is unable to find out. Too much insistence on finding out everything may result in a breakdown of communication and rapport.

The child needs a freedom for his expression that can be implemented by a willingness on the part of the therapist to provide a fluidity of use of materials and fantasy and conversation. The child may not always seem rational in his communication from an adult's point of view; and yet from the child's frame of reference, he is communicating something of real down-to-earth feeling. A therapist who is too literal-minded and who cannot tolerate a child's flight into fantasy without ordering it into adult meaningfulness might well be lost at times. Few adults have the flexibility and creative spontaneity of a child. And the use of the term "creative spontaneity" does not always mean expansive activity. In some instances, it can be seen from an adult's point of view as only an idle bit of dawdling — and yet the child's imagination and experience at the moment may bring to the child genuine affective meaning that helps him achieve a meaningful self-realization.

For example, during one series of play sessions, a little Negro boy came into the playroom each week, sat down at the table, tilted back the chair, put his feet up on the table, folded his arms across his chest, sat there with an impassive expression on his face — week after week after week. The therapist was puzzled by this behavior. When the play periods would end, the therapist would announce that time was up. The child would quickly get up and leave. Naturally, many unasked questions crossed the therapist's mind, but up to a point the therapist had not probed, interpreted, encouraged, or prompted the child to either explain himself or do something else. The therapist finally was about to speak to the child about this situation, to explain that he could play if he wanted to. However, just before the therapist broke into this situation, the boy looked at the therapist and said, "Know what I've been playing?" With eager responsiveness, the therapist replied that she did not know. With a smile and a squaring of his shoulders, the Negro boy replied, "I've been playing White Man!" Who can tell what this experience meant to that child? How can we evaluate the effectiveness of such a play experience?

If we want to provide fluidity of expression, we must keep the experience as free for associations and identifications and changing concepts as is possible. If the child picks up a toy and asks, "What is this?" our answers can determine the use the child can make of it. If we name it, we might tie it so firmly to a world of reality that the free use of it as a medium of expression is restricted. If we say (because we really mean it), "In here it can be anything you'd like it to be," perhaps we can facilitate his play. For example, sometimes we can see a tin plate change identity many times. Perhaps it starts out as a raft, becomes a flying saucer, a monster, a mother plate, a father plate, a little boy plate. Protected by the flexible self-involvement, the child can bring his feelings out into the open in such a way that he can handle them without fear and self-threat. He can always change the identity of his symbolic figures into something safe and bearable if it seems to become too big to handle.

The limitations of time and space seem important. If the child experiences consistent, predictable boundaries of time and place, he gains a sense of stability and security.

In our experiences with children who have some marked disability, either blindness, deafness, cerebral palsy, or lack of speech, we can observe children using the play sessions in ways that they adapt to their individual needs. It is with these children that we become more aware of the child's abilities to strike at the heart of his difficulties. We note that words, facial expressions, physical activities assume differing values in the relationship. We observe the common element that seems to bring about the changes in behavior that we sometimes term "therapeutic gains." This common element is the opportunity for the child to experience affectively and in exploratory fashion himself in an unrushed, protected relationship with the therapist who appreciates his integrity and personal worth, who offers an opportunity to pour out the feelings and experiences that bother him, who tries to help him achieve responsible freedom of expression so that his capacities can be utilized more constructively for himself as an individual and as a member of a group.

## Play Interview with Boy of Twelve

In closing, a brief excerpt from the play interview of a twelve-year-old boy with a record of delinquency is cited.

In the preceding session, he had asked the therapist to get him a penknife so that he could carve some balsa wood. The therapist got a three-bladed penknife. When John came into the playroom, he immediately looked on the table, found the knife, picked it up, snapped open the blade.

"Oh, you fool you," he cried. "I asked you to get me a knife to carve with and you walked into the trap. Now you've given me a knife, and I'll cut your wrists." He suddenly reached out, grabbed the therapist's hand and placed the open blade against the vein. "Now what are you going to do?" he demanded.

"It seems to me that is my question," the therapist replied. "You're the one with the knife. What are you going to do?"

"You wonder what?" John asked.

"I certainly do," the therapist said.

"What are you going to do?" John demanded.

"What would you suggest?" the therapist inquired.

"You know what will happen if I get mad enough right now?" John asked threateningly.

"What will?" asked the therapist.

"I'd cut your damn wrists. Then how would you like that? I'd cut that vein right there. What would you do? Tell me that. What would you do?"

"I'd probably bleed," the therapist answered, after some quick thinking.

"And then what would happen?" John demanded.

"I don't know," the therapist answered, after some quick thinking.

"And then what would happen?" John demanded.

"I don't know," the therapist said. "That would be your problem."

"My problem? You'd be the one bleeding to death!" John yelled.

"You'd be the one who did it, though," the therapist said.

"Why don't you try to pull loose?" John demanded.

"Why don't you let go and put away the knife?"

"You were a fool to get me this knife for in here, you know," John said. "You realize what a fool you were? You brought this all on yourself."

"You asked for the knife to carve balsa wood," the therapist replied.

"And you turn out to be the balsa wood," shrieked John, laughing hilariously. "So you'll bleed to death. Then what will you do? Tell me. What'll you do then?"

"I don't know," the therapist said. "I've never bled to death before."

John suddenly released the therapist's wrist, closed up the knife, tossed it on the table.

"Some people are too damn dumb to be turned loose," he said. "You're so stupid you could get your very throat cut and wouldn't know what happened. Why did you get this knife? Why did you give it to me?"

"You said you wanted to carve wood. I believe what you say."

Suddenly he sat down with his back to the therapist.

"Some people shouldn't be let out alone," he said. "Some people are too damn dumb. How can I fight you if you won't fight back? How can I cut your wrists if you won't even struggle? All the time here it's like this. It's not me against all the people in the world that I hate and despise. You make it turn out again and again that it's me against myself. All of a sudden I feel all my feelings — and sudden like I just wish I'm not the way I am. I wish I had a feeling of being strong deep inside of me without threats and being afraid really. I feel like I'm too little for too big a world. I don't want to always make war with myself."

John, in his way, indicated what therapists hope to induce in every child with whom they work — an increased awareness of his feelings, a sense of measuring himself against himself, a seeking for an understanding of himself that will bring with it inner peace, and a feeling of being at one with the world.

# Play Therapy:
# A Training Manual for Parents

LOUISE GUERNEY

## Why Play Sessions?

Play sessions are recommended for four to ten year old children who have problems with their own feelings and/or difficulty in relationships with others. Children often misperceive parents' intentions and feel unhappy or insecure or abused for very little apparent reason. Often the child may not be aware of his own needs and feelings, and thus parents cannot always help him in their usual w.y. Communications between parent and child on the child's deeper needs is therefore insufficient or incomplete.

One purpose of a play session is to create a situation in which the child may become aware of the feelings he has not allowed himself to recognize. In the presence of the parent, the child has an opportunity to communicate his feelings through play. The parent's acceptance of the child's feelings is essential and helps the child to come to a better understanding of how to cope with his feelings as he experiences or re-experiences difficulties in the session.

Another purpose of the session is to build your child's feeling of trust and confidence in you. If you respond to him in the manner prescribed in the play session, it will increase his feeling that he can communicate with you more fully and honestly about his experiences and feelings. This should eventually lead to more moderate and mature ways of expression, and less use of extreme and immature forms of emotional expression. He will have less fear that being open with you will lose your respect or affection.

A third purpose is to build the child's confidence in *himself*. Just as we expect you will eventually experience a greater feeling that your child trusts you, your child should experience your sense of trust in him. One goal is for him to feel more secure in making his own decisions where that is appropriate. He needs to learn to be less fearful of making mistakes. It is important for him to learn that he has choices and is himself responsible for much of what befalls him. This is very important for any child who has a problem to overcome. This means being free to make choices (including many mistakes) and experiencing the consequences, good or bad. By allowing him freedom of choice in the play session and by allowing him to experience the consequence of free choice, you build his sense of confidence. You build his confidence in himself also by giving him your complete and exclusive attention in the session. This leads to his experience of himself as a more worthwhile and likeable person, which is a key ingredient not only to self-confidence, but to good adjustment to and in relation with you and other people.

## Setting up a play session.

The following specific recommendations are essential for obtaining the desired results of closer understandings between parent and child.

### Set aside a time

(To begin with, at least one-half hour, and later somewhat longer) every week reserve time for a session with your child. Hopefully, this will be at a time and place where you are completely isolated from the rest of the family and can guarantee no interruptions. If the phone rings, let it ring. Try to have arrangements for other children so they will not interrupt this session. Your uninterrupted attention is one of the most important conditions for fruitful play sessions. Do not impede your progress by changing the time each week or cancelling a session. Such changes have undesirable effects that go far beyond what you would suppose. Whether they say so or not, children tend to feel that cancellations and changes reflect disapproval of their behavior in the previous play session. It also breeds lack of confidence and trust — the very things which we are trying to promote. If a change is absolutely necessary, it should be discussed in advance with the child. Once you begin play sessions, you should consider their availability to the child as a form of contract which you cannot break.

### Select a room

Find a room for play where there will be least concern if things get spoiled or broken. Least preferred is the child's own room, where other toys might be distracting. Water may be spilled, clay smeared, or toys dropped and broken, so a basement or kitchen floor would be best.

*The choice of toys*

Selecting toys is important to the success of the play session. Primarily, the toys should be plastic, inexpensive, or unbreakable. The following will be most useful for a beginning:

Inflated plastic bop bag (at least 4 ft. high)
Dart gun with darts
Plastic or rubber knife
Nonhardening modeling clay
Plastic cowboys, Indians, soldiers
Family of puppets
Doll family (mother, father, brother, sister, baby)
Baby bottle
Bowl for water
Crayons, paints
House box for doll furniture and family
Cups and saucers
Drawing paper
Tinker toy or similar construction toy

These toys are reserved for use in the play session only. They should not be used by another child at all, except in his own play session if you are having sessions with him. The child may not take or use toys out of the session (his own drawing or painting is an exception). Ordinarily, he may not add any of his own toys. The toys have been especially selected in order to help the child release his aggressions and to re-enact his feelings in relation to family members in a safe and accepted place.

*What to tell the child.*

It is not necessary to go into a long explanation with the child. You may simply say you want to spend more time with him. Older children may insist on further details. In this case, place the emphasis on *your* wanting to spend time alone with your child in a special play setting. *Not* that you want to help *him*, but that you want to be together, have fun, and improve your *relationship*. There is usually very little difficulty in getting the child to participate.

Some children, of course, take more time than others to feel comfortable enough to express themselves freely. On some occasions, children object to having sessions. But most of the time they enjoy the sessions and look forward to them.

### Role of the parent.

The role of the parent in a play session is to establish an atmosphere of free play and acceptance for the child. This means that the parent has to take a very unusual attitude toward the child — very different from the way you usually relate to people. You set the stage by setting the time and the few basic rules; but what the child does with the toys and what he says in the session are strictly up to him. The child may use the toys to express things he has not been able to express adequately before or express things he often expresses in a more extreme and direct manner. He may want to use the time to be very aggressive; he may want to sit and stare at the wall, unwilling to involve himself at all. He may wish to leave after a few moments. The parent has to have an open mind and be willing to follow the child's lead, whatever form it takes (including not staying). Therefore, it is important that the parent engage in:

NO criticism

NO praise, approval, encouragement, or reassurance

NO questions or leads or invitations

NO suggestions, advice, or persuasion

NO interruptions or interference

NO information

NO teaching, preaching, or moralizing

NO initiating a new activity

In short, it is important for the parent to establish a setting in which the child, and the child alone, sets the values and judgments.

Equally important, the parent must be fully involved with the child, giving full attention to everything the child says and does and feels. It is most important to be attentive to the child's mood and to note very carefully all the feelings the child is willing to reveal. This will give the child the go-ahead to begin to uncover more of his deeper feelings. If the parent is asked to participate in an activity, he should engage in it fully. But attention should be primarily focused on how the child wants the parent to participate, following his direction, and on reflecting the child's feelings. The child's play in the session need not be conventional. For example, a child may like to cheat at cards or make new rules. In such instances, the parent should reflect only the strong need to win or the child's desire to have things go his way, and the means the child uses to have things go his way, in an uncritical, warm, and supporting tone.

The parent can best demonstrate to the child that he accepts and understands the child's feelings by reflecting the child's expressed feelings and actions. This takes the form of noting aloud what the child seems to be feeling; e.g., "You're wondering what to do next." "Now, you'd like to lick the bop bag." "You wish you could shoot him dead." "You're disappointed it didn't hit the target." "That makes you mad." "You're very upset when I don't answer your questions right away." "It's annoying when it doesn't go together the way you want it to."

The child's actions are also accepted by verbal comment from the parent; e.g., "You're really beating him up." "You're going to kick him around." "It's hard to make up your mind what to do." "You love to sit on my lap." "They're all going to be killed." "You're being very careful to make it come out just right." "You're aiming very slowly so it will be sure to hit."

These are the only types of appropriate comments from the parent. Complete silence on the one hand or merely sociable conversation on the other are discouraged. In regard to the first: A child may fear disapproval when a parent is silent; so it is important to comment, letting him know that your attitude is continuously accepting. With respect to the second: social conversation leads most children to feel that they should answer questions or talk about what the parent wants to, rather than take the initiative themselves.

More important than any technique is the spirit under which this is undertaken. It is important that you try not to be mechanical, stilted, or artificial. You can avoid this best by bending all your efforts toward trying to put yourself in the child's place and understand the world as he sees it, not as you see it or wish him to see it. Try to understand the child's feelings through what he is doing and saying. Also, leave your own worries or reactions out of it as much as you can. Sometimes it will be difficult. Simply try to understand what the child is trying to express, and communicate to the child that you understand — that you know what he is feeling, and it's all right with you. You will find that some of the things the child does are distasteful or worrisome. You need not permit such behavior outside of the play session, during any other time. However, it is crucial to be very giving and accepting of any and all behavior *in the play session* (except those things mentioned below). Children quickly pick up the idea that what goes in the play session may or may not be allowed out of the play session; outside the session you can continue to be very firm about prohibiting some of the activities which are permitted in the session.

**Setting Limits**

There are few restrictions on the child's activity in the play session. These "limits" must be adhered to rigidly. If the child should "break a limit," you should point out that this particular behavior is not allowed. Warn him that if it occurs a second time, the play session will end. Make sure the child understands. Thereafter, the next occurrence ends the session. There is no warning statement or second chance. This is the one and only consequence of breaking a limit. The session ends without the parent having to get angry. The limits are:

CHILD MAY NOT HIT OR HURT OR ENDANGER PARENT IN ANY WAY. (He may not point the dart gun with a dart in it at the parent.) A similar limit on dirtying or wetting the parent may also be imposed if the parent wishes.

CHILD MAY NOT LEAVE THE SESSION FOR ANY REASON (see he goes to the bathroom beforehand) AND THEN RETURN. CHILD MAY NOT POKE THE BOP BAG WITH A SHARP IMPLEMENT.

Do not discuss these limits with the children until the need arises. And do not try to prevent or discourage a child from breaking a limit. Your task, when prohibited behavior first occurs, or is about to occur, is to let him know the consequence if he does it, or does it again. The consequence is termination of the session. If he does choose to do it anyway during that or a future session: (a) acknowledge and accept his strong desire to do what he did and (b) always, *without exception*, impose the consequence *immediately*. Remember that your purpose is *not to prevent* the behavior, but to allow him to *make the choice*, and to *experience* the consequence.

There may be one or two additional limits used at the discretion of the parent, if necessary; such as no shooting at windows or ceiling, dumping only one bowl of water on the floor (some should be allowed), and no smearing the walls. There should be *no limit* on what the child *says*, including swearing, dirty words, hostile comments towards the parent, or others.

**Children's Reactions.**

This can be a very rewarding experience for both parent and child. Some children move quickly in a direction opposite to the way they have been behaving; some at first behave like themselves but in an exaggerated or more forceful manner. Some become very aggressive; some very quiet; some may resort to very baby-like behavior; some like to order the parent around, taking complete control of the situation. Some of the children are unable to express their feelings in the beginning. Some, at first, act as though they have only negative feelings. Others may want you to make decisions; they may do things just to please you because you are spending this time alone with them. Try to reflect all of these feelings as they occur, rather than to give explanations or to make the choices for the child. You should learn a great deal about how your child feels at times toward his family and/or himself. You probably will also learn more about your own feelings towards your child.

# Therapeutic Work with Children

FREDERICK H. ALLEN

As students of human behavior we are confronted with a large dual program — one concerns the treatment of individual difficulties, and the other is concerned with those large social forces which pull human beings along in their relentless operation, and complicate, even when they do not create, many of the problems for which help is needed.

Emphasis on the individual has led to a considerable critical comment of psychiatry because of its failure to contribute more understanding of the social conditions through which we have been passing, and more interest in mass movements that will point the way to a healthier type of existence. Some of this criticism is warranted — possibly psychiatry has become too enmeshed in the intricacies of individual psychology and has neglected those large social forces needing the understanding attention which modern psychiatric thought should be able to provide.

The two large problems, the individual and the world he lives in, must continue to be understood together. Just as other aspects of medical treatment have enriched the understanding of important public health problems, so should a clearer conception of psychiatric treatment make possible a better understanding of the types of social organization best suited for growth and development of the largest number of individuals.

## Developing a Personal Approach

In no field is there more need for clear thinking and for free and frank interchange of thought and experience than in that large aspect of orthopsychiatry concerned with treatment. Our interests focus here. Research adds to our knowledge of facts in order that clinical programs may be applied with more understanding of our own and the patient's activity in therapy.

Differences of opinion are marked, even when there are clear-cut statements of points of view. Sooner or later those doing treatment come to a clearer appreciation of their own trends, and to have real conviction of what therapy consists and of some of the influences which they bring into the patient's life which allow the experience to have therapeutic value. But relatively few have formulated their points of view.

Being aware of the need of such statements, I would like to use this occasion to formulate some of my own convictions and doubts about treatment, and to test my experience against or with the experience of others. My remarks will apply particularly to the treatment of the problems of children, because it is in this field that my own point of view has developed. I do believe, however, that many of the points which I will raise will apply to the treatment problems of adults.

In doing this there is no pretense on my part that I am formulating any new principles of therapy. They have grown from my own work and from those who are closely associated with me; and in stating some steps in the growth of my own point of view, I am only trying to state what happens to other students in this field, as they move and grow and emerge with skills and points of view that have become a part of themselves.

In the past decade, the student of human behavior who has entered some section of orthopsychiatry has found a wealth of experience available for him. The large contributions of modern psychobiology, psychoanalysis, and modern medicine which have grown from the clinical experience of a wide number of people are waiting to be assimilated. How does the student select and utilize these contributions and, at the same time, come to feel that in doing so he is expressing in his developing skill, a point of view that is recognized as a part of himself? When he can use these skills with the feeling that he is not merely applying a technique but instead a point of view which has grown to be an integral part of himself, and to which he has contributed his own feeling and thinking — then his therapy becomes, not the automatic application of another point of view, but an expression of his growth and understanding. He arrives at a point when he is free to be himself in a positive sense. When this type of growth has been achieved, the therapist has moved beyond the level of identification, so important in any learning process, and is left free to utilize and to reject the contributions of others without becoming enslaved or entirely negative to them. He can even develop a new point of view and still be respected, both by himself and others who do not adhere to his principles. Thus the abundance of modern-day contributions.

I do not want to be misunderstood — I am not contending that every therapist must create a new system to which his name may be attached before he has realized his own emancipation. There are some with such an intensely individualistic drive and need to be different that they have to reject before they can create. Contributions motivated by opposition and negation rather than through the more positive unfolding of one's own self are more likely to be rooted in the prejudices of one's own personal problem, and so become warped and one-sided.

All that I have just said applies with particular force to the problems of training. The student, unless he is a very negative person, will at first try to be his teacher, to do the things he does, and say what he says. If he stops there with little capacity to develop and express himself in his therapeutic activities, the chances do not favor his becoming a good therapist. He must find from his own experience the things he can use; then he becomes free both to agree and to disagree, continuing to grow and moving beyond mere identification.

In psychiatry this growth has been retarded somewhat by a tendency to personalize schools. Frequently we designate a system of therapy by the name of the person responsible for the major contribution. The element of loyalty then enters as a factor, retarding the expressions of differences and tending to catch some at the point of identification.

Sometimes we have met with the hope that in orthopsychiatry a scientific treatment procedure could be erected that would almost apply itself. Orthopsychiatry will suffer, as it has, by any attempt to reduce treatment to formulas, standardizing technique, and in other ways, mechanizing its application. The mere copying of techniques, even with an intellectual (verbal) understanding of their purposes, does not make a therapist.

## Basic Principles

I might state as my first principle that I, as a therapist, must be myself, operating within the boundaries determined by a sound psychology, which, through training, has become an integral part of my own thinking and feeling. The progress I achieve in this direction then enables me to apply a necessary and natural corollary to this principle. I am more nearly able to respect the integrity of those who come to me for treatment, thus enabling them to come closer to being themselves in their relation with me, without the evasions and projections that have retarded their emotional growth. The capacity to accept a child or adult as he is, without an urge to recreate him or to take over his own responsibility for living, is indicative of my respect for his capacity to work on his own problem, and to achieve a healthier expression of himself through the type of relation I enable him to have with me as a therapist. I have no desire to impose my own standards upon a patient or to determine the specific attitudes toward which therapy will be directed. If I can create a relation in which the child or adult feels that he is accepted at the point he is in his own growth — rebellious, hostile, fearful, or what not — then that person has an opportunity to go ahead with those difficulties that are most concerning him. He is not kept busy defending himself against being "helped" and being remade.

The second principle that applies to myself is an outgrowth of the first. In therapy I make fewer and fewer pretenses that I am invested with certain omnipotent powers that sometimes are assumed by, sometimes assigned to, the psychiatrist. Gradually I am coming to recognize and, what is more important, accept without apology my limitations in reshaping the feelings and behavior of another. Recently a mother said to me, partly in jest but partly out of her own large sense of failure, "I expect you to perform a miracle with my son"; and I replied, "Possibly the fact that I have no illusions about myself doing such a thing may make it possible for me to be helpful to the boy." Failure to accept such limitation means that omnipotent powers are assumed. Therapy takes on a synthetic coloring with the patient, and attempts are made to recreate him in the light of the therapist's image. My willingness to accept my limitation in being responsible for "curing" allows for a quicker assumption of responsibility on the part of the patient both for himself and for the job of relating himself to his own living realities.

## The Therapeutic Relationship

Around the next point there are crystallizing some of the more important differences in therapeutic philosophy. The influence that is common to every therapeutic situation is the relationship with the therapist. This is true regardless of the use that is made of this common factor, or the name under which it is described — the authoritative director of human destinies, the moralist, the adviser, the manipulator, the attitude therapist, the analyst, the relationship therapist, etc. Regardless of what you call it, the patient, whether child or adult, has a relation with another human being to whom he has come, or to whom he has been sent, for help with problems within his own life.

The differences come in the use that is made of this relation, and in the conception of the individual being treated. I want to focus on two aspects of this, both being based upon a dynamic conception of the individual; that is, that his present behavior reactions have emerged from the experiences of the past.

One school of thought utilizes the therapeutic relation as a means of reconstructing the past, of helping the individual to re-experience the feeling of past events that have been inadequately assimilated and to which have been attached the anxiety and fear which have created the turmoil in the present. The relation has value because it becomes a symbol of something else. The therapist becomes a father, mother, and, because of the role, the emotional turmoil is re-experienced and interpreted in these terms. The therapist is of value because he becomes invested with the emotional color of another person. Therapy, then, consists in a reliving of the past, the releasing of anxiety, and the creation of insight. The present relation has value because it provides this favorable milieu to re-experience the past. The importance of content is stressed, and the reliving of specific emotionally charged memories.

The other conception of this relationship, and this forms another pillar in my own therapeutic foundation, is that it comes to have value in and for itself, as a present reality which affords the patient a clarifying milieu, not as a representation of another person, past or present, but because of what he is experiencing with me at the moment. This does not deny that the patient will behave toward me as he has to others. I accept that the feelings he will come to experience with me and toward me probably are the same feelings that he has had toward others. He will struggle to control me as he has others; he will like and dislike me as he has his mother, father, etc. Around me will revolve anxiety and fear, feelings that are rooted in the past and disguised in the present. These facts seem incontestable. I also accept that some knowledge of these background facts will enable me to have a clearer understanding of the difficulties he will have in relating himself to me.

But I am providing an opportunity for this child to experience himself in a new and present relation, and in terms of the present and not in the past. I am in a position to deal with the feeling the child expresses toward me. I can understand his struggle to control without giving in. I can understand his need to dislike me without threatening him with my own dislike. He can be friendly without being engulfed by my friendliness. I can help him to experience these feelings as his own with less anxiety, and enable him to resume growth with less anxiety and denial. In this experience I do not protect him from his own feelings, nor do I provide an opportunity for him to gratify them. He can dislike me, but he can't attack me; he can love me but, he can't fondle me. The feeling has to be accepted as arising from his own internal environment, and not as a result of the things I say or do to him. He will struggle to get me to like or dislike him, or actually to punish him in order to acquire some external justification for his own feeling. As a therapist I can help him through this without falling into the trap of giving him these reasons which act as a protection against himself.

## Interpretation

My own conviction that real therapeutic values can accrue from a relationship which deals with the patient as a present living reality naturally influences the content of my interpretative activity. I am interested in interpreting only those feelings and activities that form a part of my relation with the patient. I am interested in helping him understand and accept how he is using his relation with me and how he is feeling toward me as he struggles against the emergence of things which are real and for which he has had difficulty in assuming responsibility. I am not interested in speculating what these struggles mean in terms of the past, even though I might guess right. By doing this I feel that I would take every expression of feeling that the child experiences in his relation to me, and through my interpretation actually block the experiencing of his feeling in his present reality. I have seen many children who utilize the past as a means of protecting themselves against the emergence of feeling in the immediate relation they have with the therapist. It is my belief that it is the experiencing and being able to live with their feelings that has more therapeutic value than giving a child an understanding of his feelings largely in terms of the past.

The attitude toward content of the psychiatric interview will differ depending upon the point of view to which the therapist adheres. One point of view will stress the specific meaning of the material in the child's psychic life; the other stresses the use that the child makes of content in the relation which he comes to establish with the therapist without in any way denying the meaning that these facts may have in the child's psyche. I would like to illustrate this by a simple example. A child of six is resistive to every request of his parents, unhappy at school, and having no satisfactory relations with children. He fights with them and tries to boss them. He is friendly with no one and relates himself to everyone on an opposing basis. He brings his struggle into his relation with me. He talks a great deal about wild animals, particularly horned animals, and struggles to get me to give him some that I have in my collection. My own therapeutic interest is in the use which the child makes of these ideas to gain ascendancy over me, rather than in an interest which seeks out the meaning of the idea in his psychic past. (I accept that it does have a meaning.) After several interviews in which the struggle to gain ascendancy continues unabated, he gradually discards his wild animal fantasies as he comes closer to expressing his hostility with less fear. He finds there is less need for the reinforcement which they provided. At the same time he begins to relate himself to me on a more positive basis, finds that he can accept some strength from me without being engulfed. There is a diminishing need to oppose and be opposed. The process of relating himself to me on a more positive basis begins.

There is another point about content. I see no therapeutic value in utilizing facts that have been acquired from others in my relation with the child. A child may be stealing, or truanting, etc., facts which I have learned from school or parents. The knowledge is valuable in giving understanding of what are the child's difficulties, but I can see no value in making a child talk about these things with me unless he wants to, or in letting him know that I am acquainted with certain things.

If my relation to a child is to have any meaning to him in terms of his own growth, then he must be allowed an opportunity to develop it as his own and in his own way, subject to the limitations which involve my own rights. I respect his right to tell me what he wants to tell me, knowing that getting him to a point of being free to talk and to feel is more important, therapeutically, than what he talks about.

Children come to have a feeling that this relation belongs to them and that it has been developed through our mutual activity. Making a child aware of facts learned from outside sources only interferes with this achievement. I would adhere to this principle regardless of the age and of the number of times I am going to see the child.

## Therapeutic Use of Play

I would like to include a few words about the use of play in therapeutic work with young children. Children, particularly those under ten, relate themselves to the therapist on a basis of play. At least it usually starts on this basis. The child is given freedom to determine the type of play, but some control can be maintained by selecting the type of play materials that are available in the room. These will be selected, not because of their amusement value, but for their value as conveyors of feeling and things which children can utilize to relate themselves to the therapist, who is a part of the play situation.

Just as in other aspects of therapy, play activity can be regarded as useful from two points of view. The one stresses play as a means of bringing out the fantasies and the unconscious desires of the child. The play is symbolic of the child's repressed wishes and opens the door to the child's past. Content, with its related feeling, becomes the important thing, and therapy follows upon the interpretations and the release of feeling from the repressed material.

The other point of view stresses the value of play as providing the child with familiar tools to relate himself to the therapist. Into the play he will bring the reactions and feelings common to his relations outside. He will draw me into the play; he will shut me out; he will attempt to boss me; he will attempt to take away my toys or to destroy them; he will express his feelings of indifference toward me, and so on through a variety of uses which the child will make of play to relate himself to the therapist who is able to recognize with the child the things he is doing and the feelings he has about him. The actual content of his play becomes of less importance than the use he is making of it in relating himself to me. Interpretation then is in terms of the present meaning rather than in terms of the past.

## Generalization of Therapeutic Gains

The question then arises, suppose I have enabled the child to acquire a healthy relation with me; how does that help him with his continuing life with his father, mother, brother, sister, etc.? Does not the child have to work out these same feelings with me in terms of his father or mother before there is any real continuing therapy? Some will immediately say yes, that until these feelings are interpreted and understood by the child in terms of original sources, then therapy has fallen short of an ideal goal.

This conception of therapy which I have sketched would break down if there was not a belief in a person's capacity to assume responsibility for utilizing an experience, such as I have described, in his own living reality and in his own way. I have an increasing belief in this capacity, belief that is based on the experience of seeing it happen.

This raises the whole problem of responsibility. How far can one trust the individual to utilize an experience, within which there are healthy values, to help him to achieve similar values in other sections of his life in which I play no active role?

The whole foundation of normal growth and of sound education rests upon the principle that the individual will be able to utilize the experiences that are his, the facts that he acquires in the management of his own life, and in the relations he establishes with others. No one can do it for him, nor can anyone teach him how to do it.

So, in assuming that a child has the capacity to utilize, in the continuing relationships of his own life, a healthier expression of himself that he has developed with me, I am applying a principle which runs through all growth. The influences that are helpful in therapy are not essentially different from the influences in normal life. A child in a natural wholesome situation gradually differentiates himself from his mother, father. He acquires from this relation a sense of himself that gives him the capacity to relate himself to others and to grow. But he has not been taught to do this. He may not be aware of the influences which enable him to take on new experiences and leave the old ones.

The same principles apply in therapy. A child is subjected to influences which cause him to stumble in the process of growth. He has been unable to acquire that feeling about himself that allows an adequate estimate of himself in relation to his own reality. This will be indicated by his behavior reactions. I enable him to have a new experience within which he may gradually grow (differentiate himself). There is no assumption on my part that every child is going to be able to relate himself to a therapeutic situation on a growing basis. He may achieve a more natural expression of himself with me and then will begin to indicate, sometimes openly, sometimes in a veiled and symbolic way, that he wants to leave me. If I felt that I had to teach him how to use this experience in his continuing reality, then I would resist his desire to leave until certain he had achieved this.

However, if I apply my belief to his capacity to assume responsibility for achieving a better relation with others as he has assumed it with me, then I will utilize his desire to try himself out when he feels he is ready to do it and not view this desire to leave as resistance but as a constructive impulse, the living out of which might be the healthiest thing I can allow him. Frequently the real movement and growth come after he leaves. Treatment has helped him to achieve not only a desire to grow, but also more capacity to do so.

Activity in the treatment relation comes both from the therapist and the patient. This seems axiomatic, but in some current discussions of passivity, the emphasis has focused so much on the activity of the therapist, that there has been some tendency to overlook one of the basic purposes of treatment — to help the patient to become increasingly active on problems on which he has some concern. The activity of the therapist can either block or stimulate the achievement of this.

## On Being An Active Therapist

I have tried in the past few years — the "passive era" — to get some who use the term to tell me what they mean by it. The common reply is, "Well, the way you do in Philadelphia." Since the word was developed outside this geographical designation, that doesn't satisfy. When I press further I find a common understanding is this — *passive* means inactive — the therapist says nothing, does nothing. The patient is left to find his own way in the presence of this mummy who sits and looks and never helps. This description sometimes given facetiously carries a common understanding of the term.

The controversy hinges on what is activity and its purposes. On this point I would like to make my own position clear. There is no place in treatment for passivity, if this means inaction. Placed in the position of a therapist, I know I am expected to possess skills that are to be used and to assume a leadership in this relation. But I have no interest in keeping this leadership in the foreground or to make the individual aware of any therapeutic skill I may possess. I am more interested in helping the patient to be himself, to become more and more active on his own problem, and to come closer to his own reality in this experience with me; a reality which I know he must continue to live with after he leaves me.

I am not interested in smothering a person with my activity any more than I am interested in freezing him with studied indifference. I am interested in creating a natural relation in which the patient can acquire a more adequate acceptance of himself, a clearer conception of what he can do and feel in relation to the world in which he continues to live. There does need to be warmth and naturalness in any treatment relation, an interest in the person expressed by that subtle transference of interest that comes more from what you are than from what you say. I am not afraid to let the patient feel that I am interested in him as a person. If I feel that I must always be on my guard, watch every word, every facial movement to attain that thing which some call "objectivity" which can be "the poker face" — "the dead pan" — or the other terms used synonymous with "passivity"; then I would become not only inactive, but a confusing influence in the patient's contact with me. Passivity can be this in the hands of some individuals whose only other conception of their own activity is to tell people what to do, how to feel, and when they are ready to get along without their controlling hand.

Necessarily there are many aspects of therapy that I have not been able to touch upon in this statement. Direct treatment work with a child should, wherever possible, be carried on in close conjunction with work with the parents and with the establishment of good physical health and with efforts to modify irritating environmental factors. The fact that these other aspects of therapy have not been emphasized in this statement should not be taken as an indication that they are regarded as of lesser importance. I have full appreciation that such efforts are important and desirable to help the child to transfer into his continuing life that healthier expression of himself that he may have begun in the therapeutic situation.

## Conclusion

The next decade will require of psychiatry, and those professions closely affiliated with it, even more than the preceding decade, a clearer conception and appreciation of therapeutic principles. This will be required particularly for those problems of human behavior encompassed by the field of this organization.

Considerable progress has been made, even in the relatively short period of my own experience and those, like myself, that belong to the younger generation of therapists. There is evidence of more real respect for the integrity of people needing help and more belief in their capacity to assume responsibility for themselves. As a result, we are seeing less of that type of treatment that told people how to live, where to live, how to feel, what to feel, and so on. We are coming to see that in therapy we are providing an opportunity for a clarifying experience for the child and for the adult. This trend away from a more directive and static type of therapy has been an indication that a more vital and dynamic conception of the individual is getting applied.

It is important that this more human, natural, and dynamic concept be kept fluid and vital. Dynamic concepts can, and sometimes do, become static when the thinking that is applied to them becomes rigid and mechanized. The human being is a growing changing biological entity, not a machine consisting of a mass of mechanisms; clinics must continue to be places for understanding human behavior and not become psychological garages.

The very nature of psychiatric therapy, with the subtle interplay of feelings and with the creation of that intangible thing called confidence, means that the personal factor that the therapist introduces always will loom large. The therapist will develop that relation in a way that seems a natural expression of himself; otherwise the experience becomes strained and unnatural.

Wittels made this interesting observation in a recent book when he said, "Children place far greater importance on the person who speaks than on what that person says." This applies to the therapeutic situation; what the therapist is has a real influence on what the child is able to be in this relation. What he says may only be the confirmation in the mind of the child of what he feels him to be — a person with understanding and skill, and with the strength that comes from being himself operating within the boundaries of sound psychology, so that the child has an opportunity in this relationship to experience himself at the point in his life where he is and, through such an experience, relate himself with less fear, less anxiety, and less denial to the reality of his own life.

# GROUP

# Play Group Therapy

S. R. SLAVSON

In the application of group therapy to various personality problems, we have found that the accepted techniques of either activity or interview therapy (or group analysis) are not suitable for very young children. In the case of activity groups, unrestrained acting out without the necessary inner controls that are ordinarily present in the more mature person, leads to chaos beyond the group tolerance. The ability of any given group, as well as individuals, to withstand or absorb hostility and aggression has definite limits. Each individual and each aggregate of people has its own capacity to tolerate aggression or hostility density. When these limits are exceeded in groups, tension and anxiety set in which are expressed in hyperactivity, rowdyism or wanton destructiveness. Unless restraints are applied by some outer agency such as a parent, teacher, leader, or therapist, the group becomes severely disorganized and uncontrollable. This is true of all groups, whether children, adolescents, or adults, and is the primary reason why grouping is so important and the choice of children suitable for group therapy has been repeatedly emphasized.

It has also been observed that different members of groups are affected differently by overt boisterous behavior or by repressed hostility. The endurance for these emotions varies in individuals and is conditioned by character structure and early experiences with aggression and hostility in the family.

The superego in the young child is still unformed, and the executive functions of the ego are less effectual during the pre-oedipal and early latency stages than they are during later development. The young child is, therefore, still devoid of the controls that emanate from the repressions and inhibitions which have been only partially evolved or not at all. In view of these circumstances the function of the therapist (parent and teacher, as well) is in fundamental respects unlike that with older children. He needs to be more active and more fully in control of the group's activities as well as of the behavior of each member in it.

## Common Pitfalls of the Play Group

In group play, patterns of behavior and problems emerge that are not present in the play of one child. Interstimulation and the various types of interaction inevitably arise from the concurrent activity of several children, which is referred to as the catalytic effect — positive and negative — they have on one another. The anxiety stimulated by the presence of other children and the support they give one another in their hostility toward the adult induce hyperactivity and destructiveness seldom encountered in the play of one child. It is therefore, necessary for the therapist to be more vigilant as to the trends and possible developments in a group than in the treatment of one child and employ strategies and techniques to prevent disorganization, emotional tension, and anxiety. Since the young child's unconscious is near the surface, it is not difficult to stimulate its flow in play activity, which may have no meaning to him in terms of his specific personality problems and needs, or may be even detrimental to him at a given stage in treatment.

We have already shown that acting out has value only when it is an outcome of, and related to, the unconscious of the child and his emotional conflict.* Diffuse hyperactivity which may express hostility toward the environment, including the therapist, is in itself not therapeutic. The value of acting out lies in the relation that it has to the conflicts of the patient. Acting out of hostility by an older child, an adolescent or adult, makes him aware of the true intent and significance of his actions. This is shown in various forms of guilt manifestations such as confession, placation, submission, and restitution — all of which indicate the presence of superego formation which is still not present in the very young child. Acting out by the young child does not bring about awareness of or insight into the meaning of behavior. It, therefore, has little or no therapeutic value beyond release. Because of this absence of superego formation, low degree of guilt, weak ego structure, and basic narcissism, acting out alone does not meet the treatment conditions of group psychotherapy.

For this reason, acting out has to be limited, restrained, and directed with young children. At the same time it is necessary that the therapist

---

*Slavson, S. R., "Differential Methods of Group Therapy in Relation to Age Levels," *The Nervous Child*, April 1945.

call attention to the latent meaning of behavior. This form of interpretation has several therapeutic values. In the first place, a relationship is established akin to transference, because the child feels he is understood by the therapist. Secondly, it makes him aware of his real problems and the meaning of the hostile intent of his behavior. He becomes vaguely aware of the fact that his aggressive behavior in the group is only a substitute for aggressions he feels towards other people. In a more neurotic child, interpretation serves to bring forward repressed impulses, conflicts, and anxieties and makes the young patient aware of his real difficulties.

## The Importance of Play

When using play therapy, whether in group or in individual psychotherapy, the therapist must be aware of the significance and meaning of play in its many facets. He must recognize that play to a child is what serious, productive work is to an older person. Through play the child carries out the tasks of his life, and he uses play for many other ends as well. To review the many theories of play, such as experimentation with reality, expression of excess energy, recapitulation of the phylogenetic experience of the race, a form of mastery, an effort to attenuate reality, would take us far afield.

Play in education and in child development has been evaluated and described in an extensive and rich literature and need not be repeated here. It is necessary to call attention to the fact, however, that to the therapist play has additional meaning, as well as the developmental. He is interested in the fact that through play the child expresses traumatic fixations, conflicts, and hostilities and that he employs it as a means of communication and abreaction. The child also uses play to disguise genuine conflicts and difficulties, or he may use play to relax tension and anxiety. Of greatest importance, particularly to the group therapist, is the fact that as the young patient discharges aggression and seeks to overcome traumatic anxieties through play, it acts as a regulative mechanism. The therapist also sees group play as a possibility for overcoming narcissistic and autistic fixations for the discharging libido centrifugally through relationships with others in the group. The child discovers the advantages of such relationships, and his ego-libido drives are redirected outwardly toward his playmates and the objects he uses in his play, which are usually cathexized.

The play therapist also is aware of the importance of play as a sublimation of primary instinctual drives which in their primitive form are socially not acceptable. The service of play in finding permissible and acceptable outlets for primary impulses is of considerable value with which one must reckon. The catalytic effect of the others in a group greatly helps in this.

## Group Dynamics

The specific advantage of the group in play therapy lies in the catalytic effect that each patient has upon the other, which makes it easier for them to cut out and to bring forth in behavior fantasies and ideas. Another value of the group is that it reduces the tendency to repetition. The young child, particularly, tends to repeat the same activity. This is largely due to the limited scope of his capacities and experiences and the security that a known situation gives him. He is either afraid or unable to evolve variety in the use of play materials. While he is full of fantasy, his imagination is comparatively limited. When several children play together, their interaction and mutual support help to employ the materials progressively, rather than to become fixed at one level of self-expression. This has been observed in educational and in therapy groups and constitutes what is often referred to as a "growth-producing environment."

In play groups, and this is to a great extent also true of other groups, children assign to themselves roles which are an expression or an extension of their basic problems. In such roles one either plays out the awareness of what he is or a hopeful fantasy of that he would like to be. Thus a child playing the role of a dog may feel himself being treated with the same indifference and as impersonally as is the dog; he may seek to get the loving acceptance and protection which a pet receives in the home, or he may attribute to himself the oral strength that is usually associated with dogs. In a group such fantasies are reinforced and find easy and natural means of coming through in a variety of play forms and activity channels.

As in all psychotherapy, the fundamental dynamics are present in such groups. These are (1) relationship, (2) catharsis, (3) insight and/or ego strengthening, (4) reality testing, and (5) sublimation.

In group psychotherapy there are multilateral relations among the members of the group, in addition to the attitudes they may have toward the therapist. These relationships serve to neutralize the transference toward the therapist and aid the cathartic process. The anxiety created by hitherto unacceptable behavior is lessened by the acceptance and support the children give one another. Under these circumstances it is easy for them to express hostility toward the therapist and reveal themselves in the light of their difficulties.

## The Therapeutic Relationship

In activity-group therapy, as in psychoanalysis, the relation between therapist and patient is unilateral. Feelings are directed from the patient to the therapist, the therapist remaining neutral and to a large extent also passive.* In play therapy for young children, however, the therapist reacts to the behavior and feelings of the children, in a manner similar to case work. In the latter, as in group play therapy, the relationship is bilateral. Thus group play therapy, in its essentials, resembles individual psychotherapy, though largely modified in some secondary aspects. In both the transference is a bilateral one and the role the therapist plays in other respects is also similar.

The functions and equipment of an activity group therapist with children in latency are in many essentials different from those of a group play therapist. Though the activity-group therapist must understand the hidden meanings in behavior (as does also the group play therapist), he remains largely passive and overtly unresponsive. The group play therapist, on the other hand, responds to the acts and utterances of the patients to help them acquire insight. The element of insight is the essential difference between activity groups for children in latency and play groups for younger children.

Catharsis is an essential factor in all psychotherapy. Through it the patient is able to divest himself of conflicts and emotions fixed through traumatic experiences in early childhood that form the root of personality disturbances. Thus through play and language, layers of repressed feeling are unfolded. Play is only one means, and the most suitable means for children, for communicating the content of the unconscious and the distress that pressures of environment create; i.e., catharsis. Play under specially set conditions and in the presence of a permissive, understanding adult, is a form of communication as well as catharsis.

Concerning the factor of reality testing, tangible objects, relationships with others and actual situations constitute true reality to the child. They are more real to him than are ideas and words. Here he has an opportunity not only to experience, but also to test himself as to his powers and mastery. He has things and materials with which to work

*Slavson, S. R., "Types of Relationships and Their Application to Psychotherapy," *American Journal of Orthopsychiatry*, April 1945.

and play. He either fails or succeeds and, as a result, evolves perceptions concerning his own powers and abilities. He tests himself against others in submission-domination, anaclitic or symbiotic relationships. Through the new relationships he evolves new patterns and new attitudes. During this period he begins to realize himself as a person; evaluates his powers; measures them against the realities of his environment, and eventually adjusts his behavior in accordance with his feelings of weakness or of strength, as the case may be. Thus play activity becomes a measure of the self in relation to reality. This is the element of ego strengthening as well as reality testing.

Ego strengthening, which is so important in the psychotherapy of children, occurs in play groups through the same dynamic situations as in activity therapy groups and in all psychotherapy, for that matter. The acceptance of the child by the other children and the therapist begets the conviction that he is loved and — what is more important — that he is worthy of love. The result of this new awareness is a more wholesome self-image and perception of his worth which in turn help integrate powers and bring impulse under control. Thus the executive function of the ego as a control of impulses and the mediator between the self and outer realities is strengthened.

In psychotherapy of older persons, especially in psychoanalysis, the factor of insight is of paramount importance in this connection. Insight, acquired through release of emotional tensions and overcoming resistances to unlocking the gates of the unconscious further strengthens the ego, as well as being a source of new values and more wholesome understanding. The degrees and levels of insight that a small child can acquire, however, are subject to speculation. Through our own observation in this regard, we are inclined to believe that children are capable of a high degree of insight, though it may manifest itself in forms other than those to which we are accustomed in adolescents and adults. Theirs is a more perceptive type and less verbalized or ideationally organized, but frequently one is impressed with the uncannily penetrative remarks children make about situations, themselves, and others.

## Sublimation

One of the important values of all play therapy, especially in a group, is the fact that sublimations are ready at hand. Whatever the stage a child's libido organization may be, as he finds sublimation for it in group situations, his primitive drives are transformed into controlled socially approved patterns of behavior and more adequate adaptations to reality.

Anal-urethral cravings, for example, are expressed in play with water, paints, and clay. Genital interests are worked through symbolically in occupations such as drawing and painting, fire-setting (which should be permitted), pyrography with an electrically-heated stylus, squirting of water, shooting of guns, rubber-cupped darts, play with family dolls, toy furniture, and doll house — especially toilet equipment. Some of these toys also serve to discharge, as well as sublimate, aggressive drives, sibling rivalry, and hostile feelings. In the group each member works out attitudes towards siblings and other members of the family. Thus catharsis, reality testing and sublimation — though each having a distinct function — fuse in the play of very young children in groups, and perhaps also in all therapy groups.

Anger and aggression find numerous means for sublimation and displacement in play groups. A child may bang against things in the room, or he may hammer out a copper ashtray. To redirect hostile feelings he may destroy toys, tools, and materials, or he may hammer boards together with a view of making some useful object. Instead of directly attacking the therapist, as a substitute for a parent, he may paint or deface the walls and furniture. In the young child displacement and sublimation often go hand in hand as do transference and substitution. They may often be confused.

## Transcript of a Play Group Session

To illustrate some of the general principles in the preceding pages, we submit an abstract of a record of a group play session with three boys, five or six years old. Brief comments on some of the major dynamics of the events that took place in the group are also included.

John is the first to arrive and seems a little more friendly than during the past few weeks.

*John:* Where's everybody?

*Therapist:* They'll be along soon. (John seems to have considerable hesitation in coming to the play room where the group meets, but he finally does when the therapist says that the others are coming soon.)

*John* (immediately going over to get paper): I want a lot of colored paper. Who was here last week?

*Therapist:* Judah and Mike.

*John* (angrily): My mother said that nobody was here last week. Where is Mike?

*Therapist:* Mike will be coming.

*John* (He seems very restless.): I am going to my mother. Mike isn't here.

*Therapist:* Why are going to your mother, John?

*John:* I am going to get a nickel. My mother said nobody was here last week and now she has to give me a nickel.

*Therapist:* John, you can go to your mother after our meeting but I think you should stay here now.

John seems to hesitate and wanders around the room. He looks at the paper. He comes over to the therapist and puts his paper down.

*John:* I'm not going to stay because Mike isn't here.

*Therapist:* John, are you afraid to be here in the meeting room alone with me? (He does not answer but seems to get relief from the therapist's saying this. He relaxes immediately.)

*John:* I am going to work on my plan. (He begins to saw which he does very well.) (Speaking proudly and boastfully): Look at the thirty cents that I got from my grandfather. My girl friend Janet also gives me money. (He shows the therapist the thirty cents.)

John feels uncomfortable being alone with the therapist. This discomfort is partly due to his displaced hostility from his mother on the therapist and partly because of his sexual preoccupations in regard to the former. He substitutes the therapist for his mother, and the same anxieties that are associated with her come to the surface now.

John is disappointed that the therapist, like his own mother, has not given him siblings (playmates). She disappoints him and he is angry at her; he wants to punish her by leaving her and going to his mother, whom he plans to victimize for lying to him, which is probably his fantasy.

When the therapist interprets to John his feelings toward her, he at once relaxes and settles down to work. The therapist understood him, and since she understands him she is less of a threat. To be understood also means to be accepted, and his negative transference is at once changed into positive feelings. As a result of this rapport, John feels secure and boasts: he is liked by others as well. Even his girl friend gives him money. In this is implied a defense against his sexual impulses as well as hostile feelings toward the therapist: she is not the only one in his affections; there are others; i.e., the basic transference is a negative one.

Mike is the strongest member of the group on whom John relies and whom he fears. Mike arrives wearing a mask.

*Mike* (To the therapist): I was waiting for you downstairs.

Judah arrives wearing a mask.

*Judah* (enthusiastically): My uncle gave me this mask. He just got back from overseas, and, boy, you should see the souvenirs he brought for me. (Mike finds some candy that was left from the last meeting and grabs it.)

*John* (Trying to grab the candy from Mike): That candy belongs to me. Give it to me. Mike and John start running around the room while John keeps trying to get the candy from Mike.

*Mike:* It does not belong to you and you can't have any candy.

*John:* The candy is so mine.

*Mike:* (throws a piece of candy across the room): There you are. Run and get it.

*John* (picks up the candy): Come on, give me some more. The rest is really mine.

*Mike* (throws another piece which John runs after): and you're not getting any more.

*John:* I'm going to run out and tell my mother.

*Therapist:* Why are you going to tell your mother?

*John:* I'll tell Mike's mother.

*Therapist:* Why don't you tell Mike?

John ignores the suggestion of the therapist. Mike stops fighting him.

*Mike* (to Judah): Why don't we go out and get water for the painting. Mike and Judah go out to get water for the finger painting. John begins to work with the paper, cutting out a design on orange paper which he had crayoned black. Judah and Mike come running back into the room.

*Judah:* I am going to make a witch picture.

*Mike:* I am making a Halloween picture, too. (The boys work for a while. Then Mike tries to put paint from his hand on John. Judah follows and tries to do this also.)

*Therapist* (to Judah and Mike): Why are you boys angry at John?

*Mike:* Because John got here early.

*Therapist:* But John got here at the time he was brought. Mike, maybe you just don't like the idea that someone else is here alone with me.

*Mike:* You're right. (Mike then pretends to dab paint in John's direction without really doing so.)

*Therapist:* Mike, you just feel like acting silly now.

*Mike:* Gee, you're right again. You're becoming a mind-reader!

Both Mike and Judah are angry. It is easy to guess the cause of their anger. They act out their anger against the therapist by messing up her office, which is in another part of the building, and by depriving John of candy. Later Mike, the most disturbed of the three boys, reveals the reason for his hostility toward John. He acts out his sibling rivalry; and as the therapist helps him to understand that he is jealous of John for being alone with her, his anger abates. He pretends to throw paint at John, but does not actually do it. The therapist is somewhat defensive about John: she seems to justify, or at least explain, his being alone with her. This can be interpreted that she prefers John, which is both bad and untrue. The interpretation of Mike's feelings alone would have been sufficient. When the therapist says that Mike is just being silly, she expresses her disapproval and exercises control over him which is necessary with very young children.

All three boys go on working. Judah finishes his painting.

*Judah:* Well that's done. I guess I'll work on an airplane now. (To the therapist): Would you help me?

Mike had started several "war paintings," all at the same time. He finishes them all at the same time after working diligently. The therapist sees no design in them, although she believes that Mike is using his hands more freely and is actually finger painting rather than working the way he did last week, which was just piling paint.

*Judah* (draws an airplane on wood and comes over to the therapist): Will you saw this for me? Gee, I'm glad you got the saw you promised me.

*John* (moving closer to the therapist): Would you make me something, too?

*Therapist:* Of course I would. (John seems very pleased at this.)

*Judah:* Gee, I have an idea. Let's all make pumpkins out of wood. This is how we could do it. All we have to do is to nail pieces of wood together into a square.

*John* (to the therapist): Could you help me saw this piece of heavy wood?

Judah then starts to nail the two pieces together but has to hunt for the nails. John goes over to him and hands him a nail that he has found.

*Judah:* Thanks a lot. (John seems pleased by this.) John, come on and help me with this work. You could even start one for yourself.

The hostility felt by Mike and Judah is now sublimated in activity: airplanes and war paintings. The therapist, however, notes that Mike is much freer in his work which is very important for this boy. Judah is pleased that the therapist got the saw he wanted and, because of this warm feeling toward her, wants her to work with him. This in turn makes John jealous, and he, too, wants her help — an expression of sibling rivalry. When John gives Judah the nails and Judah in turn invites him to work with him, there is personality growth beyond narcissistic preoccupations and an expanded capacity for object relationships. John's act can be seen, however, as a placation because of his own fear of the hostile feelings he harbors toward Judah, but as Judah accepts him — i.e., forgives him — he feels relieved.

*Mike:* Let's all go now.

*Judah:* I want to finish. (He leaves his wood and takes some of the paint with which he starts to paint a picture on the wall.)

*Therapist* (to Judah): You know we are not allowed to paint on the walls of the room.

*Judah:* Oh don't worry. It will be okay because no one will know that I did it.

*Therapist:* That doesn't matter. We are still not permitted to paint the walls.

*Judah* (continuing to paint): I won't be found out. (He paints a picture of a house and one of an owl). I think it will be all right. Look at the paint that other people put on the wall.

*Therapist:* Maybe you are angry because other people use this room.

*Judah:* That's right.

*Mike* (chiming in): You're right.

*Therapist:* You see, the toy cars are ours and so is the bulletin board. . . . If you want to leave, I think we should go now. (They all want to go.) I think you should all go outside and wash.

They follow the suggestion. This is the first time that any of them have gone to wash their hands before going to eat. Because someone is in the washroom there is some delay. Mike starts banging on the door. Judah runs for a hammer and starts banging. John also participates: He kicks the door and bangs on it. They are finally able to get inside.

*Judah* (to the therapist):Would you get paper for me? I want you to lift me up so that I can get the paper for myself.

*Mike:* I want paper, too.

*John:* Me, too.

Judah and John are with the therapist. This disturbs Mike, and he suggests terminating the session. Judah does not want to go, and because the therapist did not counter Mike's suggestion, he attacks her by painting the wall. When she remonstrates with him he finds every plausible means of justifying his act; and finally he and Mike admit that they are angry because others, as well, use the room — i.e., the therapist loves other children as well as them. Judah's choice to paint a house and an owl is in itself significant.

The fact that John, a frightened and withdrawn boy, can participate in an act of such direct aggression as banging and kicking the door is very valuable to him. He could not possibly have done it when alone. The example (catalysis) of the others gave him the courage to do it.

*Judah:* Let's go down through the back stairway.

The group follows Judah's suggestion. There is no running ahead. All three walk alongside the therapist. Judah and Mike take her hand, and John takes Judah's hand.

*Judah:* Let's stop at the stationery store.

*Mike:* Yes, I see something I want.

*John:* That's a good idea. I see something, too.

*Judah:* I want a collection of books, but all the things cost too much. I only have a dime. (He gives up the idea with some difficulty).

*Mike:* Let's go now. I think we should stop and eat first, though.

Judah and John agree, and they all choose vanilla ice cream sodas and eat without playing with the ice cream the way they formerly did.

*Therapist* (while the boys are eating): What would you like to eat next week?

*Judah:* Frankfurters.

*Mike:* Yes, frankfurters.

*John:* That's right, frankfurters.

*Judah:* And please have plates, and forks and knives and mustard and flowers — daffodils — and then we'll all sing: "Here comes the bride."

*Therapist:* Who is going to be the bride?

Judah does not answer.

The back stairway is dark and has special significance for these boys as it also had for the children in other groups. They are afraid and keep together and cling to the therapist. Note that John, because of his timidity and fear of contact with the therapist, holds another boy's hand both in this instance and later on. In the discussion of refreshments, Judah brings forth the idea of a bride. Did he see himself marrying the therapist (his mother)? One can only speculate on this. When asked by the therapist who the bride would be he does not answer: He represses it.

On the way to the five-and-ten cent store, John tries to put chalk on the therapist, and Mike sort of hits her with a gun. This really takes the form of pushing the therapist from the back. Mike and Judah then take the therapist's hand, and John takes Judah's hand again. John keeps taking out his thirty cents to show how much money he has. In the store they hesitate a great deal about choosing what to buy. They look at all the various objects and Mike finally decides.

*Mike:* I'm going to buy stickers and tags for Christmas packages.

*Judah:* I want tags and stickers, too. (He decides this although he had been handling something else.)

*John:* I'm getting them, too. (John also buys crayons that Judah had picked up but didn't have the money to pay for.)

The group walks back to the office.

*Judah:* I would like to have a hundred thousand dollars and buy a big store.

*Mike:* I would, too.

*John:* So would I.

# Activity Group Therapy with Children

MARGARET G. FRANK and JOAN ZILBACH

No appraisal of current trends in group therapy with children can be adequately made unless present practice is viewed against a backdrop of the past. We propose, therefore, to review the origins and development of group therapy with children before discussing the current scene.

Since the beginning of mankind, children at the age of five or six have started to move away from the succor of their parents and to draw together to play and work in groups. Cave drawings depict in simple lines what Brueghel, centuries later, portrayed with a complexity of lines and colors in *Children's Games*. The playful pastimes of his mid-sixteenth-century Flemish children have a marked resemblance to many contemporary American playgrounds where children are engaged in hopscotch, marbles, blindman's buff, keep-away, etc.

This movement into the "society of children" heralds the "latency" phase of development, the stage of childhood that concerns us for the purposes of this presentation. Stone and Church (1957) see the school-age child as "quite a different creature from what he was as a pre-schooler and from what he will be as an adolescent. . . . One of the most striking characteristics of this age in our own and many other societies is that it forms a special, separate subculture with traditions, games, values, loyalties, roles and membership of its own. . . . Child society is a proving ground where the child learns to live with people outside the family."

The writings of Bornstein (1951), as well as Erikson, Freud, and Scheidlinger, among others, help us to appreciate the complexities of the tasks of development in the latency phase. In a recent article, Scheidlinger (1966) cogently interrelates theories of libidinal, social and ego development to point up the significance of peer life for the latency child.

When we study ego development in the latency child we see strong thrusts toward mastery. Strivings for independence, particularly from parents, typify this age. The still-needed support and sense of belonging are now obtained from the peer group rather than the family. The latency child's need to gauge the success of his developing skills finds expression in the group as child competes with child. Rituals and games become useful avenues for redirecting, containing, and sublimating the sexual and aggressive themes which are vestiges of the upheavals of the oedipal phase.

The necessary work on identity (ego and sexual) associated with this phase of development can be supported and enabled by group life as peers respond to the individual's trying on different roles for size. But just as the group can afford a child an arena for positive growth, so it can exert negative influences on some children. One need only think of the cruel, taunting voices as a group ejects an "unacceptable" child or the even more painful silent rejection felt when a child receives no attention from his peers to be aware of this potential.

There is a long history in settlement-house work and social-group work of providing latency-age children grounds and guidance for their propensity for peer group living. These groups were and are ego-supportive and ego-enhancing and in this sense should be considered generally therapeutic. However, it was not until the 1930's that the potentials for growth through the group were specifically harnessed and translated into a method of therapy for the latency child: activity group therapy.

Specifically and artfully designed to respond to the characteristic needs and tendencies of the latency-age child, the therapeutic forces of the activity group emerge from the experience of child in relation to child, therapist, materials, food, and activity. Because this is essentially an experiential form of treatment, clarification and interpretation have little place in it. The importance of activity-group therapy is not solely to be found in the specifics of the technique itself. The founder, Slavson (1943), and those who followed to refine Slavson's original stimulations (Scheidlinger, Schiffer, Hallowitz, King, etc.) have articulated some important concepts for the field of group therapy with children. If used as guides, these concepts can bring the formation and action of groups to their highest therapeutic potential. Since these concepts comprise a heritage that is all too often ignored in the present scene of group therapy with children, it would seem useful to examine them and trace their presence or absence in current practice.

## Theory of Activity Group Therapy

Activity group therapy is a noninterpretive mode of treatment designed, particularly in the first phase, to offer disturbed latency-age children an atmosphere of acceptance, non-retaliation, and nourishment in the service of encouraging benign and guided regression. In the second and third phases of treatment the therapist, responding to the children's readiness, moves the group to work on the conflicts exposed and accepted in the early phase with the goal of helping the children to acquire new modes of coping.

### Group Balance

The successful operation of these groups is, in part, dependent upon their composition. The term *group balance* refers to the totality of group composition. The child selected for a specific group is chosen not only on the basis of the clinician's perception of his need for, and ability to gain from, group therapy, but also on the specific influences that his personality, his areas of health and dysfunctioning, will have on other children in that group. What is sought in the total composition of the group is a range of ego strengths, coping capacities, and problem areas that will allow the children to activate and offset one another. One need only envisage the interaction of six children coping with the similar defense style of reaction-formation to forecast that the group would behave like a polite tea-party. But if we place together a child with little reticence about making demands on the adult with another who relies on reaction formation, we can see the potential for action, stimulation, and mutually beneficial vicarious experiences. If we enlarge the range from seeing the offsetting influence of two children upon one another to viewing the same phenomena in seven or eight children — talkers to balance the silent, doers to stimulate the immobilized, grabbers to offset those who dare not even ask — we can begin to see the potential for ego learning in a balanced group.

In addition to what the children can do for one another when selected along the lines of balance, of equal importance is the influence of group balance on the therapist's role. We have said that the therapeutic action of activity group therapy starts with a first phase in which the therapist is accepting, non-retaliatory, and nourishing. The freedom for the therapist to assume and maintain this stance in relation to a group depends in large part upon the make-up of the group. Again, if we try to envisage a group composed totally of impulse-ridden children, the nature of their problems would demand that the therapist move to set limits. While we, as professionals, may know that the limit-setting action is done to prevent chaos and to protect the frail egos of such children, the children themselves are likely initially to perceive such limit-setting as disapproval of their impulses. Had they the health to see the ego protective aspect of the therapist's actions, they would likely not need treatment. At the other extreme, in a group of children immobilized by fear of closeness to peer and adult alike, the therapist would have to move into initiating action for the children, stimulating them and actively attempting to reduce their fears.

The balance of qualities in the children can relieve the therapist of many functions he would otherwise have to carry out. Deliberately, we select a child who can approach the adult, demand, even be grabby. The therapist is free to accept this behavior because he can rely on another child to limit the grabber's behavior, albeit out of anxiety. In the face of one child's freely expressing his anger; another, fearful of the sight of it, will be mobilized to curb his peer. The therapist then is free to respond and give to both. Beyond the specific operations of this method of group therapy the theory of group balance points up sharply that the therapist's role is not only determined by his goals but by the emotional composition of his group.

### Action and Experience

A second important contribution derived from the heritage of experience in activity group therapy is the noninterpretative and essentially nonverbal nature of this technique. This is of particular importance since the basic training of present and would-be group therapists is in the talking therapies. We are taught to rely heavily upon words, ours and our patient's, as major therapeutic tools. Students of activity-group therapy universally initially doubt that actions can be substituted for words, but once they have had the experience of leading a group the power of the "corrective experience" (Alexander, 1961) takes on real meaning. All adults, even those clinically trained, move quickly to break up fights between children, but it is crucial to the therapeutic atmosphere of activity-group therapy that the therapist learn to rely heavily on the ego perceptions of the children to end their own fights. If the children appear to be overwhelmed by their impulses, the therapist learns to respond in the most nonconfronting, ego-lending fashion. The neophyte activity-group therapist is often amazed to find that his looking across the room at a fight will dissolve the tensions.

Activity, action, "acting-up," and acting-out are often and easily confused. Activity of all kinds, motoric and verbal, is important to all human beings. But the latency age child has a particular need for activity.

Motoric and muscular activity combined with the cognitive are the equipment for the latency child's acquisition of skills. Action refers to a particular goal-directed activity, either alone or in groups. The latency child will normally increase his involvement in all kinds of action if not thwarted by family, school, or the large environment. "Acting-up" should be viewed as a normal part of the activity patterns of school-age children. *Acting-out* is a term which should be reserved for a specific technical meaning; i.e., when, in the course of treatment, material which should be confined to the treatment situation is dispersed, usually by actions, and thus becomes unavailable for therapeutic work.

Activity-group therapy utilizes the activity and action patterns of the latency age child instead of battling against them as in the more exclusively verbal therapies.

### Ego Development

This leads us to a final consideration about activity-group therapy. It is a method of treatment derived from and dependent upon an understanding of ego development. This emerges clearly in the selection process. It is not enough to know the child's pathology intimately. True assessment can take place only when his disturbance is viewed within the context of the development of ego capacities. We have learned to draw ego profiles on children, viewing their learning patterns, their capacities to relate to peers and adults, their interests, their motoric (fine and gross) abilities, as well as their levels of fixation and defenses.

The very fabric of the method bespeaks an attention to and concern with ego development. The acceptance and nourishment of the first phase encourages a regression in the service of the ego. The nonintervening stance of the therapist implies his trust in the egos of the children to solve, resolve, and master on their own.

One could develop an entire paper on the rich contributions of activity-group therapy to the general field of group therapy with children. We have selected the major facets which seem to us to have particular bearing on the modifications of activity-group therapy that are part of the current trends of group therapy with children.

In 1963, Fritz Redl presented a paper in which he discussed the development of group therapy in relation to the psychoanalytic profession. He began his paper by saying that "newly emerging scientific disciplines go through a sequence of peculiar developmental phases, just as children do in the process of growing up. Some of them may have a prolonged infancy, a stormy adolescence, and then either go to pieces or settle down to mature with adult age." He suggested that the psychoanalytic profession first viewed group therapy with "suspicion and contempt." Somewhat later it reacted with "surprise ... and acceptance of some facts of group life." Following this, there evolved "the extramarital slumming party" phase of reaction. Redl pointed out that young psychoanalytic trainees are permitted, even encouraged, to "play around with therapy groups on the side provided, of course, that they (don't) take such activity too seriously." Redl continued that it is his impression that the young trainees "revel in the opportunity to do all the things their supervisors in analysis would never let them do ..." to enjoy the chance to forget about most of the hard-to-follow issues of their official training and to live in a clinical free-for-all with the security that no training analyst is going to breathe down their necks while they are at it. Redl stated that this clinical abandon has had a deplorable effect on the development of group therapy. He observed that the issues basic to all thorough clinical work turn up in therapy groups too.

### Current Trend

When we look at the development of activity-group therapy as part of the current scene of practice, it is evident that the method has not kept pace with the rest of the field. Despite the maturity of its theoretical base it is, in actual practice, an infant fighting for survival. One can count on the fingers of two hands the clinical centers offering the traditional method of activity-group therapy as part of their treatment armamentarium. Even fewer are the opportunities for professionals to get specific training in this method. The lack of sanction and time for training has been noted by Dr. Scheidlinger as a major cause for the slow development of this method.

There is no question that the lack of proper training facilities, the greater comfort with the talking therapies, and the need for specific physical settings have been deterrent to the spread of activity group therapy. But we feel that there is another factor which must be recognized. Anyone who has even a superficial familiarity with activity-group therapy is aware that this method demands of the practitioner knowledge of the growth and development of children, knowledge of the basic issues of therapy, and a strict adherence to a clinical process of thought. Nothing in this method is done without careful weighing of the implications. Selection of children, lay-out of therapy room, materials selected for use, and the therapist's behavior are all part of a highly specific therapeutic design. The therapist must be at ease with all the conflicts and impulses that emerge in the group. He must be able to give in untold ways. He must be ready to limit behavior not out of his own anxiety but prompted by a perception of the child's need. He must not allow the children to remain in the feeding stage of treatment but must move them on, shifting his own role appropriately. He must enjoy and permit identification.

It might be said that these qualities (and more) are required of all child therapists, and we would agree. But we would have to add that the requirements of the group therapist are enlarged by the very confronting of a group.

If Redl's observations about the psychiatric profession's reactions to group therapy have some truth in them, then perhaps they pertain to all the mental health professions as they contemplate group therapy. We contend that activity-group therapy in its very nature demands a rigorousness of clinical thought and action that many practitioners are not prepared to observe. We might add that in this day and age, when the enormity of the social and emotional problems confronting the mental health profession is greater than ever, the cost of activity group therapy in both training and operation seems huge, thus relegating the technique to the realm of "luxury."

**References**

Alexander, F., *The Scope of Psychoanalysis*, New York: Basic Books, 1961.

Bornstein, B., "On Latency," *The Psychoanalytic Study of the Child*, 6:279–285, New York: International Universities Press, 1951.

Grunebaum, M. G., "Phases in an Activity Group's Reaction to an 'Atypical' Member, Paper presented at the 20th Annual Conference of the American Group Psychotherapy Association, January, 1963.

King, G. H., "Activity Group Therapy with a Schizophrenic Boy: Follow-up Two Years Later," *International Journal of Group Psychotherapy*, 9:184–194, 1959.

Lieberman, F., and Taylor, S. S., "Combined Group and Individual Treatment of Schizophrenic Child, *Social Casework*, 46:80–85, 1965.

Redl, F., "Psychoanalysis and Group Therapy: A Developmental Point of View," *American Journal of Orthopsychiatry*, 33:135–147, 1963.

Scheidlinger, S., "Psychoanalysis and Group Behavior," New York: W. W. North – (1966), The Concept of Latency: Implications for Group Treatment, *Social Casework*, 47: 363–367, 1952.

Schiffer, M., "The Therapeutic Group in the Public School," In *Orthopsychiatry and the School*, ed. M. Krugman, New York: Orthopsychiatric Association, 1958.

Slavson, S. R., *Introduction to Group Therapy*, New York: The Commonwealth Fund; 1943.

Stone, L. J., and Church, J., Childhood and Adolescence, New York: Random House, 1957.

# LIMIT-SETTING

# Limits Are Therapy

RAY H. BIXLER

Restriction of behavior is one of the few universal elements in therapy. Limits have a role in all treatment methods, whether the client is adult or child, withdrawn or aggressive. It may be this very universality which accounts for the scanty material available in the literature. Obvious differences in therapy are sufficiently stimulating and threatening to hold our attention in spite of the fact that problems common to all therapies are being resolved at an equally rudimentary level. The role of limits on behavior may be more important than our current interest in them would indicate.

In the play interview the therapist will encounter children who refuse to accept limits, who kick the therapist, mar his wall, and throw his desk calendar on the floor in spite of verbalized limits and clarified feelings. The literature reveals few suggestions for dealing with this phase of play therapy. Allen (1) emphasizes the essential role of limits and stresses their importance, but omits discussion of what he does when limits are broken. Axline (2) acknowledges that limits are broken:

> Now, what about the child who breaks the limitation? Suppose he aims the block at the window and, although his feeling is recognized and he is told not to throw it there, he does so anyway. Usually the recognition of his feeling is sufficient to bring down the block; but suppose this time it doesn't? The therapist should be alert to the possibility that he may not put the block down. She should try to prevent the throwing of the block if she can do so without engaging in a physical battle with the child. But if the block should go through the window, what then? Should she lecture the child? Put him out of the playroom? Or act as though she really didn't care?

Such a situation would be a real challenge to the therapist. She could not temporarily shelve her basic principles. She would not reject the child because he disobeyed her. She would stay right there with her reflection of feelings. "It was important to you to throw it anyway. You wanted to show me that you would throw it." (2, pp. 132–133).

Again the therapist cannot help but wonder what else to do with a child who is going to attack him or permanently mar furnishings unless there is "physical battle."

The most effective method for each therapist in dealing with limits or any other problem he encounters in the interview is probably that method with which he is most comfortable. Believing this to be true, there is, nevertheless, value in understanding the approach of others. This paper is concerned with the theory and practice of limits in therapy with children. Special emphasis is placed upon the production of refusal to accept limits with accompanying illustrations.

## Limits Are Necessary

Most therapists assume that limits are essential. Verbal expression and much of other behavior may be free of regimentation, but the rights, property, and physical well-being of others must be protected. Some therapists limit verbal activity by indirect means, others protest against this, but almost all therapists set limits upon the range of nonverbal activity.

The obvious value of limits in the orderly operation of the clinic is only one of several functions that limits may serve. The therapist who protects his person and property from physical aggression has an opportunity to feel accepting of the child. The potential loss of personal possessions or the experience of physical discomfort seemingly would create pressures which operate against real acceptance of the child and his attitudes.

There may be another and even more important role in controlling behavior. The child who is allowed remarkable freedom in most of his activity but is rigidly controlled in specific areas seems to differentiate between the therapeutic experience and other relationships. Rather than giving free expression to his attitudes at home, school, or church, he seems to conform to the accepted mores of the environment of the moment. This has been observed in interview and environmental (institutional) therapy with amazing regularity. To the best of this writer's knowledge this is not equally true of children who are experiencing a passive therapy (no limits). This tentative hypothesis would seem worthy of further evaluation and may be amenable to clinical research of relatively exacting nature.

### Limits Should be Minimal

Consensus of opinion seems to indicate a minimal number of limits. If the therapist is free to plan his play therapy room for that purpose alone many limits become unnecessary. The presence of a desk with desk set, telephone, clock, papers, books, and desk drawers necessitates setting of numerous limits in order to protect property. The same is true for overstuffed chairs and other pieces of furniture which are desirable for adult interviewing. The writer has found it necessary to set limits most frequently on destruction of items associated with his desk. This condition is undesirable because of the numerous limits it places on the child as well as the previously mentioned pressures created in the therapist by potential loss of personal possessions. A play room such as Axline describes (2, Ch. 3) minimizes these dangers without eliminating the therapeutic functions of limits.

### Basic Limits

Basic limits set by any therapist will tend to differ. In therapy with the writer children are not supposed to:

1. Destroy any property or facilities in the room other than play equipment.
2. Attack the therapist in any physical sense.
3. Stay beyond the time limit of the interview.
4. Remove toys from the play room.
5. Throw toys or other material out of the window.

In addition to these rigid limits the therapist employs some relative limits which are invoked rarely and necessitated by the room in which he works. It is necessary to inhibit noise which interferes with therapeutic interviews in other offices and to keep the child from pouring excessive amounts of water on the floor, which is not leak proof. An example of the first limit and the only time it has been invoked was with a group of two children who were pushing a chair and table across the floor. Here the limit was invoked by two other staff members who found that verbal contacts were impossible in their own offices. Sound proofing, a first floor office, and isolation of the play room from other interviewing offices would minimize these limits.

### Relative versus Rigid Limits

Wherever possible it seems desirable to use well-defined limits. Both the child and therapist can achieve greater comfort when confronted with concrete demarcation between acceptable and unacceptable behavior. Such limits are easier to distinguish and are less apt to lead to insecurity on the part of the therapist. For example, there is a clear distinction between hitting the therapist and not hitting him, but the vague transition point between hitting so as to do no harm and hitting to do harm places both therapist and child in tenuous positions. Wherever degree of activity is a consideration in setting limits, therapy may suffer because the nature of demarcation is such as to place both child and therapist in the position of making decisions without criteria. It would appear preferable to limit a child's throwing a ball at the window, splashing water on the therapist, and playing with the articles on his desk on an all-or-none basis, rather than on a basis of the degree of harm to person or things involved.

No matter how hard one may try, it is unlikely that he can remove all relative limits. If for no other reason, the therapist will see many of his "rigid" limits melt before the uncanny ability of the maladjusted child. With consummate ease he manages to place himself squarely on the line of demarcation between acceptable and unacceptable behavior. What extent the therapist may go to in setting rigid limits will be determined in part by his own comfort with intangible limits. Undoubtedly some therapists work more easily with a "You can hit me, but not hard," orientation than does this therapist.

### When Limits Are Established

There seems to be little or no disagreement upon the optimal time to establish limits. Few therapists set limits prior to the child's attempt to define them. Not until the child threatens to break a limit is he confronted with the request that he refrain from so doing. This avoids a lengthy and incomplete dissertation by the therapist at the onset of treatment. A preliminary discussion of limits is apparently more disturbing to therapists than suddenly confronting the child with specific limitations upon his behavior.

There seems to be ample justification for this point of view. It is impossible for the therapist to outline all limits that will have to be set with any child before the therapeutic relationship develops. Even if this were possible, the relationship would probably be retarded by a "You can do this and that, BUT . . ." orientation. Furthermore, the initiative for developing the play sessions would be taken from the child by even the most nonauthoritative therapist.

As a result, the child learns what he is permitted to do as he explores and tests the relationship with the therapist. If the latter is oriented primarily to attitudes expressed rather than the content of the child's behavior, any negative potential which could accrue from unexpected limitations seems to be minimized.

### Mechanics of Setting Limits

With experience the therapist develops a meaningful system of dealing with behavior which exceeds his acceptable limits. It seems desirable to graduate therapeutic reactions to such behavior. The following steps may be used successfully: (1) reflecting the desire or attitude of the child, (2) verbal expression of the limit, and finally (3) control by physical means of the child's behavior. For example, a child might be angry at the therapist and want to hit him because the therapist will not let the child take a doll home with him. The gradation of limits might take place in some manner similar to the following hypothetical example.

Therapist (1). You're mad at me because I won't let you take the dolly. You want to hit me because you're mad. (To many children this is sufficient. Acceptance of their desire seems to eliminate need for the act itself.)

Child (1): (Hits at therapist, who wards off blow if possible.)

Therapist (2): You're awfully mad at me and want to hurt me. It's all right to be mad at me but you're not supposed to hit me. (The vast majority of children stop at this point.)

Child (2): (Tries to kick or hit therapist, who tries to protect self.)

Therapist (3): If you hit me again you'll have to leave the room for today. You want to hurt me because you're awfully mad at me. If you do hit me you'll have to leave for today.

Child (3): (Hits at therapist again. When limits reach the stage of Therapist (3) for the first time, the child almost always challenges this limit. In ensuing interviews it rarely happens that he will do so again.)

Therapist (3): You'll have to leave for today, John. (Stands up and opens door.) I'll see you next week — you're awfully mad at me because I won't let you do some of the things you want to do.[1]

---

1. Warning the child that he may be removed from the office may seem like threatening him. There seems to be a very real and clear-cut distinction between threatening and the procedure suggested here. The therapist is not punitive in attitude and he carries out exactly what he says he will do. When he fails to invoke this limit he actually invites more aggressive anti-social acts. The writer is indebted to Virginia H. Bixler, Director of the Vince A. Day Center, for considerable help in clarifying the role of limits in therapy. Opportunity to observe group treatment of aggressive children at the Center has played a major role in the development of this thesis.

At this point the child almost always leaves the room. Only two times in five years has the writer been forced into picking the child up and placing him outside the room. Several children, one of whom is discussed later (Marvin), have continued their attacks in the outer office to the point where it has been necessary to hold them at arm's length.

Perhaps the most significant factor in maintaining the all-important therapeutic attitude of acceptance is simply that the therapist receives very little punishment and the time involved is not excessive. Under these conditions it is quite possible to feel acceptance of the child and his attitudes while rejecting a phase of his behavior. If the therapist were to be under the influence of continual attack over a period of time in one interview, he would have to be a very strong personality to keep from rejecting the child and behaving in a punitive manner. Even if this were possible it seems undesirable to allow broken limits, especially where they involve antisocial acts.

The fact that children frequently leave the office with a sense of relief when involved in the third stage of limitations lends credence to the generally held belief that children do want to have their aggressive behavior controlled. This is further substantiated by accompanying positive changes in the child's behavior at home and in his respect for limits in therapy. Clinical experience seems to indicate that rigid adherence to behavioral limits accompanied by an acceptance of the attitudes which motivate this behavior serves as the crux of therapy with many aggressive children.

## Cases of Pat and Marvin

The following excerpts were taken from play therapy contacts the writer has had with very aggressive children. They were selected because therapy was "mussy" in spots, thus highlighting the effectiveness of sound limits when they were invoked and because they illustrate many of the extreme problems involved in setting limits.

The first is the case of Patrick Moriarity, ten years old. He was referred because of uncontrolled aggression in and out of the classroom. He had been expelled from school. In his initial contacts (the record starts with the fifth interview) his aggression was verbal or directed at the toys. In order to partially compensate for the lack of verbatim notes, comments regarding the process of setting limits are added.

5-9-47. Pat was very mad at me. He came in and kicked the ball and then with a gleam in his eyes looked around the room. He made several comments about the use of various objects in the room as weapons to be used against me. I mentioned that he was awfully mad at me and thinking up a number of ideas that would hurt me. He acknowledged this. Shortly after this it was necessary to limit his attempt to pour water on the calendar. He spent most of his time today trying to make me mad in one way or another, although it was occasionally interspersed with friendly discussion. He pinched my nose at one point and hit me at another.

It is apparent that Pat broke several limits in this interview. The therapist recognized his hostility and set the limits, but other than defending himself in a physical sense did not invoke limits to make Pat stop his aggression. It may have been desirable to have set and invoked the limit of leaving the office.

5-13-47. He started out again today to try to make me mad. First he threw the nipple out of the window, then poured the water out of the nursing bottle. He started to pour it on the table. I limited him. This intensified his trying to make me mad. He got very angry at me because I didn't get mad, but all during this he readily accepted the limits that I set. When I told him it was time to clean up, he made a few moves to do so but did not finish. He asked me what I would do if he didn't clean up. I told him that that was something I would have to clean up after he left if he didn't do it. That made him quite happy and I recognized his joy at my having to clean up the messes he made.

5-16-47. In the initial part of the period today there was a marked change in Pat's behavior. It was largely constructive. He talked about, instead of demonstrating, his aggressiveness. After a while, however, he took the nipple off the bottle, threatened to throw it out and I set a limit on him at this point. He then threw the pegs on the floor. After this episode he started to play and talk in a friendly, constructive way. I mentioned that sometimes he was mad and wanted to play and talk with me. During the rest of the period his antagonism increased, but at no time today did it approach what it has been in the past. This is somewhat difficult to evaluate at this stage in therapy.

The therapist is obviously confused. Speculation about the significance of an attitude of confusion on the part of the therapist leads to the question, "Is what ensues in later contacts a result only of the child's maladjustment, or does the therapist, because of his own uncertainty, create a subtle stimulus pattern which intensifies the youngster's reactions?"

5-20-47. Pat was very angry. As he came down the hall he struck me from behind and threw himself around the room when he came in. He took the nursing bottle and tried to break it. His attempts to break it were not very wholehearted at first, pounding it against the radiator easily for quite a period of time. I recognized that he wanted to break it. I said, "You wanted to show me that you weren't afraid. You also wanted very much to make me mad." He was pretty upset about breaking it. I recognized this and told him that he was supposed to clean it up. He began to do so and did quite a bit of the cleaning up. He got angry with me, however, much more so at this point when I didn't get mad because he broke the bottle. He was very hostile and spun my chair around. He quieted down. He asked about my writing and I told him. This upset him, too, and he didn't believe it. I recognized his feeling that I probably was giving it to other people to read. He went to the table, turned his back to me, and spent a long time there, growling. He turned to me and said, "Why do you write to yourself?" I said, "You don't believe I write these things just for myself — you feel pretty sure that I give them to somebody else to read." He responded, "Yeah, I bet you do." He talked about eating me up and other savory forms of getting rid of me. I mentioned that he was awfully mad at me and wished he could get rid of me, that he was pretty unhappy because I didn't let him do some of the things he wanted to do. At this point he came over and hit me. The time was about up and I told him it was time to clean up the water on the floor, and he asked me what I would do if he didn't. I told him, "Nothing." He said, "Who would clean it up?" I said, "I would." He threw the rag on the floor. I mentioned that it was a lot of fun to think that I would be the one who would have to clean up any mess that he left. He was pleased by this and then gradually became more angry again — apparently because I didn't get angry.

Note the intense frustration Pat experiences in his relationship with the therapist. This may be due to Pat's inability to control the therapist's emotional reactions and to the therapist's fuzzy reaction to Pat's struggle with limits.

5-23-47. Pat checked on the things he had done last time to see if they were still the way they were and looked outside to see if the nipple was there and at the back of the doll to see if it were still broken. He played quietly at the sink for awhile, then he came over to me and hit me on the head. I limited this behavior and mentioned that he was still pretty angry at me. He went over to the sink again where he played for quite a while — then he came to me for help with opening the gun. I mentioned that he was having a lot of fun playing. He was very intent on his work and a moment later I mentioned that sometimes he liked to do things to make me mad and other times he just liked to play. He played a little while longer and then came over and tried to throw water on me. When I limited him he returned and dropped the gun behind the radiator. He played quietly for quite a while. It was apparent that he was trying to destroy the doll. He was trying to tear or hurt it; and when I recognized this at the time when our time was just about up, he suddenly flew into a very intense rage and attacked me. He has become more and more frustrated because he has been unable to make me mad.

Note that the therapist seems to feel that Pat's frustration is due solely to his inability to anger the therapist.

5-29-47. Pat came into the room and immediately became aggressive. He tried to destroy the doll and was unable to. He poured water on the floor from the nursing bottle; and when he began to fill it up the second time to throw it on the floor, I told him that he could throw two bottles of water on the floor but no more; that if he poured more, he would have to leave the room. He dumped the second bottle and immediately filled it up and started to pour a third. He left readily when I invoked the limit.

This seems long overdue. Invoking of the limit was consummated while the therapist was still calm and able to accept Pat's attitudes. In the next interview Pat's mother reported marked improvement for the first time.

6-4-47. Pat refused to come in and hung around the door for ten or fifteen minutes. As soon as he came in he threw the ball out of the window. I warned him, and then he threw a doll out and I sent him from the room again.

Again the limit was invoked quickly. This approach to the therapy appears to be far removed from what is considered good counseling. Ensuing interviews and the change in behavior reported by Pat's mother would indicate that therapy is taking place.

6-11-47. He was mad today. He didn't know why or at whom and was able to say so. He spent most of his time talking in a friendly way with me. There were only two mildly aggressive acts during the period. He worked awfully hard to be good during the period and I recognized this. I said that in many ways he wanted to be good and it was pretty hard to be good. This is encouraging in light of the improvement that has taken place outside of interviews. It may be an indication that we are drawing near a close in this treatment situation.

The improvement noted at home appears for the first time in the play interviews. This is not a dramatic example of the role of limits in therapy, rather it is typical. The child as well as the adult receives much security from external control of his antisocial acts.

6-20-47. Pat was much better today. His only aggressive act during the whole period was to tear my blotter and drop it on the floor. I asked him when he thought he would want to stop coming to see me; and he was not able to answer this question at this point, saying, "I don't know."

Since this interview there has been no significant trouble at school or at home. Visiting teachers report that his behavior is exemplary. His mother called up the first week of school this fall because the principal did not want to admit him. He has been admitted and is a "changed boy." Undoubtedly more forthright limits in the earlier contacts would have brought this change about sooner. At this date, May 1948, he still retains this level of adjustment.

6-27-47. Today Pat was very constructive in his behavior. No aggressive acts towards me were apparent. He expressed some feeling about coming in, and I brought up the question of whether or not he wanted to continue. He thought at first he would like to come in three times, then he changed it to one time and finally to two times. He and I went in and spoke to Mrs. Wood and his mother about it and they decided they would come in for two half-hour appointments.

7-11-47. Pat was somewhat uncomfortable today and I brought up the fact that he would be seeing me one more time, and he growled "Yeah." I said, "Maybe you would be happier if this were the last time." He looked at me and smiled and said, "Yes." So I called Mrs. Wood to see if it would be possible to make it the last time as far as Pat's mother was concerned. She felt it would be and I told Pat, who felt very good about this. There was no evidence of hostility today. He was somewhat troubled, found it a little difficult to break with me, but at the same time maintained the improvement that he has demonstrated in the last few interviews.

Marvin was five years old. His aggressive and infantile behavior had caused a nursery school and later a kindergarten to expel him. He threw numerous temper tantrums, especially in public places. He was very fearful and used his fear to control his mother. Several contacts had preceded the first described here. These had been in the presence of his mother. (Fearful children usually can give up their parents in one or two interviews. By letting parents come with the child if he so desires, the trauma of separation is avoided by starting at the level which is feasible for the child. Marvin was unable to make this transition. An intermediate stage was initiated to let his mother see a psychiatric social worker. He was told he could come in to see me if he desired.)

2-19-47. As soon as I came to the waiting room, Marvin shouted, "I'm not going with that old stinker Bixler." I said, "You're not going to have anything to do with me. You're awfully mad at me." He did not come into my office at all during the period, but as they got ready to leave I came out and he started calling me names. He continued this for some times, calling me an old stinker, a pooh-pooh, a Mr. Grease, and other names. Twice he kicked my foot and several times made as if to hit or kick me on the shin. After I went back to my office he came back to it twice, stuck his head around, and yelled that I was an old stinker. The second time I said, "Hi," and he shouted "Mind your own business." After he was fully dressed to leave, he and his mother came back because he wanted to say good-bye to me. He stepped completely into the office and said "Good-bye, you old mind-your-own business," and shouted as he went down the hall that I was an old pooh-pooh.

Setting and controlling limits in an outer office is difficult. Where a child continues his attack it would usually seem better to separate from him at the door of the play therapy room.

3-4-47. Last week Marvin refused to come to the room and called me names when I was in the waiting room, expressing this more in a mingled anger and teasing than pure anger. About midway through our period I came out and told him that if he would like to come into the office he could come. Otherwise I was going down for coffee. He said he didn't want to see me so I went on out. He did apparently come to the office later on while I was out and was disappointed. His mother had told me that at the initial part of the contact Marvin was very anxious to come today.

Contact on 3-4-47: When I went out to get Marvin he shouted, "I'm not going in your office today." He called me an "old stinker" and several other names. I mentioned that he was awfully mad at me and didn't want to have anything to do with me; that he could come down later if he wanted to and I would be in the room. As I went to the office he followed me a short distance and stopped short of the door. He then came to the door, peeked around it, and screamed at the top of his voice. I mentioned that he was afraid to come in, yet he wanted to come in — he couldn't decide whether to do so or not. He rushed out of the room again. He returned to the door, screamed in anger, came in, and pounded on the peg board. He hit my foot at this point. I mentioned that he was afraid of me and mad at me, but that he must not hit me. He went back and hit the pounding board some more. I mentioned that he was awfully afraid and mad and when he was like that he felt like making a lot of noise. He rushed out of the room again into Mrs. Wood's (psychiatric social worker) office, then out of there and back very quickly. He started to pound, looked at me, expressing both anger and fear, which I recognized. "You B.M.," he shouted. "When you're mad at me you feel like calling me names." "You ham. I'll smash you in the jaw." I mentioned that he was awfully mad at me and would like to hurt me, and yet he was afraid of me, too. He pounded on the peg board and counted in a shout "1, 2, 3," and so on up to 10. I mentioned that it helped to make a lot of noise when he felt like he did. He said, "Shut up. None of your business," and rushed over and hit me. I again limited him.

He went to the chair on the other side of the room and said, "I can hit you if I want to." I mentioned that he wanted to hit me and yet was afraid of me. He came over and swung the mallet very close to my face and I jumped. He smiled. I mentioned that it was fun to scare me and that he was glad he could do it. He threatened time and time again to hit me at this point. I recognized his desire to scare me and at one point mentioned that he was afraid of me and wanted to make me afraid of him. He called me a snot, and then "You little snot." "You're mad at me and like to call me names because you'd like to have me get mad at you." He then rushed over and kicked me and rushed out of the room again. He returned very shortly and continued threatening me with the mallet. These threats were handled again by recognition of the anger and fear he felt.

The time was about up and I told him, "I'm glad it is." He asked me several questions at this point about the toys and then returned to his pounding, saying without any provocation, "Mind your own business, you old snot." I mentioned that he was awfully angry at me because I talked to him, and at times he got angry because I didn't. "You little snot. If you don't keep quiet, you little do-something, I'll crack your head open." When the time was up he found it very hard to leave the room.

Note that, as in Pat's case, the therapist allows limits on aggressive behavior to be broken time and time again without removing the child from the room.

The mother broke off contacts. A period of six and one half months elapsed. His mother returned two weeks before school started because she was afraid he would be expelled from school. She wanted him straightened out "in time for school." In order to get as much help as possible, Marvin was seen daily for two weeks and three times the first week of school. His fear of play situation made it impossible at first for him to come to the room without his mother.

8-20-47. Marvin was full of intense hostility. He would come into the room only because his mother came with him, threw water around the room, and very shortly after he came into the room I had set several limits and finally had to tell him if he didn't stop throwing water on the floor, I would have to send him out. He continued and I sent him out.

Maybe the therapist has learned something from his previous experience.

8-21-47. Marvin came in and spent the first part of the period having his mother read out of a comic book; then he played for a while. His play was very aggressive as it had been in the previous interview, throwing the water, etc. When I set limits about having to leave the room if he continued, he stopped. There was much less antagonism today, but the antagonism was intense.

Note the rapidity with which Marvin has altered his reaction to limits.

Summary 8-22-47 through 9-5-47: Marvin continued his aggressiveness through this period, though there have been marked changes for the better. During the next seven interviews he was able to come to my office only once by himself — that was a day when his mother had an appointment with Mrs. Wood. The last three interviews he has been able to come in by himself and play. In this period he was excluded from the room several times because of failure to meet limits, but this has diminished so that the play is much less aggressive and he meets limits much better. He continued to throw water around the room several times and to destroy things on my desk. This, too, has diminished considerably. During the last three interviews much of the time has been spent in play, rather than expressing hostility towards me. His attitude has changed from one of complete hostility to a very ambivalent attitude toward me, coming close to me many times, talking to me about things, even playing with me and asking me to do things for him. I notified him that I was going on vacation and that we would see each other three more times, and kept that up through this period.

The day of the last interview, near the end of it, he said, "Please call my Mommy and ask if I can't go to her, or if she won't come to me." He was very upset and I called her and arrangements were made. During the last three days it was not necessary to lock the door of the room in which his mother was in in order to keep him out. At first when he separated himself from his mother he would run two or three times to see her, to see if she was there, and then return to me. The last few days he has been able to stay away from the room and not run to her, the last day being the only exception and at this point instead of running to her he asked me to get her. At the conclusion of each interview he has tried to kick me. At the conclusion of the final interview on September 5, he kicked me twice, and the second time it was with sufficient vigor so that it hurt me. He kicked at me again. This time I threw my foot up to protect my shin and he kicked his shin against my heavy shoe, which put a large scratch on his leg. It hurt him considerably and threw him into a temper tantrum. Considering the fact that this was the end of our interviews for a period of time, it seemed most desirable to be with him as he worked through this temper tantrum. After all, he was not seeing me for three weeks and

I had just hurt him, which might give him a real basis for feeling rejected. The temper tantrum took place in Mrs. Wood's office, where he screamed and yelled and threw himself around. He wanted me to leave the office and was very insistent that I would. I recognized his feelings and worked with him on this. Gradually the temper tantrum receded and he began to get control of himself. There were a few sporadic outbursts after the first one, but they, too, diminished; and finally with a grin on his face he said, "I am going down to his office and pull his chair out of the room." This had been a limit which had been set in the interview and was one way of getting even with me. I recognized this desire and he rushed down to the office, pulled the chair out, put it back in, and for the next two or three minutes he tried to struggle to take the chair out of the office. I mentioned that it made him happy to try to get even with me, that he was awfully disappointed and unhappy because I had hurt him and he wanted to get back at me because of that. He seemed to be in good control of himself when he left and seemed to have worked out much of it. He was quite unhappy and sad. He was terribly sad because I was leaving and was awfully mad and unhappy because I had hurt him; yet much of the extreme tension around it had been relaxed and he was in much better control of himself.

The improvement in Marvin's behavior is faltering but marked. Marvin had actually "drawn blood" in two spots on the therapist's shin bones. Had the therapist and child separated at the office door, Marvin's injury as well as the punishment the therapist took could have been avoided. Marvin made a very good adjustment to school. The only complaint was that he did not sing when the other children sang. Six weeks elapsed between this and the following interview.

10-15-47. Marvin has made almost unbelievable progress. The first twenty minutes it was not necessary to set any limits. He was quite unhappy. I recognized this and he agreed to it. He gradually changed his unhappiness to anger and in the extremes of his anger expressed it by pounding very hard on the pounding board and screaming and yelling. He became exceedingly wild but remained within the limits of the situation, never attacking me or the permanent fixtures of the room during this period. His words became unintelligible as he shouted and screamed and pounded. Suddenly he stopped and took the nursing bottle. He began to squirt some on the floor and the wall and the windows, then he took the ball and threw it hard. I mentioned that he was awfully angry and that it made him feel good to be able to pound and yell and throw things. At this point his play took on an even more constructive aspect, and he returned to his pounding without the previous fervor. I mentioned that sometimes when he was mad he tried to hurt other people and make them mad and at other times he just pounded and yelled when he was mad. He pounded a little bit and then became quite quiet during the rest of the period, playing without any expression of hostility whatsoever. I wouldn't be surprised but that we are beginning to reach the conclusion of treatment.

Here we begin to see the closing phases of treatment. Marvin's mother again stopped treatment at this point. He maintained this level of adjustment until the end of the school strike in March 1948. Apparently the school provided some support. His mother and father are seriously maladjusted and the mother made very little progress. She has now returned for treatment and the therapist's relationship with Marvin is again very shaky.

### Limits With Adults

The reaction of children to limits, although better known and understood, is in all likelihood no different than that of adults. The staff at the Minnesota Psychiatric Institute have been trying to evaluate (clinically) the potential role of limits with adults. Although the number of cases is small and the experience too limited to be more than provocative, it would appear that limits may have a significant therapeutic role with:

1. Hysterical clients who "faint," or engage in other histrionics so as to interfere with the efficiency of the office. (Restriction of such behavior or discontinuance of contacts.)

2. Clients who seek treatment from numerous staff members, including secretaries, at odd moments and between scheduled appointments. (Setting of limit to relationship with one staff member.)

3. Clients who fail to make progress over a period of several months but tenaciously continue contacts. (Setting limit to the remaining number of appointments. We have used a limit of ten or fifteen more interviews. Results have been very encouraging and would suggest experimentation on a much wider basis.)

### Summary and Conclusion

The use of limits with adults and children seems to be most effective when the therapist's attitude is nonpunitive. It is possible to be accepting of the client's feeling or need to commit antisocial acts without permitting him to carry these feelings into action within the interview. Limits within a punitive structure apparently inhibit rather than reorient behavior. The experiences related here indicate that limits may be of greater therapeutic value than our current interest implies.

The value of limits in therapy has been minimized in the current directive-nondirective arguments. The therapist may find that the more precise his limits and the more quickly they are invoked, the easier it is for him to use them therapeutically. That limits are therapeutic is illustrated by two examples with very aggressive children. It may be that the use of limits on behavior in therapy is equally as important as acceptance of the attitudes which provoke behavior.

**References**
1. Allen, F. H., *Psychotherapy with Children*, New York: Norton, 1942.
2. Axline, Virginia M., *Play Therapy*, Boston: Houghton Mifflin, 1947.
3. Rogers, C. R., *The Clinical Treatment of the Problem Child*, Boston: Houghton Mifflin, 1939.
4. Rogers, C. R., *Counseling and Psychotherapy*, Boston: Houghton Mifflin, 1942.

# Therapeutic Intervention in Child Treatment

HAIM G. GINOTT

The literature reveals basic differences of opinion about the implication of permissiveness and the application of limits in child treatment. Some leading therapists (Rosenthal, 1956; Schiffer, 1952; Slavson, 1943) consider unconditional permissiveness and unrestrained acting out the primary requisite for effective child therapy. They strongly object to the imposition of prescribed limits by the therapist and see in it a dangerous technique that undermines the very foundation of the therapeutic relationship. They maintain that no predetermined set of limits can ever be applied in psychotherapy because "therapeutic intervention"* must always be based on insight into the needs of the individual child and must vary accordingly.

Other leading therapists feel that "the role of limits may be more important than our current interest in them would indicate" (Bixler, 1949, p. 1), that "limitations . . . are set up as prerequisite to satisfactory therapy" (Axline, 1947, p. 131), and that "without limits there would be no therapy" ((Moustakas, 1953, p. 15).

The difference between the two schools of thought is succinctly summarized in their definitions of *permissiveness*. According to the one approach, "Permissiveness means the acceptance of all behavior as it appears in the (therapy) group, be it aggressive, hostile, destructive, sadistic, masochistic, etc., without reproof, censure or restriction on the part of the therapist" (Schiffer, 1952, p. 256). To be sure, the therapist does not sanction such behavior; he only permits it.

According to the other approach, permissiveness means the acceptance of all symbolic behavior as it appears in therapy, be it

*This term was coined by S. R. Slavson in a personal communication.

destructive or constructive, without censure or restriction. All feelings, fantasies, thoughts, wishes, passions, dreams, and desires, regardless of their content, are accepted, respected, and allowed expression through words and play. Direct acting out of destructive behavior is not permitted; when it occurs, the therapist intervenes and redirects it into symbolic outlets.

These formulations of permissiveness touch on issues that strike at the very core of one's therapeutic concept and conduct. In the absence of objective research evidence, these are not issues that one therapist or one school of therapy can decide for another. At the present stage of knowledge, psychotherapists acting upon and reporting on different hypotheses will need to state their orientation, describe their practice, glean evidence from their experience, and present it for scientific evaluation.

This (paper) ... aims to provide a rationale for the use of limits in play therapy, to discuss various limits conducive to effective therapy, and to suggest techniques of limit-setting as well as methods of dealing with limit-breaking.

The following six statements are proposed as a rationale for the use of limits in individual and group play therapy.

(1) Limits Direct Catharsis into Symbolic Channels. One of the aims of therapeutic limits is to promote release through symbolic means. The unfulfillable nature of some of the children's desires makes the setting of limits on direct acting out unavoidable. Certain acts, such as murder, incest, thievery, and vandalism are absolutely forbidden in our society. Such acts may not be performed in therapy either, except in effigy. Symbolic release enables children to channel even incestuous and destructive urges into harmless outlets and to develop sublimations compatible with social demands and mores. Thus a child with oedipal entanglements may undress, hug, kiss, and make love to a mother doll. Obviously he may not act so toward his mother or his therapist. By setting limits, the therapist helps the child to change his object choice while allowing him gratification of sex interests through socially acceptable channels of playing, painting, modeling, puppetry, and discussion.

A child who is angry with his father can stab or shoot a father doll. The aggressive child may symbolically destroy his parents, teachers, and therapist over and over again in his play and games and learn from his own experience that his impulses do not actually kill anybody. The neurotic child may discover that his inner impulses can be discharged into the playroom without dooming him, thus learning that his desires are not fatal and need not be so rigidly inhibited.

(2) Limits Enable the Therapist to Maintain Attitudes of Acceptance, Empathy, and Regard for the Child Client throughout the Therapy Contacts. It is reasonable to assume that a therapist cannot remain emotionally accepting and empathic when the child attacks him, pulls his hair, paints his forehead, tears his shirt, or breaks his glasses. Such activities must be prohibited to prevent the arousal of anger and anxiety in the therapist himself. The ability of any person to tolerate aggressive attacks is not unlimited. The invoking of limits prevents the therapist from exceeding his own capacity for tolerance and enables him to remain consistently unperturbed and tranquil. To retain his role as ego ideal and identification model, the therapist must not come too close to the brink of his endurance. If the therapist questions his ability to stay calm and accepting when the child scatters mud all over the playroom, he should limit the spilling to the sandbox or to one corner of the room. If the therapist cannot tolerate the child's painting of walls, he should limit the painting to paper or toys.

It must be stressed that therapeutic controls always apply to behavior, never to words. A therapist may set necessary limits on undesirable behavior, provided that he is permitting verbal and play outlets for the expression of feelings. If the therapist cannot tolerate the children's conversation or finds it necessary to limit the symbolic content of their play, then it is unlikely that therapeutic gains will accrue. (This point is discussed more fully in another part of the paper.)

(3) Limits Assure the Physical Safety of the Children and the Therapist in the Playroom. Several common-sense health and safety limits must be set in the course of play therapy. Children may not drink polluted water, hang out the window, or set themselves afire. They also may not endanger the life or health of the therapist; they are not allowed to throw sand in his eyes, cough in his face, or dent his cortex with a mallet. For his own safety, then, the therapist may not be attacked physically. Other important reasons for this prohibition will be discussed later.

(4) Limits Strengthen Ego Controls. Many young children present behavior problems characterized by an inability to cope with socially unacceptable inner impulses. The aim of therapy with these children is not the relaxation of superego functions but the tightening of ego controls. By setting limits and invoking prohibitions the therapist becomes the external authority figure whose values, it is hoped, the child will absorb through identification and introjection. Without limits, therapy may only delay self-regulation, encourage narcissism, and lead to a false sense of omnipotence. By encountering limits on some actions in an accepting atmosphere, the child learns to distinguish between

wishes and deeds without negative consequences. He learns that he may feel all his feelings but may not act as he pleases. By accepting the child's feelings and preventing his undesirable acts, the therapist reduces the child's guilt and at the same time turns his wishes in the direction of reality controls. Thus the child comes to accept and control impulses without excessive guilt.

(5) Some Limits Are Set for Reasons of Law, Ethics, and Social Acceptability. Children may not sexually play with each other in the playroom because, among other reasons, it is socially unacceptable and against the law. A child may not deliberately defecate in the sandbox or urinate on the floor, because it is socially unacceptable. A child may utter "smutty" words in the playroom to his heart's content, but he may not yell profanities at passers-by or at the secretarial staff, again because it is socially unacceptable.

(6) Some Limits Are Set because of Budgetary Considerations. Some limits are set simply because of realistic monetary considerations. A child may not destroy expensive toys because they are expensive and clinics usually have limited budgets. Thus Bobo, the costly clown, cannot be hit with a sharp instrument; it is only "for boxing."

### Therapeutic Limits and Parental Restrictions

There is a vast difference between therapeutic limits and parental restrictions. In disciplining a child, parents and teachers generally focus on stopping undesirable actions, not on liquidating the negative feelings motivating these actions. The child is usually neither helped to bring out his troubled feelings nor provided with safe channels for catharsis. The restrictions are frequently set in the midst of angry arguing and are often punitive and inconsistent. More often than not the child is left with the sad conclusion that not only his deeds but also his feelings and wishes were disapproved of.

Therapeutic limits help the child deal both with his feelings and actions. The therapist permits all verbal and symbolic expression of feelings but limits and redirects undesirable acts. The limits are always set in a manner that preserves the child's self-respect. The limits are never punitive, arbitrary, or capricious. They are treatment-motivated and are applied without anger or violence. The child is not rejected or shamed for resenting the prohibitions. His objections to the limits and his wish to break them are recognized and respected, and harmless channels for expressing his feelings are provided.

When limits are employed therapeutically, they may lead to voluntary acceptance by the child of the need to inhibit antisocial wishes.

In this sense limits are conducive to the development of self-discipline; through identification with the therapist and the values he personifies, the child achieves greater powers of self-regulation and self-command.

## The Techniques of Limit-Setting

Both in therapy and in life, children need a clear definition of acceptable and unacceptable behavior. They feel safer when they know the boundaries of permissible action. Therefore, limits should be delineated in a manner that leaves no doubt in the child's mind as to what constitutes unacceptable conduct in the playroom. It is preferable that limits be total rather than conditional There is a clear distinction, for instance, between splashing and not splashing water on the therapist. However, a limit that states, "you may splash me as long as you don't wet me too much," is inviting a deluge of trouble. Such a vague statement leaves the child without a clear criterion for making decisions.

Limits should be stated in a friendly but firm manner. Children do not readily accept restrictions invoked with a halting and hesitant mien. When presented clumsily, limits may become a challenge to children, evoking a battle of wills and focusing therapy on restrictions rather than relationships.

Limits must be presented in a manner that minimizes the arousal of resentment in the children. The very process of limit-setting should convey a spirit of nonpunitive and helpful authority. There are different ways of phrasing specific limits. At times the following four-step sequence may prove helpful: (1) The therapist recognizes the child's feelings or wishes and helps him to express them as they are. (2) He states clearly the limit on a specific act. (3) He points out other channels through which the feelings or wishes can be expressed. (4) He helps the child bring out feelings of resentment that are bound to arise when restrictions are invoked.

This approach is illustrated in the following play therapy sequence: Johnny, age nine, wanted very much to take a gun home and made his desire known.

*Johnny:* I'm going to take this gun with me.

*Therapist:* It's easy to see, Johnny, that you like the gun and would like to take it home.

*Johnny:* Yes, I would. Can I?

*Therapist:* The rule of the playroom is that all the toys have to stay in here. But you may have the gun whenever you come to the playroom.

*Johnny:* I don't like the rule.

*Therapist:* You wish there weren't such a rule.

*Johnny:* I wish the rule was that you can take all the toys home.

*Therapist:* Such a rule you would really like?

*Johnny* (Smiling): Yeah, but then you wouldn't have a playroom.

It is not always necessary or feasible to phrase the limit in the above pattern. At times it is more effective to state the limit first and reflect feelings later. When a child is about to fire a dart gun or throw a block at him, the therapist might say — and he had better speak quickly — "Not at me — at the toys." He will do well to point to the toys in order to distract the child from himself. He might then reflect the child's wish to shoot at him and perhaps suggest to the child some harmless ways of expressing anger; e.g., "You may draw my face on the blackboard and shoot at it, or you may write my name on Bobo and punch it."

Limits should be phrased in a language that does not constitute a challenge to a child's self-respect. Limits are heeded better when stated succinctly and impersonally. "Time is up for today," is more readily accepted than, "Your time is up and you must leave now." "No shooting at each other," is obeyed more willingly than, "You must not shoot at Johnny." Whenever possible, limits should be stated in the passive rather than the active. "Walls are not for painting," is accepted with less resistance than, "You must not paint the walls," "Toys are not for breaking," is better received than, "You may not break toys."

At times limits may be set nonverbally. When a child "plays" the xylophone with a hammer, the therapist may hand him drumsticks and take away the hammer. This can be accomplished without a word, just with a smile. The child may not even be aware that a limit has been invoked. The therapist may even be thanked for providing the appropriate tools.

## Situational Limits

The materials and toys as well as the physical setting of the playroom should be so planned that they exert a "limiting" influence on children. Undesirable behavior can be prevented by removing in advance objects used for inappropriate acting out. Sharp or pointed toys should be taken out of the playroom before a session with aggressive children. Fingerpaint should not be given to overactive children; it overstimulates them and invites smearing of each other and the walls. Toys should be sturdy and hard to break. Windows, lights, and one-way vision glass should be protected with wire mesh. Floors must be water-proofed and walls readily repaintable. Office desks with stuffed drawers, overdecorated chairs, telephones, and personal books have no place in a playroom; their protection necessitates the setting of too many limits and interferes with the therapist's ability to maintain "free-floating attention."

It is advisable that the playroom be sound-proofed and isolated from clinic offices so that play therapy will not interfere with the other activities of the agency.

## Limits Conducive to Effective Therapy

*A time limit.*

A time limit is always necessary in child therapy. A play therapy session usually lasts 50 minutes. The therapist tells the child of the time limit and toward the end of the session reminds him that he has only a few minutes left to play. The therapist will say, "There are only five minutes more before time is up." He may also give the child a one-minute reminder. At the end of the hour the therapist will get up and say, "Time is up for today." With young children he may add, "Now we go out." The therapist should adhere to the time limit consistently. He should not prolong the session even if the child brings out "significant material." The child gains security from the predictability of the therapy hour.

*Toys may not be taken out of the playroom.*

Sooner or later children want to take toys home. They may want to borrow, exchange, or buy playroom toys. A limit should be set stating that "all the toys must stay in the playroom." Toys may not be taken home or to the waiting room or to the bathroom. If the child wants to show a specific toy to his mother, he may invite her to see it in the playroom. However, children are allowed to take home any painting or clay sculpture made by them during the session. The limit on taking toys home pertains also to broken toys. They too may not be removed from the playroom by the child. The reason is obvious: too many toys would be broken for the purpose of taking them home. What is the rationale for not allowing children to take toys home? Besides obvious budgetary considerations, there is a therapeutic reason for not giving toys to patients: the relationship between therapist and child should be based on emotional, not material sharing.

*Breakage.*

Children are not permitted to break room equipment or expensive toys. They may not pierce the rubber clown with a sharp instrument. They may not break the window or throw sand in the air conditioner.

Their wish will be recognized but a limit invoked. The therapist may say, for example, "You would like to cut Bobo to pieces but he is not for breaking. He is for punching," or "The air conditioner is not part of the play material. It is part of the equipment of the room."

*Physical attacks upon the therapist.*

Child therapy literature shows general consent about the necessity of prohibiting physical attacks on the therapist. Both analytic and client-centered therapists do not believe that physical attacks are helpful either to the therapist or to the child. The rationale for this prohibition is as follows: (a) It assures the physical safety of the therapists: As Dorfman (1951, p. 258) puts it, "It saves wear and tear on fragile therapists." (b) It saves the child from guilt, anxiety, and the fear of retaliation. (c) It allows the therapist to remain emotionally accepting of the child.

Some therapists (Slavson, 1952, p. 294) allow young children of preschool age to attack them physically. They interpret to the children the reason for the attack. Other therapists modify this limit to state, "You may hit me a little, but you can't really hurt me."

The writer believes that the limit against hitting the therapist should not be modified under any circumstances. There can be little therapeutic value in permitting a child to attack an adult. Effective therapy must be based on mutual respect between the child and therapist, with the therapist never abdicating his adult role. Allowing a child to dominate the relationship arouses too many insoluble problems both for the therapist and the child, and it anchors therapy outside the world of reality. Telling a child that he may "hit but not hurt" the therapist is asking him to make a too fine distinction. Such a vague limit does not contribute to the security of the child or the peace of mind of the therapist. The child is irresistibly challenged to test out the prohibition and establish the "just noticeable difference" between hitting playfully and hurting seriously.

*Physical attacks among children.*

While most therapists agree that physical aggression toward the therapist must be prohibited, there are conflicting theories regarding the value of setting limits on physical attacks among children. Despart (1945, p. 223) believes that children, especially young ones, should be allowed to fight in the playroom. According to her, symbolic acting out through toys provides children "only a limited means of release." The prohibition of physical attacks may seem to the child as "equivalent to censorship — the type of which is often the basis of his own problems."

Slavson (1943), on the other hand, believes that children, especially young ones, need external restraint when they are overaggressive. "Unless the children are checked by someone outside themselves their aggression gains momentum and increases in intensity" (p.160).

Some therapists allow aggressive fights but keep them under control by serving as referee. Axline (1947) is against this practice because "It tends to involve the therapist in a role that calls for assumption of authority and judgment which might at times appear as partiality to a certain member or members of the group" (p. 137). Axline believes that "the ruling out of physical attacks should be one of the limitations of group therapy" (p. 137).

In the opinion of the writer, there is little healing benefit in allowing children to attack each other physically. Besides the obvious danger of serious injury, such attacks merely serve to displace aggression from original sibling to substitute sibling. It is more therapeutic to channel aggressive impulses through symbolic actions against inflated clowns and family dolls and into rivalrous target-shooting and other sublimatory competitive games.

## When Should Limits be Presented?

There are conflicting opinions regarding the optimal time of introducing limits. Some therapists believe that limits should be stated at the onset of treatment because children may feel betrayed and disappointed when confronted with limits unexpectedly. That this is true of some children can be seen from the following play therapy extract.

When Eleanor, age 13, first encountered a limit, she became quite upset and voiced her disappointment openly. She said, "There isn't a place in the world without restrictions. Even this place has some. I thought that here we could do anything we wanted. Now I see that even here there is no freedom. I am disappointed because I wish there was one place in the world without any restrictions at all."

Many therapists, including the writer, are of the opinion that limits should not be mentioned before the need for them arises. There seems to be little advantage in starting therapy by invoking prohibitions on actions that may never occur. There are some disadvantages to this practice. The listing of limits may serve as a challenge to aggressive children and as catharsis-deterrent to submissive ones.

When Tommy, age 8, first entered the playroom, he was told by his therapist, "You may play with the toys any way you want to but you may not hit me or break toys." Tommy became quite upset and said, "Oh, no, sir, I'd never think of hitting you." Tommy hardly touched a toy during the next few sessions.

## When Limits are Broken

Child-therapy writers, with one or two exceptions, do not acknowledge the obvious fact that limits are sometimes broken by child patients. Few suggestions can be found in the literature for dealing with this phase of therapy. Even writers who emphasize the vital role of therapeutic limits omit specific discussion of what is to be done when a limit is broken.

In dealing with limits-breaking, Axline stresses the therapist's need to remain accepting of the child. Even when a child breaks a limit, the therapist should "stay right there with her reflection of feelings." Axline recommends that the therapist try to prevent the breaking of limits "if she can do so without engaging in a physical battle with the child."

The question is, what is to be done when the child does engage in a physical battle with the therapist? Some therapists (Bixler, 1949; Moustakas, 1953) suggest that after an initial warning, the therapist should terminate the session and put the child out of the playroom.

This writer objects to expelling a child from the playroom regardless of his transgression. Besides conveying rejection, ejecting a child is a dramatic way of telling him that he can defeat adults. This admission of failure on the part of the adult is of no benefit to the child. It may well prove to him the suspicion that he is hopeless and helpless; since he can defeat all adults, no one remains to help him. No blanket recommendation can be made on how to deal with the child's aggression, since the therapeutic reaction will depend on the meaning of the child's specific action. Some aggressive children cannot accept the therapist and his friendly overtures because they have never recognized or accepted any external authority. These children may need an experience of submission to an adult who is firm, just and strong.

When Joel, age 9, insisted on throwing a chair at the therapist in spite of verbalized limits and reflected feelings, the therapist got up and said calmly, "I am bigger and stronger than you." The boy put down the chair and started cursing the therapist, who helped him verbalize his choking anger.

It must be added that this method of limiting aggression should be applied only in specific cases when other means have failed to achieve results. However, when a child has a false sense of omnipotence, expressed in neurotic defiance, submission to the authority of an adult may be clinically indicated and may prove helpful.

Another method used successfully by some therapists is to transfer a very defiant child from individual therapy to group therapy. An aggressive child who insists on attacking the therapist and on breaking limits may be put in a group of older children. Usually, instead of continuing his defiance, such a child will seek the therapist's friendship as a protection against the actual or anticipated aggression of the other children. The older groupmates frequently are able to convey more directly and more potently than the therapist that limits must be observed. The following play therapy sequence from an article by the author (Ginott, 1958, p. 416) will serve as an illustration.

Nine-year-old George resented bitterly the few limitations set in the playroom as part of therapy. He claimed to be "superman" and seemed intent on destroying the toys, damaging the room, and attacking the therapist. When George was transferred from individual therapy into a group of older boys, he tried to continue his aggressive pattern, in the group, "superman" George met some rival "supermen."

When George threw a wooden block at ten-year-old David, the boy looked at him with surprise and in a very convincing voice, he echoed one of the playroom limitations. "This is not for throwing," he said, "only rubber toys are for throwing." When George deliberately shot a dart in his face, David became angry. He took hold of George, shook him, and said, "Look, the playroom is for playing, not for hurting. This is the law in here."

"I'm above the law," said George, "I'm superman." "Shake," said David, extending his hand, "I'm superman too." "I'm super-superman," answered George. "And I'm super, super, superman," retorted David. The boys burst out in a loud laughter. The therapist said, "Both of you are supermen and above the law?" "No," answered George, "nobody here is superman and nobody is above the law."

## A Different View on Limits

Dorfman (1951, p. 262) reports that a number of client-centered therapists use only one criterion for therapeutic intervention: They only limit activities that interfere with their ability to remain emotionally accepting of the child. Some of these therapists allow the child almost complete control over the therapy situation: The children may paint the therapist's face, take toys home, urinate on the floor, leave the playroom at will, miss sessions, or terminate treatment.

Again it must be stated that thus far there have been no published research studies on the comparative effectiveness of different practices of limit-setting. As therapists with different rationales and orientations report the result of the experimentations, the more fruitful treatment technique will become evident.

## Summary

This article proposes a rationale for the use of limits in child-centered play therapy, discusses various limits conducive to effective therapy, and suggests several techniques of limit-setting as well as methods of dealing with limit-breaking.

**References**

Axline, Virginia M., *Play Therapy*, Boston: Houghton Mifflin, 1947.

Bixler, R. H., "Limits Are Therapy," *Journal of Consulting Psychology*. 1949, 13, 1–11.

Despert, J. Louise, "Play Analysis in N.D.C.," Nolan & B. L. Parcella (eds.), *Modern Trends in Child Psychology*. New York: International Press, 1945.

Dorfman, Elaine, "Play Therapy," in C. R. Rogers (ed.), *Client-centered therapy*. Boston: Houghton Mifflin, 1951, pp. 235–277.

Ginott, H. G., "Play-group Therapy: A Theoretical Framework," *International Journal of Group Psychotherapy.*, 1958, 8, 410–418.

Hamilton, G., *Psychotherapy in Child Guidance*. New York: Columbia University Press, 1947.

Moustakas, C. E., *Children in Play Therapy*. New York: McGraw-Hill, 1953.

Rosenthal, L., "Child Guidance," in S. R. Slavson (ed.). *The Fields of Group Psychotherapy*. New York: International Universities Press, 1956, pp. 215–232.

Schiffer, M., "Permissiveness Versus Sanction in Activity Group Therapy," *International Journal of Group Psychotherapy*, 1952, 2, 255–261.

Slavson, S. R., *An Introduction to Group Therapy*, New York: Commonwealth Fund, 1943.

Slavson, S. R., *Child Psychotherapy*, New York: Columbia University Press, 1952.

# BEHAVIORAL

# Behavioral Therapy with Children

SALVATORE RUSSO

Behavioral therapy is one of the most promising developments in the treatment of children's problems. It can be used best in a residential setting where we can control many of the conditions for learning, whether the therapy consists mostly of building up adequate patterns of behavior by the use of reinforcement, or the extinction of undesirable behavior. Many of the emotional problems of children are periodic, like enuresis, encopresis, anorexia, stealing, truancy, and school phobia, and do not often appear in the child's short weekly visit at a Child Guidance Center. For this reason they cannot be worked on directly, although there are reports of problems in insect phobia (Eysenck and Rachman, 1963) and school phobia (Talbot, 1957), and other periodic behavior treated successfully in outpatient clinics. Behavior symptoms that are continually present, like hyperactivity, tics, shyness, are likely to be manifested at the clinic as well as in school and home, and hence give the therapist a direct opportunity to apply some form of conditioning to them. Since most of the children do not have an opportunity to enter a hospital for their emotional disturbances, some clinics rely on parents and teachers to conduct much of the therapy. It is true that there are many child guidance clinics that use an oblique approach and never address themselves directly to the symptoms. They expect to get results by treating the whole personality or improving the self-concept of the patient or strengthening his ego, and rely on this progress to enable the child to solve the problems that brought him to the clinic.

## Relevance to Child Guidance Clinics

There is a great need for the clinics that try to treat children's problems directly by operant learning to develop techniques that will aid the parents and teachers who are called upon to carry out much of the behavioral therapy that is planned and initiated in the clinics. Some recent experiments in therapy have been reported where the parents carried out at home the conditioning formulated for the child (White, 1957; Williams, 1959; and Lovibond, 1963), but little has been said about the training and supervision that the parents received for this work. The purpose of this paper is to report on two experiments in a conventional child guidance clinic to teach this type of activity to the parents.

Many of the problems referred to the clinics turn on the inability of a parent and child to get along. The traditional way of handling this situation is to see them individually, the child for diagnostic study and then perhaps play therapy, and the parent for counseling or therapy. This is an educational process for parent and child and each learns more about his thoughts, feelings, and modes of action. But it is left to the members of the family to apply this knowledge and skill at home and to learn to adjust to each other. They must put into practice together what they have learned separately at the clinic.

Many parents have complained that this is difficult to achieve. What they need is not only supervision from a distance, but actual experience under direct supervision. They need practice in doing at the clinic what they must implement at home. As one mother said, "I can always see what I should have done at home when I am talking to you about it here, but I need you in my kitchen when the incident is taking place." She was right. There is a difference between theory and practice and between a predicament and a problem. Discussing the situation in the office in retrospect is a verbal solution. In a predicament, one is called upon to do something about it immediately; the solution is concrete and in terms of some type of action. One can be looked upon as a dramatic crisis in life, the other more as an office discussion, however pertinent it may be.

## New Direction

Because of this difference between theory and practice and knowledge and action, we experimented with a new method — one in which both the parents and child got experience, under supervision, in behaving in the clinic the way they were expected to behave at home.* After some preliminary discussion as to our aims and methods, we took both child and parent to a playroom. During the early sessions the parent

* The experiments described in this paper were both conducted at the Wichita Guidance Center, Wichita, Kansas.

was a spectator and observed what the child and the therapist did. Soon the parent began to take part in the activity, and it became a three-way interaction. When this process was well underway, the therapist began to withdraw from the action until he became the spectator and parent and child were left to interact with each other. Only in unusual incidents did the therapist take a hand in the activities.

After each session the therapist had a conference with the parent. The first part of the discussion was devoted to playroom activity, what the feelings and actions meant, and how best to handle them in the future. The second part of the conference dealt with the activities at home and school that seemed relevant and important. This method gives parent and child practice and experience in doing the very things they came to learn to do, and has proved quite effective.

## Treatment of Sarah

The treatment of Sarah, aged six, is an example of this type of therapy. Sarah's parents brought her to the clinic because their relationship was so poor and Sarah's actions so annoying and frustrating that the mother abstained from punishing her for fear of losing her temper and harming the youngster.

Sarah had been a problem child since infancy, holding her breath and having temper tantrums. She usually battled with the older siblings, invaded their rooms, destroyed their toys, ground her teeth almost to the gums, and wet the bed. She resented her mother's attention to the other members of the family. At other times, especially with strangers, she wore a foolish embarrassed grin, was mute and resistive, and wouldn't talk about herself or her activities. At school Sarah behaved ideally. She got along well with the other children, did her work conscientiously, obeyed the teacher and showed considerable respect and affection for her.

Since she was an ideal child at school and misbehaved only at home and in the immediate neighborhood, it was obvious that the problem was related to the family constellation and its transactions with the child. Apparently her "antics" had been considered "cute" and were a cause of merriment until she became so big and strong that she was harming her sisters and becoming difficult to handle. Attempts to discipline Sarah had failed; she may have continued in her ways because of the discomfort it caused both the siblings and parents.

Sarah's mother was a competent woman. She got along well with her husband and the other children and was considered a good homemaker, had an adequate social life, and took responsibility in church activities, school affairs, and Girl Scouts.

During the early therapy sessions, Sarah was negativistic and aggressive toward her mother. The mother was reluctant to interact at first with her daughter and seemed at a loss in responding to her behavior, which was usually bossy, stormy and assaultive. Each displayed antagonism to the other in different ways.

The treatment was an example of simple reinforcement of desired behavior and the extinction of undesired behavior by lack of reinforcement. Sarah's violent outbursts, rudeness, loudness, and assaultiveness had been tolerated at home. Now the parent neither condemned nor punished her for this. Sarah became aware that the undesirable conduct did not produce any noticeable responses. Her cooperation, sociability, and friendly conduct, on the other hand, were noted verbally and encouraged by overt behavior such as joining in the activity and displaying pleasure.

At first she seemed perplexed, became angry, cried, hid, and lashed at her parent when her behavior didn't seem to have its former effect. Eventually, the maladjusted behavior appeared less frequently as it failed to provoke parental attention; the desired behavior appeared more often because it was rewarded. On various occasions Sarah resorted to her old tricks in order to attract attention, but when they continually failed, she gave them up altogether. She had learned that she could get attention and approval only by desirable behavior.

At home the parents had difficulty at first in following this plan to treat their daughter, for they thought it was contrary to "common sense." They had believed good behavior should always be rewarded, bad behavior always punished, and they didn't realize that they had unwittingly helped perpetuate her antisocial behavior by using verbal labels, punishing, and showing their disapproval, thus making it evident that she upset and annoyed them. Because it was contrary to "common sense," they needed continual practice in behaving in the therapeutic way until it became natural to them. At this point they were co-therapists.

The case was closed after nine months of therapy. Sarah had lost most of her disturbing behavior and had become cooperative, amenable, and happy. Home life had improved considerably and the parents felt that they were now able to get along with the girl at home without further help. Perhaps one should mention that the father came to therapy with his daughter about a third of the time and that all of the sisters at different times had come to the playroom to interact with Sarah.

The direct form of therapy which seems ideal for families where communication and rapport are poor may also be suitable for more disturbed cases where there are many kinds of problems present at the same time. The following is another complicated case.

## Treating a Boy with Multiple Problems

Mike was a pale, slender boy of eight whose speech was so fast and explosive that at times it was unintelligible. He was hyperactive, restless, impulsive, impatient, and anxious, with a marked facial tic. He was very bright but an underachiever at school.

He was referred to the clinic primarily because of his poor adjustment at home. He was abusive to his three sisters: he pushed one off a swing, another into the deep end of the pool, and the third off a bicycle. He was cruel to animals and did considerable damage around the house. Physicians were convinced that he suffered from brain damage. A psychologist had characterized him as an obsessive compulsive, and a psychiatrist had diagnosed him as "Borderline Ego State" with psychotic features.

Our plan consisted of seeing mother and son together in the office for fifteen minutes to discuss his behavior at home during the past week. Then they were seen together in operant play therapy for forty-five minutes, and finally a thirty-minute conference was held with the mother while Mike waited in the reception room.

The mother was a resourceful and energetic woman who immediately participated in play and was soon able to handle the play sessions without help. The therapist stood by and watched, on occasion joined in play when asked, and even left the playroom at times. When Mike played in an approved manner, his mother enthusiastically participated in the activity. When he broke the rules, she ignored him as planned, smoked a cigarette, turned her back on him and engaged the therapist in conversation, played a game with the therapist, or started a project of her own. Thus only socially approved conduct was reinforced. This brought on violent language, criticism, and stormy sessions; but eventually he learned to behave to get his mother's company and approval. Occasionally the therapist commented on activity in progress and, reminiscent of the Greek Chorus, reflected the meaning of the play activity.

In the playroom Mike tried to cheat, change the rules at will, deny his former agreements, test the limits in various ways, and manipulate his mother so that she would be like a servant doing his bidding. He always wanted to have his way and choose his own game or activity. This was very much like his behavior at home. In time this dramatic behavior subsided, and he was able to play cooperatively for long periods of time. He looked upon his mother more as a companion than as a parent, called her a pal, and seemed to enjoy the sessions thoroughly.

During some of the sessions the father came in place of the mother and the same regime was used. On various occasions the sisters were brought into the playroom one at a time. It was apparent that the girls looked upon themselves as the chosen children and on Mike as the black sheep of the family. Their provoking attitude contributed to his misbehavior in the playroom just as it must have done at home.

After twenty sessions therapy was terminated because the therapist was leaving the clinic. Mike was considered much improved. His hostility had lessened considerably, and was expressed in more socially acceptable ways. Even his teasing had become more benevolent. He had become more relaxed at home, expressed his feelings with moderation, and took better care of his person and property. He had even improved in school despite the fact that he had a very unsympathetic teacher.

The parents, too, had become more emotionally relaxed. Because of the diagnosis of brain damage, they had been tense and anxious and not able to take a firm stand or to enforce discipline. They were quite relieved when we stated that most of Mike's trouble was psychological and the result of faulty learning. His trick of turning deathly pale when threatened with punishment was a learned device rather than a symptom of encephalopathy and disappeared in time as we had predicted. In light of the substantial progress made, it is likely that if therapy could have been continued, Mike would have unlearned most of his faults and become a very acceptable boy.

## Conclusions

Since one cannot reproduce the precise control of variables in the clinic that one can in the animal laboratory, one must acknowledge that there are many other factors at work beside operant behavior, just as there are with any type of therapy in an outpatient clinic. This method of therapy differs from the other types in two ways: (1) the operant conditioning constitutes the main technique used, and (2) the parents carry out most of the conditioning necessary for therapy.

These two cases are cited to illustrate that in behavioral therapy in its strict sense or in approximations of it, parents and teachers are needed to carry out the conditions the therapist instigates, and some direct experience or training is useful to prepare them for the task.

**References**

Eysenck, H. J. and Rachman, S., *The Application of Learning Theory in Child Psychiatry* (in press).

Lovibond, S. H., The mechanism of conditioning treatment of enuresis. *Behaviour Research and Therapy*, 1, 17-21, 1963.

Talbot, M., "Panic in School Phobia," *American Journal of Orthopsychiatry*, 27, 286-295, 1957.

White, J. G. "The Use of Learning Theory in the Psychological Treatment of Children, *Journal of Clinical Psychology*, 15, 229-233, 1957.

Williams, C. D., "The Elimination of Tantrum Behaviour by Extinction Procedures: Case Report," *Journal of Abnormal (Social) Psychology*, 59, 269, 1959.

# Treatment with Child and Mother in the Playroom

JAMES H. STRAUGHAN

## Introduction

The growing list of published successes in the applications of learning theory to child therapy (*e.g.*, Patterson, 1973; Rachman, 1962) illustrate the principle that specific treatments based on known principles and specific problems are likely to be more effective than nonspecific treatment programs. Although it is true that treatment of only the parents (*e.g.*, MacNamara, 1963), the entire family (Bell, 1961), or only the child (Blanchard, 1946) may produce beneficial results, there is no good theoretical reason why one particular approach should be used on all problems. The recognition that the family constitutes the most important part of the environment of the child (Watson, 1928; Guthrie, 1938; Ackerman, 1959) does not dictate one treatment method to the exclusion of others. Effective treatment should be designed for whatever problems are recognized and should involve family members in ways that will ameliorate those problems.

## Counterconditioning Anxiety

The treatment in the case to be reported is not completely new (*e.g.*, Prince, 1961) but illustrates the use of a relatively specific playroom technique for a limited range of problems. For reasons that we did not explore, the patient's mother had developed the habit of reacting with anxiety and tension to the patient and of putting demands upon her that in turn elicited tension and anxiety on the patient's part. As far as we could tell during interviews with the mother, the behavior of the father towards the patient was not disturbed. For this reason we saw no reason to see the father in treatment but instead decided to concentrate upon the reactions of the mother and child to each other.

By carefully introducing the mother into the playroom where the child was being seen, we intended that each would learn to be more comfortable in the presence of the other. As we planned it, the process would be analogous to, or perhaps identical with, counterconditioning (Wolpe, 1958). The first step would be the encouragement of the patient's free, spontaneous play with as few rules as possible. During this time the mother would become accustomed to the situation by observation of the playroom activities and discussion with a second therapist. As soon as it seemed appropriate, we would bring the mother into the playroom, for brief periods at first, and encourage her to prompt the child's spontaneous play. We planned to terminate treatment after eight sessions at the most on the assumption that the mother would learn some skills that would generalize to the home.

## Case History

The patient, the eight-year-old daughter of middle-class parents in an urban community, was first brought to the Clinic at the suggestion of school authorities. The initial complaint was that the patient was telling tall tales and outright lies at school and home. There was no evidence of abnormal maturation.

The patient's teachers reported that she had done very well at school and that her work was neat, complete, and very accurate. However, her teacher was concerned not only by the lying episodes but also that the patient had no friends in her school room. The patient's mother reported that a friend of hers, when asked for an opinion, had said that the patient was under too much pressure at home. This friend said that the patient was told to do too many things and given her choice too seldom. The patient's mother said that this was the way she ran her household. At home the patient might mutter or mumble defiance but would continue doing what she was told.

By the time the patient was brought to the Clinic for assessment and treatment, the lying had almost stopped. The patient's mother said that she was still concerned because she had become aware that the patient was not as happy as she should be. Detailed inquiries were made about family discipline. It was learned that the mother usually took the lead in disciplining the children, particularly towards the end of the day when she became irritable. She saw herself as being too hard on the patient and had tried to be more lenient, but found it very difficult.

Doll materials were used in order to evaluate the patient's attitudes towards both school and home. In doll play, which was structured by the therapist to involve a dispute between a parent doll and a little girl doll, the patient took the role of an obedient, submissive little girl. In doll play with a school situation, the patient had her doll choose to go to the library and read rather than go out and play with the other children. These and other indications suggested to us that the patient was not a severely disturbed little girl but that she had learned to inhibit much of the free, spontaneous emotional expression appropriate to a child of eight. Instead she showed an unusual concern with accuracy, neatness, and adult approval. We also learned that she could quickly relax and play boisterously in the playroom.

## Treatment Procedures

The treatment was carried out during five play sessions with the patient. One therapist took the child to the playroom with instructions to adapt himself to what she did in order to keep her as relaxed and happy as possible. A second therapist talked with the mother and explained that the general procedures would be much as we have outlined them above. The major rationale given to the mother was that it should prove useful to know some of the procedures that a therapist used in working with a child. After the explanation to the mother, she and the second therapist went to the observation room to watch what occurred in the playroom. The fact that this observation would occur was explained to the patient and the observation room was shown to her. The knowledge that she was being watched did not seem to inhibit the child after she had returned to the playroom. In each future session the mother and second therapist made it a point to always let the child and her therapist know whenever they entered the observation room.

In the observation room the second therapist explained to the mother that in working with disturbed children it was important to keep the rules as simple as possible and to always explain the reasons for them honestly. When it appeared that the patient was playing happily and enthusiastically in the playroom, they knocked on the playroom door and explained that they would like to sit in and watch for a few minutes. The mother sat quietly to one side and did not say anything during this first time in the playroom. The two therapists talked with each other and with the child, ignoring the presence of the mother. After a very few minutes, the mother was again taken to the observation room where she and the second therapist watched the play. The mother said that she was impressed by the child's liveliness and enthusiasm in playing. Reasons for the child's greater spontaneity with therapist and the objectives of treatment with the child were discussed. It was pointed out that one of the objectives of play therapy was to find out what things bothered the child and to help her with these. A useful technique was to notice the problems as they arose in play, make guesses at their meaning in the child's life, and then discuss them without necessarily expecting the child to participate in the discussion. If something important was hit upon, the reaction of the child often showed this was so.

During the second session the procedure was repeated with the length of time that the mother spent in the playroom increased. It became noticeable that the patient was somewhat more subdued when her mother was in the room, although she still played well. This was pointed out to the mother while in the observation room and the reasons for it discussed.

During the third session, while the mother and one therapist were observing, the patient became very exuberant. The necessity of limits were discussed with the mother, not only for the sake of the child but for the sake of the adult in the situation. It was pointed out that these limits might vary depending upon the child's needs and upon what the therapist would or could accept but that honest explanations for the limits should always be given.

During the fourth session, the mother stayed in the playroom during most of the session. The patient was somewhat more subdued at first, but became more relaxed as the hour went on. An effort was made to involve the mother in the play by having the therapist remain passive while encouraging the mother to respond to the child's leads. When the mother attempted to encourage the child to perform better, the child became frustrated and turned to something else. The therapist pointed out to both of them what had happened and what the effects had been. The therapist took a more active role until the child was playing happily again.

The fifth session was also spent with the mother in the playroom during most of the hour. Again an effort was made to keep the child as relaxed and free as possible while encouraging the mother to participate naturally in the play. The effects and meaning of various interactions between them were discussed with the intent of making the effects of each upon the other as positive as possible.

## Evaluating Progress

By the end of the fourth session the mother was saying that things were going much better with the patient both at home and at school where one of the patient's teachers reported that her behavior had improved. The patient's unwillingness and inability to get along with other children had abated to a considerable extent. Since the mother was satisfied that things were going well, it was decided to discontinue treatment. A fifth session was held one week later to make sure both mother and therapist were satisfied.

In a follow-up conversation with the mother eight months later, she said that the gains had continued. What she remembered as impressing her most at the Clinic was how much freer her child was there than at home. She said that she had learned that her child had been definitely under too much pressure at home and under too much control for a child her age. Before treatment there had been nothing that the patient could do that would really please her mother. She said that she felt that the child was much better adjusted at home and that the last report from school showed that the teacher was pleased at the change. The patient had become much more relaxed at school and had made several close friends.

## Discussion

The procedure used in the treatment of this patient is certainly complex and allows for the operation of many variables. It is reasonable to suppose that direct, immediate conditioning is only one of the many factors operating. To us it seemed more likely that the child's relaxed and exuberant behavior became associated with the stimulus of the mother than that the mother became more relaxed with the child. According to the mother's report at the time and later, a very important part of the procedure was the effect of seeing the child in a relaxed, happy mood. We interpret this to mean that the mother would be better able to judge the effects of her own actions on the child and that the child's actions would act as a discriminative stimulus for the mother. Other effects probably involved imitation learning and direct teaching. The mother observed the therapist with the child during several sessions and discussed procedures with a second therapist at length. Finally, there was the effect upon the child of being brought to the Clinic. For a while the child knew that she was the center of the mother's concern without the competition of siblings.

The therapists involved with this case considered the possibility of simply teaching the mother not to do certain inappropriate things with the child. Although a comparison between these two approaches (inhibiting the mother's inappropriate behavior vs. encouraging the child's and mother's appropriate behavior) remains to be empirically presented, it seemed to us on theoretical grounds that the positive course offered more promise. Luria (1961) presents evidence showing (with children at least) that the paradigm for an inhibitory response is an overt motor response. The encouragement of a new, positive response on the part of the mother would not only be directly effective with the child but inhibitory of inappropriate responses. To merely seek to inhibit the mother's inappropriate behavior would leave the nature of subsequent behavior unsettled. We suspect that on the one occasion when we did point out to the mother that some of her playroom behavior was inappropriate, we were ineffective. The mother does not mention this incident in describing what was most helpful in the procedure. We believe that such inappropriate behavior tended to become less flagrant as the mother learned to do other things more often.

It may be useful to speculate about the conditions in which this procedure of introducing the mother into the playroom might be advantageous. First, the difficulty must primarily involve mother and child. Second, the mother must not be unduly neurotic. Third, playroom procedures must be available which will elicit the desirable behavior from the child. It seems to us that these conditions are relatively common and that, consequently, involvement of the mother in the playroom treatment offers promise in shortening some treatment.

*Acknowledgments* — The author is indebted to Robert E. Adolph of Oregon State University and Hugo Maynard of the Universtiy of Oregon for their assistance in the treatment of this patient.

**References**

Ackerman, N., *The Psychodynamics of Family Life*, New York: Basic Books, 1959.

Bell, J. E., 1961 *Family Group Therapy* (Public Health Monograph No. 64). Washington, D.C.: U.S. Government Printing Office, 1961.

Blanchard, P. "Case 1. Tommy Nolan," in *Psychiatric Interviews with Children* (ed. H. L. Witmer), New York: The Commonwealth Fund, 1946.

Guthrie, E. R. *The Psychology of Human Conflict*, Boston: Beacon Press, 1938.

Luria, A. R., *The Role of Speech in the Regulation of Normal and Abnormal Behavior*, New York: Liveright, 1961.

MacNamara, Margaret, "Helping Children Through Their Mothers," *Journal of Child Psychology & Psychiatry*, 4, 29–46, 1963.

Patterson, G. R., *A Learning Theory Approach To The Treatment of the School Phobic Child.* Unpublished manuscript, University of Oregon Psychology Clinic, 1963.

Prince, G. S., "A Clinical Approach to Parent-Child Interaction," *Journal of Child Psychology & Psychiatry* 2, 169-184, 1961.

Rachman, S., "Child Psychology and Learning Theory," *Journal of Child Psychology and Psychiatry* 3, 149-163, 1962.

Watson, J. B., *Psychological Care of Infant and Child*, New York: Norton, 1928.

Wolpe, J., *Psychotherapy by Reciprocal Inhibition*, Stanford, California: Stanford University Press, 1958.

# PART III
## Play Techniques

# Introductory Remarks

Among the play techniques and materials employed most often to date are art, clay, and drawing activities, water and sand play, dramatic play and puppet productions, free play as used by nondirective therapists, and doll play. Perhaps the most noted use of doll play is the "world picture" technique employed by Lowenfeld.* The materials consist of miniature replicas of people, animals, houses, trees, fences, bridges, etc. Water and sandtrays are provided for use with these miniature toys, and the child is directed to place the pieces as he wishes. The miniature "worlds" constructed by the child may resemble realistic models of small towns with orderly rows of houses, or they may depict a wild, fantastic scene wherein wild animals terrorize people, or they may contain no people at all. The therapist uses the content, style, and "happenings" in the child's productions to gain clues as to the degree of the child's emotional disturbance as well as the underlying dynamics.

The articles in this chapter describe the practical application of a variety of techniques and materials in the playroom. The reader will find, for example, articles discussing the therapeutic use of fingerpaints, puppets, toys, games, and stories. One of the most practical techniques for dramatic play is the storytelling technique (See articles by Gardner and Robertson and Barford). Like the other dramatic techniques, this procedure is designed to offer a "release" for pent-up emotions and to facilitate the learning of more appropriate solutions to social problems. In art therapy, drawings and paintings can be either interpreted by the

* Lowenfeld, M. "The World Picture of Children," *British Journal of Medical Psychology*, 1939, 18, 65–101.

therapist as in doll play or used as a medium for the release of underlying feelings. The article on Semantic Therapy reminds us that the science of general semantics can be applied effectively in the playroom. The many and varied techniques employed by play therapists to date reflect the richness and complexity of this exciting approach to child therapy.

Since well-stocked and spacious playrooms tend to exist more in textbooks than in clinical practice, the reader will also find in this chapter articles describing the ingenious use of suitcase playrooms, school play kits, and ordinary office equipment in play therapy. These articles leave the child therapist little excuse for neglecting play therapy due to lack of facilities or materials.

# TECHNIQUES

# Mutual Storytelling Technique

RICHARD A. GARDNER

Eliciting stories is a time-honored practice in child psychotherapy. From the stories children tell, the therapist is able to gain invaluable insights into the child's inner conflicts, frustrations, and defenses.

A child's stories are generally less difficult to analyze than dreams, free associations, and other productions of the adult. His fundamental difficulties are exhibited clearly to the therapist, without the obscurity, distortion, and misrepresentation that are characteristic of the adult's presentation. The essential problem for the child's therapist has been how to use his insights therapeutically.

The techniques described in the literature on child psychotherapy and psychoanalysis are, for the most part, attempts to solve this problem. Some are based on the assumption, borrowed from the adult psychoanalytic model, that making the unconscious conscious can itself be therapeutic. My own experience has been that few children are interested in gaining conscious awareness of their unconscious processes, let alone utilizing such insights therapeutically. Children do, however, enjoy both telling stories and listening to them. Since storytelling is one of the child's favorite modes of communication, I wondered whether communicating to him in the same mode might not be useful in child therapy. The efficacy of the storytelling approach for the imparting and transmission of values and insights is proved by the ancient and universal appeal of fable, myth, and legend.

It was from these observations and considerations that I developed the Mutual Storytelling Technique, a proposed solution to the question of how to utilize the child's stories therapeutically. In this method the child first tells a story; the therapist surmises its psychodynamic meaning and then tells one of his own. The therapist's story contains the same characters in a similar setting, but he introduces healthier adaptations and resolutions of the conflicts that have been exhibited in the child's story. Since the therapist speaks in the child's own language, he has a good chance of "being heard." One could almost say that here the therapist's interpretations bypass the conscious and are received directly by the unconscious. The child is not burdened with psychoanalytic interpretations which are alien to him. Direct, anxiety-provoking confrontations, so reminiscent of the child's experience with parents and teachers, are avoided. Lastly, the introduction of humor and drama enhances the child's interest and pleasure and therefore his receptivity. As a therapeutic tool, the method is useful in combination with traditional techniques. It is most useful for children who will tell stories but who have little interest in analyzing them. It is not a therapy per se, but rather one technique in the therapist's armamentarium.

### Basic Mechanics of the Method

Although drawings, dolls, puppets, and other toys are the modalities around which stories are traditionally told in child therapy, these often have the effect of restricting the child's storytelling or of channeling it in highly specific directions. The tape recorder does not have these disadvantages; with it, the visual field remains free from contaminating and distracting stimuli. Eliciting a story with it is like obtaining a dream on demand.

I introduce the child to the game by first pointing to a stack of tapes, each of which has a child's name clearly written on the end of the box. I tell the patient that each child who comes to my office has his own tape for a tape recording game which we play. I ask him if he would like to have a tape of his own. The child generally wants to follow usual practice, and having his own tape enhances his feeling of belonging. If he assents, I take out a new tape and let him write his name on the box.

I then ask the child if he would like to be guest of honor on a make-believe television program on which stories are told. If he agrees — and few decline the honor — the recorder is turned on and I begin:

> Good morning, boys and girls. I'd like to welcome you once again to Dr. Gardner's "Make-Up-A-Story Television Program." As you all know, we invite children to our program to see how good they are at making up stories. Naturally, the more adventure or excitement a story has, the more interesting it is to the people who are watching at their television sets. Now, it's against the rules to tell stories about things you've read or have seen in the movies or on television, or

about things that really happened to you or anyone you know.

Like all stories, your story should have a beginning, a middle, and an end. After you've made up a story, you'll tell us the moral of the story. We all know that every good story has a moral.

Then after you've told your story, Dr. Gardner will make up a story too. He'll try to tell one that's interesting and unusual, and then he'll tell the moral of his story.

And now, without further delay, let me introduce to you a boy [girl] who is with us today for the first time. Can you tell us your name, young man?

I then ask the child a series of brief questions that can be answered by single words or brief phrases such as his age, address, school grade, and teacher. These simple questions diminish the child's anxiety and tend to make him less tense about the more unstructured themes involved in "making up a story." Further diminution of anxiety is accomplished by letting him hear his own voice at this point by playback, something which most children enjoy. He is then told:

Now that we've heard a few things about you, we're all interested in hearing the story you have for us today.

At this point most children plunge right into their story, although some may feel the need for "time to think." I may offer this pause; if it is asked for by the child, it is readily granted. There are some children for whom the pause is not enough, but who nevertheless still want to try. In such instances, the child is told:

Some children, especially when it's their first time on this program, have a little trouble thinking of a story, but with some help from me they're able to do so. Most children don't realize that there are *millions* of stories in their heads they don't know about. And I know a way to help get out some of them. Would you like me to help you get out one of them?

Most children assent to this. I then continue:

Fine, here's how it works. I'll start the story and when I point my finger at you, you say exactly what comes into your mind at that time. You'll then see how easy it is to make up a story. Okay. Let's start. Once upon a time —— a long, long time ago —— in a distant land —— far, far away —— there lived a —— .

I then point my finger, and it is a rare child who does not offer some fill-in word at this point. If the word is *dog,* for example, I then say, "And *that dog* —— " and once again point to the patient. I follow the statement provided by the child with "And then —— " or "The next thing that happened was —— ." Every statement the child makes is followed by some introductory connective and by pointing to the child to supply the next statement. That and no more — the introduction of specific phrases or words would defeat the therapist's purpose of catalyzing the youngster's production of his *own* created material and of sustaining, as needed, its continuity.

For most children, this approach is sufficient to get them over whatever hurdles there are for them in telling a story. If this is not enough, however, it is best to drop this activity in a completely casual and non-reproachful manner, such as: "Well, today doesn't seem to be your good day for storytelling. Perhaps we'll try again some other time."

While the child is engaged in telling his story, I jot down notes, which are not only of help in analyzing the child's story, but serve also as a basis for my own. At the end of the child's story and his statement of its moral, I may ask questions about specific items in the story. The purpose here is to obtain additional details, which are often of help in understanding the story. Typical questions might be: "Was the fish in your story a man or a lady?" "Why was the fox so mad at the goat?" "Why did the bear do that?" If the child hesitates to tell the moral of his story or indicates that there is none, I usually reply: "What, a story without a moral? Every good story has *some* lesson or moral!" The moral that this comment usually does succeed in eliciting from the child is often significantly revealing of the fundamental psychodynamics of the story.

For younger children, the word "lesson" or "title" may be substituted for "moral." Or the child might be asked: "What can we learn from your story?"

Then I usually say: "That was a very good (unusual, exciting, etc.) story." Or to the child who was hesitant: "And you thought you weren't very good at telling stories!"

I then turn off the tape recorder and prepare my story. Although the child's story is generally simpler to understand than the adult's dream, the analysis of both follows similar principles. At this point, I will present only a few fundamentals of story analysis. My hope is that the reader who is inexperienced in dream and/or story analysis will, by careful reading of the numerous examples of story analysis to be presented in this book, become adept at story interpretation.

I first attempt to determine which figure or figures in the child's story represent the child himself, and which stand for significant people in his environment. It is important to appreciate that two or more figures may represent various facets of the *same* person's personality. There may, for example, be a "good dog" and a "bad cat" in the same story, which are best understood as conflicting forces within the same child. A horde of figures, all similar, may symbolize powerful elements in a single person. A hostile father, for example, may be represented by a stampede of bulls. Swarms of small creatures such as insects, worms, or mice, often symbolize unacceptable repressed complexes. Malevolent figures can represent the child's own repressed hostility projected outward, or they may be a symbolic statement about the hostility of a significant figure. Sometimes both of these mechanisms operate simultaneously. A threatening lion in one child's story stood for his hostile father, and he was made more frightening by the child's own hostility, repressed and projected onto the lion. This example illustrates one of the reasons why many children see their parents as being more malevolent than they are.

Besides clarifying the symbolic significance of each figure, it is also important to get a general overall "feel" for the atmosphere and setting of the story. Is the ambience pleasant, neutral, or horrifying? Stories that take place in the frozen tundra or on isolated space stations suggest something very different from those which occur in the child's own home. The child's emotional reactions when telling the story are also of significance in understanding its meaning. An eleven-year-old child who tells me, in an emotionless tone, about the death fall of a mountain climber reveals not only his hostility but also his repression of his feelings. The atypical must be separated from the stereotyped, age-appropriate elements in the story. The former may be very revealing, whereas the latter rarely are. Battles between cowboys and Indians rarely give meaningful data, but when the chief sacrifices his son to Indian gods in a prayer for victory over the white man, something has been learned about the child's relationship with his father.

Lastly, the story may lend itself to a number of different psychodynamic interpretations. In selecting the theme that will be most pertinent for the child *at that particular time,* I am greatly assisted by the child's own "moral" or "title."

After asking myself, "What would be a healthier resolution or a more mature adaptation than the one used by the child?" I create a story of my own. My story involves the same characters, setting, and initial situation as the child's story, but it has a more appropriate or salutary resolution of the most important conflicts. In creating my story, I attempt to provide the child with more *alternatives.* The communication that the child need not be enslaved by his neurotic behavior patterns is vital. Therapy must open new avenues not considered in the child's scheme of things. It must help the child become aware of the multiplicity of options which are available to replace the narrow self-defeating ones he has chosen. My moral or morals are an attempt to emphasize further the healthier adaptations I have included in my story. If, while I am telling my story, the child exhibits deep interest, or if he reveals marked anxiety, which may manifest itself by jitteriness or hyperactivity, then I know that my story is "hitting home." Such clear-cut indications of how relevant one's story is are not, of course, always forthcoming.

After the moral to my story, I stop the recorder and ask the child whether he would like to hear the recorded program. In my experience, the child is interested in doing so about one-third of the time. Playing the program makes possible a second exposure to the messages that the therapist wishes to impart. If the child is not interested in listening to the tape, then we engage in other therapeutic activities.

The therapist's attitude has a subtle, but nevertheless significant, influence on the child's ability to tell a story. Ideally this attitude should be one of pleasurable anticipation that a story will be forthcoming and surprised disappointment when the child will not or cannot tell one. The child wants to be accepted by those who are meaningful to him, and if a productive therapeutic relationship has been established, he will try to comply with what is expected of him.

Peer group influence is also important. When the child gets the general feeling that storytelling is what everybody does when he visits the therapist, he is more likely to play the game. Seeing a stack of tapes — with each child's first name prominently displayed — tends to foster his desire to tell stories "just like the other kids do." In my typical session, the mother and child are seen together for a few minutes. The mother then leaves, and the child and I start our time together with the storytelling game. The rest of the session is devoted to other therapeutic activities — most often initiated by the child. In this way, there is a pattern set down which both of us routinely follow. It is a *matter of course* that we proceed to the tape recorder (which is conspicuously placed in my play area) as soon as the child's mother leaves. If the child is disinclined to play the game he must break an expected pattern. Since this is hard for most children to do, he generally goes along with the game and finds it not only less anxiety-provoking than he had anticipated, but pleasurable as well.

### Case Illustration

Tony, a ten-year-old boy with divorced parents was brought to me because of poor school performance and hostile outbursts. His father lived in another part of the country and had little genuine interest in him, whereas his mother was more involved in dating than in spending time with her children. In the first session Tony told this story:

> There was two boys and one girl and a mother and a father, and they went out in a car about five miles out of town, and they ran out of gas in the middle of the night. And they waited there for about an hour or two and then the man said, "I'm going to go back to town and get some more gas," and he walked back. He told the other people to go to sleep and after they went to sleep the sister woke up and she heard a scratching noise on the top of the roof and then she wondered what it was and she went back to sleep. And when she woke up and she heard it again. And a police was next to the car. And the police said, "Will you please get out and walk," and she got out and walked. They said: "Whatever you do, don't look back." She kept on walking and walking and walking.

*Therapist:* Where was the rest of the family?

*Patient:* They were still asleep. And when she got about one-half mile, she just had to look back and when she looked back she saw that the noise that was scratching on the roof was the biggest brother hanging on a tree with his bloody fingernails scratching on top of the roof.

*Therapist:* So the big brother was hanging from a tree? Was he dead?

*Patient:* Yes.

*Therapist:* Upside down? I see, and his bloody fingernails were scratching on the roof. Is that the whole story?

*Patient:* Uh-huh.

*Therapist:* Who killed him?

*Patient:* That's supposed to be the mystery of the story.

*Therapist:* Uh-huh.

*Patient:* But I could make somebody up.

*Therapist:* Do that.

*Patient:* This monster and he had a big hook on his hand. There was nothing on that hand except the hook and he just takes the hook and he picked him up and he rammed it through his stomach and he took his shirt and he hanged it, and he took a rope and he hanged his feet from a tree. And then he jabbed a knife in his stomach and let him hang.

*Therapist:* I see. Now what about the cop? Where does he fit into all of this?

*Patient:* All he was doing was just telling her to get out of the car.

*Therapist:* Why did he tell her to walk away?

*Patient:* He was afraid that she would get hanged because of the man with the hook.

*Therapist:* So he was trying to protect her. What about the other people in the car? What happened to them?
*Patient:* Well, they just were sleeping, I guess. The man with the hook never saw them.
*Therapist:* What's the moral of that story —— the lesson?
*Patient:* I guess it's to get gas before you leave town. That's the first time I've ever made up the moral of that story. I just made that one up.
*Therapist:* Did you think of that story a lot?
*Patient:* Yes.

Although it was learned at the end that the story was not created *de novo* according to the rules of the television game, it is still rich in significant psychodynamic material. A repetitive fantasy is often a manifestation of powerful psychological forces, and I considered this one of equal value to the impromptu first story.

The monster represents Tony's father whom he saw as hostile because he had abandoned the patient. Before the divorce, the father had been cruel to him. The extent of the father's hostility is dramatically represented by the sadistic murder. Tony's mother is also seen as neglectful in protecting him from his father's rage — she sleeps during the murder. His sister, however, is singled out for protection from the father's wrath. She is not only spared but also ambivalently shielded from viewing the carnage. Running out of gas symbolizes the failure of both parents to provide those elements which are vital to the sustenance of the family.

With this understanding of Tony's story, I related the following:

Once upon a time there was a family. This family consisted of a father, a mother, two brothers, and a sister. And one day while they were taking a trip, when they were about five miles out of town, they ran out of gas. And they sat around and waited awhile and then the father said, "You know, I think I'd better go back to town and get some gas. I don't think we're going to meet anybody here who is going to give us any." So the mother said, "Well, it's a dark night here and there might be a lot of scary things. I hear that there's a monster with a claw who is around here." And the father said, "Yes, I heard that, too, but you keep an eye open, Mother. You watch for him. This monster is not the kind of monster that really can hurt anyone if a big person is around to protect the children." At any rate, he went away and the children started to fall asleep and the mother started to fall asleep.

The mother fell lightly asleep and the boy was sort of sleeping too, but he knew that the monster was there too. And it was he who awakened and saw the monster outside the window. He immediately got up and said, "Mother, Mother, there's a monster out there," and the mother beat away the monster. She said, "Get out of here you filthy, ugly monster." And then the cops came and took the monster away to jail.

And the moral of that story is that if there is anything around you that is dangerous, speak up, cry out, and say something about it. Talk about it, ask for help, and that's the best way to get rid of those things.

In forming my story, I realized that it would be unrealistic to introduce any elements which would have encouraged Tony to try to change his father. The latter was geographically distant and too uninvolved emotionally to be expected to respond meaningfully to any overtures or complaints from the patient. Such encouragement would only have added to his frustration and rage. His mother, therefore, was his only hope. In Tony's story she sleeps, thereby exposing him to danger but, nevertheless, she is in the car with him. In my story he wakes her up and successfully enlists her aid. As I so often do, I attempted to get the child to actively participate in improving his own life situation.

# Story Making in Psychotherapy with a Chronically Ill Child

MARY ROBERTSON and FRANCES BARFORD

Child psychotherapy seeks through play procedures to reinforce reality situations. Chronically ill children who are immobilized in hospital settings have little opportunity, except in directed play or fantasy, to act out the psychic problems connected with their situation. As a consequence, story-making psychotherapy offers the child a means of acting out in fantasy those feelings which he could not express in reality. Stories written specifically for the child in a hospital setting both (1) reflect a release of the child's feelings and (2) reinforce the therapeutic goal, which is to get well.

The stories written by the senior author, the psychologist, were read daily to the child by the junior author, the occupational therapist, and concluded one week before the child left the hospital. Before his discharge his pleasurable involvement in the reality world left less and less time for a fantasy world.

## Psychic Factors in Hospitalization

The psychic factors involved in the hospitalization of children have been described. Bakwin and others (1942) have focused attention on responses during acute illness relative to the separation of parents from their children during hospitalization. The effect of long-term hospitalization on children with chronic illness have been discussed by Beverly (1936), Bibring (1949), and others. Earlier, Freud and Burlingham (1944) focused on the personality changes due to institutionalization in infancy and early childhood. James Robertson (1962) has centered his studies on the parents' views of hospitalization of their children as indicated during interviews and in letters. MacCarthy and others (1962) have documented considerable information about the special efforts made by parents to visit the hospitalized child and the emotional reactions of the children following these visits. Vaughan (1957) reports on the beneficial effects of a special interview on admission to hospital. He suggests that there is a tendency to treat children "with little regard for their personal privacy, and to forget that they may be aware of what is going on around them and wish to understand it." The child is frequently treated as an object rather than as a human being. For example, the author received a story written by one nine-year-old hospitalized girl describing part of her medical procedure — "Groups came around at all hours with the main doctors who would say, 'Here's an interesting case.'" Hospitalization is frequently perceived as a traumatic separation from parents. The hospital is viewed as a place where children may be heard but not listened to. There are secrets in the hsopital that are often kept from the children.

The use of story making:

    a. results in more socialization and a more vivid reality as the child begins to master his feelings by overt expression of them.

    b. enables the child to act out in fantasy the feelings which he was unable to act out in reality.

## Treatment Procedure

Story-making procedure is adjusted to the individual needs of the child. The author uses his or her own empathy as a basis for going into the child's world by means of stories. The author is a "ghost writer" for the child upon occasion and an editor for the child at other times. The author uses the stories to reflect both the child's inner world and to suggest avenues on which the child can enter into a less restricted world. The present case study illustrates the process of story-making in psychotherapy with Bob. Bob's stories were designed to mirror a six-year-old's human world, to reflect the agony, to involve Bob in the delights of a fictional world, a world of fun, a get-well world.

## Case Study

For Bob, after being attached to the respirator for a year, separation from it was physically and psychologically an overwhelmingly traumatic experience. Bob became cyanotic, and his eyes reflected stark terror. Attached to his respirator, Bob was anxious and preoccupied with the possibility of irregular sounds or a cessation of sounds from the motor of the respirator. Environmental changes such as thunder storms, which might cut off the electrical current for the respirator, were repeated threats to Bob. Unable to live without the respirator, he was nevertheless fearful of living with it. It had proved its frailty by faulty functioning, temporarily stopping during an electrical storm, etc. The child's feelings of total dependency were mixed as were the staff's feelings because they found it difficult to reassure the child. The child, on one occasion, became disconnected from the respirator while asleep and continued to breathe adequately. This suggested to the staff that he might be weaned from a total dependency but he became cyanotic when removed from the respirator. Could he separate physically from the respirator? Could he make a successful psychological separation?

It was known that Bob was not motivated to separate himself from the respirator. When the story making began, Bob was primarily considered a manipulator. Subsequently, it became apparent that Bob felt himself daily to be only a manipulated object. He had to eat, have blood samples taken, be suctioned, etc.

The stories altered as Bob altered. Initially the fictional boy had no name, he was "the brown-eyed boy" but gradually, the real Bob identified the boy as himself. The fictional Bob and the real Bob then began to blend into one person. This enabled the staff, and the patient's family to know of Bob's affects and to see into the world of the six-year-old boy.

The stories functioned as a bridge between the child's view of the world and the adult's perspective of it. The story-maker could incorporate into tales the child's articulation of his world as well as mirror the therapeutic team's point of view. The use of stories as a common denominator for the adults and the child caused some adult anxiety. Were the stories feeding Bob's already considerable fantasy life? Was the friendly Green Dragon, as the central fictional character in the stories, likely to become more real to Bob than the people living in the "real" world? These were some of the questions the staff asked.

Shortly after the story-making sessions began, Bob felt sufficiently secure to reveal that he conceived of fantasy figures of many types, all more real and more harmful to him at night. He called them "witches," "boogy man," or "scary things." They had no shape except the shape of his anxieties projected into the darkness of night. They offered him no joy. The fiction contained fantasy figures also, but they were presented to him in daytime. The fictional characters had joyous experiences as well as frightening experiences. Bob saw pictorial representations of the characters in colors. The fantasy characters in the stories had more clearly defined roles; they were more life-like. Bob could enjoy them rather than be intimidated by them, as he was by the nighttime fantasy figures of his own anxious imagination.

The main character of the stories, "Friendly Green Dragon" was "no bigger than the palm of your hand." Bob related to "Friendly Green

Dragon" quickly. The dragon had many difficulties to overcome but each time succeeded in overcoming adversity. Bob believed in him to the extent that he desperately wanted to capture "Friendly Green Dragon." He asked his doctor to "Make a dragon trap to catch Friendly Green Dragon." On one occasion when he was undergoing weaning from the respirator, Bob jumped from his wheel chair and inspected some marks on the playground. "The dragon has been here." he observed. "I see his running tracks."

A system of rewards or surprise gifts was used to separate Bob from the respirator with the Green Dragon designated as the giver of the reward. Bob could respond therefore to the surprises without having to admit that he had separated voluntarily from the respirator.

A continuity of story-making was assured to Bob by means of a nonsense rhyme placed at the end of each story such as:

"If you want to know what happened next
    put on a red and blue vest"
or
"Walk ten steps to the West"
or
"Wait another day."

The occupational therapist read the stories to Bob each day and reported the child's responses to the story-maker. The story-maker accompanied the occupational therapist each Friday and herself read the story to Bob, thereby becoming a visible member of the team. During the weekly team conference, the story-maker reflected Bob's point of view as he portrayed it in his responses to the stories. For example, Bob commented one day, "I'm not afraid of anything, of blood tests, of having my trachea tube changed, or even of ghosts." Subsequently, the fictional characters spoke of their fears and of how they combatted fear. The fictional Bob initially denied fear but eventually admitted experiencing it.

These stories were structured for a six year old. The animal characters in the stories were used to convey feelings in a variety of ways and used to express change in feelings as Bob changed emotionally. For example, Secret Squirrel, one of the fictional characters, at first was very secretive but became more open in his expression of feelings as Bob became more open.

In the stories, reality situations could be dealt with as well as fantasied concepts. For example, in one story the altered medical procedure was discussed:

"I wouldn't like things changing all the time," said Friendly Green Dragon.

The story book Bob nodded and said, "I want to cry whenever the nurses or doctors use something new."

"It's scary," said the dragon.

"Yes, said Bob of the story, "and I had a dream, and in my dream the doctors, the nurses, and the ladies who clean the floor, all called out to me, 'We are trying something new, Bob. Do what we tell you to do.'"

"But," said the story book Bob as he turned to the dragon, "I'm going to get well and I'll never have to have a tube down my nose and have them take my blood."

"And," said Friendly Green Dragon, "You'll run, and you'll play in the woods."

"Yes, said the story book Bob, "I will."

The story thus did not deny the medical procedure but it recognized the feelings occurring because of it; and at the same time, the goal of "getting well" was reflected.

Bob's fluctuating levels of health were incorporated into stories. The stories became a means whereby the "story-book" Bob moved closer to the Bob in the hospital. Bob separated from his respirator for longer periods of time, interacted with other children more, and began to assimilate the therapeutic goal — "Get well. — Leave the hospital." It was at this time when, psychologically, Bob appeared ready to separate permanently from the respirator that he suffered tracheal obstruction; his life was endangered; and he was hastily moved to the Intensive Care Unit. Subsequently this near-death experience was reflected through the stories composed for him.

For example, Bob said, "Write a story about when they stuck the tube down my nose," and he continued, "I had bad dreams. A giant lizard was choking me and I couldn't breathe. Write about the bad dreams." He smiled, "Put in about pills too." (The pills he related would make him giant size so that he could "Crush the giant lizard.") The trauma of this child's near-death experience was reflected in "bad dream" stories. When the first of these stories was read to him, he asked for more stories in which the death of an animal was a common occurrence.

A week later, Bob still on the respirator, was frightened by a thunderstorm . He sought physical closeness from the nurse, occupational therapist, and others in his environment. He reminisced about fictional characters in the stories. Bob recognized his dreams as a part of the medical crisis of his near-death experience, and not as a permanent feature of his sleep, for many of his fears had been successfully transferred to the make-believe characters in the stories. His doctor separated him from the respirator at this time for he was ready for the separation. He showed anxiety, and he sought reassurance, but he did not need stories. The world outside the hospital ultimately became a place where he could function. He continued to stay off the respirator, and as the time of his separation from the respirator increased, Bob became more involved in activities in the occupational therapy workshop, in the pediatric play area, and in the environs of the hospital. Discharge from the hospital occurred shortly thereafter.

After Bob returned home, he still remembered stories of the "Friendly Green Dragon," and other fictional characters. When seen for one year follow-up, he requested more stories. Will Bob, when he is twenty-one years of age, still view his long hospitalization period as a series of traumas, or has the use of stories to mirror his psychological condition diminished the trauma?

## Conclusion

Prolonged hospitalization of a child tends to cause mental as well as physiological complications. The stories enabled the child to act out in fantasy what he was unable, for some months, to act out in reality. The stories incorporated the child's expressed concepts, and also the concepts of the team, so that eventually the child was able to involve himself psychologically and physiologically in the world beyond the hospital. The narratives recognized and embraced a six year old hospitalized child's world and by so doing they diminished his isolation and loneliness.

**References**

Bakwin, R. M. & Bakwin, H., "Care During Infancy and Childhood," *Psychologic Development*, Appleton Century, New York, 1942.

Beverly, B. I., "Effect of Illness and Emotional Development," *J. Pediat.*, 8, 533, 1936.

Bibring, G. L., "The Child First," *Long-Term Care of Children*, Report of Bi-Regional Conference, published by Arizona State Department of Health and Public Welfare in cooperation with the Children's Bureau, 1949.

Freud, A. & Burlington, D. T., "Infants Without Families," International Universities Press, New York, 1944.

Robertson, James,"Hospitals and Children," International Universities Press, New York, 1962.

MacCarthy, D. & Morris, L. M., "Children in Hospital with Mothers," *Lancet*, March 24, 1962, pp. 603–8.

Vaughan, G. F., "Children in Hospitals," *Lancet*, June 1, 1957, pp. 1117–20.

# Finger Painting in the Psychotherapy of Children

JACOB A. ARLOW and ASJA KADIS

Originally introduced as a form of play and a medium for artistic expression, finger painting is now a recognized psychotherapeutic technique. Shaw (1), who invented the medium, was quick to see how it enabled her pupils to overcome their inhibitions and permitted fuller expression of their fantasy life. Painting out hostile fantasies served as a means of catharsis for conflicts.

In addition to the therapeutic possibilities as a play technique, which it shares with the graphic arts (2), finger painting has several peculiar advantages. It is a socially sanctioned form of playing with mud. Both Spring (3) and Mosse (4) emphasized the utilization of the anal regression. Finger painting requires little technical skill and permits the use of larger muscle groups. Fleming (5), working with adult neurotics, related the character of the painting movements to personality types. Other authors have attempted to interpret finger painting through a universal symbolism of form and color, even suggesting that specific colors are related to definite clinical entities (6). Shaw and Lyle (7), who use the medium to encourage fantasy expression in children, warned against the danger of arbitrary interpretation of finger paintings.

## Finger Painting Procedure

In the work which forms the basis for the present paper we attempted to integrate finger painting with the total psychotherapeutic situation, using the medium as a form of projective play, as a study of motility, and as a source of fantasies and free associations. No attempt was made to analyze the paintings by themselves; at all times they were viewed within the context of the therapeutic situation.

We described the process of finger painting to our patients, but in order to avoid the suggestion of any technique, it was not rehearsed in practice. No suggestion was made concerning colors or themes. Unlike other authors (4), we did not leave the room while the patient painted. We adopted instead an attitude of passive objectivity, observing the patient in the same spirit as an analyst observes the patient, taking note of the patient's behavior as well as the content of his productions. As much can be learned from the approach to the new situation of painting as from the drawing and the fantasy. Finger painting gives the painter liberty to create as well as to destroy his creation, without actually being destructive. From the same material he is able to obliterate and create again and again, and is spared the humiliation of asking for fresh material.

If the patient is not observed during his experimentation with the medium, important material is missed by the observer which the patient may conceal with a stroke of the palm. Conversely, the metamorphosis of forms often reveals the condensations and distortions which are used to disguise the expression of conflicts and wishes. For example, when a patient with a few strokes of his fingers converts a rabbit into a small child, one may anticipate that the rabbit and child may unconsciously have been equated. We thus observe at first hand a graphic presentation of the dream work.

Although the medium properly used may give rise to intriguing designs and artistic patterns, we have not found it necessary to praise or encourage the patient's efforts. After a relatively short period of time, he comes to appreciate finger painting as a medium of self-expression and uses it accordingly. In this respect finger painting commends itself to children because no great skill or experience is required, and is a distinct advantage over other forms of drawing or painting. The painter is not discouraged by experiencing failure or inadequacy.

While the patient paints we observe how he applies himself to the task, the rate and rhythm of his work, the colors he employs, types of lines, etc. After the child feels that the picture has been completed, he is asked to tell the story of the painting. Then we inquire whether he is reminded of anything by the painting. How the material is used depends primarily upon the level to which the therapeutic process has advanced. The following case reports will demonstrate how the material is integrated with treatment.

Case 1: Harry S., a ten-year-old white boy, was brought to the clinic by his mother as a behavior problem. Presenting the clinical picture of a mild Froelich's syndrome, with an undescended testicle on the left side, he had been receiving endocrine therapy but with little result. His testicle remained undescended and his weight continued to increase. His mother complained that Harry was completely unmanageable. He was involved in endless quarrels with his mother, usually nagging her over some exorbitant demand which she had not fulfilled. His misbehavior would begin shortly after his mother had denied a request. Requests ranged from a watch, a football, a young dog, to a younger brother. During these periods of frustration the boy's appetite became insatiable. He would descend upon the icebox and gorge himself with all it contained. The fluctuation of his weight curve on the clinic chart was one of the surest indicators of his behavior during the week. School behavior was similarly disturbed so that performance on tests ranged from excellent to extremely poor. Intelligence was slightly above average.

The mother's attitude toward the boy was characterized by extreme ambivalence, the result of conflicting rejection and guilt. If not for the patient, she would have left her husband for whom she felt temperamentally unsuited. She sometimes indulged the boy's every wish and on other occasions denied the most modest request. For example, for a while she had considered placing the boy in an institution, yet a few months later she applied at a foster home agency for a child in order to satisfy Harry's intense wish for a baby brother, which she was unable to satisfy because of a hysterectomy.

Harry's behavior in painting was characteristic of his general attitude. He could not get enough of anything nor could he get it quickly enough. He used too much water and too much paint; he mixed the colors indiscriminately in massive quantities, resulting in an unpleasant brown or gray effect. He spread the paint well beyond the limits of the paper on to the linoleum used to protect the table. As often as not his picture extended right on to the lineoleum. His movements were rapid, restless, and definitive, giving the lines of his drawing a bold character. Despite this turmoil the content of the drawing was always something very simple — something this frustrated little boy desired: a football, a pipe, etc.

### Wish Fulfillment

The following two instances illustrate how unexpressed wishes or even unconscious wishes can find expression in painting.

1. During the period when Harry's feelings of inadequacy about his small genitalia and undescended testicle were being discussed, he kept making drawings of a tremendous football which he wanted his parents to get for him to replace an old small football which he had lost. In the play room he modeled a human figure out of clay and then made a large

penis which he placed in the appropriate position. Smiling, he removed the penis, placed it in the figure's mouth explaining: "It's a cigar." Immediately after, he drew a large male face with a tremendous cigar in the mouth, a very clear example of symbolization and displacement from below to above. (One of his problems was smoking.)

2. Among the many things which Harry demanded of his mother was that she present him with a younger brother. He also wanted a puppy but she refused because it would entail too much work. Harry painted a picture of a boy seated in a chair, arms outstretched to receive his dog. The dog, however, was not pictured on the floor but in the air at the level of the boy's arms, revealing the obvious intention to hold it as one holds a child. More interesting, however, is the fact that a year earlier Harry drew practically the same picture as a pencil sketch for another examiner. There were two differences: in the earlier sketch the dog was on the floor, but his head was unmistakably that of a child. Thus Harry's wish for a baby brother transformed into the desire to get a puppy found expression in identical drawings on two separate occasions more than a year apart. This illustrates what we have found to be true in our experiences: that the pictorial productions and fantasies which the patient creates about them are characteristic for him and undergo relatively minor modification with the passing of time.

Case 2: Paul O., a fourteen-year-old Italian-American boy, was brought to the clinic by his mother. When asked what was wrong, he burst into tears and complained that "things are phoney, I don't feel real. I don't feel like myself." He was unable to leave the house unaccompanied. When an attack overcame him at school he would either run home or return to his "home class" where in the presence of his male teacher his anxiety would abate. The feeling of complete unreality and the feeling of body change which he experienced during the attacks were the most disturbing symptoms.

Paul appeared short and young for his age, which was a definite family trait. He had two older sisters and a younger brother. Many symptoms pertained to the younger brother, of whose whereabouts Paul had to be assured constantly. He felt no antagonism toward any members of his family and was unaware of any interpersonal conflict.

## Expression of Conflicts

It was Paul who took the initiative in incorporating finger painting into the therapeutic process. While trying rather unsuccessfully to explain how he felt during an attack, he suddenly turned and reached for the painting which he had made a few minutes earlier. In pale yellow he had drawn two indistinct figures at opposite ends of a road. He pointed to the more distinct one, and said: "I'm this person. But during an attack I feel that I may be this one (pointing to the opposite figure). Or I'm here and sometimes I feel that I'm there. During an attack I don't know who I am or where I am." Using the painting, he thus gave us not only a graphic description of his sensations during an attack, but also an invaluable clue to its psychological significance, for we later learned that identification with another person was a most important dynamic factor in his illness.

Paul's manner of painting was characteristic. In a series of over fifty paintings he deviated only two or three times from his customary approach. After mixing his colors, he spread the paint over the paper in smooth, even strokes, then stopped and stared at the paper in a sort of trance. Following this he would draw in a very deliberate manner, changing, erasing, and adding, then stop suddenly and say: "It's finished." He explained that he always knew when a picture was completed because a certain feeling of uneasiness within him disappeared.

Following the original drawing, Paul painted a series of twelve to fourteen pictures, all of which were related by two closely connected themes: either a young child was lost or killed, or the smaller or younger of two objects or persons was destroyed. He was unaware that his paintings and fantasies told an identical story in an almost compulsive manner, until it was brought to his attention when he related several dreams, of which the following two are typical.

Paul dreamed that he was helping his brother up a mountainside when the brother lost his grasp and plunged down the mountain. He woke from his dream in one of his attacks. He dreamed that he was offering condolences to a neighbor who had lost the younger of her two sons. In explanation of this dream Paul stated: "She really has three sons but my mother has two, myself and my younger brother."

At this point, with the aid of his own drawings, we were able to demonstrate how an unconscious thought may act in a dynamic fashion and force itself into his creations and his behavior. He showed genuine amazement when we demonstrated to him the persistent recurrence of these themes in his paintings. He insisted that he never knew beforehand what he was going to draw. We questioned him on many occasions in order to ascertain that this was so and in order to eliminate the possibility that the theme of the painting had been suggested by us.

The next turning point in treatment occurred when the patient became aware that he was not only thinking of his younger brother's death, but was wishing for it to take place as a result of his own efforts. Once again this was made clear by the paintings. Paul drew a picture of the body of a young boy and a ball lying at the foot of a tree. In explanation he said that the boy had climbed into the tree to retrieve his ball. Having gotten it, he lost his footing and fell to the ground injuring himself seriously. Paul was ready to leave discussion of the painting, when he was asked whether the picture reminded him of any specific events in his life. After a few moments two childhood incidents occurred to him which he had forgotten. Both events occurred in the country where his illness began. In the first situation the younger brother had climbed into a tree to retrieve his dog. Paul, standing on the ground, urged his brother to throw the dog to him. When the little boy refused, the patient threatened. The intimidated youngster finally yielded to Paul's demands. Paul, however, permitted the dog to fall to the ground. He was immediately overcome by guilt and remorse, feeling that the dog had been killed. In the second incident, Paul threw his younger brother out of the tree under the pretext that he was not coming in for lunch promptly enough. Fortunately the boy was not injured, but Paul responded as on the previous occasion, with guilt and remorse.

These revelations were followed by a series of paintings in which Paul kept rescuing his younger brother from danger. Then he produced a painting in which the tree reappeared. This time a small chipmunk was in the branches while below stood a young boy poised to kill the animal with a stone. To this Paul associated the many times when he had killed frogs, squirrels and rabbits, and felt guilt later. He finally renounced this destructive pastime and felt only extreme gentleness and solicitude for animals. Having already equated the little animals with his brother, his unconscious wish to kill his younger brother was now apparent to him from his own drawings. We were further able to point out that the sequence of drawings in which the theme changed from overt hostility to stories of rescue, recapitulated Paul's attitude toward animals and toward his younger brother: first destruction, then extreme solicitude.

In a drawing which he made sometime later, the patient revealed that, out of guilt, he had identified himself with the object of his destructive wishes. In this painting two boys are walking on a road in which an excavation is so covered over with leaves that travelers are unaware of the danger. Paul explained the picture: "My brother and myself on a road in the forest, the pit is like an animal trap. One of the boys falls in." (Which one?) Paul remained silent for a moment, then smiling very sheepishly, meekly said: "I fall in." He explained that he had meant to say the brother fell in, but had changed his story when he became aware that the pit reminded him of a grave. (Prior to the painting we had been discussing Paul's first acquaintance with death — the funeral of his grandfather.) He continued by saying that the structure at the bottom of the pit, which he had noticed during his explanation of the picture but about which he had made no comment, reminded him of a coffin.

The painting thus demonstrated to Paul how, on becoming aware of his death wish toward his brother, he substituted himself for his victim. This sequence of events, now made conscious, was used to explain the genesis of his attacks in which Paul felt that he was dead or dying. As in the painting, so in the attack; Paul felt impending death only after he had first thought of or fantasied the death of some other person.

We have presented the above case in some detail because the observable content of the drawings reflected very closely the content of the fantasies which the patient created about his paintings. This correlation of drawing and fantasy is not always the rule. Younger children, particularly those under five years of age, are more likely to use finger painting to gratify their need for emotional outlet in the form of overt motor activity. As a medium of expression this relates finger painting closer to dancing than to the graphic arts. We might say that our patients "danced with their fingers" on the paper, expressing in their movements the mood at the time of painting.

Some of our patients assaulted the paper, smearing the paint about in swift, aggressive strokes, often tearing the sheet. One girl, on the other hand, after evading discussion of her bed wetting, painted like a dilettante, flicking the paint about with the nail of her little finger in a thoroughly supercilious manner. She thus made known to us beforehand that her resistance to discussing bed wetting would not be overcome through painting.

Sylvia, a fourteen-year-old girl, ordinarily painted with deliberation and planning, and her drawings were usually organically related to her productions. After a quarrel with a friend, however, she expressed her mood in a purely motor form. She poured a generous amount of brown paint on the paper and kept rubbing with both hands, making ceaseless, vigorous, circular movements. Nothing appeared on the paper but two boldly drawn, overlapping circles, concerning which she stated: "This drawing is a forest. There are brown leaves all around. My friend is a forest. There are brown leaves all around. My friend is dead and I am burying her and burying her. I am so mad with her, I could kill her." This regression to a more immature way of using the medium, unusual for a girl this age, may be related to the fact that Sylvia was inhibited in verbal expression by a stammer.

The cathartic value of this particular painting technique is quite apparent. A combination of the use of motor activity and drawing content for cathartic purposes is clearly seen in the case of an eight-year-old boy who, shortly after being admitted to a children's institution, kept painting and destroying a "bad man" over and over again. He related the "bad man" to the enemies of his country, but also to his father who had been instrumental in having him institutionalized.

## Reflection of Ego Strength

The correlation between the observable content of the painting and the patient's fantasy story about it, we have found to be an almost infallible index of the degree of ego development; in children, it is a measure of the progress of treatment. The restless, aggressive child finds it difficult to inhibit his motor activity long enough to plan and execute meaningful forms in his finger painting; he has already abandoned formal language when he begins to express his conflict in the form of misbehavior and symptoms. Following psychotherapeutic treatment more formal means of speech and behavior are adopted. There is also a greater degree of self-criticism which results in increased appreciation of the environment. The child relates himself more objectively to his surroundings and begins to use patterns of speech, behavior, and drawing which are more meaningful to the observer. This process has been observed in several badly disturbed children.

Case 3: When Allan, age four and a half, came to the clinic, he raced through the halls at top speed, shrieking loudly, and slamming doors. In the play room he ordered the other children about and climbed on top of the toy chest. At home he had thrown food out of the window, smashed dishes, and started several fires. Because of his marked restlessness a diagnosis of post-encephalitic behavior disturbance was entertained for awhile.

On the first day of finger painting Allan made no picture at all; he got so excited he fell into the pail of water that was used to moisten the paper. Later, when he did paint, his creations were meaningless jumbles of lines with no discernible form, pattern, or organization. His verbal productions in relation to these drawings were at first equally incoherent and unintelligible. After months of treatment he was able to tell stories about the paintings which made sense, but the paintings themselves remained without form or meaning. These stories, which usually centered about a sinister and threatening figure called "the Shadow," led to the youngster's fear of his cruel and abusive father. As Allan was able to discuss his problem, in part, his mood became more tranquil. This turn in the treatment was reflected in a short time when he was able to draw an easily recognizable pair of green curtains. A well-executed boat on a blue sea followed soon after. This improvement in his ability to express himself in drawing was paralleled by concurrent improvement in his symptoms.

Case 4: Bernice, a seven-year-old girl, was first observed when she was at the height of a sexual affair in which she masturbated a 16-year-old boy. Her symptoms consisted of disobedience, begging and stealing, exposing herself and masturbating in public. Her excitement never abated. When asked to relate some incident or tell a story, she produced an incoherent mixture of fact and fantasy.

Her early finger paintings were equally incoherent and the fantasies concerning them equally senseless. As in the previous case, the story the little patient told about the pictures became intelligible long before the painting showed any discernible patterns or forms. Bernice would point to some part of the maze of twisted lines and say: "This is a bad man with a big knife, who is chasing the little girl to her house." Man, knife, girl, or house, could be recognized nowhere in the drawing. The theme of impending assault persisted, however, and the patient was not able to express any other fantasy in relation to her paintings. Finally, through her drawings, we became aware of her sexual behavior.

As treatment was continued and the problem discussed, her anxiety and excitement began to abate. The progress of treatment was clearly recorded by the finger paintings. Soon a man, a knife, a girl, and a house could be recognized in the drawings. The threatening man characteristically appeared in the same part of the painting each time. Bernice showed her readiness to renounce her interest in the object of her sexual play when she spontaneously blotted out that part of her painting which the threatening man usually occupied. Liberated from this all-encompassing interest, the compulsion to tell the same story about each painting disappeared. The choice of subjects for her paintings was now much wider and varied over the range of a child's normal interests. She was able to paint with greater ease, using fewer movements, better planning, and several distinct colors, instead of an over-all mixture of many colors.

## Painting and Resistance

In the dynamics of therapy, finger painting may be used by the patient for purposes of resistance as well as overcoming resistance. We have cited several typical examples of children who were aloof and indifferent to their creations, as if to indicate that they felt only distantly related to their paintings. This attitude may be expressed both in the manner of painting and in the content of the picture. Other children, or the same children at other times, may paint with obvious emotion. In such instances, even before the content of the drawing or the fantasy are made known, the intensity of the patient's movements and his application to the task foretell the revelation of significant data. Often it was possible to circumvent a patient's resistance during an interview by shifting from conversation to painting.

In Case 2, while discussing the death of his grandfather, for example, Paul became aware that he could think of nothing further to say. At this point it was suggested that he paint. Though unable to talk, he was able to paint, and produced the picture with the hidden pit in the road. The painting plainly revealed the cause of his resistance. During the discussion of his grandfather's burial, Paul was struggling with a fantasy of burying his brother. The painting thus acted like a dream "made to order" for the purpose of overcoming the resistance.

When resistance is strong, the patient may become completely inhibited; that is, he may be unable to paint at all, and experience uneasiness and anxiety. This situation may persist for a varying length of time but is usually dissipated because the patient finds a discharge for his anxiety in the motor activity of the apparently meaningless smearing movements. These early movements of spreading the paint, so aimless and neutral, seem very "safe" to the patient and help to assuage his anxiety.

The conflict between the resistance and the emerging unconscious wish is often dramatically acted out by the patient while he is trying to paint. This was obvious in the case of Paul. After having spread the paint over the sheet, he was unable to proceed. Several times he moved his fingers toward the paper, but withdrew them. He then drew an animal, but instantly marked it out. Again he stood before the sheet unable to proceed, appearing very tense. He finally drew the animal and completed the picture by drawing a young boy pursuing the animal with a stick. When he had completed the painting he said: "I have a very funny feeling." Later he explained that he had tried very hard not to draw the animal, but try as he might, nothing else would come to his mind and he felt compelled to return to the theme of the fleeing animal. On only one occasion was this patient completely unable to paint. This occurred after his wish to do away with the younger brother was clearly revealed. Naturally, the question arose: What possible motive could he have for such an impulse?

Paul failed to keep his next appointment. At the following session, after preparing his sheet he was unable to paint. He turned to the examiner after a painful pause and said: "I can't paint today . . . I don't want to paint . . . You tell me what to do. . . . " Since this was a departure from his usual practice he was asked to explain. He explained that while traveling in the subway to the interview, he had thought of the dream he was going to tell. In his dream, he and his younger brother are escaping from some danger. They come to a picket fence. He gets by successfully, but the brother does not. Then for the first time he thought in advance of a possible subject for his painting. It occurred to him that a picket fence and a small boy would be a good theme. Suddenly there flashed into his mind the thought: "No, don't! That would be giving too much away." The patient thus confessed that he did not trust himself to paint for fear of revealing too much repressed material. As it developed, the picket fence dream and painting were a repetition of an almost identical event which served as the precipitating incident of the neurosis.

At some period in treatment almost every patient produces a characteristic painting which we have come to recognize as a "resistance painting." Such a drawing consists of a simple design repeated over and over again so as to cover the sheet completely. The wish to "cover up" is acted out. The children themselves learn the implication of these paintings very quickly. One little patient after completing such a painting, looked at it, laughed and said: "I guess I'm not going to do much talking today." This was true.

Very frequently abstract forms are painted by the patient with such persistence that one suspects important material with emotional coloring is hidden behind a screen of abstract designs. In such instances, if the patient is left undisturbed, he may ultimately gather enough courage to commit himself in a painting. A nine-year-old boy persisted in drawing abstract forms about which he could produce no fantasy. The intensity of his movements, however, suggested that something very disturbing was hidden behind the abstractions. At last he painted a picture of a dancing girl but threw the painting out of the window before he thought anyone had seen it. In explanation he stated that he had been thinking of something which no good boy should ever do. Later interviews revealed a conflict over masturbating to the fantasy of dancing girls.

The manner in which the finger painting and the fantasy express resistance to therapy is very similar to that of the dream. As a matter of fact, the parallelism between dreams, painting, and fantasy is most striking in relation to the problem of resistance. One patient, for example, was quite surprised when one of his paintings pointed to his sexual experiences. The interpretation of the painting was confirmed by a dream which the patient had had the previous night which he had intended to withhold. The themes of the dream and the painting were identical, but a slight change of locale in the painting led directly to the interpretation of the traumatic situation. This unexpected revelation apparently came upon an insufficiently prepared patient. He did not keep four of the next eight appointments. He was much disturbed, trying to decide whether to continue treatment. During this period of indecision he made the following paintings.

1. A boy arrives at a fork in the road; cannot decide which way to turn.

2. An armed guard is protecting a precious storage tank against sabotage by enemy spies. The tank he associated with gas tanks near the Mental Hygiene Clinic.

3. Two boys are on a road which winds endlessly toward the horizon. This painting was made twice. He identified the two figures as himself and his illness. The road to recovery seemed long and endless.

The ending of this period of resistance was foretold in another painting in which a boy comes upon a huge stone which blocks his path. At first he is undecided whether to walk around the stone or to tackle it directly and roll it away. The decision in the fantasy to roll the stone away indicates the patient's readiness to talk about his sexual problem. The painting part of the session was terminated and in the ensuing interview the patient finally resumed discussion of his sexual conflict.

We might say briefly that almost every dynamic mechanism of defense observed during psychoanalysis has some counterpart in the patient's relation to his finger painting.

## Meaning of Color

The choice and use of colors proved of singular importance. The particular color selected was an almost unfailing index of the mood of the patient and the theme of the painting. One girl used light blue for a painting, the "Ship of Success" coming into port; green for a study of music and the musical instrument which she hoped would bring her recognition; brown for the burial of a faithless friend; black for a drawing of bars which reminded her that living in an institution was like being a prisoner.

Paul (Case 2) once made two companion paintings on the same day. The first, a young boy at the bottom of a pit, unable to escape and doomed to die, was painted in black. The second was that of an older boy at the top of the pit having successfully evaded death, which was painted in light blue. The color selections were made quite unconsciously; even before he knew what he was going to draw he searched through the jars saying: "Where are the darker colors?" This infallibly predicted the type of painting. Death was invariably executed in black; themes of hostility or aggression were executed in brown or black.

As a rule this was true of all our patients. A young refugee boy, who had been through the London blitz and had developed a severe neurosis upon separation from his parents, could paint nothing but fighter planes crashing to the earth in black, brown, and red. His theme and selection of colors never varied. Conversely, bright colors were chosen for happy scenes.

An interesting use of color was made by Muriel, age eleven, who was a bed wetter. She identified herself with the color yellow. She was a middle child who resented the attentions showered on her younger brother, the only boy. The one occasion which he had not spoiled for her was the only birthday party her parents had given her, for which they had bought her a bright yellow dress. Her paintings repeated the theme of three siblings quarreling with each other; and whether these were pictured as animals, flowers, or humans, she was invariably identified with the yellow one.

Very few children chose red as the sole color for a painting. A notable exception was a six-year-old boy, who was on a fire-setting spree. A few enuretic girls also drew burning houses repeatedly in red.

Younger children, age four to ten, preferred to use several colors, usually the primary ones, which they frequently employed in striking combinations. Their reactions indicated immediate color appreciation, showing a very primitive pleasure of color. As a rule they did not mix colors to produce any of the intermediate shades. Older children preferred to use a single color, usually an intermediate shade, apparently centering their interest on the form and content of their paintings. Inhibited, frightened, and insecure children were partial to the darker colors and, in the younger groups, used only one color as a rule. Such children may be unable to adapt themselves to finger painting as such; instead they may dip an individual finger into the paint jar and use the finger as a pencil or crayon, thereby indicating reluctance to avail themselves of the less formalized means of expression which finger painting permits. Those children who fail to cover the sheet completely with paint may be suspected of being inhibited or frightened. Conversely, the inability of a child to limit himself to the paper is important diagnostically. Such a child may be suspected of being too aggressive or insufficiently inhibited. He can no more limit himself in painting than he can in other life situations.

## Value of Finger Painting

The habits and technique employed during finger painting reflect very accurately the personality and habits of the painter. Together with the fantasy material which is elicited with relative ease in relation to these paintings, we are afforded quick and valuable insight into the organization of and the conflicts within the personality. The parallelism observed between the dream life and the fantasies concerning finger paintings is consistent and striking. It demonstrates clearly the significant role played by unconscious forces in the elaboration of day dreams and in the process of artistic creation. We hope through finger painting to make a further study of this problem.

Shaw (1) has suggested that the neurotic child, by repeatedly painting his fears onto paper, may discharge his anxiety and free himself from his symptoms. We have not found this to be the case. Although finger painting may be used as a locus for displacement of anxiety, it does not relieve the anxiety per se. The way in which the anxiety-producing fantasy reappears and is elaborated in finger painting is most impressive. The fantasy persists in an almost compulsive manner restricting the patient's productivity and interests until the underlying conflict is resolved either by life or by psychotherapy. Our case material has demonstrated that it was the resolution of the underlying conflict which caused both the persistent fantasy and the related symptom to disappear. Getting the child to express his fantasies during finger painting is therapeutically futile unless his productions can be related to the traumatic life situation from which they have originated. In other words, the experiences derived from finger painting must be integrated with the developing ego.

In personal conversations we have heard the opinion expressed that finger painting may prove to be further destructive to a disintegrating ego which has already begun to abandon reality, by encouraging fantasy formation and facilitating the appearance of more symbolic rather than more concrete forms of expression. The feeling is that on a psychological plane finger painting fosters chaos. The premise upon which such a fear is based is incorrect. Like other forms of behavior and expression, finger painting is but a manifestation of the capacities and organizational strength of the ego. A disturbed personality will produce chaotic finger paintings. As the individual responds to therapy, the paintings become more explicit. The cases of Bernice and Allan illustrate the course of events. When these two very severely disturbed children were finally able to cope with their fears, they were also able to paint explicitly, using concrete symbols in well defined patterns. Often only through finger painting were we able to discover the disintegrating element in the personality.

In our experience the consistent use of finger painting has proved very valuable in treating children with behavior problems and neuroses. Within the framework of a controlled situation it permits observation of personality and motor patterns. It facilitates the emergence of fantasies and personality trends. The finger painting acts both as a record of the psychotherapeutic experience and as an objective measure of the progress of treatment. Above all, it affords an excellent means of confronting the individual with trends in his own creations. Since these productions are recorded in paint in his own unmistakable style, the young patient finds it very difficult to repudiate them. He "sees" what he has been doing.

References
1. Shaw, R. F., *Finger Painting*, Little, Brown, Boston 1938.
2. Bender, L., and A. G. Woltmann, *Play and Psychotherapy*, Nervous Child, 1, 1, 1941–1942.
3. Spring, W. J., *Words and Masses*, Psychoanal. Quart., 1935.
4. Mosse, C. P., *Painting Analysis in the Treatment of Neurosis*, Psychoanal. Review, Jan. 1940.
5. Fleming, Joan, *Observations in the Use of Finger Painting in the Treatment of Adult Patients with Personality Disorders*, Character & Personality, June, 1940.
6. Obendorf, C. P., Quoted by Mosse (cf. 4).
7. Lyle and Shaw, *Encouraging Children to Express Their Phantasies*, Bull. Menninger Clinic, 1, 3, Jan. 1937.

# Theraplay Technique

ANN M. JERNBERG

The problem of providing psychotherapy to a group of emotionally disturbed children, too many in number, too poor in economic circumstances, and too lacking in easy verbal expression of feelings has faced many of us who attempt to provide psychological services to schools. It is difficult enough to make reliable diagnoses (of intelligence or anything else for that matter). It is far more difficult to treat. Among obstacles which lie in the way of available and effective treatment are the discrepancy of worlds from which the treator and the treated often come and the treatment reality itself. The fifty-minute hour must be a highly valued concept in order for a (possibly already overburdened) mother to agree to bring her child once or twice a week (often with other children in tow, and sometimes far across the city) just so that doctor and child can "talk."

## Helping Teachers Cope

This paper proposes to discuss one way in which this problem has been tackled in one city-wide school program. From the parents' point of view initially, at least, the kind of therapy described probably makes little more sense than "talking" therapy. From the administrative point of view it allows many children to be helped, often by people who understand their life-styles, for relatively little money, in relatively few sessions and on their (the children's) own home base.

In 1967 the contract for providing psychological services to the Chicago Head Start Program was awarded to Worthington, Hurst and Associates, Incorporated, a private psychological consulting firm. The WHA proposal promised to serve the 5,000 children in the program at that time (last year there were 7,000) by giving help to the teachers in recognizing and coping with the somewhat problematic child. It was assumed that all children with more pronounced emotional difficulties could be referred to existing mental health facilities. It was not long, of course, before it became evident that high quality facilities for the immediate treatment of little children were virtually non-existent. More often than not, in-take procedures, staff screenings, case conferences and long waiting lists all took priority over the initiation of treatment. In many instances school was out before the first therapy session had even been scheduled.

In 1968 WHA undertook to expand its psychological services to Head Start by providing its own psychotherapy component to be included as an adjunctive branch to the already established consultation unit. One therapist was hired on a trial basis to treat those H.S. children referred by the psychological and psychiatric consultants. Treatment was carried out at the child's own school — often in his classroom. The number of referred children soon exceeded the number who could be seen once, twice or three times a week for thiry to forty-five minute sessions by this one therapist alone. Other therapists were trained and hired.

### Theoretical Basis

Theraplay, the therapy method used by WHA therapists in the Chicago H.S. program (and several area private school programs) is based on the theory of Austin DesLauriers. It was DesLauriers' theory that a deficiency in emotionally positive infantile sensory experiences could lead to later emotional problems. The cause of the deficiency may lie within the parent or it may lie within the child. A parent may be depressed, emotionally unavailable, hostile or just not given to tickling, cooing, and piggy-back rides. Unbeknownst to a mother or father a child may be born with an almost biological barrier against stimuli so that it may take an inordinate amount of stimulation before he senses what other babies would more easily feel. The parent, feeling unresponded to, might decrease his efforts in turn. Or he, himself, may turn off the stimulation which is offered in order to defend himself against the accompanying hostile tone. In any of these three cases he misses out on the stimulating experiences which are so necessary if he is to develop a good sense of who he is, what he can and cannot do, what he looks like and where his body leaves off and the rest of the world begins. Having missed out on the physical stimulation and on the emotionally warm context within which it is ordinarily provided, he fails to develop a sense of confidence in himself and of trust in others. By the time he arrives in school he appears withdrawn, he acts out, or in some other way he becomes a worry to his teacher. The method of treatment developed by DesLauriers is designed to undo the original damage, to fill the initial void. The Theraplay technique provides to the understimulated child the stimulation he should have received when he was little.

## Treatment Procedures

Even though he is now four, five, six, or ten years old his treatment consists of having his hands washed and his feet tickled, being carried piggy-back and being played with in many of the other body contact ways which are so pleasurable to and so demanding of eye-contact from a one-year-old. The therapy is fun-filled and includes elements of surprise such as putting his shoe on his head and his hat on his feet. Even older children enjoy peek-a-boo with an unself-conscious therapist. Through this intense, pleasurable personal experience the child soon gains a newfound sense of self as someone whose skills and body boundaries he knows well and who can have fun with another person. Viola Brody, at the University of South Florida, working with children with school achievement problems, found that this same concrete sense of self is soon followed by a more abstract one (improved human figure drawings) and this, eventually, by improved symbolic functioning (reading and writing) and higher IQs.

## Therapist Training and Selection

It is evident from the foregoing description of the Theraplay method that neither the PhD nor the psychiatric residency are necessary for the effective functioning of the Theraplay Therapist. Indeed too much knowledge of theory and experimental method often gets in the way. For the effective therapist must be creative, spontaneous, optimistic, and comfortable about physical closeness to his patient-child. Yet creativity and optimism alone will not suffice. The skilled Theraplay Therapist knows when to demand, when to wait, when to include the parent in the interaction, when to increase the frequency of sessions and when to prepare the child for termination. The skilled Therapist knows how to handle the almost inevitable negative phase which so often follows the appearance of too-early trust.

In order to learn these skills the beginning Therapist is trained in a group. Beginners learn to develop their own new Theraplay techniques with one another. Each defines "normal" and "abnormal" parenting behavior by observing interactions between "normal" and "abnormal" parent-child pairs. The beginning Therapist is assigned one "normal" infant and one "normal" child, and he practices the Theraplay technique with each under the critical eye of his classmates and supervisors. Throughout, he has been observing experienced Theraplay Therapists at work with their own caseload of referred children. Eventually he joins in at these sessions, and finally he receives his own assigned "problem" child and works with him under supervision. The training, of course, does not end there.

The intense effort to help a troubled child is always demanding. It is for this reason that Therapists in the Chicago Head Start (and other) programs meet weekly as a group and even the most experienced ones (and incidentally this same principle applies to the professional consulting staff) are encouraged to call for observation by or consultation with a colleague whenever the need is felt.

## School Acceptance

Needless to say, there was considerable initial resistance on the part of teachers and school principals. The method is boisterous and even though it often seeks to incorporate a child's playmates into the sessions as quickly as possible, still it does give a great deal of "attention" to one child. School personnel at the onset feared its potential for "spoiling" children, rewarding already bad behavior, disrupting classrooms, undercutting teachers, teaching behavior (such as running with bare feet or jumping into the therapist's arms from a table) which is inappropriate to the schoolroom. It has taken many years to gain the kind of acceptance the WHA Theraplay program has at present. The extra long list of child referrals and of parent volunteers for Theraplay training, which comes directly from Board of Education teachers themselves, attests to it.

## Summary

This paper has attempted to describe Theraplay, a method of child therapy, which has been used in several Chicago school programs over the past five years. Since it takes place within the school, is short term and is taught primarily to people not required to have professional degrees, Theraplay would seem to be the method of choice for areas having large numbers of school children with emotional problems, few good local child facilities and the desire to train and utilize their own human resources. Extensive follow-up evaluation on the long-term effectiveness of Theraplay is necessary now, of course. The two children in the film, *Here I Am*, which documents the Theraplay method, were refilmed and retested three years after their termination. At that time their gains had been maintained both in testing and in their school behavior.

# Diagnostic Family Interviews

IBRAHIM N. ORGUN

The contribution of family interviews to the diagnostic understanding of the family and the identified patient is well established. However, the role of younger children in family interviews conducted on a verbal level has not attracted much attention. Those familiar with children and child development are well aware of the difficulty and discomfort that children younger than ten years of age experience in family interviews that are conducted in an office, where the primary mode of communication is verbal and on the adult level. These same children, however, find the playroom and play material conducive to communicating their conflicts and feelings. This consideration, combined with the aforementioned concerns, makes the playroom an ideal setting for interviewing families with children ten years of age and younger. In our experience with seventy families, even some children between ten and twelve years of age felt more comfortable in a playroom setting.

## Review of the Literature

Having a parent, especially the mother of the child patient, in the playroom is not new. Schwartz described the psychoanalytic treatment of two children while their mother was in the playroom (1). Pappenheim and Sweeney treated a child with the mother in the playroom because of the separation anxiety that both the child and the mother experienced (2).

Others included home visits in the diagnosis or treatment of children. Bornstein treated a two-and-a-half-year-old child by visiting the patient at her home (3). Freeman found home visits to be very valuable in diagnosing children (4).

Drechsler and Schapiro (5) described a three step family interview-procedure that included: (1) a psychiatrist's interviewing a family in a playroom while a psychologist observed through a one-way screen; followed by (2) a ten-minute period when the family was left alone while the psychiatrist and psychologist observed through the one-way screen; and (3) a final period when the psychologist introduced a questionnaire and remained with the family as they answered it while the psychiatrist observed through the one-way screen.

Augenbraun and Tasem (6) described two different techniques of family therapy for preschool children and their parents in a play-therapy room. Differences in techniques were related to the makeup of the parents, specifically whether they were neurotic or borderline and psychotic. Bergel and associates (7) presented the use of play materials in conjoint family therapy. Ackerman (8) aptly dealt with the importance of the child's participation in family therapy and suggested techniques to ensure it.

Our approach comes close to the techniques described by Augen-braun and Tasem (6) and by Bergel and associates (7). However, it differs from theirs in that it uses the child's play and activities as a starting point and focuses on the child's communication. In short, communication through play activity and material constitutes the primary communication mode, at least for the children.

## Family Interview Technique

The diagnostic family interview is part of the diagnostic process, which also includes interviews with the parents, individual interviews with the child, psychological testing, and, when indicated, electroencephalography. During their individual interviews with a social worker and a child psychiatrist the parents and the child are each told that they will be seen as a family so that the diagnostic team can get to know how the family functions. The family diagnostic interview is held about a week after the child's psychiatric interview. The social worker and the child psychiatrist meet with the entire family in the playroom. The child, who is familiar with the clinic setting, is frequently asked to lead his family there; his handling of this task offers diagnostic clues.

Our playroom has enough chairs for adults and teenagers. The family members choose their seats; how they seat themselves gives clues about the sidings and groupings in the family. Once the older members of the family are seated, the members of the diagnostic team place themselves among the family in a way to make it possible for each of them to observe and interact with all members. We have found that if the team does not initiate the interview by making a verbal statement, there is a better chance for the interview to proceed on play and activity levels; any verbal statement from the team tends to communicate that the interview should proceed on an adult verbal level. However, in cases where prolonged uneasiness and anxiety are experienced, the original statement that the team wanted to see the family together is repeated. In the majority of cases, the child patient or the siblings have begun playing and the interview has proceeded smoothly. If the children did not play or interact with each other and the adults, we have found that it was more revealing and effective to explore the reason for this with the parents than to encourage the child to play. An example follows.

*Case 1.* A ten-year-old boy, Michael, who was referred because of poor school work, throwing away his books, general disobedience, and running away from home, was seen in the playroom with his divorced mother and his eight-year-old sister, Nancy. Both children sat rigidly, without moving; they glanced at their mother. When this was pointed out, the mother indicated that the children never did anything unless she told them they could. With her permission they started to play, but even then they waited for her nonverbal cues as they moved from one activity to another.

As an interview proceeds the social worker and psychiatrist move around and, if invited, join in the children's play. They interact verbally with the older members of the family inquiring about their reactions, feelings, or interpretations of the child's interaction or activity. They may encourage the older members of the family, especially the parents, to join in the children's activities. The interaction in these instances is quite revealing.

*Case 2.* A six-and-a-half-year-old boy, John, his four-year-old sister, Judy, their mother, and their stepfather of a few months were interviewed. At one point the stepfather complained that he wanted to do things with John but that the boy rejected his offers. A few minutes later, John asked him to play a game. First the stepfather, who accepted this offer, remained seated in his chair while the boy sat on the floor. This created a gap and made it uncomfortable for both.

At one point both of their playing pieces landed on the same square, the stepfather's arriving last. The stepfather told John that he had to go back to the start. The boy insisted that the rules contained no such move, but the stepfather would not accept this.

One of the diagnostic team members suggested that they might want to read the rules. However, the stepfather did not take this suggestion, the boy stopped playing, and communications broke down. At this point, the mother took the game cover that contained the rules and read them. Realizing that her husband was wrong, she seemed to become very angry. But paralyzed with anger, she put the cover back without saying a word.

Frequently the child psychiatrist interacts with the children and a social worker interacts with the parents. However, these roles are switched as often as the team sees it is necessary during the fifty-minute interview. As the interview proceeds, the play and verbal interactions among the members of the family are observed and scrutinized.

While observing John and his sister Judy, mentioned in case 2, one of the team members overheard Judy say to her brother that she had the white wooden doll. (They were both playing with different colored dolls; there was only one white doll.) As soon as Judy said this, John grabbed the white figure. The little girl began crying and protesting. The mother, not realizing that Judy had initiated the interaction, scolded the boy. In this instance, we should see the little girl's manipulation and understand why the boy struck out at his peers and those adults who tried to control him.

The team comments on the nature of divisions, sidings, and conflicts among the members of the family. At the end of the interview they attempt to relate the presenting problem of the patient to the family and to explain its functioning.

## Findings and Conclusions

Two years of experience have shown that use of the playroom for diagnostic interviews of families with young children leads to the unfolding of more diagnostic data in a much less stressful atmosphere than an office setting. The children find the play material conducive to revealing information, some of which may be important.

Case 3. In a family interview that included the patient, Larry, age twelve, his sisters, ages ten and five, and their separated mother, the ten-year-old created a violent fight between the mother and father puppets. At the end of the fight the mother puppet asked the father puppet to leave and to take the children with him. Since the mother had told us she did not know why her husband had left her, this piece of play activity was very revealing.

By meeting in the playroom, the adults communicate their willingness to listen to the children. They enter the child's world and meet him on his level. Meanwhile the diagnostic team observes the interaction between the parents and children and among the children themselves, which is very much like that that in everyday life. In an office setting we only hear about this interaction or, at best, listen to its verbal aspects.

> *Case* 4. At the beginning of this family diagnostic interview centered around a six-year-old boy named Richard, who was known to have coordination and learning problems, his father asked him to draw his (the father's) picture on the blackboard, thus setting a goal that could not have been attained. As the child struggled, the father made manifest his disappointment on the one hand and his inability to accept the child's limitations and to support him on the other.

Since the material revealed by the children is through play and activity, the examiner can choose not to focus on it in order to keep the child from becoming anxious. In contrast, the child cannot be protected from discomforting anxiety in an office-type interview. When an anxiety-provoking situation does take place in the playroom, the play material is available to help the child deal with his anxiety.

> Judy (cited in case 2) found the little girl and father puppets helpful in dealing with her anger and anxiety over the disagreement between her brother John and her stepfather about the game rules. She made the little girl puppet hit the father puppet, saying, "Don't hurt my brother."

Playroom equipment offers situations that may be helpful in understanding the parents' personalities as well. For instance, parental reaction to finger paints and aggressive toys like guns provides us with opportunities for better understanding that could not be duplicated in an interview held in an office setting.

> *Case* 5. After observing her son's attraction to a toy gun, the borderline mother of four-year-old Jimmy, who was referred because of aggressive behavior, expressed her disapproval and with it her own problems with aggression. She reproached the child psychiatrist, saying that the gun and darts explained why her son had told her that he liked the doctor following his individual interview. When she recognized her feelings, she admitted that she would never allow toys like darts or guns in her house.

*Case 6.* Another mother, who had had psychotic episodes, used an alligator puppet with large sharp teeth to interact with her three-year-old daughter. Speaking for the alligator, she brought the mouth of the puppet to the child's, saying, "I want to kiss you." Her confusion about love and aggression could not have been better expressed.

Almost all parents welcomed the family interview. They felt, as did the diagnosticians, that it would provide a better picture of the family and the identified patient. Furthermore, they liked the idea of meeting the child psychiatrist with whom they otherwise would have had no contact.

We felt that meeting in the playroom had one more distinct advantage. Most parents have difficulty understanding play interviews and play therapy. The usual interpretation is that they are suspicious or jealous of their child's relationship with the therapist. Nevertheless, in some cases, if not in all, this question is realistic and justified. One cannot think of a better way to acquaint the parents with play interviews than to have them observe and participate in them.

The family's functioning in the diagnostic family interview is the most helpful prelude to family therapy. It can be used effectively in deciding the mode of therapy for the family.

**References**
1. Schwartz, H., "The Mother in the Consulting Room: Notes on the Psychoanalytic Treatment of Two Young Children," *Psychoanal Study Child* 5:343-357, 1950.
2. Pappenheim, E., Sweeney, M., "Separation Anxiety in Mother and Child," *Psychoanal Study Child* 7:95-114, 1952.
3. Bornstein, B., "Phobia of a Two-and-a-half-year-old Child," *Psychoanal Q* 4:93-119, 1935.
4. Freeman, R. D., "The Home Visit in Child Psychiatry," *J Am Acad Child Psychiatry* 6:276-294, 1967.
5. Drechsler, R. J., Schapiro, M. J., "A Procedure for Direct Observation of Family Interaction in a Child Guidance Clinic," *Psychiatry* 24:163-170, 1961.
6. Augenbraun, B., Tasem, M., "Differential Techniques in Family Interviewing with Both Parents and Preschool Child," *J Am Acad Child Psychiatry* 5:721-730, 1966.

7. Bergel, E. W., Gass, C., Zilbach, J. J., "Role of the Young Child in Family Therapy," in *Progress in Group and Family Therapy*, (eds) Sager, C., Kaplan, H. S., New York: Brunner/Mazel, 1972, pp. 385-399.
8. Ackerman, N. W., "Child Participation in Family Therapy," *Family Process* 9:403-410, 1970.

# Puppets in Child Psychotherapy

LAWRY HAWKEY

## Introduction

During the development of child psychotherapy certain play materials have become well established and are now in general use in nearly all clinics. Among these are the sandtrays and "world" materials introduced by Lowenfeld (1939). Even where Lowenfeld's method is not followed, modifications of this material are usually found. In addition, paints, paper, chalks and crayons are usually provided as well as various objects for water play. Dolls, sewing materials, dolls' houses, building bricks, trains, cars and guns are also common. These materials and many others have been in use since the early stages of play therapy.

## Use of Puppets

More recently sets of puppets and puppet theatres have appeared in some of the British clinics, and a good deal of work has been done in America on puppets in group therapy.*

In Switzerland, Rambert (1938) has used puppets as an extension of the play-therapy technique, and in Paris, Marcus (see Wall, 1950) uses puppets in both diagnostic and therapeutic work with children.

My own experience of puppets has been entirely in individual treatment. I have never used them alone nor emphasized them to the exclusion of other play material. They have been kept in the playroom with sand-trays, paints, dolls and other materials mentioned above. On looking back over the play of the children I have treated since introducing puppets into my playroom, I have come to the conclusion that they make

*E.g. at the Bellevue Hospital, New York.

a valuable addition to the other material in a child guidance clinic. They are particularly suitable for the expression of fantasy and are popular with children of varying ages. There are also various ways in which they can be used in individual treatment.

The majority of my patients who have used puppets have given shows in the usual way, playing out their own fantasies. When they do this I am the audience and watch the show. Many of the children ask me to take it in turns with them to give the show. This method of taking turns can be used by the therapist as a means of interpretation. Instead of discussing the material in the child's show I sometimes follow it with one of my own, in which I bring out more clearly the problems contained in the child's fantasy.

In other cases conversation is carried on between the therapist manipulating the puppet and the child in the audience, or vice versa. In this way children who are too shy or inhibited to give a show of their own often begin to produce fantasy material.

## Stealing by Boy of Twelve

One boy of twelve was attending the clinic on account of peculiar behavior at home. He frequently stole property from his adoptive mother, and always hid what he had stolen in a hedge near home. He was expecially inclined to take shoes and shoe-laces, and would also hide these in various places in the house. On one occasion the mother found that he had put on a pair of girl's knickers under his trousers. Although he was quite friendly when he came to the clinic there was at first nothing that he wanted to do. He would sometimes talk quite normally about school, but could never discuss his symptoms nor any emotionally toned material. He disliked drawing and painting, had no dreams and could remember nothing that had happened to him except in the last few years. All attempts to get at his fantasies failed until he was encouraged to use puppets. Even then he stood behind the curtains for a long time and said nothing. I tried to encourage him to do something, saying that it didn't matter what it was like. He then asked if it mattered if the puppets didn't talk. I said it didn't, and he just made them appear. This did not seem to be leading anywhere, so I asked if I could talk to them. He agreed to this, so I began by asking who they were and where they were going, etc. With this assistance he soon developed a fantasy of his own and introduced conversation himself. In the first fantasy all the animals had been bewitched and turned into different things by the witch. In the next show the snake was chasing the wolf because the latter had bitten off the snake's tail. But the wolf explained that he hadn't really done this and said he was a friend of the snake. The witch had made an imitation wolf, and this was the one that had bitten the snake. The animals joined together and killed the witch.

These fantasies were relevant to the boy's problems. The adoptive mother had actually behaved like the witch. She was a woman of good social status who had adopted an evacuee child from the slums and tried to turn him into something different. The fantasy of the snake's tail suggests a castration complex and was connected with the abnormal interest in shoes and with the wearing of girl's knickers.

After this the boy began making his own puppets. He became much more open and talkative and was very enthusiastic about coming to the clinic.

## Overdependency in Boy of Eleven

Another way of using puppets was introduced by David, a boy of eleven. He never used the theatre, nor gave a show in the ordinary way. He began with a boy glove puppet on one hand while I had a woman. They began talking to each other, David's puppet being called "David Prank" and mine "Mrs. Prank."

David was himself very good at home but was extremely nervous. He was very frightened of the dark, and when in bed would keep calling down to his mother. She said that he got in such a state if left alone that she spent most of the evening sitting upstairs in his bedroom. If she did not sit with him she would often find him under the bedclothes soaked with perspiration. David was very intelligent but he was backward at school, was frightened of going to school, and was bullied by other children. He also stammered and suffered from attacks of asthma.

In his play with puppets he began by making "David Prank" disobey "Mrs. Prank." The mother puppet sent the boy to bed. He kept calling down to her and being naughty. In the game he was not frightened but was just a nuisance. As the game developed the boy puppet became more and more aggressive, openly attacking the mother. This play was continued and developed over a period of many months. It became clear that "David Prank" was a representation of the inferior or "shadow" side of David's personality. As Jung (1940) says: "I have called the inferior and less commendable part of a person the *shadow*. We have met with this figure in literature, for instance, Faust and his shadow — Mephistopheles."

The boy David was extremely attached to his mother, was much too dependent on her and was unable to stick up for himself. The puppet David was aggressive and rude to his mother, refused to obey her and developed into a thoroughly delinquent character. He bullied other children in a most sadistic way, robbed banks and committed murders.

The majority of the aggression, however, was directed either against "Mrs. Prank" or against mother substitutes in the form of "Mrs. Prank's" charwomen.

Through this play with the puppets David gradually became aware of the "other" side of himself. He came to realize that behind his fear of the dark was a desire to dominate the mother. We discussed the relationship with his own mother in connexion with the David Prank games. At first David was afraid to stand up to his mother at all and was in danger of being swallowed up by her. The danger was also shown in his fears at night, which were mainly of prehistoric monsters which would devour him. I pointed out to him that he had in him the power to stand up to his mother in the way that "David Prank" did to "Mrs. Prank." He liked playing at "David Prank" but did not want to become like him, and was at first a bit afraid that he might do so. This was the fear of being swallowed by the shadow (Jung, 1940). However, this reversal did not take place. David was able to project the "bad" side of his personality on to the puppet, but in doing so he became aware of this other side of himself. He was gradually able to integrate some of the previously unconscious aggressiveness, and to become better able to stand up for himself. He was also able to free himself from his dependence on his mother. The asthma and fears disappeared, his appetite improved and he got on much better at school. The one symptom which remained when he stopped treatment was the stammer. This was variable and had improved considerably, but had not gone altogether.

The following case study shows another way in which puppets have been used by a child for the expression and development of his fantasy.

## Aggressive Boy of Six

Peter was six when he started treatment and was of average intelligence. He was an extremely aggressive child, and was reported to the clinic because of very bad behavior at school and at home, as well as for petty pilfering. When he first came to the clinic he was distractible and could not concentrate on any play. During the first seven months of treatment he was very destructive and spent a good deal of his time swearing at me and throwing things about. He was always on the defensive and seemed unable to make a relationship with me. He was very demanding and often took home the toys from the clinic. If we played in the garden he would throw stones at passing cars, and if I told him not to do this he would attack me. When any interpretation was attempted he became even more aggressive.

When he had been attending for seven months I had a new puppet theatre in my playroom. When Peter first saw this he didn't know what it was and was scornful about it. He tried climbing on it and nearly broke it. (It was not as strong as would have been desirable.) He wanted to know what it was for, so I showed him the puppets and gave a small show for him to see. Peter was very pleased with this and sat watching quietly except for comments of appreciation and requests for me to repeat bits. I asked him to do one himself, but he refused. He asked me to promise to do the same show again next time.

At the next interview he asked me to do another show and again refused to do one himself. However, he soon began to produce his own fantasies by telling me what to make the puppets do. He wanted one about a witch so I asked if he could think of a story. He told me to do one about a boy called John who was naughty to his Mummy. The sister was good. The boy was taken away by a witch and was killed. Father then killed the witch. When I began playing this he altered the story and said that John was to kill the witch. Animals had to come to frighten him, but he killed them all. After this the boy was good. A doctor brought the witch to life. She left the boy alone now that he was good.

The next time he again asked for the puppets and told me what to make them do. The boy was naughty and his sister was good. In the play the boy was captured by the witch. He killed the witch and all the nasty animals. At this interview Peter himself tried using the puppets after I had done his play. His own show consisted entirely of making the puppets fight and of banging their heads together.

During the next two interviews he was again unsettled and aggressive and did not have the puppets. He returned to them subsequently with the same story of the boy being captured by the witch and killing her. This time a man kept bringing her to life and she was killed again by the boy.

This recurrent theme was a statement of Peter's own problem and of the reason for his aggressive behavior. Peter himself was a naughty boy and he had a sister a year younger who was usually good. The witch is the devouring mother (Hawkey, 1947). Being devoured by the mother is a "state in which the child is too much mothered and kept infantile, is unable to stand on his own feet and becomes fixated to his mother, with the result that he tries to overcome her by outbursts of rage and by actual attack, or, alternatively, becomes a compliant weakling completely dependent on his mother and inseparable from her" (Fordham, 1944).

In Peter's case he tried to free himself from the devouring mother by the method of attack. Similarly in his fantasy the naughty boy kills the witch. But this is no permanent solution as she keeps coming to life again. In other words, Peter has been unable to free himself from the mother.

This theme was developed in later puppet shows. On one occasion Peter joined in from the audience and asked if he could be a member of

# Costume Play Therapy

IRWIN M. MARCUS

During the years of development and maturation, there are changes in the child's motivations, dynamics, and methods of play. A number of excellent papers have been concerned with various aspects of the theory of play; among them are those of Sigmund Freud (1920, 1923), Anna Freud (1936, 1944, 1946), Erikson (1937), Waelder (1933), Ernst Kris (1934), Piaget (1945), and Peller (1954).

Fantasy life underlies all human activities and retains its basic themes, although during the course of healthy development reality issues will have a stronger influence upon the individual. Whereas the younger child can express his fantasies spontaneously with whatever material is available, the older child is less free in this repect. The latter may show initiative and creativity on an independent basis, yet he tends to require the cooperation of others for role playing and support in his more formalized imaginative games. Thus, the older child prefers real materials and more true to life situations, or stories he has seen or experienced in other ways. The limitations placed upon the type of communication an older child will permit, either in play or directly is a reflection of his defenses and his fears of the fantasy content.

Experienced and skillful therapists are able to work with the various disguised manifestations of underlying mother-child or child-father and sibling relationships and conflicts. The transformations are seen in the child's sports, hobbies, secret clubs, and his intense feelings over winning and losing the great variety of structured popular games. Play behavior in the latency period is characterized by defenses that veer toward games which lack spontaneity, and tends to be conventional and competitive, with relatively little emotional content. The older child is gradually moving away from the disappointments and frustrations of his earlier about the first session at which he did not swear at me. The aggression and rudeness were now becoming contained in the puppet shows where the anal theme continued to develop. He now omitted the play about collecting the money and spent all the time on the puppets. The whole of the fantasy was Peter's although I again manipulated the puppets and he watched. This time the black "Sambo" joined the gang. First he had to fight the parrot to show he was strong enough. He did this and won. Then he had to fight "the little tough guy" (the sailor boy). The sailor won, as "he's the strongest of all," but Sambo fought well and was taken into the gang. He asked if he could live with the gang forever, but was told that *"first he must go and kill his mother."*

This fantasy is very significant. It is reminiscent of the passage from Barlach's drama *Der tote Tag* quoted by Jung in *Psychological Types* (1936):

> And there about my bed stand the lovely forms of a better future. Still are they yet, but of radiant beauty, still sleeping — but he who shall awaken them would make for the world a fairer face. A hero would be who could do it.
> *Mother.* An heroic life in misery and dire need!
> *Kule.* But perchance there might be one!
> *Mother.* He first must bury his mother.

In *Psychology of the Unconscious*, Jung (1916) says:

> The onward urging, living libido which rules the consciousness of the son, demands separation from the mother. The longing of the child for the mother is a hindrance on the path to this, taking the form of a psychological resistance which is expressed empirically in the neurosis by all manners of fears, that is to say, the fear of life .... The fear springs from the mother, that is to say, from the longing to go back to the mother, which is opposed to the adaptation to reality. This is the way in which the mother has become apparently the malicious pursuer. Naturally, it is not the actual mother, although the actual mother, with the abnormal tenderness with which she sometimes pursues the child, even into adult years, may gravely injure it through a wilful prolonging of the infantile state in the child. It is rather the mother imago which becomes the Lamia. The mother imago, however, possesses its power solely and exclusively from the son's tendency not only to look and to work forwards, but also to glance backwards to the pampering sweetness of childhood, to that glorious state of irresponsibility and security with which the protecting mother-care once surrounded him.

Thus, before Sambo can become a permanent member of the gang he has to "go and kill his mother," that is, he has to free himself from his attachment to his mother.

In Peter's fantasy Sambo went home to his mother and she wasn't good to him. He said he was going to kill her. She begged him not to do this and gave him her watch. She promised she would be good to him, so he gave her another chance. She gave him whatever he liked for supper. But she didn't go on being good to him and so he killed her. When she was dead he hit her in the face, then he went back to the gang and left her there. After this the wolf came and found the mother. He fetched a book of magic and brought her back to life. She couldn't remember what had happened.

The wolf found Sambo and said he'd brought the mother to life. Sambo was cross and said he'd killed her. The wolf followed Sambo, who climbed into a house through a window. Sambo hid in the house and the wolf tried to find him. Sambo kept popping out and pulling the wolf's tail. Eventually Sambo and the wolf had a fight. Sambo killed the wolf and threw him in the river. Then he went home again to kill his mother. This time she promised she really would be good to him. He went off in the woods with the gang and his mother said it didn't matter what time he came home. He could stay out as late as he liked.

In this fantasy the boy has actually killed the mother but the wolf brings her to life. However, she is now less possessive. Sambo is allowed to go out with the gang and to stay out as late as he likes. He has gained a certain amount of independence.

At the following interview the wolf wanted to join the gang. He had to have fights with the parrot and the "little tough guy," to show he was strong enough. Peter was the "little tough guy," and spoke for him part of the time. The episode of pulling the wolf's tail was repeated and then he was allowed to join the gang. He said he was going off to kill Sambo's mother, but this never actually happened. The magician came in swearing about "arse holes" and "lumps of shit." Peter began shouting out at the magician, "You're made of shit." "You've got a big arse hole." He came and punched the magician on the face. He continued to be aggressive himself until the wolf killed the magician.

In the next show a girl was in the house alone. She was going to bed and a ghost came and frightened her. The boy hid in a cupboard and killed the ghost the next time it came. He threw it out of the window. After this all the bad characters came in turn to get the girl. Each time the boy came out and killed them. Gradually other members of the gang arrived and also hid in the cupboard. This time Peter was "Sambo" and was the best fighter. The devil (magician) was again the one to say "shitbugger," etc. Whenever he appeared, Peter began shouting this out, and this became the devil's name. Apart from this there was no swearing. At the end Peter pretended to kill the devil and he went off quietly.

The next time he came in in an aggressive mood. He threw paint jars on the floor and was very cross because he got his clothes splashed with paint. He swore at me and said, "I'll kill you." He said he wanted a puppet show, but I was to make it up. As Peter's mother had been away to stay twice recently I began with the boy's mother saying she was going away and that he was to look after his little sister. Peter immediately joined in and said for the boy, "How long are you going to be away?" I said for the mother "A fortnight." Peter objected to this and said he'd kill his sister if his mother was away as long as this. I made her offer to come home in a week. He said this was not long enough, she must stay away a week and two days. The mother agreed and went away. The boy then fetched the baby. Peter said he must look at her "arse hole" and then at her "cock." After this the boy went out with his pals. The witch came. Peter said she was to stick her nose up the baby's "arse hole." She did this and Peter said for her "it's lovely and soft." Peter then said he would be friends with the witch. She went home to "Market Square" and took the baby with her. She put her nose in the baby's "arse hole" again and went to sleep. The boy went home and found his baby sister was missing. Peter told him what had happened and told him to go to "Market Square." He did this and saw the witch with her nose up the baby's "arse hole." He went in and put his nose up the witch's "arse hole." Sambo then had to appear. Peter told him what the others were doing and that the wolf was coming to put his nose up Sambo's "arse hole." The wolf arrived and went to the baby's "arse hole." Sambo fought him. He allowed him to put his nose up the baby's "arse hole" for a little while, but then killed him and threw him out of the window. The others woke up. There was more about the noses up "arse holes," and then they all went home. After this Peter asked for the girl again. She was to be frightened like the last time. Sambo was in the cupboard. He said he would look after her. The ghost came to look at the girl's "arse hole," and Sambo killed him. Then the devil came and began to put his nose in the girl's "arse hole." Sambo killed him. All the bad ones and the animals came in turn to do this to the girl and Sambo killed them all. The witch and the devil came to life and came a second time. After killing them Sambo did it to the girl himself. Then Peter said for him "Now I'll do you." I made the girl ask what that meant.* Peter said it was putting his "cock" in her "arse hole." When he had done this he killed her with a penknife.

During this fantasy there was much emphasis by Peter on the niceness of the feeling when one of the puppet's noses was in either the

---

*I have been told by other children that the expression "I'll do you" means sexual intercourse.

witch's, the baby's or the girl's "arse hole." At these times he often said "it's lovely and soft." He did not say this when the nose was in the wolf's or another boy's "arse hole." Sometimes two characters would do it together; e.g., the witch's nose in the boy's "arse hole" while his nose was in hers. There was a good deal about wanting to look at each other's "arse holes." Once the boy asked to look at the witch's "cock." He said "Oh, it's lovely!" then he went off to fetch a stick. He came back and pushed it up her "cock." "All piss" came out over the stick. He did it again and this time she didn't "piss."

Once he began telling me to put a puppet's "cock" up another's "arse hole", but altered "cock" to nose. Clearly in the whole of this fantasy the nose is a substitute for the penis.* Throughout this interview Peter sat masturbating while he told me what the puppets were to do. This fantasy shows the overlapping of anal and genital eroticism. The appreciation of the girl's "holes" which are "lovely and soft" indicates a development from the anal to the genital level, but this is not yet complete. The play reveals a good deal about the sexual fantasy of the child and also about the material which lies behind his swearing and aggression.

The next time he returned to the same theme. The baby and the girl were in bed. Sambo was in the cupboard. The bad ones came and put their noses up the baby's and the girl's "arse holes." Sambo fought them and also did it himself. The red devil came and said "Shit-bugger." Sometimes Sambo put his "cock" in the witch's and the girl's "cock." He also got a knife and stuck it up the witch's "arse hole." During this play Peter sucked his finger instead of masturbating.

All the bad ones and the animals were killed by Sambo. After this Peter wanted a different show. This began with mother, father and Sambo. Sambo had a "magic touch." He could make food by clapping his hands. He made a meal of egg on toast. Father asked Sambo to teach him how to do it. Sambo did, and then father could also make food. Mother also asked and Sambo taught her as well. Mother said she wished she could get a bicycle. Sambo said he could make anything they wanted. He made a bicycle for his mother and then a racing bike for himself. He raced the wolf. The wolf bet him £90 he wouldn't win. Sambo won and had the £90. Then the wolf bet him £100 he wouldn't win again. He did and got the £100. He went home with the money in his pockets. His mother saw his pockets bulging and told him to empty out that rubble. She was cross with him for having his pockets full. She was surprised when she saw the money. The same scene was repeated with the father. After this Sambo

*There is also the idea of the nose smelling the dirt.

raced the wolf once more and won £1000. The parents were again cross when they saw his bulging pockets.

Here again the relationship between faces and money is significant. Jung (1916) says (see also Freud, 1909):

> Children bring to the act of defaecation and the products of this an esteem and interest which later on is possible only to the hypochondriac. We do not comprehend this interest until we learn that the child very early connects with it a theory of propagation. The libido afflux probably accounts for the enormous interest in this act. The child sees that this is the way in which something is produced, in which something comes out. . . . In this way one can make what one wishes, and the thing made is the thing wished for.

In the next puppet show the witch was in the woods and was killed. Someone tried to pull down the boy's trousers. They did not succeed, but the boy pulled down theirs and killed them. This was repeated with different puppets. I asked Peter if he did this. He said "We pull down the girls' knickers at school. We hide in the trees and jump on the girls. I do it to Jane."

Next the girl was killed by the witch. She had a cut on her "arse hole." Sambo brought her to life. Sambo went home and said "Bugger." The girl told the mother and she told father. Father was angry. He had a fight with Sambo, who killed him. Sambo went off on his bicycle. Mother followed him but couldn't catch him and she went home. Sambo came home and killed the girl and the mother. The girl came to life and she brought her mother and father back to life. Sambo swore again and threatened to kill his father.

After this there was another show in which Peter pretended he could do magic and make gold. He pretended to teach Sambo to make gold, but this was only paper gold. Sambo went off to buy a bicycle but hadn't enough money. Peter pretended to give him a lot of gold. Then he was able to buy a bicycle.

This was the last of the shows about making money and he did not return to the "arse hole" theme. He began playing much better with the other materials, and the puppet shows changed to stories about Roy Rogers and his cowboys. By this time the most destructive phase was over and Peter was no longer pilfering.

During the early part of his treatment Peter was extremely uncooperative and seemed unable to make a good relationship with anyone. He had no friends, and his only approach to children or adults was an aggressive attack. It appeared from the puppet shows that this inability to make relationships was connected with his fixation at the anal-sadistic level. In the fantasies the anal interest was gradually superseded by interest in the "gang" and in Roy Rogers and the cowboys. In these fantasies there was definite co-operation between the different cowboys, and by this time Peter himself had become much more friendly, both with me and with other children. His general behavior continued to improve and regular treatment was stopped after a few months.

Until this boy became interested in the puppets he had been unable to express his fantasies in any constructive way. His aggressive and destructive behavior was apparently related to his fixation at the anal level. However, he was at first unable to express his anal fantasies because of the feeling of guilt attached to them. As Freud (1913) says:

> Children are proud, as it were, of their own excretions and make use of them to help in asserting themselves against adults. Under the influence of education the coprophilic instincts and inclinations of children give way to repression; they learn to keep them secret, to be ashamed of them and to feel disgust at the objects themselves.

For the same reason he was unable to make the puppets act himself. The method which he developed, whereby he produced the ideas and I manipulated the puppets, was a way of overcoming the guilt. However "bad" the action he suggested, I myself made the puppets perform it. In this way I shared in the fantasy with him and was able also to share in the guilt.

The "bad" fantasies in this case were concerned mainly with the anal-erotic system and with the desire to look at and to play with excreta. There was also seen to be a close connexion between these fantasies and those about money and the magic production of gold. Freud (1908) says:

> The connexions which exist between the two complexes of interest in money and of defecation, which seem so dissimilar, appear to be the most farreaching . . . — wherever archaic modes of thought predominate or have persisted — in ancient civilization, in myth, fairy-tale and superstition, in unconscious thoughts and dreams, and in the neuroses — money comes into the closest relation with excrement.

## Conclusions

In my experience puppets are particularly valuable for certain types of cases, for the following reasons. First, there is the boy of eleven or twelve (cf. case 1) who finds difficulty in expressing his fantasy. Children of this age often think when they first come to the clinic that they are too old to play with toys. On the other hand, they may not be mature enough to be treated through dream analysis and discussion of problems alone.

Drawing and painting are used a great deal with children of this age, but there are some boys and girls who definitely prefer and respond better to puppets.

Secondly, children of any age who find difficulty in formulating their fantasies seem to be stimulated by the appearance of the puppets. Ordinary dolls are, of course, invaluable and are used especially for working out problems connected with early childhood and attitudes to baby brothers and sisters. But the fact that puppets can be more readily used as either adults or children, men or women, and the presence of animal puppets, witches, ghosts, etc., encourages the child in the projection into them of a large variety of material.

The fact that all three cases which I have chosen for discussion are boys is not without significance. Elsewhere I have described the play of two girls, both of whom used puppets during their treatment (Hawkey, 1945, 1947). However, I have not yet treated a girl who has concentrated on puppets to the exclusion of other play material, nor in whose treatment the puppets played such an important part as they did in the cases discussed here. When the girls have used puppets they have had them as another means of expression in turn with dolls and pretending games. Probably the reason for this is that girls can play with dolls, whereas a number of boys think it babyish to do so. Fortunately, this attitude does not extend to puppets. Even big, adolescent boys are able to use these without feeling that they are being childish or girlish.

The last case which I have discussed here illustrates the value of puppets in acting out the child's "bad" fantasies. In this case the child was especially concerned with anal erotic material, with examining and playing with faeces and anuses, and with the magic production of money and gold. Puppets are particularly useful for the expression of fantasy, as they can be made to do anything, however "bad." To a young child the puppet seems to be "real,"* and the guilt he feels about the fantasy is projected on to the puppets. It is the puppets who are doing the "bad" things, not the boy himself. Because they are puppets they are not permanently harmed by their bad deeds. Even if they are killed they can always come to life again.

In the analysis of adults Jung and his followers lay stress on the value of "active-imagination." In *Mythology of the Soul*, Baynes (1949) wrote:

> . . . the saving means clearly lies in creating a new avenue by which the inturned fantasy-activity can become objective.
> The essence of psychotherapy consists in this operation: it effects a means whereby the vague, subjective, unsizable, inverted

---

*Cf. Peter's remark, p. 209: "It's a real witch."

activity of the libido can gain objective form and expression. This may be achieved by talking, free association, discussion and interpretation of the dream, fantasy or other products of autonomous mental activity: in a word creating one's own myth.

For the child the use of puppets can be another means to this end.

### References

Baynes, H. G. (1949), *Mythology of the Soul*, London: Methuen and Co. Ltd.

Fordham, M. S. M. (1944), *The Life of Childhood*, London: Kegan Paul, Trench, Trubner and Co.

Freud, S. (1908), "Character and Anal Erotism," in *Collected Papers*, 2, London: Hogarth Press (1949).

Freud, S. (1909), "A Phobia in a Five-year-old Boy," in *Collected Papers*, 3, London: Hogarth Press (1949).

Freud, S. (1913), "The Excretory Functions in Psychoanalysis and Folklore," *Collected Papers*, 5, London: Hogarth Press (1949).

Hawkey, L. (1945), "Play Analysis — Case Study of a Nine-year-old Girl, *Brit. J. Med. Psychol.* 20, 3.

Hawkey, L. (1947), "The Witch and the Bogey," *Brit. J. Med. Psychol.* 21, 1.

Jung, C. G. (1916), *Psychology of the Unconscious*, New York: Moffat Yard and Co.

Jung, C. G. (1936), *Psychological Types*, London: Kegan Paul, Trench, Trubner and Co.

Jung, C. G. (1940), *The Integration of the Personality*, London: Kegan Paul, Trench, Trubner and Co.

Lowenfeld, M. (1939), "The World Pictures of Children," *Brit. J. Med. Psychol.* 18, 1.

Rambert, M. L. (1938), "Une nouvelle technique en psychoanalyse infantile: le jeu de guignols, *Rev. franc. Psych. anal.* 10.

Wall, L. V. (1950), *The Puppet Book*, London: Faber and Faber.

# Costume Play Therapy

IRWIN M. MARCUS

During the years of development and maturation, there are changes in the child's motivations, dynamics, and methods of play. A number of excellent papers have been concerned with various aspects of the theory of play; among them are those of Sigmund Freud (1920, 1923), Anna Freud (1936, 1944, 1946), Erikson (1937), Waelder (1933), Ernst Kris (1934), Piaget (1945), and Peller (1954).

Fantasy life underlies all human activities and retains its basic themes, although during the course of healthy development reality issues will have a stronger influence upon the individual. Whereas the younger child can express his fantasies spontaneously with whatever material is available, the older child is less free in this respect. The latter may show initiative and creativity on an independent basis, yet he tends to require the cooperation of others for role playing and support in his more formalized imaginative games. Thus, the older child prefers real materials and more true to life situations, or stories he has seen or experienced in other ways. The limitations placed upon the type of communication an older child will permit, either in play or directly is a reflection of his defenses and his fears of the fantasy content.

Experienced and skillful therapists are able to work with the various disguised manifestations of underlying mother-child or child-father and sibling relationships and conflicts. The transformations are seen in the child's sports, hobbies, secret clubs, and his intense feelings over winning and losing the great variety of structured popular games. Play behavior in the latency period is characterized by defenses that veer toward games which lack spontaneity, and tends to be conventional and competitive, with relatively little emotional content. The older child is gradually moving away from the disappointments and frustrations of his earlier dependency upon his family. With developmental changes, he is ready to seek the pleasures and security of new object relations through identifications with peer group and parentlike figures. The desire of an older child to play the usual games considered appropriate for his age helps him to defend against his earlier family conflicts by clinging to impersonal activity and shifting his competitive feelings toward his peers. However, this quality of ego development can be a real barrier to communication between a child and therapist when the child dedicates himself to concealing his feeling and is ashamed of his daydreams. Furthermore, the latency period is the time when adults expect the child to conform, to accept limitations, to develop good learning and study habits, skills, and group behavior. Thus, his anxieties are often met with reassurance, logical arguments, or ridicule which fosters the child's defenses against communication of his fantasies.

## Stimulating Spontaneous Play in Older Children

Utilizing the knowledge of play theory, this project explores the *possibility of deliberately stimulating a more spontaneous play pattern in older children.* The intent was to revive the imaginative play of the earlier years in a manner that would diminish the defensive embarrassment frequently produced by the usual play materials. Play patterns of the younger child allow vivid communication and the participation of others, but the grade school child *prefers props to support his role in the fantasy.* Therefore, costumes were provided in abundance for the purpose of setting the stage for dramatic play. In turn, this reopened an avenue that was once so pleasurable and useful for expressing emotional and conflictual experiences. Thus, the costume technique is designed to combine the advantages of the situational method and free play. Children who are disturbed because they have had to endure experiences of a traumatic magnitude can work toward mastery through playful repetition of more digestible portions of these events. By changing roles, children who were passive victims can become active aggressors. Their feelings of painful helplessness can be re-experienced with a happier, stronger, and successful conclusion. Although play is usually not complete abandon, there is sufficient relief from both reality and the conscience to allow for a display of the child's fantasies about himself and others. Play enables the ego to deal with the external pressures of reality and with the intrapsychic impact of impulses and conscience. With more complete emotional involvement in the fantasies of play, the child has a greater outlet for his anxiety and can experience the pleasure of wish fulfillment.

A striking aspect of costume play therapy is the ease with which older children can act out vital unconscious material without sufficient awareness to intensify anxiety and thereby resistance. The complementary role assigned to the therapist by the child allows the therapist to engage in meaningful responses, which promotes further communication and fosters problem solving. If the child is suffering from a neurotic illness, the interpretive possibilities open to the therapist are well known to those with experience in the field. The fantasy play may be linked with the significant episodes and figures in the child's real life; or the therapist may call attention to resemblances between play situations and the real relationships in a manner that allows the defenses to be worked upon. Metaphoric interpretation may be used when the assessment of the child's ego strength suggests that a distance must be maintained between the fantasy and the conscious awareness of the child — although, of course, the therapist must eventually bring the known conflicts into consciousness. When regressions are already present or easily evoked, as in the borderline and psychotic states, tenuous object relations can at least be maintained by confining interpretations to the patient's own regressed language (Ekstein and Wallerstein, 1956). Repetitious play on the regressed level, as long as the contact remains, provides a foundation for later, more mature identifications and the emergence of secondary-process thinking.

In therapy, the traumatic experience, conflict, and anxiety must be externalized and brought into the child-therapist relationship. As Anna Freud (1946) noted, fruitful work in child therapy requires a "positive attachment." Since the specific play roles become the chief avenue for communication, the context of the emotion is more readily recognized and handled, thus permitting the therapist to sustain his position as the child's ally. *A trusting and meaningful relationship evolves from the ability to communicate understanding* to the child, rather than from friendly playful activities as such. Costume play therapy allows the therapist to communicate with the child on whatever level the child presents. "Playing out" fantasies, feelings, and traumatizing situations through "make-believe" emphasizes the demarcation between reality and fantasy while bridging the gap with communication and understanding. Thus, the therapeutic nature of the costume play is promoted through sharing the disguised experience and mood, through closeness, mutuality, good communication, and understanding of the specific anxieties which accompany the fantasies. In all the techniques of play therapy, varying roles are explicitly or, more often, implicitly assigned to the therapist and assumed by the patient, depending upon the child's needs at the time. However, part of the difficulty in practicing and teaching play therapy is precisely the problem of understanding the child's communications through play. Unfortunately, this factor may impart in the minds of parents, student therapists, and others a mystical and esoteric quality to the direct treatment of children. Costumes as a stimulus for imaginative play clarify the explicit nature of the role and utilize the child's need for motility, activity, and defensive disguise.

Anyone who wishes to relate to children must know how to play or converse with them. Therapists are at times "kept in the dark" and at a considerable distance in the relationship because a child may reject playing with dolls or puppets and would rather play a game or color a picture than paint freely or play with clay. Costumes are natural equipment within the current experiences of both the child and the therapist. The therapist at varying times throughout his life will "dress up" for costume parties or events as a not infrequent experience in social "fun" activities.[1] In costume play therapy the therapist does not dress up, nor, in my experience, does the child require this. The costumes are for the patients. The therapist remains an adult with his reponses geared to the reality of therapy, and he should not slip into acting out his own unresolved or revived conflicts. However, the ability of a therapist to be an adult who can understand and still be with the child in his fantasy play is a unique and essential quality of child therapy. The basic principles are no different with the costume play therapy technique. The child's need for the therapist to accept a role is more dependent upon the therapist's response than the latter's appearance in a costume. The therapist's anxiety about "what does this mean?" when viewing certain other play activities is diminished and replaced with the increased security of feeling a sense of mastery through improved contact and communication with the child.

---

[1] The basic premise of this paper is easily observed among adults in New Orleans during Mardi Gras. I am analyzing a married woman who has a frigidity problem. She reported that prior to therapy she dressed as a "baby,"her regression from the oedipal conflicts. In a later phase, she spontaneously selected the role of a "flapper." A patient who had to fashion a costume for his "date" at a party created a "nun's outfit" for her, and in analysis recalled he once heard someone say she was promiscuous, but he rejected the idea because of his affection for her. Another woman, with sexual frustration as one of her problems, repeatedly dressed in skin-tight leotards as a "devil." A homosexual man once dressed as a "bum," but with a very large nose, whereas another homosexual patient could never decide what he wanted to wear, reflecting his identity problem. A Jewish man in conflict with his religious identity selected an Arab costume. Finally, there are always a number of adults who dress as the opposite sex whenever costumes are permitted for an occasion, an obvious revelation of unresolved conflicts.

Although "dress-up" games are part of oedipal period play, its Anlage may be seen in the early imitation and identification activities, when the child experiences the pleasure of closeness with mother and father through clumping around the house in their shoes and decorating himself with any other item of apparel he can snatch from the household. The popularity of the box of old hats sometimes included in a nursery school setting is an example of the natural attraction of children to "dress-up" games. It is an activity which is permissible at times in all ages, and thus resistance to this play is less likely to occur. The mutual pleasure of costume play enhances the likelihood of the child's returning to the same materials for more consistent working through of disturbed feelings and conflicts. In contrast, the anxiety or hostility displayed in activities of play where there is less pleasure and the therapist's role is more vague in the child's mind may contribute to the disruption of play.

The study was initiated with three children, a girl and a boy both ten years old, and an eleven-year-old boy. All three were photographed in black and white 16 mm. movie sound film during the early phase of their individual therapy. The introduction to costume play and samples of the technique and interaction during therapy were edited in a twenty-minute reel. The camera and professional observers were concealed in another room and viewed the therapy through a one-way mirror. Sessions were conducted weekly, for about forty-five to fifty minutes, with the author as therapist. The costumes included the following: those appropriate for a baby, mother, father, doctor, superman, witch, devil, clown, skeleton, ballerina, and three large pieces of colored cloth for a self-designed outfit.

## Case of Evan: A Multiple Problem Boy

The method is illustrated in the following example: Evan, aged almost ten, was referred by the Welfare Department because he was a slow learner and about two years behind in schoolwork. He seemed confused and incapable of following directions. Teachers complained of his daydreaming and inability to concentrate. He was effeminate in his mannerisms and submissive in his relationship to his fraternal twin brother. His constant and pervasive lying included serious distortions about his teachers, friends, and other adults. He stole, but accused others when objects were missing and later found to be in his possession.

In psychological testing Evan achieved an I.Q. on the Verbal Scale of 94, on Performance 92, and on the Full Scale of 92. It was difficult for the examiner to understand his stories on the Apperception Test, but one could grasp his sadness, feeling of loneliness, and fears that his mother would kill him. Both he and his brother showed ego disorganization. His schizophrenic mother had been hospitalized for several years, and since the age of two he had been in institutions and foster homes.

Treatment was initiated in May 1963 and terminated in December 1964. Evan was shy and reluctant about selecting a costume from the many hanging in open display and denied having any memories of play with costumes. In low, hushed tones he recalled various situations in which he was deprived of a variety of toys and play materials. His actions and communications were highly inhibited and constricted. He preferred to find a chair, sit down, and stare with a blank expression — a response that frequently causes therapists to become bored and frustrated. However, the theapist's sympathetic responses to Evan's past and present situations and continued encouragement to try making up a play with the costumes gradually succeeded. Evan cautiously examined each costume and finally selected the mother's outfit. He began playing the role of a teacher, asking the therapist to be the principal, and at other times the teacher's husband. He prepared large meals for the family, gave his children money for food, and in the school play he instructed the children, using a nearby blackboard, and assured them that they would pass.

The theme of a good mother who fed her children well prevailed for many sessions. The therapist commented on Evan's great concern that the children be fed. He responded by recollecting that others had told him his mother was sick and could not take care of him, and that he longed for his mother. In time the therapist mentioned that sometimes children are very angry about their mothers leaving them. Evan seemed to have a minimal response to this comment, but the sessions gradually shifted into a detective story. He reported a woman murdered because she murdered her children. However, the good woman who punished the bad mother would in turn be punished by the police. We talked about people being afraid to say their angry thoughts because of fear of being punished. The therapist interpreted that sometimes very sad children have very angry thoughts that frighten them, because they are afraid they will be punished by having to live away from their homes. During this phase of the play, Evan interjected thoughts about the fantasized cold weather in the play and of how he hated to be "out in the cold."

Evan later switched into the role of the ghost of the bad mother (stimulated by his selecting the skeleton costume during this phase) who had been murdered in previous sessions. There was much anxious and excited play about coffins and a ghost seeking revenge. In the end, the ghost was defeated by the therapist, who was assigned the role of policeman. Evan began to show overt warmth toward the therapist at this stage, being reluctant to leave at the end of the sessions, hugging the therapist upon leaving and arriving, and expressing eagerness about the next visit of his social worker who would transport him. He became more responsive and communicative with her during their time together. The sessions shifted to his playing the wife in a loving marriage. During this phase, among his many comments, he exclaimed, "Darling, darling, darling, hold me in your arms." In these periods we were able to talk about his fantasies about his father (who had deserted them), his wishes to have his father back, his fears about whether his father had hurt his mother, his fears about being hurt himself, and his fantasy that the only way a boy could be loved is to be like a girl. However, he had another solution to being loved which became apparent in the following sessions when he selected, for the first time, the baby costume. In the baby role, he arranged the chairs into a bed and curled into the fetal position, made goo-goo sounds, engaged in rocking motions, and sucked his thumb. The satisfaction and regression on this level of play were so intense that for a while he was inaccessible to contact. However, in coming out of the baby role, he was exuberant, smiled happily, and seemed much more relaxed.

The therapist did not appear to have any specific role during the foregoing, other than to allow Evan the gratification of his longing for the fantasied pleasures of being an infant again. This time he could imagine starting life with a new parent figure, the therapist. The therapist commented on how children who are unhappy wish to be a baby again and have new parents who will take care of them: to love and be loved. Evan responded very strongly with memories of a foster family he loved before he was shifted into the institution. I commented on his disappointments in the past and concern about trusting each new person in his life, including the therapist. His costume play then vacillated between the role of baby and that of a mother, re-enacting a cruel mother who hated her baby, whom he named for his brother. During these sessions he expressed a great deal of hostility toward his brother, and verbalized his feeling of being hated by his mother. With self-designed costumes from the pieces of colored cloth, he became a cruel queen and captured an explorer (the therapist) who had landed on "her" planet. The explorer was tortured in many ways, whipped, shot with ray guns, and made into a weak, submissive man.

His fantasy patterns showed marked sadomasochistic features. There were many variations of his fears of being injured, his self-image of being castrated, and his desire for and fear of inflicting destruction. His castration anxiety and sense of helplessness were translated into the fears of the explorer, and the resemblance of the cruel queen to a hated and feared mother were interpreted. His image of women as castrated, vindictive, dangerous torturers of men necessitated concealing his own masculinity. In response to the therapist's query about what made the queen so mad, he replied that "her face had been burned off by old men." He later remarked about women having to be cut open to take their babies out. Periods of decreased anxiety followed as the foregoing was repeatedly worked through. In later sessions he assigned the doctor role to the therapist to repair the damaged queen.

After several months of therapy, progress reports prepared by his social worker indicated that he had become more aggressive and defended himself in a physical encounter with another boy. His effeminate behavior diminished, and he showed improved ability to tolerate frustration, to accept discipline and disappointments. He became more demonstrative in expressing affection for the worker. After a year of therapy, his academic work began to show real improvement. His intense interest in the costumes gradually diminished, his communications became more direct, and he manifested a growing interest in typical organized boys' games.

The history of Evan was one of severe neglect early in life. His instinctual life could not be combined with the pleasurable sensory stimulation of good mothering. He experienced too much real deprivation and frustration which impaired the adequate development of his ego. Combining instinctual tensions with only fragmented perceptions causes a child to produce distorted fantasy perceptions of his environment. The result is a diminished attentiveness to the outside world, greater absorption in unconscious fantasies, gratifying daydreams, and impaired reality testing. With his ego organization thus disturbed, Evan's instinctual tensions were frequently relieved through primary processes resulting in "nonsense" and "silly" talk and behavior. His energies were dissipated by these conditions and a severe learning and behavior problem was inevitable. His hunger for a mothering relationship caused him to cling to primitive, distorted identifications with mother figures and to be submissive and dependent upon his brother and other boys.

Evan was very responsive to play opportunities provided by the costume technique. He quickly constructed a plot around a family setting, and, as expected, he played the mother role. Play forms may combine or merge with one another, and *preoedipal play*, with its preoccupation with mother, was present for a prolonged period. He dramatized the role of a mother figure, his teacher, and displayed his wishes for the good mother who would be loving to her children and husband. He presented a fusion of mother and teacher, playing both roles; in addition, he demonstrated his wish to be like her, to have her with him at all times, and to replace her in order to achieve closeness with father. During his preoedipal play he was characteristically very serious. His rage and anxiety in relation to mother gradually unfolded in the murder plot, as he tried to get rid of the bad mother and retain the good mother identifications and introjects.

Guilty reactions appeared in the punishment scenes wherein the police apprehended the good woman who killed the bad one. Fantasies of the magical power of bad mothers, corpses, and ghosts who can destroy their children reflected the delusional fear of the absent mother and provided opportunities for the therapist to play the policeman (institute-therapist-social workers, and benevolent conscience) who will protect him and diminish his fears and guilt. His rage and guilt were also felt toward his brother and were concealed behind a submissive reaction formation, but these feelings were ventilated in the baby-mother scenes. On the baby level he gratified and expressed his dependency needs and fantasies without having to defend against them with denial or repression. By the maintenance of the therapeutic relationship through the most regressive periods of the play, the primitive transferences became a bridge for reopening avenues of identificatory processes.

In later play he was more oedipal and assumed the role of the powerful omnipotent adult (queen) and happily controlled the therapist (child). During this play, he displayed his feelings about people who lied to him — the facts about his family and his own origin. On another level, he relieved his oedipal conflict by controlling father and (possessing) being mother. His castration anxiety was an important theme throughout this phase.

As the pressures of his intrapsychic conflicts were played out, his relationship to the therapist grew more positive and new identifications occurred, his attention to reality improved, as did his ego organization, and learning again became available to him. His ability to separate from mother attachments and develop his own individuality developed gradually and he became more assertive with his brother. Identifications with male figures became more acceptable and effeminate behavior diminished. The strengthening of the ego was also apparent in his increased tolerance for frustration and discipline.

## Summary and Conclusion

Older children tend to be more defensive about their feelings and avoid communication about fantasies and daydreams. Their play preference is for conventional, competitive games. Costume play therapy is designed to stimulate deliberately an imaginative play pattern. In earlier play patterns the children prefer props to support their roles in the fantasy; therefore, a variety of costumes was provided to set the stage for spontaneous fantasy productions. Thus the costume technique combines the advantages of the situational or structured method and free play. The method may be employed in certain phases of child psychotherapy and analysis. It is conceivable that, as a projective instrument, the method may be useful for research into self and body imagery.

Examples of the technique were edited in a twenty-minute, sound, 16 mm. movie. A striking aspect of this method is the intensity and pleasure experienced by the children in acting out their vital unconscious material with relatively less resistance and thereby less interruption of play. The complementary role assigned to the therapist by the child allows the therapist to engage in meaningful therapeutic responses and diminishes the amount of speculation sometimes necessary in certain other forms of less communicative play.

Costumes are enjoyed upon occasion in all ages and are less likely to be considered too babyish by older children during therapy. Costume play therapy appears to be a worthwhile addition to child therapy, especially in older children who are less spontaneous in communication. The materials represent the only addition to the therapy. The therapeutic technique is essentially the same as we know it and interpretive work proceeds gradually to more mature levels. The goal likewise remains unchanged: to help the child understand reality in keeping with his developmental capacity.

References

Ekstein, R. & Wallerstein, J. (1956), "Observations on the Psychotherapy of Borderline and Psychotic Children," *The Psychoanalytic Study of the Child*, 11:303–311. New York: International Universities Press.
Erikson, E. H. (1937), "Configurations in Play: Clinical Notes," *Psychoanal. Quart.*, 6:139–214.
Freud, A. (1936), *The Ego and the Mechanisms of Defense*, New York: International Universities Press, 1946.
———(1946), *The Psychoanalytical Treatment of Children*, New York: International Universities Press, 1959.
———& Burlingham, D. T. (1944), *Infants Without Families*, New York: International Universities Press.
Freud, S. (1920), "Beyond the pleasure principle," *Standard Edition*, 18:7–64. London: Hogarth Press, 1955.
———(1923), "The Ego and the Id," *Standard Edition*, 19:12–66, London: Hogarth Press, 1961.
Kris, E. (1934), "The Psychology of Caricature," *Psychoanalytic Explorations in Art*, New York: International Universities Press, 1952, pp. 173–188.
Peller, L. (1954), "Libidinal Phases, Ego Development and Play," *The Psychoanalytic Study of the Child*, 9:178–197. New York: International Universities Press.
Piaget, J. (1945), *Play, Dreams and Imitation in Childhood*, New York: Norton, 1951.
Waelder, R. (1933), "The Psychoanalytic Theory of Play," *Psychoanal. Quart.*, 2:208–224.

# Use of Checkers in Therapy

BORIS M. LEVINSON

The virtue of a game like checkers is that it does not carry for the testee the implications of a diagnostic exploration. Checkers is a game, not a test. It may thus open communication and permit exploration in depth. I have introduced checkers into a therapeutic setting to facilitate meaningful interaction. It may be introduced when the child is uncommunicative or as a shock absorber. It may also become an integral part of the therapy session when the child knows the therapist and is comfortable in his presence.

This game, as any other, may be utilized to give the therapist a chance to observe and evaluate the child's ego strength and his adherence to reality. The therapist may vary his own game. He may permit the child to win or to lose after a long or short struggle. The child may thus win by the "skin of his teeth." In playing the game the child must keep in mind its rules and in a realistic manner meet the onslaught of reality (therapist's aggressive moves). In a sense then checkers may represent structured life space in which the child's defenses in the course of the game may become clues to the defense structure; viz., method of playing and reactions to victory and defeat.

## Personality Reflections

The start of the game may indicate child's attitudes toward therapy and the therapist. What is the style of the child's game? Is he daring? Does he assume a defensive or an offensive posture? Does he select black or red checkers? Does he have "lucky" colors? Does he request the therapist to make the initial move? If so, does he imitate the therapist's moves or does he have a stereotyped approach to the game? Does he move the checker defensively protecting it in the palm of his hand while considering his opponent's response? Does the child think through his approach or does he act impulsively and haphazardly? Does he show foresight and ability to act and to think quickly and accurately under pressure? What are the child's verbalizations and expressions of feelings about himself and his game?

How does the child react when he wins? How does he feel? Is he happy because he won from a hated adversary? Is he sad because he discovered that another strong figure in whom he had implicit confidence is not as strong and protective as he thought he might be? Is he afraid that the therapist might feel affronted and will punish him by denial of love? Is he afraid to win and loses by making "stupid" moves when on the verge of winning? If the child wins because of "aggressive" moves, does he feel guilty?

How does the child react to defeat, to initial reverses? Does he give up in despair or fight tenaciously until the last man? Does losing a game mean a further self-devaluation? Does he refuse to play another game? Does he attempt to refashion reality more to his heart's desire or to deny reality by "cheating;" i.e., unobtrusively taking off the therapist's checkers or by putting on additional ones for himself? Does he change the rules of the game "midstream" to his advantage because this is the way he "plays" with his friends?

# Use of Checkers in Handling Resistances

EARL A. LOOMIS, JR.

Resistance has been defined by Freud as "anything that interferes with the course of analysis." While the rediscovery of lost memories and the disclosure of the contents of the repressed constitute indispensable aspects of the analytic process, this disclosure will be facilitated and the analysis will be enhanced if concurrently the resistances are analyzed and overcome. In fact, the more emphasis we place upon character and ego problems, the more we are concerned with resistance analysis.

In this brief communication I will attempt to demonstrate some of the types of resistances and character problems uncovered in checker play with children in analysis or psychotherapy. In addition, examples will be given from some uses of checkers as a means of disclosing content, handling resistances, and introducing interpretations.

### Fear of Winning

An eight-year-old boy had from the beginning seemed entirely too comfortable and symptom-free in his relations with the therapist, too blissfully agreeable to participation in therapy, and apparently possessed of too little anxiety to motivate his really being willing and able to think about his troubles. Treatment proceeded several months without significant change. The patient's parents acknowledged no alteration in his symptoms at home (anxiety, enuresis, shyness, and mild school phobia). When checkers were casually introduced, the patient accepted the possibility of playing without obviously being threatened. He proceeded to lose every game, however, despite his prior experience with checkers. His losses were neither simply accidental nor careless, but seemed calculated to defeat the analyst's attempts to play as an appropriate opponent of an eight-year-old. When the therapist and the patient became aware of what was going on, the patient could express for the first time his fear of winning, of triumphing, or of successfully competing in anything. His passive, agreeable veneer began to crack, and the underlying aggressive needs and competitive drives became apparent as the therapeutic situation — more particularly the checker games — provided a neutral and safe context of acceptance and understanding in which could be worked out in microsphere some of his fears of his drive to strive successfully.

"But I don't need to win." "I mean, I don't want to win." "I don't care if all boys want to win at least part of the time!" "What do you mean I'm too good a player to lose?" "You mean I try to lose?" "What do you mean I use my head to lose rather than to win?" "No, I don't think you'll be mad if I would beat you." "I don't care if some boys do fear people will get mad sometimes when they beat people." "I just don't want to beat people." "Let's play checkers." (The interpretations between these remarks here telescoped are probably obvious.)

The next step for the therapist was to reintroduce the subjects of ambivalence and internal conflict as ways in which the lad's self-defeat came about. He got what I meant when I suggested that he was fighting the checker game inside his head rather than on the checkerboard and that not I but rather he himself was his opponent. The final and crucial tying-up with reality experiences of past and current life situation and behavior was an essential stage of the boy's therapy, but is not relevant to the topic of this paper.

Here checkers offered a boy an opportunity to see his resistances and character defenses, to play with leaving behind one or another aspect of them in miniature, to retreat into the play *with* checkers rather than to talk about them, but in so doing to give himself and the therapist a convenient and useful symbol to summarize and communicate a complicated intrapsychic conflict. Hence again and again in this boy's analysis he could turn off painful material by saying, "Let's play checkers," to which the analyst could acquiesce by saying, "Perhaps the game will make the checker feelings less hard to talk about," or "Perhaps today we talk less with words and more with checkers."

### Fear of Losing

In another eight-year-old the fear of losing so dominated that he devised his own checker game: "Larry-checkers." This consisted of rules which he created somewhat as follows: "Red checkers on red squares, black on black. Checkers move on an angle, staying on their own color, but jumping straight ahead onto another square of their own color. They may, however, jump over the end and back to their position in taking a man on an end row, or they may jump in a diamond pattern around a man and return to this own square or any square of the diamond. You get "kings" by jumping a lot or by bringing a man on top of another man close to him. If a king wants to, he can move two squares on an angle or can jump two squares of his own color forward. Another way to take men is to pass by them as the king moves his two squares forward." Usually by reserving the right to move first and through launching an attack from the start, he could win overwhelmingly. When on occasion I managed to beat him at his own game, he would usually anticipate this and change the rules abruptly before the last move, only to trap and defeat my nearly victorious army. Rarely he would actually allow me to win. In these cases he insisted that alongside the score which was religiously kept be recorded: "Dr. Loomis won only because Larry let him." Interpretations of his fear of losing, his dread of not having everything under control, and his displacement and projection of fears reinforced material and experiences from other areas including the school, the home, and the history. Larry is still fighting the battle of his fears of inner anarchy, inner insanity, and inner aggression, but he has learned to see sometimes that his foes are as often inside as out, and Larry-checkers has helped him to see this. In fact, a leading remark of his led me to predict to him that "Sometime you will let me teach you 'Earl-checkers.' " His answer, "O.K., when I get Larry-checkers out of my system," led me to believe my prediction would be fulfilled.

## Paranoid Mistrust

Fears of winning and losing, of dominating or being dominated, are not the only resistance creators which checkers may disclose. A more serious paranoid distrust with ill-concealed hostility first made its appearance to the therapist in the course of highly competitive games compulsively played and competitively scored by a fourteen-year-old boy. At first I felt that he was "merely" eager to win, normally competitive for adolescence, and busily attaining to the state where he could teach his elders. (He did in fact teach me most of what I know about competitive checker playing.) Yet as we went along from game to game and from tournament to tournament, it became evident that Will was not just trying to keep me in my place: he was trying to humiliate me — more, to destroy me. In the course of the checker games he would allude to "strangleholds," "head-locks," "jujitsu," "bayonet practice," "judo," "hand-to-hand combat," and "ambush or attacks from the rear." The anxiety warnings which had much earlier left me puzzled now fitted together to justify concern for this boy's reality judgments, defenses against homosexuality, and ego integrity. Attention to the threatened fragmentation of civilized veneer disclosed through checker games (and no other discernable place at first) led me to take more appropriate steps in his handling. Checkers here served as catalyst to delusional and hostile breakthrough — again, thank fortune, on the level of "only a game!"

## Silence as Resistance

Awkward silences may or may not constitute resistances. Usually, I think they do. Techniques that work with adults too seldom yield results with young children or adolescents. Checkers offers a communication medium that can continue through the verbal blackout both to reassure the patient that the therapist is still "in there pitching" and also to keep the therapist in touch with possible changes in the meanings of the silences.

Naomi, a thirteen-year-old girl with a tic-like compulsion, talked freely with the therapist one hour out of twelve, sparsely one hour out of six, and maintained all but total silence on more than one occasion. During these periods of affective and communicational inertia, checkers frequently broke the vicious circle of silence begetting silence and question begetting monosyllable. Throughout the game the eyes flashed with excitement, the muscles tensed with expectancy, and the dry and occasionally caustic wit appeared. On occasion mercy would be implored through tender, longing glances, and on others grace would be gratuitously proffered. I did not play silently and Naomi did not speak often. Yet we communicated: I through words and she through checkers — sometimes, both of us through checkers. Naomi's fears partly stemmed from the sex difference of the therapist; yet even after she had been transferred to a woman physician, checkers served to provide an occasion for conversation — at least by the doctor. For example: Naomi is sitting, staring straight ahead. "Would you like to play checkers?" "I really can't be sure if you are silent, perhaps we won't go far wrong if we assume that silence gives consent." Medium smile from Naomi. "I guess this means you are glad." Broader smile. "But I can understand smiles only a little and shrugs even less. Sometime when you can tell me in words how you think and feel, we can understand together even better." And so on into the game. . . .

For another boy, Pat, eleven, asthmatic, and shy, checkers revealed content, history, feeling, and transference in a fascinating manner. I knew that he was lonely, that his real father died when he was three, that his stepfather frightened him. I knew that his mother was overprotective, almost parasitic upon him, and that his grandmother fought to get in on the act too. Yet I had never been able to help him voice just how he felt when in the middle of the night he would choke up and feel he was going to die. He could never bring himself to relate how he felt then and after his mother came to his bed. Usually as he sat talking of trivia he would be comfortable. As his associations led him into tension areas, he would gradually tighten up verbally, become anxious, and begin to wheeze. He lost his ability to talk at this point and only gradually regained it. In time we both learned that if at a moment when he first began to choke up he would ask for a checker game, the attack would pass.

One day he said, when I had asked him again what checkers meant, "Checkers feels like it does when I'm going to have an attack at night and mother comes to me and brings me a drink of water and my medicine and puts a cool cloth on my forehead and lies down beside me and stays with me till I fall asleep." From then on his request "Let's play checkers!" became more meaningful to both of us and we grew to use the phrase "the checkers feeling" as shorthand for the cravings to be protected and loved.

As his confidence and insight grew, he came to use checkers in other ways, and as each stage of meaning developed and was clarified, a new understanding of his character, his life situation, and the transference emerged. Only resistance aspects of this symptom have been considered here.

From these five examples the role of checkers in disclosing the presence of resistances, aiding in analyzing them, and helping to discover their inner meaning is illustrated. The advantages of the game to the child analyst and child therapist are its flexibility, variety of personal meanings (as projective technique), and its wide range of therapeutic applicabilities. Thus it can be seen that checkers is flexible far beyond the obvious form of the medium (a competitive game).

## Summary

Five clinical examples of ways in which checkers illuminated or facilitated therapy and analysis of children have been presented. While I personally find checkers particularly valuable in the uncovering and analysis of resistances and character problems, I am sure that similar applications are being made with many other games and modalities. The advantages of checkers are the facts that it is widely known, is familiar to most latency children and adolescents, and is unusually appropriate as a game between adult and child which does not require any condescension on the part of the adult. This paper covers only a few of the special attributes and possibilities of checkers. It is hoped that it will stimulate the uncovering and sharing of other uses of the game, together with the examination of other types of therapist-child activities from similar points of view.

# Semantic Play Therapy

SALVATORE RUSSO and HOWARD W. JAQUES

Several articles on the use of semantics in psychotherapy were included in *Papers from the Second American Congress on General Semantics,* published in 1943. Psychiatrists, psychologists, counselors, and social workers reported on their use of general semantics in their therapeutic work and gave the impression that we were on the threshold of a new era in psychotherapy. This approach that seemed so promising thirteen years ago, however, has borne very little fruit, for a perusal of the *Psychological Abstracts* did not disclose a single semantic article on individual therapy since the Congress was held in Denver.

The lack of development in this field may be due in part to the expressed attitude of many of the therapists who pioneered this work that, while all therapists use semantics to some extent, general semantics is not an adequate or even a useful method by itself. Dr. Campbell wrote, "As a general statement one can say that general semantics is emphatically not a psychotherapy in itself. It is an adjuvant, an accessory method."[1] He also said that the principles of general semantics are best used piecemeal according to the progress of the case rather than "employing them as a system." Their indirect and auxiliary use, nevertheless, he believed, was valuable since it materially shortens the length of psychotherapy. This attitude that general semantics cannot be fashioned into a sufficient or complete mode of psychotherapy may have discouraged interested therapists from trying to develop actual techniques.

[1]Douglas G. Campbell, M. D., "Neuropsychiatric Foundations and Clinical Applications of General Semantics," in M. Kendig (ed.), *Papers from the Second American Congress on General Semantics* (Chicago: Institute of General Semantics, 1943), p. 133. (This volume will hereinafter be referred to as *Papers.*)

The accounts of semantic therapy that were presented at the Congress were sketchy and fragmentary. The writers usually gave hints or general suggestions, rather than actual details of their work. One got the impression that the therapist was experimenting and had not arrived at definite methods. The general principles or aims were clearly stated, such as training in map-territory or language-fact relationship, levels of abstraction, extensional devices, etc., but the actual procedures were absent. In those instances where some substantial account of the case was given, much more space was devoted to the results achieved than to the details of the method employed.

The generalities in which most therapists at the Congress were content to speak are illustrated by the marital counselor, for instance, who felt he could condense his technique into a single sentence: "I try to find out what symbols the subject is clinging to, help him evaluate them extensionally, retain those that are adequate for his adjustment, and discard and supplant with useful symbols those which are causing the trouble."[2] Dr. Campbell pointed out that "the crucial technique is a training in the proper order of evaluation brought about principally by the use of the extensional devices" (Papers, p. 130). Another therapist said he showed a man how to build up generalizations and conclusions and go to a higher order of inference. The reports made interesting reading, and gave hope that the use of general semantics could help us in our therapeutic work, but the effort seems to have spent itself.

It is possible that the extravagant claims, moreover, caused therapists to look upon general semantics with suspicion. Dr. Scarbrough claimed that he had found general semantics "workable" in cases of homosexuality, mild manic-depression, simple schizophrenia, severe anxiety, alcoholism, mild depression, migraine headaches, impotency, frigidity, etc.[3] One therapist claimed he had cured a person who had been a homosexual for twenty years in three weeks.[4]

None of the cases reported apparently dealt with general semantics in the psychotherapy of children. Two cases of children with problems were discussed, but the semantic treatment was with the parents and not with the child. Our article deals with the direct use of semantic play with a child and may be the first case of its kind to be reported. The use of

[2]Donald McLean, "Use of General Semantics in Marital Counseling," Papers, p. 307.
[3]Hartwell E. Scarbrough, "General Semantics in the Practice of a Consulting Psychologist," Papers, pp. 300 ff.
[4]Papers, p. 305.

semantics was direct and became the basic mode of treatment rather than an auxiliary one; thus we found the need to coin the expression "semantic play therapy." The details of each play session are summarized so that one can follow our work step by step.

When the child whose treatment will be the subject of this article was accepted for treatment we had no intention of using semantic play. We resorted to it because we were desperate and felt that we needed a treatment out of the ordinary. The boy had been diagnosed in the usual fashion, as will soon be discussed, and given the usual permissive type of play that is used in many child guidance clinics. After ten sessions of play therapy we were confronted with the strong possibility that the parents would terminate the case if we could not produce results in the near future. The following account touches briefly on the first ten play sessions and deals mostly with our experiment with semantic play therapy. It might be noted that the semantic play sessions have a rationale. In the first one Larry was presented with an objective and impersonal situation unrelated to his immediate problem; in the last one he had arrived at a point where he had to deal with a problem parallel to his own on a human basis.

## Case of School Anxiety

Larry was just eleven years of age and in the sixth grade when he was brought to the Wichita Guidance Center. He had been referred the summer before by a school counselor, who had described the boy as unhappy in school, not achieving, shy, unwilling to recite in class, and showing his resentment of school by crying and fretting.

The mother described him as quiet, serious, and worried about people's faults and world problems. He worried so much about school work that he developed insomnia. He was very critical of himself and easily discouraged. When he was criticized, he "cried like a baby" and then complained that he was afraid that people knew he cried. He liked to paint and draw, was not interested in sports, and was too sensitive to swim in the nude at the YMCA.

Larry was jealous of his younger brother's academic achievement and brooded a lot over insults and injuries. He had taken a profound dislike to a man who was a neighbor and tranferred his hate to the man's daughter, who played daily with the younger brother and visited the home often. Despite his hostility the neighbor girl remained friendly and tried in vain to win him over.

A diagnostic study was made. The study indicated that the parents had established very high and rigorous standards which caused him to develop a feeling of failure and inadequacy. His tests showed that he had made some compulsive attempts to achieve and had reacted to failure by being hypercritical of himself and others, and had learned to avoid threatening situations by childish means, such as negativism, weeping, and begging to be excused from the situation. He was not considered to be a seriously disturbed boy, but an unhappy one who was dissatisfied with everything and everyone, and who would respond favorably to play therapy with a male figure.

A conventional play therapy was used for ten consecutive weeks. He seemed very agreeable during these sessions and engaged in a variety of self-chosen activities: he made model planes, a bean-shooter, a bracelet; played with water guns, modeling clay, mumble-peg; he accompanied the therapist to the drug store for a soda. But while he was quiet, passive, non-communicative in play sessions, at home he resisted coming to the Center as violently as he resisted going to school.

The mother had been seen concurrently by another member of the therapeutic team. She reported weekly his refusal to go to school and to come to the Center. He said that they weren't going to get anywhere because he didn't want them to make him better, and that they didn't ask him anything sensible or important, and that they could never make him like going to school or to the Center. In defense of his position he said that the mother's therapist did not like him, and that his own therapist was nice to him just so that he could do his work. He said that if his parents expected him to be nice at home by coming to the Center they were just wasting their time, for he would never be that way. At home he had become more antagonistic to the neighbor girl, and began to chase her away from the home.

While Larry had never intimated his great resistance to the Center to his therapist, he resisted so much at home that his family asked for help in this matter. Should they continue to force him despite his growing refusal, or should they allow his treatment to be terminated? The decision to terminate is usually left to the child, and in such instances most of them choose to continue when they are given the right, but in this case it was decided that he needed help and that he should be brought to the Center even against his will.

## Dichotomous Thinking

It was at this point that the therapeutic team felt that the boy might profit by some form of training in semantic play, since his problem appeared to us as basically a semantic one. It seemed that his difficulty lay in his pervasive dichotomy of the world and his allegiance to his categories. He clung so rigidly to his categories that he was enslaved by them. *Everything to him was either good or bad, everyone was either for or against him.* He couldn't understand how his parents, who liked him, could punish him or make him unhappy. When his stubborn use of categories became frustrating or painful, he could not realistically reconsider the situation, but resorted to sulking, crying, or temper tantrums.

It was apparent to us that he was reacting not to the realistic environment but to the world created by his own faulty and pervasive generalizations. He was projecting his preconceived dichotomy on the world and forcing all experience to fit it. Larry had no insight into his problem. We felt that we would have to help him escape from his perceptual chains, for unless he could be freed from his harmful thinking, improvement was not likely. Hence the decision was made to have him continue to come to the Center and get some basic experience in the classification of experiences and abstracting to arrive at a more realistic manipulation of his world. This need for semantic play therapy arose from a consideration of his conduct outside of the playroom.

For the next seven weeks he was given experience in a prearranged, highly structured situation. These seven sessions are described below. At the end of that time he was given the opportunity to decide for himself whether he wanted to terminate or continue his activities at the Center.

## Play Sessions

*First Session.* Larry entered the playroom and found an object-sorting test scattered on a table. The therapist commented that someone must have left them out but that he knew what they were for. He said it was some sort of game and that they could play it if they wanted to. Larry sat on one side of the table and the therapist on the other. He was asked to select an object and place it in front of him. He selected a pair of pliers. Then he was asked to put all the objects with it that belong with pliers. He selected all the tools, and was told it could be called the tool pile, since they were all tools. He was then asked in what other way he could sort them, and he replied that he didn't know. It was suggested that he could choose all the metal ones. He agreed to this and the sorting continued. After a while the therapist chose an object, and Larry added all those that belonged with it; the next time Larry chose the master object, and the therapist chose those that went with it. Larry caught on very rapidly to the different ways objects could be classified and vied with the therapist to see if he could find more classifications than the therapist did. At the end the therapist put all the objects together and had him classify all of them in several groups, which the boy did successfully.

*Second Session.* The next week the therapist brought in three large wooden boxes that were used to store toys in the play room. They contained a great diversity of toys, such as dolls, blocks, cars, planes, and tanks. Larry was asked if he recalled the game he had played last week; he replied that he did. He was told that they were going to continue it, but that it was going to be a little more difficult. Each day they would play with something more advanced. The problem was to classify all of the objects into *three* groups, one group for each box; the objects must be so classified that each box could be labeled. Larry dumped the material out of the boxes and began to sort them into three groups. He discussed the classification while he worked. He first divided them into metal, rubber, and wood. But this broke down. Then he tried to classify them by the nature of the toys. This broke down, too, partly because he needed a classification for "junk" consisting of parts of objects. Then he used classifications of those that run on land, fly in air, or go in water. After many attempts and compromises he arrived at three large categories that seemed practical. The therapist printed the labels and they were pasted on the boxes.

*Third Session.* The therapist brought the same three boxes. Larry examined them and discovered that the contents had been mixed up. The therapist commented on this fact. Larry separated the objects and sorted them out and put them back into the boxes according to the old classification. When he had finished this, he went to all the other play rooms and brought out the boxes and worked on them. This time he made the labels and put them on the other boxes and worked on them. Thus he classified all the toys for all of the play rooms.

*Fourth Session.* Larry asked what they were going to do that day. Therapist had brought a large stack of cards with pictures of animals on them cut from various magazines. He explained that this was a more advanced study of classification. Larry started the classification by making two piles, those that had fur and those that didn't. He put most of the birds and insects and four-legged animals in the fur class. The therapist discussed the fitness of placing both pigs and birds in the fur category. Larry argued that birds had fur under the microscope. This was the first time that he defended his sorting. He was told that since we didn't have a microscope we couldn't use that argument, thus pigs and birds wouldn't fit. Then he divided the animals into those that were edible and those that weren't; then into birds and non-birds. He had trouble with bats and insects. They could fly but weren't in the class of birds. At this point for the first time he talked to the therapist about not wanting to come to the Center. He asked how much longer he would have to come. He said that he didn't like to come to the Center because he preferred to play at home. He also preferred home to school.

*Fifth Session*. The same cards were used again for classification. This time he sorted the cards into four piles. He still ran into a lot of trouble in his fourfold classification. Early in the hour he said he didn't want to come to the Center. He was told that the therapist would meet him anywhere Larry wanted to go. Larry replied that he just wanted to be with his friends. The therapist set up the classification of friends and non-friends. Larry insisted that everyone was either his friend or not his friend. He discussed a couple of boys who were his friends and some who were not. Did the therapist come under the category of friend? He answered that he did not know. He was asked if he had ever acted like one of his non-friends who disliked to bathe; he denied it.

*Sixth Session*. Larry came in with tears in his eyes and his usual persecuted air. When asked what was wrong, he said that he did not want to come. The therapist discussed his usual method of resisting, and asked him why he persisted in using the same method if it didn't work. Therapist talked to him about the things he could do here. Larry replied that he could do things at home. But it was only once a week. Larry replied that he could have a good time at home once a week. Therapist talked to him about his wanting his own way. Larry said he always wanted it. He was asked if his younger brother always had his own way. No. Did his parents always get their own way? No. Did he want to be different from everyone else? He didn't answer. It was suggested that if his parents didn't let him do everything he wanted to do, it was because they liked him. If they didn't care about him they would have ignored him. This made him thoughtful and he suggested they go to the drug store for a soda.

*Seventh Session*. Showed him the film *Angry Boy*. Larry said that it was a good movie but there wasn't any resemblance to him. When the similarity was pointed out he agreed. The film has two admirable scenes of play therapy. In one of them the child is provoked into shooting the therapist on the head with a dart gun because of persistent questioning. The child apologizes by saying that he was sorry, the gun slipped. But the therapist ignores the proffered reason and uses this as an occasion to discuss the relationship of people and their acts. He gets the boy to see that an instance of anger or hostility is not co-extensive with the whole person, because people who like you sometimes hurt you, and you sometimes hurt people you like. Both the people in the film had just acted that way. Larry was able to understand this argument as well as the boy in the film.

When asked if he put up the usual fight coming, Larry said he hadn't, or he would have gotten a real spanking. He talked about the problem while he pounded modeling clay. When asked if he would continue to come if given a choice, he said no.

The mother was told of the boy's decision, and she agreed to the termination. She felt that he had improved greatly, and said the neighbors had spontaneously commented on the fact. An aunt who had visited the home had spoken of the difference in the boy. The mother thought that Larry had a better sense of responsibility and was talking more freely about his feelings to his parents. The strong antagonism he had had for the neighbor girl had lessened considerably. The mother felt that they had the situation well in hand, and would like to see if it wouldn't continue to improve without forcing him to come to the Center.

This case is reported in order to encourage the use of semantic play therapy with children. It may be that there have been other attempts similar in nature that have not been published. The reviewing of this case has caused this team to wonder why we hadn't used this method more often, and it has stimulated us to want to use it again in the future. We plan to start using this method from the very beginning by selecting at intake cases that we feel would profit by such a method. We realize that it falls far short of a complete example of semantic therapy, and has some of the limitations of the other cases reported, but we have confidence that it could be developed into a therapeutic device that might have wider application in psychotherapy with children.

Readers may have thought of — and some may even have had experience with — other ways in which the principles of general semantics can be actualized in the form of therapeutic techniques. If this paper stimulates the publication of descriptions and results of other experiences with general semantics in psychotherapy, it will have achieved its main purpose.

# FACILITIES
# AND MATERIALS

# Use of Ordinary Office Equipment

M. B. DURFEE

Reports of play therapy in recent years include mention of dolls, puppets, interpretive dancing, finger painting, and the like. One easily gets the impression that the ordinary office and its equipment are ill suited to such work. Here are reported some observations in the use of ordinary office instruments which encourage verbal play. These include the typewriter and telephone, but the dictaphone is our major interest here, an instrument long used in this way by Dr. J. P. Molloy, director of the Houston Mental Hygiene Bureau.

The adult feeling that these are ill suited to children's play arises from a perception involving the connotations of use, cost, complexity, and inventive skill. The machine-age child merely sees "the phone" or "that thing you make records on."[1] It is our experience that adult instruments often outlure childish playthings.

A ten-year-old boy, very poorly emancipated, had to be taken forcefully from his mother. Angrily refusing all proffered toys, he sobbed over and over that he wanted to go to mother. The dictaphone immediately captured his attention. In ten minutes he imitated several radio programs, (revealing some of his interests), verbally assassinated a "cranky teacher," (release of hostility), and established a lasting rapport.

### Telephone

The telephone offers less novelty, but gives insight into the child's approach to others, e.g., the frequent indications of hunger for affection.

[1] Adroitly expressed by Ogden Nash in *Baby, What Makes the Sky Blue?*

The ten-year-old girl who anonymously phones and heckles adults reveals some of her hostility for those who thwart her at home and school. For some of the more underprivileged youngsters, ours is their first telephone. In learning to use it they derive a feeling of equality with more fortunate playmates. We have helped timid children build up friendly relationships with semi-hostile playmates through phone conversations in which we occasionally participated and in which the patient had a feeling of our support.

## Typewriter

The typewriter is often too distracting, but occasionally offers a convenient retreat into activity to the child who finds himself talking too openly for eye-to-eye conversation. Children to whom phonetics and spelling are a nightmare often make a new approach through the fun of typing. Carlson has shown the particular function of the typewriter in the education of children suffering from cerebral palsy (1).

Many children enjoy dictating to our typing. In some instances we have used this for releasing hostility, the patient composing sadistic, unmailed letters. In other instances actual correspondence is dictated to parents or others, important to the child but not available to the clinic. Through feigned misunderstanding of the dictation, slightly altered restatements, and attention reward for such improved expressions, the child is helped to new attitudes. Interesting results often come not only from the child, but from the parent so approached.

One boy, too compulsively submissive to make open suggestions to authority, used the typewriter as a sort of intermediary, typing off "Let's play outdoors," then turning the machine to face us with this appeal. This illustrates a general value of the fact that the impersonality of the machine encourages freer expression. A ten-year-old girl, unable to discuss her relationship to her father, often telephoned detailed accounts of his visits to relatives who necessarily knew these details. The phone offered her an indirect way of informing us of these things. One boy passed through a stage of refusing to answer all questions, however benign, until we spoke them into the dictaphone, whereupon he dictated his answers. It is as though the child felt, "If I tell this person he may disapprove, but this machine will have no opinion. Then, if he disapproves of what the machine tells him, it, and not I will receive the disapproval."

## Dictaphone

This release of expression is shown on another level in the case of Clyde, an epileptoid of four years, whose responses to us at first were

almost exclusively echolalic. This repetition continued in dictaphone
play, which he enjoyed at once. However, when the dictaphone played
back the questions and their echoes, the boy answered the machine,
replying to both our interrogations and his own repetitions. The
following is an excerpt of the dialogue between the boy and the
dictaphone.

> Dict: Who makes you the maddest? (Our question)
> Clyde: Phillip.
> Dict: Who makes you da maddes'? (Clyde's repetition)
> Clyde: Phillip.
> Dict: What do they do to you? (Our question)
> Clyde: He hits me.
> Dict: Wat do dey do ta you? (Clyde's question)
> Clyde: He's alla time hittin'me.
> Dict: What would you like to do to them? (Our question)
> Clyde: Hit him.
> Dict: Wat you like to do to 'um? (Clyde's question)
> Clyde: Hit his face. Knock 'im down. KICK 'IM!

The fervor of this last was a far cry from the defensive echolalia of a
few minutes before, and after listening to the record two or three times,
conversation became easy.

This possibility of immediate repetition of the identical expression is
uniquely offered by the dictaphone. The child often listens over and over
to his productions and occasionally to ours; e.g., the five-year-old
enuretic who was fascinated by our expression that he was learning to be
"boss of the water," playing this section five or six times. For the child
this offers the learning effect of repetition; for us the child's selection of
favorite passages offers insight. If a child fears the cylinder it may be
played by others, and he is allowed to resurface the cylinder, a
reassurance which seldom requires repetition. Typically, he wishes to
save the record; often he brings his parent in to hear his production, and
occasionally we are asked to play it for other children, sometimes for
therapeutic effect — "Maybe it will help those kids." Obviously, for those
who prefer verbatim records, the dictaphone offers not only the words,
but the pauses, emphases, and tone of voice.

## Hostility Release

If we avoid family figures, active hostility release often begins in the
first interview. In these "stories" or "radio programs" teachers are
immediately attacked with mimicry, scolding, and physical violence. A
first-grader, who hated his "sissy" pageant costume, joyously had the

teacher shot, yelling, "Come on, you kids. You don't have to stay in here any more. She's dead." A ten-year-old boy insisted on spending a second interview developing a sequence of buttings of the teacher by a trained billy goat. A six-year-old had his story hero granted the wish to be an elephant for a day. This animal jumped up and down on the roof of the school till it collapsed with terrific sound effects and "killed the ol' teacher and all the kids." Turning aside to us he beamed, "Isn't that a swell story?"

Domineering playmates and hostile neighbors are also promptly and easily attacked, but as we approach deeper hostilities, more symbolization is often required, particularly with the child who slips over into using "I" and "me" in place of the story character.

Peter, a very submissive seven-year-old, easily lashed out against the teacher but could not say anything against his sadistic stepfather. He greatly enjoyed constructing a story of a "little bear" who became angry and shot a lady (teacher symbol?) and then "he shot a — a — a big old bear, (father symbol?) and then the little bear shot himself" (punishment for death wishes?). We intruded to save the little bear and introduce him into the house of a big old — a big old what? Peter decided on a big old horse. We had the horse threaten the little bear with physical violence. Peter, speaking for the bear, could offer no retorts but begged helplessly to be spared . This paralleled the relationship between the boy and his stepfather. The little bear fled, but the horse pursued him into his own house . Finally the little bear began to stand his ground, insisting that it was his home and that in it he had the right to be left alone. He was reluctantly led into annihilating the horse, but once this had been accomplished, Peter was greatly delighted and obviously relieved at the outcome.

Typically we have observed diminution of hostilities after release in dictaphone play. Sometimes this is directly stated; in other cases the play reveals the change.

As nine-year-old Clara's hostility toward young males began to subside, she made up a dictaphone story of a little girl, who completely outdid, out-talked, and outwitted a boy. Suddenly Clara saw there was but little of the cylinder left and exclaimed, "Oh, hurry! We've got to get it fixed up before it gets to the end and it's too late for them to make up." Dictating rapidly, she raced to a happy reconciliation. It is not surprising that her former hostility is now more easily directed into scholastic and athletic rivalry without anxiety or tension.

In some cases the dictaphone is particularly revealing of fantasy life. This may be done without symbolization, as in the case of the boy who acts as radio announcer, broadcasting great feats of athletic prowess with himself as hero. Others involve easily identified personnel, the identifications being strongly comparable to those seen in doll play.

William, whose family was badly disrupted, enjoyed dictating stories about a family which, like his, consisted of father, mother, brother and sister. In this fantasy family the parents loved each other and were very fond of the children. Brother and sister were sickeningly gracious toward each other. William, suffering feelings of hostility, guilt and rejection over being the only one in the family placed in an institution, had the boy in his fantasy family leave home of his own choice because he "got turned into a little devil."

Melvin, a more deeply introverted child, dictated entire cylinders without interruption, consisting of dialogues between two boys. One boy constantly suggested stealing pecans, digressing from the homeward path to see a wreck, disobeying orders to remain indoors, neglecting school work, or frankly truanting. Another boy argued against this with varying success. It was not surprising to learn that life for Melvin was an endless struggle against sin. He dared not go to movies, "Cause you cain't tell when Jesus is coming, and you'd sure hate to have him come and find you a-settin' in a picher show."

Five-year-old enuretic Freddie puzzled us for a time with lengthy scolding at a boy called Froggie. While listening to the record, he shouted retorts to these same scoldings. Stresses in Freddie's life included feelings of rejection from his foster home placement, guilt over sex play, inferiority from being the smallest in his social group, a strong feeling of genital inferiority, and a castration fear amplified by the experience of having chopped off one of his toes. Boasting and flight into activity were inadequate defenses against anxiety. In this situation he invented this fantasy self "Froggie," whom he scolded in the dictaphone, but by whose name he went in neighborhood play. As Bender and Vogel (2) indicate, fantasied companions "represent an effort to compensate for some lack or deficiency in the child's experience or in his relationship with the world." Froggie, in the dictaphone accounts, was very bad. He hit everybody. He did bad things with girls. "Him got the bigges' penis in the whole worl'." Thus Freddie ambivalently extolled and repudiated all those lurking desires on which his heart smiled and his conscience frowned. As Freddie "Jekyll's" emotional difficulties subsided, so did Froggie "Hyde." At the close of treatment, enuresis was gone, and Freddie announced, "there ain't any Froggie any more."

In the face of an excellent relationship and the use of several play approaches, the therapeutic value of Freddie's dictaphone play cannot be estimated. At least it yielded us considerable insight, offered Freddie some release effect, permitted him to formulate some of his feelings, and gave him a chance to hear this conflict material coming from a source outside himself. The dictaphone thus became a sort of verbal mirror for the child.

One boy aged nine, referred because of odd fantasy behavior, demonstrated that dictaphone play may be contraindicated. He avoided outdoor and social play, restlessly paced the floor for hours muttering to himself, frequently bursting into unexplained laughter. The dictaphone revealed his mutterings to be memorized humor from movies, radio, and dime-store cartoon books. The dictaphone was too attractive for this child, too much in line with his non-social recreation. Play in a small group yielded gratifying results. However, we were indebted to the dictaphone for revealing the nature of this bizarre conduct.

## Story Telling

Where fantasy situations are created for the child in the game of the alternately-told story, we are given some insight into the child's reaction tendencies in emotional or problem situations. Typically the youngster wishes to dictate a radio thriller, and more often than not we are asked to start the story. In this it is our feeling that we are adopting much the same as David Levy's (3) or Solomon's (4) approach, except that possibly the child has more of a feeling that the idea is his rather than something thrust upon him.

It is our practice, when asked to start the story, to look perplexed and ask if a story about such and such will be all right. Our manner indicates that this is an impulse of the moment. It is thus conveniently possible to create a situation of fear, wishful thinking, vengeance, compensatory success, or whatever seems pertinent to the child's case apparently at his suggestion. Haunted houses, wishing rings, villainous bullies, overbearing teachers, etc., become appropriate story material as the case may indicate. The hero figure is usually easily identifiable with the patient, although some cases call for more remote symbols.

The range of individually-different responses brought out by a given story situation is considerable. In the boy-runs-away-to-sea story (rebellion against home authority) we have heard such attacks as the following. The stowaway demonstrated such courage and ability that he won the high regard of the captain and crew. A patient who was superior in intelligence, but several years behind his normal grade placement, offered a very rebellious stowaway who sneered at the captain's orders and loftily announced that he was not going to be bullied into doing any work but was going to enjoy himself. An extremely submissive boy was able to express no more rebellion than to select the South Pole as the destination of the ship; i.e., as far as possible from home. Another patient attempted to thwart all efforts to return the hero home, sinking the home-bound ship, grounding a returning plane, running an ambulance into the ditch. When the runaway was met by parents protesting their affection, the patient retorted for the hero, "That's a lot of baloney, I'm going back to the ship." (This precociously emancipated boy clearly understood his mother's continued wish that he were a girl.) Another patient's stowaway was frightened most of the trip, took precautions against numerous dangers, managed his money carefully, and cabled his parents to come and get him.

Often enough the conduct of the story character can be evaluated by the child with effective ease. The boy whose story hero depended heavily on his parents was next worked into a story of a boy maintaining himself unaided in the woods. The patient contributed only threats, such as snakes, bogs, alligators and drowning to the story. However, he inserted our very tentative suggestions, which he was made to feel had been his additions to the story. Afterward the patient talked easily about the story character's stupid lack of self-reliance. We encouraged this identification with an ideal of self-dependence and in later clinic visits both the boy and his parents pridefully reported each new step in emancipation.

A somewhat different function is performed when the hero figure occupies a position opposite of the child in his problem situation. Usually these reversals occur in dictaphone repartee rather than story construction and arise spontaneously. When created by us they often produce an initial awkward hesitation, but by avoiding any forcing of the issue, none fails to enjoy the game in the end. Many of these are reminiscent of Allen's patient, whose participation in therapy once took the form of announcing himself the doctor, about to cure the bad therapist (5).

Many children have become the patient teacher, persuading us, the maladjusted student, to a happier attitude. One boy spontaneously reversed himself into bellowing orders to his probation officer to get out of bed, stop stalling, wash all over again, stop teasing the girls, etc. A hypochondriacal child impulsively became the sly physician, pointing out the obvious mechanisms in our mountain of somatic complaints. After leading us into a better attitude of triumphing over these complaints, he pronounced, "That's the way I like to hear people talk."

The amount of embarrassment shown in such reversals seems to be some measure of the emotional charge involved. A girl who had largely

overcome her feeding problem laughed delightedly in the role of
disciplinarian, with us as the evasive, resistive child. In contrast, Jennie,
whose parents condoned stealing and hated "the law," blocked somewhat
on finding herself constructing the story of a burglar robbing a little girl
of jewelry resembling the patient's. The judge (by us) turned the burglar
over to the little girl for punishment. Only after the patient thought of
sentencing the burglar to a vast amount of housework, did she begin to
relax and laugh. Ease became complete when the burglar and little girl
became great friends. It may or may not be significant that in her foster
home the patient had shown unusual zeal in helping with the housework.

That there was a most gratifying change in the above child is hardly
ascribable to any great change in the child's super-ego resulting from
such play. The relationship situation in this instance was particularly
fortunate, and much was done for the child outside the clinic. However, it
is still true that in the milieu of this relationship the child experienced
some imitation of the desirable feeling and attitude. Speaking in a quite
different connection Oberndorf (6) has said that "identification leads to
imitation rather than vice versa, but imitation plays an important role in
the integration of characteristics initially acquired through identification." Even though our imitation experience and imitation attitude do
not accomplish this, they appear to soften some of the child's hostility
toward his opposition. We feel that something is gained by the child's
sponsoring mature conduct, repudiating more infantile behavior, by
experiencing therein a pleasure enriched by our relationship.

Many children do not choose the dictaphone as a plaything. Many
who do offer us little beyond songs, imitations of animals, sound effects
for air raids and the like, which we have not felt capable of endowing with
symbolic value. However, many children find the instrument a
convenient and helpful means of expression in the therapeutic situation,
as the following example demonstrates.

### Handling Anxiety Through Dictaphone Play

Jimmy, age seven, was brought in because of stuttering and anxiety
symptoms. Prominent among these latter was extreme fear of thunder
and lightning. It is the handling of this anxiety we consider here.

There were no somatic complaints, physical examinations findings
were normal, the boy was popular in his social group and above his
fellows in athletic prowess. Binet findings rated his IQ at 121. So far as
we could learn home life was reasonably happy and parents well adjusted,
despite the fact that both worked and the wife was suggestively the
superior earner and executive of the two. The home was not operating

under financial stress, in fact was expanding into better quarters. There were no siblings, no neighborhood problems, and no morbid religious atmosphere, except that the Negro maid believed in an actively vengeful Jehova.

An obvious superficial answer to the boy's anxiety in connection with lightning was furnished in the statement that he had seen his mother frightened by thunder storms. Before coming to the clinic she had steeled herself to pretending she enjoyed the beauty of lightning, and during the first hour with us Jimmy spontaneously and rather too emphatically informed us that he thought lightning was beautiful and that it didn't frighten him.

While the dictaphone play was by no means the only approach used in this case, the boy took a strong fancy to playing with the machine and this play filled the bulk of all interviews after the first. In his first conversation he told us something of a resentment of punishment at home and the domineering by older boys. He talked easily about enjoying fantasies of vengeance on these bigger boys, openly discussed his annoyance at mild quarreling between his parents, and unhesitatingly stated that if given authority he would punish daddy and mother for this quarreling by spanking them and putting them to bed without any supper. While it is true some of this was brought out in an atmosphere of jovial nonsense, it is still true that the later emerging connection between these hostilities and his anxiety symptoms was already displaced. It is of further interest that the association was revealed to us and to the boy through dictaphone play, without which we might have been satisfied with the easier interpretation on the basis of his mother's fear of thunder storms.

In the second interview the boy immediately chose the dictaphone and was led into a fear-situation story. It dealt with a boy who dressed as a ghost and went about scaring "some big kids." This aroused little interest. The story character then went home and (with Jimmy dictating) greatly frightened his father. Jimmy enjoyed this tremendously. It was obvious that more affect release occurred in relation to punishing a father symbol than in attacking older boys.

Having thus broken the ice, we introduced the stowaway story. When the captain roared, "What's the idea in running away from home?" Jimmy interrupted: "I know, let me do it."

He took the mouthpiece and dictated, "I ran away because those kids are always mean to me, and daddy and mother are always going places and not taking me along." We should mention in connection with this second hour that the boy stammered much less than in the first hour.

In the third hour Jimmy wished to resume the story game. We again introduced a fear situation atmosphere with a story about a boy in a haunted house. Jimmy spontaneously added that the boy was running away from home and explained it was because "Daddy and mother are always going out to movies and other places and not taking me along." Did the boy think they ought to be punished for that? Yes, Jimmy thought they ought to be punished pretty hard. Was the boy pretty angry at his daddy and mother? Yes, he was. Did he sometimes hope that something really terrible would happen to them? Yes, sometimes he did.

*At this moment Jimmy spontaneously introduced thunder and lightning into the picture.* In the story situation we developed the fact that to Jimmy an angry God sent them to punish the boy for thinking such murderous thoughts about his father and mother. As this meaning of thunder and lightning emerged, the boy's stuttering became markedly worse.

After this impersonal emergence of death wishes the boy informed us that, like the boy in our story, he too had felt abandoned when his parents left him at home while they went out to have a good time. He was led into talking about the maid's ideas of religion and into formulating his own differing viewpoint.

In the fourth interview Jimmy wished to continue and furnished his own story setting. His story was about a boy who was angry because his father would not give him a pony. Wisely or not, we intruded here and had the boy wish his parents would always let him have his own way and give him everything he wanted, even if it did spoil him. The parents immediately interpreted this to mean the boy did not love them or he wouldn't act that way. Jimmy had the little boy laugh and inform the parents he was only joking. Later in the story we placed the boy deep in the woods on his pony and had him suddenly discover a — "a what?"

"Oh, I know. There was a pretty little girl. She was lost in the woods because a rattle snake had bit her horse."

Jimmy dictated a gallant rescue and a handsome reward of a hundred dollars. While glancing with slight embarrassment at us he had the little girl reward the boy with a kiss.

It was then our turn. We started the boy and girl off to the movies to spend some of the reward money. They chose to see Donald Duck and Gene Autrey, Jimmy's favorite movie performers. Immediately the father and mother intruded, demanding to be taken along, refusing to accept the explanation that they wouldn't like this kind of picture. They insisted that the boy's refusal to take them along meant he didn't love them any more. "What did the boy say?" For the first time in all this play, Jimmy could not think what the boy should say. When we offhandedly broke the impasse by dictating the retort, "Aw nuts," Jimmy laughed aloud, suggestively more with relief than with amusement. Tension over this point vanished and did not reappear during subsequent auditions of the story.

Later in the hour, while engaged in handwork, Jimmy ended a period of quietness with, "Gee, sometime I would like to take girls to the movies and spend some money and get to do it all by myself."

The family decided to discontinue the interviews. We certainly doubt that the boy's stuttering benefited greatly from so brief a contact. However, the anxiety concerning lightning and thunder is still absent. We do not minimize many other items contributing to this result, but it does appear that the dictaphone play bridged the displacement between hostility and anxiety, minimized both of these affects, and helped the boy project a more mature self as his ideal.

## Summary

Observations on verbalized play therapy using the telephone, typewriter, and dictaphone have been presented, indicating several minor uses and some general considerations. Among the latter are the following. The impersonality of the machine encourages freer expression. Such play is more applicable to children near or over ten years, particularly boys, than is play with more childish toys. The dictaphone, in particular, furnishes a medium for revealing fantasy thinking, makes conveniently available records of the child's exact expressions, and uniquely offers an objectification of the child to himself and a repetition effect having obvious values.

A procedure is outlined for leading the child into vicariously living through any selected type of problem situation by means of such play. A case is presented to show some of the application of such an approach.

It is our feeling that such mechanical devices are more appropriate to the play of children accustomed to a machine culture than our sentimental memories might lead us to believe.

References
1. Carlson, Earl Reinholdt, Born that way, New York: The John Day Co., 1941.
2. Bender, Lauretta, and Vogel, B. Frank, "Imaginary Companions of Children," Am. J. Orthopsychiatry, XI: 1, 1941.
3. Levy, David M., "Trends in therapy: III: Release Therapy," Am. J. Orthopsychiatry, IX: 4, 1939.
4. Solomon, Joseph C., "Active Play Therapy," Am. J. Orthopsychiatry, VIII: 3, 1938.
5. Allen, Frederick H., "Trends in therapy: IV; participation in Therapy," Am. J. Orthopsychiatry, IX: 4, 1939.
6. Oberndorf, C. P. "Discussion of Identification as a Socializing and Therapeutic Force," by Orgel, Samuel Z. Am. J. Orthopsychiatry, IX: 1, 1941.

# The Suitcase Playroom

SYLVIA CASSELL

Mount Sinai Hospital and Medical Center of Chicago has a problem it shares with hundreds of other hospitals throughout the country: overcrowded facilities. With our outpatient psychiatric facilities as overworked as they are, it is impossible to allocate space for a play therapy room. Yet play therapy is a primary mode of treatment for young children and as a teaching hospital it is important for the psychiatric residents to become familiar with the treatment of young children by this method.

As the hospital could not have a permanent playroom, a portable "Suitcase Playroom" was devised. Basic play materials and a small portable doll house and puppet stage were assembled so that the therapist could pick out the variety of materials he wished by bringing the appropriate suitcase along with the patient to the therapy room. The collection of suitcases and materials used at Mount Sinai cost less than $100 and by judicious spending, a more limited Suitcase Playroom could be assembled for about $50.

The materials to be described all were chosen for their possibilities for basic emotional expression by the children, child appeal and, wherever possible, economy. As only one of the therapy rooms has a washbowl, it was considered necessary to exclude a few important psychotherapeutic play materials such as regular clay, finger paints, and watercolor or poster paints. Other artistic materials, however, were included.

## Play Materials

The play materials used come under three rather general headings and were assembled as such: psychotherapeutic toys and artistic materials, hand puppets and portable stage, and portable furnished doll house. Toys and art materials fill the largest suitcase, measuring 20½ by 7 inches. Toys are placed in boxes in the main part of the suitcase and art materials in a zippered compartment in the suitcase lid. Two smaller suitcases, 16½ inches by 5½ inches, are used for the hand puppets. One suitcase has a black family, plus other puppets, and the other contains a white family and ancillary puppets. The doll house, with handle, is 15 inches by 9 inches closed, 25 inches by 9 inches open, so it fits the small tables in the therapy rooms. A small portable stage completed the playroom equipment.

All of the materials, with the exception of the suitcases, the two cuddly puppets (the skunk and the bear), and the Lego blocks, can be purchased at Constructive Playthings, 1040 E. 85th St., Kansas City, Mo. 64131. "Childplay" of New York, 43 E. 19th St., New York, N.Y. 10003, also carries the family puppets, which are difficult to buy except through special mail order houses such as these. "Childplay" also carries a sack of multishaped table top blocks for $4.00 and a set of 119 American brick blocks for $4.00. The large vinyl suitcase can be bought for about $7.00 or $8.00 in a wide variety of stores. The zippered lid type is helpful in keeping the materials in order and easily found.

In our large suitcase are several boxes which fit the inside. One small box contains fifteen miniature cars and trucks, including an ambulance, police and fire equipment, tow truck, other trucks and passenger cars. Also included in the box are a set of small flexible doll house scale dolls (scaled to fit the Fisher-Price play house) representing parents, several children and a baby.

One of the two larger boxes has a large set of small interlocking Lego blocks. Included in the box are a set of standing wooden figures (tallest six inches). The figures comprise two families of five members each, one set black and one set white, plus community figures such as police and firemen, postman, construction worker and delivery man. The doll house dolls and the wooden figures are placed with the cars or blocks simply to keep everything in place and readily available without having to rummage throughout the suitcase to find something.

The other large box contains army green plastic war toys. There are about three dozen soldiers in assorted postures; e.g. prone or shooting from a standing position. There also are four tanks, four trucks, two jeeps, and assorted small field guns. A doll house bathroom with tub, toilet, and washbowl completes the suitcase interior.

The zippered lid contains the art materials. There is a large pad of newsprint, several packages of non-toxic crayons, a set of eight different colored felt tip pens, one pound of plasticene, and two clay boards. The latter are simply two 12 inch square masonite boards which keep the therapy room table tops from getting oily. Children who use the plasticene are asked to wash their hands before putting on their outer clothing to go home. An experiment was made earlier using regular potter's clay, which is softer, but it was found that the clay rapidly seemed to get distributed on the children, their clothes, and the floor so it was eliminated for our particular flexible needs.

The two small suitcases, 5½ inches by 10 inches, contain the puppets. The contents of the two suitcases, which are of different colors to make it easy to select the desired case, are essentially the same with the exception that one suitcase has a black family and the other a white family. All of the puppets are hand puppets. The primary puppets are a family; in this case the white family suitcase will be described. (Some of the animals and community workers vary between the two suitcases.) The family puppets consist of a father, mother, boy, girl, and baby and the set costs $9.25. These puppets have plastic heads and cloth bodies and hands for easy manipulation (and washing!). A much-used feature of the baby puppet is that he has a small plastic nursing bottle with removable nipple (with hole) which can be filled with water. Other plastic-headed cloth body puppets are a doctor in a white coat and a workman in blue suit with matching cap. (The other suitcase has a nurse in white uniform and a policeman in navy blue with a matching plastic hat with white star.)

The remaining puppets are all animals. Among the least expensive are the felt "talking" puppets. (The puppets have large mouths that open and close rather than arms or legs.) The felt puppets are $2.00 apiece, or six for $10.00 from Constructive Playthings. The ones we have chosen, from a wide selection of those available, are ones which we feel make it easier for the young patient to express his feelings or to identify himself with the puppet. We have a fierce looking green crocodile with pointed white teeth and scowling eyebrows, a happy tan lion with fringed brown mane and dark brown nose, a little brown bear with black nose and yellow muzzle, a rather silly looking gray elephant with long upturned nose and a tiny orange tuft on the top of his head, a proud green rooster with bright red comb, and an appealing pink bunny with large pink ears. Constructive Playthings also sells plush animal puppets at $3.00 each or six for $15.00, and "talking" plastic-headed, cloth-bodied puppets representing mostly animals, but also Santa Claus and a clown. Either of these types of puppets (plush or plastic) come in a wide variety of animals. The plastic puppets are $1.95 each or six for $10.00

Department store additions to the puppet suitcases include a very cuddly, thick plush skunk with a red ribbon at his neck, a small pink tongue and a tiny red cap with a white pompom, probably one of the children's favorites along with the crocodile. Completing the puppet suitcase is a furry brown bear with shoe button type eyes and the same gay ribbon and cap as the skunk. Each of these two puppets costs $3.00. Other puppets which are well used by children are all the plastic "talking" puppets from Creative Playthings, Princeton, New Jersey 08540. These "big mouthed" puppets include a whale, duck, wolf, frog and dragon and are 9½ inches long. They are sold for $2.95 each.

Creative Playthings used to carry a fine inexpensive puppet stage but Constructive Playthings now offers the only inexpensive one we found. It's a convertible stage for hand puppets or marionettes and sells for only $5.75.

The portable dollhouse, manufactured by Fisher-Price, is ideally suited for a modest, portable play program. Closed (with handle) it measures 9 by 15 inches, and open it is 9 by 25 inches, particularly ideal for our needs. This "play house" as it is called, sells for about $12.00 at department stores or $16.00 at Constructive Playthings. It is a complete toy with furniture and a dowel-type family of parents, children, and dog. As the dolls are quite stylized and unrealistic looking we added an additional set of flexible Flagg family dolls. Although relatively expensive, $8.50 for a family of five, the realistic qualities of the dolls and accurate minute details make them favorites over the other dolls.

As the Suitcase Playroom has five pieces (three suitcases, a play house, and cardboard stage) the therapist generally should start by using the large suitcase and possibly one of the small suitcases appropriate for his patient. Then as the child makes his interests known, e.g. playing with the wooden figures, the puppet stage or play house might be substituted for the unused collections in the large suitcase.

We have found that this collection of material, while obviously lacking many of the fine large pieces of equipment, e.g. sand table or the punching bag clown which need more space, does include materials to meet most of the expressive needs of the children.

# Use of a School Play Kit for School Adjustment Problems

DONALD A. LETON

Since the pattern of school adjustment is substantially established in preschool and early school years, it becomes important that parents, teachers, and other school personnel handle wisely the problems which children experience in their school adjustment. The child's functioning, initially as a pupil, later as a student, and eventually as an adult, may be influenced permanently by the emotional experiences he encounters in his early school environment. Perhaps the most important task for the nursery school, kindergarten, and primary grade teachers is to stimulate children to respond in a particular manner appropriate to the school setting.

Unfortunately, however, a number of children at these age levels do not respond in the manner prescribed by the school. Many also do not behave in a manner acceptable to their parents and their peers. In spite of this critical importance of the early school experience, with implications for later adjustment, teachers have relatively little time available to work with individual children on their school adjustment and behavior problems. The situation which prevails is that teachers generally persist in their efforts to develop positive attitudes and adjustment for the majority of the pupils, but they cannot devote time to the study and elimination of undesirable traits in maladjusted children. Even though the classroom atmosphere may be friendly and conducive to learning for the majority of the pupils, nevertheless, there are still some children whose anxieties will interfere with their school participation; and there are other children whose feelings of aggression and hostility will prevent their cooperation with school controls.

The use of play techniques for studying and helping the child in general adjustment has had wide application in clinics for child guidance. The early studies in this field (4,5,6) relied on psychoanalytic theory and concepts to interpret children's play. The psychoanalytic interpretations were detailed and involved, and thus this approach was limited to a few clinics. The wide acceptance of play therapy followed the development of nondirective and noninterpretive techniques developed by Axline (1,2). Other variations of play therapy were introduced by Levy (7) and by Solomon (9). These latter techniques are directive from the standpoint of purpose; i.e. release therapy and structured play. At the present time, clinical practices in play therapy vary widely. Few therapists rely on one system to the exclusion of others. Almost every therapist has devised his own system of observations and procedures. As yet none of the authorities in this field has proposed an eclectic approach; however, this may be the theoretical position held by many of the play therapists.

## The Diagnostic Problem

At the present time there are no adequate instruments to measure school adjustments in the primary and intermediate grades. Teachers are inclined to assign the causes for poor school adjustment to factors in the home or to early child experiences. On the other hand, parents, who are naturally defensive about their child's behavior, tend to relate the maladjustment to school factors. Neither position is, of course, completely accurate or inaccurate. School maladjustment should no longer be viewed as unique to that setting, neither in cause nor effect. It should be regarded as part of a total problem of social adjustment. It was the lack of adequate diagnostic instruments and therapeutic materials that led to the development of the School Play Kit.

## Use of the Kit for Diagnosis

The School Play Kit is a set of materials designed to represent the average classroom. It consists of miniature school furniture, black-boards, bulletin boards, miniature books, some plastic materials, and the teacher and pupil dolls. The number of dolls may vary with the age level of the child. Certain other materials such as miniature rugs, blocks, and plasticene clay may be included for kindergarten children. The kit was devised and assembled with a two-fold purpose in mind: first, for the diagnosis and treatment of school adjustment problems in kindergarten and primary grade pupils; and secondly, to help preschool children to form realistic concepts and positive attitudes toward school.

The purpose of this experiment was to evaluate the play kit in the diagnosis of school adjustment. The subjects for the study were twenty children, chosen from two kindergarten classes. The teachers were asked to rank their children on the following variables: (1) Relationship to teacher, (2) Responses to school routines, and (3) Relationship with peers. These rankings were summarized into a single score, and the five children in each class with the best school adjustment and the five children with the poorest school adjustment were selected for the experimental samples. They were then referred in a random order for individual play sessions. The psychologist had no previous knowledge of their adjustment classification. He was not provided with any of their school records, nor could he utilize supplementary interview techniques in the play sessions. At the end of a single play session, ranging in length from thirty to fifty minutes, the psychologist attempted to identify the category and nature of their school adjustment. A summary of the rankings on school adjustment and the psychologist's identification is shown in Table I.

## Table I
### Scores on Adjustment Rankings and Psychologist's Identification

| Well Adjusted Samples | | | |
|---|---|---|---|
| Class | Pupil's Rank | Score | Adjustment Identification |
| I | 1-G | 3 | Well |
|  | 2-G | 8 | Well |
|  | 3-B | 11 | Well |
|  | 4-G | 11 | Well |
|  | 5-B | 12 | Well |
| II | 1-G | 5 | Well |
|  | 2-G | 6 | Well |
|  | 3-B | 9 | Well |
|  | 4-B | 13 | Poor*** |
|  | 5-G | 13 | Well |
| **Poorly Adjusted Samples** | | | |
| Class | Pupil's Rank | Score | Adjustment Identification |
| I | 21-G | 64 | Poor |
|  | 22-B | 68 | Well** |
|  | 23-B | 70 | Well* |
|  | 24-B | 71 | Poor |
|  | 25-B | 72 | Poor |
| II | 22-B | 64 | Well** |
|  | 23-B | 65 | Poor |
|  | 24-G | 70 | Well** |
|  | 25-B | 71 | Poor |
|  | 26-B | 75 | Poor |

*the letters B and G indicate boy or girl.
**indicates a false negative diagnosis
***indicates a false positive diagnosis

## Experimental Results

The result of the experiment shows an accurate identification of fifteen of the twenty pupils. Four of the inaccurate identifications were false negatives and one was a false positive. One of the most difficult tasks in validating clinical judgments is for the clinician to identify the signs used in making the judgments. In order to obtain some insight into the diagnostic process involved in using the play kit, the protocols of the play sessions were reviewed.

This study may be considered an exploratory study in that an attempt was made to identify the signs or cues in the school play from which the school adjustment could be inferred. The characteristics of play associated with poor school adjustment seemed to be relatively easy to identify. The following notes were taken from these protocols: needs assistance in setting up school play; impulsive changes in play activities; inappropriate combining of materials (chalk in clay, clay on globe, etc.); frequent tipping over of furniture; over-excitement, flighty actions, and frequent shifting of ideas in play; dolls fighting; random aggressiveness; rejection punishment or aggressiveness directed against other pupil and teacher dolls; slow recognition of materials as representative of classroom; reticence to handle materials; and prolonged questions about the materials.

In this study the identification of the pupils who were well adjusted seemed to be a much easier task than the identification of the poorly adjusted. The interpretations of the protocols for good school adjustment included the following: accurate knowledge of school routines; easy projection into roles of teacher; realistic imitation of teacher behavior; play centered on school activities; attempts at orderliness — distributing materials, putting books away, display of achievement skills; writing name; reading books; satisfaction with achievement; alliance with other pupils on tasks.

Perhaps the most consistent behavior in the sessions of the well-adjusted pupils was the display of achievement skills. On the other hand, the pupil with poor school adjustment who was erroneously classified as well adjusted displayed excellent achievement skills. Even though this appeared to be the most reliable sign for the well adjusted, it also led to the one false positive diagnosis. This child was a gifted child who tended to dominate the other children in group activities. In the school play session this domination was misinterpreted as leadership rather than social aggression. In the same protocol a cue about toilet routine was overlooked. This subject showed some concern about "proper" school behavior. This was misinterpreted as a knowledge about appropriate pupil behavior rather than a concern about his own poor behavior.

The four pupils who were erroneously classified as well adjusted did not display sufficient deviant behavior to justify either classification. In each case the judgment might have been suspended until further sessions, however, the purpose of the experiment was to test the effectiveness of the kit in a single play session.

Two of the variables which should be considered in establishing the validity of the diagnosis are the base rate in the population and the expectancy rate in the diagnostician. The incidence of school maladjustment is ordinarily limited to a minor percentage of children. Most of the pupils in the experimental group with poor school adjustment would not be regarded as clinical cases. The expectancy rate in the diagnostician would also not necessarily coincide with the base rate. Other important factors which deserve further study are the characteristics of the play materials. One set of materials which may be diagnostic and therapeutic for maladjusted pupils may not be useful in detecting variations on a continuum of school adjustment within the normal range.

## Use of the Kit in Treatment

The most common use of the kit in treatment up to this time had been with cases of school phobia. This condition is one in which the child exhibits mild or extreme fears of school. It is frequently associated with psychosomatic illness and withdrawal from a variety of social settings. Although the symptoms are displayed in the school setting, the causes usually reside in the earlier emotional development of the child.

A secondary use of the kit has been to help children gain an objective view of the classroom and of their own behavior as a pupil. In this respect the play kit represents a stage for sociodrama. The exchange of pupil and teacher roles can be accomplished more readily in the play setting than within the classroom.

A third use of the materials has been for expressive release. There are many restrictive and inhibiting factors operating in most classrooms. These are not always repressive, but rather are necessary for normal routines in crowded schools and classrooms. It is not often possible to identify these factors, much less to define their influence on personality. There have been sufficient case materials to indicate that many children need some expressive release for the conflicts and problems they encounter in school.

References
1. Axline, Virginia M., *Play Therapy*, Boston: Houghton-Mifflin Co. 1947, 374 pp.
2. Bloomberg, C. M., "Experiment in Play Therapy," *Child Education*, 25: 177–180, 1948.

3. Conn, J. H., "Play Interview as an Investigative and Therapeutic Procedure," *Nervous Child*, 7: 257-286, 1948.
4. Erikson, E. H., "Studies in the Interpretation of Play," Genetic Psychology Monographs, 22: 557-671, 1940.
5. Harms, E., "Play Diagnosis: Preliminary Consideration for a Sound Approach," *Nervous Child*, 7:233-246, 1948.
6. Klein, Melanie, *The Psychoanalysis of Children*, London: Hogarth Press, 1932.
7. Levy, D. M., "Trends in Therapy III, Release Therapy," *American Journal of Orthopsychiatry*, 9:817-736, 1939.
8. Moustakas, Clark E., "Children in Play Therapy," New York: McGraw-Hill Book Co., Inc., 1953.
9. Solomon, J. C., "Active Play Therapy," *American Journal of Orthopsychiatry*, 8:479-498, 1938.

# Play Equipment

HELEN R. BEISER

In the past twenty years a large volume of literature has accumulated both on play therapy and on various specialized techniques for interviewing children for purposes of diagnosis or research, but in the papers on play therapy it is difficult or impossible to discover just what physical equipment was provided for the interviews. Melanie Klein (4), in a brief description of the play materials she uses in child analysis, mentions such items as human and animal figures, various conveyances, paper, scissors and pencils, but she does not discuss the basis of selection. Psychoanalytic literature, as a whole, while it emphasizes interpretation of the play, has offered no enumeration or evaluation of the materials used.

Other literature on play equipment falls into several categories. First, there have been studies on individual types of toys such as puppets, or family dolls, or special equipment as described by M. B. Durfee (2). Closely related to these studies are the investigations into children's drawings or paintings, such as the work of Alschuler and Hattwick (1). In another category are those studies in which a child is asked to give a certain performance in a structuralized situation and the interpretation of this production or behavior is made according to the theoretical leanings of the observer. Lowenfeld (5) and Erikson (3) both described studies in which a variety of figures and building materials is provided and both have developed methods of recording the interviews for future study and comparision. This technique is very closely allied to the various projective tests of the psychologist. Solomon (6) gives an excellent summary of present play techniques with an extensive bibliography of pertinent clinical and experimental studies.

## Problems in Toy Selection

The inexperienced diagnostician and therapist, then, is confronted with a considerable problem in choosing play equipment for clinical use. He has a tendency to use everything that has ever been shown to be useful until his experience demonstrates which toys or what materials seem to tell the most about a child. The writer experienced this problem quite sharply when appointed to the responsibility for purchasing play equipment for the Institute for Juvenile Research. The tradition of this clinic fitted most closely the play technique of Melanie Klein; that is, children were invited to play freely with a selection of toys. Upon investigating available play materials, I discovered that the choice of toys offered by manufacturers is almost unlimited and ever changing. Many toys cannot be duplicated even after a few months' time. Instead of the relatively few simple toys described by Melanie Klein, our playrooms were filled with mountains of toys, frequently scarred and broken beyond use, and of whose value no one was quite sure.

After much trial and error it was felt that toys could perhaps be selected on the basis of some general categories, to overcome the problem of rapid shifts in manufacturing. In searching the literature for help toward this end, the study of Dorothy Van Alstyne (7) on the choice of play materials for children in nursery schools groups was found valuable, although not directly applicable. A clinical study along similar lines was clearly indicated. This present paper deals with a controlled study of the diagnostic interviews of 100 children, based on a free choice of a wide variety of children's toys.

Although interpretations may be similar, diagnostic interviews present fewer problems of study than therapy interviews. Besides, the first contact with a child is a more critical test of a toy's communication possibilities. In this paper no consideration is given to any intrinsic therapeutic value of play, and toys are evaluated only as aids in the professional understanding of a child's personality.

Before discussing the study itself, it might be helpful to describe some of the problems peculiar to the Institute because of its size and structure, and how they were solved. In outlying clinics, play interviews may be held in offices ordinarily used for other purposes, and the toys kept in a bookcase, cupboard, or closet which can be opened when the child is seen. In the headquarters clinic in Chicago, special rooms are set aside for play interviews. Here a system has been devised which provides for fundamental stability and ease of maintenance, with sufficient flexibility for individualization. Each room contains table and chairs, sink, sandbox, dollhouse, tool bench, and clean-up equipment. To such a room each examiner brings a box containing a doll family, unstructured materials such as paper, crayons, paints, clay, paste, scotch tape, etc. This box of toys broadens and enriches the basic equipment already present in the playroom and, in outlying clinics without permanent playroom space, furnishes a "portable play-room."

The toy boxes have found their most interesting function, however, in giving some individualization to therapy. Each child is provided by his therapist with his own toy box which is kept for him alone as long as treatment continues. At the beginning of therapy the equipment is the same as that used for diagnosis, but items can be added or removed with the changing needs of the child. Occasionally, other toys may be used in therapy which are too large or too expensive for individual boxes. Games, construction projects, larger doll-play accessories, etc., are kept in a closet accessible to all the playrooms.

To be sure, it would be advantageous for each examiner or therapist to have his own equipment in his own office, with perhaps more individual variations than have just been described, but we believe that the method as devised provides for some flexibility in the toy box, while still keeping within the necessary limitations of a large and complex organization.

The problem remained, however, of checking these traditional or intuitive choices objectively. One of the outlying clinics was chosen for our study because of greater ease in maintaining controlled conditions. No data could be obtained here on sand or water play or special therapy equipment such as games, but it was felt more important to get information on toys not needing any special physical environment.

## Study of Toy Preferences and Use

The following study was made in a city of 100,000 population in Northern Illinois. It is a prosperous industrial city in the heart of a well-to-do farming area. Most referrals to our clinic are by social agencies, but the clinic in this region has been established long enough so there are some direct referrals by parents as well as by local physicians. The range of cases, therefore, is broad in relation to social level and community environment, as well as type of problem.

Our study in this particular clinic was made on 100 consecutive cases over a period of approximately two years. Clinics are held four days each month and the same psychiatrist sees all cases except on very rare occasions when a junior psychiatrist may accompany the team for training purposes. The room used was a moderate-sized office with desk, filing cabinet, telephone, and bookcase with toys. The child's chair was placed between the interviewer's desk and the bookcase. The interview was conducted as follows:

The child was brought into the room and the appropriate chair pointed out to him. A short time was allowed to see if he would play with the toys spontaneously, and, if not, he was invited to play. Free play was permitted until such time as further material did not seem to be developing, or when the play became repetitive and did not seem likely to shift. The child was then interviewed verbally, although if play continued during the verbal interview it was not interfered with. Occasionally children were found who felt free to play only after some conversation had been started. There were also, of course, situations in which the child did not want even to enter the room, and special methods had to be used to get him into the room and to invite him to play. There was, hower, very little urging used, so that the results can be considered on the basis of free choice.

The age group of the cases ranged from two up to twelve. As in most child guidance clinics the boys outnumbered the girls, there being seventy-nine boys in this group. There were fourteen children with IQ's below 70, but the largest group, thirty-six, had IQ's of between 85 and 100. As a whole, the intelligence range was broad, from grossly retarded up to superior.

At the time the study began, the approximate cost of the play items was $15. The arrangement of toys in the bookcase is shown in Table 1. These items can usually be obtained in inexpensive variety stores and the names are for the most part self-explanatory. Both white and colored paper was provided. The clay was of the type which can be re-used indefinitely. The trucks and planes were plastic and of various sizes. A small plastic locomotive was included with the trucks. The gun was a cowboy cap pistol. The large baby doll was an inexpensive one with painted rompers. Doll families are the most difficult to buy at any price and the Institute buys them in large lots whenever they are available. This one was of hard plastic with movable joints and with the clothes painted on. A bottle could be inserted into the baby's mouth. The goose was a large, metal one which jumped when wound up with a key. The Nok-Out Bench is now made by several companies with slight variations. The main features are a wooden bench with a hidden central passage and a number of cylindrical pegs. The pegs are pounded into the top opening with a wooden mallet, and when the central passage is full they are ejected by a spring from an opening on the side. This toy presents a problem to a child in its manipulation and in discovering its mechanism.

Notes were made during the interview as to which toys a child played with or touched in any way, and what he did with them. From this

## TABLE 1. ARRANGEMENT OF TOYS

| Top Shelf | Second Shelf | Third Shelf | Bottom Shelf |
|---|---|---|---|
| clay | trucks | large baby doll | Nok-Out Bench |
| scissors | planes | telephone | blocks |
| paste | gun | doll family | ball |
| pencil | soldiers | furniture | goose |
| crayons | farm animals | | |
| paper | | | |

description the following data could be obtained for each interview: (1) which toys were used at all, (2) which toy was first choice, and (3) in a general way, the manner in which the toys were used.

On a much more subjective level the examiner then tried to determine what sort of dynamic information could be interpreted from the play. This sort of information depends to a large extent on the training and experience of the examiner and might vary in interpretation, perhaps, between different examiners. However, I believe that for the purposes of this study the subjective impressions of this examiner could be used as a basis for comparing the value of the various toys used. A total of 11 interpretations was made including both impulses and defenses. For example, play with the gun would indicate direct aggression if the child shot the gun at some definite object, whereas if he merely shot the gun as if examining the mechanism, this was considered indirect aggression as well as curiosity. Castration fear was interpreted when a child was anxious concerning a defect in the toy or noticed that some part of equipment was missing. It was surprising how many young boys became very anxious because only the locomotive was present and not the rest of the train; or, they picked up minute defects in a very tiny plastic airplane, defects that would not ordinarily be noticeable.

## Play Interview

The following is a sample play interview, with interpretations. The verbal portions have been largely deleted and enough historical material is given to show how it may relate to the play.

> *Interview with D.* This seven-year-old boy came readily to the office and began a conversation in a mature fashion. However, as soon as he became aware of the toys next to him, he picked up the gun, remarking that he had one like it, and pulled the trigger to see how it worked. He touched the trucks briefly and then played for some time with the doll family and furniture. He wiggled the joints of the father doll, stating that he didn't think he would ever stand up, and then set him on the couch with the boy doll next to him, but

almost immediately separated them with the girl doll. There followed much replacing of all members of the family. Finally, he separated the father from the group and said angrily that he would never be able to walk. He made a tight grouping of the family, furniture, soldiers, and airplane "so they won't get out," but when the father doll fell off the chair he broke up the group, lined up the furniture, made some bizarre remarks about the planes' making the furniture fly, and grabbed the gun, holding it tightly as he talked of his plans to go out West. After some further conversation which included complaints about his father and brother, he became interested in crayons and began to draw, saying he would show me how to draw "a new kind of girl."

*Interpretation.* The trucks in this sequence were only of passing interest and no interpretations could be made from them. The crayons were used to produce on paper a drawing with fantasy content. The drawing, with his description of it, was interpreted as his wish to identify with the opposite sex. The other toys were used together in a rather poorly organized fantasy. The use of the airplane is not clear, but may be symbolic of the wish to fly away, which he later verbalized in his plans to go out West. Certainly his tight holding of the gun indicates that he has considerable separation anxiety concerning such a wish. His hostility is covered up or controlled, being demonstrated indirectly by a random shooting of the gun and the angry complaints against the inadequacies of the father doll. When the father doll accidentally fell over, he compulsively lined up the furniture. The interchanging of dolls could be interpreted as his confusion about sex, but as this was not clear, only sibling rivalry seemed conclusive.

*Correlation with historical material.* D is the older of two boys by fourteen months. His mother stated he had strong feelings of being displaced when his brother was born. D has been asthmatic from early age and mother is very overprotective of him. Father is a farmer and prefers the younger boy because D's allergies prevent his participation in farm work. D has expressed his problem mainly by failing to learn in school (IQ 101), and by occasional petty stealing. Without further detail, I think one can understand D's play as the reaction of a boy who feels left out and inferior, is angry with his brother and father, but is afraid to express himself openly, using compulsiveness, control of aggression, and feminine identification as his defenses, apparently because of marked separation anxiety. These defenses are not completely satisfactory to him as they are not sufficient to prevent stealing, but are too inhibiting to allow for free learning in school.

## Toy Categories

In studying the total results, the toys were first categorized according to some general characteristic as Van Alstyne (7) did. For example, there were toys which definitely stimulated doll play, or were an adjunct of doll play. Then there were other toys which could be considered a stimulus to motor activity in some way, or which, in themselves, suggested motor activity. The bench with the pegs is in a category by itself. It actually has a certain pattern which the child must discover in order to make it work. The mechanical goose was put in the group largely to see whether mechanical toys had any greater interest for children than those with less obvious stimulating power. The remainder can be classified as unstructured. In other words, the potentialities of their use depend far more on the child than on the toy itself. (The toys are listed in their categories in Table 2.) Thus it was felt that the toys offered to the child presented a broad range, although perhaps somewhat heavily weighted in the doll-play and unstructured groups. These two categories quite obviously were felt intuitively to be the most important when the study was begun.

### TABLE 2. CATEGORIES OF TOYS

| Doll Play | Motor | Pattern | Mechanical | Unstructured |
|---|---|---|---|---|
| gun | trucks | Nok-Out Bench | goose | clay |
| soldiers | planes | | | scissors |
| farm animals | ball | | | paste |
| large baby doll | | | | pencil |
| telephone | | | | crayons |
| doll family | | | | paper |
| furniture | | | | |

## Popularity and Therapeutic Value

Each toy was then individually tabulated according to how many of the children had played with it in any way, how many times the play developed into fantasy, and how many of the dynamic characteristics were shown. First, as to popularity, somewhat surprisingly, the dollhouse family ranked first. The most popular toys and the percentage of children who played with them are listed in Table 3. The gun was the most frequent first choice. The least popular toys are listed in Table 4.

Although reasonable popularity is important for a toy's usefulness, we want to know much more about what its use can tell us. One method of obtaining this information was to tabulate each interpretation of dynamic significance which could be made from the play with a toy. A comparison could be made between the popularity of a toy and a roughly quantitative measure of its dynamic communication. A ratio was worked out between the popularity and total dynamic interpretations which I will call the communication value. A communication value of 1 would signify that the popularity and the total dynamic interpretations were the same. The average communication value for the whole group was .72. Those toys with highest and lowest communication values are listed in Tables 3 and 4.

Another method of attempting to evaluate what a toy tells us about a child is to determine how often such a toy stimulates fantasy play. Occasionally dynamic interpretations cannot be made of such fantasy, but if recorded, might become extremely meaningful in therapy. Consequently, the number of times a toy stimulated a child to fantasy-play in relation to being played with at all was determined for each toy. The toys stimulating the most and least fantasy are listed in Tables 3 and 4. The percentage figures refer to the proportion of fantasy play in the total use of that toy.

TABLE 3. HIGHEST RANKING TOYS

| Popularity | Communication Value | Fantasy Stimulation | Dynamic Spread | Combined Total |
|---|---|---|---|---|
| 64% doll family | 1.41 Nok-Out Bench | 55% doll family | 11 doll family | doll family |
| 62% soldiers | 1.14 doll family | 54% paper and crayon | 10 animals | soldiers |
| 60% gun | 1.13 gun | 48% clay | 9 planes | gun |
| 55% Nok-Out Bench | 1.00 soldiers | 46% blocks | 8 clay | clay |
| 51% trucks | .88 paper and crayons | 43% planes | 8 trucks | paper and crayons |
| 50% goose | .83 clay | 39% soldiers | 8 gun | animals |
| 46% telephone | .79 large baby doll | 35% animals | 8 Nok-Out Bench | planes |
| 46% animals | .65 animals | 29% trucks | 8 goose | Nok-Out Bench |
| 46% planes | | 29% furniture | | trucks |

One other factor was considered to be of significance. How broad, in the dynamic interpretations listed above, was the significance of an individual toy? In other words, how many of these interpretations could be made on a single toy, not necessarily as used by a single child, but when the entire group was totaled? This factor I have called the dynamic spread. Of the 11 possible interpretations, the doll family is the only one on which all had been made. The other toys with the highest and lowest dynamic spread together with the total number of interpretations made are listed in Tables 3 and 4.

One effect of the ratings must be taken into consideration — the influence of the grouping on the shelves of the bookcase. This factor is somewhat difficult to evaluate because all the toys on the top shelf were of the same category and might be unpopular anyway. However, it was noted that in the group under five years of age the toys on this shelf were chosen only half as frequently as in the older age groups. The top shelf was slightly above the eye level of the older children. Otherwise the choices on the second, third, and bottom shelf seemed to be pretty much made according to the popularity of the individual toys.

TABLE 4. LOWEST RANKING TOYS

| Popularity | Communication Value | Fantasy Stimulation | Dynamic Spread | Combined Total |
|---|---|---|---|---|
| 3% pencil | .0 pencil | 0 pencil | 0 pencil | pencil |
| 8% scissors | .2 crayons (only) | 0 ball | 1 paste | paste |
| 9% paste | .26 furniture | 9% Nok-Out Bench | 3 scissors | scissors |
| 13% blocks | .26 telephone | 11% paste | 4 blocks | ball |
| 13% ball | | | 4 ball | |

Taking all of the above factors into consideration, a combined total rating can be given to individual toys. Two toys were prominently ranked by all four criteria. These are the doll family and the toy soldiers. The doll family far outranked any other toy, being first in all categories except communication value. Other toys of highest and lowest total rankings are listed in Tables 3 and 4.

An attempt was then made to see if the evaluation of the individual toys had any relationship to the previously described functional categories. This was difficult because two categories had only one representative, but also because an individual toy might overlap several categories. For example, the mechanical goose had its own category of a mechanical toy but also had other aspects, placing it in the doll-play group, because of its obvious structure. I believe that it is its animal qualities rather than the mechanical aspects that rated it so high in dynamic spread and communication value. There is likewise a large doll-play quality about the trucks and planes, and they were frequently used as adjuncts in doll play. The unstructured materials were occasionally fashioned into objects which then fell into different categories.

In order to determine if any specific category of toy seemed to be more important in communication value than any other category, the rankings of the various toys in each category were averaged so that the categories themselves could be rated. The overlapping described above was ignored for this purpose. The results are listed in Table 5. This would lead one to believe that doll-play materials are the most valuable for understanding a child, and unstructured materials the least. However, I do not believe that this would be a valid judgment, owing to the wide spread of individual toys in these categories. For example, there is wide variation within the structured category from paper and crayons, which rate fourth among the toys taken individually, to the scissors, paste and pencil, which were lowest in rank. Because of this finding it is felt that, unfortunately, categories of toy materials are not nearly so important as the consideration of the possibilities of an individual toy, and the problem remains of trying to duplicate from the manufacturers' stock those toys which have been found valuable.

TABLE 5. RANKING OF TOY CATEGORIES

| Popularity | Communication Value | Fantasy Stimulation | Dynamic Spread | Combined Total |
|---|---|---|---|---|
| pattern | pattern | doll play | pattern | doll play |
| doll play | doll play | unstructured | mechanical | pattern |
| mechanical | motor | motor | doll play | mechanical |
| motor | mechanical | mechanical | motor | motor |
| unstructured | unstructured | pattern | unstructured | unstructured |

## Discussion

It is felt that from this experience certain general principles of setting up a playroom can be established. It is apparent that communication of important material can be obtained from the use of a wide variety of toys. For the inexperienced examiner or therapist, however, it would seem advisable to set up as simple and standardized a play setting as possible. By doing so, the examiner is able to compare within his own experience the behavior of different children in the same setting and in reaction to the same toy stimuli. The toys in this study are not necessarily the only toys that could be used, but have been found to be useful and inexpensive. They are adaptable to any room, from the elaborate playroom constructed especially for that purpose, to a small box of play materials which can be transported easily and which can be used as a standard of stimuli for the interview situation in any physical setup. It would be perhaps difficult to find a pattern toy small enough to be easily transportable, but in many ways the toy box itself is a pattern, and its investigation or lack of investigation can be looked upon diagnostically in the same manner.

In setting up this study it had been hoped that certain general criteria could be established for choosing toys. As already discussed, the categories used here have not been very valuable. One cannot even conclude that the value of toys depends on the ability to stimulate fantasy of the "doll-play" type, because of the very high rating of the Nok-Out Bench which stimulates very little fantasy. Another surprise was the relatively low rating of the unstructured materials. Van Alstyne (7) found these to be most popular among normal preschool children.

Consequently one wonders if lack of interest in these materials is part of the disturbance in children brought to a clinic. At the same time she found pattern toys of little value, whereas the definite pattern toy in this study had very high popularity as well as communication value. Further study is planned covering in more detail the influence of degree of disturbance, age, sex, and intelligence on play patterns.

In a more general sense, however, we are interested in interviewing a child to find out what his problems are and how he is handling them. We depend largely on the parents' information to determine the *why* of the child's problem, at least for diagnosis. Therefore we are interested in providing material which stimulates the production of fantasy by which we hope to learn the content of the problem, and also material which will give us some insight into the child's modes of operation. I believe it is because of what it shows about the child's reaction to his problem that the Nok-Out Bench had such a high rating. The doll family, as would be expected, was the best toy for stimulating highly important fantasy content to provide the answers for the *what* in the child's problems. It could be concluded that adequate diagnostic studies could be done using only these two toys. However, I believe this leaves out consideration for the range of a child's activities and for an estimation of the degree of his defenses. For example, a bright older child may be quite aware that play with a doll family reveals problems which he wishes to conceal. He may feel free to reveal problems of interpersonal relationships only through the more disguised medium of impersonal soldiers, animals, or such inanimate objects as cars or airplanes. On the other hand, the Nok-Out Bench may be too complicated, or the hostile aspects (hammering) too frightening for some children and simpler patterns may be seen in the manipulation of the telephone, or even in the bouncing of a ball.

The unstructured toys really combine both elements. They provide certain material which is to be used in a given way to obtain the desired results. One hopes, however, that the resulting product will have some sort of content which has the same value as a fantasy. It is quite possible that it is a special strain on the capacity of the disturbed child to master adequately both the disturbing content and the skills necessary for an integrated production, at the same time. But this is a subject for further investigation.

In conclusion it is suggested that a fairly broad selection of toys and materials be provided for diagnostic and therapeutic play interviews, at the same time keeping the total play environment relatively simple and stable.

**References**

1. Alschuler, Rose, and LaBerta Hattwick, *Painting and Personality*,Chicago; Univ. of Chicago Press, 1947.
2. Durfee, M. B., Use of Ordinary Office Equipment in "Play Therapy," *Am. J. Orthopsychiatry*, 12: 495–502, 1942.
3. Erikson, E. H., "Sex Differences in the Play Configurations of Preadolescents," *Am. J. Orthopsychiatry*, 21: 667–692, 1951.
4. Klein, Melanie, *The Psychoanalysis of Children*, London: Hogarth Press, 1932.
5. Lowenfeld, Margaret, "The World Pictures of Children," *Brit. J. Med. Psychol.*, 18: 65–101, 1939.
6. Solomon, Joseph C., "Play Technique," *Am. J. Orthopsychiatry*, 18: 402–413, 1948.
7. Van Alstyne, Dorothy, *Play Behavior and Choice of Play Materials of Preschool Children*, Chicago: Univ. of Chicago Press, 1932.

# Toys for Nondirective Play Therapy

DELL LEBO

One of the important considerations in play therapy is the types of toys needed in the playroom. The problem of selecting proper play materials becomes apparent when only a limited budget is available. When a minimum of toys may be purchased, it is essential that toys making the greatest contribution to the therapeutic process are selected. When ample funds are available: "The inexperienced diagnostician and therapist . . . had a tendency to use everything that has ever been shown to be useful until . . . experience demonstrates which toys or what materials seem to tell the most about a child" (5, p. 761). A basis for selecting toys for therapy would seem to be desirable in either case.

## Selection of Toys

One of the first factors to be considered when purchasing toys for a playroom is that they should be selected, rather than accumulated. The importance of a "quantity and variety" of toys advocated by one nondirective play therapist (24) is in sharp contrast to the few toys utilized by Anna Freud (7). However, a psychoanalytically oriented play therapist indicates that the tendency to surround the child with toys is not singular to nondirective play therapy. For she reports finding "playrooms . . . filled with mountains of toys . . . of whose value no one was quite sure" (5, p. 762). Another psychoanalyst advocates "offering an ample choice of objects . . . fitting for every age level from preschool to teen age" (14, p. 11). Therapist of different schools, then, may be guilty of gathering, rather than collecting, toys.

## Objective Method

Another factor that merits the most careful consideration is the basis for selecting toys. The process of selecting toys should be an objective one. In this way the method, rather than the toys indicated by the method, may be applied in a variety of situations under numerous conditions. If toys are selected subjectively, it seems to the present writer that only the toys selected, and not the method of selection, can be empirically tested. That is to say, the toys will stand or fall when tested under different conditions. However, when the method of selecting toys is an objective one, then this method can have multiple application as well as revision.

One of the most objective accounts of psychotherapy is the verbatim protocol. David Levy, in discussing psychotherapy in adolescents, remarked on the necessity of the therapist exposing "his method verbatim . . . so that we might know from the record itself what went on from session to session. Such knowledge seems essential in assaying a case" (34, p. 14). The word-for-word account gives prominence to speech. The worth of talk in therapy would, then, seem to be a valuable consideration.

## Value of Talk

Recent years have seen an emphasis on the value of talk in the psychotherapeutic relationship. For example, a comparative investigation of the psychoanalytic and nondirective schools revealed that in both of these methods the client did more than seventy percent of the talking (11). In play therapy talk has been afforded similar prominence. One play therapist has reported that those children who can verbalize some insight as to the reason for their coming into the play situation "show the best progress" (1, p. 101). Another investigator seems to have raised talk to the status of a *sine qua non* in play therapy. He wrote: "Those children who transfer . . . the insolvability of their problems into the play situation . . . need to be induced . . . to reconsider, on a more verbal level, the constellations which have overwhelmed them in the past. . . . (31, pp. 71-72).

Several factors are probably responsible for such considerations being given to talk. In the first place, Freud, the perennial of the bibliographies of psychology, had much to say about speech. He showed the role of speech in analysis as a means of facilitating the patient's efforts to grasp physical or psychical reality. Later he indicated the importance of speech in bringing internal events into consciousness (28).

A second factor was the rise of objective investigations into the process of psychotherapy for teaching and research purposes. The importance of speech has been increased by such interests (17, 27). For, typewritten verbatim style records of therapy could be completely and accurately obtained, and evaluated at leisure by a variety of nonsubjective methods. Hence, much of therapy, in text and experiment, has become almost synonymous with speech.

Such was not always the case. There are many kinds of psychotherapy, now largely of historical or anthropological interest, that do not require the patient to talk (10). Words are actually late developments of expression and communication. In the cultures of antiquity, the word is said to have served as the elucidation of gesture and posture. "Scholars agree that voice language is . . . a substitute for body language" (26, p. 572).

Despite Freud's pronouncements on the value of speech and his employment of verbatim style protocols (8), the young child frequently remains a nonverbal creature. Indeed, Vigotsky (32) intimates that children may prefer to conceal their feelings and fantasies in unvoiced speech. Many play therapists, consequently, have come to share the sentiment that it can be good for a child to be properly and truly silent in the playroom. One therapist has noted that some children "show remarkable improvement in their symptoms and behavior when there has been a minimal amount of . . . conversation about their problems or their inner thought processes" (29, p. 591).

However, an examination of such cases, i.e., children who do not speak in play therapy, reveals that such children "are usually presented . . . in the guise of a unique, single case history" (21). It is to be noted that play therapy and not play diagnosis is being discussed here. In play diagnosis speech is not important. The history of play diagnosis stretches into antiquity, when actions truly spoke louder than words. A play diagnosis by "all the wise men of Egypt . . . and the angel Gabriel . . . disguised as one of them" may serve as an example. These experts diagnosed the behavior of a three-year-old, Moses, according to an account based on the *Canticles Rabba* of the sixth century, as he placed Pharaoh's crown on his own head. The king and his attendants were terrified as they feared this act presaged the usurpation of Pharaoh's power. Gabriel proposed a diagnostic play situation involving a minimum of easily available equipment, i.e., an onyx stone and a live coal. These objects were placed before the child Moses. Hypotheses were proposed and accepted: (*a*) If the child grasped the onyx he would be shown to act with purpose. Hence, his seizure of the crown would have been a meaningful act. (*b*) If he seized the live coal he would be diagnosed as an impulsive, but witless babe.

Moses tried to seize the cold stone, but Gabriel, wishing to influence the outcome and arrive at a predetermined diagnosis, placed the child's hand on the live coal. Moses, apparently now operating from the cue furnished by the examiner, touched the coal to his mouth and burned his lips and tongue. Thus, he lived, but all his life was slow of speech (9, pp. 272-274).

Other examples, methodologically more sophisticated, of play diagnosis are discussed elsewhere (23). Although play has interested people of many lands and cultures since the time of Aristotle (20), play therapy cannot be said to go further back than Rousseau's *Emile* of 1762 (18). Play therapy, then, is of much more recent origin than play diagnosis and generally has come to involve conversation. For the latter reason, children who do not speak in play therapy are unique.

The real problem of determining what is happening to the child who does not speak has been clearly indicated by Axline. She recounted the story of a little Negro boy who, week after week, sat down, tilted back his chair, propped his feet on a table, folded his arms, and just sat. Naturally, many unasked questions crossed the therapist's mind. Just before the therapist was about to prompt this child, the boy smiled, squared his shoulders and remarked, "I've been playing White Man!" Axline poignantly asks, "Who can tell what this experience meant to that child? How can we evaluate the effectiveness of such a play experience?" (4, p. 6).

It is possible for play therapy to be therapeutic even though the child does not speak. However, as Axline's queries suggest, it is as yet impossible to evaluate the process in such cases. Hence, in establishing a method to select toys for play therapy nontalking children cannot yet be included, even though they are encountered in nondirective play therapy. An empirical formula cannot admit subjective elements into its composition.

## Age of Children

Another factor that must be considered is the age of the children who will respond in the play therapy situation. A review of the literature on the suitability of children at different ages for play therapy, appearing in this Journal (21), revealed that most investigators set twelve years as the upper age limit for successful play therapy. A study of success in child therapy, not reported in those previously cited, indicated that: "Therapy with children over the age of twelve was conspicuously less successful than with children under twelve" (6, p. 175). This important finding was based on seventy children treated by eight different therapists.

Unfortunately, for present purposes, the writer did not indicate what type of child therapy was employed, other than that it was "individual treatment." The present writer (21), utilizing nondirective play therapy, has reported that twelve-year-old children did not seem to respond to current nondirective methods with the same verbal vigor as younger children. In view of the quite general agreement that play therapy, presumably of all schools, can be of benefit to children twelve years of age, that age would still seem to be suitable as an upper limit for subjects in a study designed to develop a method of toy selection. The lower limit of age may suitably be established at approximately four years. It has been noted that the three-year-old child finds it difficult to talk and act simultaneously (13). Since the present interest is in play therapy, rather than in play diagnosis, talking becomes objectively important. The four-year-old child can perform two simultaneous motor acts (13). Hence, children of that age make suitable younger subjects for an investigation of a method of selecting toys.

## Attention Span

Sex and age have for long been regarded as important considerations in investigations of children's play. Many investigations utilized the concept of attention span, i.e., the length of time a child will concentrate on a play task. In general, previous studies gave the impression that attention span varied with sex, age, and with type of play material. A recent and well formulated study, reported in this Journal (25) tends to negate these earlier concepts. Moyer and Gilmer found "no regular increase of attention span from year to year" (25, p. 196). The authors conclude that the concept of attention span is meaningless since its measure depends on selecting the right toy or play material for the right age. The much investigated concept of attention span may be less appropriate for indicating the therapeutic value of toys than a procedure involving the child's conversation.

## Value of Toys

There is no doubt that the playroom should be supplied with materials of proven value from a clinical point of view (12). Yet there have been few psychotherapeutic evaluations of material presented (5, 19).

Van Alstyne (30) undertook to discover what differences would be observed in the use of certain play materials in nursery school and kindergarten free play situations. She found that certain materials appeared to have considerably more conversation value than others. The materials highest in conversational value seemed to be: dishes, hollow blocks, doll corner, wagon, parallel bars, telephone, blocks, colored cubes, balls, crayons, and clay. She reported further that the similarities between boys and girls in regard to their choice of play materials were greater than the differences.

A study of the contribution of toys to psychoanalytic diagnosis, not therapy, has recently appeared. The subjects consisted of seventy-nine boys and twenty-one girls ranging in age from two to twelve years, and in intelligence "from grossly retarded to superior" (5, p. 753). As has been noted, speech is not particularly important in play diagnosis, hence, it is not surprising to find that the investigator was not concerned with speech. The examiner's notes indicated: (a) which toys were used, (b) which toy was first choice, and (c) the manner in which the toys were used. "On a . . . subjective level the examiner then tried to determine what sort of dynamic information could be interpreted from the play" (5, p. 764).

Since the writer herself concludes that these categories "have not been very valuable" (5, p. 769), extended comment on her investigation would seem to be unwarranted. Even so, it should be noted that because of the conditions of the study no data on sand or water play could be obtained.

Three other papers (19, 22, 23) on the question of toys have seemed to indicate that the kinds of toys used in nondirective play therapy have been established by inference rather than by investigation. If this were true it would mean that the published lists of toys recommended for the playroom would not necessarily be helpful in selecting the most advantageous toys. Evidently the quantification of a problem formerly treated largely on an intuitive basis would be a desirable step.

## Experimental Method

One of the papers on toys (19) used the Borke Categories to analyze 4,092 statements made by children in nondirective play therapy. The categories were also rated on the basis of their expressiveness. A one-to-five scale was employed by three judges experienced in play therapy. A rating of *one* indicated the judges regarded the category as being very revealing of the child's feelings and attitudes. A rating of *three* meant that the judges considered the category as being neither revealing nor unrevealing of the child's feelings. A rating of *five* meant that the category so rated was held to be very unrevealing.

The development and reliability of these categories have been presented elsewhere (15, 17). Categories *A* through *W* have been published in full in this Journal (17) and a brief description of Categories *A* through *U*, with the judges' mean rating, are available (19). Category *V*, i.e., sound effects, received a mean rating of *four* and Category *W*, i.e., mumbling or talking to self, was rated as *five*. It does not seem necessary to present the overlapping information here.

A previous investigation (19) used more than 60 different types of toys and play materials. Some of the toys were recommended in published lists. Other toys either did not appear on the lists or were specifically negated. For purposes of that experiment it was necessary to tabulate and categorize the statements by each child as he played with various materials. These data were not published.

It has seemed to the present writer that a consideration of those unpublished data would afford an empirical indication of the expressive value of toys in nondirective play therapy.

## 1. Subjects

The verbatim style statements utilized in the present investigation were those of 20 children selected as being chronologically, socially, and intellectually satisfactory. A child considered chronologically representative could not vary more than four months from the age of four, six, eight, ten, or twelve years. There were two boys and two girls at each age level. Normal social adjustment was determined by an examination of cumulative records and by interviews with the children's teachers. To be considered intellectually satisfactory a child's Stanford-Binet IQ score could not vary more than one sigma from an IQ of 100. The last two requirements were established in an attempt to circumvent the possible influence of serious behavior problems and extremely high and low intelligence on the types of statements children might make and the activities in which they might engage.

## 2. Therapy

Three, one-hour, individual nondirective play therapy sessions were held with each child by the same therapist, in the same room, with the same toys (or similar ones) available for each session. To simulate the actual nondirective play therapy process, the children were not informed in advance that the contacts would be limited to three sessions.

## Research Results

All of the toys were ranked on two bases. These bases were the total number of statements made while the children used particular toys and the variety of categories into which the statements fell. For example, children made 533 statements while playing with the doll house, family, and furniture. The nature of these statements was described by nineteen different Borke Categories. This item ranked as one in number of statements, and as 1.5 in category variety.

A rho comparison of the statement and category ranking of all the toys resulted in a figure of .96. This figure was significant at better than the one per cent level of confidence. It indicated a very dependable relationship between the rankings. It suggested that it made little difference whether the toys were ranked as to the frequency of statements made while they were used, or by the variety of categories the statements fell into.

However, it is quite possible that toys not among those presently considered might encourage a large number of statements that could all fall into a limited number of categories. For instance, a fascinating mechanical toy could be very attractive to children. Most of the statements made while using such a toy might be requests for information. Such statements would be classified as $P$. Category $P$ has been rated as 4, or unrevealing. Use of another toy might result in a few statements spread over a wide range of categories.

Ranking by number of statements or by variety of categories does not seem to be adequate. Therefore a method was devised which took both factors into consideration. This method is called the verbal index, or VI. The formula is:

$$VI = \frac{\Sigma VRS}{1} + \frac{\Sigma RS}{2} + \frac{\Sigma Nu}{3} + \frac{\Sigma U}{4} + \frac{\Sigma VU}{5}.$$

The EVRS stands for the sum of the very revealing statements; ERS for the sum of the revealing statements, etc. The sum of each of these types of statements is divided by the judges' rating of the categories into which such statements fall. This formula considers both the number of statements and their expressiveness. For instance, when the number of statements made while playing with water pistols was considered, that toy had a rank of 37. Yet it only had a verbal index of 2. When ranked by VI it was in the 47th place.

Twenty-eight toys with a VI of 10 or above are listed in Table 1. The published source of each toy is also indicated.

The toys in Table 1 would seem to offer the "quantity and variety" deemed advisable by a recent nondirective play therapist (24, p. 207). It is to be noted that six of the toys in the list of toys with the highest VI have appeared on none of the published lists of playroom toys utilized in the present investigation. One of the toys, the checker game, has even been cautioned against (3). Yet, an empirical investigation revealed that the checker game has a slightly superior VI to the highly recommended toy soldiers.

Other toys appearing in published lists have even lower VI's. Such toys, with VI's of 7 to 0, include cups and saucers, pencil, boats, rubber knife, clothesline and pins, airplanes, pegboard, rubber hatchet, paper dolls, spoons, mallet, telephone, water pistols, cloth or rags, broom, doll bedding, doll bed, and scissors.

## TABLE 1

Rank Order Arrangement of 28 Best Toys of the 62 Toys Empirically Examined:
Toys Are Ranked on the Basis of Their Obtained Verbal Index

| Toy | Rec. By | VI |
| --- | --- | --- |
| Doll House, Family, and Furniture | A, Ax, M, W* | 212 |
| Poster Paints, Brushes, Paper, Easel, and Jars | A, Ax, M, W | 186 |
| Sandbox | Ax, M | 99 |
| Blackboard and Colored Chalk | ** | 80 |
| Cap Guns and Caps | A, Ax, M. W | 59 |
| Coloring Books | None | 43 |
| Hand Puppets | Ax, M | 36 |
| Balloons | M | 36 |
| Nursing Bottles | Ax, M | 34 |
| Films and Viewer | None | 34 |
| Water in Basin | Ax, M | 32 |
| Pop Guns | A, Ax, M, W | 29 |

*A — Arthur (2), Ax — Axline (3), M — Moustakas (24), W — Watson (33).
**While blackboard and chalk are not specifically recommended, they are similar to crayons, paints, and paper which are all highly recommended.

| Toy   Rec. By   VI | | |
| --- | --- | --- |
| Bubble Gum | None | 26 |
| Coffee Pot | None | 24 |
| Cord, Rope | None | 23 |
| Animals | A, Ax | 18 |
| Wood, Asso. | M | 16 |
| Balls, Asso. | None | 17 |
| Crayons | A, Ax, M, W | 16 |
| Baby Dolls | A, Ax, M, W | 16 |
| Bow and Arrows | W | 15 |
| Clay | A, Ax, M, W | 14 |
| Cars | A, Ax, M | 13 |
| Checkers | None | 12 |
| Shovel | M | 12 |
| Masks | M | 11 |
| Toy Soldiers | A, Ax, M, W | 10 |
| Water Colors | A, Ax, M, W | 10 |

Toys with obtained VI's of 1 or 0 are: Comic books, cloths and rags, doll bedding, broom, play money, man's sweater, paper pumpkin, scissors, doll bed, ladies' shoes, and washboard.

There is a sprinkling of recommended toys appearing in this last list. These toys evidently contribute very little to encouraging expressive verbalization in the nondirective play therapy room.

## Uses of the Formula

1. The VI formula can be used to determine the verbal expressive value of toys currently in the playroom. As can be seen from an examination of the above lists of toys, some toys highly regarded by nondirective play therapists do not contribute much to encouraging the child to verbally express himself. The toy telephone, for example, has been highly regarded. It is prominently listed among essential playroom equipment by modern nondirective play therapists (3, 24). The telephone would appear to be particularly valuable as an expressive toy. The development of verbalized insight was of particular importance in client-centered therapy with adults (16). In nondirective play therapy the assumption was that use of the telephone would encourage the child to make his feelings and attitudes known verbally. Such verbalizations by the child should furnish the nondirective therapist with splendid opportunities for therapeutic reflection.

Yet the telephone appears among the toys with a VI of 7 or less. It would seem that while the toy telephone has a high "theoretical" value it has a negligible empirical value. Other recommended toys in the above lists of toys could perhaps be profitably removed from the playroom.

2. The VI formula can be used to determine whether or not a newly purchased toy will carry its own weight in the therapeutic playroom. Simply by taking verbatim records of the statements made by children while playing with the new toy as well as the toys already in the playroom, the VI of the new toy may be compared with the VI of toys known to be successful. If the VI was not up to the average of the other toys the new toy might be removed immediately. Such usage of the VI formula would prevent a playroom from becoming crowded with useless toys.

3. Specific types of toys can be contrasted by means of the VI formula and the best toy selected. For example toy guns are well recommended (2, 3, 24, 33). Yet it is not specified whether cap guns, pop guns, or water pistols are meant. As can be seen from an examination of Table 1 and the above lists of toys, cap guns have a VI of 59, pop guns a VI of 29, and water pistols have a verbal index of less than 10. Cap guns are obviously superior in the present study. It would seem to be necessary to specify cap guns rather than use the generic term, toy gun in selecting playroom toys.

4. The VI formula may also be used to select an absolute minimum of toys for a visiting teacher's or psychologist's traveling kit. The toys in the suit case recommended by Axline (3), with the exception of the toy telephone, all have a VI of 10 or above.

## Summary

A formula was presented enabling the selection of toys for nondirective play therapy on an objective rather than an inferential basis. This formula was called the verbal index and considered both the number of statements made while a particular toy was used and the expressive variety of the statements. Use of the verbal index formula was suggested for:

1. Determining the verbal expressive value of toys presently in nondirective playrooms.

2. When deciding upon including new toys in the playroom.

3. In selecting specific kinds of toys rather than general types of toys.

4. In selecting a minimum of the most verbally expressive toys. Twenty-eight types of play equipment receiving verbal indexes of 10 or above were enumerated. They are suggested as the toy nucleus of a nondirective playroom. Eleven toys receiving verbal indexes of one or below were listed. It was suggested that such toys be avoided even though some of them have been recommended in published lists.

**References**
1. Alexander, F. S., "A Panel Discussion on Diagnosis and Therapy Through Play," *Trans. N. Y. Acad. Sci.*, 1953, 15, 99-101.
2. Arthur, H., "A Comparison of the Techniques Employed in Psychotherapy and Psychoanalysis of Children," *Amer. J. Orthopsychiat.*, 1952, 22, 484-498.
3. Axline, V. M., *Play Therapy*, Boston: Houghton Mifflin, 1947.
4. ———. "Play Therapy Procedures and Results," Paper presented to the Amer. Orthopsychiat. Ass., New York, March, 1954. (Mimeographed.)
5. Beiser, H. R., "Play Equipment for Diagnosis and Therapy," *Amer. J. Orthopsychiat.*, 1955, 25, 761-770.
6. Durham, M. S., "Some Observations Concerning External Criteria of Success in Psychotherapy," *J. of Psychol.*, 1952, 33, 175-181.
7. Freud, A., *The Psycho-Analytical Treatment of Children*. London: Imago, 1946.
8. Freud, S., *Collected Papers, Vol. 2, London: Hogarth, 1953. (Pp. 147-289.)*
9. Ginzberg, L., *Legends of the Jews*, Vol. 2, Philadelphia: Jewish Publication Society, 1913. (Pp. 272-274.)
10. Grazia, S. de., *Errors of Psychotherapy*, New York: Doubleday, 1952.
11. Gump, P. V., "A Statistical Investigation of One Psychoanalytic Approach and a Comparison of It with Nondirective Therapy," Unpublished master's thesis, Ohio State Univ., 1944.
12. Hambidge, G., Jr., "Structured Play Therapy," *Amer. J. Orthopsychiat.*, 1955, 25, 601-617.
13. Hamilton, G., *Psychotherapy in Child Guidance*, New York: Columbia Univ. Press, 1947.
14. Hellersberg, E. F.., "Ego Deficiency in School Age," *Psychoanalysis*, 1954, 2, 2-16.
15. Lebo, D., "The Relationship of Response Categories in Play Therapy to Chronological age," *J. Child Psychiat.*, 1952, 2, 330-336.
16. ———, "The Development of Client-Centered Therapy in the Writing of Carl Rogers," *Amer. J. Psychiat.*, 1953, 110, 104-109.
17. ———, "Quantification of the Nondirective Play Therapy Process," *J. Genet. Psychol.*, 1955, 86, 375-378.
18. ———, "The Development of Play as a Form of Therapy: from Rousseau to Rogers," *Amer. J. Psychiat.*, 1955, 1. 2, 418-422.
19. ———, "The Expressive Value of Toys Recommended for Nondirective Play Therapy," *J. Clin. Psychol.*, 1955, 11, 144-148.
20. ———, "The Relationship of Play to Play Therapy," *J. Educ. & Psychol.*, Baroda, 1955, 13, 114-121.
21. ———, "Age and Suitability for Nondirective Play Therapy," *J. Genet. Psychol.*, 1956, 89, 231-238.
22. ———, "The Contribution of Toys to the Nondirective Play Therapy Process," *J. Child Psychiat.*, (in press).
23. ———, "The Question of Toys in Play Therapy — An International Problem," *J. Educ. & Psychol.*, Baroda, 1956, 14, 66-73.
24. Moustakas, C. E., *Children in Play Therapy*, New York: McGraw-Hill, 1953.
25. Moyer, K. E., & von Haller Gilmer, B., "Attention Spans of Children for Experimentally Designed Toys," *J. Genet. Psychol.*, 1955, 87, 187-201.
26. Reik, T., *The Search Within*, New York: Farrar, Straus, & Cudahy, 1956.
27. Rogers, C. R., "The Use of Electrically Recorded Interviews in Improving Psychotherapeutic Techniques," *Amer. J. Orthopsychiat.*, 1941, 12, 429-434.
28. Solomon, J. C., *A Synthesis of Human Behavior*, New York: Grune & Stratton, 1954.
29. ———, "Play Technique and the Integrative Process," *Amer . J. Orthopsychiat.*, 1955, 25, 591-600.
30. Van Alstyne, D., "Play Behavior and Choice of Play Materials of Preschool Children," Chicago: Univ. Chicago Press, 1932.

31. Van Der Spuy, D. S.,"Play as a Therapeutic Measure for the Readjustment of Youthful Personalities with Behavior Problems — A Study at the Municipal Play Centres of Johannesburg," Unpublished magister's dissertation, Univ. Pretoria, Pretoria, 1948.

32. Vigotsky, L. S., "Thought and Speech," *Psychiatry*, 1939, 2, 29-54.

33. Watson, R. I., *The Clinical Method in Psychology*, New York: Harper, 1951.

34. "Direct Psychotherapy in Adolescence — Symposium," 1941, *Amer. J. Orthopsychiat.*, 1941, 12, 1-41.

# PART IV

# Clinical Experiences

# Introduction

The articles in this chapter emphasize the practical, clinical application of the major theoretical approaches described in Chapter Two. The reader will find in this chapter a wealth of useful information, including such insights as how to introduce a child to the therapy situation, the course of play therapy with a schizophrenic child, suggestions for adapting play techniques to the needs of the individual child, and a view of play therapy from the eyes of a child. The articles in Chapters Two and Four are intended to give the reader a comprehensive picture of how therapists from widely divergent orientations actually utilize play for therapeutic purposes.

Several articles in this chapter highlight the current trend towards employing a wide variety of professionals and nonprofessionals as play therapists. The reader will find, for example, articles in which nurses and parents function as play therapists. This trend reflects the growing awareness that what happens to the child outside the therapist's office — e.g., the child's social interactions at home and in the community — may be even more important than what transpires between the child and the therapist in the traditional fifty-minute hour. Recognition of the importance of involving the child's family in the therapeutic process has also led to an increasing use of conjoint play therapy wherein disturbed parent-child interactions are the prime focus of the play therapist (See articles by Johnson and Brown; Forehand and King).

Another trend that is apparent in this chapter is an increasing emphasis on the early remediation of a child's problems by play sessions at home and in school (See articles by Fuchs and by Alexander). Typically, parents and teachers have waited until the problem has become chronic and intolerable before they have requested professional assistance. This reluctance to consult with child therapists stems both from the traditional advice of pediatricians that the child will "grow out of it," and the social stigma that our society has attached to consulting with mental health professionals. Hopefully, the current trend towards short-term intervention for incipient problems will develop into a major thrust towards prevention rather than remediation of childhood disorders.

Finally, it seems important to note the differential use of play by therapists from the several theoretical orientations. The most striking difference between the theorists pertains to whether they use play merely as a medium for effective therapist-child interactions or whether they use play as a technique in which purposeful use is made of the content and/or processes of play. As the article by Despert suggests, play itself has definite diagnostic and therapeutic purposes when used as a technique. In contrast, the behavioral, limit-setting, and group therapists tend to employ the playroom simply as a stage for applying other principles, such as learning theory, group processes, and discipline. Whether one uses play as a medium, a technique, or both, the therapist will undoubtedly be more effective if he or she is thoroughly familiar with the basic readings on the psychology of play.

# PSYCHOANALYTIC

# The Search for Ego Controls

PETER D. KING and RUDOLF EKSTEIN

Genuine play requires a certain maturation of ego organization and is possible only where achievements of maturation are fairly stable and not excessively invaded by more regressive precursors of thinking. It is a stage in the hierarchy of ego development, lying between impulse on the one hand and secondary process thinking on the other. Ekstein and Friedman have discussed these concepts and illustrated them with clinical material from the treatment of a neurotic, delinquent, adolescent boy, and from work with psychotic children. It is the purpose of the present communication to present and discuss clinical material from the treatment of a schizophrenic boy in which is seen a comparable progression of rudimentary play during psychotherapy, from chaotic impulse to a compulsive quasi-order.

## Treatment of a Schizophrenic Boy

George was a nine-year-old schizophrenic boy who had apparently been psychotic since early childhood. He was from an eccentric, chaotic Jewish family. His self-employed paranoid father often withdrew; at other times he exploded with profanity. His mother stated that her life was devoted to George and she read everything she could about emotionally disturbed children, yet was seen trying to manipulate him like a large mechanical doll. George spoke of himself in the second and third person, was manneristic, and wore a bandanna around his neck, apparently to collect the spittle that drooled from his mouth, which gave him a most bizarre appearance.

George had been unwanted and unplanned, his conception occurring ten years after the birth of his one sibling — a bright but emotionally unstable brother. He had been a normal full term baby who had had no separations from his family. His physical examinations, skull films, EEG, and Phenylpyruvic test were all within the normal range.

George had been brought to the clinic one year before starting treatment because of "nervousness" which referred to a number of symptoms, including head tic, crying, talking to himself, fear of loud noises, learning difficulty, fear of the dark, drooling, withdrawal, destructiveness, choking other children, and possibly hallucinations.

The examining psychologists wrote:

> One of the outstanding things is George's intense and pervasive fearfulness. Of the things which frighten him, feelings of anger are prominent, leading to a sort of immobilization with perseverative, nonadaptive responses ... Fearfulness also interferes with his ability to function intellectually with more structured material. Thus he failed to respond to the questions "What scratches? What bites? What stings?" He performs best on intellectual tasks which permit him to apply perceptual and motor skills on impersonal objects with minimal social implications. ... It is evident that his potential level of intellectual functioning is at least average although he obtained an IQ of only 80 on sensorimotor tasks.

The examining psychiatrist ended his summary by saying: "The patient seems overwhelmed by his impulses which force his return to the completely controlling parent who would aid him in suppressing ... those impulses. His behavior and verbalizations are consistent with a diagnosis of psychotic reaction." He was a given a diagnosis of schizophrenic reaction, childhood type, and after one year's wait was begun in psychotherapy, three times weekly.

## Chaotic Impulses

At first George's behavior was quite chaotic. For example, in the interview he would masturbate against the table, display his penis to the therapist (and others if he could), smash toys, scream, attempt to smash windows, try to cut the therapist with scissors or jab him in the eyes, and suddenly run out of the room into other rooms to break toys or attack other people. The therapist attempted to circumscribe the limits in terms of what George could or could not do. For example, he was restrained from breaking windows, going into other rooms or seriously hurting the therapist, while the therapist made comments like "Poor George, is afraid that he will be hurt, so he tries to break things and hurt other people." There was a driven, counterphobic quality to George's behavior, and it seemed that his crazy activity was an exaggeration saying, in effect, "look how badly I need to be controlled." At the same time it expressed his concern over the integrity of his body and, more specifically, his castration anxiety; thus he would display his penis and cry, "Look, Dr. King!" On several such occasions the interpretation was made that George was really afraid he would lose his penis, while it was also pointed out that his behavior was an attempt to provoke violent control. Gradually therapy became more circumscribed in that George made fewer attempts to attack others and enter other rooms, although chaotic behavior continued within the limits of the therapy room.

## Compulsive Quasi-Order

Following this first chaotic phase, George would use a dictating machine by means of which he transcribed various sounds, songs, and profanities. Then he had the therapist play it back while he ambled around the room, masturbating against the table, fingering toys, and humming with intermittent, chaotic, destructive outbursts. Later he had the therapist use the dictating machine to transcribe a continuous description of everything he did. This was interpreted as his wish to make some kind of order out of the discontinuity he experienced. Thus in one early session:

> George inserted a cylinder into the dictating machine and asked me to record everything he did. I said I guessed he didn't understand all the different things he did, and having me dictate was like having somebody understand and make some order out of it. He looked pensively at me, started sliding around the floor on a cart, and then rubbed his penis against the table. Suddenly he stopped to pull apart a plastic mannikin and break a toy airplane, but he returned to his masturbation. I said what he had just done was sudden and frightening to him and he couldn't understand why he did things like this. He looked at me and said "God damn it!" which I repeated into the transcriber. He said he had to "make sissy" and took down his pants and began inspecting his penis. I took him to the bathroom where he urinated and wiped his penis with a handkerchief. After zipping up his fly, he dashed out into the parking lot and began climbing on top of the nearest car. I lifted him down and brought him back into the clinic to my room, but he ran into another room interrupting another therapist and her patient. I took him out and brought him back to my room where at his request I again recorded

his activity. He asked me suddenly if I made sissy and I answered that
I was sure he had many questions about me. He wanted to know
when I urinated and I said I guessed he felt that telling him things
about myself and even showing him my penis would prove that I
liked him. He went to the table and began to masturbate again, then
came over and attempted to masturbate against my leg. He picked up
a plastic house and asked if he could take it home. I said he could if he
would bring it back, but he lost interest in it. He wanted to play my
record of his activity, but he was tempted to abuse the apparatus
first. I had previously threatened to remove it if he mishandled it and
pointed out to him that he wasn't really sure if I meant what I said.
Then he played the record until the end of the hour.

There was gradual progression to a new phase in which George had
the therapist play a "doctor game," George being the patient and the
therapist being the doctor. In this play George's chaotic behavior was
mostly confined to the game, which began by George's official signal,
"give on." The therapist was to respond "ready, aim, fire," dash across the
room, and grab George, carrying him to the "examination table" to inflict
an "examination" in the exact sequence dictated by George. If at any time
during the play George said, "give up," the therapist was to stop
immediately. The therapist pointed out that by this play George made
the "doctor" do all kinds of things he was afraid of, yet he was in complete
control of the situation since he could say "give up" whenever he wanted
to stop.

George introduced variations to the "doctor game" making it
increasingly dangerous, as can be seen from one of the sessions:

George came in, put his clock and keys on the desk, and began to
order me around in an imperious voice. He smiled with pleasure as I
carried out his instructions, getting out the key, unlocking the
cupboard to fetch his pillow, and setting up the "doctor" instruments. Then he had me hit myself on the head with the reflex
hammer, varying the pitch of the resultant sound by opening and
closing my mouth at his direction. I said, "You know, George, it must
be fun to have a Dr. King puppet. I'm like a big puppet who does
whatever George tells me to do. Wouldn't it be nice if you had a
Mommy puppet and a Daddy puppet and a big brother puppet so you
could tell Mommy to do this and do that. You could say, 'Mommy,
give on' and she would do whatever you wanted; then you could say
'give up, Mommy' so she would stop and George would be in total
command of the situation." George looked pensively at me, then

indicated that we were to play the "doctor game" with a series of punishments if he swore. He instructed me to yell "Why did you say that?" beat him with a stethoscope, shine a light in his eye, stick him with a "lockjaw needle," pour poison in his mouth to burn out the nasty words, cut his buttocks with a knife, and make him look in a microscope at all the dirty words, while I said "Look, look at all those nasty, dirty, filthy words." Then whenever he said "fuck," "fuckalucka," or "stick it up your ass" I pretended to inflict the series of punishments with some variation in their sequence and severity, according to his instruction. I interrupted this play to say, "George, I see what you're doing. What you want to do is control all the dirty, nasty things you feel are inside of you. You think that the punishments will work better if they are more severe and more complicated. That's why you tap your left hand then your right hand, shrug your left shoulder and then your right shoulder and do things in such a way that you think will keep all the bad, nasty, dirty things inside and even make them go away by magic." George indicated that we were playing a game, so I sighed and shrugged my shoulders saying "that's right, you want me to stay a puppet and not tell you things about yourself, so we'd better go back to our game," which was continued for the little remaining time.

George increased the severity of punishments through stabbing, shooting, and electrocution to embalming and burial in a cemetery. Then he introduced a series of vicious dogs who scratched him, bit him, and tore him to pieces; but they also carried him, gave him presents, and drove him around in their cars. Thus during one session:

George told me not to talk to him but leave the room and send in Wolf Dog. I saluted him, salaamed, and said "Yes, oh George, I Dr. King-puppet will do whatever you tell me," pretended to leave the room and come in snarling as Wolf Dog to attack him, scratch him, pick him up and spin him around, and take him in the car to Alaska if he swore. Promptly he said "fuck" so Wolf Dog carried out the punishments as instructed. The sequence was varied, with trips back and forth from Alaska to the clinic, but always with much snarling, shaking, and spinning around, during all of which George cried out "fuck" over and over again, until Wolf Dog collapsed into the chair. He picked up the toy telephone and called "Dr. King" to tell him how George had made him carry him and spin him over and over until he was all tired out. "Dr. King" explained to Wolf Dog that George was trying very hard to control himself, but George quickly interrupted telling Wolf Dog to call in a meaner, more vicious dog. Wolf Dog ended his telephone conversation with "Dr. King" and called Bull Dog, who promptly came over to replace Wolf Dog. Bull Dog was much more vicious than Wolf Dog as he snarled, scratched, shook and twirled George whenever he swore. Soon Bull Dog was tired out too, so George had him send for Tiger Dog; but again, despite his ferocity, he too finally fell exhausted into the chair. George told Tiger Dog that he was to summon the meanest, most vicious dog in the whole world — Lion Dog. But Tiger Dog was skeptical and when he talked to Lion Dog on the phone, he said that George was so full of dirty, nasty words that even Lion Dog himself might not be able to make him stop. Then he added that really he himself and all the dogs — even Lion Dog — were created by George in his attempt to control himself. But Lion Dog promptly told Tiger Dog to be quiet since George did not like to hear comments about himself. Lion Dog also failed to stop George's swearing and shortly after this the hour ended.

This theme continued over several sessions until in one:

I said: "George, what shall we do? You've made me into the meanest doctors and the most vicious animals in the world. Even your mother, your father, and the head of this clinic have not been able to stop you from doing crazy things. Do you think this (burying) will work?" Then I pretended to bury him, but George soon asked, "What's gonna be if I swear?" I slapped my hand to my forehead in feigned exasperation, saying, "Oh, no, don't tell me it didn't work. Do you suppose that nothing is going to work?" George stopped himself in the process of saying a "dirty word" and looked very pensive for a while. He went to the table and began to masturbate, then he came over to me and said again, "What's gonna be if I swear?" I then suggested that a nice big, strong St. Bernard that helps people and protects them might work, but he cried, "No! No! Be vicious!"

The next stage in the progression of George's material occurred when George played both himself and the examining doctor:

George said to himself, as if he were talking to a patient, "I am going to examine your bones, rub your bones, and examine your head." Then he lay on the table and conducted an imaginary physical examination similar to what he had me pretend to perform in previous sessions.

In this play George displays a partial identification and projection of his own distorted conception of the therapist. This theme continued during this hour when he gave himself an imaginary electroencephalographic examination, encouraging himself by saying, "That's a good boy. I'm going to put these things on your head to see if your mind is all right," also voicing for the first time some fragment of insight into the fact that he was ill. Similarly during his session the next day he said "crazy, crazy" and tapped his head.

## Summary and Conclusions

George's material shows a progression from disorder to rudimentary ego control, a transition from chaotic acting out to enlarging segments of play, yet much inner chaos remains. Within his fragmented productions can be seen many meanings, prominent among which is a poorly organized search for order and control. In his attempt to find them, he summons controlling goblins from within and projects them onto his surroundings. Thus his identification with the therapist is also a misidentification which distorts him into an instrument rather than an object, a puppet rather than a person — the psychotic reversals of his mother's unsuccessful manipulation of him. At the same time it inflicts an actual and symbolic revenge upon an ungratifying world — a sort of punishment to fit the crime. Thus earlier in his acting out, and later in his play, others are maneuvered into the exhausting role of inflicting the rigid, sadistic control which he had never really been able to achieve by himself.

In the psychotic transference, George creates an omnipotent sort of genie in his attempt to make order out of discontinuity. But it is the product of chaos, the projection of inner megalomanic narcissism which will not allow the therapist to be a real genie; thus, instead of being the helping St. Bernard, the therapist must play the vicious Wolf Dog. Nevertheless, George has created genii who, although manipulated by him, are identified with order, control and the acceptance of the fact of his illness. The genii present a tenuous bridge to the outside world and to the real therapist — a modest hope for further progress toward continuity and appropriate inner controls.

# Play Therapy

J. LOUISE DESPERT

## Introduction

In several earlier publications the writer has dealt with a number of problems relating to the subject of play therapy, among which are those of physician-patient relationship and physical set-up used in this form of therapy. A few additional formulations are presented at this time.

## Some General Considerations

Methods of play therapy, already numerous and diversified, have been, even at this early stage of development, widely applied to a variety of child (and even adult) psychiatric problems, and extensively reported upon. Nevertheless, the presentation of the total clinical experience, of its evolution in the course of treatment, and its far reaching effect on the subsequent adjustment of the individual, remains fragmentary.

The complexities of personal interrelationships are considerably greater in child than adult therapy. The dependence of the child on his parents, themselves often emotionally disturbed, introduces elements of behavior interplay which account for some of the complexities. It is also impossible to isolate and study the part played by the normal growth process which continues, modified though it be by the thepeutic situation. If analysis, as rigidly applied to the biological sciences, seems difficult of application here, the responsibility must lie with the very subject matter, and the limitation be reckoned with, and perhaps accepted without reservations.

In view of the great variety of approaches used in the treatment of children's behavior and neurotic problems it seems puzzling, on superficial examination, that very similar results are obtained by applying such divergent points of view. However, in all approaches, a common denominator is found, which is the therapist-patient relationship. This is utilized in different ways, in accordance with the individual training of the therapist, at various levels of expression and interpretation.

Any given moment of behavior contains and reflects the child's total life experience. While this is also true of the adult, there is in the child a striking fluidity of expression which makes for further complexity, but also opens additional avenues of approach to the task of interpretation. A child may bring up a fantasy as a conglomerate of dream material, partial or full recollection of a life event, and expression of a wish, together with symbols and emotional overtones relating to any or all of these, and to the current situation as well. A child engages in a game, independently of, or in participation with the therapist; this game may be developed and interpreted by the therapist in terms of the actual situation, and the therapist-child relation, or in terms of symbols of the unconscious, or any intermediate expression between the two extremes, because the game itself contains and reflects all of them. It is this multi-faceted quality which gives each therapist, with his specific point of view and training, his special opportunity to work with the child patient at any particular level. Changes in the neurotic personality structure occur, which may appear very dissimilar, but in any case a realinement of affective forces is induced, and a mobilization of anxiety takes place. How each therapist deals with the anxiety is a matter of individual methods and even personalities. The point emphasized here is that the great variety of approaches in child psychotherapy is evident, not only when comparing one method with another, or one individual therapist with another, as exemplified in the literature; it is also very striking when considering the total experience of any one therapist.

In looking over the records of several hundred children brought for diagnostic evaluation and treatment, one is impressed with the diversity of patterns which unfold in the course of individual therapeutic work: some children lead the therapist rapidly into deep areas of conflict, crowded with symbols pressing for interpretation, while others may remain at fairly superficial levels of behavior expression, or simple, direct abreacting situations. Over a span of five to ten years follow-up, it has not been apparent that there were significant differences between the two groups, when considering long term adjustment. In this sense the child truly *leads* the therapist, though this is not to imply that the latter plays only a passive role: the patient offers material at different levels of expression (often simultaneously) and the therapist, in dealing with this material, must be able to recognize at any given moment which expression is more readily accessible to elaboration and interpretation. A child may have been, at a given interview, in the midst of working out a deep sexual conflict, and come, the next day, all excited about a moving picture he had just seen, an incident which has just taken place at home, or even a test anticipated at school. It would be poor judgment to press the child about the unfinished business of the earlier interview, even if there had been then evidenced a great need for bringing out the conflict, and relieving the anxiety associated with it.

In many accounts of therapeutic interviews, the impression is gained that trends are followed, and areas of conflict resolved according to a more or less systematic plan, in keeping with the clinician's conception of therapy and of the child's therapeutic problem. The textbook picture of psychotherapeutic methods is of necessity oversimplified, especially with regards to children. Clinical experience shows that two cases, however similar from a psychopathological point of view, may, in the course of treatment, unfold widely divergent patterns, in ways which, in certain cases, are not even approximately predictable. Post factum, the divergences can usually be explained in terms of additional pressures due to life events which involve the child or the family; but the "unpredicta-bility" remains a significant factor in the evaluation of each new case, as well as a challenge, which is attached to child therapy itself. It is the sort of challenge which makes it imperative for the therapist to be keenly alert to any minor variation in the child's behavior and emotional expression, while he participates in his play. If the extreme fluidity of the child's life experience, as projected in the therapeutic situation, is not to baffle him, he must at once be an active participant, an astute observer, and an objective interpreter.

## Practical Considerations

*Introducing the therapeutic situation:*

In the initial phase of treatment, much depends on the degree of wisdom shown by family and psychiatrist in bringing the child to treatment. Some children have been threatened with psychiatric treatment and hospitalization because of their "bad" behavior, others were led to believe that they were visiting a teacher, or a friend of the family. The father of a very disturbed girl of ten years introduced the writer as "a business associate." (He was an accountant). He had planned the whole approach in his own way, even after indicating his willingness to follow suggestions carefully discussed at the first interview with both parents; it thus became evident that he had no intention at any time to carry them out. The father said he had come to "say just a few words" to his business associate, and was going to leave the child "for a few minutes, while I'm going on an errand." The physician would not take any part in the deception and the father later insisted that it was this lack of cooperation which had caused the child to be upset and resistive. While such attitudes are very revealing of habitual techniques used by parents in the handling of their children, they are so damaging to the first contact as to make further contact difficult, if not impossible.

Since the child almost never asks to be taken to a psychiatrist, it is up to the therapist and the parents to pave the way for the anticipated experience. Frequently, the parents have given thought to the matter, some have had a tentative talk with their child, most parents ask for suggestions. After the anamnesis has been taken, the patient's complaint, as interpreted by his environment, is more or less clearly delineated. In particular, it is then known what specific manifestations have been openly mentioned and discussed in the family. The stress at this point is on the child's *awareness* of his symptoms, rather than their severity. A child may be more distressed by the fact that he "cannot make friends" than by the concomitants of associability and poor reality contact, or by his avowed fears rather than his aggressive, anti-social behavior.

Thus, the parents are advised to start from whatever specific complaint has been brought up on previous occasions and explain to the child that he can be helped, and that, in order to achieve this end, they plan to take him to a man (or woman) whose job is to do precisely that, help children with such problems. In the older age group, there is no reason for not referring to the anticipated visit as a visit to a psychiatrist, even if the reference arouses some resistance. In the face of the discomfort experienced by the child, any step taken toward alleviation is frequently welcomed. In the lower age group, however, the very mention of a doctor — and especially an unfamiliar one — may bring on such a severe reaction in an anxious child, that it is preferable first to let him become acquainted with the therapist: during the first interview, the question is raised "Do you know my name? . . . Dr. ——." By this time, he has learned a good deal about the new category of experience. The young child frequently expresses it in very revealing spontaneous comments, such as "You're a funny doctor . . . a different kind of a doctor . . . a doctor that doesn't give you needles . . . how come you don't examine me?" etc., all of which provide additional opportunities to make clear the therapist's function.

Another point relating to the first interview is the separation from the parent, generally the mother who brings the child. It is clearly indicated beforehand, that only one parent is to come, as separation is thus more easily achieved; in a total experience of several hundred first interviews there have been a few instances of two parents, alone, or together with one or two siblings, and even in one case, his whole family accompanied a patient, despite earlier recommendations; while such occurrences are highly significant of the family as a whole, they are quite destructive. A separation which lingers, with additional hugs and "one more word before I leave you" comments on the part of the parents, is a poor introduction to therapy, and is best avoided through a thorough discussion of its devastating effects on the child, at the time of anamnesis taking. The child feels the more insecure about the strange setup as his parent manifests more reluctance to leave him here.

Although in the early stages of child guidance practice, parents and child were frequently seen together by the therapist, this approach is not common now. Play therapy precludes the presence and participation of the parents in the situation. In the writer's experience, there have been only a few exceptions to this rule, when it was thought advisable not to attempt the separation: in the several cases, the child was very young and acutely disturbed. One of them was treated for a number of months with the mother in the playroom, a fact which added complexity to the therapeutic situation, as it required a constant unobtrusive interpretation to the mother of the child's behavior, as well as reassurance, regarding its most severe manifestations.

In recent years, the technique has been adopted by the writer to ask that the child be left at the office, with the mother returning later to pick him up, rather than waiting in an adjoining room. This change was prompted by the anxiety of some children, about their mother being within hearing distance, especially those in the middle and older age groups (approximately six years and above). This was not actually the case, since there were two intervening doors, as they had been informed, but they wanted to know further if the doors were locked, or if their mother could listen. In the case of the younger children, the close proximity of their mother led them to request more frequent visits to her than was possible to handle. So, for all age groups, it has been found that the complete removal of the mother from the setup works out better when straightforwardly presented to the child, even at the cost of arousing a little more anxiety at the initial interview. It is made clear to the younger children that their mother is available and can be reached if they feel the need to see her before their time is up, but very few children have availed themselves of the opportunity.

*Using the first interview:*

It is of practical importance as soon as possible to ascertain the nature of the therapeutic problem, and evaluate approximately the duration of treatment. As a rule, the first interview gives enough insight into the nature of the conflict to be a decisive one, as regards future plans; this, provided certain areas are searched, more or less systematically, by utilizing the words, gestures, feeling tones and other expressions demonstrated during the first contact. First memories, dreams, early fears, past and present, family relationships are brought to light, not in answer to direct questions regarding these particular points, but through the interpretation of the child's spontaneous activities in the playroom.

Again, one is impressed with the infinite variety of patterns shown by the patients, in spite of which a common characteristic is found in all cases, namely that the first interview gives the needed clue to the child's conflict, whether the medium is a reported dream, a first drawing, an early memory, or a spontaneous bit of play. To illustrate the point, several cases are briefly quoted:

A boy of twelve years, four months was brought to treatment shortly after it was discovered that he used women's underwear, preferably his mother's, in the performance of sexual activities (at least the family surmised), which had considerably disturbed the people in his close environment. It was suspected that the activities had taken place over a period of months, possibly years; the informants — the mother and her (female) cousin — did not know what the activities were but feared that they might involve the younger sister. They were only sure that their underwear disappeared in large numbers, later to be found soiled, torn, often in inaccessible hidden spots, and that the boy would "get frantic" if he could not secure the feminine apparel; to this end, once, he had broken into the garage and broken the trunk lock of a visiting female relation. He was a boy of superior intelligence, the older of two children in a family of high economic status. His sister was three years younger. When he was seven-and-a-half years old, his father committed suicide, and a maternal female cousin then moved, literally, into his father's bed. The mother was a psychopathic individual, and a chronic alcoholic. Marital relations had been poor, and the mother-relation to her cousin was strongly suggestive of homosexual adjustment. The first interview illuminated the dynamics in this case with no delay: the boy was not interested in toys, his first drawing showed a "volcano and smoke," with the smoke in the shape of a spermatozoan, head upward, a short distance above the crater of the volcano. He was freely communicative, but in a superficial way, until asked *early memories*.

He recalled his father's death, recalled in particular having been confused by the conflicting explanations given, and by the avowed contempt of his mother for her husband's family; he recalled very little regarding his sister's birth, but one memory was quite vivid in his mind: this first memory became the clue to his transvestitism; as reconstructed later, through the identity of the nurse, and the description of the house, both of which he gave with accuracy, the experience recalled had taken place when he was less than two years old: his mother had left, on a long trip, he was standing in his crib, crying, when the nurse put his mother's girdle on him, he stopped crying, and felt "funny" (obviously referring to erection). He had sought the repetition of this experience, intermittently, following this episode. At times of stress, he put on feminine underclothes, three to six samples of each item, and masturbated while fantasying that he was his mother, or some attractive woman resembling her. The first memory, promptly brought up, presented a multifold interest in that the specific details recalled ("the thin nurse, not the fat one ... the one who beat me, etc. ...") set the time of the episode accurately, although no one in the family was in a position to have known of its occurrence.

The record of another patient illustrates a different introduction to therapy: this was a boy of eight years and two months, at the time of admission. He was brought to treatment because of asociability, emotional immaturity, and schizophrenia-like behavior, in which phantasy and reality were often confused. He was extremely fearful, did not let his mother out of his sight, did not engage in any play with other children and had, as a realistic life-companion, a huge teddy-bear with whom he slept, whom he addressed as a living person, etc.; on the other hand, he fought constantly with his only sibling, a younger brother. His I.Q. was over 150 and he attended a class for exceptional children where he had considerable difficulties owing to his day dreaming, and poor contact. He was an omnivorous reader, selecting classics, and "books of knowledge" which he absorbed at top speed during any hour he was free from school. A verbal child, he talked freely during the first interview, although he was manifestly anxious. In a high-pitched voice, and with blunted affect, he talked mostly about imaginary characters, some of them taken from radio programs and comic strips. Looking the toys over, he expressed his contempt for "that baby stuff," but kept glancing sideways at some of the dolls. Reassured that boys also played with the dolls sometimes, he selected two large dolls, a girl and a baby, and began a play theme which was very revealing: he used the baby's diaper as a flowing cape tied at the neck, calling this doll Superman, and the other doll Lois, both well known comics characters. His story, however, differed from the Superman story: over and over, Superman and Lois "fought" in violent physical attacks upon one another, then lay side by side on the floor. "They're tired, they're going to sleep." When first asked regarding Lois, he had stated that she was "his girl friend" (Superman's). The *symbolism of the play* was so clearly evocative of the primal scene and a child's reaction to it that after he had laid the dolls down once more, a comment was made to the effect that they behaved more like man and wife, than boy and girl friend, besides what were they fighting about? It was not long before the boy referred to his own parents in a puzzled, questioning way. Later, upon checking with the mother, it was learned that several years prior to admission, and before the brother's birth (which would make his age as under four years), the patient had once come to the parents' room, at night, and witnessed sexual intercourse. At least, they now surmised that he had been there for some time when first seen; he had stood in the doorway, "like in a trance,"; the mother had brought him back to his bed, and no one had ever referred to the episode, then or afterward.

A third case which presents differences from the two cases referred to above, was also different from the large majority of neurotic children seen, in that the child stepped directly into the area of conflict on his first contact with therapy. This was an only child, a boy of eight years and four months, who was referred for severe anxiety manifestations, refusing to go out on the street, alone or accompanied, "he was petrified;" he also had reading and spelling difficulties, in spite of superior intelligence, and satisfactory achievements in other subjects. Nightmares had marked the onset of anxiety manifestations, at 6 years, following a performance of Hansel and Gretel. He had become increasingly difficult to manage owing to his fears and inhibitions. Both parents were neurotic: the father, a compulsive individual, was undergoing psychoanalytic treatment, and the mother, insecure, vague, circumstantial, had been under psychiatric treatment, intermittently, for several years. As later developments confirmed, the child's conflict was in the nature of castration anxiety, and in the first contact presented itself with *little symbolization or complexity of expression*. The boy drew "a lady and a man," both armless, then when asked if he knew why he came to see the therapist, he said that people, men and women, "come when my father and mother are away at night," (fears which prevented him to sleep), that he had nightmares, dreamed of "drunken men and crazy men," then added, "will you please tell me the difference between a drunken and a crazy man?" He said he'd feel easier if he "only could know the difference in the street." A drunken man might come, kidnap him, and kill him or "do worse things than that": this, he would not elaborate upon, but, as he talked, he rammed one plane inside another, and said, "they're going under each other." The association with the drunken man was clearly brought out when he said that he did not actually know any drunken man, "except my father but he never got drunk."

Sometimes, a child, although seemingly interested in the play setup and the toys, gives the clue to his emotional problem through his behavior, rather than his use of the toys: an only child, a girl of four-and-a-half years, very precocious, was brought to treatment because of anxiety, clinging to her mother, and feeding difficulties. The parents were divorced, and she lived with her mother, who had been under analysis for nearly two years. When she gave the history, it became apparent that she was acutely hallucinating (she had placed a screen between the child's bed and her own, fearing she might harm the child, as she saw her rising from her crib, in mid-air.) The father, passive, effeminate, immature, had been under analysis himself for several months, at the time of admission. Although the mother appeared frail, and the child was well able to walk, she carried the little girl to the office, hugging her passionately, and holding on tightly to her. The child was upset, screamed, stamped her feet, but the absence of tears was striking. After her mother had left (this was not as difficult for the child as had at first been assumed) she stood in the middle of the room, sucking her thumb, making obvious efforts not to seem interested in the toys, though at intervals she made forward motions toward the shelves. "No, I don't want to do anything. . . . " She was afraid to get involved with the strange person and the strange setup. When the therapist took from the shelves two beds to make a bedroom arrangement, the child volunteered that she had "only one bed," and that she had "scary dreams . . . a man kills a girl . . . and lions to eat her. . . ." She then made significant statements regarding her actual unhappy experience. "I want my daddy and my mommy together again . . . sometimes, I'm alone . . . no daddy, no mummy. . . ." Throughout her treatment, of several months duration, in weekly visits, she chose the type of *direct play* which involved almost no toy equipment. There was considerable body contact, climbing over the physician, or on her lap; at intervals, being quite aggressive towards her. She assigned definite roles to her (father, mother, child), with complimentary identifications for her own part, so the play patterns were varied and showed great fluidity. Her selection was the more conspicuous as she was a young child, and one who had had considerable opportunity for play with toys (in nursery school, and with young cousins who were frequent companions). Her anxiety, her ambivalent attitudes toward both parents were largely resolved; on the other hand, while the home situation was to a great extent clarified, it could hardly be made happier, especially as the mother,early in the treatment, had to be hospitalized.

Material from the few cases referred to above was selected and may be sufficient to give some conception of the diversity of reactions shown, even if only the first interview is considered. Examples could be multiplied, they would only further emphasize the high degree of individuality and differentiation encountered in play therapy with children.

One point of some importance relates to the taking of notes, while the play is in progress or even as the physician takes part in it. This needs to be explained early to the child. The majority of children accept that the therapist could not possibly remember everything about every child, that it is important to remember, not to confuse one child with another, and that the notes are entirely for her own use. Several children have been known to ask: "Do you show them to my mother?", but as a rule, even they can be reassured on this point. Very few children (possibly one out of a hundred) seem concerned regarding note taking and in these few exceptions where blocking is manifest as a result, it has seemed advisable to discontinue the practice, even at the cost of losing valuable associations.

## Aspects of Communication

As regards the question of communication between parents and therapist, the parents are advised not to send notes via the children (a common practice if it were not checked), as the latter usually want to know re. the content, as a rule not meant for their perusal. The children are also informed that the therapist, at intervals, sees their parents (if that is to be the case); it is explained that whatever *understanding* doctor and child have gained regarding the child's difficulties can be passed on to his parents. Stated in simple terms, the communication is accepted by most children.

Another aspect of communication deserves to be mentioned briefly: almost universally, children choose not to tell others about what is going on in the playroom. As a matter of routine, following the first interview, the parents are asked what the child reported about his first visit. The parents usually express their disappointment that the patient was willing to say so little, even when they questioned him (some of them show unwanted persistence in this respect, and may thus arouse antagonism in the child). The query serves two purposes: one is to ascertain the child's reaction, expressed to his close environment, and also to demonstrate to the parents that the child's reticence expresses his own choice, although it is also psychologically sound, a point which is thus brought up for discussion. This reticence toward the visits and their content is noted, not only in relation to the parents, but also toward other relatives and friends. It has been possible for nearly two years to conduct the simultaneous treatment of two first cousins, though they were closely associated in their family life, without either of them telling the other of the experience. An interesting incident took place when the therapist's name was mentioned accidentally by a teacher in the midst of her group. One boy was under treatment, a girl had been discharged several months earlier. The girl began to refer to "a friend" of hers who had been "treated there." The boy reported the many details she gave regarding the therapist and the setup, not suspecting that the girl might have been the patient, both children were eleven years old. Similarly, when siblings are simultaneously or successively treated, each may be very inquisitive about the other, but refuse to divulge his experience in the office. Even very young children show this tendency, indicating that the segregation of emotional experiences is manifested very early in the psychological economy of the personality.

The child must be assured that his "secrets" are protected, even as the understanding gained through their coming out is to be imparted to his parents. Throughout the period of treatment the therapist must sift what can be emotionally accepted by the parents, what they can handle without setting off neurotic explosions: their new knowledge of the patient's inner feelings may, at intervals, act destructively in their own relation to the child. The time at which one or the two parents should be referred for treatment is often determined by the neurotic parent's reaction to the child's progress in therapy. This indeed may bring up feelings of anxiety and hostility in the parents, which need clarification and resolution, if adjustment in the family is to be successful.

# Play and Cure

ERIK ERIKSON

Modern play therapy is based on the observation that a child made insecure by a secret hate against or fear of the natural protectors of his play in family and neighborhood seems able to use the protective sanction of an understanding adult to regain some play peace. Grandmothers and favorite aunts may have played that role in the past; its professional elaboration of today is the play therapist. The most obvious condition is that the child has the toys and the adult for himself, and that sibling rivalry, parental nagging, or any kind of sudden interruption does not disturb the unfolding of his play intentions, whatever they may be. For to "play it out" is the most natural self-healing measure childhood affords.

## Psychoanalytic Terms

Let us remember here the simple, if often embarrassing, fact that adults, when traumatized, tend to solve their tension by "talking it out." They are compelled, repeatedly, to describe the painful event: it seems to make them "feel better." Systems designed to cure the soul or the mind make ritual use of this tendency by providing, at regular intervals, an ordained or other-wise sanctioned listener who gives his undivided attention, is sworn not to censure arbitrarily or to betray, and bestows absolution by explaining how the individual's problem makes sense in some larger context, be it sin, conflict, or disease. The method finds its limitations where this "clinical" situation loses the detachment in which life can be reflected, and itself becomes a passionate conflict of dependence and hostility. In psychoanalytic terms, the limitation is set by the tendency (especially strong in neurotics) to transfer basic conflicts from their original infantile setting into every new situation, including the therapeutic one. This is what Freud meant when he said that the treatment itself, at first, becomes a "transference neurosis." The patient who thus transfers his conflict in all its desperate immediacy becomes at the same time resistive to all attempts at making him see the situation in a detached way, at formulating its meaning. He is *in resistance;* in a war to end all wars, he becomes more deeply embroiled than ever. At this point, nonpsychoanalytic therapeutic efforts often end; the patient, it is said, cannot or does not want to get well or is too inferior to comprehend his obligations in treatment. Therapeutic psychoanalysis, however, begins at this point. It makes systematic use of the knowledge that no neurotic is undivided in his wish to get well and of necessity transfers his dependencies and hostilities to the treatment and the person of the therapist. Psychoanalysis acknowledges and learns from such "resistances."

## A Case of Play Disruption

This phenomenon of *transference* in the playing child, as well as in the verbalizing adult, marks the point where simple measures fail — namely, when an emotion becomes so intense that it defeats playfulness, forcing an immediate discharge into the play and into the relationship with the play observer. The failure is characterized by what is to be described here as *play disruption* — i.e., the sudden and complete or diffused and slowly spreading inability to play. . . . I shall now introduce a little girl who, although she came for diagnostic purposes only, led me through a full cycle of play disruption and play triumph, and thus offered a good example of the way in which the ego, flooded by fear, can regain its synthesizing power through playful involvement and disengagement.

Our patient is Mary. She is three years old. She is a somewhat pale brunette, but looks (and is) intelligent, pretty, and quite feminine. When disturbed, however, she is said to be stubborn, babyish, and shut-in. Recently she has enriched her inventory of expression by nightmares and by violent anxiety attacks in the play group which she has recently joined. All that the play group teachers can say is that Mary has a queer way of lifting things and has a rigid posture: and that her tension seems to increase in connection with the routines of resting and going to he toilet. With this information at hand we invite Mary to our office.

Maybe a word should be said here about the thoroughly difficult situation which ensues when a mother brings a child for observation. The child has not chosen to come. He often does not feel sick at all in the sense that he has a symptom which he wishes to get rid of. On the contrary, all he knows is that certain things and, most of all, certain people make him feel uncomfortable and he wishes that we would do something about these things and people — not about him. Often he feels that something is wrong with his parents, and mostly he is right. But he has no words for this and, even if he did have, he has no reason to trust us with such weighty information. On the other hand, he does not know what the parents have told us about him — while God only knows what they have told the child about us. For the parents, helpful as they may wish to be and necessary as they are as initial informants, cannot be trusted in these matters: the initial history given is often distorted by the wish to justify (or secretly punish) themselves or to punish (and unconsciously justify) somebody else, perhaps the grandparents who "told you so."

In this case, my office was in a hospital. Mary had been told that she was coming to discuss her nightmares with me — a man whom she had never seen before. Her mother had consulted a pediatrician regarding these nightmares and Mary had heard the mother and the doctor argue over the possible indication for a tonsillectomy. I had hoped, therefore, that she would notice that the appointments of my office indicated a strictly non-medical affair and that she would give me a chance in simple and straightforward terms to acknowledge the purpose of her visit, to tell her that I was not a doctor and then to make clear that we were going to play together in order to get acquainted. Such explanations do not quite settle a child's doubts, but they may permit him to turn to the toys and do something. And as soon as he does *something* we can observe what he selects and repudiates in our standard inventory of toys. Our next step, then, will be guided by the meaning thus revealed.

Mary holds on to her mother as she enters my office. When she offers me her hand it is both rigid and cold. She gives me a brief smile, then turns to her mother, puts her arms around her, and holds her close to the still open door. She buries her head in her mother's skirt as if she wanted to hide in it, and responds to my advances only by turning her head to me — now with tightly closed eyes. Yet she *had* for a split moment looked at me with a smile that seemed to convey an interest — as if she wanted to see whether or not the new adult was going to understand fun. This makes her flight to her mother seem somewhat dramatic. The mother tries to encourage her to look at the toys, but Mary again hides her face in her mother's skirt and repeats in an exaggeratedly babyish voice, "Mommy, mommy, mommy!" A dramatic young lady: I am not even quite sure that she is not hiding a smile. I decide to wait.

Mary does make a decision. Still holding on to her mother, she points to a (girl) doll and says several times quickly and babyishly, "What that, what that?" After the mother has patiently explained that it is a dolly, Mary repeats "Dolly, dolly, dolly," and suggests in words not understandable to me that the mother take off the dolly's shoes. The mother tries to make her perform this act herself, but Mary simply repeats her demand. Her voice becomes quite anxious, and it seems that we may have tears in a moment.

Now the mother asks if it is not time for her to leave the room and wait outside as she has told Mary she would. I ask Mary whether we can let her mother go now and she, unexpectedly, makes no objection, not even when she suddenly finds herself without anybody to lean on. I try to start a conversation about the name of the doll, which the mother has left in Mary's hand. Mary grasps it firmly around the legs and suddenly, smiling mischievously, she begins to touch various things in the room with the doll's head. When a toy falls from the shelf, she looks at me to see whether she has gone too far; when she sees me smile permissively she laughs and begins to push smaller toys, always with the doll's head, in such a way that they fall too. Her excitement increases. With special glee she stabs with the doll's head at a toy train which is on the floor in the middle of the room. She overturns all the cars with growing evidence of a somehow too exciting kind of fun. As the engine overturns she suddenly stops and becomes pale. She leans with her back against the sofa, holds the doll vertically over her lower abdominal region, and lets it drop on the floor. She picks it up again, holds it over the same region, and drops it again. While repeating this several times, she begins first to whine and then to yell, "Mommy, mommy, mommy."

The mother re-enters, sure that communication has failed, and asks Mary whether she wants to go. I tell Mary that she may go if she wishes but that I hope she will be back in a few days. Quickly calmed, she leaves with her mother, saying good-bye to the secretary outside as if she had had a pleasant visit.

Strangely enough, I too felt that the child had made a successful if interrupted communication. With small children, words are not always necessary at the beginning. I had felt that the play was leading up to a conversation; and at any rate the child had conveyed to me by counterphobic activity what her danger was. The fact of the mother's anxious interruption was, of course, as significant as the child's play disruption. Together, they probably explain the child's babyish anxiety. But what had she communicated with this emotional somersault, this sudden hilarity and flushed aggressiveness, and this equally sudden inhibition and pale anxiety?

The discernible mode content had been *pushing* things, not with her hand but with the doll as an extension of her hand; and then *dropping* the same doll from the genital region.

The doll as an extension of the hand was, as it were, a pushing tool. This suggests that she may not dare to touch or push things with her bare hand and reminds me of her teachers' observation that she seemed to touch or lift things in her own special way. This, together with the general rigidity in her extremities, suggests that Mary may be worried about her hands, maybe as aggressive tools.

The transfer of the doll to the lower abdominal region followed by her strangely obsessive and repetitive dropping leads to the further suggestion that she was dramatizing the loss from that region of an aggressive tool, a pushing instrument. The attack-like state which overcame her at this point reminds me of something which I learned long ago: severe hysterical attacks in adult women have been interpreted as dramatizations representing both partners in an imagined scene. Thus, one hand in tearing off the patient's dress may dramatize an aggressor's approach, while the other, in clutching it, may represent the victim's attempt to protect herself. Mary's attack impressed me as being of such a nature: by dropping the doll several times, panicky and yet as if obsessed, she seemed to be inexorably driven to dramatize both the robbed and the robber.

But what was to be stolen from her? Here we would have to know which meaning is more relevant, the doll's use as an aggressive tool — or the doll as a baby. In this play hour the dropped doll had first been the prolongation of an extremity and a tool of (pushing) aggression, and then something lost in the lower abdominal region under circumstances of extreme anxiety. Does Mary consider a penis such an aggressive weapon, and does she dramatize the fact that she does not have one? From the mother's account it is entirely probable that on entering the nursery school Mary was given her first opportunity to go to the toilet in the presence of boys and visits to the toilet were said to be occasions for anxiety.

I am thinking of the mother when she raps on the door. She has left the child, now quite composed, outside to come back and add something to Mary's biography. Mary was born with a sixth finger which was removed when she was approximately six months old; there is a scar on her left hand. Just prior to the outbreak of her anxiety attacks, Mary had repeatedly and urgently asked about this scar ("What that, what that?") and had received the routine answer that it was "just a mosquito bite." The mother agreed that the child when somewhat younger could easily have been present when her congenital anomaly was mentioned. Mary, the mother adds, has recently been equally insistent in her sexual curiosity.

We can now understand better the fact that Mary feels uneasy about the aggressive use of her hand, which has been robbed of a finger, and that she may equate the scar on her hand and her genital "scar," the lost finger and the absent penis. Such an association would also bring into juxtaposition the observation of sex differences in the play school and the immediate question of a threatening operation.

Before Mary's second visit, her mother offered this further information: Mary's sexual curiosity had recently received a specific blow when her father, irritable because of a regional increase in unemployment which threatened his means of livelihood, had shown impatience with her during her usual morning visit to him in the bathroom. In fact, he had shoved her out of the room. As he told me later, he had angrily repeated the words, "You stay out of here!" She had liked to watch the shaving process and had also on recent occasions (to his slight annoyance) asked about his genitals. A strict adherence to a routine in which she could do, say, and ask the same thing over and over again had caused her to feel "heartbroken" over the consequent exclusion from the father's toilet.

We also discussed the fact (already mentioned) that Mary's disturbed sleep and foul breath had been attributed by a pediatrician to a bad condition of the tonsils, and that the mother and the physician had engaged in a discussion in front of Mary as to whether she needed an immediate operation or not. *Operation,* then, and *separation* are seen to be the common denominators: the actual operation of the finger, the anticipated operation of the tonsils, and the mythical operation by which boys become girls; the separation from her mother during playschool hours, and the estrangement from her father. At the end of the first hour of play observation, then, this was the closest we could come to the meanings on which all of the play elements and biographic data seemed to converge.

## Play Satiation

The antithesis of play disruption is play satiation, play from which a child emerges refreshed as a sleeper from dreams which "worked." Disruption and satiation are very marked and very clear only in rare cases. More often they are diffused and must be ascertained by detailed study. But not so in Mary's case. During her second appointment she obliged me with a specimen of play satiation as dramatic as that of her play disruption.

At first Mary again smiles bashfully at me. Again she turns her head away, holding on to her mother's hand and insisting that the mother come with her into the room. Once in the room, however, she lets her mother's hand go and, forgetting about the mother's and my presence, she begins to play animatedly and with obvious determination and goal-mindedness. I quickly close the door and motion the mother to sit down, because I do not want to disturb the play.

Mary goes to the corner where the blocks are on the floor. She selects two blocks and arranges them in such a way that she can stand on them each time she comes to the corner to pick up more blocks. Thus, play begins again with an extension of extremities, this time her feet. She now collects a pile of blocks in the middle of the room, moving to the corner and back without hesitation. Then she kneels on the floor and builds a small house for a toy cow. For about a quarter of an hour she is completely absorbed in the task of arranging the house so that it is strictly rectangular and at the same time fits tightly about a toy cow. She then adds five blocks to one long side of the house and experiments with a sixth block until its position satisfies her (see Figure 10).

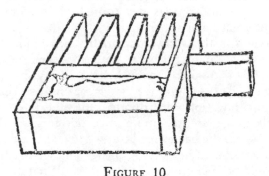

FIGURE 10

This time, then, the dominant emotional note is peaceful play concentration with a certain maternal quality of care and order. There is no climax of excitement, and the play ends on a note of satiation; she has built something, she likes it, now the play is over. She gets up with a radiant smile — which suddenly gives place to a mischievous twinkle. I do not realize the danger I am about to fall victim to, because I am too fascinated by the fact that the close-fitting stable looks like a hand — with a sixth finger. At the same time it expresses the "inclusive" mode, a female-protective configuration, corresponding to the baskets and boxes and cradles arranged by little and big girls to give comfort to small things.

Thus we see, so I muse, two restorations in one: The configuration puts the finger back on the hand and the happily feminine pattern belies the "loss from the genital region" previously dramatized. The second hour's play thus accomplishes an expression of restoration and safety — and this concerning the same body parts (hand, genital region) which in the play disruption of the first hour had appeared as endangered.

But, as I said, Mary has begun to look teasingly at me. She now laughs, takes her mother's hand and pulls her out of the room, saying with determination, "Mommy, come out." I wait for a while, then look out into the waiting room. A loud and triumphant, "Thtay in there!" greets me. I strategically withdraw, whereupon Mary closes the door with a bang. Two further attempts on my part to leave my room are greeted in the same way. She has me cornered.

There is nothing to do but to enter into the spirit of the game. I open the door slightly, quickly push the toy cow through the opening, make it squeak, and withdraw it. Mary is beside herself with pleasure and insists that the game be repeated a few times. She gets her wish, then it is time for her to go home. When she leaves she looks triumphantly and yet affectionately at me and promises to come back. I am left with the task of figuring out what has happened.

From anxiety in the autosphere in the first hour, Mary had now graduated to satiation in the microsphere — and to triumph in the macrosphere. She had taken the mother out of my space and locked me into it. This game had as content: a man is teasingly locked into his room. It was only in connection with this playful superiority that Mary had decided to talk to me, and this in no uncertain terms. "Thtay in there!" were the first words she had ever addressed to me! They were said clearly and in a loud voice, as if something in her had waited for the moment when she would be free enough to say them. What does that mean?

I think we have here the consummation of a play episode by way of a "father transference." It will be remembered that from the moment Mary came into my room at the beginning of the first contact she showed a somewhat coquettish and bashful curiosity about me, which she immediately denied by closing her eyes tightly. Since it can be expected that she would transfer to me (the man with toys) a conflict which disturbed her usually playful relationship with her father, it seems more than probable that in this game she was repeating with active mastery ("Thtay in there") and with some reversal of vectors (out-in) the situation of exclusion of which she had been a passive victim at home ("Stay out of here").

To some this may seem like a lot of complicated and devious reasoning for such a little girl. But here it is well to realize that these matters are difficult for rational thinking only. It would indeed be difficult to think up such a series of play tricks. It is even difficult to recognize and analyze it. But it happens, of course, unconsciously and automatically: here, never underestimate the power of the ego — even of such a little girl.

## Self-Curative Processes

This episode is presented to illustrate the self-curative trend in spontaneous play; for play therapy and play diagnosis must make systematic use of such self-curative processes. They may help the child to help himself — and they may help us to advise the parents. Where this fails, more complicated methods of treatment (child psychoanalysis)* must be initiated — methods which have not been discussed in this chapter. With advancing age, prolonged conversation would take the place of play. Here, however, it was my purpose to demonstrate that a few play hours can serve to inform us of matters which the child could never verbalize. Trained observers, in the possession of numerous data, can see from a few play contacts which of these data are acutely relevant to the child, and why. In Mary's case, her play disruption and her play satiation, if seen in the framework of all the known circumstances, strongly suggest that a variety of past and future, real and imagined events had been incorporated into a system of mutually aggravating dangers. In her second play hour, she disposed of them all: she restored her finger, reassured herself, reaffirmed her femininity — and told the big man off. Such play peace gained must, however, be sustained by new insight on the part of the parents.

Mary's parents accepted (and partly themselves suggested) the following recommendations. Mary's curiosity in regard to her scar, her genitals, and her operation required a truthful attitude. She needed to have other children, especially boys, visit her for play at her home. The matter of the tonsils called for the decision of a specialist, which could be candidly communicated to the child. It did not seem wise to awaken and to restrain her during her nightmares; perhaps she needed to fight her dreams out, and there would be opportunity to hold her lightly and to comfort her when she awoke spontaneously. The child needed much activity; playful instruction in rhythmic motion might relax some of the rigidity in her extremities, which, whatever the initial cause, may have been at least aggravated by fearful anticipation since hearing for the first time about the mysterious amputation of her finger.

* Anna Freud, *Psycho-Analytical Treatment of Children*, Imago Publishing Co., London, 1946.

When Mary, a few weeks later, paid me a short visit, she was entirely
at home and asked me in a clear, loud voice about the color of the train I
had taken on my vacation. It will be remembered that she overturned a
toy engine on the occasion of her first visit: now she could talk about
engines. A tonsillectomy had proved unnecessary; the nightmares had
ceased; Mary was making free and extensive use of the new play
companions provided in and near her home. There was a revived play
relationship with her father. He had intuitively made the most of Mary's
sudden enraptured admiration for shining locomotives. He took her for
regular walks to the railroad yards where together they watched the
mighty engines.

Here the symbolism which has pervaded this clinical episode gains a
new dimension. In the despair of play disruption, the toy engine
apparently had a destructive meaning in some context with phallic-
locomotor anxiety: when Mary pushed it or, she apparently had that
awesome "Adam, where art thou" experience which we first observed in
Ann. At the time, Mary's play relationship to her father had been
disrupted, and this (as she could not know or understand) because of his
worries over a possible disruption of his work status. This she seems to
have interpreted entirely in terms of her maturational state and of her
changes in status: and yet her reaction was not unrelated to the
unconscious meaning of the father's actions. For threatened loss of
status, threatened marginality, often result in an unconscious attempt by
more stringent self-control and by purified standards to regain the
ground lost or at least to keep from slipping any further. This, I believe,
made the father react in a less tolerant way to the little girl's exploration,
thus offending and frightening her in the general area which was already
disturbed. It was, then, this area which appeared in her play in a
condensed form, while she attempted, from the frightfulness of
isolation, to work her way back to playful mutuality. Thus do children
reflect and, where play fails, carry over into their own lives, the historical
and economic crises of their parents.

Neither Mary's play nor the insight it provided could assuage this
father's economic worries. But the moment he recognized the impact
of his anxieties on his daughter's development, he realized that from a
long-range point of view her anxieties mattered much more than the
threatened change of his work status. In fact, actual developments did
not confirm his apprehensions.

The father's idea of taking walks to the engine yards was felicitous.
For the real engines now became symbols of power shared by father and
daughter alike and sustained by the whole imagery of the machine
culture in which this child is destined to become a woman.

Thus at the end of any therapeutic encounter with a child the parent must sustain what the adult patient must gain for himself: a realignment with the images and the forces governing the cultural development of his day, and from it an increased promise of a sense of identity.

# RELEASE

# Release Therapy

DAVID M. LEVY

Since the time allowed for this paper is too limited for a needed introduction to the method to be described, I shall state simply that before the employment of this or any other psychotherapeutic method with children a proper history of the case has been taken and all necessary examinations, including physical and psychological studies, have been completed. When the form of treatment named "release therapy" or "abreaction therapy" is selected, it is assumed that the child is the primary consideration in a therapy limited entirely to procedures in the office. The mother is seen whenever she wishes. She is not excluded in any sense from contact with the psychiatrist. It is implied merely that the problem presented by the child can be treated in a relatively short period of time without relation to the family situation; since, as an exclusive therapy, it is used especially in cases in which the problems are primarily of the child and not of the mother or other members of the family. What proportion of children can be treated by this method is still to be determined. The more that can be included the better, since the results appear to be satisfactory and are accomplished in a relatively short period of time.

By release therapy of young children is meant a psychotherapy in which the primary concern of the therapist is to create or facilitate the creation of situations by the use of play methods in which the anxieties of the child are given expression. Though abreaction, the psychoanalytic term for this procedure, is part and parcel of psychoanalysis, and most varieties of psychotherapy, the reason for this special name is because of a limitation practically to that procedure. Two forms of this type of therapy can be differentiated. One may be called a specific release therapy, since it relies on various forms of restoring the situation out of which the anxiety and its accompanying symptoms arose. The other form, general release therapy, is utilized typically when symptoms have arisen in the child because of excessive demands or prohibitions made upon it at too early an age.

Brevity requires limiting illustration of the essential features of the method to but two cases. Before doing so, it is important to state that no method of treatment is better than the results it produces. No matter how logical or how beautifully formulated any psychotherapy may be, the test of its value is in the results it achieves. Follow-up studies are therefore an essential function of treatment, for the purpose of determining the results, as also the dynamics of the therapy.

## Specific Release Therapy

As an example of specific release therapy, I am selecting a boy age two years and two months. He was referred because of difficulties of about one week's duration, namely, stammering and a general fearful attitude. He looked as though at any moment he might be scolded or hit. His speech had developed rapidly from the age of fifteen months. He had a larger vocabulary than usual, and up to the onset of his difficulty there had been no speech abnormalities. The difficulty was related to an event which took place in the nursery school. A boy hit him, slapping and scratching him, on two occasions, the first occasion a week, and the second a day before the stammering began. This was the child's first experience of this type. He appeared "indifferent" and did not hit back.

It is unusual to have a child referred for treatment whose difficulties are of such recent onset. I was interested in seeing how quickly the child could overcome the anxieties aroused by this situation. The therapeutic device was simply to restore the situation in which the patient was attacked, releasing the anxiety that was occasioned by it, repeating it to the point where the fears could be discharged in aggression — in other words, to enable the child to complete an act which had been blocked presumably by fear.

There were four sessions in all. In the first he entered the playroom very readily. He showed no overt over-attachment to the nurse who brought him. I showed him the play cabinets. He busied himself with various toys. His activity at first was quiet, busy, handling and looking at various objects. Later he began to name the objects he was playing with. I showed him some clay, which he manipulated, though with some caution. In general, the first session was devoted chiefly to a developing familiarity with the playroom. In the second session, after his spontaneous play, he brought a big piece of clay to me and said, "Break it." I broke it into little bits as I had done for him in the first session. He heaped them all on top of a doll and then said, " 'Nuf. 'Nuf. Play train." I opened some drawers and he picked out a train. I resumed taking notes. He ran the train on my pad of paper. I said, "I'll play with you." He said, "Play with me." He continued to play with the clay. H put some between my lips. I did the same to him. At first he refused. Later he did it himself. While playing in this manner, I asked him what the boy at school did to him. He answered by making a slapping movement at his cheek. I asked, "Where else did he hit you?" He then made a slapping movement at the other cheek. I took two dolls and tried to reproduce the situation, saying, "This one is Paul (using his name) and this is the one who hit you," butting the head of one doll into each cheek of the other. Paul said, "Here, too," pointing to the head, which I then also hit. I said, "Now what does Paul do?" He made a move to hit the doll, stopped, and then went to the door and said, "I want to see Nelly." Nelly is the name of his nurse. He could not open the door and cried. I distracted him by filling a mouse with water, etc. He got interested and played until the end of the hour. Judging by his expression in the play with the dolls, there was no anxiety until he made a move to hit. I have left out numerous details, since my purpose is to illustrate the essential point of reproducing the situation out of which, presumably, the difficulty came. Therapeutic skill was involved in gauging the time of the introduction and, if you wish, the amount of dilution of the experience in order not to exceed the child's point of tolerance.

In the third interview, after about thirty minutes' play in which certain bits of aggression were given expression, the play of the dolls was repeated. At the moment when the slapping movement had been previously inhibited, he now hit the other doll hard, threw it on the floor and stepped on it. Then he said, "Nelly," turned to the door but made no further movement in that direction. He continued playing with clay and then with water at the sink, throwing objects down and finally trying to squirt me. The next session consisted of freer activity along the same lines. It was after the third session that the mother reported that the stammering and the fearful attitude were no longer in evidence. The therapy consisted in helping the child overcome anxiety aroused by the situation in very quick order. It probably facilitated what the child would have done for himself. It is prophylactic in the sense that it made sure of this process. For follow-up study, the child was seen on two occasions — one year and two years following the treatment. The stammering had not returned. Information from the mother, the father, the nurse and the school indicates a normal, healthy development. In general, the experience with specific release therapy applied to symptoms arising out of a definitely known traumatic episode is quite gratifying.

## General Release Therapy

As an example of general release therapy I am selecting a girl age two years and three months, the younger of two children, referred because of severe temper tantrums, lack of demonstrable affection for the parents or the four year old brother, general negativism, sulkiness and tenseness. The tempers were of the normal variety, that is, they consisted of lying on the floor, kicking and screaming. When allowed to pursue their own course they would last about two hours. The child was an "easy" baby until twelve months of age when bowel training was instituted. There was a battle every time she was put on the pot. Bowel control was established within a few months, bladder control by twenty-five months. A history of the case revealed that the difficulty was related to an intelligent but severe disciplinary nurse. In the early interviews the child showed difficulty in handling the clay. Her general resistive behavior also made it appear that a general release method was worth trying. She was seen on ten occasions. In her case, a follow-up investigation was made by letters and telephone yearly for four years. There was an added advantage in that the mother recorded her observations of the child's behavior after each interview. Since the mother was not told what had occurred, they were especially valuable in studying changes in behavior in immediate response to the therapeutic process.

In the first session she refused to come in alone, holding onto the mother's skirt. I asked the mother to come in with her. I put various toys on the floor. She made a few forward movements, walking a step towards them, then retreating, still holding the mother's skirt tightly. I took a gun and shot at some clay figures and then said, "Who shall I shoot?" She pointed to her mother at whom I shot and then at me. After this she left her mother to play with the toys, sitting down near them. As I came closer she hid under a chair. I passed toys to her while she remained there. She would push each one away. After six such attempts she came out from under the chair, walked to her mother and stood close behind her, though not holding onto her skirt. I threw various objects down on the floor and she laughed. In the interview I tried to overcome her refusal to enter into the play. It seemed to be due to negativism rather than to fear of a stranger. I hoped to release her own destructive behavior by preceding it with my own performance.

The second interview continued essentially as the first. For ten minutes she stood near the mother but showed interest in my activities. At one point she said she wanted to go to the toilet. The mother took her along; when she returned I beckoned the mother to leave, meanwhile placing some clay in the child's hand. The mother left. The child played with the clay, forming it into "babies," but each time after making a baby she would lift up her finger to have me flick off the clay. This latter became a kind of game. She looked into various toy drawers and took out material freely. Before leaving she put each toy back in the drawer from which she took it.

In the third session she refused to come in alone. With the mother present she played with clay material as previously. At a certain point I beckoned the mother to leave. The child continued her play and then began to collect material from the various drawers of toys. She still handled the clay gingerly, not shaping it easily with her hands but holding her fingers to be wiped before touching the clay again. It was a careful, light holding and manipulating activity. Again she put each toy back in its drawer before leaving. In this interview there was laughter and generally easier play activity. In the several sessions following she had some clay babies sit on potties, others stand near them, depicting a recent experience in which she tried to urinate standing up like her brother. This she verbalized quite freely.

In the fifth interview for the first time she shaped clay freely and put pieces of it in a dish. Presumably they were meant to represent a bowel movement, though when I asked her what it was she looked up at me, smiled, but gave no answer. The day following this interview she soiled herself. When the mother asked her why she did it, she said, "I like it." The soiling became frequent, several times daily. I told the mother to allow the child to indulge in it and not to discipline her for a while. After soiling herself she would sit that way for over an hour and then she wanted to be cleaned. In the eighth interview there was an increase in destructive behavior, tearing paper off crayons, pulling her clay babies apart, throwing them about the room and the like. The day following this session at home she smeared herself with her own feces. On that day the mother telephoned to me in despair and I advised her to use what methods she wished to overcome the soiling. The period of regression to soiling had so far lasted 15 days. The mother went to the child after the telephone conversation with me and told her that she didn't like little girls who soiled themselves, that other children didn't like it, that if she wanted to play with other children she would have to be clean. The child said she wanted to get clean. It stopped that day and has not recurred since. The mother observed that the child had a wonderful time that way, was perfectly content, "loved it," and would grin at you when you looked at her. It is interesting that the ninth session which followed by a week the establishment of her bowel control, was featured by smearing of clay, picking some up and putting it into her mouth, licking her lips and putting it back on the floor.

Changes in behavior were noted after the third interview, consisting of "sudden and unusual display of affection" which would come and go. There was a decided lessening of negativism, more affirmative answers, freer play with other children and generally less tension and disobedience. This seemed to go hand in hand with changes occurring in the office, consisting of lessened anxiety about destructive tendencies, about dirt and about orderliness. The general change was described by the mother in the form of "a gayer and lighter child." The play method presumably enabled the resolution of anxiety engendered by a discipline that was stamped in too soon or too severely or both. The release of the repressed infantile tendencies, a kind of therapeutic regression, made the new modifications more tolerable. The word "release" seems especially applicable. The child blossomed when "released" from constricting influences through a method that freed activity along lines marked out by her own anxieties. In the four years that followed there is evidence that growth in her social and intellectual life has proceeded favorably.

Further theoretical implications of the method cannot be elaborated now. In general the younger the child the sooner can results be achieved. The need of the short psychotherapy is obviously clear enough. This paper is presented as a contribution to that end.

# Play Therapy at Home

NATALIE ROGERS FUCHS

There are times when even the happy and healthy child may develop nagging fears or persistent hostilities. At such times we parents do our best by loving, cajoling, rewarding and punishing. Parents do not usually think in terms of therapy for the normal youngster, and if we did, we might not think of ourselves as possible therapists. A recent experience of mine, however, persuades me that reasonably intelligent, sensitive parents can help their children over some of the rough spots of growing up by using the techniques and attitudes of a play therapist.

## Child with a Specific Fear

Two years ago our first daughter, Janet, developed fears about having her bowel movements. Although Janet is basically a very happy, outgoing child, this one problem made our lives temporarily difficult. The correspondence with my father, Dr. Carl R. Rogers, tells how this problem was handled.

Dear Dad,
I wish you had time to visit us and to see your cute, blonde granddaughter, Janet. At the age of one-and-a-half she is running circles around me (literally), has quite a large vocabulary, and is beginning to put some of her big words together into short sentences. But she does have one rather overwhelming difficulty about which I would like to ask your advice. She is terrified at having to do her bowel movements and does everything she can to hold them back. She fusses and cries every time she has any peristaltic action; she hates to have her diapers changed and cries, "no diapers,

no wipe-wipe, no lotion," every time I start to change her. When she thinks she does have to eliminate, she strains, turns red-and-blue in the face and obviously gets all upset about it.

We have been giving her mineral oil as our pediatrician advised but now she can hold back from having a bowel movement for two or three days even with an adult dose of mineral oil in her. Since she will only do a little smear at a time it takes two or three of these episodes a day for her to complete her elimination. This is getting to occupy a great part of our day and is changing her from an outgoing, happy child into a constantly worried and whiney person.

I can understand how this developed but our problem is trying to cope with it. As an infant she was constipated and had some pain on occasion when she eliminated. Also, two or three times in infancy she had some fissures in her rectum which must have caused discomfort. I discussed this with our pediatrician and she helped us help Janet by controlling her diet and adding prune juice to her menu.

Now her fear is out of all proportion to any possible pain. For a long while, Larry and I thought there *must* be something physically wrong with her intestinal tract for her to make such a fuss. Our pediatrician was quite sure there was no organic trouble but said if we wanted to be positive we could send Janet to the hospital for a barium enema and X-rays. We finally decided to do this, if only to reassure ourselves that there was no physical defect. The specialist at the hospital had a nice chat with us before we left Janet. He said he had seen this happen time and time again and that there was almost *no* chance there was anything organically wrong with Janet. He was very appreciative of our concern, however, and after discussing it some more, Larry and I decided we, as parents, couldn't have a relaxed attitude about Jan's troubles until we were one hundred per cent sure there was no internal difficulty. So we admitted her to the hospital for 48 gruesome hours (for us, anyway). I don't know who suffered the most, she or we, but I hope we never have to go through anything like that again!

The results were as the doctors had predicted. There is no physical difficulty. We breathed a big sigh of relief, but now we must think of constructive ways to attack the problem from the psychological angle.

You know I have read about play therapy and probably you remember that I had a little experience dealing with children in a therapeutic situation at College. So I am wondering if you think I could help Janet myself. We have thought of going to a psychologist but I would prefer to do everything we can ourselves before seeking outside help. Do you think it is possible for a mother to be a therapist with her own child? If so, how should I go about it?

Dear Natalie,

I woke up early this morning, got to thinking about you and your difficulties with Janet and decided to get this off to you. First, is this a problem in Janet, or in you? She seems to have had real pain in infancy and reacted to it, but now the problem comes in double strength without any direct cause. While no doubt she felt the return of the fear for some reason, I guess I feel the situation couldn't have reached its present pitch without you being involved at least as much as she. I could be wrong, though. Since it is easier to write letters to you than to her, I'll start by thinking about the part you might be playing. Is it that this is Janet's only, or best way of getting attention? This seems unlikely. Could it be that you have a hard time in your own *feelings* — not your intellects — letting her be a separate person to the extent of bearing her own pain? This seems one possibility. It is very hard to let a child feel frustrated and alone when put to bed, or to feel hurt from a skinned knee without wanting to bear these unpleasant feelings for him. But to that extent we all do have our private worlds, and I can't carry for you the distress you feel about her — though I would be willing to — and you can't bear for her the fright she feels about her bowel movements.

I guess I feel that if the parents living with her had feelings such as the following, the problem wouldn't last so very long. "I know that for some reason you need to feel fright and terror and pain about your b.m.'s even though there is no physical necessity for any of those things. I don't share it, but I can certainly understand that you feel it and I am willing to let you feel it as long as it exists." The question is — how does one *acquire* this attitude? Because pretending it won't help much.

I think your suggestion about play therapy is a good one and it would give Janet an opportunity to express her fears and you a chance to show her you understand, though you cannot bear her pain and fright for her.

You might get a small batch of suitable play materials; some smallish furniture and dolls, including a mother, father, older child and a baby doll (the dime store variety would do). A toilet, a potty-chair, and any other things that might reproduce the frightening situation such as cotton or toilet paper should be included. Also a regular nursing bottle, something "ooshy" like plasticine or clay, and something to pound on. Don't get too much.

Then it might be helpful if at a special time each day, in a special place, you let her play with these things and then put them away afterward. While she is playing with them be the best therapist you can — *never* initiating anything yourself, trying to understand and follow her feelings as they exist, accepting her *feelings* even if you have to limit her *behavior*. I would feel that it was important in this situation never to focus on the toilet more than she does and never to avoid it or the feelings she may have about it.

You might like to re-read Virginia Axline's book, *Play Therapy*, to refresh your knowledge. The verbatim case material she includes is lively reading and shows how to create the atmosphere important to therapy. This is really more important than the toys. Play therapy is not just a gimmick to get children to talk. It is a time when the therapist in all genuineness tries to see and understand the world exactly as the child views it. It is an atmosphere in which the child feels free to explore feelings he may have been afraid to admit to himself. Concentrate on Janet's play in a way that will let her know you understand what her actions and feeling mean to her.

I will be interested to know if you find it difficult to be a mother-therapist. I hope you do go ahead and try your luck with this procedure. Let me know how things develop.

## Mother-Therapist

Dear Dad,

It has been ten days since my first play-therapy session with Janet and I'm anxious to tell you of our progress. I bought the toys you suggested and the first day I told Janet I had some new toys — some special ones. She opened the bag and I sat on the floor to watch her and concentrate with her. We played on the dining room floor where there is no rug to worry about. Also, I felt this would help create an atmosphere different from our usual play in her room. She opened the toys and immediately tried to sit on the tiny toilet and toy potty-chair (was I surprised!). I held them so she could actually try to sit on them. She played at this for ten minutes or so. She didn't seem afraid but acted like it was a good game. Yet I had the feeling that beneath this carefree attitude she was feeling: "perhaps I really should do it like other people." I merely reflected her obvious actions and attitudes, such as, "Janet would really like to sit on the toy potty." She continued at this for a while, then turned to the other furniture and played house. After about 40 minutes I told her we would put them away in her closet and take them out again the next day. She didn't like this at first. My reaction was: "I know you don't *want* to put these away, but these are special toys and we will get them out every day for awhile and when we are through they will go back on your closet shelf." After this first session she was helpful in putting them away and later insisted on putting the toys in the bag all by herself.

This type of play went on for several days. Usually it involved the potty or toilet. Then I added some brown plasticine to the toys. (I hadn't been able to find any in the stores before this.) At first I was almost sorry I had bought it as she spent all of her time in the next few sessions just pinching off pieces of clay making "cakes for Daddy and Mommy." She didn't touch any of the furniture or play with the dolls but continued with great earnestness to make cakes and more cakes. It happened that the day I bought the clay she had found a piece of her own bowel movement in her diaper and had brought it to me. We had examined it, discussing what it was. I thought she would take one look at the brown clay and make the connection. But if she does, she won't admit it at this stage. Perhaps she is thinking it all over while she makes one cake after another.

Also, for several days she concentrated on diapering the baby doll. For this she had me get her own baby oil and cotton and diapered the doll saying, "b.m. hurt you! b.m. hurt you!" She was quite emotional and concerned while playing this out and at first avoided looking at me when I reflected with real concern in my voice that "the baby thinks the b.m.'s really hurt very much." This happened on several occasions. Then eventually she got up courage to watch my face and look in my eyes while I was reflecting her feelings. I tried hard to sense the way she was feeling in each aspect of her play, and to put into my words the way it seemed to her.

Her behavior outside the play therapy has changed quite a bit. Within two days of our first play-session she stopped fussing about being diapered. This makes life a lot easier for all of us!

I certainly plan to continue with the play and will let you know what happens. I do notice that it is good for me, too, to sit and pay full attention to her some time during the day. Not just reading to her or initiating any kind of play but just looking at the world from her view.

Dear Dad,

Janet's last few play-therapy sessions will interest you, I think. A week ago she started putting the clay in the toy potty-chair and

said she was putting "cakes in the toilet." She put it in the toy bath
tub and the little bed she calls Daddy's bed. After several days of this
she called it "b.m." and wanted me to eat it! I said: "I know you'd like
me to eat the b.m., but I can't do that. It would give me a tummy ache.
But I can pretend to eat it if you want me to." She accepted this and I
munched at it in a make-believe fashion. She was quite preoccupied
with the idea that "b.m.'s come from my tummy."

During this time (about three weeks of play-sessions all
together) she has changed her attitude a lot about the toilet outside
of playtime. She asked me to sit on the big toilet, which she does a
couple of times a day now, though she never does anything in it. And
she has tried out her own potty-chair. Before this she wouldn't go
near either and the suggestion to do so was always emphatically
turned down. Though I don't think I have been over-anxious to
toilet-train her at this age, I had originally bought the potty-chair in
the hope that she would sit down to eliminate, making it easier for
her. This approach didn't succeed. In fact it boomeranged and made
the toilet and potty-chair places to dread.

Yesterday she got the clay and dumped it all in her own potty-
chair (the real one) and said: "These are b.m.'s" Today she put some
of the clay in the toilet and flushed it down, commenting on it.

The amazing thing is that she seems to have really conquered
her fears in the past few weeks and it certainly shows in her
behavior. She no longer makes any fuss when she does her own
bowel movements. She doesn't say "hurt me" or strain while she is
doing them. I have stopped giving her mineral oil and she gets along
nicely without it. It is hard for me to believe after so many months of
trouble with this problem that she has been able to work it out in this
fashion, and in so short a time. We hope it lasts!

Janet is now three and a half years old. Several things that have
happened make me want to share our experience with other parents.
First, Janet's troubles over her bowel movements have vanished
permanently. Our results were so startling that my first reaction was, "it
won't last." But it has. And there have been several times when I felt
Janet *might* regress to her original fears. She was very upset when I made
a middle-of-the-night trip to the hospital for an emergency appendec-
tomy. Also, she might have regressed to her earlier fears when her baby
sister arrived on the scene. Instead, Janet has continued to work out
anxious feelings about doctors and hospitals, jealous feelings toward
baby, etc., through the continued use of the special toys.

Another reason I wish to share my experiences is that I have found
friends whose children have similar, if not identical, problems. These

children are basically happy, secure individuals who, for some reason or other, have developed very strong emotions or fears in one particular area. Talking to a mother whose child had similar anxieties about having bowel movements and also fears about water and bathing we discussed the use of play therapy.* She felt she wanted to try helping her daughter, Ellen, using these techniques and attitudes.

Until the day the mother started therapy, Ellen was cautious about water and insisted that towels, toy fish, and other toys be removed far from the tub so that they wouldn't get wet. Six days later, during her special-play Ellen washed the fish for ten minutes, floated him, then submerged him, laughing all the while. Then she took a towel, started by wetting one corner, then dunked the whole thing. She wrung it out and soaked it again and again. At one point, Ellen, eyeing her mother's reaction, filled the sink until it was almost overflowing. She was apparently testing herself and the permissiveness of her mother.

In discussing this with Ellen's mother I realized that there are special problems concerning limits of play during therapy that a mother must face. Play therapy is going on in the home where there is furniture that cannot be harmed, toys that shouldn't be broken and general rules of the household. A mother-therapist does not have a special playroom where the child can do damage or feel free to express his emotions by creating an unusual mess. So the mother must be able to find ways of setting permissive limits within the confining boundaries of home. Since we are discussing play therapy with normal children (not deeply disturbed ones) the problem is not insurmountable.

The special toys will be the only objects which the child can treat differently than his usual play things. The child quickly senses that this atmosphere is different from the usual mother-child relationship and seems to comprehend that the special toys can be broken, thrown about or mutilated. If the child includes household furnishings in his dramatic play, as Ellen did when she took her special toys to the bathroom and used real water and the sink, limits must be established which will be acceptable to the mother's standards of housekeeping. A mother can reflect feelings and at the same time set the limit.

*Virginia M. Axline. *Play Therapy.* Houghton Mifflin, Boston, 1947. Dorothy Baruch. *New Ways in Discipline: You and Your Child Today.* McGraw-Hill, New York 1949. Elaine Dorfman. "Play Therapy." In: *Client Centered Therapy,* by Carl R. Rogers. Houghton Mifflin, Boston, 1951. Clark E. Moustakas. *Children in Play Therapy.* McGraw-Hill, New York, 1953.

To Ellen, the mother might say, "You are wondering whether or not you'd *like* to let the water go over the top of the sink." Ellen may look to mother, then to the sink, debating whether she dare flood the floor. The mother could interject: "I guess you might like to flood the floor but I can't let you do that. It would ruin our kitchen ceiling." If Ellen does flood the floor, the mother must turn off the water herself, though she can still understand and reflect the child's feelings in wanting to break the limit.

The general thought about limits might be that anything which would cause the mother to be upset or unhappy later should not be allowed. If the mother does get disturbed by her over-permissiveness, the child will undoubtedly sense this and feel guilty. The rule is applicable to a child who would like to hit his mother during special-play. Some mothers might not object to a physical attack by their offspring but I know that I don't allow it. I feel this gives a sense of security to me and my child since neither of us would be happy if things got out of hand.

It is interesting to me that my own child, and Ellen in her play too, immediately felt the special-play hour was different. No lengthy explanations were needed. When a mother eliminates all value judgments, does not praise or condemn, suggest or divert her child's behavior, the child *knows* this is different. For a mother to listen carefully and watch her child's most simple play or complex emotions is probably a new and rewarding experience for her, too. Until one has tried it, it is almost impossible to realize how unusual it is simply to try to understand the child's feelings as they seem to the child without making any judgments about them. It is so unusual that a mother may find that changes have taken place within herself as a result of play therapy. After my experience I found I had greater patience with Janet and was willing to really listen to her before responding in our every day routine. I also found that while I was more capable of accepting her feelings I was also more free to express my own attitudes to her. I felt I was able to establish my own rights as a person without feeling I was neglecting my child.

It is difficult to say just how or why children (or adults) respond to the therapy situation as they do. With Ellen, after about two weeks of play-therapy her attitudes about her bowel movements improved greatly (as well as those of fearing water) although she never discussed bowel movements or played out her feelings on the subject. A letter from my father put it this way: "I can speculate to my heart's content as to what caused Janet's difficulty and what, specifically, cured it, and at the end will have to admit I don't know. It confirms my feeling that though we do not know all that might be known about the process, we do know how to establish the conditions which facilitate therapy; warmth, interest, and intent to understand empathically, a willingness for the individual to have his own feelings, and in this way to be a separate person."

My experience confirms this statement. I do not entirely understand what went on in Janet's mind, or in Ellen's. I only know that as a mother I was able to provide enough of the conditions of play therapy so that my child responded most constructively. Perhaps this possibility will be a useful one for other mothers to consider.

# Play with a Five-year-old Boy

MARY LOU BYERS

It is well known that permanent alteration of body image and function presents long term and complex problems to children, their families, and the health professions. In many institutions, the trend is toward short term hospitalization. An attempt is made here to learn more about the problems and crises children encounter and try to master during brief stays in the hospital. In this way, the nurse's helping role may be more clearly defined.

In the normal course of family development, preschool age children are involved in a psychosocial developmental crisis. This crisis intensifies and becomes more complex when illness or accidental injury occurs. The child discussed in this paper was a five and one-half year-old boy who was hospitalized for eleven days. His chief health problem was smoke inhalation. He had small second-degree burns on both feet and on one hand. None of these problems was severe enough, in the physical sense, to lead to permanent disability.

During Robby's hospitalization, two major themes were identified in his play activities. One theme concerned his injuries, the fire, and the medical equipment used for treatments. The second theme seemed to be related to Robby's concerns about his family, their interrelationships, and their separation from each other.

Around 7:00 a.m. on a Saturday, the Adams' two and one-half year-old daughter had awakened and climbed into bed with them. Robby was asleep in the children's bedroom. The Adamses smelled smoke. When they opened their bedroom door, the hallway was filled with smoke and flames. Both Mr. and Mrs. Adams were burned trying to rescue Robby, but they were not able to reach him. Mr. Adams jumped from the second floor bedroom window and caught his daughter and his wife when they jumped. Meanwhile, two neighbors heard Mr. Adams' cries for help and were able to enter through the front door of the apartment. One man ran through the flames and rescued Robby.

## Hospitalization of Robby

Mr. Adams' burns involved about eight percent of his body, and Mrs. Adams' burns involved about sixteen percent of her body. The burned areas of both parents were located predominantly on their arms, and they were hospitalized in the same room on the adult service for eleven days. Robby was hospitalized in pediatrics. His sister was hospitalized for observation, and released the next day in the care of her grandfather.

Polaroid pictures were taken of Robby and of his parents, and exchanged so that each could see the condition of the other. As soon as the rigid protective isolation was discontinued, Robby talked with each of his parents on the telephone at least once a day.

Robby enjoyed painting, and almost every day a painting was sent to his parents. In return, Mr. Adams sent drawings of mazes to Robby. They were drawn with great precision and accuracy on 8 x 11-inch paper. The contents of these mazes were interesting. Each maze alluded to a main character exposed to dangerous and fearsome creatures. The first one had pictures of a ferocious-looking lion with gaping jaws, a snake coiled, ready to strike, and an alligator with many sharp teeth. The caption with that drawing read, "Quick, Tarzan, back to the treehouse, but watch out for snakes, lions and alligators." The second drawing included an underwater scene of a shark with teeth, an octopus with large, ominous-looking tentacles, a giant crab with great pincers, and a treasure chest, partially buried by sand. A ship, named "The Good Ship Robby," was drawn on the surface of the sea, and the caption directed, "Find the treasure from the Good Ship Robby."

A red, white, and blue suitcase which contains a variety of items, such as small family figures, small toys, a soft rubber baby doll, play dough, crayon, and paper, is kept on our unit for special work with children. Articles pertinent to an individual child's hospital experience may be added. For Robby's play interviews, intravenous equipment, a stethoscope, tongue depressors, material for dressings, and a rubber doll figure of a fireman were included in the play materials.

Six days after Robby's admission, a nurse colleague and I conducted our first play interview with him. My colleague provided the help Robby required, and I acted as the recorder. The play interviews were utilized in an effort to learn more about Robby's concerns, and to help him assimilate the injury and the hospital experiences.

At this time, Robby was not permitted to be out of bed, and he eagerly anticipated our arrival. Prior to the play interview, we had asked not to be disturbed for thirty minutes. We had spoken with staff and placed signs on the door in an attempt to discourage visitors. In spite of our precautions, we were interrupted four times, but Robby continued his play.

## Play Interviews

Upon seeing the suitcase, Robby asked the nurse, "Can you open it?" The nurse tried to limit her actions, verbal and otherwise, as much as possible, as she assisted him in unhooking the fasteners on the suitcase. He called out excitedly, "Hey! Even paper. Put it right here. Here's a nurse!" Robby picked up a small nurse doll for an instant and then put it down again. He set a doll bed on the table, and commented, "Here's a bed for a child — put it there." In a quiet tone, he said, "Nice place for a child."

Robby picked up the fireman figure and placed it on the doll bed. The doll's legs extended at least one inch beyond the end of the bed, as the bed was smaller than the figure. He was very particular about the placement of these items. He picked up a small, round, green wooden pig with "good luck" printed on it, and exclaimed, "Oh, it's a pig with a round nose."

Robby pointed to the five-yard gauze rolls, and asked quizzically, "What's this?"

The nurse replied, "Bandages, like we use on your burns."

He picked up the stethoscope, and said, "Here, hear the heart." A small hand puppet was included in the suitcase. Robby pointed to the puppet, and said, "I want to hear inside of him." He placed the bell of the stethoscope on the puppet's chest, and murmured, "Hey, that sounds funny." Robby listened to the fireman doll. "Oh, oh, too much air." He listened to the nurse figure. He nodded his head slightly from side to side, and stated. "Don't hear anything. Might be empty."

His attention focused on the bottle of water, and he asked, "What's in water?" He did not wait for an answer, but immediately took the fireman figure, and called loudly, "Spit out as much as you can. S-p-p-p-p-." He dunked the head of the fireman doll in the medicine cup in which he had poured water.

In a firm, direct manner, Robby said to the nurse, "You're going to be the nurse for the play!" He looked at the adhesive tape, and asked, "Is this real tape?"

The nurse responded, "Yes, it's real."

Robby exclaimed, "This case even has scissors in it."

His grandfather entered at this time, and sat down next to him.

Robby called casually, "Hi, Poncho," looked up briefly, and continued to concentrate on his play. "This fireman's in bed, he has a beard. I'm a doctor." (Robby's father had a beard.) "He's got a cut on his forehead. He kind of got burned." (Robby has a small superficial burn on his forehead.) Robby cut a small piece of tape with scissors, and placed it on the doll's forehead. He turned to his grandfather, and held up the stethoscope. "You can really hear, listen," he announced excitedly.

Grandpa became interested, and started to direct Robby's play. Robby quickly tired of this arrangement, and exclaimed, "Do you know what? They have puppets here, like I do."

At that moment some of the intravenous fluid flowed through the tubing and onto the paper. Robby moved out of the way, and his grandfather quickly took a piece of cloth to wipe it dry. Robby said, pensively, "That fireman, his hands are burned. His soles are burned, too." (There were no soles on the boots of the fireman doll.)

His grandfather asked, "How can you patch him up?"

Robby replied, "I don't know. He's too big for the bed. His feet both stick out. If he gets up, he'll fall on his head. Yes, he did. That's how he hurt his forehead. Better lay down."

Robby looked at the intravenous equipment, and at the scalp vein needle set, and said, excitedly, "Can I use that? Oh, look at all that stuff." He removed the needle shield from the needle, and exclaimed, "There! Hey, how do we stick that in? We could tape it. Oh, a needle! Will it go through him? I think it will." Grandfather helped him to insert the needle into the fireman doll. Robby heaved a sigh of relief. "There! Whew, there it goes, you can turn it on." The intravenous fluid ran down and out of the fireman doll's soleless boots. Robby laughed, in a forced, artificial way. He continued, excitedly, "See any water coming out of the boots? Get the tape! Funny, goin' to be funny. WOW! There's some out of the boots, out of the heels. Oh, yeh, look how much! I think he had too much to drink. He's small." Quietly, Robby said, "I have to go to the bathroom," but he continued to play.

At this time, his grandfather left. Robby listened to the fireman doll with the stethoscope. He exclaimed, "He really does have a heart. I'll listen again. He's not the one." As he looked at a male doll figure, Robby said, "It's that man over there." He took the needle, and said, "How can I stick it into him? Right there?" As the small male doll figure was of hard rubber, Robby used considerable force to insert the needle. "Now lay down!" he declared.

Robby moved about on the chair, and in an urgent, irritable manner, said, "I have to go to the bathroom, quick!" Mrs. Adams had reported that Robby had always had urgency, and that this behavior had existed prior to his hospitalization.

He looked at the fireman doll, and said, sadly, "He has two burns on him." (Robby had one wrist and one foot bandaged). "He has holes in his boots and got burned on his feet. He's better now."

After a few moments of silence, I queried, "How did he get better?"

Robby replied, "He had to have an I.V. He rested in bed a lot."

"What about the bandages?" I asked.

Robby explained, "It was hard to put his bandages on. It was hard to cut the tape."

I questioned, "Robby, were his bandages changed?"

Firmly, Robby replied, "No, he had to keep them on."

I continued, "I thought he had to have his bandage changed every day to help his burns get better."

Quizzically, Robby said, "What?"

"And each day, the bandage gets smaller and smaller, and soon he won't need a bandage because his skin will be healed."

Robby retorted, "Oh, he's all better now. Oh." He paused a moment. "No. We need a bandage on." Pensively, he added, "Yeh, then we'll be able to go home like the fireman." Robby's mouth formed a wide oval as he imitated a loud siren, "Woo-o-o-o!"

He took the large, soft rubber baby doll and put it on top of the gauze roll. "Yeh-h-h-h, take her here." He removed the needle from the other doll. "O-o-o-o, she's crying. Wha-wha-wha, she needs a bed. Sure do hurt. She needs an I.V. She's going to feel scared." Confidently, he continued, "The needle isn't going to hurt very much for long. Wait a while, and it won't hurt." Robby inserted the needle in her thigh, and simultaneously cried, "Wha-wha-wha." The needle slipped out. He continued the examination of the doll. "Oh, no holes in her feet. Her hands are O.K. Her forehead is O.K. She'll need a little fluid." He took a small plastic nursing bottle, unscrewed the cap, and started to fill it with water. Inadvertently, he spilled water on a small piece of linen, and he immediately seemed to become uneasy.

I said to him, "That's all right, Robby, it'll dry."

He continued his play. "Here's the needle. Wha-wha-wha." With conviction, he announced, "This baby needs help!" Robby picked up the stethoscope again and placed the ear pieces in his ears. He placed the bell on the doll's genital area, and listened intently for several seconds. Then he moved the bell up to the doll's chest. "Nope, nothing there. No heart." He tried to give the doll some water with a medicine cup. He continued to rummage through the toys in the suitcase.

I told Robby that we would leave soon, but that we would come again and bring the suitcase. He said, "Please keep the big I.V. bottle with it."

He gathered the toys together, and placed them in the case. Pensively, he said, "We're moving, aren't we? Into another building with our things."

"Yes," I replied. "Mother, Daddy, Sister and you will be moving together to another apartment when it is time to go home from the hospital."

In the treatment regime, at this time, Robby's dressings were changed daily. These dressing changes were stressful, and he cried vigorously each time this procedure was done. He was placed in a bath tub twice a day, and was encouraged to walk. His shrieks of terror and agony filled the ward when bath time was imminent. He was convinced that he could not bear his weight or walk. He pleaded, "Get me the wheeler chair, please. I'm afraid to walk. I can't. I can't."

It is difficult and painful for the staff to be with the burnt patient during this particular treatment because of the extent and appearance of the patient's wounds, and, also, because of the patient's screams of fear and pain. I was glad that Robby could tell us how difficult walking seemed for him, and I told him I knew it was hard. I said that we were going to help him to learn to walk again, and that right now we knew that he could not do it by himself.

Robby cried out, "I'm afraid you'll drop me."

"We're very strong," I replied, "and we know just how to hold people, so we don't drop them."

He insistently questioned, "Are you as strong as a wheeler chair?"

"Stronger," I replied, with much conviction.

He continued to scream for several minutes. Then I said, "I know we can do this together, Robby, and we're going to start soon!"

In a harsh but firm voice, he retorted, "I'm ready now!"

At first, we held him so that his feet scarcely touched the floor. Over a period of days, the amount of weight he could bear increased, and Robby was able to ambulate. He was thrilled as he mastered his body functions again, and chattered joyously to his visitors about his accomplishments.

The second play interview was held on the ninth hospital day. Robby rummaged in the suitcase and removed the intravenous equipment, syringe, needle, and alcohol sponge. "I didn't get through with the little baby," he remarked. He held the intravenous needle, and said, "Where is the hole? Where did I put this? I'll put it there. Is the water going in? I'd better listen to her heart. Don't talk to me while I have this thing in my ears." Robby looked at the intravenous tubing, and, his eyes wide with surprise, he said, "I see a leak. Oh. Something shuffling around in her."

The nurse asked, "What is it?"

He shrugged his shoulders, and said, "I don't know, maybe it's water.

I better give her a shot." He looked at me, and asked, "How'd you like a shot?"

I asked if he thought I needed one.

"No," he replied, matter-of-factly, "at least, not in the leg." Robby looked at the bandage, which was similar to the one used each day for his dressing change. "Is this real?"

"Yes," the nurse replied.

"Kids shouldn't play with things doctors use."

"Oh, it's O.K., Robby; this stuff is for playing."

He immediately refocused on the syringe. "Where is the shotter? Here it is!" He manipulated the needle cover, and exclaimed, "Hey! I got it off by myself." He stuck the needle into the doll's leg. "How do I get it out of there? Why are there children's toys in here? (In the suitcase.) There's a little of everything. They've got everything. Look at the cars. I know what these are — tongue depressors. Oh, they're used."

The nurse remarked, "Just wet."

Robby continued, "Oh, this one's O.K. Stick out your tongue and say, 'Ahhhh.' "

A short period of silence followed. I asked Robby, "What did you see?"

Seriously, he replied, "One of her bones wiggled around. We have to take her to a doctor who has casts." He picked up a band-aid, and asked, "I forgot how to do this. Which side do you stick? Oh, that's the side. Oooo, that sure is long. Have to wrap it around her arm. I have to listen to her heart once. Nothing wrong with it." Robby picked up the tourniquet, and exclaimed, "I don't want this on me. This must be a real doctor's case. This fireman isn't real." He looked at the doll, and said, "Now I think she knows what time it is. Wrap-around time. Fix that elbow (which was really a knee). I don't know what happened to her knee, but she does need it fixed." He cut some tape with the scissors. He nodded toward the doll, and said, "It isn't for you. You aren't going to get cut with these." He looked at the nurse knowingly, and remarked, "She thinks it's for her. Hey! What's this glove for? When it's cold?" He thoughtfully continued, "Oh, yeh, I remember." Robby's doctors used gloves each day when they changed his dressings.)

As Robby poured water into a medicine cup, he muttered, "Have to be careful." He took the syringe and needle, and tried to aspirate fluid into the syringe. The nurse suggested that he place the tip of the needle in the cup. Enlightened, he said, "Oh, yeh. It's for the baby. Oooooo. She needs more in her eyes. It doesn't hurt. Don't get it on her clothes." He transferred his attention to the small male doll figure. "This one has a little bed. It's big enough for him. He's kind of sick. We need an I.V. for

him. He needs the same kind of shot." Robby filled the syringe and
expelled water, drop by drop, into the male doll figure's eyes. "Uuu-ooo-
p, I did something wrong. I can't let him fall off the bed. He needs a little
more." He placed little drops of water all over the male figure. The sound
of the air as it was expelled from the needle caused Robby to exclaim, "It
sure does sound funny when it comes out. I feel like I have an I.V. in."

After a pause, I asked, "Can you tell me how that feels?"

"It hurts when it goes in and it hurts when they take it out, too."

During the last few minutes of the interview, Robby poured water
from one vessel to another, cleansed the baby doll, and gave her shots. He
requested that we bring some animals the next time we came to play with
him.

Robby worked laboriously to paint a picture of a Dodo bird behind
bars. This painting was almost identical to a picture of a Dodo bird in a
book. Each person who commented about this painting called it a Dodo
bird (pronounced "Doe Doe"). Robby laughed and laughed, in a
hysterical, superficial way that sounded forced, and said, "That is a 'Due
Due!'" Perhaps Robby's painful ambulation contributed to his desire to be
a bird, even a bird called a "Due Due," and to fly away. He could not
escape, however, because, like the bird, he was in "jail." It was also noted
at this time that Robby's play with family figures was minimal. Play with
animal figures seemed to be a safer mode for the expression of his
concerns.

The final play interview included the same suitcase of toys, plus a
large basket of rubber animals of various types. When we went into
Robby's room, he was awake and rocking back and forth in his bed. He
got out of bed, focused all of his attention on the animals and the low
wooden fences we had brought, and rejected the suitcase entirely.

Robby was attracted to the giraffes. He took two of them, and stood
them nose to nose inside the fence. He looked at me, as if he had just told a
risque story, and said. "They're giraffes; they're kissing." He giggled and
giggled. "These are elephants. There's the king of the jungle! Hey, I need
gates for them." He picked up a gate that was broken. "Hey, this one is
kind of too little. Oooops, (looking at a broken section) that's why." He
looked back at the giraffes. "Hey, they don't have a baby!" He picked up a
cow, and remarked, "There is only one of them. Uuuu, I only have one
gate left." He took a dog, and said, "You don't belong there; get out of
there." Excitedly, he added, "There's a lion baby. If these animals get
away out of that broken fence, watch out!"

Robby looked at the giraffe, and said, "Oooo, she's got a broken leg.
She needs to wash every day two times, cause she's dirty."

He had heard personnel mention that his burns were dirty, and he was placed in the bath tub twice a day. Menacingly, he cautioned, "Nurses will give you shots." As he looked at the fence, Robby said, "Uuuuu, the animals can run out!" He placed two giraffes together, and said, "They keep hugging." When two of the long rubber legs collapsed, he exclaimed, "Ohhh, two more broken legs. What a boring giraffe she is. She was shot in the jungle. I found her out in the jungle laying in the water. There, she's a patched giraffe." He fixed the legs with adhesive tape, and placed the giraffes in a standing position. Confidentially, he said, "She's kissing. Ever see a giraffe kiss laying down?"

"No," I replied.

Robby continued quietly, "I don't see her baby."

After a pause, I asked, "I wonder where it is?"

"Maybe she zipped her pouch up. Oh," he said, with an exasperated tone, "it's kangaroos who have pouches."

This play interview terminated abruptly when Robby urgently stated his need to go to the bathroom. Upon his return to the room, the evening meal was served.

Robby was discharged the following day with his parents. A week later, a home visit was made. Mrs. Adams stated that the hospital stay was the best vacation Robby ever had. He sat next to me on the couch, and volunteered detailed information about the fire and the location of the flames. He took the suitcase, showed his parents the intravenous equipment, and listened to their hearts with the stethoscope. He and his sister played fleetingly with the animals, then asked eagerly to go outside. Robby thought it would be fun to have his picture taken in his favorite tree, and we all enjoyed this activity.

Mrs. Adams stated that Robby continued to manually rotate his left foot, even though he seemed to have full range of motion in his ankle joint. She was also concerned about his vision. The parents planned an appointment with the ophthalmologist. Some of Robby's play involved eye washing. Whether an eye injury occurred was unknown.

Robby's efforts to work through the stress caused by his injuries, hospitalization, and treatment were apparent. His articulation and manual dexterity were exceptional. His creative use of personnel and materials aided him toward successful mastery of a crisis situation.

# RELATIONSHIP

# Play Therapy as Described by Children

VIRGINIA MAE AXLINE

Therapists have their intentions in therapy clearly defined in their own minds. They have their theories and goals and methods of evaluating the outcomes of therapeutic experiences. In all likelihood there would be general agreement among all therapists that a "successful" therapeutic experience for a child would bring about marked and noticeable changes in the child's behavior — physically as well as psychologically. For example, reports from parents at the conclusion of "successful" therapy for the child include observations that the child is more relaxed, eats better, sleeps better, shows improvement in his coordination, no longer manifests overt behavior symptoms of tension or anxiety such as nail-biting, bed-wetting, hair-pulling, or any of the other possible symptoms that he may have had prior to the therapeutic experiences. Usually the child is reported as being more cooperative, happier, more spontaneous in all of his behavior. In other words, the descriptions given of the child at home and at school indicate that the child has achieved adequate adjustability so that he functions with ease and enjoyment both individually and in groups. He has become a happy child in harmony with his world. From such observational evaluation, the therapist draws up a picture of what has happened to the child during the period of his therapeutic experience.

There are differences of opinion as to the dynamics that are in operation which facilitate these observable changes. Theories and explanations of process are varied. The perceptions of different therapists are often at variance. The question that is raised frequently is one that is a challenging and provocative one: What element or elements in all successful therapeutic approaches are the essentials that bring about these changes? Are the changes that are observed immediately after the termination of therapy lasting changes?

Speculation alone does not provide the answers, but research, follow-up studies, and investigations from various angles into the process might throw additional light in this direction.

## Follow-Up Study

As has been stated above, the therapists have their intentions in therapy, but how do the *children* perceive and experience the play therapy sessions? And what is the significance of this experience to them? How does the child size up the situation while he is participating in it? How does the child describe the experience at a later date? What would be indicated by follow-up studies of children who had completed therapy which had been evaluated as "successful" by parents, teachers, and therapists?

The study reported here attempts to explore possible answers to the above questions.

Out of thirty play therapy case records evaluated as successful, twenty-two of the clients were available for a follow-up study. The other eight children had moved away and there were no forwarding addresses.

The procedures used in these interviews were as follows: The therapist met the child in an interviewing room and asked one introductory question, "Do you remember me?" There were no probing questions, suggestions, or directing of thinking other than those quoted in this paper. The purpose was to get any reactions the children might have had to their therapeutic experiences.

In the cases where letters were sent to the children, a copy of the following handwritten letter was sent to each child not contacted in the school personally.

Dear————:
We are interested in finding out what if anything you remember about the experience you had when we met in the playroom at (name of school or clinic) in the (date — season and year).

We would appreciate it very much if you could come in for a little talk with me — about that experience and about what you are doing now.

Will you please call (telephone number) and make an appointment so we can talk together again. — Or write on the enclosed card when it would be convenient for you to come in.

If you cannot come in, will you write me a letter telling me what, if anything, you remember about the experience?

It is quite possible that you have forgotten all about it. It has been a long time ago. If that is the case, will you just write on the card, "I don't remember anything about it," and mail it to me?

Thank you so much for your kindness.

Sincerely yours,

. . . . . . . . . . . . . . . . . . . . . . . . . . . . . . . . . . . . . . . . . . . . .

Name of Therapist

In all of the twenty-two cases referred to in this report, the child was the only one in the family who received therapy. The parents were not receiving any kind of treatment.

These cases were selected because first of all they were considered "successful" cases according to evaluations immediately following the termination of therapy and also at follow-up studies a year later. The reason for confining this study to "successful" cases only was to attempt to gain some insight into the children's perception of the experience, their interpretation of it, and their memory of it. Those cases wherein the child was the only recipient of therapy were selected to keep to a minimum any reactions to the therapeutic experience by other members of the child's family. If no other member of the family had had a therapeutic experience they were not likely to influence the child's impressions of it by their conversation; so that the attitudes toward the therapy which the child expressed would be the child's own attitudes.

## Children's Comments During Therapy

The first group of quotations from the children are drawn from recorded material during the play therapy sessions — those spontaneous comments that came forth unsolicited as the children were experiencing the therapeutic play sessions.

Betty, aged four, was referred for play therapy because she was "a feeding problem, had nightmares, had temper-tantrums, could not get along with other children because she was so bossy and scrappy" according to the mother's report. Betty was seen by the same therapist twice a week for a period of fifteen weeks. She was seen individually during one of her weekly sessions and at the other time in a group of three. Betty was told that each week for the group meetings she could bring with her two other people. One of the significant developments in her therapeutic experience emerged from her selection of the other two members. During one of the group sessions at which time she had brought two girls — one her age, the other girl a year older — the children were finger-painting. Each child had a complete set of colors but Betty continually reached over for the paints the five-year-old was using. The five-year-old protested once in a very mild manner and then accepted Betty's behavior apparently not being very concerned about it. Finally Betty stopped pushing her fingers through the paint, rested her hands in the middle of the paper and said, "I wonder why I want every jar of paint she has? I wonder why? It isn't the color because I have red, too. And it isn't because I haven't got any because I have just as much as she has. I guess it's just because she's got it and I wanta take it away from her and I wonder why I do that." She looked straight into the therapist's eyes for a long time. "I never thought about why I do what I do before," she added slowly.

At another time during Betty's individual play therapy session she encountered the limitations that had been set up by the therapist. She fussed and argued and expressed her feelings quite vividly. The therapist reflected back to Betty the emotionalized attitudes that she was expressing. Then suddenly Betty stopped storming around and said angrily to the therapist, "You don't care if I feel mad. You don't care if I feel glad. You don't care if I don't feel anything I do believe! All right then! I'll feel all my feelings any old way they are!"

Jerry, aged seven, had just been indulging in creating a mess in the playroom — spilling water on the floor, throwing sand around. This was a new expression of Jerry's feelings. When he had begun therapy his behavior had been rigid, repressed, fearful. Suddenly he stopped pouring the water on the floor and cried out joyfully, "Oh every child just once in their life should have this chance to spill themselves out all over without a 'Don't you dare! Don't you *dare! Don't you dare!'*"

During a contact several weeks later he said to the therapist, "It used to be I thought everybody was out to get me but I guess I been wrong. All people aren't bad people. *Some* people are *good*. You're good. Sometimes I'm good. Maybe — Say, listen — Maybe *all* people are some good and some bad just like me. Maybe you are. Maybe *even Mom!*"

Harold, eight years old, had been a behavior problem. He had spent several weeks in "destructive" play in the play room. On this particular day he rushed across the room and threatened to break the window — then as suddenly he stopped. "No," he said to the therapist. "I don't have to break that window. I don't have to go on acting like I always have. I don't have to do *everything* just because I get the idea to do it. I don't *have* to hit people just because I feel like hittin' 'em. I guess it's because I didn't know before I could just feel mad and in a while it would go away — the bein' mad and I would be happy again. I can change. I don't have to stay the same old way always because I can be different. Because *now I can feel my feelings!*"

These brief excerpts are examples of the child's present awareness of his experiences — are examples of his coming to terms with himself. He has stated himself in his play. He has seen himself in a different perspective. He seems to be developing a different self-concept as a result of his experience. This would seem to indicate that "insight" is the result of a personal experience wherein the child sees new meanings in his feeling reactions.

Joe, aged eight, suddenly stopped in the midst of his play and walked up to the therapist demanding, "Why do you just say what I say and think only what I think? I guess I can guess why you do. I'm the little me and you're all of the other people in the world. You're my big shadow that I can make move this way and that and I can see just what I am being."

Mike, aged seven, cried out in sheer ecstasy, "Oh what fun this is to have bought up the whole world and owned it all for a whole hour on one day every week!"

Joan, aged five, had been very timid and shy and withdrawn. As the therapy progressed she gained courage to be herself and one day cried out, "It's *me* saying 'I will!' It's *me* saying 'I won't. It's *me* saying *everything* I think about and no slaps. Do you know who I am?"

"Who are you?' asked the therapist.

"I'm a little girl just five years old who can stretch up so big I reach clear around my world and hug it up in my arms." (She swept out her arms and gathered up the family of dolls, the little car, the toy animals — every little toy she could manage to scoop up.) "And I can shrink down to be a baby and suck on my bottle and crawl around." (She dropped the toys, grabbed the nursing bottle, sucked on it and crawled.) "Little and big. Grow and shrink. And feel glad inside out!"

Then there was John, seven years old, not knowing how to handle his freedom. He stood just inside the playroom door and mumbled nervously, "What'll I do? What'll I do?" He was told that in here this hour he could do what *he* wanted to do with the toys and materials — that he could play or not play, which ever way he felt. But John was not able to make a choice and he repeated in a louder voice, "What'll I do?" Then he yelled at the therapist angrily, "Why don't you tell me what to do? Why do you let me just *stand* here? *You tell me what to do!"*

"So you want me to tell you what to do! Well in here, John, it's up to *you* to decide what you want to do."

John screamed at the therapist. "But I'm *telling you to tell* me what to do!"

"Yes," said the therapist. "You want me to tell you what to do and I am telling you to decide whether you want to stand there or do something else."

John's face grew red with anger. "I don't want to just stand here," he cried. "And I don't want to do something else. I want *you to tell me* (sobs) what — I *should* — do —"

"There isn't anything that you *should* do in here, John, That's why I don't tell you what to do. Because it doesn't make any difference what you *do* just so it's what you want to do."

John's voice dropped to a whisper and he said. "I'm afraid."

"Are you afraid, John?" the therapist said gently.

"Yes," John whispered. He came closer to the therapist and took her hand. *"Mommy* always tells me what to do," he said.

"I see, John, Mommy tells you what to do and when someone else tells *you* to make up your own mind, then it scares you?"

"Yes," John said. There was a long silence. Finally John said, "Would it be all right if I played with that little red car?"

"Yes, if you want to," the therapist replied. John edged over to the little car and began to play with it.

Five months and twenty-one contacts later John spontaneously referred to this first contact.

"Do you remember that scared silly little kid who was afraid of letting himself do what he really wanted to do?" he said to the therapist. "I can hardly remember that *baby.* 'Tell me what to do,' " he mimicked. "Scared as a rabbit then, that was me. But not any more. 'Cause now I know what I can do — what I want to do — what I will do."

These children's references to the experiences they were having at the time this new self-awareness was emerging occurs quite often during therapy. The manner in which the children express such thoughts — the tone of voice, the gleam in their eyes, the spontaneous gestures and expressions indicate that the play therapy experience is an emotional experience that brings about reorganization of meanings, concepts, feelings, self-understanding. It indicates that so-called intellectual insight is the child's awareness of these emotional experiences and that that insight which is effective in bringing about such reorganization always follows the emotional experience of sharpened awareness of the nature of his emotional expression. It raises the question of the relative position of importance between intellectual understanding of cause and effect as determinants of present behavior and the immediate emotional experience the individual has during therapy as the essential dynamic in the process of reorganization of the self.

Are these experiences significant to the children? How might one determine their significance? If we assume that significant experiences are those experiences that change attitudes and behavior; if we assume that they are remembered vividly long after the experience has passed; then it seems we might be able to judge whether or not such experiences are significant to the child. Changes in attitudes and behavior were the criteria upon which the evaluation of the therapy as "successful" had been made. The attempt was then made to do follow-up interviews with some children several years after the therapy had been completed. The therapist who had conducted the therapy sessions personally did the follow-up studies. She had not seen any of the children between the termination of therapy and the follow-up interviews. Quotations from these interviews are presented here for the reader's contemplation. Does it seem to have implications for studying the nature of emotions, personality structure learning theories, educational practices?

*Tom*, whose complete therapy experience was reported in play therapy [1] was interviewed in his school five years after the termination of therapy. Tom was twelve years old when the therapist first saw him. He was seventeen years old at the time of the follow-up. According to school records, Tom was well adjusted and one of the leaders of his class. His health was excellent. He was planning on entering college after his graduation. He recognized the therapist immediately and said, "Oh, you're the puppet-lady!"

"So you remember me as the puppet-lady, do you?" the therapist commented.

"Yes!" Tom laughed. He sat down across the table from the therapist in a small office.

"Yes," Tom said. "I don't think I'll ever forget it. It was a real turning point in my life — although for the life of me I can't figure out why. It's been one of the big mysteries in my life because — well, I never could understand why I did what I did or what happened to me. But I know one thing. It gave me a great deal of satisfaction to make up those puppet plays and put them on for those little kids. I really enjoyed it. And then one day — I remember so plainly — one day right in the middle of one of my plays I thought, '*What the heck am I doing here playing with dolls?*' Because all of a sudden Ronnie lost all his life. Up to that time he was more real than I was and *I* was more like the puppet. And then I thought, '*What the heck! One of me is enough in this world and that's going to be the real me and not a doll.*'"

"So you stopped being a puppet and became a real person, hm?"

"Yes, but it was fun. And yet it wasn't fun. Do you know what I mean? I can remember it as plain as if it was yesterday. Sometimes during those plays I felt really unhappy — and I used to go home and — well, I'd think a lot. Especially about my stepfather and my sister. Incidentally, my sister and I get along fine now. I get along all right with Pop, too. Right now I'm planning on going to college. I can't quite make up my mind what to major in. I'd like to be a doctor — but I can't decide whether to be a human doctor or a horse doctor!" Tom laughed. "Then, of course, there is the problem of the Army. They may get first choice." And Tom continued talking about his plans for the future.

In this follow-up interview the therapist did not ask any questions related to the therapeutic experience — did not initiate any mention of the puppets. However, Tom seemingly remembered the experience vividly even to the name he gave the puppet and recalled it as a significant experience in his life.

## Poor Readers Five Years Later

Five years ago a group of thirty-seven children who were nonreaders were placed in a class with a teacher-therapist to experiment with a therapeutic approach for poor readers [2]. The follow-up study on this group was made by the teacher who visited the school these children were attending. Out of the thirty-seven children in the original class, twenty-four were available for follow-up studies. Five of these children were "honor roll students," having a record of "straight A's." Edna, Nancy, Ronald, Balcolm and Roger had secured that record. In a city-wide scholarship test Ronald and Balcolm scored first and second place. With the exception of Blair, Kenneth, Rollo and Jamey, the other children had attained reading skill that was adequate for their grade placement.

When the therapist visited the classroom at a time five years after the experiment the classroom teacher asked the children if they recognized the visitor. All of the children who had been in the remedial class immediately indicated that they did. The following conversation was stenographically recorded.

Nancy: "I know you. You were the teacher who taught us how to read with hammer and saws."

Balcolm: "I remember the family of dolls and our doll house. We had fun."

Jack: "I remember one day we buried all the mother and father dolls." (Laughter).

Ann: "Remember the puppet shows we put on? I won't ever forget that funny show Blair put on about the principal!"

Bill: "I think the music we had then was wonderful. I could float way out into space on it."

Dick: "I remember that year. It was the only time in my life I ever felt happy where I was." (He still had a tense voice and a pale unhappy face). "I remember we could pound and pound and pound."

Delores: "The paintings we did with our hands."

Arlene: "You were good to us. You let us do what we wanted to do."

Dick: "It didn't last though."

Blair: "Nope. But it was fun while it did last."

Then the talk veered away from the past experiences and into the present.

The therapist then asked each child who had been in that class to write the one thing they remembered best about that semester.

The children wrote brief comments.

Jack — Freedom.

Leonard — We could play.

Bill — Everybody was nice to one another.

Donald — We could do what we wanted to do.

Jerry — I learned to read.

*Edna — I found out I could make friends and I stopped being afraid of everything.

Mack — I learned to read.

Tommy — I liked to go to school then.

Allen — We played together and had fun no matter what we had to do.

Ann — The music.

Delores — To play.

Roger — So many many interesting things to do.

*Dick — I lost my feeling of being lonesome and I felt that I wasn't all bad and that some people liked me and didn't shove me away.

Ronald — We were always doing something.

Blair — We could move without being yelled at and do things kids like to do.

Arlene — I loved the clay and paints and the stories.

*Jim — I remember how I came to feel like I was worthwhile.

Balcolm — I liked the wood-working we could do.

Barbara — We had so much fun.

Jamey — There were so many things to do. Not just lessons.

Burt — The chance to choose and plan our own time.

Becky — Always something exciting to do.

*Jenny — I was afraid of everything and everybody but I got

over being an afraid person because I wasn't afraid of anybody in there like I used to be.

All the children seemed to recall their experiences in that classroom vividly. They remembered for the most part the things they did, the activities they engaged in, the things they learned. However, the four children (*) who had had individual play therapy sessions after school described the experience in terms of personal feelings or attitudes toward themselves. This is a very brief sampling, but the discrimination of the experience as related by the four children who had had individual play therapy indicates that the important element to them was not the use of the materials but an awareness of changing attitudes toward the self.

### Sam — A Case of Social Isolation

*Sam* was twelve when first seen by the therapist. The reasons for his referral were "failing in school although very bright and an excellent academic record behind him. Daydreams, sleeps most of the time, or reads or goes to the movies. Eats continually, wets the bed, has no friends, never talks to anyone, just briefly, almost rudely answers questions and then turns his back on the person. Seems very unhappy. Careless about his clothes. Always losing things."

Three years later at the age of fifteen Sam came in for a follow-up interview.

"Talking and whittling a piece of wood — that's all I remember doing. Telling you about stories I had read, shows I had seen, what I had eaten, how I liked eating and sleeping and being by myself. Telling you that and all the time thinking something else. That here I was preferring to keep awake and talk to you — to talk about anything at all just to be able to come there and talk to you — and saying something else to myself all the time. Saying to myself that I didn't really like the way I was living away off in a corner of the world by myself — burying myself in a book — or in a movie — or dreaming — or sleeping. What did I do it for then? I asked myself. This time I spent talking to you was the most wonderful important experience I ever had. Why did it seem like that to me? I asked myself. Certainly the things I told you weren't important or wonderful. It was a kind of mechanical talk that I didn't even listen to myself. The important thing was that I was *talking* to someone. I was *doing it*. And I got up early in the morning to keep that appointment. I spent two hours on the train coming and two hours going — five hours all together of real hard effort in all kinds of weather and I never missed once. Why did I? Because I wanted to get away from that dead-alone person I was and I wanted to be a together-person in a real people's world." And the follow-up immediately following therapy indicated that he had achieved that goal. He made friends, stopped going to the movies so often and discontinued the excessive reading. He began to diet. He went out with his friends to a neighborhood Boys Club and started a hobby of leather-tooling. He stopped wetting the bed.

Sam maintained these gains.

## Maryellen — A case of Pseudo-Retardation

*Maryellen* was fourteen years old when she was seen by the counselor. She was referred by a physician who questioned the diagnosis of "progressive feeble-mindedness" which had been given to her by two psychologists and a psychiatrist. She was a seriously disturbed young girl who took no initiative in anything, had dropped out of school, who had no friends, who sat and either sulked or giggled, who refused to get up in the mornings and who behaved in the helpless manner of a very dependent five-year-old. During her counseling contacts she painted with the finger paints and gradually dropped the superficial giggling and meaningless chatter. There followed long periods of uninterrupted silences. Finally she began to talk to the counselor. After six months she was back in school, making friends, conversing intelligently with other people, adjusting satisfactorily at home and at school. When the therapist called her to make an appointment for a follow-up interview, Maryellen said she was working after school and couldn't come in but she would write a letter to the counselor about her memory of the experience. The follow-up was three years after the conclusion of therapy. Here is a copy of the letter she wrote:

Dear Friend:
 I remember you because you were the first person who ever believed in me — who didn't think I was all bad — who didn't think I was silly — who took the time to try to find out how I felt about things. And you never dug into me like I was a person without feelings. You let me have my own world my own way and did not try to snatch it away from me without first making me feel strong enough to go live in another world or to seek a new world or to go without a world for a while until I found a new one. It was as though you said to me you can hate and you can be sad and you can feel cheated by your mother because that was the way I felt. And so I didn't have to lie to you or feel ashamed because I was me. I painted pictures all the time because then I could think in peace. And the quietness was around both of us like a clean white shawl giving us

warmth but not smothering. I washed myself clean in that silence. I crept back bit by bit into the world of color. It had been all black and grey before. I wasn't being sullen when I was quiet with you. I wasn't being hateful that day when I finally said I felt hate. I remember saying it deep inside myself, with the tips of my fingers scratching on the slippery paper. This is hate I feel. It had been a numbness but it was not really numbness. It was not no-feeling. It was *hate* so big I was afraid of it. But that day I let the word creep outside of me that first time and it scared me. But it didn't scare you. I remember it because it struck me like a bolt of lightning. I am a hater, I thought. This is wicked and bad. Then they separated — the feelings and me. I thought you must *know* I have good reasons for my hate even though I hadn't told you then. Another time I mentioned my fear. It was then that I learned that a feeling was a changeable thing because I *felt* it change — in my heart, in my arms, in my head, in my legs. It came out and twisted and turned and lost its sharp edges. From that day on I was a free person because I could separate my feelings from the people I felt about. Then I began to look at myself and try and figure myself out. I got so I liked myself better. I got so I liked people. I got so I liked the world. I think this all happened to me because you gave me a chance to believe in *me*. And then I felt I *was* worthwhile. I have grown up since I saw you last. As I think back about it you didn't seem to do a thing but be there. And yet a harbor doesn't do anything either, except to stand there quietly with arms always outstretched waiting for the travellers to come home. I came home to myself through you.

Your friend,
Maryellen

## Summaries of the Children's Comments

Considering the material that has been presented in this paper, the following observations, interpretations and inferences are presented for the reader's evaluation.

In each case the child gave evidence of remembering the play therapy experience vividly and in detail. Also, the therapist noted that although she had had dozens of child clients during the past several years she too remembered as vividly as the child and recalled minute details of his play activities and expressions when once again face to face with the child. This indicates that there was a high degree of concentration and focus on the individual child during the therapeutic sessions.

There is also obvious self-reference in each case indicating an awareness of a changed attitude toward the self. The children in recalling the therapeutic experience explained it as an experience that brought with it sudden awareness of what they were feeling and thinking.

In the excerpts from the original play contacts the children's explanations, pulled out of context for illustration, present this coming to terms with the self in the children's own words.

"I never thought about why I do what I do, before."

"I'll feel my feelings any old way they are."

"Oh, every child just once in their life should have this chance to spill out all over."

"I don't have to stay the same old way always because I can be different. Because I can feel my feelings."

"I'm the little me and you're the big me. I'm all of myselves and you're all of the other people in the world."

"Oh, what fun it is to have bought up the whole world and owned it all for a whole hour on one day every week."

"It's *me* saying 'I will.' It's *me* saying 'I won't.' It's *me* saying everything I think about and no slaps."

"Do you remember that scared silly little kid who was afraid of letting himself do what he really wanted to do? I know now what I can do — what I want to do — what I will do —"

In the follow-up studies the children give their perceptions of the experience at a later date. There is nothing to indicate that the children had the insight and self-awareness during the therapy which they ascribe to it at a date several years later. However, the play therapy experience was recalled with sufficient accuracy in their recital (as was checked by examination of the records of the therapy for confirmation or refutation) to justify the conclusion that the later interpretations stemmed from the feelings that the experience created. Perhaps the feelings were not clarified by the children at the time they experienced the therapy. In retrospect, perhaps, the rational explanations emerged — especially in the cases of Tom, Sam, Maryellen, and Dibs.

The relationship between the experience and the children's interpretation of it are more apparent in the follow-up interviews. Each quotation is from an interview with a different child.

"And then one day — I remember so plainly — one day right in the middle of one of my plays I thought, 'What the heck am I doing here playing with dolls?' Because all of a sudden Ronnie lost his life. Up to that time he was more real than I was and I was more like the puppet. And then I thought, 'What the heck! One of me is enough in this world and that's going to be the real me and not a doll.'"

"I guess I found out that I could be what I wanted to be and how I felt was more important than how I looked. I couldn't do that though until I believed it myself by the way I felt."

"But once I broke loose I could do anything I wanted to do."

"I was *afraid* to really *do* anything. But it was nice to sit there and think maybe I could."

"What was it stopped me so I couldn't be a doing-person?"

"Maybe I was playing out my war with my mom and pop."

"I wanted to get away from that dead-alone person I was and I wanted to be a together person in a real people's world."

"It was then that I learned that a feeling was a changeable thing because I felt it change — in my heart, in my arms, in my head, in my legs. It came out and twisted and turned and lost its sharp edges. From that day on I was a free person because I could separate my feelings from the people I felt about."

"And the feeling I got before I was through — a feeling that meant a lot to me — a feeling that to you and to me I made sense and I was a person worthwhile."

"I built my world there . . . I was afraid because I didn't know what you would do . . . I didn't know what I'd do. But you just said, 'This is all yours, Dibs. Have fun! Nobody's going to hurt you.'"

This verbatim material from the children presents data that could be studied and analyzed and interpreted in different ways. It would be interesting and helpful to do a similar study interviewing children whose therapeutic experiences had been of a different type than that which had been employed with the children in this follow-up study.

It would also be interesting to do a similar study interviewing children whose therapeutic experiences had been evaluated as failures.

Certainly every therapist can cite examples of "other ways" the play situations might have been handled. Perhaps the use of different techniques during the sessions might have brought forth different results. The therapists who stress the importance of interpretation might think it would have been an important addition to the therapeutic experiences.

However, instead of focusing attention on the "might have beens" there is a great need for us to record completely and analyze as accurately and objectively as is possible with our present research tools, or other tools we might devise, what actually *has* happened and by comparing the results of all our research hope to improve our understanding of the therapeutic process and devise more effective ways of conducting the therapy sessions.

## Conclusions

One might conclude that the therapeutic experiences for these children were emotional experiences that sharpened their awareness of themselves as "feeling" individuals — and through these "feeling" experiences they gained an understanding of themselves, of their emotional natures — and with this understanding came a control over their emotions and feelings. It might be interpreted as sudden change in self-perception — an instantaneous reorganization so that Maryellen, and Sam, and Tom, and the others not only experienced a change in their concept of themselves but were aware of the change and could go beyond "thinking what I might do" and "do it" — could stop dreaming in a passive world and become active in a living world — could stop being an unreal person and live effectively in a realistic world — become "real persons in a doing-world."

If we define adjustment as being free to act spontaneously, free to be one's self, "a doing-person," "a real person," "a together-person in a real world," a person who "can feel their feelings," we might say that these children had achieved adjustment by achieving a synthesis in self-awareness, self-acceptance, and self-actualization.

In the cases which were referred to in this paper the role of the therapist had not been clearly defined to the children. This therapist in an attempt to establish the kind of relationship with the child that stressed noncritical acceptance of the child from the beginning of the therapy did not explain the situation as anything other than a play experience. As a matter of fact, this therapist regards "play therapy" as *a play experience that is therapeutic because it provides a secure relationship between the child and the adult so that the child has the freedom and room to state himself in his own terms exactly as he is at that moment in his own way and in his own time.* Therefore, since the child has had no explanation of the therapist's role he is free to interpret it as he will. The children's comments in regard to the therapist are interesting. She becomes symbolic of "other people in the world," of "the big me," of "my big shadow that I can make move this way and that and I can see just what I am being," of "grown-ups," of "freedom," of "the first person who ever liked me or who ever was kind to me," as "someone to talk to," as "the first person who ever believed in me — who didn't think I was all bad — who didn't think I was silly — who took the time to try to find out how I felt about things," as "The Sand Lady," as "the lady of the wonderful playroom who said, 'This is all for you. Have fun . . . Have fun. Nobody's going to hurt you.'" This seems to indicate that these therapeutic experiences were immediate, active experiences for these children — and that it was not necessary for them to clarify their "problem" and so to work out a logical, rational solution to the problem because this was not "problem solving" therapy. The case of Sam and the case of Martha give some evidence of this. Sam spent his time during the therapy sessions talking as "mechanically" as he could so that he could *experience* to the fullest the *relationship* with the therapist. Martha did not recall what, if anything, had been discussed. She was aware only of impressions and feelings. And Maryellen's letter to the therapist is a sensitive description of an adolescent girl's emotional awakening. "And the quietness was around both of us like a clean white shawl giving us warmth but not smothering. I washed myself clean in that silence. I crept back bit by bit into the world of color. It had been all black and gray before."

And so it seems that we might better be able to answer some of the questions that tease and tantalize so many psychiatrists, social workers, psychologists, and educators today if we study carefully the objectively recorded interviews of many children during therapy and in follow-up interviews. For it seems that we are not studying material that is of interest only to therapists but to all those people who are interested in learning more about the child — of how he thinks and how he feels and how he learns. There is an honesty and a frankness and a vividness in the way children state themselves. A consideration of this kind of material might add to our studies of human behavior and personality development that might give to us all ways of understanding how feelings can "twist and turn and lose their sharp edges" and perhaps bring a bit of functional psychology to bear upon the problems of all interpersonal relations — and make a contribution that will enhance the efforts of educators who are beginning to think of ways of implementing theories of building and living in a world community.

**References**
1. Axline, Virginia M., *Play Therapy*, Boston: Houghton Mifflin, 1947.
2. Axline, Virginia M., "Nondirective Therapy for Poor Readers," *J. Consult. Psychol.*, 1947, **11**, 61.

# Participation in Therapy

FREDERICK H. ALLEN

The child's participation in a therapeutic experience designed to help with his emotional and behavior disturbances is the subject of this paper, which is not concerned with various theories regarding how these difficulties arose. I shall confine this discussion to the child's own participation and the steps and stages many of them go through as this experience comes to have meaning to them.

It is difficult to generalize on a situation that is used so differently by children who have different needs and capacities to utilize a relation with another for their own development. But in spite of the difficulties, there are certain elements, common both in the structure and in frequent patterns of response and movement. It is the discussion of some of these common patterns that seems possible and useful, and from which might accrue a somewhat clearer picture of the child's participation in achieving change through a specially designed relationship.

It is not possible to evaluate and understand a behavior problem in a child as existing apart from the important relationships of his life. It is equally difficult to think of therapeutic work with a child unrelated to the more complete living picture that makes up the child's reality, and out of which emerges the emotional turmoil requiring help.

The understanding of the growth picture is acquired through knowing the dynamics of the living structure within which the child moves toward achieving a separate self. Since therapy takes place within a relationship and is a unique growth experience, the process can be better evaluated as the dynamics of its structure are understood.

American child guidance clinics have found that the best therapeutic work with children follows where both parent and child participate in the process. They come to a clinic together to work on a problem which, in varying degrees, involves both of them. Usually the child is *brought* and has participated very little in the starting of this new experience, which involves meeting and going off with a new and strange person. He comes in the setting of his own emotional turmoil and with various types of explanation. But usually he is brought with the implication that he needs to be changed and that this new place and person will be the means of bringing that change about. When he arrives, he finds that it involves going off by himself and leaving the mother.

## Dynamics of Separation

From the start the child meets a new separation experience — leaving behind of his usual supports. He begins this new relation with what he has in himself, which allows him to come to grips with what he is in himself. These factors give this unique relationship a significance from the start that is closely associated with the growth turmoil which made treatment necessary.

A brief tracing of five interviews with a young child will illustrate some of the dynamics of the structure in which the therapeutic process moves. A two-year-old boy, caught in a determined struggle with his mother, begins treatment in the midst of a deadlock in which he would not allow the mother to leave or do anything which did not include him. Two determined people, mother and child, come together for help, and peacefully they are together in the waiting room before they leave for their separate appointments. There is little protest the first time over leaving the mother when the child goes with the therapist. A half hour follows, with the child having little to do with the therapist but determined to go when he wants, which he is unable to do because he cannot open the door. He fights the door, but does not ask for help, which is not offered until his time is up. The next time, mother and child leave for their separate appointments together. This evokes a vigorous protest which is carried on before and after leaving the mother. Then he yields, has a few contented minutes, and is reunited with the mother. The third hour, as the mother prepares to leave him, he fights against letting this happen, again yields, has a very happy time and includes the therapist in all he does, following which he is taken back to the mother. The fourth hour finds him starting to leave without protest, then protesting mildly but comes along, and a natural period follows. The fifth and last time, he allows the mother to leave for her appointment, comes to his period in a natural way, and leaves in a way that clearly indicates he is through. There was a quick change in his behavior reactions, and his relation with the mother was established on a growing basis.

The structure provides an experience in separation — allowing both assertion against and yielding around the person of the therapist. This structure is important in all work with children and provides the framework, guided and directed by the skill of the therapist, but made dynamic by the feeling which the child is able to bring to it, and by the understanding and guidance the therapist can give.

Viewed from the child's participation in the building of this structure, it can be divided into three parts which provide a natural sequence. It begins with the child entering and becoming engaged in this relation. Following, is the use he can make of this experience for his own self-differentiation within the relationship established. Finally, there is the child's participation in bringing this experience to a close.

Irrespective of the philosophy and technique of the therapist, every child undergoing treatment around his emotional turmoil will go through these three phases, each of which has therapeutic importance. The value of the first is frequently overlooked because of regarding it as a preliminary to therapy rather than an important aspect of therapy. And the growth value of the last phase is probably the least understood and the least utilized because of the common feeling that it is the therapist who determines ending and lets the child go because of the feeling he has finished.

## Beginning Phase

The child is taken at the point he is at in his own development and he will react with his own feeling to meet this experience. It may bring out the overt fear that emerges around each new experience which requires leaving behind the supports he never has been able or willing to let go. He may enter this relation with a guarded, cautious attitude that allows little if any participation. He may attempt to assume complete control by an assertive, aggressive attitude which may be directed against the therapist or be a part of his activity which aggressively shuts him out. He may try to establish a side of himself that is completely adequate and then show he needs no help from anyone. He can do all his own changing, or even prove those changes have occurred before he came. But the important fact to be understood is that the child starts this experience with his own feeling, whatever form it may take, and, in putting his own feelings into it, the experience immediately takes on a significance that links it with his growth problem. The therapist then has the opportunity to give meaning and direction to this new growth experience because he is a part of it. He is in the position to give immediacy to the child's turmoil and help him to a more livable balance as this relation is established, as it moves and, finally, as it ends.

He begins to discover certain unique features of this new experience. Here he may be afraid without having efforts made immediately to remove his fear. He has met with a person who understands and accepts both his need and his right to be afraid without melting before it. He finds that he can be aggressive and hostile and, at the same time, finds a person who can both accept the feeling and give limits to its expression. He finds a person who is interested in what he says, in what he is, and is not trying to squeeze him into a preconceived mold. He can have his own power without having it overwhelmed by the greater power of another. He comes expecting to be changed and finds a person interested and related to what he is now. Truly, this is a unique experience which is started with himself in the center of it.

This beginning period, which cannot be clearly demarcated from the second, may be very short. The child may never get beyond it, but the child who can bring a good deal of feeling into his first hour or hours is usually the one who quickly feels himself a part of this new relation and, through focusing his turmoil, there begins the second period of treatment. On the other hand, a more deeply disturbed child who either feels too complete in himself or too broken up, may throw himself very quickly and totally into this experience and move very slowly toward a more livable balance.

## Middle Phase

In various ways a child begins to use this new experience he has moved into, and the skill of the therapist in guiding that use to a better integrated self, constitutes the important material of this second period. The child establishes himself on whatever basis he can, but always on the feeling and activity that he puts into it. He does not put this feeling into a vacuum but into a real relation, given direction and meaning by the therapist's skill to allow the child a real expression of himself with one who can maintain his own realness and is not swept away by the child's projection, his fear and his struggles to control.

The child begins to move with a variety of reactions, of which I can mention only the more common. The child comes with the implication that he is to be changed, which may be associated with a feeling of wanting that to happen. But the participation in change so that it has the realness which can only come from within may be where the therapeutic difficulty arises.

The most natural reaction is for children to set their own strength or will against this external threat or force. Then they discover an individual who is not trying to change them, which leaves them with more participation in the process of their own change. But that may serve to focus the struggle and make it more intense through the child's projecting all the cure or change on the therapist and retaining the struggle against that which has been projected. For example, a fighting, negative child with very neurotic eating habits and clinging tenaciously to his mother, maintains in his therapeutic relationship this type of projection: "You tell me why I don't eat better. You are the doctor, and it is your job to cure me." This is a more blatantly maintained projection than is usually encountered and spread over most of his activity. He fights against accepting any responsibility for himself.

Many children move toward a more responsible feeling about themselves as they are able to put so much struggle into this experience, and through finding both the value and limitations of their power. Many can reach a point described by one child who, early in treatment, described this projection when he emphasized, "You understand me," and his own part in being changed by that understanding. But he moved on with this when he said, "When I first came to you, I thought the most important thing was to get things out to you. But now I know the important thing is to get them back in me." The mere release or getting out of feeling has little value therapeutically. It is the incorporation of that feeling into himself and the ability to be responsible for its use and direction that constitute growth. The boy has found from his own experience that this is true.

The phenomenon of projection takes other forms and provides further illustration of how a child can use this experience for his own natural growth. The child frequently identifies the therapist as being his projected bad self which he has had difficulty in assimilating into his own more complete feeling about self. The cure is then directed toward this projected side of himself as an external. For example, a six-year-old boy with many fears associated with being left alone, going to school, etc., has struggled hard against some of the realities of growing up. In the midst of this difficulty, he starts treatment and, at the beginning, experiences a good deal of anxiety which he handles by saying, "I will only stay a minute and then go back to my mother." He is able to stay, even though afraid, and as he goes on he begins to be afraid, not of coming, but of the fact that he is beginning to like the therapist. He needs to reassure himself that he likes his mother better. Then he says, "I have been seeing you enough. I will go and stay with my mother." But his desire to stay is stronger than the impulse to go. After about four interviews he has really gotten into this experience and has begun to be much more assertive and demanding. In the midst of the struggle, he announces he has become the doctor and that the therapist is the bad person whom he is going to cure. This had been preceded by his own ability to be a little bad and by associating bigness with badness. "Big boys are bad." Also, he was moving toward bigness against which so much of his struggle has been directed. "A long time ago I was a baby, and now I am a big boy."

When he begins to assert and prove his bigness by his desire to control and fight against limitations, he reverses the role and makes the therapist the sick person, and no one but himself knows what the trouble is. For several weeks he actively maintains this projection, insisting, "You are the bad boy." Even while being able to experience some of his own assertiveness (badness) he fights any interpretation that accepts the badness as his own. His activity was the indication of the taking back into himself of that side which at the start he had had to disown.

Through the testing out of his own power he had found that he could accept his own difference from another power that could be bigger than his own. And, around the growth toward a more real feeling of his own bigness, he was ready to take part in the ending of a relation in which he had found himself.

I have not said much about the content that the child brings in. Verbal and motor expressions of himself in play and conversation may be directly concerned with immediate realities and the whole experience may be carried on the content of his immediate hour. Other children reveal through a rich phantasy life the feelings about themselves and the use they are making of this relation to acquire a more livable unity in themselves. Others may use outside experiences and relations to handle their relation with the therapist. Their play may be a means of maintaining control, and a projection of their feeling as an external symbol of themselves. It may be their means of maintaining an isolated totality that tries to shut out any invasion of a force that may break it up. Or the activity may be the medium that not only allows a freer experiencing of self but, at the same time, brings the therapist into closer rapport. Naturally, it is the skill and sensitivity of the therapist that takes whatever content the child is able to bring out and gives the growth value to what is going on.

The changes that children see and feel in themselves through this second phase, stir both puzzlement and anxiety. A child may come for treatment struggling against being changed and, through such struggle, begin to feel change. It seemed a little like magic to one child who had struggled a good deal to maintain his own separateness. In the midst of this he brought out the fact that he was feeling better and added, "But you don't do anything." It is this not "doing anything" that is sometimes incorrectly called passivity, whereas it is a very active process, active in terms of meeting the child's own feeling, not in putting one's own force or interpretation and urge into it.

## Final Phase

Just as it is the child's participation in the beginning that gives significance to that aspect of therapy, so it is his participation in bringing it to a close that makes this phase significant as an aspect of the therapeutic movement. At the start the child goes through the experience of separating from his old supports and relations. In the ending phase, he goes through the experience of bringing a meaningful relation to an end and separating from it.

During treatment, a child moves toward a more responsible feeling about himself. He has found what he can begin to be within himself and can maintain and live out that feeling in this unique relation. Ending signalizes a more complete acceptance of this responsibility and may stir some of the same feeling that characterized the beginning.

It is common for children to react to ending with an ambivalent attitude — a readiness and desire to end and a struggle against it. A child can indicate in various ways his readiness to move on. The therapist's skill and belief in the meaning of that material helps the child to act. His wanting to act stirs the uncertainty and fight against letting it happen. "I will come fifty more times," is the frequent reaction of a child ready and anxious to finish in two or three more visits.

Some children relive the whole experience around ending. In this way, they seem quickly to recapitulate all that they have gone through as a means of being surer where they are. They may do this by going back to forms of activity and behavior prominent in the first interviews. I will give one example that is particularly revealing of how a child makes the ending a significant experience rounding out his movement.

A very seriously disturbed boy of seven went through a rather long treatment period. He brought an unusually rich and disturbed phantasy life characterized by an emphasis on old things and everything being destroyed. He had become a very much better organized child and was ready to end treatment. Around ending, he went back to his earlier type of play which he had left for a more constructive type of play. Then he recalled more specifically his first visit and wanted the date, and mentioned for the first time that he had come because he couldn't get along with the kids — "Now I can."

In the last interviews, he wanted to go back over what he had done in the first ones. So, with the record, I went back with him. It would be difficult to give you the feeling the boy put into this and the significance it had for him. After a half hour he announced, "I know what I want to do," and proceeded to duplicate the activity of his first hour when he had built an old dilapidated house which was falling to pieces. There is a baby in the house and, as the roof falls in, someone grabs the baby and saves it. The mother stands there and just as it falls a rich man comes along and saves them. He is carrying them away when a robber comes and starts to rob them. The rich man grabs the gun, kills the robber and the family is as happy as they have always been. The rich man throws the gun away because he will not need it anymore. A moment later he says goodbye.

In therapy, if we can be sensitive to what the child brings to this experience and ready to respond in terms of our own values and understanding, we are in a position to make this experience real for the child and one that can lead to a more livable, organized self. We do have to start where the child is, and maintain our basic orientation to the uses that he is able to make of this experience. When we lose that and turn our preoccupations to the child that was, we take ourselves out of the essentially dynamic element which is our relation to him and what he is moving toward as a result of his capacity to make this relation a living and real experience.

# School Centered Play-Therapy

EUGENE D. ALEXANDER

There were times when Chucky sat in the corner with his back to other children. Sometimes he would stand up and shake his hands as if they were foreign appendages stuck onto his body. There were occasions when he would desperately hug the teacher's leg and hide his face in her dress. At other times he had a faraway look in his eyes and would not respond at all when spoken to. Often when you talked to him he would answer in irrelevant, unrelated sentences. Yet somehow he was learning to read and much of the time he would sit in his seat trying to take part in classroom activities. There were even occasions when he was seemingly able to share openly in activities with the other children. His teacher had warm feelings for him. She was concerned and worried. She talked with his parents and found that they rationalized his different behavior. The parents also indicated that they did not have time and were not interested in taking him someplace for help. The teacher was desperate. She felt deeply for this child. She knew that he was profiting from his school experience. She wanted to keep him in her class, yet she feared that if he did not get some help very soon it might become more difficult for him to function in the school situation. What was she to do for Chucky? She guessed that he needed some psychotherapeutic help.

## Rationale for Play Therapy

Psychotherapy is most often practiced in either the hospital or the clinic setting. In the hospital the children are usually very severely emotionally disturbed and are treated as medical cases. In the clinic setting it is almost mandatory that the parents participate actively. There are very few facilities available to the relatively mildly disturbed youngster or to the youngster whose parents are accepting of help for their child but not willing to participate. To fill this gap there have been recent attempts to help the child in the school situation. In the school setting it is not necessary to involve the apathetic parent. It is also possible to help the disturbed child who is manageable in the classroom, without upsetting his immediate academic situation. This relieves the load from the other facilities so that they can concentrate upon children with more intensive difficulties. This paper describes one approach to play therapy in the school setting.

Play therapy in the school has a somewhat different emphasis from the way in which psychotherapy is usually conceived. It is an integral part of the educational program and like the rest of the educational program, is not medically oriented. The general goal of education is to increase the individual's knowledge and understanding of the universe and of himself. Educational play therapy concentrates on the latter aspect of this task.

Most children who come for play therapy are referred because they have problems in their relationships with other people. The teacher finds them hostile, withdrawn or possessed of an atypical perception of their environment. Through the one-to-one relationship in the educational play therapy setting the child is given the freedom to express and to explore himself in an accepting climate. Educational play therapy as here conceived is not a method but an attitude. Through creative listening (an involved alertness to underlying feeling and a sensitivity to the meaning of this feeling in the child's existence) and intense empathy the therapist is able to share the fundamental inner experience of the child. By responding in terms of this inner experience, the therapist helps the child struggle through to a better self-concept.

The therapy relationship has the basic essentials of any genuine human relationship. It differs only in that the therapist is able to give his undivided self completely to the child and is totally alert and sensitive to the child's feelings. The therapist shows complete acceptance, faith, hope and trust in the child. This frees the child to express himself openly and to allow his feelings of fear and distrust to emerge. He is able to examine those aspects of his self that he regards as negative as well as the ones he regards as positive and to see them both as meaningful aspects of existence.

This approach to children has been referred to as Relationship Psychotherapy by Moustakas (1959b). In this approach the child is not regarded as mentally ill. There is no effort to change the child, to manipulate him, to categorize him, to adjust him to society. The child is seen as an individual in his own right. It is assumed that he has his own goals, his own needs, his own mode of perceiving and these are respected. Therapy creates a free situation in which the individual is given the opportunity to self-actualize. The basic human tendencies that Maslow (1954, 1962) describes are allowed to emerge. The child needs to expend less energy in defending and protecting himself and can devote more effort in exploring and expressing his potential as a being.

There are times when a sensitive, responsive teacher is able to have a therapeutic relationship with a child. This is frequently quite difficult for teachers because of the large number of children in the class and the teacher's lack of awareness and experience with the possibilities of such an experience. The school play therapist can offer his undivided attention for a 50-minute period once a week. There are no other children demanding the therapist's attention, there are no academic requirements limiting the relationship, and the therapist has been highly sensitized to respond to the feeling tone of the child.

Fortunately for Chucky, (the child mentioned at the beginning of this paper), his school system was one of the few that employed a child therapist as a regular member of the staff. Chucky's teacher discussed his situation with her principal and the school therapist. They decided that psychotherapy would be a helpful experience for the child.

The psychotherapist set a regular time for him and Chucky to meet. The therapist's mode of operation was unique to the public school environment. He worked in several schools and had no permanent room. He carried toys in a suitcase and spread them out in any reasonably quiet room that might be available. He knew that it was the relationship, not the toys, that was the key to emotional growth.

## Therapy Begins

Chucky entered the therapy situation with suspicion and wariness. He did not look directly at the therapist. He went to the corner of the room and began to shake his hands in the air. Then he went to the toys, examined them for a while, and walked to the other side of the room. The therapist said, "You don't feel like playing with the toys today." Chucky looked at the therapist with a surprised expression. He spent most of the rest of the session alternately looking at the therapist and just standing with his inner thoughts. The therapist sensed Chucky's feelings and said, "You're not quite sure what to make of all this. You're surprised that there are not things you have to do." The therapist said very little during the first session. He shared the silence attentively with Chucky. He was alert to Chucky's being. Even though little was said, Chucky and the therapist felt closer to each other by the time the session was over.

The therapist is different from most adults the child has experienced. He listens attentively to what the child has to say and responds with real understanding. He is honest with the child and the acceptance the child experiences is an active one with sincere encounters when limits are reached. The child does not find the therapist demanding of him or threatening, but waiting attentively to share and to explore those things most important to the child.

Chucky began to talk a little bit more each session. A little of his talk hinted about things that raised his anxiety. The walls of the building, storms, big animals, time, all seemed to disturb him. Most of his talk was about irrelevant, unimportant things that had little meaning in his life. Often he would just sit and stare at the clock or at the therapist's watch and call off the time. Soon he was able to sit close to the therapist and to hold onto his watch hand for comfort. This seemed to make him feel more secure and he began to pour out his anxieties. Would the next minute follow this minute or would time stop? Would the walls fall in? How could you be sure that they would stay up? Would a big snake come and eat him? Would the wind blow the building down? The therapist did not try to minimize these fears or to reassure Chucky. He shared Chucky's worries and tried to feel them the way they appeared to Chucky. He made such remarks as, "You want to be sure that the next hour will come," "You are still afraid of the room," "When it is raining outside you want to hide from the storm," "You are afraid of animals you do not know." But primarily the therapist tried to concentrate his whole being on the inner experience Chucky was having. He tried to let this sharing be communicated by the minimal cues that Chucky had learned from his incidental everyday experience.

A play setting is provided because it is in play that the child has been most familiar and comfortable in expressing himself. The toys give the child a means of acting out feelings and experiences which he is incapable of expressing verbally, due not only to their threatening emotional content, but also because of the child's limited experience with the language. The play setting also facilitates the exploration of experiences not accessible to awareness and in fact the greatest growth most often takes place at this level. The child can explore his feelings through the toys until he is ready to explore them more directly in his relationship with the therapist. Toys, in their very existence, usually represent a freeing, playful atmosphere. They are the one means available in everyday life by which the child can escape the restrictions and distortions of the adult world. To find an adult that can enter and share the playful world of toys helps to build up a trusting relationship.

Before Chucky was able to come over to the therapist and to explore his watch, he spent much time examining a toy watch and placing it on a doll's wrist. After he had tested the watch on the doll, he was able to explore the therapist's watch. This examination of the watch initiated a physical closeness to the therapist. This physical closeness in turn initiated a closer relationship that gave Chucky enough security to make a more involved exploration of the toys. At first he spent most of his time arranging the toys in neat order. As he began to feel more free, he started to use the toys more expressively. He shot the guns, moved the cars, played with the toy soldiers and even fed the baby doll. He became less concerned about the neatness of the toys and left them strewn around the room. He even began throwing some of the toys and on several occasions hit the doll. Later on he began to focus on a male puppet. He called it names and would alternately hit it and run from it. Still later he began to call the therapist names and pretended to hit him. On other occasions he came over and sat on the therapist's lap, putting his head on the therapist's shoulder.

The child finds himself in a situation with a very minimum of limit from which he can branch out and discover his true feelings. The limits serve as a superstructure from which he can build rather than a fenced-in enclosure from which he cannot escape. By struggling through the limits the therapist and child come closer to each other and the child gains security in knowing where he stands. The limits emerge from the requirements of the situation and are not arbitrarily imposed in terms of external values. This in itself is a learning experience. The child learns to appreciate realistic structure.

**Testing of Limits**

During the third session Chucky wanted to leave early. The therapist pointed out that he had to remain the full time limit if he came, but did not have to come at all if he so desired. The next session Chucky not only asked to leave early, but tried to sneak out. The therapist had to stand by the door to prevent this. When he came for the following session, Chucky belligerently stated, "I am not going into that old room." The therapist acceptingly said, "If that is what you wish Chucky, it will be all right. You may go back to your classroom if you want." Chucky looked at the therapist in disbelief. The therapist actually had to reassure Chucky that he was free to go. Chucky went back to his classroom. Nevertheless this was the last time that he challenged the time limit. He came promptly and never missed another session for reasons other than illness. The therapist sensed that Chucky was so used to being ordered to do things that a real feeling of freedom was necessary before growth could take place. This resolution of limits also had the effect of bringing the therapist and Chucky closer together. They had faced an issue together and had remained friends.

After Chucky was at ease in the therapy situation and had begun to play freely with the toys, other kinds of limits were necessary. Because the toy budget was small, the therapist could not let the children break toys randomly. Chucky began to toss the toys all over the room. Then he began to jump on them. He smashed one of the little plastic cars. The therapist explained, "I can understand the fun you have in smashing that car, but the school doesn't have enough money to buy new toys. I'll have to ask you not to smash any more toys." Chucky began to smash another car and the therapist again set the limit. Chucky refused to listen and continued to break the car. The therapist quietly said, "Chucky, if you try to break one more toy, that toy will have to be put away." Chucky tried and the therapist removed the item. This continued until half of the items were placed in the suitcase. Chucky then stopped playing with any of the the toys and glared at the therapist. Angrily he said, "You are a mean man. I hate you. I'm not going to come to this dirty old place any more." The therapist sympathized, "I certainly can understand your anger, Chucky. It is natural to feel hurt and angry when you want to do something very much and someone stops you." He added, "You are especially angry at me because I let you do so many other things. You are afraid that my stopping you means I don't like you." Chucky got even more angry and stamped his feet. He again began to throw toys around, but being careful not to break any. The therapist continued to accept Chucky's anger. Finally Chucky tried to break another item and the therapist took it away also. This really aggravated Chucky and he struck the therapist. The therapist held Chucky's arms to prevent Chucky from striking him again. Chucky stamped his feet, screamed and cursed the therapist. "I hate you! I hate you! I hate you!" Still holding Chucky, the therapist said, "You are terribly angry with me and you are being honest about your anger. You have to feel the way you feel and I understand." Chucky relaxed a little and the therapist continued, "I have to stop you from breaking toys and hitting me, Chucky. That has nothing to do with whether I like you or don't like you." A little while later the therapist added, "I know saying it might not mean very much, but, Chucky, I like you very much." After a while Chucky quieted down and sat fingering some toys. He left the therapy session without saying a word.

## Exploring the Relationship

Something had taken place in this session that brought Chucky and the therapist still closer together. They had a real encounter and Chucky discovered that the therapist could accept him even when he was at his angriest. He expressed physical aggression toward the therapist and he was still accepted.

Significant growth does not take place only in the therapeutic situation. The therapeutic situation actually serves as a demonstration experience exposing the child to the possibilities that can emerge from a sincere relationship. It is a guidance experience with the real growth frequently taking place outside of the therapy hour. The therapy experience helps the child to free himself to more open and trusting relationships in everyday life. In therapy he discovers himself to be a worthwhile individual, a person others can like and respect. He begins to have warm relationships with other individuals and each relationship in itself by its very existence is therapeutic. The child has less need to defend or to withdraw. He learns to value the truly human aspects of relationships.

Chucky lost interest in the toys and focused completely upon his relationship with the therapist. He began to approach the therapist physically. He touched all parts of his body, occasionally pinching or twisting, but always stopping when the therapist asked him to. Later he sat on the therapist's lap and hugged him. He began to talk about his family. For several sessions he talked in a hostile manner about his father. He said, "I hate my father." Then one day he told how he had climbed up on his father's lap and how his father had accepted him. His attitude toward his father showed a gradual change and it was obvious from his verbalizations that he was having much more of a mutual sharing relationship with his dad.

Therapy may help the child to become better adjusted to his life situation. On the other hand he may refuse to adjust to those aspects of his life situation which he senses as destructive to his integrity and to his humanity. In this sense a child may emerge in some aspects as more maladjusted after therapy than before. Nevertheless, such maladjustment can be seen as the most wholesome way to respond to an environment that is detrimental to his creative self-actualization.

From Chucky's conversation it appeared that much of his anxiety was related to his father's attempt to control and mold him. Several conversations with Chucky's father confirmed this. Through his interviews with the father the therapist was able to help him become more accepting of Chucky. It was a very difficult experience for both Chucky and his father when Chucky began to assert himself. For the first time they were confronting each other in an open and honest way. Slowly Chucky learned to accept the love that his father had for him and at the same time his father learned to accept Chucky as an individual in his own right who could not be molded into something he was not.

Chucky's new confidence in himself helped him to insist upon his rights, and his father's glimpse of understanding helped him to accept what first appeared to him as defiance.

## Therapist and the Teacher

The therapist does not work in isolation from the rest of the school program. He attempts to create a therapeutic attitude throughout the school system. He relates in an accepting, respecting attitude with other school personnel. He realizes that both the teacher and the parent spend a much longer time with the child and as a result often influence a child's behavior more significantly than the therapist. The therapist shares experiences with the teacher. Because of his on-going relationship with the child he can really share with the teacher in a very concrete way rather than in the more abstract way usually occurring if he were to function in a consultative capacity. By this very intimate sharing he can relate closer to the teacher than he could if he saw the child only occasionally. It is through this sharing that the therapist is able to help the teacher explore herself in relation to all her students to help her develop a more therapeutic attitude toward them.

Chucky's teacher, though warmly concerned about him, was confused and upset about his behavior. Reassurance that Chucky could be lived with, and that she would eventually be able to communicate with him in a more open manner, was not enough. Knowing that the therapist was actively involved in helping the child gave her real security. They were two people deeply involved with Chucky who could mutually share concrete feelings about him. When the teacher talked about Chucky's reluctant attempts to touch her, the therapist knew the deep feelings involved, for he too had lived with them. When the teacher voiced anxieties over Chucky's new ability to be hostile, the therapist shared the development of Chucky's aggressiveness as it was expressed in therapy. As a result, the teacher could see Chucky's hostility was actually a positive expression for him. She could then feel more at ease and accepting of his hostility. This strengthened her interpersonal relationship with him and she was able to make the classroom experience more therapeutic for Chucky. There were also times when the confidence and hope of the teacher helped alleviate the therapist's own shadow of despair. The teacher-therapist relationship as it developed became mutually supportive. Each helped the other with his struggle to help Chucky. In sharing their beings, Chucky, the teacher, and the therapist each became a little more human in his own way. This was reflected in all their other interpersonal relations.

Moustakas (1959a, p. 343) describes this approach to the teachers. "He listened to encourage further exploration on the part of the teacher, but also to understand and learn for himself from the experiences of the teacher; he encouraged the individual teachers to maintain positions they felt were right and valid, but tried to do this without minimizing the value of majority opinion or suggestion; he expressed his point of view from time to time; but encouraged others ... to maintain their own perceptions and convictions; he directly supported individuals ... when he felt their integrity and self-respect were being threatened or destroyed; he encouraged teachers to experiment and try out new ideas that came to them ... and he tried to show his belief in the worth and dignity of each teacher ... his belief in their potentialities as a creative teacher and his acceptance and empathy in response to each expression."

Thus the play therapy program in the schools must reflect the therapist's accepting attitude toward the teacher's experience as well as the experience of the children. Though the school therapist may work with parents, he focuses upon the teacher-child relationship. The therapeutic relationship between therapist and child can act as a catalyst to a therapeutic relationship between teacher and child. The therapist is able to support the teacher in her struggle to accept and to understand the child while he is helping the child learn to relate more comfortably with people in general. The child is helped to make an emotional reorganization to his school environment as a step toward emotional growth at home and in his everyday life.

**References**

Maslow, A. H., *Motivation and personality*, New York: Harper, 1954.

Maslow, A. H., *Toward a Psychology of Being*, Princeton, N. J.; D. Van Nostrand, 1962.

Moustakas, Clark E., "A Human Relations Seminar at the Merril-Palmer School," *Personnel Guid. J.*, 1959, **37**, 342-349. (a)

Moustakas, Clark E., *Psychotherapy with Children, the Living Relationship*, New York: Harper, 1959. (b)

# Filial Therapy

BERNARD G. GUERNEY, JR., LOUISE F. GUERNEY
and MICHAEL P. ANDRONICO

## Historical Introduction

The traditional practice in treating emotionally disturbed young children has been to separate distinctly the child's own therapy sessions from the counseling or psychotherapy offered to the parent. The treatment procedures, regardless of any verbal reassurances to the contrary, have tended to suggest to the parent that his potentials as an ally for ameliorating the child's problems were not taken seriously and that the role he played in the development and continuation of the problem was the important factor.

Filial therapy is a new method for treating emotionally disturbed children up to ten years of age. In contrast to the orientation just depicted, it uses parents as allies — in fact, the agents — for effecting therapeutic change in the child; delegating to the parents functions that have traditionally belonged to therapists. Because of this reversal of the traditional picture, it seems to many an abrupt and startling change. Viewed as a total system, the change is admittedly a radical one; but in addition to having partial historical precedents all the way back to Freud himself, which we cannot go into here, it can be viewed as one of the logical extensions of several historical trends in relation to the theory and practice of psychotherapy (Fidler, Guerney, et al., 1964). In order to place the filial technique in this perspective, we will now briefly describe these trends.

As do professional therapists, the medium that the parents use in filial therapy to effect change is play sessions with the child. The idea that play affords a salutary outlet for troubling emotions has been traced at least as far back as Aristotle (Mitchell and Mason, 1948). In the early

1920's, the systematic utilization of play to facilitate the treatment of emotionally disturbed children was developed independently by Sigmund Freud's daughter, Anna Freud (1946), and Melanie Klein (1950), who was also a Freudian psychoanalyst. The former initially used it largely as a means of facilitating a positive and influential emotional relationship between the therapist and the child. Melanie Klein viewed the specific content of the child's play — for example, the way in which a child made use of toys, the stories a child acted out in playing with dolls — as comparable in many ways to the free associations or dreams of adult psychoanalytic patients, and she directly interpreted the child's actions to him in terms of their hitherto unconscious meanings.

Today, professionals engaged in what has come to be called "play therapy" would agree with their predecessors that the fantasies of children do reflect those emotional concerns that have had and are having the greatest impact on the formulation of the child's personality. They also agree that in his play with others — particularly under the special atmosphere that can be created in play therapy — the interpersonal patterns the child displays reflect important dimensions of his own emotional needs and his perceptions and expectations of other people. They would agree that under the permissive conditions of play therapy the child often returns to events, wishes, or types of interpersonal interaction that have become laden with anxiety or with undischarged emotions of the past, and that the child can use play to release these tensions and emotions in a more satisfying way. In this way he can learn gradually to express and master his emotional responses to experiences that previously frightened him and needed to be repressed — kept outside of his present experience and perceptions.

But many such professionals, possibly the majority, no longer feel that the major benefit to be derived from play therapy is to be achieved by imparting an intellectual understanding to the child as to the "true" meaning of his behavior in the play sessions. There is less reliance, too, in modern thinking, on explaining to the child how events of the child's past are linked to those of the present. There is, instead, an emphasis on the importance of the *relationship* between the therapist and the child as the critical factor in psychotherapy. This conceptual change is traceable to the theories of Rank (1945) that were applied to play therapy by Taft (1933) and Allen (1942).

The development of client-centered therapy by Carl Rogers (1951) supplied more specific methods by which the therapist could foster the type of relationship believed to be especially therapeutic, and at the same time provided a consistent theoretical framework for understanding its importance in the therapeutic process. Work in play therapy consonant with or derived from Rogers' views has been carried out and enriched by such people as Axline (1947), Dorfman (1951), and Moustakas (1953). Central to the client-centered method was the idea that what the therapist needed to impart to the child (or adult) "client" was the feeling that he was completely respected, understood, and deeply and warmly accepted as a worthwhile person by the therapist; that no view or feeling expressed by the child would change this permissive understanding and accepting attitude. This attitude, conveyed to the child, was the essential element that would enable him to choose those paths of self-expression and interpersonal behavior within the therapeutic situation that would enable him to overcome his emotional difficulties and most fully develop his potentialities.

According to this more recent (but by no means universal) view, the therapist's function thus becomes not one requiring knowledge and facility with respect to Freudian psychodynamics, nor, in fact, complicated psychodynamics of any sort. Rather, his function under this orientation is to be able empathically to understand and accept the ideas, wishes, and feelings of the child at any given moment, and to convey this understanding and acceptance to the child. Moreover, Carl Rogers and his followers have carefully described the nature of the therapist's task and his verbal responses. Thus, this type of therapy can be more readily taught than many other types of therapy.

We now go back to Freud and his immediate followers to trace the second historical change that has occurred in orientation toward psychotherapy. The dimension we are concerned with here is the locus of the problem of an emotionally troubled child. One's conception of this locus determines the target and nature of the treatment effort. Following the medical and scientific models prevalent in his time, Freud's emphasis was on the stresses and conflicts that existed within the individual, rather than between individuals. It was the individual's own psyche and the patterns of interaction among the differing aspects of the psyche — id, superego, and ego — that absorbed most of the energies of the Freudians in theory construction and treatment. The patient was, in effect, studied in a state of isolation. Contact with associates of the patient and with family members of patients was kept to a minimum for fear that such contacts would be harmful to the treatment process.

In more recent years, especially since the Second World War, the conceptual focus of psychotherapy with adults has expanded, so that much more attention has been paid to *interpersonal interaction:* relationships between people. Such broadening of theoretical horizons has been reflected in the development of new modes of psychotherapeutic treatment: individual therapies stressing "ego psychology" and interpersonal relations, group psychotherapy, conjoint therapy sessions with husbands and wives, and family group therapy.

The third trend to which we wish to call attention is the increasing realization that the traditional therapeutic techniques based on a one-to-one contact between a professional therapist and patient via hourly sessions spread over many months or years, cannot hope to resolve the mental health problem the country faces. The supply of such people, using such techniques, could not conceivably keep up with the need for mental health services. It is increasingly realized that new techniques are needed that afford the professional therapist greater leverage in the use of his time, and indeed, the physical facilities at his disposal.

These trends are what have encouraged the conception of filial therapy. The first suggested that the highly intellectual, expensive, and prolonged training in psychodynamics theory was not essential in learning to play a therapeutic role. The second suggested that with emotionally disturbed people, and particularly with children and their parents, one should attempt to modify directly the *relationship* between people and not only its psychic representation as it exists separately in the minds of each. The third trend provided the sense of urgency and necessity that energizes experimentation, and influenced the formulation of a technique that involves very high leverage in terms of the professional time and facilities.*

## Rationale for Using Parents

In addition to the potentially high leverage it provides in the use of professional time and resources, the rationale for the use of parents as therapeutic agents was based on a variety of considerations (Guerney, 1964). As a minimum, it was felt that the extra and undivided attention the child would be receiving would alone have some degree of positive effect in enhancing the child's sense of belonging and worthiness, and make him feel somewhat less negative and more "giving" toward the parents. But much more important, it was reasoned that if the parent could be taught to execute the essentials of the role usually taken by therapists, the parent would conceivably be more effective than a professional. This was taken to be so because the parent has (a) more emotional significance to the child, (b) anxieties learned in the presence of, or by the influence of, parental attitude could most effectively be unlearned, or extinguished, under similar conditions, and (c) interper-

---

*A fourth trend that has influenced the development and rationale of the technique is the increasing realization that the application of general learning theory can help us to better understand and to improve psychotherapy.

sonal mis-expectations should be efficiently corrected if appropriate delineations were made clear to the child by the parent himself as to what is, and what is not, appropriate behavior according to time, place, and circumstances.

It was further assumed that an approach that made it very clear to the parent that his good intentions toward the child could be harnessed to directly benefit the child would provide a strong motivation for the parent to undertake a therapy program and to continue treatment for the necessary time. It was felt that the parents would learn to play the role required of them sufficiently well, because they would be asked to play it for only short periods of time under special conditions, and while receiving feedback and encouragement from the therapist and other parents making the same attempt. The very difficulties that the parent encountered in trying to adopt such a role might prove illuminating to him with respect to his general pattern of relationships with the child. The fact that the parent would, through his learning of a new role for the sessions, deliberately break certain previous patterns of interaction for at least a limited amount of time, might also be expected to enhance his ability to explore and adopt new patterns outside of the sessions. With these considerations in mind, the following technique was developed.

## The Filial Method

The age of ten is ordinarily the upper limit for the maximum effectiveness of a play format for psychotherapy. When a child below ten is deemed, after diagnostic testing and interviewing, to have an emotional problem (as opposed to, say, an intellectual or neurological one), the general nature of this problem is explained to the parent. Such problems arise in large measure, and with differing specific patterns in each case, from a lack of self-confidence on the part of the child, from a lack of sufficient feeling on the part of this child that he is accepted as a worthwhile individual by the parents, from the child's fear of, and consequent need to hide, certain kinds of significant feelings from other people and from himself, and from a lack of communication and understanding between parents and child that would enable the child to express his needs in such a way as to allow these difficulties to be overcome. This is explained to the parent in a manner that fits the individual case. It is then explained that we can teach the parent a specific way of interacting with his child, at special times, and in a special place set aside for this purpose. This special interaction we expect will enable the child to express his feelings and needs more freely and adequately, and build his sense of worthiness and confidence. It should also help the parent to understand better the previously hidden or distorted inner needs and feelings of the child, and thus enable him to respond more appropriately to the child.

If, after full discussion, the parent accepts the recommendation for this type of help, the mother and/or father are placed in a group of six to eight other parents also beginning filial therapy. A group may be comprised of mothers, of fathers, of spouses, or of mothers and fathers of different families. The parents then attend a group meeting with the therapist every week thereafter until the parent terminates therapy, which is usually between six and eighteen months thereafter.

The first two or three group sessions are devoted to explaining further to the parent the nature and purpose of the role he will be asked to assume in the weekly sessions he will be having with his child. The parent's role is modeled as closely as possible after that taken by a client-centered play therapist. The basic things that the parent must learn are: (a) to be empathic with the child during the sessions — to make every effort to understand how the child is viewing himself and his world at the moment and what his feelings of the moment are; (b) to be fully understanding and accepting of the child — i.e., his feelings and thoughts, whatever their nature; (c) to leave the directions that the play sessions take (within certain clearly defined limits to be discussed later) completely to the child; and (d) most of all, to *convey* this understanding and acceptance to the child. It is explained to the parent how the creation of these conditions will tend to allow the child to express more freely his previously repressed feelings and needs. It is explained to the parent that the repressed needs and denied feelings that contribute to the child's difficulties continue to press on him for expression and realization, but because he has learned through earlier experiences to fear them, the child denies them. This leads him to distort personal and interpersonal realities and/or to satisfy his needs in devious and ultimately unsatisfactory ways. As his anxiety about losing status in the eyes of his parent and in his own eyes diminishes and he reveals his true feelings, he can come to grips with these feelings more and more effectively — mastering them rather than denying them or being overwhelmed by them. As this anxiety goes down and the child experiences his true range of feelings while remaining fully accepted by the parent, his sense of worth and confidence and his desire to give to others increases, while his frustrations and concomitant hostilities decrease.

But were there not legitimate reasons for his not expressing some such feelings openly in the past, and even now? The answer to this question is contained in a consideration of time, place, and mode of expression. The emotionally disturbed child for whom both the traditional and the filial mode of therapy is appropriate is in trouble largely because: (a) he has *over*learned certain inhibitions — now overextending restrictions originally placed on overt *behavior* to the experiencing of the related *emotions* as well; and/or (b) he has *under*learned the need to restrict the expression of certain feelings, and instead acts on them directly and overtly without restraints appropriate to the time and place. The latter circumstance brings us to consideration of limitations, mentioned parenthetically above, that are imposed on the child during the session.

These limitations are very modest by ordinary standards, and most of them become relevant only after the child has come to realize the freedom of the sessions, and expresses feelings such as anger very strongly and directly. The child is not permitted to extend the time of the session; he is not allowed to break a certain (expensive) toy of those that are provided him to play with in the sessions; and he is not allowed to physically hurt his parent. There are a number of reasons for imposing these "limits" aside from the obvious practical ones. Prominent among them are the following two. First, the essential ingredient of the sessions is the empathic understanding felt and conveyed by the parent. Professionals do not expect themselves to be able to fully maintain this attitude while being physically abused, nor do we expect it of parents. Second, parents as parents — especially parents of the children with underlearned behavioral restraint — benefit from knowing and practicing the art of setting firm limitations on their children's *behavior* while nevertheless accepting the child's feelings as real, and while continuing to convey a sense of valuing the child as a person. When parents successfully practice that art, children derive a sense of security and safety — knowing that they cannot go too far — as well as learning what is socially appropriate.

All of the above matters are not taught in lecture fashion. The parents are encouraged to express their own feelings and ideas, and often arrive at certain of these principles themselves, through group discussion.

Next, the therapist, using children not under treatment, conducts two or three play sessions himself as demonstrations for the parents. The parents observe these sessions through a one-way screen and later discuss what they have seen from the point of view of technique and from the point of view of what meanings the behaviors of the therapist and the child held for the child. Then each of the parents brings in his own child and conducts sessions under observation by the therapist and the rest of the group, followed by discussion as just described. When the parents and therapist feel they are ready — usually two to three months after the meetings began, after two practice sessions under observation, and after having observed some fifteen or twenty sessions — the parents begin to conduct their sessions at home. Every so often, sessions are again conducted at the Clinic under the observation of the group. The parents use the most appropriate room they have — a basement, garage, kitchen, or bedroom, perhaps — and a prescribed set of toys designed to permit expression of certain basic psychological needs, interpersonal fantasy, or role-playing. The toys include, for example, a "Joe Palooka" punching bag, a baby bottle, a family of dolls, a family of puppets, a toy gun, clay, crayons, and paper. This particular set of toys is available to the child only during his sessions. Other young children in the family are also given sessions. Originally, the session is once a week, and a half hour in duration. Later, if practical and appropriate, the sessions may be extended to forty-five minutes and up to several times a week. This time is devoted exclusively to the child — to the extent of not answering the phone, etc.

In the continuing weekly meetings with the therapist, a description of the home session by each parent serves as a starting point for discussion. Problems of technique and interpretation of the meaning of sessions, and the parents' emotional reactions to the sessions, are given high priority. However, the parents are free to go into other matters of emotional significance to them or their child. The work of the therapist, then, is a combination of a didactic role with respect to the home sessions and a more traditionally therapeutic one in dealing with emotional concerns of the parent, as in other forms of group therapy (Andronico, Fidler, et al., 1965).

The fact that the parents are all striving to play a similar role in their home sessions provides an extra dividend with respect to their group sessions in that it gives the members of the group a standard situation — a common framework — in which to view their children's problems and reactions and their own problems and reactions. This facilitates mutual comparison and understanding among them. The home sessions and the group sessions seem to make both separate and mutually facilitating contributions toward helping the parent and child establish a better relationship and adjustment.

## Case Illustration

The particular case to be presented was chosen for several reasons. The obvious ones are that it proceeded according to our expectations, was successful, and rather dramatic in content; which, of course, is not always the case. But, in addition, it is particularly interesting because the mother, who was the parent selected to be trained to work with the child, was regarded — to quote from summaries of the diagnostic and interpretive interviews before therapy began — as "a challenge to the limits and capacity of filial therapy to motivate parents...." This guarded assessment of the mother's capacity for conforming to the required role was based partly on her personality, and also on her strongly expressed feeling that "the idea of interacting with the child in a play situation is emotionally repulsive." Further, Mrs. S's attitude toward psychology and psychiatry was quite negative. Because of a previous brush with someone in an allied field, she regarded persons in these professional areas as meddlers who are looking for things to criticize, under the guise of presenting an individual with insight about himself.

Her boy, Fred, was a seven-year-old referred to the Rutgers Psychological Clinic by the county mental health clinic. It was reported that he was a nervous child, had frequent headaches, ate poorly, was enuretic, had nightmares, masturbated excessively, bit his nails, and manifested tic-like throat clearing. Socially, he was quiet, easily offended, with no friends. He feared physical aggression, and took flight from play with peers when games of this sort were introduced.

Tests of personality revealed that he perceived his home life as highly uncomfortable. He perceived his mother as directing and assertive, always guiding, warning, and protecting, in a most unwelcome way. Father was seen as a hostile figure. There was some indication that the mother was regarded as the more threatening figure "behind the scene," but Fred refused to acknowledge hostility in himself or his mother. The examiner's summary pictured Fred as a bright, anxious child, developing compulsive behavior and manifesting many nervous symptoms. Fear of physical aggression and some hypochondriacal behavior were also present.

Mrs. S. was a very bright, well-read woman in her late thirties. She was rigid and controlling in all phases of her life. She injected herself into all phases of Fred's existence, demanding appreciation for all that she did. She constantly instructed and moralized. She was in awe of authority figures she respected, very scornful toward those she did not. Because of space limitations, we will not discuss the father's personality, except to say that it was relatively bland.

Mrs. S. initially reacted against the idea of being a member of a group. She found the other members' comments rather worthless, and felt that only the psychologist's statements had any real meaning. She particularly disliked one group member and attacked her from time to time in terms of how people like her made the group idea a poor one. Mrs. S's criticisms were handled as reflective of her personality rather than a realistic appraisal of the group approach. Ultimately, Mrs. S. confessed to the group that she did, after all, see value in a group approach, because she felt that she had gained as a person in learning to be more accepting of antagonistic views, in contrast to her previous need to attack them. She regarded the behavior of the therapist, which served as a model in this respect, as inducing this change in herself. Toward the end, more than once, she led the group in relating how the group discussions had benefited them.

With respect to the play session technique, Mrs. S. asked meaningful questions from the beginning. She doubted the wisdom of simply reflecting the child's own feelings, and felt that directing and interpreting his behavior would be more productive. However, she was willing to give the approach a try, and learned to play the role required in the play periods very well. Her biggest problem was in refraining from asking leading questions, which she did control for the most part. While she did not achieve the ultimate in empathic attitude, she became fairly warm and relaxed, and even had a genuinely good time during the play periods — joining in play, as requested by her boy, in a goodnatured manner with no airs of adult superiority. Fred accepted the sessions with enthusiasm, and kept up a high level of interest in them until close to the end, when he could take them or leave them. (When problems diminish, motivation to work on them generally lessens as well.) Some of his play periods read like textbook sessions. He expressed, and apparently worked through, Oedipal feelings, castration fears, ambivalence toward his parents and himself, conflict over aggressive feelings, and self-destructive impulses; and, in the end, genuine positive feelings toward himself and his family emerged.

Fred entered into the play situations eagerly, and centered most of his activity for the initial sessions around the Joe Palooka "bop bag" (which bounces back and allows the subject to feel he is really fighting). He commented that he did not want to try to make anything with the Tinkertoy for fear that it would turn out badly. Until Session 4, his mother's special role did not fall under his scrutiny. At Session 4, he seemed to be annoyed by the style of her comments and made various critical remarks about them. This abated after a few weeks, when he apparently realized she was not going to change her behavior, and because she handled these remarks by reflecting and accepting his annoyance. Thus, he learned that his mother could tolerate his criticisms — and aggression — and in turn respond uncritically, and even sympathetically.

By Session 6, Fred was able to assemble Tinkertoy objects without fear of making mistakes, and used them quite creatively. However, in quantity and dynamic quality of play, Joe Palooka continued to remain the focus. In the course of the sessions, this punching bag was at times labeled with his father's nickname and soundly beaten. As Father, Palooka had his penis cut off with a rubber knife (no penis actually appears on the figure). As Mother, it was beaten, stabbed, shot, hugged, and told Fred loved it. As Sister, it was killed, "with blood gushing from its head."

Early in the sessions, Fred had accidently hit Mother with the punching bag. He then received a warning that hitting Mother in any form would not be permitted, and would cause the session to end. A few weeks later he did it again; the session was ended. The next week, Fred asked Mother to be sure to tell him when he had one minute left. Mother did, and Fred immediately walloped her with the punching bag. She pointed out that he seemed to have been wanting to do that all of the session (as indicated by various remarks), but that he had waited until the end. He explained that this way he lost only one minute and was still able to hit her. This system he devised continued from this time until Session 45. After that, on the rare occasions when Joe Palooka or some other object hit her, it seemed to be truly an accident.

In puppet play, his family was wiped out by crocodiles, storms, huge monsters, Nazis, etc. Father was always first to go — with the son looking after Mother usually until the last minute, when everyone was killed.

Around Session 40, a different tone began to emerge in Fred's play. He included Mother in more activities, wanted her to join him in beating up Palooka, help him by giving him clay bombs to throw, play cards with him, and the like. More often Joe Palooka was Mother, whom he hugged, kissed, and said, "I adore you," etc. However, there was an increase also in the amount of hostility directed toward her. As Palooka, Mother's nipples were bitten off after he sucked them. He named her the daughter of Frankenstein, and made Palooka into this daughter and bombed her with clay bombs. He drew war pictures with swastikas, which he knew from experience outside the session she did not like, sat on her lap like a baby, and then stuck his tongue out at her. She came into focus as the main figure of interest, and great conflict about her was revealed. He loved her, wanted her, needed her, etc., but could not do so unconditionally. Strong negative feelings were present as well, and feelings of anxiety about his aggressive feelings toward her.

In addition to providing catharsis for the child, this play made it possible for the mother to see that he reacted to her with a variety of feelings, depending on his anxiety level, most pressing emotional needs, etc. It was easier to see why in real life she did not see consistent devotion, obedience, etc., but that these positive feelings were actually present. She was able to adjust her expectation of his emotional commitment to her to more realistic levels, saving herself from disappointment when he was not all "love." This, combined with newfound ability to resist being manipulated by him in the hope of "buying his appreciation" made their relationship much more satisfying to both.

By the time fifty-five home play sessions were held, all symptoms were completely removed or greatly diminished. After eleven more sessions, Mrs. S. decided that though he was still somewhat introverted she could accept this degree of introversion, and therapy was terminated.

Toward the end, the sessions were calmer and less emotional in content. More of them were devoted to simple play-poker, target games, etc. However, Palooka was still important. Fred usually played the role of world champ and beat him up soundly. (At this point, he started wrestling with Father in real life.) Finally, after it was announced to Fred that sessions would end after two more, he had a very symbolic session where he staged "pretend temper tantrums" and then assumed his normal voice and laughed. Mrs. S. remarked that "Big Fred is laughing at Baby Fred," and he agreed. He seemed to be exorcising the babyish element in himself in this way, bidding it goodbye goodhumoredly, because he was ready to do so.

## Status of Research

Evaluated from the point of view of preliminary clinical experience — with about a dozen groups completed or under way — most of the assumptions underlying the technique seem to hold up, and the technique seems an effective one; for us, more effective than more traditional approaches. We are fully cognizant, however, of the role experimenter enthusiasm and bias inevitably play in making such judgments. At the same time, the problems presented in attempting to subject the effectiveness of psychotherapy to rigorous experimental test are extraordinary. They range from the philosophical and ethical through complex problems of measurement to the practical matter of the enormous expense involved in seeing sufficient numbers of subjects in a reasonable span of time. For such reasons, the practice of psychotherapy in general rests on clinical experience and evidence, and not quantitative experimental evidence. An enormous amount of work remains to be done before this situation can be effectively reversed. Much of our present effort is viewed as being along lines of trying to develop more efficient therapy by clinical methods and evaluation. If more efficient methods can be developed in this way, experimental methods of evaluation will then become more feasible.

At this time, we are trying to evaluate qualitatively and clinically the effects of different types of parent groups and the types of parents and children most amenable to the technique; and we are trying variations in the technique with the idea of improving it further. On the quantitative side, we are trying out certain measuring instruments and attempting to adapt or develop others appropriate to young children. In the area of process (as opposed to "outcome") research, an experimental research project is currently being carried out by the senior author and Mrs. Lillian Stover, part of which objectively and quantitatively tests the assumption that parents can learn and apply the prescribed role. Preliminary results comparing trained parents and children with a similar group of untrained parents and children indicate that they can. Moreover, the children begin to respond to that role in ways predicted by client-centered theory as early as the second training session.

We regard the essence of the filial technique to be that of systematically tapping a relatively neglected but potentially powerful resource: the energy of parents in working for the betterment of their children. We have hope that this principle can be applied also to other age groups of emotionally disturbed children and also to different types of problems. We are hopeful, for example, that underprivileged children's educational motivation and scholastic skills might be increased by applying the same sort of positive orientation to the use of parents, with appropriate modifications of the method of working with the parents and the skills the parents are taught. In the future, we hope to be able to conduct research along these lines as well.

**References**
1. Allen, F. H., *Psychotherapy with Children*, New York: W. W. Norton, 1942.
2. Andronico, M.P., Fidler, J., Guerney, B. Jr., and Guerney, Louise F., "The Combination of Didactic and Dynamic Elements in Filial Therapy," paper presented at the 1965 American Group Psychotherapy Association Convention.
3. Axline, Virginia M., *Play Therapy*, Cambridge, Mass.: Houghton Mifflin, 1947.
4. Dorfman, Elaine, "Play Therapy," in Rogers, C. R. *Client-Centered Therapy*, Boston: Houghton Mifflin, 1951.
5. Fidler, J. W., Guerney, B. Jr., Andronico, M. P., and Guerney, Louise, "Filial Psychotherapy as a Logical Extension of Current Trends," paper presented at the Sixth International Congress of Psychotherapy, London, 1964.
6. Freud, Anna, *The Psychoanalytic Treatment of Children*, London: Imago, 1946.
7. Guerney, B., Jr., "Filial Therapy: Description and Rationale," *J. Consult. Psychol.*, 1964, 28, No. 4, 304-310.

8. Klein, Melanie, *The Psychoanalysis of Children*, London: Hogarth, 1950.
9. Mitchell, E. D., and Mason, B. S., *The Theory of Play*, New York: A. S. Barnes, 1948, p. 77.
10. Moustakas, C. E., *Children in Play Therapy*, New York: McGraw-Hill, 1953.
11. Rank, O., *Will Therapy*, and *Truth and Reality*, New York: Knopf, 1945.
12. Rogers, C. R., *Client-Centered Therapy*, Boston: Houghton Mifflin, 1951.
13. Taft, Jessie, *The Dynamics of Therapy in a Controlled Relationship*, New York: Macmillan, 1933.

# GROUP

# The Therapeutic Play Group
# — A Case Study

LILLIAN ROTHENBERG and MORTIMER SCHIFFER

Jose was left on the "doorstep" of the guidance office by a distraught teacher on the very first day of school. He stood there — a small, thin, solemn boy. His clothes were worn but clean. His face was immobile; his eyes were without expression. Every day thereafter, and sometimes several times a day, Jose showed up because his teacher could not manage him. In the classroom he made strange sounds, crawled on the floor, hid in the clothing closet, and sometimes ran around the room in a frenzy, throwing over chairs and tables. At other times, strangely enough, he played quietly with toys or drew pictures of monsters. At no time did he do any school work.

Jose lived in a low income housing project bounded on one side by a river and on the other by an old, stable community of private houses. No hospitals or community mental health agencies were located in this neighborhood. Besides, Jose's mother was too rejecting of the boy to accept clinical help even if it were available. She chose, instead, to be angry at the school for "picking" on Jose.

In his seven short years of life, this child had already experienced violent upheaval in life's routines, severe deprivation, and open rejection. His confusion and low self-esteem were once dramatically stated in the remark "I was born in a garbage can." The father, whom he had never known, was in "the army, navy, or air force," depending on Jose's mood or need. At times he described a variable number of sisters, brothers, and even mothers. He expressed fears of death, illness, and violence. Woven into his fantasies were pertinent observations about his life situation. At times, he seemed surprisingly bright. He seldom smiled; but when he did, the contrast was remarkable. His face would light up and he was strikingly handsome.

Jose's mother was a tall, attractive woman who spoke English fairly well. When interviewed, she told of her marriage at fifteen years of age, desertion shortly thereafter by her husband, and her journey to New York with seven-month-old Jose. After her arrival in New York City, she was employed a few hours each day as a houseworker. One day she left Jose unattended in a furnished room to go out to a job. On the way to work, she fainted and was hospitalized. Jose was found a day later, hungry and dirty. He was taken to a foundling home and eventually claimed by an uncle. His mother was placed in an institution.

During the following years, Jose was shunted back and forth between relatives, then to his mother after her discharge, and finally to his aunt. When Jose was with his mother, he witnessed her violent emotional outbursts and severe asthmatic attacks. During this time he lived with her and several of her common-law husbands. She threatened, bribed, and beat Jose and on rare occasions fought for him. Several times, in desperation and disgust, she "gave" Jose to his aunt but kept her other children.

Jose's aunt had two young children of her own. Because she lived in a city housing project where the "extended" family was strictly discouraged, she had to hide Jose. Her income was barely sufficient to support her own family. She tried to control Jose by fear and mystical beliefs. Despite these difficulties, she clung to him.

Jose had suffered from repeated dislocations, shock, and rejection. He had no roots, no identity. No trauma could be more disabling and threatening in the emotional development of a child. In planning to help this boy within the school, it was necessary to provide an experience that would offer security and a sustained, consistent relationship with an adult over a long period of time. It was decided, therefore, to place him in a therapeutic play group which the counselor was forming as one of the guidance services used with emotionally disturbed children.

## The Therapeutic Play Group

The therapeutic play group was devised by the second author, Mortimer Schiffer. He modified a clinical practice in group psychotherapy so that it could be used on a practical level as part of guidance in elementary schools. In New York City during this year, thirty-five therapeutic play groups were meeting in fourteen elementary schools.

In February, 1959, this play group was brought together for its first meeting. It met one hour a week during the following three and a half years. The play room contained several children's tables and chairs, blocks, paint, clay, crayons, drawing paper, games, toy autos, books, and a large inflatable plastic "Bop" bag. The four other boys in the group had also been carefully screened. They were of the same age and from the same grades but in different classes. Lester was referred because he was immature, aggressive, and demanding. Ronald was extremely withdrawn and suspicious. James was passive and uncommunicative. Martin was disoriented, provocative yet frightened.

In the play group the counselor group leader is permissive in the sense that children are enabled to bring out conflicting feelings with which they have been struggling for a long time. Because the leader of the group accepts this behavior without questioning, the children learn to trust. The leader's technique is to stay marginal to the group, but she is always ready to help them. Since such complete acceptance is novel and satisfying to the children, it throws them off balance psychologically, for other adults have not treated them this way. Because of this doubt, they test the adult. They do a good deal of acting out to see if the leader will continue to accept them. The play group eventually becomes psychologically like a family in which the children unconsciously relate to the leader and to the other children as if they were parent and siblings. The basic difference is that there is no repetition in the play group of earlier, damaging, growth experiences.

More importantly, it gives the children an opportunity for positive, rehabilitative experiences. All counselors who use the play group process are given intensive training which is continued through supervision.

## Reaction to the Group Situation

Jose's behavior in the playroom was infantile from the beginning. He smeared paints, threw toys, used colorful language, wrestled with Lester, and teased and taunted the other children. When overstimulated, he ran around the room aimlessly. He told many fantasies. Every group meeting was recorded in detail, and the leader met regularly with the consultant for supervision.

Since Jose was so emotionally disabled by the severity of early deprivation, it was necessary that the leader help him manage some of his impulsive behavior. In a sense, it was as if the permissiveness (love) of the leader was "too rich a dose" for Jose in the beginning, after his having been deprived of security and love during his earliest formative years. It was added that Jose, without the support of the therapeutic experience and the emotional tie to the leader, could not possibly continue in school. In the meantime, it was suggested that he be given diagnostic psychological tests and that a social worker see the aunt to help her apply for approval from the housing authority to keep Jose in her apartment and to get additional financial assistance from the department of welfare.

During his first year in the play group, Jose vacillated between periods of quiet, isolative play and unpredictable, excitable, angry behavior. At the beginning of each meeting, he removed his shoes and ran around the room gleefully like a delighted two year old. Sometimes he would tell involved fantasies about his father or other members of his family. He was confused as to their names. He built elaborate block structures on flimsy foundations which he would then knock over. He made intricate figures out of clay which he stabbed or cut up. He lashed out verbally at the other children, cursed, and made slurring references to other races. At snack time, he grabbed for food, taking second and third helpings. In this very diffuse way, Jose exhibited his primitive behavior.

Yet, he would consistently come to the leader to have his shoes tied, his sleeves unrolled, his tie fixed, or his face wiped. In the classroom, he continued to present serious problems. He still made no attempt to learn or to conform. It was arranged for Jose to attend school for a shorter day to help him manage the regular class routines.

A social worker succeeded in getting financial aid for Jose's support and approval from the housing authority. Psychological and psychiatric examinations revealed much scatter in intellectual functioning, with responses ranging from very low to very high; he had no real concept of himself; he had fantasies of death and desertion; he was extremely anxious and fearful. Jose was not psychotic but was very seriously disturbed. It was recommended that he continue in the play group and, in addition, that he visit with the social worker each week.

## The Second Year

During the second year of the play group, Jose's massive dependency on the group leader began to lessen and he became increasingly aware of the needs of the others. He formed a close relationship with James. They improvised circuses and did stunts that called for a good deal of jumping and chasing. Jose's sudden, angry moods disappeared entirely. He began to notice when other children were absent, and he was more observant of changes in the setting. He began to speak more freely of his feelings about his family. At times, he still had fantasies; and on occasions, he spoke morbidly about his death. The consultant suggested various techniques by which the leader could limit excessive fantasy and keep him more in contact with the real experiences in the group. This was done by stimulating his interest in sculpture and art in which he was quite skillful.

Without notice, Jose's mother suddenly left one of his half sisters with the aunt. Jose reacted to this by behaving like a baby at home. He destroyed things, played all the time, and ran around the apartment. His aunt still did not permit him out of the apartment after school, despite the fact that she was no longer fearful of the housing authority. Now she was afraid he would get into trouble. Jose told his aunt, "Mommy, if you die, I'll sit by your grave and never leave you."

Jose still attended school part time. During the summer, arrangements were made for Jose and his cousin to go to camp for two weeks. Strangely enough, when this deprived child returned home, he said that camp was "junky." He added he did not like being away from home.

## The Third Year

During the third year in the therapeutic play group, Jose acted out less and less and became more friendly. He joined in and sometimes organized group play. He helped to mediate some of the arguments that would develop in the group. Some of his morbid fantasies changed to dramatic play about doctors and operations. While he continued to taunt Lester, he no longer wrestled with him. There was general improvement in his relationships with children.

Once again Jose's mother left the half sister with the aunt and returned to Puerto Rico. Jose told the play group, "My mother went to Puerto Rico. I hope her plane crashes." His behavior in the classroom took a turn for the worse, and his teacher now demanded that he be suspended from school. Because of the manifest progress this boy had made and the imminent threat of having the therapeutic process interrupted through a suspension or transfer to a school for delinquents, the counselor arranged for a trial transfer to another class in the same school.

Fortunately, Jose responded well to the new teacher who was able to capitalize on some of his talents. He described her as being like his aunt and brought her a present. At this point, for the first time in his school career, Jose began to make efforts to learn. Recently, in speaking of this teacher, he said, "She gave me back my brains."

## Results of Therapy

During the last stage of the therapuetic play group, the leader's role becomes much less permissive, and reeducation becomes primary. The children have greater tolerance for frustration because the lengthy and sustained therapeutic experience in the group satisfies many emotional needs. They are much more responsive to the leader, who now takes a more direct part in helping them adjust to the demands of the group life.

After ninety-eight group meetings during a period of three and one-half years, the play group was being prepared for termination. Jose had attended ninety-four out of the ninety-eight meetings. Since the four absences were caused by illness, it is fair to say that this boy's attendance was perfect and a reflection of the meaning the play group had for him.

On the first day of school after the next summer vacation, Jose walked into the guidance office. He had grown several inches and looked well. In a loud voice, he said to the counselor, "I got your letter from India, the one with the elephant on it." He grinned broadly. This was not the end of all of Jose's problems. Jose had been told that after the play group was terminated, he could visit the counselor whenever he had the need to do so. A few days later his teacher complained about his behavior. Jose later explained that he did not want to share his reader with a girl. When another boy intervened on behalf of the girl, Jose hit him. Later, the teacher confirmed this incident without embellishment or fabrication, as he formerly would have done.

Jose continued to stop by to see the counselor on one excuse or another every day before he went to class. He requested information or asked for envelopes for his books. Sometimes, he would just poke his head in and wave. Once he helped in moving blocks out of the cabinet and placed them on the shelf. He began to work enthusiastically but soon became distracted. The counselor went over to help and chat with him. In a few minutes, the job was done. Jose said, "I betcha I was the fastest one to do this. It only took five minutes." She nodded and said, "I remember when you were in the second grade. Those were the good old days." Jose shook his head soberly in denial, "These are the good old days."

As Jose's behavior became more positive, the adults around him responded accordingly. They now seem more patient and more sensitive to his needs. They anticipate an occasional need on his part to "fool around" and try to divert him.

Jose's teacher described an interesting incident. She was teaching a lesson in which the children were asked to put words in a sentence. The room was very quiet. Jose came up to her and in a whisper said, "I'll tell you the sentences and you write them down for me." She did. With a big smile she added, "and he got 100 percent!" She added that Jose has been playing ball, and he is thrilled with his success. He is now reading at the third grade level. He needs help with mathematics and spelling. He still resists doing homework. This was more than fair progress for a child who formerly did no work at all.

Jose is back at the guidance room "doorstep," but in a far different way. His experience in the therapeutic play group remains a bond. He is far more reality oriented and seems eager to achieve. He takes pride in his accomplishments. Jose continues to need support and reassurance.

In our schools there are many Joses and yet no rehabilitative "short cuts." The impoverished personality development of early formative years can yield to a certain extent to a well planned and implemented therapeutic program involving the child and other adults with whom he has meaningful contact during school years. Otherwise, in the absence of corrective experience, our Joses are destined for continuing deprivation which will be manifested through more severe emotional disorders and antisocial behavior.

# Activity Group Therapy

S. R. SLAVSON

In the present paper an attempt is made to present a few *specific* processes in activity group therapy.[1] The need to study and understand intragroup processes and the nature of adaptations that individuals make to groups is deeply felt. Recreationists, and especially some group workers, are becoming increasingly concerned by the lack of knowledge as to what actually occurs in groups. When this knowledge becomes available, both official education and informal programs will be strengthened in their efforts toward developing better integrated individuals and a more balanced social milieu. At present precise information in this field is sadly lacking, a dearth that impoverishes family life, school education, recreation, and therapy.

We are accustomed to thinking of individuals in relation only to other individuals. When speaking of interpersonal relations we often have in mind what would more correctly be designated as interindividual relations. Interindividual relations are bilateral, i.e., an emotional process is present between two persons. But as soon as the infant emerges from his earliest stages of vegetative existence, he becomes involved in relations with people other than his mother. He responds to a number of persons who are in definite relation among themselves. The infant too, becomes one of a complex of emotional threads and positive, negative, and ambivalent attitudes. This maze of emotionality and intellectual congruence and conflicts widens and becomes more intense as he grows older and is forced to assume an active role in it. School, friends, play groups extend even further the relational areas of a child. Such

[1]A detailed account may be found in S. R. Slavson, *Introduction to Group Therapy*, Commonwealth Fund, New York, 1943.

relationships we have described as multilateral. Even the most enlightened writers on family and education omit the group aspects. They concentrate upon interindividual (bilateral) attitudes and underplay the group (multilateral) aspects and dynamics in personality growth and character formation.

This omission, perhaps even shyness, to deal with these areas arises from their complexity and amorphous nature. The mathematical probability of interpersonal attitudes in groups is very great as shown in the possible combinations described later in this paper (Figure 3). This complexity, however, is not only mathematical or quantitative. The variations in the qualitative outcome of emotional and intellectual interaction of a number of individuals is equally confusing. To this must be added also the *intensity* of emotional quantum in group life. Thus groups must be studied from the point of view of three unknowables: quantity, quality, and intensity of reactions. The product can be shown to be not three dimensional as would first appear, but four dimensional, and therefore difficult to comprehend.

It is not the intention of the present discussion to enter into the most abstruse facets of group life. Rather, this is an attempt to throw some light upon *separate* elements of a specific group. It may be advisable to describe briefly the setting of an activity therapy group. Seven or eight children come on invitation to a meeting place at a specified time. The children are carefully grouped on the basis of their personality characteristics and problems so that they will have a therapeutic effect upon each other. The importance of proper grouping cannot be overemphasized. The very foundation of this type of group treatment, its value, and effectiveness, are determined by a proper combination of clients. This is true for all types of group therapy with children, adolescents, and probably with adults.

Tools are provided for metal work, wood work, painting, clay modeling, basket making, and similar activities. Included also are individual, pair, and group games such as quoits, checkers, handball, and ping pong. After a period of free undirected work, the children partake of a meal which is at first prepared by the worker and later by the members themselves. The atmosphere is permissive; children may use materials, tools, and the total environment, in whichever way they wish. They may be destructive or constructive, isolate themselves, or enter into relationships with fellow members. They may work or idle, do their homework, read funnies, play or fight, eat with the group or by themselves. At appropriate times this simple and attenuated reality is extended and modified through changes in the meeting room, materials, personnel of the group, change of worker, visits to restaurants, trips, picnics and excursions.

The five elements in the treatment process to be described are:
1. The "knowable" nature of the group.
2. The role of the adult.
3. Social fixity versus social mobility.
4. Levels of identification.
5. The phenomenon of nodal behavior.

## "Knowable" Nature of the Group

All groups are threatening to all individuals at some time. This postulate is easily confirmed by introspection and observation. One source of fear is the unpredictability of group reactions. When one understands the character and mechanisms of a person one can predict with some degree of certainty his response to a given stimulus. It is quite different with groups. Even if one understands the character of each individual in a group, one cannot be certain how he will respond in a group situation. Each member present goes through a process of partial deegotization. One will submit where in ordinary relations he would be dominant; another controls his usual hilarity and is quiet and withdrawn; still another abreacts to a feeling of discomfort by humor and volubility; while a fourth who may be gentle in individual contacts becomes overbearing. Even more confusing to the observer or leader is that one person may react in different ways to different situations or persons in the group and to the total situation at different times. In addition, an integral physiognomy of the group — its specific group culture — emerges, and entity to be dealt with apart from the individuals composing it.

Early association with the family is another source of threat to each one of the members. It is not likely that any one has been reared in a "wholesome" family. Families can be only less or more pathogenic. Unconscious cruelty and resentment concomitant to sex intercourse, open or covert hostilities, ambivalence, struggle for dominance, sibling and other rivalries, discrimination, rejection, drives, and conflicts are ever present in greater and lesser degree. Later in life a group arouses conscious misgivings and, what is more important, are the unconscious and repressed feeling tones associated with the family that each brings to the group situation. Each member has the perception of the danger of being hurt, rejected, discovered for what he thinks he *really* is and about which he feels guilty. As a result of these fears some take on definite social amenities, others reject the group by attacking or withdrawing from it. The more wholesome the relations in the family, the more ready is the individual for constructive and easy multilateral relations in a group.

Fear of group association is also engendered by the basic feeling of isolation and loneliness that most people have and are unwilling or unready to give up. Each assumes a protective mantle to prevent hurts. Exposure to the gaze of a group, laying oneself open to analysis, criticism, and censure is a threatening situation. The need to be accepted (social hunger) is the strongest need in man. Groups can easily destroy one's ego by fair means or foul, and isolation, therefore, is a means of self-protection.

A therapeutic group must be free from all these threatening possibilities. It must give each individual security as to status and acceptance, release the blocking to expression, and free him of fear of relationships. The elements which make this possible in a therapy group are: (a) respect by the worker of the individuality of each member; (b) absence of rejection and persecution by other members (through careful choice of clients); (c) consistent positive attitude by the worker; (d) emphasis upon the constructive rather than negative in achievement and social status; (e) substitutes for the lack of gratifications in earlier life.

The most important single element that makes for a therapeutic atmosphere is its *knowable nature.* An activity therapy group has a definite pattern. No changes are made or variations introduced for a long time. The same room, the same physical set up, the same worker, and the same co-members prevent fear of the unexpected, the unpredictable. The disturbed child who is unable to make adaptations and is easily frightened about his ego survival and group status, need have no misgivings. He knows what he will find when he comes to the meetings, he has made adjustments and is no longer afraid. Changes are introduced when the children have gained a sufficient psychic strength and are less rigid to adaptations.

### Role of the Adult

The role of the adult in an activity therapy group is essentially different from that in a social club or in most types of groups. In the latter the leader occupies a prominent role where he is the central person. He is the source of security to the members since they are aware, consciously or unconsciously, that problems will be settled by him. Behind the activity and effort of members of these groups, is the awareness of the leader's superior powers, abilities, and resources which gives each member a sense of security. At the same time, there exists a common relationship on the part of the members of the group that all share the leader, which serves as a unifying or integrating element.

The relationship between member and worker in a therapy group is quite different. Here the leader is not the source of security nor does he guide the group through the maze of conflicting emotions which may arise. By his neutral and comparatively passive role, the members of a therapy group are led to dissociate him from authority or support. Through conscious strategies and techniques the worker withdraws from participation in interpersonal conflicts and relationships among the children. He confines himself to helping the members with their work in arts and crafts when they need or ask for it.

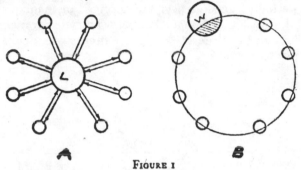

FIGURE 1

In Figure 1, A illustrates schematically the interindividual (bilateral) relations existing between the leader, and each member of an ordinary club in addition to the relation existing among members. The leader (L) is the central person here. The interpersonal (multilateral) relations existing in an activity therapy group are shown in B. This illustrates that the worker is only partially included in the group circle in conformity with his "neutral" role.

The aim in activity group therapy is to strengthen the autonomous trends in children rather than to feed their dependence. This role of the worker becomes necessary because, among other things, clients chosen are children who were made dependent and insecure by overprotection and coddling, or through excessive and unreasonable rejection and deprivations. Some of these children need a personal relation with an adult and are referred for individual treatment, or a Big Brother or Big Sister. In the group, however, the child cannot monopolize the adult. Group treatment addresses itself rather toward eliminating dependence and helping the child find security within himself.

A client who is incapable of object relationships is not ready for any type of group treatment. The withdrawn and frightened child needs to have his anxieties reduced, and the one with self-protective aggression must become basically more secure. This is accomplished through relations with other children. The adult deflects whatever ties appear toward him away from himself and toward other members of the group. However, emotional weaning cannot be direct or the client will feel he is not wanted, or rejected. In grouping, an effort is made to place children together who may serve as supports to each other, thereby reducing their need for the worker.

We have so far described the relationship between client and therapist from the point of view of the adult. The child, however, does come to the group with definite attitudes toward adults which he inevitably projects upon the group therapist. The dependent child will go through a period of dependency, the deprived or inadequate will seek praise, and the weak will demand support. The worker meets the needs of each, but without encouraging further dependence or strong emotional ties to himself.

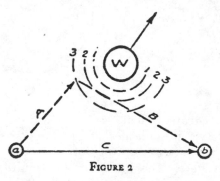

FIGURE 2

Figure 2 is a schematic representation of the "deflective process" the worker employs to help the child establish relationships with his contemporaries. At first line *A* was extended to *W*. The worker however withdrew gradually as shown by arcs 1-1, 2-2, 3-3, until (*a*) found it necessary and was able to relate to (*b*). Line *B* is the "deflective relational line." Later (*a*) is able to relate to (*b*) directly, line *C*, omitting the worker (*W*).

The worker is only partially involved in the group situation. He is there physically and meets the needs of the client. Emotionally, he remains neutral, and his physical participation as well must gradually decrease as the children become more mature and emotionally stronger. This he tests out by leaving the room for a time and observing how the children behaved during his absence. When direct questions are addressed to him concerning matters of conflict or group behavior, he informs the children that the "club" is theirs and they may run it as they please. Through these direct statements and the worker's subtle strategies the children become aware of their responsibilities and that they are on their own.

The role of the worker is vastly different in interview group treatment than in therapeutic play groups. In the former, the worker is active both emotionally and physically. Each member has a transference relation with the worker, which is encouraged and utilized in treatment. The worker is the central figure, and the group is a tool in treatment. This is especially true of adolescents. In activity group on the other hand, the worker's part is a "recessive" one.

## Social Fixity Versus Social Mobility

The major reason why boys and girls who fail in regular groups but make adjustment to a therapy group lies in the fact that the latter are mobile rather than fixed groups. Groups evolve social crystallizations, rigidities, codes, and pressures. Each member is expected to adopt its mores, manners, ideas, and convictions. Divergence from the group norm is tolerated only to a degree to which the group morale is not threatened. Pressure of the other members on a divergent individual forces him to conform or his survival as a member of the group is made impossible.

Such groups can be described as groups of *social fixity*. Their ideology, modus operandi, codes of behavior, concepts of loyalty, and expectations of self-control are fixed. To be accepted, the individual must adapt himself to the group climate, must give up or limit his mechanisms and behavior to conform with group pressures. To a considerable extent this involves partial deegotization, flexibility or, better still, an absence of rigidity of which only a fairly well integrated person is capable. The neurotic or otherwise disturbed individual persists in his own pattern of behavior, retains his individuality and uniqueness which tend to place him in conflict with the group. Success in group membership is, therefore, closely tied up with the capacity to fit into an average or norm.

In a therapy group no such norms exist. If and when they spontaneously arise, they are minimal and the pressure for conformity is either absent or very slight. The integrative processes, the common goals, authority of the leader, and the symbiotic relationships existing in ordinary group formation are absent. There are no common goals here; there is no similarity in the attitudes toward the leader; there is no ideological aim. In activity therapy groups, especially, no specific behavior is expected or imposed. Common interests, such as a place to visit or the kind of food to buy, arise spontaneously and soon vanish into limbo. The total atmosphere and setup of the group permit individuals a fairly autonomous existence. Contacts, friendships, conflicts, and compromises frequently occur and have great therapeutic value, but their value lies in the fact that they are spontaneous and arise from actual situations meaningful to the participants.

Since there is no external imposition or pressure in the early life of the group, the child has no need to conform or live in fear of offending the leader or members. Each child does whatever interests him, and cooperates with others only as he is ready. Because deviant or disturbing behavior is accepted by the adult, other members of the group do not curb it too violently unless it threatens another child directly. Conversation, working together, and combining in subgroups are quite spontaneous and arise in a desultory rather than an organized manner.

As a result of this permissive atmosphere, the child's autonomous needs are not curbed. He can behave on the level of his own development without being stigmatized, have a feeling of being different, or suffer from rejection and retaliation. There is free choice of association, temporary or permanent; a child can either remain in isolation or attach himself to an individual on a basis of comfort, mutual fitness, support, or any type of relation he may need. There is no group action as such, but there is individual work with tools and materials, and also free physical movement. Such a group may be described as one of *social mobility*. It is in every sense mobile. The opportunity to live out or act out one's real self leads to release of suppressed and hidden impulses, an expansion of the quantum of inner life through which new powers, talents, and abilities come to the surface. Activity catharsis combined with the example set by the worker and other members of the group beget new perceptions of self and of the world and its nature.

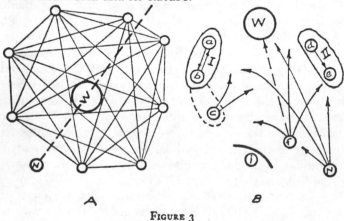

FIGURE 3

*A* illustrates schematically the compactness of a "fixed" group. Lines representing relationships emanate from each one of the members to every other. The worker (*W*) is in the center. The newcomer (*N*), must cut through — adapt or force through — the maze. It may require considerable flexibility (partial deegotization) or inner strength to make his way into the group through domination or adaptation.

*B* is a schematic representation of a "mobile" group. In configuration I there is a strong relation between the two individuals (bilateral) in the solid ellipse, (*c*) having a loose and partial relation with (*a*) and (*b*). He also moves about freely, as shown by the arrows, and relates himself to all or some co-members at different times (multilateral relation). II is a configuration of a bilateral relation permitting little or no invasion. *I* illustrates a *symbiotic* relation where (*a*) and (*b*) depend upon each other; *II* on the other hand, illustrates a *supportive* relation, where (*e*) is the support of (*d*); (*f*) is a "free-floating" individual who may or may not attach himself temporarily to different persons or configurations. He is shown here as having a strong attachment to the worker, which for therapeutic reasons he must be helped to resolve (Fig. 2); (*i*) is an isolate who works by himself and has little or no contact with the other members of the group. (*N*), the newcomer, need not cut through "lines of relationships" to feel acceptance and comfort. There are many possibilities for him to establish relationships.

Social fixity can also be expressed mathematically. The law of permutation operates here and the formula $S = n (n - 1), (n - 2), (n - 3) \dots (n - n + 1)$ can be applied. Such density of attitudes and social solidity makes it impossible for a weak, disturbed or anxious person to fit into a group.

Disturbed persons need groups of social mobility where they can feel free and develop relationships at their own pace. It is this basic dynamic that makes therapy through a group possible. Pressure groups are not therapeutic except, perhaps, for very specific clients who fall within the diagnostic category of psychopathic personalities. It must also be noted that in interview therapy groups the degree of social fixity is higher than in activity groups.

## Levels of Identification

Identifications are on a considerably lower level in an activity therapy group than in an ordinary club, let us say, which in turn is on a lower level than in an interview therapy group. Because of basic differences among the members and because they are heterogeneous psychologically and socially as compared with an ordinary club, assimilation and integration into the group do not take place until much later in treatment. In fact, the capacity to identify is very weak in many of our clients because of early experiences in relationships. As image distortions because of distrust and fear are overcome, capacity to identify is increased. Important is the growing ability on the part of each client to accept the co-presence of other persons and to work out with them some method of living.

Too much emphasis upon developing relationships in an activity therapy group would be an error. What we seek is to develop a *capacity* for relationships. This is largely due to the fact that activity group therapy centers around the ego strengthening of the individual rather than upon his libido development. In interview therapy of adolescent girls, for example, libido factors are ever present, but not so in the group treatment of children in the latency period and puberty. We deal in the latter predominantly with the nonsexual social drives or the desexualized libido.

Although the majority of our clients are referred to us because of faulty "social" development, this condition is largely due to youth and character structure, rather than gross sexual distortions. As the child becomes secure, accepts himself and gains confidence in his abilities, he is able to relate himself better to other people. However, we utilize in this process the love needs which drive every individual toward other persons. We designate these needs as "social hunger." Thus, in group therapy the ego and libido — the *self* and the *group* impulses — run parallel and develop simultaneously. The point must be made that in activity group therapy the ego is much more involved than is the sexual libido. This is not the case to the same degree in interview group therapy for adolescents. From the little work we have done in this field it seems to us that relationships among adolescent girls in the groups are strongly charged with erotic content. The girls talk about each other's appearance, they are interested in one another's shapes and clothes, and are preoccupied with boys and sex. They often hug each other, comb one another's hair, and put make-up on each other's faces. There is definitely a personal interest with sexual connotations. Interest in each other's love affairs and petting parties, too, would indicate that sexual interest is present.

The attitude toward the worker in interview groups is more sharply defined, very much like toward a mother. In activity group therapy workers function as parent substitutes and some of the children refer to them as "mamma," "papa," or "unk." Because of the nonparticipatory role and the unilateral relation that exists here, it is not consummated into a close personal (libidinal) relationship. Since one cannot affect any area of the personality without at the same time affecting other areas to varying degrees, it is understandable how girls in our interview groups have gained greatly in ego strength as well. Here they are with friends who like them, accept them, listen to their opinions, and take them seriously. In other words, "they belong," a feeling which these adolescents have not had either at home, in school, or in their recreational and free time associations.

Friendships established in the groups for adolescents are carried on outside indicating that identifications in these groups are much more intense than they are in activity group therapy. One reason lies in the nature of the group activities. In one case the manual occupations form the center of interest, while in the other, this center is the other members of the group. Thus both identification and mutual transference are set up more intensely in the latter. Another element to be considered is the age of the children. The drive of adolescents toward each other is greater than among younger children. Adolescence is a time when group awareness and the identifications with others is accelerated. Another factor is that identifications among girls is stronger than among boys. Still another factor is that the worker's emotional and verbal inactivity does not encourage personal interaction, transferences, and identifications. In interview groups these processes are helped and stimulated by the worker's activity as they are also in individual treatment.

What has been said here does not mean that relationships are absent in activity groups. They are continually in operation. Identifications are also set up, but what is important here is not to exaggerate their significance. The center of treatment is the situation which helps to overcome psychological blockings, release internalized repressions, build up self-restraint through compensatory gratifications as a result of being recognized, accepted, and having status. The fact that the adult in charge does not press, criticize, or punish, and that the atmosphere in the group is warm and friendly, help the child gain new and wholesome attitudes.

## Phenomenon of Nodal Behavior

The children in an activity therapy group feel strained and act subdued during the early meetings. Comparatively little overt aggressiveness occurs. They seem afraid to reveal themselves. They work with materials more or less avidly and have very little contact with one another. This period of acclimatization and quiescence is longer where the members have not previously known each other. Previous acquaintance shortens initial insecurity, the warming-up period is briefer, and release occurs sooner. The presence of outgoing or aggressive children also accelerates the warming-up period.

Groups alternate between stages of equilibrium and disequilibrium. Conflicts, fights, playful hilarity, and destructiveness are followed by periods of quiet and constructive activity. These cycles have a definite rhythm. At first they are more frequent during the eating period, contributed by the anxiety associated with food and the closer intimacy around the table. Habitual behavior similar to that of the home, such as fighting and hilarity, may also be a factor as well as the stimulating effect of food. The period of hyperactivity or group disequilibrium will be referred to as *nodal* behavior, while the stages of quiescence and equilibrium as *antinodal* behavior (Fig. 4).

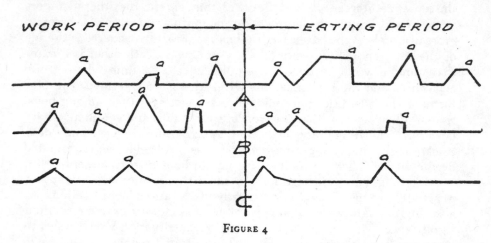

FIGURE 4

As the children become more acclimatized to the situation, hyperactivity (nodal behavior) occurs more frequently during the work period than during the eating period. Even after a boisterous meeting, boys and girls can bring themselves under control and settle down to a quiet meal. Conflict or hilarity, if any, are confined to individual or small subgroups and do not involve the group as a whole. This is indicative of increased security and freedom, increased preoccupation with and interest in each other and the worker. Gradually the distribution of nodal and antinodal behavior are equally distributed, indicating general improvement and greater ease in the group.

Food anxiety is also gradually decreased and there appears a better relationship among the children. An equal distribution of cycles also indicates a growing inner poise which after many months, leads to complete disappearance of cyclical behavior. The group now functions more evenly.

The social therapeutic process occurs at the point where hyperactivity is transformed into a state of equilibrium; self-control, compromise, mutual understanding and other neutralizing factors are set up which help the individual grow psychologically. Our opinion is that the transition from the nodal to the antinodal state is the growth-producing situation in activity group therapy, the point where personal integration, maturity, and emotional growth take place.

In a group where there is constant or too frequent eruption of hyperactivity with inadequate or infrequent transition to equilibrium, little therapy can be expected. The group is in constant turmoil, conflict, and anxiety which affects every member. The neurotic child grows even more anxious and may stop coming to meetings. Other children either become more secure in their undesirable behavior or feel threatened by it. The child whose infancy has been prolonged finds an operational field that meets his desires only too well, but his needs for growth are not met by such a group. On the other hand, in a quiet group that maintains a constant state of equilibrium, little interpersonal process occurs. Each is preoccupied with his own manual interest and continues in the same state of development with which he came. In such groups little or no intrapsychic changes can occur. Therapy occurs where the group follows the pattern of alternate nodal and antinodal stages, for psychological changes usually accompany the transition from disequilibrium to equilibrium.

$A$ indicates the greater stability of the group during working time than during the eating period at the early stage of group life. This state is reversed later, as shown in $B$. $C$ represents schematically the behavior of the group after prolonged group treatment. The frequency and intensity of nodal behavior is more or less the same in both periods. The $a's$ represent stages of transition from nodal to equilibration when self-control, compromise, and group restraint set in.

The value of *instigators* and *neutralizers* in a group becomes apparent; the former activate the group and the latter bring it under control. However, both instigators and neutralizers must possess the capacity to move toward more balanced personality integration. Thus the more active child must have the capacity to bring himself under control through the group. If he does not, he continues to activate the group to a point from which it cannot make the transition to the quiet (antinodal) state. On the other hand, the neutralizers should not be repressive and prevent the hyperactivity and release by the other members.

Nodal and antinodal behavior proceed from a number of sources. Infectiousness of mood is one of the elements. The mood of the stronger children is taken on by the others. Present also is the mechanism of interstimulation common to all animals as well as man. One child may begin to play boisterously or grow hilarious and soon others who had been working, or who are normally self-contained, also lose self-control. This reacts upon the others who, in turn, act to intensify each other's mood. Thus there is an endless chain of interstimulating acts which may reach a point of group hysteria.

Most of the children who come to us have had their activity impulses and self-expressive drives inhibited. In a favorable situation, such as a therapy group, they are released. From the point of view of mental hygiene, this period of egress of emotion and activity catharsis is very important. Repressive authority has in the past impeded expression to a point where serious intrapsychic tensions have set it. Before the children can establish a psychic balance they first need to divest themselves of these tensions. The instigator, who may be a child with no conflicts about his behavior, has the beneficial effect of releasing the inhibitions of the others. The neutralizer, on the other hand, applies social controls and helps the integration of personality through the group situation and interpersonal reactions.

# Activity Group Parameters

CHARLES SEMONSKY and GLORIA ZICHT

The major sources of referral in most child and adolescent psychiatry clinics are schools, parents, and our liaison disciplines. One large group of children we all see for evaluation and for whom treatment planning always presents difficulties are latency and preadolescent boys referred for significant behavioral disturbances. This paper is a description of the initial efforts in our facility to treat eight such boys in an activity group in an outpatient clinic setting. It outlines our experiences and our findings.

A comprehensive evaluation of the patient is a necessity in the responsible selection of an indicated therapeutic modality. Significant factors include constitutional endowment, early rearing experiences, the family constellation, past and present conflicts, resolutions of developmental issues, and the social and cultural conditions which define the transitions of development into adolescence (Berman, 1957; Buckle, 1969; A. Freud, 1965; McDonald, 1965; Slavson, 1955, 1960; Stone and Church, 1957). While the difficulties in achieving such a comprehensive evaluation are all too common, we know that all are relevant factors in understanding a child's predicament and developing purposeful planning for him.

At the same time, we are confronted with our own economic considerations in terms of financial, professional, and, in crowded clinics, spatial factors which demand effective use of professional time and clinic facilities. Our responsibility is to provide the maximum therapeutic benefit to as many patients as possible without compromising the effectiveness of our work with any one of them.

For some years, we have known that group activities during latency and adolescence provide an effective means of modifying behavioral expression. Previous workers have demonstrated the importance of activity groups in the treatment of latency age boys. The technique was developed by Slavson in the 1930s and later modified according to the needs of different age groups and degrees of pathology (Slavson, 1943, 1945).

Scheidlinger (1960) and his coworkers (1959), using Slavson's approach as a model, describe work with lower socioeconomic group children (aged 8 to 18) who manifest severe ego disturbances. He emphasizes the importance of a "benign familylike setting," controlled gratification and regression," and the separation of reality from fantasy. Coolidge and Grunebaum (1964) discuss the combined use of individual and activity group treatment. In their case presentation, individual therapy is discontinued in favor of group therapy. They stress the importance of the group as the "proving ground where the child learns to live with people outside the family." This transitional aspect of the group in effecting healthy adaptation potentials and modifying character traits is noted by many workers (Frey, 1962; King, 1959; Patterson et al., 1956; Sager, 1960; Schulman, 1959). It is predicated upon the ability of the child to internalize a consistent sense of self and the capacity for independent functioning.

In 1945, Buxbaum stated, "The peak of group development is reached in pre-adolescence and adolescence" (p. 351). She relates the phenomena of socialization and peer identification developmentally to unresolved dependency strivings in conflict with the need to negotiate object ties from the family to the outside world. It is logical to use this normal path of resolution in the service of therapeutic goals. The importance of group therapy with latency and preadolescent children depends upon its utilization of developmental processes and defenses appropriate to that age group.

## Group Composition

The group members were chosen from our clinic waiting list. They are representative of a large number of older latency and preadolescent children evaluated annually and having certain characteristics in common.

All of the children were referred because of severe behavioral difficulties. Most of the referrals were initiated by local schools because of concern about the child's aggressive behavior, defiance of authority, and poor academic performance. The ability of the school to maintain these children within its facility was frequently in question and often conditional upon the child's receiving psychiatric help.

The children themselves show a remarkably similar behavioral profile representing severe disturbances in ego development. They are characterized by restlessness, lack of control over aggressive impulses, inability to tolerate frustration and delay gratification, conflicts with adults (especially those representing authority), poor academic performance, and use of denial and projection as major defense mechanisms.

Some, a minority, function at the opposite end of this spectrum. Passive patterns of aggressive expression are substituted for overt patterns. Withdrawal, sullenness, and compliance are prominent features. Dependent strivings are more overt and fostered to variable degrees by a maternal figure.

Characteristically, these children also share a lower socioeconomic background with a high incidence of broken homes. Concepts of the nuclear family and average expectable environment do not seem applicable. Fathers are generally not present in the homes with any constancy, and, when present, set examples of antisocial, psychopathic, and deviant behavior. In addition, the primary mothering figure is often variable, leading to inconsistencies in identification and expectation. The developmental progression leading to a positive sense of self with tolerance for frustration, delayed gratification, and healthy patterns of social interaction has been significantly undermined.

## Member Selection

The original members consisted of eight black males ranging in age from ten years, ten months to thirteen years, ten months. The social behavior of the boy was a primary referral concern in all cases. Five of the original eight members were referred directly by schools because of provocative and aggressive behavior, and of the remaining three, two were sources of concern expressed to the parent by the school. One boy (Michael) had evidence of minimal brain dysfunction. He had not previously been on medication, and because of his approaching adolescence and ability to integrate into the group, we elected to continue him without medication. Evaluation diagnosis according to GAP formulation (1966) placed most of the boys in the range of personality disorder or less severe pathology. Psychological testing raised the possibility of a fundamental ego defect in one boy (Anthony), and when this turned out to be the case, it was necessary to arrange a different treatment disposition. We replaced him with another boy from the waiting list.

A common and unifying characterisitc of all these boys was their disorganized family. None had a stable and satisfying relationship with his father, and five experienced at least two mothering figures before the age of five. None of the boys described satisfying peer relationships with mutual respect and sharing of gratifying experiences.

*Vincent*, age eleven years, ten months, was referred by his school because of his immature and aggressive behavior: he was suspended three times in two years. Vincent is an only child. His mother never married but lived with two men at different times, both of them heavy drinkers. These affairs were tumultuous, with final separations occurring when Vincent was two and seven years old. Vincent's mother is both overprotective of him and dependent upon him for companionship.

*Anthony*, age thirteen years, nine months, was referred by the Pediatric Clinic because of his frequent temper tantrums and threats of physical violence to his mother. Anthony is an only child, unwanted and born out-of-wedlock. His mother is openly rejecting of him. She describes only the difficulties and problems he has caused her. Anthony never knew his father, nor did he ever experience a long-term relationship with any man.

*Guy*, age thirteen years, ten months, was referred by the Orthopedic Clinic because of infantile behavior and sexual preoccupation. Guy was born with a moderate scoliosis and wears a corrective brace. His parents have been separated for seven years. Even though Guy sees his father every month, he is bitterly aware that his older brother is the favored child. Guy's mother has overprotected and infantilized him to the point of sharing the same bed with him until he was ten years old.

*Milton*, age thirteen years, two months, was referred to us by the Pediatric Clinic because of his mother's expressed concern that he was too inhibited and shy. Milton's parents divorced when he was ten years old. Prior to that, their marriage was marked by frequent fights, physical as well as verbal, and several short-term separations. Milton adopted the role of protector of his mother and two-year younger brother. He does not see his father at all now. At the time of referral, he had no close friends or activities outside of the home.

*Percy*, age eleven years, one month, was referred by the school because of disruptive behavior characterized by frequent fighting, whining, and demandingness. Percy's parents separated when he was four years old. His mother, a chronically depressed woman and heroin addict, has undergone two psychiatric hospitalizations. Three years ago Percy moved in with his maternal grandmother, who has since become his legal guardian.

*Michael*, age twelve years, three months, was referred by the school because of belligerence and immature behavior. Michael is an unplanned and unwanted child. He was raised by his grandmother from the time of birth until the age of nine. When Michael's grandmother became ill, he was sent from the South to live with an aunt and uncle. Within two years, both his grandmother and his uncle died. His aunt has not remarried and there are no other children. He has seen his mother only infrequently and not at all in the past year.

*Kevin*, age twelve years, seven months, was referred by his mother because of his frequent fighting at home and in school. Kevin is the second youngest of four children. After a long history of marital conflict, his parents divorced when Kevin was eight years old. Kevin's father continues to provide support for the family by court order but visits only infrequently, and even then the visits are marked by continuous arguing with Kevin's mother. The mother, a strong-willed and determined woman, has kept the family unit intact. Kevin's older brother and two sisters seem well adjusted.

*Nat*, age ten years, ten months, was referred by his maternal grandmother. She was concerned about his jealous, demanding behavior at home and reports from school that he was fearful of joining in play with boys his own age. Nat's parents separated when he was four years old. His mother sent him to live with his grandparents when he was six. The following year his grandfather died. At the time of referral, Nat spent most of his time engaged in solitary activities and had few friends.

*William*, age eleven years, two months, was referred to our clinic by his school because of aggressive behavior and declining school performance. William was seven years old when his parents separated. It was necessary for William's mother to get a court injunction against her common-law husband in order to effect the separation. She is now seeing a man with an alcoholic problem and has had occasion to call the police when he became abusive.

## Group Process

Our expressed goals in working with these children were to utilize their available capacities and strengths to foster positive interactions among themselves and with the group leaders. The group as a unit would provide the matrix within which the now obsolete responses to earlier conflicts and deprivations, often preverbal, could be met, pointed out, confronted, and altered.

Simultaneously, the individual's self-esteem would be enhanced by activities, interactions, and support perceived as gratifying by the child. The alternatives to maladaptive patterns which we hoped to offer were: delayed gratification in lieu of immediate gratification; control and sublimation instead of overt and direct aggression; assertiveness instead of submissiveness; independence instead of dependency; identification with group norms instead of suggestibility; and active participation instead of withdrawal.

As therapists, we saw the need to establish a nonverbal alliance which would allow regressive and deviant behavior, but within the tolerance limits of our own capacity and that of the group. It would be important for the child to recognize that someone in authority could set limits without being punitive, could be consistently firm and at the same time accepting, could gratify without bribery or seduction, and could ultimately care about him.

We set up our group based on Slavson's model (1945), utilizing Scheidlinger's modifications (1960) for children with serious ego disturbances. We added the further modification of male and female cotherapists.

Meetings were held in one of the offices of the outpatient clinic of the Division of Child and Adolescent Psychiatry at St. Luke's Hospital. Before each meeting, personal effects and breakable objects were removed and tables and chairs arranged in a large circle. Games or models were set up before the members arrived. Toward the end of the first year, members who arrived early helped in setting up the room.

The group met once a week after school for an hour and a half. Our first meetings were structured around an activity that was individual in nature and yet gathered the members around a table to share materials. The grouping of the members created an atmosphere for socialization. Plastic models and leather kits proved useful. They were easy to assemble, gave the members a common experience to talk about, something tangible to take home, and a sense of accomplishment.

Even so, some of the boys (Milton and Nat) were uneasy with this much interaction and found it necessary to leave the table under one pretext or another. We encouraged them to return, but did not force them. After several meetings their anxiety diminished and they were able to remain with the group.

From the start, the boys were permitted to yell, run, climb, argue and wrestle. They were not allowed to attack others, deface or throw objects, or inflict pain. We identified hostile and destructive behavior to the individual member and described the consequences of that behavior. We supported the boys' attempts to verbalize feelings rather than act on them.

Following the activities, we provided sodas and doughnuts, the high point of the meeting. The boys' behavior and feelings about our buying food for them pervaded the entire meeting. Sodas were hidden under jackets and behind curtains. We were questioned repeatedly about the time for refreshments and the rules governing their distribution. There were frequent struggles between members to ensure even distribution. If one member was absent, the group focused attention on the extra food available. Two of the more withdrawn members (Milton and Nat) who could not interact competitively with the others began arriving late — too late to participate in activities, but just in time for refreshments. Therefore, we reversed the group format and began with refreshments, followed by activities. Thereafter, the tension which had pervaded the entire meeting and which focused on food lessened. We also observed that it was easier for members to share materials at the table. Our fear that they might want to leave early proved unfounded.

By the end of session 8, it was clear that the group had coalesced. Friendships established within the group carried to the outside. Some members began to arrive early regularly, anxious for "their group" (in distinction to other groups in the clinic) to begin. If a member did not appear, the others expressed concern about him rather than turning attention to the extra food which would be available. Between sessions 10 and 12 we were able collectively to establish rules of conduct which allowed for equitable sharing within the group. When this happened, we felt the group was sufficiently stable for more active interventions and for limit settings.

Because our group met within a clinic, it was necessary to emphasize the group's responsibility to others. Repeated descriptions of the effects and consequences of running up and down the hall, picking up the telephone, and of opening and closing office doors gradually altered their behavior. In "talk sessions" we emphasized the importance of the clinic to others as well as to ourselves and the fact that if we did not respect others' needs, they would not respect ours. These explanations were effective in the long run. From talking with secretaries and patients in the waiting room, the boys learned about other groups which met in the clinic.

It is interesting that they never asked us directly about other groups and our possible involvement with them. Rather, there was a sense of one-upmanship in their telling us about the other groups and sundry functions of the clinic. At one meeting, we discussed a possible schedule change. A time segment was suggested by one of the members which conflicted with Dr. S.'s schedule. When he told the group it was not possible to meet at that time, Percy, with animation and self-satisfaction, announced, "I know why, Dr. S. It's because you meet with them little kids." Kevin corrected him, "He doesn't meet with them little kids; the other doctor does." Undaunted, Percy continued, "You see, Dr. S., we know what goes on around here, too." It seemed fair that if we could probe into their lives, they could and would probe into ours.

Members showed an increasing tendency to exert controls on each other and to express concern not only for the group members but for other patients as well and for the clinic as a whole. A good example happened during session 18, when Michael was exceptionally loud, boisterous, and provocative with Dr. S. As spokesman for the group, and only after considerable effort to help Michael control himself, Kevin asked that we adhere to our previous agreement that anyone who persistently disrupted the group leave. The other members agreed, and Michael left, making it clear he was doing so only because the group wanted him to and not out of any submission to Dr. S.

In this example, the strong and positive identification with the group as a whole and the peer identifications among the members balanced the negative feelings experienced toward the male therapist. We shall come back to this important transference reaction in a moment. Suffice it to say, we did work to avoid power struggles with the members, and when confronting them with a particular behavior, did so in a manner which offered simultaneous support or allowed a face-saving exit. It was important that we not reinforce their expectation of authority figures, especially males, as hostile, belligerent, exploitative, condescending, and demeaning individuals.

There had been very little discussion of problems, behavior, or concerns outside of the group itself. Isolated instances, for example, when Guy's mother shaved his head because she did not approve of his Afro, led to affectively charged exchanges of material reflecting their chaotic backgrounds and genuine fears. At best, these exchanges were brief and gave every evidence that the members were not yet able to deal with them on a verbal level. We decided therefore to concentrate primarily on the group experience, and to look for generalizations from this focus.

One activity which proved helpful in linking the group experience to the child's daily environment was an enamel jewelry-making set. It required the sharing of materials, the chance for imaginative creation, and, most important, attractive decorative objects which could be shared with family. The materials were inexpensive enough for the members to make dozens of pendants, cuff links, earrings, etc. At first they were very concerned that there be enough pieces; in fact they looked like animated Christmas trees before the day was over. Their self-concern, as with the food at earlier meetings, was obvious. Soon, however, they brought back stories of how their relatives enjoyed the jewelry made for them and how their friends, too, admired their creative works. With this positive response and enhancement of esteem, they were then able to concentrate more effectively on the task at hand, creating intricate designs and multiple layering effects. In short, their ability to concentrate, to endure frustration, and delay gratification was enhanced by the presence of a positive motivation: feedback from parents and peers and in association with authoritarian support, guidance, encouragement, and approval.

Returning now to an earlier point, we wish to consider one of the most interesting behavioral patterns acted out in the group, namely, the manner in which the members related to the two therapists. The difference was striking: the members were more comfortable dealing with the female therapist than with the male. They initially looked to Mrs. Z. for nurturance and caring, and also for discipline and control, giving her in effect attributes of dual gender roles — both father and mother. For example, during the first several weeks Mrs. Z. could effect far more verbal limit setting than could Dr. S. Questions and requests for help went first to her, and only when she referred them to Dr. S. would the individual members use his help. This was especially true of the more active members. Percy expressed it rather well when he said, "Mrs. Z., if you want to stop us from acting bad, what you need to do is get a big black woman in here." Not only did the group look to Mrs. Z. for limits, but even the presence of Dr. S. had a disquieting effect. Assuming a passive role, he was challenged and provoked by the more active members. It was in working through these behaviors and attitudes toward gender-differentiated authority that the cotherapy structure was most helpful.

The racial difference between the white therapists and black members did not impede group cohesion or the identification process. We expected that we and the members would invest in the group and that the the fabric of cohesion would consist of qualities which transcend racial difference. Racist terms such as "white trash" and "nigger," the most frequently used animadversion between members, were seen as cowardly "cop-outs" to avoid the conflict of the moment. As such, their use signaled defeat, and, understandably, they were used infrequently.

The relationship of the cotherapists was warm and friendly and characterized by mutual respect. The members, however, saw it as a sexual relationship. For example, they wanted to know what we were doing in the room before they arrived and made many allusions to our having sexual relations. These notions were met by comments such as, "I'll bet you think that's all men and women do together," and, "Here we go with the old sex routine again!" We felt their initial expectation of a sexually based relationship between therapists reflected the circumstances of their rearing, where adult men were often experienced primarily as sexual intruders. The constant belligerence toward the male therapist gradually became attenuated over a period of several months, primarily through the intervention of the female therapist. She was able to describe the interaction of the members in relation to the male therapist and point out the discrepancy between their expectation and his intent. One of the more dramatic examples of an intervention occurred when Michael repeatedly provoked Dr. S. by punching him in the arm, and taunting him to retaliate. Attempts to resolve the conflict verbally did not succeed. Finally, Dr. S. took hold of Michael and held his hands pinned to his sides. Meanwhile, Mrs. Z. explained to Michael that he was being held only until he could establish his own controls; that Dr. S. did not want to fight with him; and that if something made him angry, it could better be talked out than fought out. Michael was able to take in this clarification and to exert his own control, and later after leaving the room and calming down, to discuss his anger. By the end of six months, the feeling of the group about Dr. S. was such that he was sought out for advice and approval. Michael frequently championed his cause.

## Evaluation of Group Treatment

At the end of one year, we concluded that three of the nine members selected for group treatment either could not be maintained in the group or did not profit by the group experience:

*Vincent*, a passive-aggressive personality type locked in a passive-dependent relation with his mother, adopted an immature "baby" role. He was an only child. His attachment to and identification with an infantilizing mother were stronger than the outward identification fostered by a group experience. Fighting and truancy in school continued and led to expulsion.

*Anthony*, referred because of disruptive behavior in school and frequent arguments with his mother, was not able to maintain relationships with peers or adults except by dominating and controlling situations. Within the first two months of the group, it became evident from his behavior that his ego strengths were insufficient. He became frankly psychotic and required placement.

*Guy*, referred because of demanding behavior and sexual preoccupation, was the oldest member of the group. His advanced age, physical maturity, and exhibitionism proved too much for the group to handle. He was transferred to an older adolescent group. Follow-up a year later showed that Guy could not be maintained in a group setting. A reevaluation disclosed more significant pathology than was first suspected with a diffusion of ego boundaries and the use of paranoid defenses.

The other members, however, made substantial gains through association with the group experience.

*Milton*, referred because of shy, inhibited behavior in school, had great difficulty making friends. His mother was very protective of him and did not encourage socialization. In the group he withdrew at first, but with support and encouragement and by association with another member (Nat), he became more assertive. After five months, Milton decided to stop coming because "there was too much fighting." After leaving the group, he joined the Boy Scouts. Milton returned to visit the group the following year. He had remained with the Boy Scouts, was doing well in school, and was active in the local community center.

*Percy*, referred for disruptive behavior and poor peer relations, was originally sullen, negative, and demanding. The group confronted his infantile behavior and gradually accepted him as that behavior modified. At the end of the year, Percy was more assertive and less negativistic and demanding than he had previously been. His improvement was substantiated by reports from home and school.

*Michael*, referred by his school because of immature and aggressive behavior, was one of the most negativistic members, and had the greatest conflict dealing with male authority. At the end of the year, he was strongly invested in the group and returned the following fall, saying, "We had a lot of fights last year, but this year there won't be many " And that is how it has been. In addition, there are no complaints from school, and his aunt states he is getting on better at home and in school.

*Kevin*, referred because of frequent fighting at home and in school, was the least troubled and most independent of the members. He adjusted quickly with relatively little of the regressive behavior evidenced by the other members. His behavior at home and school and his school performance improved during the year.

*Nat*, referred because of jealous demanding behavior at home and excessive shyness in school, was the most withdrawn member of the group. He frequently removed himself from activities. Gradually, and with encouragement, he became more assertive and verbal. At home, he became less dependent and demanding. A report from school, however, indicated little improvement there.

*William*, referred because of aggressive behavior at home and in school together with declining school performance, adjusted well to the group. He related primarily to Kevin and Dr. S. By the end of the year, there was considerable improvement in his behavior at home and in school. Academic achievement returned to a satisfactory level.

## Discussion

One of our questions when the group was organized was the feasibility of treating these children in a group within a hospital clinic setting. Previous workers have described their success with similar children, but their work was done within a community setting or family agency. We found that while we could work effectively in a clinic, the initial disruptiveness of our group and the members' difficulty in leaving the clinic created tensions among the staff members which required sensitive handling. At one point the survival of the group was in question. The conflict with the staff was very real and necessitated an awareness and sensitivity to others in the clinic. It was a potent cohesive force for both the therapists and members. By making minor adjustments in scheduling and by dealing with the problems as they arose in the group, we resolved these difficulties. Still, a community-based program geographically separate from the hospital and more flexible in activities and time, seems more desirable. To be effective, however, the group must experience its relationship and responsibilities to other elements of the program.

We thought at first that group treatment of these boys would offer an attractive economic advantage over individual treatment. That this did not prove to be the case was due in part to the cotherapy model. Nevertheless, cotherapy offered significant advantages with these children, and we strongly support it. Additional time required for the preparation of each session, buying materials and food, setting up the room, putting it back in order, discussion of group process and strategies, and maintaining contacts with families and schools resulted in a time investment fully equivalent to the treatment process using the diadic relationship. The choice of treatment modality, then, should be determined by the effectiveness expected of the treatment, and not by arguments of possible economy.

The cotherapy model was useful in two ways: not only did the individual therapists become objects for the transference, but their relationship took on transferential qualities. The multiplicity of interactions and conflict manifestations and their resolutions provided the substance of our therapy and the *raison d'etre* for the group.

In addition, the cotherapy model buffered the intense counter-transference reactions experienced by the therapists. We agree with Kassoff (1958) that "the tremendous emotional demands of such deprived boys are really too great for one therapist" (p. 71). The mutual support of the therapists, especially during the settling-in phase of the group, was an important factor in the group's success.

There still remains the question of why this particular treatment approach is effective and what the actual effects on the individuals are. The answers to these questions lead into a theoretical discussion beyond the scope of the paper. Nevertheless, a dynamic perspective is helpful in understanding and containing the anxieties of such a group.

The regression of our members to points of oral and anal fixations with subsequent integration at higher levels of organization is similar to the work described by Alpert (1959) with preschool children. However, the fact that our members enter treatment at a different developmental level makes for significant differences. The establishment of the diadic relationship, with its dependent manifestations and strong emotional attachments, is now too strongly defended against. Attempts to treat these boys on a one-to-one basis are notoriously unsuccessful. In a group setting, the situation alters.

Members relate simultaneously to both the leaders and the group members. In Alpert's (1959) context the development of an "*exclusive, need-satisfying* relationship" and of "regression to the *point of traumatic fixation*" (p. 181) is no longer possible. In fact, it is doubtful that the latter phrase has relevance to this group of boys who were undoubtedly traumatized from the day of conception. What the group experience does offer is an alternative perception of the world and themselves, a perception altered by partial satisfaction of dependent yearnings and reinforced by peer validation.

The common denominator in the lives of these boys is their broken, often chaotic family life and the effect it has had on their character formation and defense system. The negotiation of the oedipal conflict with development into and through latency, the consolidation of the superego as a discrete psychic structure, and the use of defenses important for socialization and increased reality testing are in a very fluid state. To quote Sarnoff (1971), "The potential stability of the state of latency in a child is defined in terms of the strength of the ego structures related to the production of latency" (p. 402). At the same time, consolidation depends upon the child's identification with a parental model, the internalization of an ideal to which he aspires, and the cultural and social reinforcements he experiences.

The creation of a family model in an activity-oriented group affords a second chance for the development and reinforcement of defenses characteristic of latency. The capacity for sublimation and reaction formation in the service of increased reality testing was significantly limited in all these boys at the time of referral. It remained limited for those boys who did not profit from the group. They were not able to use the therapists as models for identification or interact appropriately with the other members. Those who did profit gave evidence of using the experience constructively and incorporating it into the fabric of their developmental progression.

It is not possible to estimate the ultimate effects of this work on personality structure. Our own thinking is in accordance with that of Weil (1953) that "a remaining deficient personality structure" exists in spite of the clinical improvement. But it is nonetheless significant that clinical improvement does occur and that these boys functioned at a higher and more satisfying level of integration as a result of their group experiences.

**References**

Alpert, A. (1959), "Reversibility of Pathological Fixations Associated with Maternal Deprivation in Infancy," *The Psychoanalytic Study of the Child*, 14:169-185. New York: International Universities Press.

Berman, S. (1957), "Psychotherapy of Adolescents at Clinic Level," in *Psychotherapy of the Adolescent*, ed. B. H. Balser. New York: International Universities Press, pp. 86-112.

Buckle, D. F. (1969), "Mental Health Services for Adolescents," in *Adolescence: Psychosocial Perspectives*, ed. G. Caplan & S. Lebovici. New York: Basic Books, pp. 363-371.

Buxbaum, E. (1945), "Transference and Group Formation in Children and Adolescents," *The Psychoanalytic Study of the Child*, 1:351-365. New York: International Universities Press.

Coolidge, J. C. & Grunebaum, M. G. (1964), "Individual and Group Therapy of a Latency Age Child," *Int. J. Group Psychother.*, 14:84-96.

Freud, A. (1965), *Normality and Pathology in Childhood*, New York: International Universities Press.

Frey, L. A. (1962), "Support and the Group: Generic Treatment Form," *Soc. Wk.*, 7:35-42.

Group for the Advancement of Psychiatry (1966), *Psychopathological Disorders in Childhood*, New York: Group for the Advancement of Psychiatry, Report No. 62.

Guerney, B., Jr. (1964), "Filial Therapy," *J. Consult. Psychol.*, 28:304-310

Kassoff, A. I. (1958), "Advantages of Multiple Therapists in a Group of Severely Acting-out Adolescent Boys," *Int. J. Group Psychother.*, 8:70-75.

King, C. H. (1959), "Activity Group Therapy with a Schizophrenic Boy: Follow-up Two Years Later," *Int. J. Group Psychother.*, 9:184-194.

McDonald, M. (1965), "The Psychiatric Evaluation of Children," *This Journal*, 4:569-612.

Patterson, G., Schwartz, R., & Van Der Wart, E. (1956), "The Integration of Group and Individual Therapy," *Amer. J. Orthopsychiat.*, 26:618-629.

Sager, C. J. (1960), "Concurrent Individual and Group Analytic Psychotherapy," *Amer. J. Orthopsychiat.*, 30:225-241.

Sarnoff, C. A. (1971), "Ego Structure in Latency," *Psychoanal. Quart.*, 40:387-414.

Scheidlinger, S. (1960), "Experiential Group Treatment of Severely Deprived Latency-Age Children," *Amer. J. Orthopsychiat.*, 30:356-368.

———, Douville, M., Harrahill, C., King, C. H., & Minor, J. D. (1959), "Activity Group Therapy for Children in a Family Agency," *Soc. Casework,* 40:193-201.

Schulman, I. (1959), "Transference, Resistance, and Communication Problems in Adolescent Psychotherapy Groups," *Int. J. Group Psychother.* 9:496-503.

Slavson, S. R. (1943), *An Introduction to Group Therapy,* New York: International Universities Press, 1954.

———(1945), "Differential Methods of Group Therapy in Relation to Age Levels," *Nerv. Child,* 4:196-210.

———(1955), "Criteria for Selection and Rejection of Patients for Various Types of Group Psychotherapy," *Int. J. Group Psychother.,* 5:3-30.

———(1960), "When Is a 'Therapy Group' not a Therapy Group?" *Int. J. Group Psychother.,* 10:3-21.

Stone, L. J., & Church, J. (1957), *Childhood and Adolescence,* New York: Random House.

Weil, A. P. (1953), "Certain Severe Disturbances of Ego Development in Childhood," *The Psychoanalytic Study of the Child,* 8:271-287, New York: International Universities Press.

# LIMIT-SETTING

# Experiences in Group Therapy with Latency-Age Boys

NORMAN EPSTEIN and SHELDON ALTMAN

The Children's Psychiatric Center, in its development of groups to service latency-age children (nine to eleven), initially attempted to utilize the model of nonverbal activity group therapy as a therapeutic modality. Central to the concept of the activity group is the high degree of permissive behavior tolerated by the therapist who presents himself in a consciously passive role and utilizes a minimum of verbal interventions. As the name of the group implies, the children are engaged in a selective variety of craft activities that serve as a springboard for eliciting feelings and encouraging peer interaction. The underlying concept of therapeutic effectiveness is based on the belief that when children are given the opportunity to express feelings in and through activity, the resultant catharsis results in a breakthrough of repressed impulses and affect with subsequent changes in behavior. Peer interaction is viewed as resulting in corrective modifications of interpersonal modes of behavior, with the former being subtly encouraged by selective, nonverbal interventions on the part of the therapist. The process of growth is enhanced when the leader does not serve as an object of negative emotions but does provide the permissive atmosphere within which the child's identification with the therapist occurs.

When this type of group therapy for the latency-age child was implemented at the Children's Psychiatric Center, the program was soon threatened with total collapse because of the apparent inappropriateness of activity group therapy for the type of youngster we were attempting to service. There appeared to be a mismatch between the therapeutic modality employed and the type of child we were attempting to serve. In effect, we were endeavoring to fit a round ball into a square hole. Despite a variety of therapeutic strategems on the part of the therapist, the element of contagion generated the lightning spread of acting-out behavior in the group. The dedication, warmth, sensitivity, and therapeutic skills of the therapist appeared to be irrelevant when confined by the classical approach of activity group therapy to an emphasis on activity and limited therapist interventions.

In evaluating the youngsters in the group, it became increasingly evident that they were not repressed, fearful, and withdrawn children requiring therapeutic interventions which would encourage expression of inner feelings and conflicts but, instead, were children who exercised a full repertoire of power techniques which were seemingly impervious to adult interventions. Schools are prone to refer such children for therapy because they exhibit difficulties in exercising behavioral self-control and constitute a serious threat to classroom management, and the children themselves are often quite ingenious and successful in applying an intricate host of behaviors devoted to the frustration of a teacher's efforts to maintain discipline. Our earlier tendency to view the behavior as reactive to underlying feelings of inferiority and powerlessness was the result of questionable formula thinking which reflected a resistance to accepting the reality of power strivings that were exercised and displayed with resolute force on the part of the child. Upon re-examination we could find little evidence to support the contention that these children suffered from feelings of "powerlessness" in their dealings with adults and peers.

A latency-age activity group, in existence for several months, produced no discernible positive change in the behavior of these boys. Parents were questioning the usefulness of treatment; teachers were showing signs of losing patience with the behavior of the boys in the classroom; and the therapist was becoming disillusioned with the effectiveness of group treatment of children with poor inner controls. We were faced with the choice of either looking for new insights and skills or giving up using the group as a medium of change for this type of youngster.

## Setting Limits

The introduction of verbal content represented a first step in what eventually developed into a total restructuring of the group. We introduced and insisted upon structure in the form of limits and expectations for behavior, initially doing this in connection with the serving of treats. We moved in this direction out of a recognition that a permissive atmosphere, the therapist's benign presence, and play materials such as tools, paints, and other craft materials used to stimulate expression of internal conflicts worked against ego integration and toward the encouragement of random, regressive, acting-out behavior. Our aim was to initiate a process that would involve each boy in evaluating his behavior in terms of self-perceptions and provide a means by which he could move toward the goal of greater behavioral control.

We decided to use the feeding time portion of the activity group session to initiate changes, not only because this was usually the most difficult period in the group session, but also because the boys were seated around a table and this was conducive to talking. The boys were told that "hacking around" with the treats would no longer be permitted, that unacceptable behavior would be the focus of discussion, and that treat time was the time for the boys to talk about difficulties at home, in school, and with peers. The therapist identified unacceptable behavior as any distraction that interfered with the main purpose of the group, which was to help the members learn how to use their heads to stay out of trouble. The therapist "demanded" that the boys remain in their seats, refrain from walking about the room, or engage in any other activity that would distract from talking together. When one of the youngsters reacted by running about the room, the therapist forcefully returned the youngster to his chair as a visible demonstration to the group that infantile behavior would not be tolerated. When a second youngster began to throw food around, the therapist invited group censure of this boy by pointing out the babyish quality of this behavior. The fact that the boys joined the therapist in censuring one of their peers suggested that there was a facet of these children that still sought to identify with the adult and wanted his approval. It was decided to use this phenomenon to begin the establishment of a new group culture.

## Common Sense Club

We decided to push for a reconceptualization of the purposes of the group in the minds of the boys. The therapist deliberately became the dominant figure. He suggested that the group be called "The Common Sense Club," which was explained as a club where "boys grow up by figuring out how to get along with people." The emphasis was on helping the youngsters develop greater skill in social interaction by questioning their existing inappropriate behavior styles. The therapist utilized the process of confrontation wherein each boy was faced with the therapist's conceptualization of the infantile, unproductive pattern of his behavior. The other members of the group were invited to verbalize their perceptions concerning each other's behavior. It was interesting to note that there was a very close correlation between the therapist's and the group members' observations. The therapist's verbalizations and attitudes placed a heavy premium on the ability to figure out alternate forms of response to difficulties in school and at home. The concept of the development of self-control was fostered as the highest attribute of masculinity and growing up. We thus attempted to create a culture counter to the one which prevailed in the lives of the youngsters.

The initial response to our introduction of verbal content and structure was one of disbelief, and the boys engaged in their usual behavior of hacking around. We responded to this by reaffirming the firm limits and expectations previously outlined. The boys were told quite clearly that we would not tolerate "hacking around," and the therapist indicated a readiness to utilize physical restraint if necessary. He repeatedly reminded the boys that they were members of "The Common Sense Club," a unique organization to help boys manage their lives more effectively. It did not take long for the boys to refer to the group by this name.

The overall reaction to this change in the group's nature was encouraging enough to give rise to a decision to give up the activity room and have the group meet in the therapist's office. It was found that the therapist's office encouraged verbal interchange as it provided a smaller, more intimate setting and greater physical proximity between the therapist and group members. The therapist was able, for example, to reinforce positive behavior by patting a member on the back when the boy made a significant verbal contribution to the discussion. The boys were encouraged to report difficulties that had occurred during the week, and the therapist verbally pushed boys to discuss how a group member might have handled a particular situation differently and more effectively. Utilizing this process, we learned a great deal that we incorporated into our techniques. Our handling of one boy within this framework illustrates our experiences.

## Case Illustration

Steven, a nine-year-old, was on the brink of expulsion from school. His judgment and controls appeared to be so primitive that he had his parents, teachers, and previous therapists, relating to him as if he was "crazy," a helpless victim of his impulsivity, driven by forces outside of his control. Perceived in this manner, Steven dictated to his environment and his omnipotence was rarely challenged. He was in an indisputable position of power and control. This situation did little to help or motivate

Steven's ego to gain mastery over his "crazy" behavior. Steven reacted to the therapist's initial attempts to restructure the group during snack time by picking up a bottle of carbonated soda, shaking it, and spraying the contents on the other boys. The therapist unceremoniously removed the bottle from Steven's clutches and emphatically stated that babyish behavior would not be accepted in the group. The therapist then focused group discussion on Steven's infantile behavior by inviting individual members to comment. Steven blurted out that he was not a baby and offered to fight several boys to prove his point. Only physical restraint by the therapist kept the peace. Steven rationalized that he was just having some fun. Pushed by the therapist to differentiate between fun and acting like a "nut," Steven argued that he was as smart as any kid in the group and added that he was going to be a scientist when he grew up, as if to lend credence to his claim. The therapist stimulated the boys to talk about what it takes to become a scientist by encouraging them to think about what is required to reach one's goals. The group slowly began to participate in its first serious discussion, taking its lead from the quiet, deliberate tone set by the therapist.

In the sessions that followed the boys appeared to be pulled between infantile and more mature behavior. However, they increasingly took over the responsibility of reminding Steven to "use his head" whenever he was acting "babyish." The therapist consistently stimulated discussion of Steven's beliefs that he had the stuff to become a scientist and contrasted this with his actual performance in significant areas of his life. For example, in one session we discussed the space program in terms of the control and confidence that the scientist on the ground must demonstrate to the astronauts. We then compared this with reports of Steven's behavior in the classroom which had earned him the reputation of the class clown. To our satisfaction, there were dramatic changes in Steven's group behavior, and, more significantly, his parents and teachers reported that he was displaying much better controls. His homeroom teacher commented that because Steven had "calmed down," the school was investing the money to replace a couple of door hinges that Steven had worn out.

Steven was subsequently discharged, and one year later, at the invitation of the therapist, returned to a new and strange group as a visiting expert on the subject of learning how to "use your head to stay out of trouble." This is not to suggest that all was smooth-sailing with the group but, rather, that our experience convinced us that latency-age boys with control problems could talk about their difficulties and help each other in the group.

## Parent Participation

Since our initial departure from the traditional activity group, we have added other innovations to maximize the impact of treatment. Most recently, we have included parents in at least one group session during each month of treatment, and this has evolved into a crucial component of the group's functioning. Parent-child confrontations have enabled us to quickly deal with distortions and blatant fabrications. They have also served the purpose of giving the parents an opportunity to have meaningful interchanges focused on mutual problem-solving with their child. The parent is encouraged to listen to the child's description and explanations of a situation that is presenting difficulties. The child is then encouraged to listen to the parent's perception of the same situation. The therapist discourages recriminations and threats, constantly verbalizing the idea that solutions to the difficulty can be found. The parent is often gratified to discover that his child can be a deliberate human being.

The child's knowledge that, through the therapist's interchanges with the parents, new sources of information will be available constitutes a critical arena for interaction. The interchange can be utilized to open new avenues of praise and recognition by the parent for the child which serve as a reinforcement of acceptable behavior.

In a recent session, a mother revealed her complete frustration in attempting to handle her nine-year-old son who had been forging her name to notes sent home by his teacher. The mother was amazed when her son responded to prodding by the other boys by tearfully saying that he did not want to be a drop-out. She had always viewed her son as being very tough and unconcerned about his future. A probable solution was opened up when another boy announced, with an air of finality, that he knew what Mark's problem was. Encouraged by the group, this boy said that Mark wanted an education, wanted to be somebody, wanted to have a good job, but did not want to work for these things. The implication was that acting the clown was easier than developing the discipline to reach one's goals. The therapist highlighted that, in growing up, there is a reluctance to give up more babyish ways of dealing with situations and to develop self-control as a means of achieving future goals. He finished with the prediction that Mark would be a drop-out if he did not learn how to use his head. By this time, both mother and son were very distressed, and each sat without saying a word. The therapist directed the discussion toward ways in which Mark and his mother could live together with less friction. With help from all the youngsters, a plan was worked out to get Mark started on his homework which included the parents' setting of structure and realistic expectations. Mark left this group meeting feeling that he had his mother's understanding and support, while his mother left the session with a different view of her son's aspirations and concrete suggestions for helping him. A by-product of this dramatic interchange was the growing confidence of the boys that they could be of help to each other in developing ways of coping with their difficulties.

## Role of The Therapist

A further observation about our experiences has to do with the role of the therapist. As indicated in the clinical material, the therapist activates the group by setting the structure and then mobilizes discussion around how the boys use the group. It has been our experience that the boys gradually move to wanting to please the therapist, and they begin to imitate his style. There is open competition for who gets to sit in the therapist's chair. We have used this to support a boy's progress. For example, in the earlier described session the therapist praised the boy who summed up Steven's problem by inviting him to take over the therapist's chair. This process of identification with the therapist is encouraged and viewed as a legitimate growth stimulant in the latency-age child. The act of propitiating the therapist is not viewed as an act of mere submission but, rather, as a normal developmental phenomenon for this age group. The process of identification with the aggressor (therapist) is a deliberately sought-after phenomenon. The seeking of approval on the part of the child is viewed as a basic process in growth which in turn must be reinforced by the therapist's verbalizations and recognition. It is the therapist, to a greater extent than the group, who serves as the model for behavior. The child who is initially convinced that behaving with dignity and control is beyond his personal repertoire often mistakenly equates counterattack to provocation from others with a quality of masculinity and strength. Consequently, we attempt to teach alternate methods of response to provocation from peers.

Our experience with latency groups has indicated that verbal interchange is not beyond the scope of the young child and, indeed, can constitute a deeply moving therapeutic experience.

Therapy with the latency-age child, as indeed with all patients, becomes ritualized and loses meaning if not based on a pragmatic attitude that leaves room for experimentation. The methodology we have evolved is geared to the diversion and rechanneling of energies spent in unremunerative power ploys. The method is based on an awareness that the child clings to inappropriate uses of energies because of the satisfactions they bring in spite of overt turmoil and seeming failure in relationships and academic performance. The child often sees no viable alternative to maintaining the same ploys because adults in his environment inadvertently cling to their perceptions of the subject as a weak, helpless being who is the victim of forces over which he cannot exert control. We have attempted to develop a view of the acting-out child as capable of assuming responsibility for his behavior and involving himself in a verbal process of identifying areas of difficulties and developing skills to cope with the tasks of growing up in a more efficient manner.

# Most and Least Used Play Therapy Limits

HAIM G. GINOTT and DELL LEBO

## Introduction

All child therapists use limits in play therapy. Generally the limits pertain to physical aggression against the therapist or the equipment, socially unacceptable behavior, safety and health, playroom routines, and physical affection. It would be of interest to know which limits are considered useful by all therapists and which by few therapists.

## Questionnaire Study

Answers to a questionnaire on limits were received from 227 play therapists (100 psychoanalytic, 41 nondirective, and 86 adherents of other schools). The therapists indicated whether or not they regularly used the following limits in play therapy with emotionally disturbed children aged three to ten years:

1. Taking home a playroom toy
2. Taking home a painting he made
3. Taking home an object he made of clay, etc.
4. Refusing to enter the playroom
5. Leaving the playroom at will
6. Turning off the lights for a long while
7. Pouring a generous amount of water in sand box
8. Spilling sand any place in the room
9. Spilling as much sand as he wants
10. Painting inexpensive toys
11. Painting expensive toys
12. Painting or marking walls or doors
13. Painting or marking furniture

14. Prolonging his stay at the end of the session
15. Bringing a friend
16. Bringing drinks or food to the playroom
17. Lighting matches brought with him
18. Smoking
19. Starting small fires
20. Reading books he brought with him
21. Doing his school work
22. Breaking inexpensive toys
23. Breaking expensive toys
24. Damaging furniture and fixtures
25. Breaking windows
26. Opening door or window and talking to passers-by
27. Using terms such as Nigger, Mick, Kike, etc.
28. Verbalizing profanities in the playroom
29. Yelling profanities at passers-by
30. Writing four-letter words on blackboard
31. Drawing, painting, or making obscene objects
32. Painting his face
33. Painting his clothes
34. Exploding a whole roll of caps at once
35. Climbing on window sills high above the ground
36. Hitting you mildly
37. Squirting water on you
38. Painting your clothes
39. Throwing sand at your shoes
40. Throwing sand at your person
41. Throwing rubber objects around the room
42. Throwing hard objects around the room
43. Tying you up playfully
44. Shooting suction-tip darts at you
45. Attacking you with some force
46. Sitting on your lap
47. Hugging you for long periods of time
48. Kissing you
49. Fondling you
50. Completely undressing
51. Masturbating openly
52. Drinking polluted water
53. Eating mud, chalk, or fingerpaints
54. Urinating or defecating on the floor.

## Results and Discussion

Table 1 shows the percentage of therapists of each of the three orientations using particular limits.

The most used play therapy limits pertained to protection of playroom property, child's safety, and the therapist's attire. Over 90 percent of all therapists regularly set limits on breaking windows, drinking dirty water, and painting the therapist's clothing. Over 80 percent of all therapists prohibited the child from yelling profanities at passers-by, and over 70 percent prohibited him from forcefully attacking the therapist and painting walls and doors.

Breaking furniture and fixtures was prohibited by more than 90 percent of analytic and "other" therapists and by over 80 percent of nondirectivists. Urinating and defecating in the playroom and climbing on high window sills was prohibited by more than 00 percent of "other" therapists and by over 70 percent of nondirective and psychoanalytic therapists.

The least used limits pertained to symbolic expression of socially unacceptable behavior and to playroom routines. Only 10 percent or less of all therapists set limits on using racial slurs, on speaking profanities, writing four-letter words, drawing or making obscene objects, throwing rubber toys in the room, and taking home paintings made there.

Twenty percent or less of all therapists prohibited the child from painting his face. Taking home clay objects was prohibited by 10 percent or less of the psychoanalytic therapists and by 20 percent or less of the nondirectivists and "others." Bringing food into the playroom was prohibited by 10 percent or less of the psychoanalytic therapists and by 30 percent or less of the nondirectivists and "others."

Reading books in the playroom was prohibited by only 10 percent or less of the psychoanalytic and nondirective therapists and by 20 percent or less of the "others." Allowing the child to sit on the therapist's lap was prohibited by 10 percent or less of the nondirectivists and "others" and by 20 percent or less of the psychoanalytic therapists.

A child's refusal to enter the playroom was honored by many therapists. Only 20 percent or less of the nondirectivists and 30 percent of the psychoanalysts and "other" therapists invoked a limit requiring the child's entrance. Painting inexpensive toys was prohibited by 20 percent or less of the psychoanalytic and nondirective therapists and by 30 percent or less of the "others."

**TABLE 1**
THE PERCENTAGE OF THERAPISTS OF THREE ORIENTATIONS USING PARTICULAR LIMITS

| % | 1 | 2 | 3 | 4 | 5 | 6 | 7 | 8 | 9 | 10 | 11 | 12 | 13 | 14 | 15 | 16 | 17 | 18 |
|---|---|---|---|---|---|---|---|---|---|----|----|----|----|----|----|----|----|----|
| | | | | | | **Limit Number and Therapeutic Approach** | | | | | | | | | | | | |
| 0-10 | | X | PA | | | | | | | | | | | | | PA | | |
| 11-20 | | | ND OT | ND | | | | | | PA ND | | | | | | | | |
| 21-30 | | | PA OT | | | X | PA ND | | | OT | | | | | | ND OT | | |
| 31-40 | | | | PA ND | | | OT | | | | | | | ND | | X | | |
| 41-50 | | | | OT | | | | X | X | | | | | | | | | |
| 51-60 | | | | | | | | | | | PA OT | | | PA OT | | | | ND |
| 61-70 | PA ND | | | | | | | | | | ND | PA | PA | | | | | PA OT |
| 71-80 | OT | | | | | | | | | | | | X | ND OT | ND OT | | | |
| 81-90 | | | | | | | | | | | | | | | | | | |
| 91-100 | | | | | | | | | | | | | | | | | | |

*Note*: PA = Psychoanalysts, ND = Nondirectivists, OT = Others, X = The Three Approaches.

**TABLE 1** (*continued*)

| % | 19 | 20 | 21 | 22 | 23 | 24 | 25 | 26 | 27 | 28 | 29 | 30 | 31 | 32 | 33 | 34 | 35 | 36 |
|---|----|----|----|----|----|----|----|----|----|----|----|----|----|----|----|----|----|----|
| | | | | | | **Limit Number and Therapeutic Approach** | | | | | | | | | | | | |
| 0-10 | | PA ND | | | | | | | X | X | | X | X | | | | | |
| 11-20 | | OT | | | | | | | | | | | | X | | | | |
| 21-30 | | | PA ND | | | | | | | | | | | | | | | |
| 31-40 | | | OT | X | | | | | | | | | | | PA | ND | | |
| 41-50 | | | | | | | | | | | | | | | ND OT | PA OT | | PA ND |
| 51-60 | | | | | | | X | | | | | | | | | | | OT |
| 61-70 | PA ND | | | | PA | | | | | | | | | | | | | |
| 71-80 | OT | | | | ND OT | | | | | | | | | | | | PA ND | |
| 81-90 | | | | | | ND | | | | | | X | | | | | OT | |
| 91-100 | | | | | | PA OT | X | | | | | | | | | | | |

**TABLE 1** (*continued*)

| % | 37 | 38 | 39 | 40 | 41 | 42 | 43 | 44 | 45 | 46 | 47 | 48 | 49 | 50 | 51 | 52 | 53 | 54 |
|---|----|----|----|----|----|----|----|----|----|----|----|----|----|----|----|----|----|----|
| | | | | | | **Limit Number and Therapeutic Approach** | | | | | | | | | | | | |
| 0-10 | | | | | X | | | | | ND OT | | | | | | | | |
| 11-20 | | | | | | | | | | PA | | | | | | | | |
| 21-30 | | | | | | | | | | | | PA | | | | | | |
| 31-40 | | | | | | | | | | | | ND OT | | | | | | |
| 41-50 | | | | | | ND | PA OT | | | | | | | | | | | |
| 51-60 | | X | | | | PA OT | ND | | | | PA | | | | X | | | |
| 61-70 | PA ND | | | X | | | | X | | | ND OT | | PA OT | PA | | | PA | |
| 71-80 | OT | | | | | | | | X | | | | | ND OT | | | ND OT | PA ND |
| 81-90 | | | | | | | | | | | | | | ND | | | | OT |
| 91-100 | | X | | | | | | | | | | | | | | X | | |

## Summary and Conclusions

Responses to a questionnaire on limits from 227 play therapists revealed that the most widely used limits pertained to protection of playroom property (breaking windows, furniture, and fixtures and painting walls or doors), child's safety (drinking dirty water and climbing on high sills), therapist's safety (attacking the therapist or painting his clothing), and socially unacceptable behavior (urinating and defecating on the floor and yelling profanities at passers-by).

The least used limits pertained to symbolic expressions of socially unacceptable behavior (racial slurs, speaking or writing profanities, and making obscene objects), and to playroom routines (bringing food to and reading books in the playroom and taking home paintings or clay objects made there). Most therapists also allowed the child to throw rubber toys, paint his own face, and sit on their laps.

Two patterns emerge clearly from this study:

1. Child therapists show great permissiveness in some areas that are prohibited in society at large. They allow children to verbalize profanities, to write four-letter words on the blackboard, to draw, paint, and make obscene objects, and to use racial slurs. Aware of society's attitude, therapists do not allow children to yell profanities at passers-by.

2. Blatant physical aggression is not tolerated in the playroom. Children are not allowed to destroy costly furnishings and ruin equipment or physically to attack the therapist.

# BEHAVIORAL

# The Reduction of Overactive Behavior

STEVE G. DOUBROS and GARY J. DANIELS

## Introduction

Operant techniques are presently employed in an increasing number for the diminution and control of disturbed human behavior. The application of behavioral learning principles to problems of psychopathology is constantly increasing and the results have been more than encouraging.

Traditionally, overactivity* is assumed to be one of the personality traits of subnormal, mentally-retarded children especially those with a definite CNS defect. Although systematic observation and experience with this population does not bear this out completely, Strauss and Lehtinen (1951) view most defectives as behaviorally erratic, driven, uninhibited, perseverative and catastrophically anxious. Parenthetically, the term "mental subnormality" is not a unitary concept. It refers to a heterogenous condition at best describing individuals that differ among themselves along a number of dimensions (i.e. genetic, physical, hormonal, psychological, etc.) of varying nature and degree. Viewed within this context, overactivity is not a uni-dimensional entity but a class of responses having differential etiologies and being maintained by an often unspecified number of environmental consequences. Unquestionably, overactivity — whether verbal or motor — is a "wrong" response leading to poor social discriminations and subsequently, inappropriate courses of action. It interferes with the child's meaningful transaction with his environment and may become quite disruptive in terms of ward life and routine. It is therefore, important that the

*The terms overactivity and hyperactivity are used interchangeably throughout this paper.

therapist make a systematic effort to bring this behavior under some sort of environmental stimulus control.

With respect to etiological factors, we like to assume that increased activity in the playroom is the outcome of ill-defined stimulus variables with organic deficits simply lowering the threshold of responsiveness in the situation — the variables may be thought of as releasing mechanisms with respect to accumulated tension. It may also be, that they present attempts at self-stimulation having been learned at critical periods during early childhood. Scott (1962) has presented this point lucidly whereas, Denenberg (1964) postulates a monotonic function between adult personality composition and pre-weaning stimulation in infancy. The function seems to decrease with easy tasks and increase with difficult ones. An inverted "U" shape relation is hypothesized to occur when the situational tasks are moderately within the individual's level of competence. An extension of this point would imply that toy novelty at the play-room should be controlled over the period of therapy, since it may be related to the degree of difficulty experienced by the child as he manipulates materials of various types.

Following the first attempt by James (1963) to manipulate hyperactive behavior by the deliberate programming of the teacher's social interaction with the child, a number of investigators turned their attention to the same problem. Anderson (1964) was successful in modifying the same behavior of a ten-year-old, brain-damaged boy by reinforcing first by materials (i.e. candy) and later by social means (i.e. praise) attending responses within the classroom. A similar study by Patterson (1964) yielded comparable results. In an apparent attempt to replicate these findings, Patterson *et al.* (1965) followed an almost identical procedure in conditioning another brain-injured, hyperactive boy in the same situation. Despite the effectiveness of the procedure used, one may question some aspects of these studies in terms of uncontrolled social reinforcement (i.e. the classmates were told about what the Es were attempting to do with the boy) and conditioning awareness (i.e., these instructions were apparently given at the presence of the boy in class). An effort was made in the present study to control these factors as much as possible.

In so far as material reinforcement is a valid principle of learning, it was predicted that (a) overactive behavior will be reduced and, (b) play activity will become more constructive following the conditioning process. The study is exploratory in nature.

## The Differential Reinforcement Procedure

### Subjects

The subjects were six mentally-retarded boys whose ages ranged from eight to thirteen years with a mean of 11.5 years and S.D. 2.64. Five of the subjects were assumed to function at a Measured Intelligence Level II and one at a Measured Intelligence Level I, according to the classification scheme set forth by Heber (1961). The types of retardation represented by the six children were Down's Syndrome, cerebral defect due to unknown prenatal influence, retardation associated with emotional disturbance, and three subjects classified as mentally retarded due to unknown cause with the functional reaction alone manifest. These six children were selected for this study because they were reported to be the most hyperactive in one cottage. None of the subjects were on medication at the time of the study; however, medication was discontinued with two of the boys for the purpose of this study.

### Apparatus

The playroom was approximately 12 x 16 ft. A table, 3 x 6 ft, and a chair were placed in the middle of the room. The subject was seated, facing a one-way glass screen. The examiners were seated in an observation room having a complete view of the playroom via the one-way glass screen. A toy cabinet was located to the right of the child, approximately five feet from the table. Placed on top of the cabinet was a remote controlled token dispenser. The dispenser was contained in a cardboard box approximately one foot square to eliminate distracting noise. A 3 x 5 in. opening on the side of the box allowed the subject to retrieve his tokens at the end of each session. The dispenser was also equipped with a buzzer and a small electric light which were activated simultanously with each token dispensal. The dispenser, light and buzzer were controlled by a manual switch which was operated by one of the examiners seated in the observation room behind the one-way glass screen.

### Procedure

Prior to the actual study, each subject was observed in the playroom for fifteen minutes per day over a two-week period. These observations were used to construct a check list of hyperactive behavior. The responses chosen for the checklist were those emitted most frequently and deemed hyperactive by the examiners. Four general classes of behavior comprised the checklist: stationary body movements (i.e. scratching, mouthing objects, shuffling feet, etc.), locomotive behavior (i.e. walking, crawling, climbing on fixtures, picking up unassigned toys, etc.), destructive behavior (i.e. kicking, throwing away toys or materials, pounding toys, etc.) and communication (i.e. talking constantly, shouting, whistling, etc.).

The actual study consisted of fifty-six sessions in which the subjects were observed individually. The sessions were divided into four groups: pre-conditioning (baseline) for eight days, conditioning for thirty days, phasing-out four days, extinction for eight days and follow-up for six days. Both observers tallied responses during the pre-conditioning and extinction phases. During the conditioning and phasing-out stages, one observer operated the token dispenser switch and the other tallied responses. To check the conditioning effect beyond the immediate post-conditioning phase, a follow-up period of six sessions was conducted three weeks after the last extinction trial. A session was a ten-minute observation period. Timing of a session did not begin until a subject had been seated and given the instructions. The instructions for the pre- and post-conditioning phases (extinction and follow-up periods) were similar:

> "Sit over here —. Do you see all these things on the table? You may play with whichever you like to play with. I'll be back in a while."

The instructions for the conditioning phase were:

> "Do you see all those things on the table? You may play with whichever you like to play with. Do you see that machine over there? Every time you hear a clanking noise, that means you are doing well and you are getting a token. When the session is all over, you may exchange the tokens for candy. Remember, the more tokens you get, the more candy you are going to have. I'll be back in a while."

The toys on the table consisted of four types: quiet-type toys, noise-producing toys, puzzles, and drawing materials. Approximately ten toys, representing the four types, were placed on the table each day. Specific sets of toys were used to control the possible "novelty effect" produced by new or unfamiliar stimuli. The sets were alternated every eight days; therefore, the toys used during the preconditioning and extinction periods were exactly the same.

A hyperactive response was tallied every time it occurred during a thirty-second interval. Therefore, it was not possible for any subject to receive more than twenty tallies for any one response during a session. Some of the items on the check-list were not independent of each other, so it was possible for the subject to receive multiple tallies within the same time interval for related responses, e.g. standing up and walking around the room would receive two tallies. If the boy pumped his legs, whistled and swayed the body all at the same time, three tallies were scored and so on. Some responses, such as verbalizing, mumbling, and playing with a noise-producing toy had to persist for thirty seconds before they could be tallied.

The schedule of reinforcement employed was similar to a fixed, differential reinforcement schedule of other behavior (DRO), with a thirty-second time-hold of continued absence of hyperactive behavior after a single fifteen-second interval at the beginning of each play session. If the studied activity was shown during the limited time-hold period of the original fifteen- or subsequent thirty-second intervals, the stopwatch was idled and it was not reset until the hyperactive response ceased. During the phasing-out stage, the beginning time-hold period remained at fifteen-second intervals for trials 39 and 40 but were lengthened to thirty seconds for trials 41 and 42. The subsequent time-hold intervals were forty-five seconds on trial 39, sixty seconds on trial 40, seventy-five seconds on trial 41, and ninety seconds on trial 42. Any constructive use of time during the absence of behavior operationally defined by the hyperactivity checklist, was reinforced.

Social reinforcement was controlled by (a) presenting the same instructions to each boy by the same examiner at the same tone of voice, and (b) eliminating any other verbal comments that may be possibly considered as social reinforcers. There was no other person in the playroom throughout the ten-minute sessions except the subject involved.

## Results of the Experimental Approach

In order to assess the degree of agreement between the two observers on the hyperactivity checklist before and after conditioning, two statistical computations were carried out: (1) an overall Spearman's rho ($p$) coefficient comparing the total mean response for each S across the eight-day pre- and post-conditioning periods and, (2) interitem comparisons from observer to observer on the combined responses during these periods. In the first case, agreement was very high with a Spearman rank-difference correlation index of 1.0 indicating that the two observers judged Ss in the same way with respect to total frequency of hyperactive responses. In the second case, the item to item analysis on blocks of eight days revealed individual correlation coefficients ranging from .83 (the lowest) to .98 (the highest). This implies that the observers were also in relative agreement between themselves regarding the tally on individual items on the check list. It is possible that these correlations have been somewhat over-estimated due to the fact that independence between or among certain items on the checklist was not complete.

The absolute rate of response during baseline performance, conditioning, phasing-out, extinction and follow-up periods was 17.32, 6.69, 4.67, 4.14 and 4.33, respectively.

A comparison of group means in terms of absolute frequency of response between the pre-conditioning (base-line) and extinction periods indicated a highly significant difference (T=O,P<.01, Wilcoxon sign-ranks test, two-tailed). It is interesting also to note that response variability was reduced substantially during the extinction period in comparison to the same period before conditioning (F=6.21, d.f./=6, P<.05).

In an effort to determine the extent of response stability within the baseline and extinction periods, separate statistical manipulations were performed comparing the total number of response output between the first four days of baseline period with that of the last four days of the same period. This difference was significant (P<.05, Composite-rank method, Wilcoxon) indicating a substantial amount of discrepancy in hyperactive output between the two periods with Ss being more active at the last four days immediately preceding the conditioning process. A similar type of analysis between the two day-blocks of the extinction period showed the difference to be negligible (P>.05). Apparently, response output was more stable during the latter period. The significance of this fact will be discussed later in the study.

The actual curve representing mean frequency of overactivity during pre-conditioning, conditioning, phasing-out, extinction and follow-up periods is shown in Fig. 1. The function appears to be negatively decelerated as it is the case with most learning curves plotted along these two dimensions. It is evident from this curve that strong tendencies towards response acquiescence (i.e. reduction in hyperactivity) took place early during the conditioning period (i.e. on the first twelve days) with improvement continuing at a relatively low pace afterwards.

A graphic presentation with respect to frequency of use of play media or materials during the pre-conditioning and extinction periods is indicated in Fig 2. As it can be seen from this graph, "grasshopper" play activity (i.e. continuous use of numerous toys one after the other) was reduced considerably following conditioning. The decrement is more noticeable on the noise-producing toys (such as motorcycles, cars with sirens, drums, whistles, peg-board, etc.) than those of the quiet-type (such as stuffed animals, rubber human figures, miniature house displays, house furniture, blocks, etc.). Whereas such constructive use of time as solving puzzles, drawing, writing and so on, increased to a moderate degree during the latter part of conditioning as well as the extinction period, numerical evidence cannot be presented since the

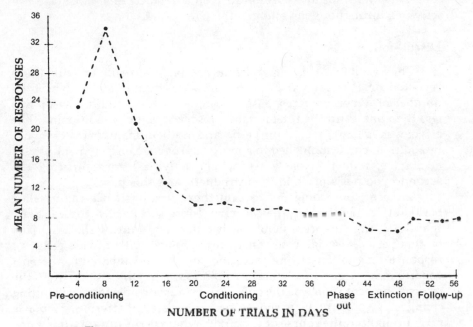

Fig. 1. The effective control of motor and verbal overactivity as a function of conditioning.

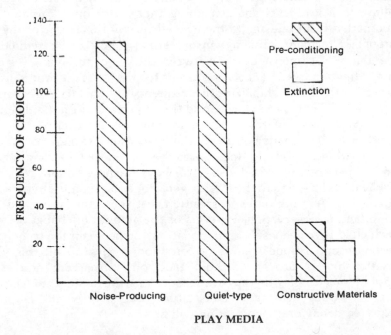

Fig. 2. Absolute frequency distributions of use of play media and materials drawn in comparative form between the baseline and extinction sessions.

observers were not in a position to keep a detailed time table of these activities throughout the study.

## Discussion

The results of this study are in complete agreement with those reported by Patterson *et al.* (1965) in a classroom setting. The total number of hyperactive responses during extinction and follow-up was less than one-third the total number observed before conditioning. The effect was evident on both the verbal and motor domains of overactivity. In addition, conditioning led to a more appropriate employment of play media (i.e. reduction of "grasshopper" activities) substantiating the second hypothesis made in the introduction of this paper.

Chance alone could not explain these findings since the baseline period offers evidence to the contrary. More specifically, the very fact that the youngsters were significantly more active during the latter part of this period, as Fig. 1 demonstrates, coupled with a wide range of response fluctuation during the same period (as compared to the post conditioning situation) would strongly support the notion that the reinforcing operation was the only variable responsible for the resulting changes. Two of the boys showed an inconsistent pattern of response rate throughout the course of the study, whereas the other four became more predictable as a function of conditionability with rate of response falling to a low level and remaining there with only a minimum of fluctuation from one day to the next. Probably this is one of the most important incidental findings in our study. The sizeable reduction in variability of response output between the pre-conditioning (s = 63.52) and extinction (s = 25.48) periods seems to imply that the procedure used was also effective in stabilizing the frequency of hyperactive responses at a low level. That is to say, the conditioning treatment not only lowered the total *frequency* of the behavior in question but it also reduced the *variability* of hyperactive output within the group to a significant degree.

Another interesting finding was the presence of a strong tendency on the part of the most hyperactive boys to show a more remarkable behavioral change than those who were not as high on the hyperactivity check-list. A rank-order correlation between the pre- and post-conditioning observations in terms of the amount of change shown by each child revealed a substantial relationship between the frequency of response and responsiveness to conditioning (p = .60). If this sort of relationship is proven to hold true on subsequent studies, the implications for play therapy are self-evident; the higher the incidence of the obnoxious demeanor under study, the greater the amount of expected behavioral modification will be.

It was very difficult in this study to select a control group from the hospital population to match in exact form the characteristics of the experimental group in terms of such variables as chronological age, presence of hyperactivity, intellectual functioning, possibility for withdrawing medication, etc. The heterogenous aspect of the hospital's retarded population with all the ensuing differences in CNS pathology and emotional personality composition prevented the selection of such a group. In future studies, however, an attempt will be made to institute a control group if possible.

Within the experimental group, the factor of "pure stimulus novelty" was well controlled since the same number and type of toys and materials were used throughout the study with different sets from day to day (to prevent satiation or boredom) but with the overall totals remaining constant across each phase of the study. This control in stimulus novelty is very important since it has been shown to have a definite conditioning effect in certain instrumental learning situations often acting as a temporary reinforcement variable (Cantor and Cantor, 1964). As a result, conditioning appears to develop faster with respect to novel than familiar materials. By holding toy novelty at a constant level, the possibility of this condition occurring was minimized considerably.

Apparently, the wider the stimulus-toy field within which overactivity is operative, the more difficult it will be to bring it under control. As a matter of fact this seems to be the key difficulty in classical therapy situations. No attempt is being made to control the specific behavior in question; instead the therapist's efforts are directed to "personality dynamics" in the belief that the behavior can be dealt with only when the underlying personality complex is altered. No need for such a notion is indicated here. Once the field becomes more narrow in the sense that a newly established discriminate stimulus provides a basis for the reward of constructively employed behavior, overactivity is reduced to the point where it can no longer interfere adversely with a person's life.

An unexplored area of play therapy is the effect that reinforcement has on particular types of activities in the playroom, primarily those of educative value. Although inspection of the present data revealed that time spent on such activities as drawing, puzzle-solving, writing, etc. increased as a function of the conditioning process, the exact nature of this relationship remains obscure. It will be interesting to examine the bearing of reinforcing operations upon specifiable materials (i.e. human figures, mechanical toys, etc.) once the main behavioral problem has been effectively controlled in the situation. The traditional ways of play therapy will have to be modified greatly if the projective expression of feelings and attitudes at play can be directed along certain lines through a planned program of systematic material and social rewards.

Unquestionably, overactivity is a self-defeating technique in many everyday situations. If one adopts the medical model and assumes that this form of behavior is irreversible because organicity (i.e. a chronic brain syndrome, extrapyramidal injury, etc.) is rarely amenable to environmental-psychological manipulation, then any approach exclusive of medical interference is doomed to failure. The present results strongly indicate that irrespective of the origin or etiology of retarded mental growth, psychological treatment by operant techniques is not only possible within the play-room setting, but it can be very effective in reducing those obnoxious behavior patterns that have been traditionally thought of as an exclusively medical problem.

## Conclusions

The small number of children taking part in this study does not allow any general or far-fetched conclusions. The results do point, however, to certain directions regarding the effectiveness of an operant procedure within the playroom. It was shown that (a) overactivity can be reduced considerably, and (b) play can acquire a higher level of organization and meaningfulness for the child. Under these circumstances, the traditional ways of play therapy should be reexamined and reevaluated.

### References

Anderson D. (1964) *Application of a Behavior Modification Technique to the Control of a Hyperactive Child*. Unpublished M.A. thesis, University of Oregon.

Cantor, G. N. and Cantor J.H. (1964), "Effects of Conditioned Stimulus Familiarization on Instrumental Learning in Children," *J. Exp. Child Psychol.* 1, 71-78.

Denenberg, B. H. (1964), "Critical Periods, Stimulus Input and Emotional Reactivity: A Theory of Infantile Stimulation," *Psychol. Rev.* 71, 335-351.

James, C. E. (1963), *Operant Conditioning in the Management and Behavior of Hyperactive Children: Five Case Studies,* unpublished manuscript, Orange State College.

Heber, R. (1961), "A Manual on Terminology and Classification in Mental Retardation," Monograph Supplement to *Am. J. Ment, Defic.,* 2nd ed.

Patterson, G. R. (1964), "An Application of Conditioning Techniques to the Control of a Hyperactive Child." In *Case Studies in Behavior Modification* (Eds. L. U. Ulmann and L. Krasner), Holt, Rinehart & Winston, New York.

Patterson, G. R., Jones, R., Whittier, J., and Wright, M. A. (1965), "A Behavior Modification Technique for the Hyperactive Child." *Behav. Res. & Therapy* 2, 217-226.

Russo, S. (1964), "Adaptations in Behavioral Therapy with Children," *Behav. Res. & Therapy* 2, 43-47.

Scott, J. P. (1962), "Critical Periods in Behavior Development," *Science*, New York: 138, 949–958.

Siegel, S. (1956), *Nonparametric Statistics*, New York: McGraw–Hill.

Skinner, B. F. (1953), *Science and Human Behavior*, New York: McMillan.

Strauss, A. A., and Lehtinen, L. E. (1951), *Psychopathology and Education of the Brain-Injured Child*, New York: Grune and Stratton.

# Producing Behavior Change in Parents

STEPHEN M. JOHNSON and RICHARD A. BROWN

## Introduction

The focus of research reports on operant behavior modification appears to be changing as the field continues to develop. It no longer seems necessary to demonstrate that modification of behavioral contingencies can produce changes in the behavior of individuals who have shown marked behavioral deficits or excesses. It has also been documented that nonprofessionals with very limited training can serve as effective contingency managers (Allen and Harris, 1966; Allyon and Michael, 1959; Davison, 1965; Gericke, 1965; Risley and Wolf, 1966). In general, however, the methods necessary to effect change in these agents of contingency management have not been adequately described. Because writers have focused on changes in the target behavior of patients, few have given adequate information on how the new behaviors of the agents of change were produced. In our work with disturbed children and their parents, producing meaningful change in the parental component of the parent-child interaction has become the central therapeutic problem. The case reports which follow involve the examination of learning techniques used in producing effective contingency management behavior in the parents of disturbed children. The first report represents an example of parental instruction using many learning techniques more or less simultaneously. The second report represents the examination of only one learning technique in effecting parental behavior change.

Many of the learning techniques which are reported here have been used by other investigators in various combinations. One of the most common involves directing parental behavior during parent-child interaction (O'Leary, O'Leary and Becker, 1967; Sanders, 1965; Welch, 1966). Some investigators have followed up this initial direction with some form of social reinforcement to the parents when they engage in effective contingency management on their own (Hanf, 1968; Wahler *et al.*, 1965). Although it has been infrequently recognized as a source of training, a number of endeavors in parental behavior change have included parental observations of child-therapist interaction (Hanf, 1968; Risley and Wolf, 1966; Russo, 1964; Straughan, 1964). While all of the above studies have employed some kind of didactic training and simple instruction, only the recent report by Walder *et al.* (1967) emphasizes and describes these procedures. In all other studies, the role of traditional interviewing techniques and the role of cognitive understanding of contingency management principles remain unclear.

The first case is presented to illustrate a wide variety of learning techniques in parental training. The case dramatizes rather well the problem of ascertaining the effective ingredients in an effective treatment.

## Case Report: The Use of Multiple Techniques

*Background*     Judy was two years nine months when she was first referred for examination. Judy had been adopted shortly after birth and her parents felt that her development had been slower than average, especially in the language area, as she could say only two words. The child's most prominent behavioral difficulty was intense over-activity. Her mother was unable to control her during interviews prior to treatment and she responded with loud crying to every attempt by her mother to restrain her. At home she required constant supervision and control. Along with these difficulties, Judy's parents were most concerned about the fact that their daughter was not socially responsive. They reported that she would not respond to affection or punishment in any noticeable way and was oblivious to people around her.

A complete neurological was given the child and the results were negative in all respects. A Cattell Infant Intelligence Scale was attempted, but its validity was questioned due to the child's over-activity and her unwillingness to co-operate. The examiner's best estimate of I.Q. score was in the range 60–70.

Judy's family included her parents, a nine-year-old brother and a grandmother. The father was employed as a white collar worker and this was an average middle-income family. Since the grandmother played an important role in the child's care, it was decided to involve her as well as the mother in the therapy program. The father was not directly involved in the treatment.

## Procedures

*Observational diagnosis*    Treatment began with two diagnostic observational sessions in which Judy, her mother and grandmother participated. Each session was divided into three periods. In period 1, the mother was asked to get Judy to play with her in a playroom. In period 2, grandmother was given the same task. In period 3, both mother and grandmother were asked to converse together and require Judy to play by herself. Each period lasted 5 min. Systematic observations were made by the therapist from behind a one-way mirror. Past experience with over-active children suggested the following classes of behavior for observation:

1. Child changes activity — Every instance of redirection of activity (e.g. change from playing with a doll or running across the room). Changes within one activity area (e.g. doll play) were not noted. One unit score was given for each instance of such behavioral redirection.
2. Child interacts — Child engages in the same activity as the adult within close proximity to the adult. One unit score for each ten-second period of such interaction.
3. Parent directs, pushes, holds, or carries child — Each instance of parental attempt to verbally or physically change the child's activity by directing, pushing, etc. In addition to one unit for each instance of such behavior, one unit was recorded for each ten-second period of continued restraint of the child.
4. Parent rewards child — Each instance of parental social praise to the child (e.g. "Good girl," "That's right," etc.).

Observations were made as they occurred and dictated into a dictaphone. Timed variables (interaction and continued restraint) were measured by operating stop watches.

Figures 1 and 2 present data on these observations throughout the entire treatment course for period 1 (five minutes in which interaction was required between mother and child). Examination of the data for the first two baseline sessions clearly reveals that the behavior classes "child changes activity" and "parent directs, pushes, etc." are of high frequency, while the behavior, "child interacts" and "parent rewards" are almost non-existent. In baseline session 1, mother depressed Judy's over-activity by restraining her for a three-minute period. Judy yelled and cried during this time. The data on grandmother and Judy were very similar in baseline sessions although the grandmother had a slightly better relationship with the child.

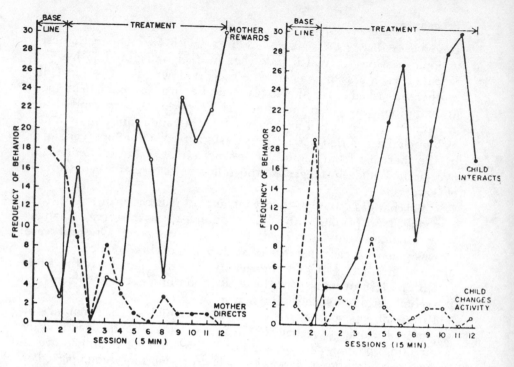

Fig. 1. Frequency of mother's recorded behavior in 5-min mother–child interaction (period 1) over sessions.

Fig. 2. Frequency of child's recorded behavior in 5-min mother–child interaction (period 1) over sessions.

*Formulation*     In the first two baseline sessions, both adults spent a good deal of time chasing Judy, picking her up, returning her to the play area, and restraining her. All through this they talked to Judy, never harshly but rarely with approval. Judy received almost constant attention from the adults but it was non-contingent and undifferentiated. It would have been extremely difficult for Judy to discriminate wanted from unwanted behavior under these circumstances. The adults were told this at the beginning of treatment session 1, and were shown recorded data. They were told further that their pursuing and restraining behaviors appeared to be ineffective because:(1) Parents were giving attention to Judy for undesired behavior and thus were probably reinforcing it; (2) Parents were rarely punishing, as clear-cut disapproval was hardly ever communicated; and (3) Parents did not label those behaviors which were desired. The child seemed to do as she pleased in those periods when she was allowed to play by herself and it was clear that, as mother had reported, Judy did not find interaction with these adults particularly rewarding.

Based on these observations and formulations, the immediate goal of the treatment program was to reduce parental pursuit and restraint, and to increase parental reward for desired behavior (interaction) in the child. Both adults were given a simple explanation of the formulations and goals before the program began. Treatment sessions were given twice weekly and lasted approximately one-and-one-half hours. The program consisted of the following techniques.

*Direct instruction*     Parents were introduced to the central principles of learning theory and the presenting problems were placed in that context. The presentation of the therapist's formulation represented one instance of direct instruction, as did subsequent discussions of reinforcement, shaping, schedules of reinforcement, and modeling. As part of the instructional program, the adults read programmed instruction materials on the principles of contingency management presented by Patterson *et al.* (1966). This programmed material has proven valuable in short-cutting and clarifying the direct instruction process. The instruction appeared to facilitate the realization by Judy's mother that chasing her daughter had become a "way of life" for the family. This recognition occurred in treatment session 2 and preceded one of the mother's first dramatic behavior changes — her ability to completely ignore Judy's over-activity. Both adults seemed to grasp all the essential points of contingency management by treatment session 2 and most of the didactic training was completed by the end of this session.

This direct instruction was among the less discrete and specifiable techniques in our treatment of this and similar cases. Experience seems to indicate, however, that all or most of this instruction could be effectively done through sophisticated programmed instruction. The existence of such materials would not only facilitate greater ease in this instructional step but would also provide research tools to test the role of conceptual and theoretical understanding in effecting appropriate contingency management behavior.

*Group discussion*     Judy's family was seen together with another child's family, to whom the same general principles and behaviors were being taught. All instruction and discussion were done in the group context. Each of the parental groups observed the formal behavioral training of the other and discussed it after the session. The group's discussion of punishment seemed most valuable in opening Judy's family to the use of some mild aversive stimuli with her. Before treatment, it was very apparent that she was rarely made aware of those behaviors which were not desired. The parents of the second child provided a strong influence and probably accelerated learning in this area and others. Group discussion appears useful in spreading the base of social influence to produce parental behavior change. In this case, for example, the report of an experienced parent concerning the use of appropriate aversive control was of particular value to Judy's parents who had been unable to show even clear-cut disapproval to their child.

*Behavioral direction*    The formal behavioral training took place in repeated sessions structured in the same manner as the baseline sessions. Period 1 of each session involved mother – child interaction for five minutes. Period 2 involved grandmother – child interaction for five minutes. Period 3 involved conversation between both adults with the child present, for the purpose of teaching the child to play by herself without demanding adult attention. Behavioral direction was used only in the first two treatment sessions. The therapist, using a red light, signaled the adults to reward Judy when he felt it was appropriate. At first, parents were signaled to reward Judy whenever she approached them. By treatment session 2, Judy was required to interact with the parents before receiving reinforcement. For the first four treatment sessions, candies (M & M's) were used and were always paired with verbal social rewards. About fifty percent of the social rewards were accompanied by candy in these periods.

In many cases, behavioral direction appears to hasten parental learning by immediately raising the level of appropriate parental contingency management. When this occurs, the child may often begin to immediately reward such parental change by better behavior. In addition, this procedure may be of particular utility in the first stages of treatment where the parents must reward only approximations of the desired responses. Shaping procedures are perhaps among the most difficult to teach parents, and until parents understand behavior theory and have experienced some success with its techniques, it may be more useful to rely on behavioral direction.

*Behavioral reinforcement*    Behavioral reinforcement was employed in sessions 3 – 13 and consisted of signaling the parents by means of a signal light when they rewarded their child appropriately as well as when they missed a good opportunity to reward her. Thus, the signal light communicated the therapist's approval or disapproval of the adult's social reward behavior immediately after its occurrence. The light was not optimally effective, however, as the adults often missed seeing it. A device for administering an auditory stimulus to parents through a small receiver placed in the parent's ear may be used to eliminate the error experienced in this case (Welch, 1966).

Behavioral reinforcement has become a major technique in establishing effective contingency management behavior in parents. While other techniques may be valuable in eliciting appropriate contingency management, we believe that both specific behavioral reinforcement and generalized social reinforcement are vital in sustaining this new behavior over time. Of course, when the parental behavior becomes effective in maintaining desired behavior in the child, reinforcement from the therapist should no longer be necessary.

*Modeling*     In treatment sessions 3 - 13 modeling sessions preceded the formal treatment interaction periods. During the modeling sessions, the therapist would attempt to play with Judy and demonstrate the desired behaviors to the parents who observed from behind a one-way mirror. During these periods, the therapist attempted to emphasize labeling the child's desired and rewarded behaviors, to accentuate positive affective expressions during reward, and to demonstrate a wide variety of socially rewarding behaviors including physical contact, etc. Although systematic observations of these periods were not made, the therapist was able to engage the child in play for the entire five-minute period on most occasions. In addition to these opportunities for modeling, a number of other opportunities were included in the treatment program. Both adults had the opportunity to observe the other in interaction periods with the child. In addition, they viewed the formal treatment sessions of the other child and his parents. Modeling seems to be particularly useful in increasing the initial frequency and variability of contingency management behavior in parents. The rationale for this hypothesis will be discussed in the presentation of the second case.

## Discussion

Judy's case is rather typical in that improvement came suddenly and dramatically after a period of slow progress and change in parental behavior. This is reflected in the data on the mother-child interaction presented in Figs. 1 and 2. The data on the grandmother-child interaction are very similar although this interaction was somewhat better at all treatment stages. The results are of considerable interest for the striking agreement between verbal report of behavior, and the behavior shown in treatment sessions. A very real change in the problematic behaviors was evidenced in treatment session 4, which began with an excited report of changes in Judy's behavior at home. It was reported that she was talking more and interacting with others more readily. Grandmother felt that Judy actually enjoyed playing with them and enjoyed receiving social rewards. In addition, she reported that Judy seemed to be affected by mild disapproval and punishment as never before — "It seems to hurt her feelings and she seems more sensitive to it." The adults reported that Judy had initiated numerous interactions with other people in various settings during the past week. Mother reported that her daughter was following many more direct commands and stated, "Before this, I really didn't think she understood what we said." While Judy interacted with her mother for only two minutes in this session, she interacted for the full five minutes with her grandmother. It seemed clear that the child-grandmother interaction was a much smoother one, and an additional five-minute session was added to involve child interaction with both adults. In this session, and those which followed, this period produced interaction at or near the five-minute maximum. Session 4 marked the first time when difficulty was experienced in the period in which the child was required to play by herself. She made bids for the adults' attention; and when she did not receive it, she became visibly frustrated and cried. This behavior is interesting in view of the fact that this child had previously been oblivious to others and not interested in interaction with them. After 3 sessions in which Judy's bidding for attention was ignored, it extinguished. In treatment session 5, progress was further consolidated and mother further improved her relationship with Judy. In this session, mother indicated that her child was "more fun to live with" and stated "she seems more intelligent than we had thought." Sessions 4 - 6 showed marked improvement in all respects and this was a period of high optimism and rising expectations for the adults. Sessions 7* and 8, however, were characterized by a clear-cut reversal in progress as indicated by the behavior in the clinic and the adults' report of Judy's behavior. Although surprising at first, it quickly became apparent that the adults were requiring responses of which Judy was incapable, and thus, opportunities for rewarding success were infrequent. The parents indicated that they were once again disappointed by Judy's inability to do things usually expected of children her age. In short, the parents' expectations rose too rapidly. The adults were frustrated and communicated this to Judy through reducing the frequency and meaningfulness of their rewards. These points were discussed in session 8 and the adults clearly agreed with and contributed to the above formulation. By session 9, they appeared to have adjusted their expectations to a more realistic level and the quality of the interaction returned to its former level.

Between sessions 11 and 12, the therapist visited the home during the morning hours. Judy was observed playing quietly by herself and

*Data unavailable due to mechanical failure.

intent on one activity. Her mother and grandmother were both successful in joining her play and interacting with her. The only behavior
which upset the otherwise unremarkable observation of Judy and her
parents was her repeated attempts to sit on the therapist's lap and relate
to him.

The clinical observations of parental behavior change in Judy's case
and others like it suggested that the modeling procedures used were
quite powerful in contributing to successful outcome. Modeling seemed
to be particularly valuable in effecting rapid initial change in parental
behavior. There are a number of reasons to expect the success of
modeling procedures in problems of this kind. Among the most apparent
is the fact that, with most parents who require such training, the desired
behaviors are of very low probability. Even when they can be evoked by
instruction, they are often quite ineffective. Social rewards, for example,
may be quite stereotyped, flat in affective tone, or they may be long and
complex statements which make little sense to a small child. If the
behavior problem constitutes parental over-involvement with the child,
an instruction to ignore undesired child behavior may well lead to
cessation of verbal harangues, but intensification of non-verbal
attention from parent to child. Thus, learning through behavioral
direction and reinforcement alone may simply help to perpetuate
ineffective behavior. Another powerful aspect of modeling would appear
to be the vicarious reward provided the parent by his child's response to
the model's behavior. It seems that many of these children respond in the
desired ways more quickly to a strange model's contingency management behaviors than to those of his own parents. Thus, modeling
procedures may strengthen the desired responses in the parents through
vicarious reinforcement, when direct reinforcement is likely to be
delayed. These clinical observations are consistent with the more
systematic research on modeling which indicates that learning may often
be greatly facilitated by observation, and that this facilitation may be far
greater than that which is provided by additional learning trials (Adler,
1955; Hayes and Hayes, 1952; Rosenblith, 1959). The following case of
David and his mother provided an opportunity to check the power of the
modeling procedure used independently.

## Case Report: The Use of Modeling

*Background*     David was a six-year-old child with a long history of poor
development and adjustment. He was adopted at fourteen months and
reportedly was rarely allowed to leave his crib during this first year. At
the time of adoption he rolled constantly, crooned to himself, and
stiffened when touched. He was unable to walk, but soon learned to do so

in his new home. Although his parents had considerable trouble in raising him, he was not referred for professional evaluation until it became apparent that he was unable to function in a regular school program. His school teacher reported that he was over-active, distractible, tense, excitable, and given to frequent outbursts. He had attacked other children in school and was "defiant of authority," frequently responding to commands with "No, I won't," etc. David was dismissed from school because he was "too unpredictable to be safe." His behavior at home was also clearly problematical in that he was excessively demanding and manipulative, to the point that the organization of the household was largely determined by him. This process can be more readily understood by illustration than general description. The following excerpt of ongoing behavioral observation in the home will indicate the nature of the problem.*

David, mother, (Sue twelve-year-old adopted sister), and baby brother are all in the family room in the basement. David annoys Sue and Sue complains to mother about David. Mother says to David, "Behave yourself." David complains in a whining voice, "The baby is wrecking my train set." Mother says, "No, he isn't." David whines and says, "Take him upstairs." Mother: "David, I'll take him if he bothers, I'll take him." David whines again, "Do it now." Mother asks, "Are you going to work on your trains now?" David replies in the affirmative and mother says, "Okay, I'll take him up." Mother then goes upstairs with the baby and David and Sue are left in the family room. David gets a small piece of rubber tubing, puts one end of the tubing in his mouth, goes up to Sue and blows air on her. Sue says "Stop!" in a loud annoyed voice. David does it again. Sue says "Stop!" again, but David continues. Sue yells upstairs to mother, "David has a tube in his mouth and he's blowing air in my face." Mother goes down into the family room and tells David to stop that, sharply. David does it some more. Mother says to David, "I thought you were going to play with your trains, I took the baby upstairs so you could play." Mother leaves the room. David stays in the family room with Sue; he does not play with his trains, he keeps the tube in his mouth, but he doesn't bother her any more. He then goes into the laundry room. When David does this Sue calls, "Mother, David is going into the other room." Mother comes into the family room and says to Sue, "Let *me* handle that." Sue replies, "You always tell me to tell you when he goes into the laundry room." Mother talks to David in the laundry room and then takes him upstairs into the kitchen. Mother cooks in the kitchen and David fills a glass with soapy water

*The writers are grateful to Robert Phillips for his permission to use this excerpt of his observation.

and blows bubbles with his piece of tubing. Mother: "David, I said no bubble blowing." David laughs and stamps his feet in glee. Mother repeats in a stronger voice, "I said no blowing." David replies, "I didn't hear." Mother becomes angry and says, sharply, "Yes, you did." Mother then gives David a short lecture on bubble blowing.

In this, and a number of other observed interaction sequences, two relationships became apparent: (1) David's demands were very freqently followed by his mother's compliance which was frequently followed by further demands. (2) Behaviors by David which others found annoying almost always brought him attention. Following such attention, his annoying behaviors appeared to increase in frequency.

Psychological testing and a neurological examination were included in this child's evaluation. He earned an IQ score of 97 on the Stanford-Binet Intelligence Scale. Immaturity in visual-motor skills and absence of well-developed laterality were noted in the examination. The neurologist rejected the diagnosis of minimal brain damage while noting an element of immaturity in the functioning of the central nervous system. No chemo-therapy was recommended.

Enrollment in a day school for boys with severe behavior problems followed completion of this diagnostic study. His classroom was one in which contingency management principles were used extensively and it conformed in general design to the classrooms engineered and described by Birnbrauer et al. (1965). In addition, David's parents were seen in group treatment which could be described as fairly didactic in nature and oriented toward teaching the principles of contingency management. They had participated in this weekly therapy for a period of eight months before being referred for further individual intervention. During this time, David's behavior at school had improved considerably, but his behavior at home had been only minimally affected.

David's family included both parents, a twelve-year-old adopted girl, and a one-year-old non-adopted boy. The mother had a high school education and was not employed. The father was college educated and employed in a profession. This was an upper middle income family.

## Procedures

*Parental interview*     The child's mother was interviewed twice prior to observational diagnosis procedures. She indicated that she was very concerned because her son was "emotionally disturbed" and "sick." She was unable, however, to specify many of the behaviors which upset her, other than indicating that her boy would sometimes wave his arms when excited, and that he became overly involved with mechanical gadgets. At times he would withdraw for long periods to engage in this play. When pressed for more specific instances she reported that David would refuse to get ready for, or go to school, and that he would refuse to do simple assigned household chores. At these times mother would either "keep after" him, or do for David what he would not do for himself. She further reported that David could not tolerate having company in the home. This resulted in an almost total absence of visitors. In these and many other instances, mother revealed that she was not responsive to her son's undesired behaviors and compliant to his demands. She also manifested considerable resistance to the suggestions given her in the treatment group regarding the possibility of her ignoring David's undesirable behavior. She indicated that she felt it necessary to be constantly responsive to her son in order to avoid his becoming even more "out of control" and bizarre in his behavior. As the material on this child and his family accumulated, it became more apparent that his interaction patterns conformed rather closely to what Patterson and Reid (1968) refer to as "coercive interaction." In this pattern the behavior of the coercive member of the dyad is maintained by positive reinforcement (e.g. demands produce compliance), while the behavior of the coerced member is maintained by the withdrawal of an aversive stimulus (e.g. compliance produces the cessation of demands, whining, bizarre behavior, etc.) It was also apparent that the coerced member of this mother-child dyad (mother) was most reluctant to give up her habitual attentive and compliant behavior, due to her very reasonable fear that such a change would result in the exacerbation of her child's coercive behavior, which she found so unpleasant.

*Observational diagnosis*     In order to create a situation which might elicit the problem behaviors, mother was asked to enter a room with David and was instructed to play with him for two minutes with a favoured toy. She was then signalled to require him to do arithmetic problems for a five-minute period. This was followed by another two-minute play period and another five-minute arithmetic period. The arithmetic problems presented were well within his capabilities as determined by his teachers. Meanwhile, the therapist (T1 and T2) observed the interaction in the arithmetic periods for twenty seconds at a time, followed by ten-second breaks for recording the following behavior classes:

1. Mother rewards on-task behavior: Any verbal praise given to David for doing the arithmetic.
2. Mother criticizes off-task behavior: Any clearly critical remark by mother to David for his failure to do the arithmetic.
3. Mother attends to off-task behavior: Any non-critical verbal behavior by mother emitted when David is not doing arithmetic.

4. David's time on task: The cumulative time spent by David on arithmetic.

The observer agreement on the first three measures was computed by counting the agreements on the occurrence and non-occurrence of behaviors. Over the first four sessions (two baseline and two treatment) composed of six five-minute arithmetic periods, observer agreement on mother's rewards was 100 percent. Mother's attention to off-task behavior yielded 97 percent agreement, and mother's criticism of off-task behavior, 95 percent agreement. T1 observed the child's cumulative time on task in each session but no observer agreement was obtained on this measure.

Figure 3 shows that the average percent of mother's attention to off-task behavior was 98 percent over two baseline sessions composed of four arithmetic periods. The average percent of mother's criticism was 12.5 percent. The child's cumulative arithmetic time, in these periods, was always below thirty seconds, and mother rewarded on-task behavior only twice in four sessions. When mother asked her son to do the arithmetic, a barrage of non-arithmetic behaviors was elicited. The first among these were, "I want a drink. . . . I have to go to the bathroom. . . . I won't do them with the lines on the paper. . . . How many do I have to do?" etc. Mother responded to all these statements and many others like them, and little arithmetic was completed in the baseline sessions. While it was very easy for David to direct his mother's attention in these ways, it was observed that he could get even stronger responses from her by acting in more unusual ways, such as sucking his thumb, pouting, head banging, making machine-like noises, crawling on the floor, etc.

*Formulation*    The findings of the observational diagnosis further confirmed the formulation already outlined — namely that David's undesired behaviors appeared to be maintained by mother's compliance to his demands, and her rather intense attention to his unusual and manipulative behavior. In line with this formulation, the goal of intervention was the cessation of her compliance and attention. Weekly directive counselling and didactic group discussions had been employed to this end for eight months with limited success, and other measures seemed to be called for. It was decided to employ only the modeling procedure for a brief period for the purpose of producing the desired change. These treatment sessions were given twice weekly and lasted approximately one hour.

*Modeling*    In treatment sessions 1 and 2, T1 accompanied David into a room where he took him through the play periods and arithmetic periods just as mother had done. Meanwhile, mother and T2 observed the interaction and both made systematic behavioral observations as already

outlined. It was believed that this recording would direct the mother's
attention to the relevant cues and model behaviors and thus facilitate
learning.* She proved to be an accurate observer. Observer agreement in
treatment sessions 1 and 2 were as follows: $T^1$ rewards, 98 percent
agreement; $T^1$ attends to off-task behavior, 90 percent agreement; $T^1$
criticizes, 82 percent agreement.

$T^1$ engaged in contingency reversal procedures in the arithmetic
periods and the child's time on task was noted. David's time on task was
4.5 min in the first arithmetic period during which $T^1$ rewarded on-task
behavior, gave minimal criticism for off-behavior, but otherwise did not
respond to the child. The child's time on task was 0.5 min when $T^1$
responded to off-task behavior but did not reward on-task behavior or
criticize off-task behavior. These results were observed by the mother
and the data was shown to her immediately after the sessions. The
therapist did *not* draw any conclusions from the data, nor did they require
any conclusion from the mother. She was then sent into the room with
her son and asked to use whatever methods she though appropriate to
get him to do the arithmetic. The same procedure was followed in
treatment sessions 2, except that $T^1$ attended to off-task behavior in the
first arithmetic period, and rewarded on-task behavior with minimal
criticism for off-task behavior in the second period. Under these
conditions no reversal of the child's behavior was obtained.

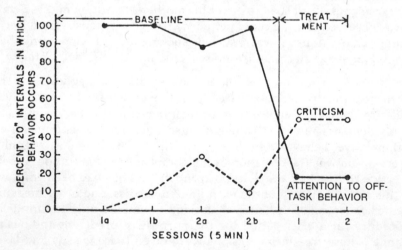

Fig. 3. Per cent of mother's attention to off-task behavior and criticism in 5-min baseline and
treatment sessions.

*Miller and Dollard (1941) found, for example, that when observation aided the subject in
attending to relevant stimuli, learning was facilitated, but when observation led the subject
to miss important cues, learning was retarded.

As can be readily seen in Fig. 3, the mother's attention to off-task behavior dropped from an average 98 percent in the baseline session to an average of 21 percent over the first two treatment sessions. Her critical comments rose from an average of 12.5 percent in the baseline sessions to an average of 50 percent in the treatment sessions. T[1] had modeled critical behavior at an average of 25 percent and the child's mother apparently responded to the modeling. As treatment progressed, however, it became apparent that such criticism was ineffective in producing compliance even when used minimally. In later treatment of this child mother was taught to restrict her use of verbal criticism. Her rewards of on-task behavior were at a uniformly low level through these first sessions. David's on-task behavior was very infrequent in these sessions, thus giving mother minimal oportunity for appropriate reward.

*Extended treatment*     Having established the desired parental behavior through modeling procedures, the focus of the therapeutic interventions shifted slightly at this point in the direction of strengthening those behaviors and maintaining them, until the child himself could provide the needed reinforcement to sustain them. Two extended sessions with T[1] and David were carried out in which T[1] remained consistent in his contingency management behaviors. T[1] gave verbal approval for working on arithmetic but gave no attention for other behavior. Mother and T[2] observed these sessions and recorded T[1]'s behavior. T[1] required David to stay in the situation until he had attended to the task for five minutes. In the first treatment sessions of this kind, forty-seven minutes were required for the child to reach this criterion. In the second sessions fifteen minutes were required.

The next 4 treatment sessions included mother-child interaction with David required to do arithmetic. The time required to reach the five-minute on-task criterion in each session was thirty minutes, fifteen minutes, 9.5 min, and thirteen minutes, respectively. In the final two sessions, David completed all the problems presented to him in ten minutes and fourteen minutes, respectively.

David's mother achieved very meaningful behavior changes during this time, both in and out of formal sessions. As in Judy's case, however, there was a good deal of fluctuation on the mother's part at various stages. Because procedures varied in the latter phase of treatment, it is impossible to determine which treatment ingredients helped maintain the new, more effective maternal behaviors. As in case 1, direct instruction, discussion, modeling and social reinforcement were used to support mother's new behaviors and facilitate generalization to the home situation. In addition to the eight treatment sessions for which behavioral data is reported, the mother was given eight more counseling sessions to facilitate the effect of the behavior change program in the home and to assist David's re-entry into public school. As she became more successful and positive in her relationship with her son she appeared more relaxed, and expressed feelings of confidence in "teaching" other family members more effective ways of interacting with David. Five months after the modeling procedure was initiated, David was successfully placed in a regular public school classroom.

## Discussion

The present case serves to demonstrate the effectiveness of brief modeling procedures in producing effective and novel contingency management behaviors in the parent of a disturbed child. It is significant that the success with modeling followed the relative failure of other more directive and instructional methods designed to produce such change. This fact seems to greatly enhance the interpretation that the modeling procedures were responsible for the changes observed. It is also interesting to note that, at the end of the treatment, David's mother perceived modeling as the most helpful technique in the treatment program.

The vital problem in this case seemed to be the maintenance of the novel maternal behavior until the time when the child began to reinforce such behavior himself. Modeling was effective in producing behavior change; the maintenance of that change over this critical period then became the central problem. Because multiple techniques were employed to that end, the effective ingredients of this latter phase of treatment cannot be systematically ascertained.

The isolation of the modeling technique served to demonstrate its utility in effecting parental behavior change in the present case. Much more systematic research is required, however, to ascertain what effect each of these techniques may have in producing meaningful change in inter-personal behavior. In addition, follow-up data on cases such as these is vital to the continued development of the field.

## Summary

Out-patient clinic procedures for changing problematic parent–child relationships were described. These procedures were illustrated by the presentation of two cases in which parental behavior change was effected with resulting improvement in the parent – child interaction. Standard interactional situations were developed in each case in which a set of behavior demands were made on the parent and the chid. These demands elicited the problematic child behaviors for which treatment was required. Systematic behavioral observations were taken establishing a quantifiable measure of problematic child behaviors and related parental behaviors. Measures were then taken to modify the nature and frequency of parental behaviors while systematic observations on both parent and child continued. The techniques used in the parental training were described and their uses illustrated in the development of parental behavior change. The results indicated that these procedures can be effective in producing desirable changes in problematic parent-child relationships and that they are worthy of continued exploration.

References

Adler, F. A. (1955), "Some Factors of Observational Learning in Cats," *J. Gen. Psychol.* 86, 159-177.

Allen, Eileen K. and Harris, Florence R. (1966), "Elimination of a Child's Excessive Scratching by Training the Mother in Reinforcement Procedures," *Behav. Res. Ther.* 4, 79-84.

Allyon, T. and Michael, J. (1959), "The Psychiatric Nurse as a Behavioral Engineer," *J. Exp. Analysis Behav.* 2, 323-334.

Birnbrauer, J. S., Bijou, S. W., Wolf, M. M. and Kidder, J. D. (1965), "Programmed Instruction in the Classroom," in: *Case Studies in Behavior Modification* (Edited by Ullmann, L. and Krasner, L.), New York: Holt, Rinehart & Winston, pp. 358-363.

Davison, G. C. (1965), "The Training of Undergraduates as Social Reinforcers for Autistic Children," in *Case Studies in Behavior Modification* (Edited by Ullmann, L. and Krasner, L.), New York: Holt, Rinehart & Winston, pp. 146-148.

Gericke, O. L. (1965), "Practical Use of Operant Conditioning Procedures in a Mental Hospital," *Psychiat. Stud. Proj.* 3, 2-10.

Hanf. C. (1968), "Modification of Mother-Child Control Behavior During Mother-Child Interaction in Standardized Laboratory Situations," paper presented at meeting of the Ass. Behav. Ther., Olympia, Washington.

Hayes, K. J., and Hayes, C. (1952), "Imitation in a Home Raised Chimpanzee," *J. Comp. Physiol. Psychol.* 45, 450-459.

Miller, N. E., and Dollard, J. (1941), *Social Learning and Imitation,* New Haven: Yale University Press.

O'Leary, K. D., O'Leary, S., and Becker, W. C. (1967), "Modification of a Deviant Sibling Interaction in the Home," *Behav. Res. Ther.* 5, 113-120.

Patterson, G. R., Krodsky, G. D., and Gullion, E. (1966). *How Did It Happen to Us and What Can We Do About It?* unpublished mimeographed book, Eugene, Oregon: University of Oregon.

Patterson, G. R., and Reid, J. B. (1968), "Reciprocity and Coercion: Two Facets of Social Systems," unpublished manuscript, Eugene, Oregon: University of Oregon.

Risley, T., and Wolf, M. M. (1966), "Experimental Manipulation of Autistic Behavior and Generalization into the Home," in: *Control of Human Behavior* (Edited by Ulrich, R., Stachnik, T., and Mabry, J.), Chicago: Scott, Foresman, pp. 193-198.

Rosenblith, Judy F. (1959), "Learning by Imitation in Kindergarten Children," *Child. Dev.* 30, 69-80.

Russo, S. (1964), "Adaptations in Behavioral Therapy with Children," *Behav. Res. Ther.* 2, 43-47.

Sanders, R. A. (1965), "Behavior Modification in a Two-Year-Old Child," paper read at Midwestern Psychological Convention, Chicago.

Straughan, J. H. (1964), "Treatment with Child and Mother in the Playroom," *Behav. Res. Ther.* 2, 37-41.

Wahler, R. G., Winkel, G. H., Peterson, R. F., and Morrison, D. C. (1965), "Mothers as Behavior Therapists for Their Own Children," *Behav. Res. Ther.* 3, 113-124.

Walder, L. O., Cohen, S. I., Breiter, D. E., Dacton, P. G., Hirsch, I. S., and Lievowitz, J. M. (1967), "Teaching Behavioral Principles to Parents of Disturbed Children," paper read at Eastern Psychological Convention, Boston.

Welch, RK. S. (1966), "A Highly Efficient Method of Parental Counseling: A Mechanical Third Ear," paper read at Rocky Mountain Psychological Convention, Albuquerque, New Mexico.

# Pre-School Children's Non-Compliance

REX FOREHAND and H. ELIZABETH KING

## Problem

A number of case studies[4][5][6] have demonstrated that teaching parents to use differential social reinforcement for desirable behavior of their deviant child is often not sufficient to reduce oppositional behavior. However, when attention for desirable behavior is paired with time out for deviant behavior, child compliance has increased. Hanf[1][2] recently has reported a program which systematically teaches parents to first reinforce desirable behavior by their child and, subsequently, to punish deviant behavior by time out.

This study examined the effects of a laboratory parental training program on the deviant behavior of preschool children. To be applicable in many applied settings, a treatment program often has to be both brief and immediately effective. Consequently, the present investigation limited the number of treatment sessions (mean number = 6.2 sessions). The format of the treatment approach was basically derived from Hanf[1][2][3] in that each parent was first taught to reinforce positive behavior (Treatment A) and, subsequently, to punish deviant behavior by time out (Treatment B). However, the present study differed from Hanf's work in that abbreviated precedures, a shorter duration of treatment, an abbreviated coding system, somewhat different definitions of recorded behaviors, and less stringent criteria for successful behavior change were used.

## The Parental Training Program

*Subjects.* The Ss were five male and three female preschool children (age range of three to six) referred for treatment because of behavior problems. The problem behaviors involved a wide range of responses that generally could be classified as noncompliance. For example, fighting, disruption and disobedience were reported by most of the parents. Only the mothers of the children were involved in the treatment program. Although an attempt was made to include fathers in the program, this was typically not feasible because of time; however, fathers usually attended one session in which the program was explained.

*Setting.*      The setting was a therapy room equipped with a table, chairs, several toys, and a bug-in-the-ear (Farrall Instruments). In addition, an observation room with a one-way window was adjacent to the therapy room. From the observation room, the experimenter could both observe and hear the parent-child interactions as well as relay messages to the mother by way of the bug-in-the-ear.

*Behaviors Observed.*      Three parent behaviors and one child behavior were recorded. The parent behaviors were verbal rewards (attention to child by describing or approving his activity), commands (an order, demand, direction or suggestion requiring a motor response), and questions (interrogation or suggestion requiring a verbal response). The recorded child behavior was compliance (initiated obedience of parental command within five seconds).

    Reliability was obtained during eighteen percent of the sessions. The following mean percentage inter-observer agreements [agreements/total observations] were obtained: rewards 89 percent; commands 81 percent; questions 82 percent; and child compliance 88 percent.

*Procedure.*      Prior to treatment, three ten-minute baseline sessions were held for each mother-child pair. During each baseline session, the mother was instructed to play with her child under two conditions: for five minutes to play whatever game her child wished to play (Baseline for Treatment A), and for five minutes for the mother to determine the game to play and the rules of the game (Baseline for Treatment B). During the initial situation, only the three maternal behaviors were recorded while in the latter situation two maternal behaviors (commands and rewards) and child compliance were coded.

    Each parent-child pair was treated individually during sessions which were typically held twice a week. Sessions during Treatment A (reinforcement) typically involved the following steps: A five-minute data collection period consisting of observation of the mother and child interact in whatever game the child chose to play; discussion with mother concerning her use of reinforcement in the preceding five-minute period and at home; modeling of appropriate techniques by the therapist; role playing of the situation by mother and therapist; and a practice period for the mother to implement her new skills with the child. During the last phase, the mother would wear the bug-in-ear and receive instructions and feedback concerning her behavior. Similarly to Hanf[3], during the reinforcement sessions mothers were also taught to reduce commands and questions. The purpose of such a reduction was to eliminate behaviors that were incompatible with rewarding the child.

The sessions emphasizing time out (Treatment B) typically involved the same procedures as during reinforcement sessions, except that the initial data collection period consisted of an observation of the mother and child for five minutes in the activity chosen by the child and for five minutes in the activity chosen by the mother. The time out procedure was similar to the one described by Hanf[3]. The mother was taught to give direct, explicit commands and to verbally reward compliance. If compliance did not occur, a warning (if - then statement) was given to the child. If compliance still did not occur, the child was placed in a time out chair in a corner of the room. If the child left the chair, he was warned that a spanking would occur the next time and was then returned to the chair. If he subsequently left the chair, he received two quick spanks on the rear and was placed again in the chair. Following approximately two minutes in time out, the child was returned to the uncompleted task. Completion of the task was followed by verbal reinforcement from the mother.

## Results of the Short-Term Treatment Program

Table 1 summarizes the findings. It is apparent that within a short-term treatment program both mother and child behaviors can be rapidly changed in the laboratory setting. During the reinforcement phase, the mothers demonstrated a significant increase from baseline in rewards and a significant decrease from baseline in questions and commands. During the time out phase, child compliance and parental rewards increased significantly from baseline. Perhaps most impressive is the significant increase in percentage of child compliance [complies/commands] and percentage of parental rewards relative to number of child compliances [total rewards/total compliances].

Table 1. Rate Per Minute and Percentages of Mother and Child Behaviors

| | Baseline | Treatment | $p^*$ |
|---|---|---|---|
| Reinforcement Phase | | | |
| Rewards (rate) | .7 | 4.4 | .005 |
| Commands (rate) | 1.1 | .1 | .01 |
| Questions (rate) | 1.8 | .4 | .005 |
| Time Out Phase | | | |
| Rewards (rate) | .8 | 2.3 | .005 |
| Commands (rate) | 4.0 | 3.2 | NS |
| Child Complies (rate) | 1.7 | 2.6 | .03 |
| Compliance/Commands | 43% | 81% | .025 |
| Reward/Compliance | 45% | 89% | .025 |

*Determined by the Wilcoxon matched-pairs signed-ranks test.

These results indicate that child noncompliance is a behavior that is amenable to a rapid behavioral treatment program in a laboratory setting with the parent as the primary therapist. With the present mother-child pairs, methods to generalize the laboratory gains to the home situation were implemented. Data were obtained in the home with two parent-child pairs: with one pair immediately following treatment termination and with the second pair one month after treatment. In each case, the child's compliance at home was higher than his treatment mean in the laboratory as one child increased from 87 percent to 100 percent and the second child increased from 84 percent to 96 percent. Parent behaviors remained consistent with the means obtained during laboratory treatment. The data from these two cases as well as positive parental reports indicate that generalization from the laboratory to the home did occur.

### Summary

This study examined the effects of short-term behavioral treatment on non-compliant children. Eight parents of behavior problem children were trained in a laboratory setting to reward desirable behavior and punish deviant behavior with time out. The results indicated that parent behaviors and child compliance changed significantly from baseline. Furthermore, in two cases measures were obtained in the home. In both cases generalization from the laboratory to the home occurred.

## References

1. Hanf, C., "Facilitating Parent–Child Interaction: A Two-Stage Procedure," unpublished manuscript, University of Oregon Medical School, 1972.
2. Hanf, C., "Presentation in Workshop on 'Research in Altering Mother-Child Interactions,'" at American Orthopsychiatric Association, June, 1973.
3. Hanf, C., "Shaping Mothers to Shape Their Children's Behavior," unpublished manuscript, University of Oregon Medical School, 1970.
4. Lavigueur, H., Peterson, R. F., Sheese, J. G., and Peterson, L. W., "Behavioral Treatment in the Home: Effects on an Untreated Sibling and Long-Term Follow-Up," *Behav. Ther.*, 1973, 4, 431-441.
5. Wahler, R. G., "Behavior Therapy for Oppositional Children: Love is Not Enough," paper presented at Eastern Psychological Association, 1968.
6. Wahler, R. G., Winkel, G. H., Peterson, R. F., and Morrison, D. C., "Mothers as Behavior Therapists for Their Own Children," *Behav. Res. Ther.*, 1965, 3, 113-124.

# Acknowledgments

## Part One

1. Sutton Smith, B., "The Role of Play in Cognitive Development, excerpted from *Young Children*, 1967, 6, 364-369. Reprinted with permission.
2. Pulaski, M. A., "The Importance of Ludic Symbolism in Cognitive Development," in Magary, J. F., Poulson, M., & Lubin, G. (eds.) *Proceedings Third Annual UAP Conference: Piagetian Theory and the Helping Professions*. University of Southern California Press, 1974. Reprinted by permission.
3. Frank, L. K., "Play in Personality Development," *American Journal of Orthopsychiatry*, 1955, 25, 576-590. Copyright (c) 1955 by the American Orthopsychiatric Assoc., Inc., Reproduced with permission.
4. Florey, L., "An Approach to Play and Play Development." *American Journal of Occupational Therapy*, 1971, 25, 275-280. Reprinted by permission.
5. Frank, L. K., "Play is Valid," *Childhood Education*, 1968, 32, 433-440. Reprinted by permission of the author and the Association for Childhood Education International. Copyright (c) 1968 by the association.
6. Walder, R., "The Psychoanalytic Theory of Play," *Psychoanalytic Quarterly*, 1933, 2, 208-224.
7. Slobin, D. I., "The Fruits of the First Season: A Discussion of the Role of Play in Childhood," *Journal of Humanistic Psychology*, 1964, 4, 59-79. Reprinted by permission.

## Part Two

8. Klein, M., "The Psychoanalytic Play Technique," *American Journal of Orthopsychiatry*, 1955, 25, 223-237. Copyright (c) 1955 by the American Orthopsychiatric Assoc., Inc. Reproduced with permission.
9. Freud, Anna, "The Role of Transference in the Analysis of Children," excerpted from *The Psycho-Analytical Treatment of Children*. London: Imago Publishing Co., 1946; New York: International Universities Press, 1955. Reprinted with permission.
10. Hellersberg, E. F., "Child's Growth In Play Therapy," *American Journal of Psychotherapy*, 1955, 9, 484-502. Reprinted by permission.
11. Levy, D. M. "Release Therapy," abridged from the *American Journal of Orthopsychiatry*, 1939, 9, 713-736. Reprinted by permission of the author.
12. Hambridge, G., "Structured Play Therapy," *American Journal of Orthopsychiatry*, 1955, 25, 601-617. Copyright (c) 1955, by the American Orthopsychiatric Assoc., Inc. Reproduced with permission.

13. Axline, V. M., "Play Therapy Procedures and Results," *American Journal of Orthopsychiatry,* 1955, 25, 618-626. Copyright (c) 1955 by the American Orthopsychiatric Assoc., Inc. Reproduced with permission.
14. Guerney, Louise., "Play Therapy: A Training Manual for Parents," Mimeographed Report, 1972. Reprinted with permission.
15. Allen, F. H., "Therapeutic Work with Children," abridged from the *American Journal of Orthopsychiatry,* 1934, 4, 193-202.
16. Slavson, S. R., "Play Group Therapy for Young Children, "*Nervous Child,* 1948, 7, 318-327.
17. Frank, M. G. & Zilbach, J., "Current Trends in Group Therapy with Children," abridged from *International Journal of Group Psychotherapy,* 1968, 18, 447-460.
18. Bixler, R. H., "Limits are Therapy," *Journal of Consulting Psychology,* 1949, 13, 1-11. Copyright (c) 1949 by the American Psychological Association. Reprinted by permission.
19. Ginott, H. G., "The Theory and Practice of 'Therapeutic Intervention' in Child Treatment," *Journal of Consulting Psychology,* 1959, 23, 160-166. Copyright (c) 1959 by the American Psychological Association. Reprinted by permission.
20. Russo, S., "Adaptations in Behavioral Therapy with Children," *Behavior Research and Therapy,* 1964, 2, 43-47. Reprinted with permission.
21. Straughan, J. H., "Treatment with Child and Mother in the Playroom," *Behavior Research and Therapy,* 1964, 2, 37-41. Reprinted with permission.

## Part Three

22. Gardner, Richard A., "Mutual Story telling Technique," excerpted from *"Therapeutic Communication With Children. The Mutual Storytelling Technique."* New York: Science House, Inc. 1971. Reprinted with permission.
23. Robertson, M. & Barford, F., "Story-making in Psychotherapy with a Chronically Ill Child," *Psychotherapy: Theory, Research and Practice,* 1970, 7, 104-107. Reprinted with permission.
24. Arlow, J. A. & Kadis, A., "Finger Painting in the Psychotherapy of Children," *American Journal of Orthopsychiatry,* 1946, 16, 134-146. Copyright (c) 1946 by the American Orthopsychiatric Assoc., Inc. Reproduced with permission.
25. Jernberg, A.M., "Coming Alive through Theraplay." paper presented at the American Personnel and Guidance Association Convention, Feb. 9-15, 1973. Reprinted by permission.
26. Orgun, I., "Playroom Setting for Diagnostic Family Interviews," *American Journal of Psychiatry,* 1973, 130, 540-542. Reprinted by permission.
27. Hawkey, Lawry, "The Use of Puppets in Child Psychotherapy," *British Journal of Medical Psychology,* 1951, 24, 206-214.
28. Marcus, Irwin M., "Costume Play Therapy: The Exploration of a Method for Stimulating Imaginative Play in Older Children," *Journal of Child Psychiatry,* 1966, 5, 441-452. Reprinted with permission.
29. Levinson, B. M., "Use of Checkers in Therapy," *Psychological Reports,* 1972, 30, 846. Reprinted by permission.
30. Loomis, E. A., "The Use of Checkers in Handling Certain Resistances in Child Therapy and Child Analysis," *Journal of the American Psychoanalytic Association,* 1957, 5, 130-135. Reprinted with permission.
31, Russo, S., & Jaques, H., "Semantic Play Therapy," *ETC: A Review of General Semantics,* 1956, 13, 265-271. Reprinted by permission of the International Society for General Semantics.
32. Durfee, M. B., "Use of Ordinary Office Equipment in Play Therapy," *American Journal of Orthopsychiatry,* 1942, 12, 495-503.

33. Cassell, S., "The Suitcase Playroom," *Psychotherapy: Theory, Research and Practice*, 1972, 9, 346-348. Reprinted by permission.
34. Leton, D. A., "The Use of a School Play Kit in the Diagnosis and Treatment of School Adjustment Problems" *California Journal of Educational Research* 1960, 11, 14-18. Reprinted by permission.
35. Beiser, H. R., "Play Equipment for Diagnosis and Therapy," *American Journal of Orthopsychiatry*, 1955, 15, 761-770. Copyright © 1955 by the American Orthopsychiatric Assoc., Inc. Reproduced with permission.
36. Lebo, D., "A Formula for Selecting Toys for Nondirective Play Therapy," *Journal of Genetic Psychology*, 1958, 92, 23-24. Reprinted by permission.

## Part Four

37. King, P. D. & Ekstein, R., "The Search for Ego Controls: Progression of Play Activity in Psychotherapy with a Schizophrenic Child," reprinted from the *Psychoanalytic Review*, 1967, 54, 639-648, through the courtesy of the Editors and the publisher — National Psychological Association for Psychoanalysis, New York, N. Y.
38. Despert, J. L., "Play Therapy. Remarks on Some of Its Aspects," *Nervous Child*, 1948, 7, 287-295.
39. Erikson, Erik H., "Play and Cure," Excerpted from his book *Childhood and Society*, 2nd Edition, New York: W. W. Norton & Co. 1963. Reprinted with permission.
40. Levy, D. M., "Release Therapy in Young Children," *Psychiatry*, 1938, 1, 387-390.
41. Fuch, N. R., "Play Therapy at Home," *Merrill Palmer Quarterly*, 1957, 3, 89-95. Reprinted by permission.
42. Byers, H. L., "Play Interviews with a Five-Year-Old-Boy," *Maternal Child Nursing Journal*, 1972, No. 2, Summer. Reprinted by permission.
43. Axline, V., "Play Therapy Experiences as Described by Child Participants," *Journal of Consulting Psychology*, 1950, 14, 53-63. Copyright (c) 1950 by the American Psychological Association. Reprinted with permission.
44. Allen, F. H., "Participation in Therapy," *American Journal of Orthopsychiatry*, 1939, 9, 737-742.
45. Alexander, E. D., "School Centered Play-Therapy Program," *Personnel and Guidance Journal*, 1964, 43, 256-261. Copyright (c) 1964 by the American Personnel and Guidance Association. Reprinted by permission.
46. Guerney, B. G.., Guerney, .L. F., & Andronico, M. P., "Filial Therapy," *Yale Scientific Magazine*, 1966, 40, 1-6. Reprinted by permission.
47. Rothenberg, Lillian & Schiffer, Mortimer, "The Therapeutic Play Group — A case Study," *Exceptional Children*, 1966, 32, 483-486. Reprinted with permission.
48. Slavson, S. R., "Some elements in Activity Group Therapy," *American Journal of Orthopsychiatry*, 1944, 14, 578-588.
49. Semonsky, C. & Zicht, G., "Activity Group Parameters," *Journal of Child Psychiatry*, 1974, 13, 166-179. Copyright 1974 by the American Academy of Child Psychiatry. Reprinted by permission.
50. Epstein, N. & Altman, S., "Experience in Converting an Activity Group into Verbal Group Therapy with Latency-Age Boys," *International Journal of Group Psychotherapy*, 1972, 22, 93-100. Reprinted by permission.
51. Ginott, H. G., & Lebo, D., "Most and Least Used Play Therapy Limits," *Journal of Genetic Psychology*, 1963, 103, 153-159. Reprinted with permission.
52. Doubros, S. G., & Daniels, G. J., "An Experimental Approach to the Reduction of Overactive Behavior," *Behavior Research and Therapy*, 1966, 4, 251-258. Reprinted with permission.

53. Johnson, S.M. & Brown, R. A., "Producing Behavior Change in Parents of Disturbed Children, *Journal of Child Psychology and Psychiatry*, 1969, 10, 107-121. Reprinted with permission.

54. Forehand, R. & King, E., "Pre-School Children's Noncompliance: Effects of Short-Term Behavior Therapy," *Journal of Community Psychology*, 1974, 2, 42-44. Reprinted with permission.

# Index

# Index